John Simpson is the BBC's World A............ He has twice been the Royal Television Society's Journalist of the Year and won countless other major television awards. He has written several books, including five volumes of autobiography: *Strange Places, Questionable People*; *A Mad World, My Masters*; *News from No Man's Land*; *Not Quite World's End* and a childhood memoir, *Days from a Different World*. *The Wars Against Saddam*, his account of the West's relationship with Iraq and his two decades reporting on that relationship, encompassing two Gulf Wars and the fall of Saddam Hussein, is also published by Pan Macmillan. He lives in London with his South African wife, Dee, and their son, Rafe.

§

'A very fine journalist'
Nelson Mandela

'At one point, Simpson lists "the most extraordinary journalists of the century . . . George Orwell, Richard Dimbleby, Ed Murrow, Martha Gellhorn, Bill Deedes". Who but the most resentful can seriously doubt that he, too, belongs on that list?'
New Statesman

'A first-rate writer and funny with it'
Sunday Telegraph

'Inspirational, anecdotal, humorous and chilling. Simpson's unbiased accounts are riveting'
Bob Geldof

'The doyen of foreign correspondents'
Spectator

*Also by John Simpson
and published by Pan Macmillan*

Strange Places, Questionable People

A Mad World, My Masters

News from No Man's Land

The Wars Against Saddam

Days from a Different World

Twenty Tales from the War Zone
(A World Book Day Quick Read)

Not Quite World's End

JOHN SIMPSON

UNRELIABLE SOURCES

How the 20th Century Was Reported

PAN BOOKS

First published 2010 by Macmillan

First published in paperback 2011 by Pan Books
an imprint of Pan Macmillan, a division of Macmillan Publishers Limited
Pan Macmillan, 20 New Wharf Road, London N1 9RR
Basingstoke and Oxford
Associated companies throughout the world
www.panmacmillan.com

ISBN 978-0-330-43563-5

Printed in the UK by CPI Mackays, Chatham ME5 8TD

Visit **www.panmacmillan.com** to read more about all our books
and to buy them. You will also find features, author interviews and
news of any author events, and you can sign up for e-newsletters
so that you're always first to hear about our new releases.

To those who told the truth

Contents

Introduction

A journalist who writes truthfully what he sees and knows on a given day is writing for posterity. The scepticism and criticisms that I met in some quarters during the Spanish conflict made me feel at times that I was working more for the historical record than for the daily reader.

Herbert Matthews of the *New York Times*,
'A World in Revolution' (1971).

Reporting is an art form which has sometimes been mistaken for a science. People who read the news in the paper or on a website, who listen to a radio bulletin or who watch television news, usually imagine they are getting something approaching the truth. Instead, they are merely getting a version of what has happened. Anybody who has witnessed an event, and then come across a news report of it afterwards, knows how inaccurate the reporting can be. There are mistakes of fact, of understanding, of interpretation. Journalists are like portrait painters: their work will be accurate and fair, or inaccurate and distorted, according to their individual capability.

So a book about the way journalists reported the events of the twentieth century is likely to be a detailed study of human inadequacies. Sometimes these are great, sometimes surprisingly small. Occasionally, very occasionally, someone will be found to have been exactly right about something he or she has reported. Those are times to celebrate; but for the most part this book will not be a celebration. All the same, it certainly does not set out to be a wholesale condemnation either. Perhaps because I am one myself, I have not started with the assumption that all journalists of the twentieth century must automatically be establishment hacks, bigoted, lazy, and blinded by their class and ethnic limitations. There are, indeed, plenty of those in the pages that follow, but, to use Oscar Wilde's phrase, there are also marvellous exceptions.

And so, reading through the narrow columns of print from past decades, peering at awkward photocopies, I found that most reporters were much like the journalists I have known in my own time; just limited human beings trying to find their way through a dense forest of uncertainty, with the light fading and a deadline approaching fast. I found it hard to be too judgemental, having been stuck in the same forest so many times myself.

These journalists are not emotionless recording machines, or supermen, or psychics. They are simply doing their best to puzzle out what on earth is going on, then trying to fit their interpretation of it all into an unrealistically small number of words, before spending a disproportionate amount of time working out the technicalities of getting their material transmitted back home. As everyone who has ever done the job can testify, reporting, especially from abroad, isn't so much a first draft of history as a form of escapology.

All the same, there are plenty of villains in this book: journalists who through laziness or conceit or ideological tunnel vision chose not to find out what was really going on. There is Bennet Burleigh of the *Daily Telegraph* who, without actually bothering to go and check out the facts, assured the nation that there was no truth in the stories that Boer women and children were dying like flies in the British concentration camps in South Africa. There is the charming yet unlovable Beach Thomas of the *Daily Mail*, who knowingly lied about the terrible disaster of the first few days of the Battle of the Somme. There are correspondents who preferred not to notice the activities of Hitler's or Stalin's thugs, who saw cruelty and violence close up but said nothing because it might put people off the cause they themselves believed in. There are tabloid journalists of our own day who make up stories because they are pretty sure no one will sue, and who sometimes wreck people's lives in the process.

But there are others who managed to let us know something of what was really going on, in spite of censorship or the fear of official retaliation. Philip Gibbs tried to report on the reality of the Somme and Passchendaele, rather than parroting the official version.

Ellis Ashmead-Bartlett managed almost single-handedly (he was helped by, of all people, the father of Rupert Murdoch) to put a stop to the disaster of the Dardanelles campaign. The man from the *Daily Mail*, of all papers, revealed to people in Britain the brutality of the Black and Tans in Ireland. The man from the *Daily Express*, of all other papers, reported with great courage about the cruelties being visited on the Jews in Hitler's Germany. In 1979 the *Daily Mirror*, at the urging of John Pilger, devoted an entire edition to reporting on the horrors of Cambodia, and – such is the desire that people sometimes demonstrate to understand what is really going on – every single copy of it was sold.

So alongside the acts of moral and intellectual cowardice, the laziness of thought and action, there are also clear signs from time to time of a stubborn determination to tell people honestly and openly what is really going on. It shines out of the browning pages of the newspaper files and the transcripts of broadcasts right down to our own times. I wish there were more instances than there actually were; though I have had to leave out some of them. Sadly, too, I have not been able to refer to the work of some of the journalists I personally most admire. Being mentioned here is not at all like being mentioned in despatches.

There are plenty of depressing elements in twentieth-century British journalism: the baleful influence of many of the big press barons, from Northcliffe and Rothermere to Rupert Murdoch; the implosion of once vibrant titles like the *Express*; the rise of celebrity news, and the day of the blogger. Yet by and large neither the trade of journalism nor the position it occupies in the national life seems to have changed a great deal in the course of a century. Prime ministers in the 1920s and 1930s tried to keep on the right side of Lord Rothermere; now they go on their knees to News International.

And there are those ludicrous incidents which always seem to hover round journalists, like flies in a souk: how Hitler raised a cricket team to play an English eleven, for instance, but decided that the game was too soft; or how a star Fleet Street journalist arrived to cover the Spanish Civil War with his brand-new wife and a Siamese cat, and left after twenty-four hours to report a massacre which hadn't actually happened. Evelyn Waugh's *Scoop* remains as accurate an account of journalism now as it was when it was first published.

To write an account of the journalism of a century in a single volume is a big undertaking, and I have sadly found it necessary to focus on a number of specific subjects, ignoring many important and fascinating events altogether. It has been a humbling experience. Compared with many of the people whose work I have examined, my career has mostly been spent in the shallows, covering small wars, forgettable politics, and toytown presidents and prime ministers. The heroes of this book, and there are quite a few of them, were giants who saw far more and far worse things than the correspondents of my time have had to endure. By comparison with them, my generation and I have had it easy. For that, and for much else, I honour them.

This is a journalist's book, which has largely been written on the road. I have got up at impossible hours of the morning in Tehran, Mexico City, Johannesburg, Urumchi and Kabul in order to peer at the photocopies my peerless researcher, Kathryn Beresford, has sent me by post or email, and tried to make sense of British politics, Irish troubles or Nazi thuggery – or why on earth Tony Blair should have helped to invade Iraq. I bashed away on my laptop late at night during a power cut in the Chimanimani mountains of Zimbabwe, when my colleagues and I had slipped illegally across the border to report on the problems of the present. Great drops of sweat landed on my keyboard in an army hut in Basra with the temperature at 115 degrees. None of it has made the writing of this book any easier, and it can't possibly have made it any better; but it has certainly made it more atmospheric. Ellis Ashmead-Bartlett, Alan Moorehead and (most especially) Martha Gellhorn would, I hope, have approved.

§

My long-suffering producer Oggy Boytchev had to work around my inattention and my late appearances in various part of the world. Kathryn Beresford worked marvels to send me the newspaper extracts I needed, and struggled through the various chapters to check that I had got my facts right. If I haven't, the fault is mine alone, though I should add one caveat. Until the 1930s newspaper headlines generally ended with a full stop, but some papers persisted in the habit until much later. Apparent inconsistencies are thus, in fact, faithful reproductions of what actually appeared. Ann Baker was extremely helpful in digging out extra material when Kathryn was overloaded with the research. My dear colleague Dr Joanne Cayford was full of helpful ideas and advice, and so was Jeff Walden, the archives researcher at the BBC's written archives centre at Caversham. Professor Jean Seaton, with whom I had a memorable lunch in the garden of the Chelsea Arts Club, gave me some excellent leads, all of which have their results in this book. Two good friends, Dr Mark

Billinge of Magdalene College, Cambridge, and David Reddaway, the British ambassador to Turkey, came up with a number of valuable ideas (and cups of tea) in the idyllic setting of a Sicilian villa overlooking Mount Etna.

My long-term friend, the author and journalist Andrew Taylor, was kind enough to read through the manuscript, suggesting cuts and changes and pointing out some of the especially boring parts. Vin Ray, the head of the BBC's Journalism College, gave me the benefit of his thoughts, some of which I have passed off as my own here. My colleague Malcolm Balen, with great dedication, read through the manuscript to check that I had not diverged from the BBC's rules of balance and fairness, and made a number of suggestions, each of which was an improvement on the original; I incorporated them all. My agent, Julian Alexander, was full of help and ideas, and looked after me with the greatest of care; as ever, ours is an enjoyable partnership and I owe him a great deal. Georgina Morley was, as ever, a powerhouse of support, and proved very forgiving as (in best journalistic tradition) I missed successive deadlines.

My wife Dee (once a reporter herself) had to endure two years of my ramblings about reporters and reporting, and I think I can honestly say I took every piece of advice she gave me. As for my four-year-old son Rafe, he was sheer delight: chattering away while I was trying to write, accompanying me to the London Library (where the staff treated him, and me, with remarkable tolerance and care), and everlastingly trying to lure me away from my laptop to come and watch DVDs of Charlie Chaplin or Spongebob Squarepants with him. Whenever I caved in, I confess I preferred it greatly.

London, November 2009

1

THE VOYAGE OF THE *DUNOTTAR CASTLE*

As the RMS *Dunottar Castle* sailed out of Southampton on the afternoon of Saturday 14 October 1899 and headed for the Atlantic, there was one overriding fear on board: that the war would end before the ship could reach Cape Town. Sir Redvers Buller, the general in command of the British forces, sixty years old, bluff, reserved and energetic, was travelling with his staff, 1,500 soldiers, and half a dozen war correspondents, each accredited by the War Office to cover the fighting in South Africa. All were anxious to get the two-week voyage over quickly, so they could play their part in the fighting and get whatever share of the credit might be available. The correspondents, like journalists in general, were a mixed bunch. One, H.S. Pearce of the *Daily News*, had only just managed to catch the ship in time. The previous afternoon, according to an admiring article in *Harper's Magazine* of New York, 'English War-Correspondents in South Africa', published in the July 1900 edition, he had strolled late . . . into his office. 'Things are looking more serious in South Africa. You had better get out as soon as possible.' 'I'll just have time to catch the train for the South-African mail,' he replied. He caught his train, and within three weeks was in the battlefields of Natal.

Most of the other journalists on the *Dunottar Castle* had covered the small colonial wars which Britain had fought over the previous decades. They knew how fast the British army could move, and how effective it usually was against an inferior colonial enemy. The general opinion among the war correspondents, and among General Buller's staff, was that the Boers would be little better than the various native armies Britain had fought and defeated. The experience of the First Boer War, in 1880–1, did not seem at all conclusive. The Boers had defeated the British at Majuba, but it had happened more because of the failings of the British commander than because of the Boers' military skills. Before the defeat could be avenged, the incoming prime minister in London,

W.E. Gladstone, who was deeply opposed to colonial adventures, halted the British column under Roberts as it marched against the Boers, and agreed a peace deal instead.

The most famous journalist on board was the youngest and least experienced of them all: the glamorous, showy, yet oddly unselfconfident Winston Churchill, at twenty-four the accredited correspondent of the *Morning Post*. He was well-connected socially, and was closer to many of Buller's staff in terms of class and age than were the other correspondents, and the officers found him easy to talk to. Churchill's fame had grown with his unsuccessful campaign to win a parliamentary seat at Oldham, three months earlier. In the days immediately before the *Dunottar Castle* sailed, it had increased as a result of the release of pre-publication copies of his highly opinionated but impressive second book, *The River War*, about the Sudan campaign in which he had taken part. Its scheduled publication date was 6 November, a week after the *Dunottar Castle* was due to arrive at Cape Town. He called it, grandly but with his usual touch of self-mockery, 'my magnum opus (up to date)'.

In spite of his notorious pushiness, Churchill was a pleasant travelling companion. Before leaving, he had proclaimed loudly that the *Morning Post* was paying him £250 a month, for a guaranteed minimum of four months. This was astonishingly high for a man so young: the largest amount, probably, that any newspaper had ever paid a war correspondent. Yet once aboard the *Dunottar Castle*, Churchill managed to get on good terms with the other journalists. They were older, mostly middle class, and instinctively suspicious of aristocrats, of flashiness, and of other journalists who put on airs.

The correspondent of the *Manchester Guardian*, John Atkins, got on well with Churchill and later gave the impression in his autobiography *Incidents and Reflections* that Churchill shared his stock of brandy, Bordeaux, Scotch and Rose's lime cordial with him and the other correspondents on board. (He may even have occasionally shared the information he extracted from his sources on Buller's staff.) Atkins described Churchill on the *Dunottar Castle* as '. . . slim, slightly reddish-haired, pale, lively, frequently plunging along the deck . . .'

Despite his salary, and all the attention he received, Churchill still wrote home like a young boy.

17 October [1899] Madeira
en route
South Africa

My dearest Mamma,

We have had a nasty rough passage & I have been grievously sick. The roll of the vessel still very pronounced prevents my writing much, and besides there is nothing to say. Sir R. Buller is vy amiable and I do not doubt that he is well disposed towards me. There are a good many people on board – military or journalistic – whom I know and are all vy civil – but I cannot say that I am greatly interested in any of them . . .

Ever your loving son,
Winston

Privately, Churchill was less concerned than the other correspondents about the need for haste. He was sure that Buller would not be in any great hurry when he reached South Africa. On Wednesday 25 October, eleven days into the voyage, he wrote to his mother to tell her of a briefing he had received from one of Buller's staff officers.

The main campaign – as I learn on the best possible authority – for who can foresee such things – will begin about the 25th December and we should be at Pretoria via Fourteen Streams and Bloemfontein by the end of February.

This was one piece of information Churchill did not, apparently, share with the other journalists on board.

A war artist for the *Illustrated London News* was travelling on board, and during the voyage he sketched Buller and his ADC, both dressed in civilian clothes, in deep discussion on the promenade deck. Churchill, wearing a cap, is standing behind them, listening to another staff officer. Perhaps this was the moment when he heard about Buller's plans.

Another *Illustrated London News* artist on board was a difficult, self-promoting character called Melton Prior. At fifty-four, he was one of the longest-serving, most battle-hardened journalists out of the lot. Short, bald, with a shrill laugh and a high-pitched voice, Prior was known at the

Savage Club in London, where he held court, as 'the screeching billiard-ball'. He had first met General Buller during the Ashanti campaign twenty-six years before. After that Prior followed and sketched almost all of the colonial wars the British army had fought, together with the Russo-Turkish War, the Graeco-Turkish War, and revolutions in Latin America.

Between 1873 and 1904 he only spent an entire year, 1883, in Britain. As happens with so many foreign correspondents, his private life was badly affected by the unstructured nature of his work, and his marriage eventually broke under the strain. Prior always had two sets of suitcases and equipment ready packed at home; he called them his 'hot and cold outfits'. If his editor asked him at short notice to go to Novaya Zemlya or Timbuctoo, he once said, he would simply wire his servants to deliver the appropriate set of cases to Charing Cross railway station in time for the next available train to the Continent, and he would head off. It would save an entire day's packing.

Like the young Churchill, Prior was a convivial travel companion, and the *Illustrated London News* equipped and paid him lavishly. He was one of the few journalists covering the war in South Africa who were paid anything like as much as Winston Churchill. His editor at the *ILN* once called Prior 'the Illustrated Luxury', and he had brought with him, as ever, large amounts of whisky and even larger quantities of tins of Moyer's Irish stew. According to his carefully phrased obituary in *The Times*, in 1910, he was a 'Rabelaisian humorist [with] a certain roughness of metaphor in his own speech'.

Translated, this seems to mean that Prior's language was coarse and loud. Yet by the time he boarded the *Dunottar Castle* for South Africa, in October 1899, Prior represented a phase of British journalism which was fast coming to an end. The press camera, together with better methods of reproducing photographs on the page, were heralds of a new era, which was to last throughout the entire twentieth century. War artists were beginning to seem faintly anachronistic: the *Daily Mail*, one of the most advanced newspapers in the world, no longer had a full-time war artist on its staff. Yet for the time being they had an important function to perform, since it was still very difficult to take usable photographs in the height of action. As a result Melton Prior's sketches provided the *ILN*'s readers with a much better sense of a battle or a grand occasion than any photograph could. His coolness under fire was legendary – not least because he told everyone about it – and he had developed an impressive speed in first sketching and then refining a drawing for engraving, transmission to London, and printing on the *ILN*'s cover.

The sketchpad was well suited to the small-scale colonial wars which men like Prior were used to covering. The situations were easy to grasp, and usually limited in scope; in most cases, a single battle fought in one location, which brought the entire campaign to a successful close. The large-scale war which was just starting across the full expanse of southern Africa would prove to be far harder to cover in the fashion that newspapers had adopted during the previous half-century: a single report of several thousand words by a correspondent and one or two page-sized drawings by a war artist. The Boer War would demand new approaches to reporting.

War reporting was changing in other ways. When, in 1904, Prior went to Japan to cover the war with Russia, the military authorities in Tokyo would not allow him anywhere near the front line. He left Japan in disgust: a war artist who was not allowed to see the war for himself had, he felt, no part to play in its coverage. Prior increasingly seemed like a figure from the past. There had been no moral or intellectual question about most of the wars he had covered. There was only one side that mattered, and that was the British side. He was more than willing to take up a gun and use it against the enemy, since he saw himself as being as much a part of the war effort as the soldiers themselves. Guns were a necessary part of the war correspondents' equipment: during the Zulu War, for example, they had to ride long distances alone through hostile territory, in order to reach some isolated centre of civilization from which they could transmit their report. The journalist, under these circumstances, was in no sense an objective onlooker, but also a participant.

The man who invented the profession of war correspondent, William Howard Russell, had shown an impressive independence of judgement during his reporting of the Crimean War. Russell liked to spend his time with the junior officers and the ordinary soldiers, rather than with the generals and their staff; and he often showed as much sympathy for the sufferings and privations of the Russian soldiers as he did for those of the British. But the onward march of imperialism during the nineteenth century hardened the attitudes of newspaper correspondents. By the mid-1860s, new men were taking over from Russell and were setting a different tone: more opinionated, and increasingly more nationalistic. Russell's great rival, Archibald Forbes, for instance, the hero of dozens of dashes on horseback, skirmishes with the enemy, exciting escapes, and subterfuges, legitimate or otherwise, introduced a more personal style, in which the adventures of the reporter off the battlefield as well as on it began to play a much greater part. Many people grumbled that Forbes was too often the hero of his own reporting, and he was sometimes accused by his colleagues of stealing their stories. He usually scooped them (the noun 'scoop' was already in use by the 1870s, as was its synonym, 'beat') by his sheer energy and his clever use of the available technology.

Forbes's patriotism was noisier than Russell's. He was usually accurate, even if he had borrowed some of the facts from his colleagues; but he had none of Russell's instinctive sense of balance and objectivity. Everything he wrote was intended to further the national cause; he saw his reporting as essentially a patriotic duty. If the British forces behaved discreditably, or failed in their task because of the incompetence of their superiors, this would not appear in his reporting; not, at least, in the way they had in Russell's despatches from the Crimea a generation before. Then, the British public had become angry at the incompetence in the command structure, and the army's entire approach to warfare had been reassessed. The success of Forbes's style of reporting changed things. The tone of war reporting in the last quarter of the nineteenth century became unquestioning, even fawning.

Archibald Forbes was sixty-one in 1899, seven years older than his friend Melton Prior, but he did not head off to South Africa with him to cover the Boer War. He was critically ill back in London, and died five months later. Forbes's death closed the door on an entire era.

Probably the only non-imperialist on board the *Dunottar Castle* was the *Manchester Guardian* correspondent, J.B. Atkins – the man who drew a favourable pen-portrait of Churchill walking along the deck. He had been hand-picked both for his views and his journalistic skill by his redoubtable editor, Charles Prestwich Scott, who had made the *Manchester Guardian* a strong, though balanced, opponent of the war in South Africa. Scott had impressed upon Atkins that the *Guardian* was the voice of calmness, accuracy and truth, at a time when the British press in general had been hijacked by lies and pro-war hysteria. For Atkins, as for Scott, the Boer War was symptomatic of everything he most disliked: in particular the growing influence of unscrupulous plutocrats, expressed through the excitable and unreliable journalism of newspapers like the

Daily Mail, which had been founded only four years earlier. Such papers, Scott believed, stirred up the masses to irrational, jingoistic hatreds by demonizing Britain's enemies instead of promoting a calmer, clearer understanding of them.

Nevertheless, once the war had begun, Scott treated it as something which, while regrettable, had to be got through as quickly and humanely as possible. He was clear that Britain must win the war, but the editorials in the *Manchester Guardian*, which he either wrote himself or approved personally every evening, insisted that clear and specific political aims were required. Inevitably, he and his newspaper came in for a great deal criticism as a result. The Unionist government (a coalition between the Conservatives and Liberal Unionists, elected in 1895), which had manoeuvred Britain and the Boer Republics into war in order to extend British power to the whole of South Africa, regarded Scott and the *Guardian* as particular enemies, especially after Scott became MP for Leigh in 1895. In the 'Khaki election' of 1900, a year after the war began, an anonymous pamphlet was circulated, apparently by the local Conservative Party office, accusing him of being pro-Boer and anti-British, and of encouraging President Kruger of the Transvaal to resist British demands before the war began. Scott did not sympathize with the Uitlanders who were demanding greater democracy in the Transvaal, the pamphlet said, 'because, of course, they were only Englishmen, and not Mr Scott's friends the Boers'.

In addition, Scott received a large amount of hate mail from the ordinary public. Someone who claimed to have been a *Guardian* reader for twenty-five years told him to 'go to Hell'. Someone else said the *Guardian*'s leader showed a 'continued disloyal line'. More aggressively, someone who signed himself 'A Yorkshire Lad' wrote: 'I dare not shoot you, or blow up your premises, as you deserve, so I will punish you in the only way I can . . .' – presumably by refusing to buy the newspaper any more. None of this had any effect on Scott.

On board the *Dunottar Castle*, his chosen correspondent, J.B. Atkins, knew that his editor would be watching his despatches with particular interest. Yet once the war began, Scott allowed Atkins to show a broad support for the war effort. In South Africa, Atkins's reporting would never be shrill, and he stuck faithfully to the facts even when they did not necessarily suit the C.P. Scott approach. He was a man of quiet, pleasant humour and a disciple of William Howard Russell, whose biography he later wrote. His account of the siege of Ladysmith, published the following year, was the best and most balanced of a slew of books by eyewitnesses there.

A few correspondents were still willing to blur the distinction between being an onlooker and being a participant, but there was a growing disapproval of journalists who were willing to fight alongside the troops. Several of Winston Churchill's fellow-reporters criticized him for carrying a gun, and for badgering Buller into allowing him to take an officer's rank in a South African regiment, while he was an accredited reporter for the *Morning Post*.

With a new century approaching, journalism was starting to change in many ways. The Boer War, fiercer and longer than any other war the British army had fought since the Crimea, would shortly witness as great a revolution in reporting as it would in military affairs.

§

The Boer War was the first twentieth-century war, and not merely in chronological terms. It lasted for more than two years instead of the expected weeks, and required mobilization of troops from around the world. It employed new weaponry and new strategies looking forward to the First World War rather than back to the small colonial wars of the later nineteenth century. It developed into a fierce guerrilla war which led to new and deeply controversial counter-insurgency tactics. Civilians were no longer innocent onlookers; they played a part in the fighting, were duly targeted by the soldiers, and died in concentration camps in appallingly large numbers. The war became a major focus for anger in the rest of the world, and there were popular demonstrations from Paris, Berlin and St Petersburg to New York and Sydney, of a kind that would become familiar much later in the century.

The British themselves were bitterly divided by the war, even though its outright opponents were few in number. As it progressed, it proved to the outside world, and to the British themselves, that their superpower status was on the wane. It was the first war to be fought out in full view of the mass media. And it was to be an early test bed for a new kind of reporting.

As the nineteenth century drew towards its close, the British press felt itself to be at its peak. The great editors of the period, men like J.L.

Garvin and C.P. Scott, insisted that the press had established its complete independence, and now constituted the 'fourth estate of the realm'. Yet in practice most newspapers noisily echoed the patriotic, imperialist and unionist values of the Conservative government. For the first time in British history, the opinion of the masses was becoming a dominant factor. The press delivered the support of public opinion, right across the class spectrum, for the Boer War.

'The new journalism' was first introduced in the 1880s by a group of pioneering and crusading editors, of whom the most enduring was W.T. Stead of the *Pall Mall Gazette*. It reached its full flowering with the Harmsworth newspapers in the 1890s, and created a new mass market among the increasingly better-educated, more prosperous lower-middle and working classes. The established press still devoted immense, carefully crafted articles, sometimes 15,000 or 20,000 words long, to serious subjects, but these needed long hours of concentrated reading by people with plenty of leisure. Such newspapers had little attraction for the new readers, who were attracted to the new journalism: short, emotive articles with catchy headlines, illustrated with line drawings or, increasingly, with photographs. Bright, sharp, opinionated, full of what newspapermen called 'colour', they proclaimed that they were produced for 'the busy man'. They made the news more comprehensible and more palatable.

Alfred Harmsworth, who was born in Ireland of an Anglo-Irish family, began as a magazine publisher, bought the *Evening News* in 1894, and founded the *Daily Mail* in 1896.

Among the innovations he introduced in the *Daily Mail* was the banner headline which ran right across the front page, instead of merely across a single column. Human interest stories, usually avoided by the more traditional newspapers, abounded. Their snappy headlines were designed to intrigue: 'Was it Suicide or Apoplexy?', 'Another Battersea Scandal', 'Bones in Bishopsgate', 'Hypnotism and Lunacy', and 'Killed by a Grindstone'. There were features for women about cooking, entertaining, clothes, the care of children, the management of domestic finances, but the *Mail* was aimed primarily at lower-middle-class men, clerks and office workers in London and the other big cities. Lord Salisbury, the Conservative prime minister, looked down his nose at it and said it was run by office boys for office boys. The established editors disapproved too, but the sales showed that there was a big and growing demand for this kind of journalism.

Sometimes Harmsworth's pursuit of the sensational led his correspondents and editors to get too far ahead of the truth. In July 1900, for instance, when the Boer War seemed for a time to be over and there was a need for some other exciting source of news, the *Daily Mail* reported an entirely fictional massacre of white men, women and children in Peking. This kind of thing gave his newspapers a reputation as scandal-sheets among more serious newspapermen. But the *Mail*'s readership was unaffected. At its height during the Boer War it sold 989,255 copies, and never dropped below 713,000. Harmsworth at first allowed his newspapers a degree of political independence. But as the crisis in South Africa unfolded, the *Mail* became stridently imperialistic. So, to a greater or lesser degree, did almost all the main London newspapers.

§

On 10 October 1899, four days before the *Dunottar Castle* sailed, the British government had received the text of an ultimatum from President Paul Kruger, the elderly, homespun but crafty president of the Republic of the Transvaal. He was certainly not against the idea of fighting a war. If the British could be defeated, as they had been at Majuba nineteen years earlier, they could perhaps be driven out of most of the territory they controlled in South Africa.

But more immediately the crisis had been engineered by the British, and more particularly by a coalition of interests that included Joseph Chamberlain, the colonial secretary in the Conservative government of Lord Salisbury, Cecil Rhodes, whose meteoric career had brought him immense riches from the diamond mines of Kimberley and the premiership of the Cape Colony, and Sir Alfred Milner, the British proconsul in South Africa. Milner, an effective intriguer who nevertheless possessed a startling degree of honesty and self-awareness, had a fierce disdain for the kind of jingoism those in politics and the press (who most supported his policy towards the Boers) were inclined to show. All three men wanted to see Britain extend its control over South Africa and absorb the two Boer Republics of the Transvaal and the Orange Free State. The gold mines of the one and the diamond fields of the other were, naturally, major incentives to press ahead with the enterprise.

Again and again the *Guardian* challenged the government's version of the origin of the war, which was that the Boer Republics had unreasonably resisted Britain's demand that the foreign settlers in Johannesburg ('Uitlanders' in Afrikaans) should be given the vote in the Transvaal and thereby end Afrikaner rule in the Transvaal. The Uitlanders were mostly English-speaking settlers, attracted to the Rand by the lure of gold. The *Guardian* was the only leading British newspaper to point out regularly that whenever the Boers had tried to compromise over the British demands, the British pro-consul in South Africa, Sir Alfred Milner, had changed the demands. According to the *Guardian*, Sir Alfred had wanted war right from the start.

For the most part, though, the British press had accepted the official government view that this was a war for the democratic rights of the Uitlanders. A poorly planned effort in 1895, headed by Rhodes's close friend and follower Dr Leander Starr Jameson, to invade the Transvaal from across the Bechuanaland border and establish a pro-British regime in Johannesburg failed humiliatingly. President Kruger, having defeated the Raid, sent Jameson for trial in London rather than in Pretoria. It was a clever move. All sorts of unsavoury details came out in court about the advice and support Jameson had received from Rhodes, whose career as prime minister of the Cape was finished as a result.

The entire episode was imperialism in its rawest form: the annexation of valuable territory, occupied by an inferior, even mongrel race, for the greater good of Britain. It was justified on the grounds that British citizens were being denied the political rights they demanded. And it received the full support of British society and press. Rhodes at first asked the *Times* correspondent Captain Francis Younghusband to lead the Raid. Wisely, he refused.

Even W.T. Stead, who later became a fierce supporter of the Boers, approved of the Jameson Raid in his *Review of Reviews*. Imperialism was a broadly based national enterprise, and the romance of it all enthused large numbers of people back in Britain. The idea that war was an integral part of the great national adventure of the British people is inescapable in the writings of most of the leading journalists who reported from South Africa in the early stages of the crisis.

In 1895 this feeling was at its height; and the correspondents of the British press, many of whom were leading devotees of the imperialist ideology, spread their gospel through their reporting. The year before, in 1894, Germany's gross domestic product had overtaken Britain's, and although this received relatively little attention at the time, it contributed to a faint background sense that things were not entirely going Britain's way. It is not difficult to detect a distinct sense of anxiety in the hectic outpouring of joy and loyalty when Queen Victoria celebrated her Jubilee in 1897. The weaknesses were there, and the Jameson Raid had shown them up. The only way to compensate for the humiliation of the Raid would be to go through with the job of annexing the Boer Republics.

In the aftermath of the Jameson Raid, Chamberlain, deeply embarrassed, sent Alfred Milner to South Africa as Britain's high commissioner. Both of them wanted to extend British control to the Boer Republics, but Milner was more single-minded about it than Chamberlain, and clearer about the methods required. He understood that the only way to make it happen was through war, and set about manoeuvring the Boers into a position where war would be inevitable. In the end, President Kruger provoked it himself by issuing an ultimatum which he knew the British would not accept, so that he could strike the first blow by invading British territory.

In a remarkably frank letter to Field Marshal Lord Roberts at the end of the first phase of the war, on 6 June 1900, Milner confessed his part in the affair: 'I precipitated the crisis, which was inevitable, before it was too late. It is not a very agreeable, and in many eyes not very creditable piece of business to have been largely instrumental in bringing about a big war.' Apart from the *Manchester Guardian* and one or two smaller newspapers, the British press showed no interest in analysing the real reasons for the war. Yet, sometimes, even among some of those who were most vocal in their support for British imperialism in South Africa, there was an understanding, even if half-smothered, that cruder and greedier motives were involved.

The young Winston Churchill, for instance, was a firm believer in the rightness of Britain's imperial mission. Churchill thought he was destined to die early, as his father had four years earlier, and he felt a need to make his mark on history quickly. Self-centred, more than a little unscrupulous, and a lifelong romantic imperialist, he could have been expected to proclaim that this was a war for principle, rather than for territory, diamonds and gold, as the war's opponents insisted. Yet seven months later, in May 1900, when he stood beside the bodies of eighteen Gordon Highlanders laid out for burial after British troops had stormed the ridge at Doornkop outside Johannesburg without the help of covering fire, Churchill admitted he could not help 'scowling at the tall chimneys of the Rand' where the gold-bearing ore was treated.

In other words, he understood perfectly well what lay behind the decision to go to war with the Boers, and the manner in which he wrote made it clear that he knew his readers would understand what he meant too. Yet it would not have occurred to him to put such thoughts into his reporting. Neither his editors nor his readers would have approved, at a time when imperialism was the dominant political ideology in Britain, and the army was not doing well in the war.

For the *Daily Mail*, to question the war was a betrayal of the soldiers who were fighting and dying on the front line. It was the voice not just of imperialism but of jingoism, condemning as unpatriotic any doubts about Britain's right to impose her control throughout South Africa, regardless of the opposition. The *Mail* was noisy and aggressive. This is a typical quotation, from 18 September 1899, a month before the *Dunottar Castle* left for South Africa:

> The outcry of the Little Englanders awakens no response in the heart of the people. The time has come to show the world and Mr Kruger that we are as good as our word – that when we have put our hand to the plough we do not turn back because the soil is stony and difficult.

More than the *Daily Mail*, indeed more than any other newspaper, *The Times* had encouraged and nurtured the war. And, remarkably for the 1890s, its policy was run by a woman. Flora Shaw, a senior executive on the paper, was forty-six when the war broke out. She had received no formal education, and had started out as the author of a number of books for children. Her strength was her powerful intellect, yet she was highly sociable and a pleasant dinner companion, and had a number of well-placed friends – among whom was John Ruskin. Another friend, the novelist George Meredith, suggested that she should take up journalism. As a result she began writing for the *Pall Mall Gazette*.

In 1888 she went to Egypt to work as the Cairo correspondent for both the *Gazette* and the *Manchester Guardian*, and came to know the *Times* correspondent there, Charles Moberly Bell. He admired her intelligence and force of character. 'If you were a man,' he told her, 'you would be Colonial Editor of *The Times* tomorrow.' When he was called back to London to become the paper's assistant manager he was in a position to make this happen. Flora Bell wrote a series of highly influential reports for the paper from South Africa, going down into the gold and diamond mines to interview the miners, and meeting the leading British and Afrikaner politicians. In particular, she established a firm friendship with Cecil Rhodes.

Impressed by Flora Shaw's despatches and by Moberly Bell's assessment of her abilities, *The Times* offered her a place on its permanent staff in London, with the title of Colonial Editor and a salary of £800 a year. This made her the only female newspaper executive in Britain, and one of the best-paid women journalists anywhere. In 1897, though, her close involvement with the Jameson Raid proved damaging for her and for *The Times*. She was called to appear before a House of Commons select committee investigating the Jameson Raid, and had to face some difficult questions about the highly revealing telegrams that had passed between her and Cecil Rhodes, some of which had been found when Jameson's papers were abandoned at the time of his capture.

It seemed clear that she had been the link between Rhodes and Joseph Chamberlain in the planning of the Raid. But she answered the MPs' questions well, and nothing was proven against her. The press, for the most part lacking any experience of, or appetite for, investigative journalism, chose not to take it further. Editors and proprietors did not see it as the function of their journalists to look into the motives or practices of government, and their readers would almost certainly have disapproved.

Yet if the British press had brought itself to examine the details of the Jameson affair more critically, and had placed the blame for it where it belonged, there would have been a major scandal, and the Boer War itself might not have been fought. But with only the radical press to question the origins of the Raid, and all the mainstream newspapers following *The Times* in supporting it, the British government was not held to account. When war came, the authoritative and outspoken support of *The Times*, as well most of the rest of the press, ensured that it would be popular with the public, and would remain so even after the early disappointments and disasters.

§

Battlefield reporting was a very different matter from political reporting. Dozens of journalists from around the world were heading for the front line, and their reporting – fast, racy, opinionated – would be of a completely different order from anything that had gone before. With them went a revolutionary, if still entirely experimental, form of technology. The Boer War gave the infant British newsreel industry, which would one day metamorphose into television news, its first opportunity to operate from the front line.

Below decks on the *Dunottar Castle*, in second class, was stored the Biograph camera, an immense, imposing and cumbersome affair made of mahogany, leather and brass. When fully mounted, it weighed a thousand pounds. Cinematographic cameras had been in existence only since Thomas Edison started making films seven years before, but during that time the art of film had made remarkable advances. After some discussion with the War Office, and with the reluctant agreement of General Buller, the Biograph team had been given permission to sail on the *Dunottar Castle*.

The role of director, producer and cameraman was performed by William Kennedy-Laurie Dickson, an Englishman who had spent much of his life in the United States and had previously worked with Edison. In 1888 Edison had appointed Dickson to be a leading experimenter for the Kinetoscope, which he described as 'an instrument to do for the Eye what the phonograph does for the Ear'.

Dickson was soon to prove himself adventurous and brave on the battlefield, always conscientious in trying to get as close as possible to the action. But he was not a domineering figure like Melton Prior. In the presence of British officers he seemed awkward and naive, and more than a little ingratiating. When the *Dunottar Castle* reached Madeira, for instance, he and his team went ashore to stretch their legs and do some filming. Coming back, they shared a boat with some of General Buller's staff.

> . . . [A]s we were about to shove off, a native, without any apparent authority, stopped the boat and demanded that the payment should be made to him and not to the boatmen. As he was very insolent the officer nearest to him shoved him into the water, when the fun commenced . . . It would make a very funny picture to sketch the man being caught by the throat as he was about to step into the

boat, and being thrown overboard, while underneath the sketch
should be written the remark made by his victor: 'Go and get a
wash, you filthy beast.'

No doubt Dickson shared the same sense of humour as the officer; but
he also had professional reasons for laughing so ingratiatingly. When they
reached South Africa, Dickson, with his unwieldy equipment and his
team of three, would be entirely dependent on Buller and his staff. He
would need a huge, slow-moving Cape bullock-cart to get his camera
from one place to another, and he had to have the army's help to move
around. Without Buller's specific approval, the Biograph team would not
be able to go anywhere near the front line; and if Dickson could not
obtain film of the battles that lay ahead, their entire effort would be
wasted. He could not afford to offend any of the officers in Buller's team.

On board the *Dunottar Castle*, he kept a diary which went towards
The Biograph in Battle (published in 1901). Its tone was obsequious, as if
he were already getting into practice for keeping in with Buller. He quotes
the ship's barber ('our tonsorial friend'), who had just cut Buller's hair,
as saying 'the General is a gentleman, sir, and as kind as he can be'. Some
days later, the *Dunottar Castle* sights another ship, and Dickson wants to
film her, or 'Biograph' her as he puts it.

We quickly got the 'Bio' in position, but finding the lighting rather
poor I asked the Captain, would he change the course of the boat,
so that we should pass the steamer on our left instead of on the
right; and, as usual, he accommodatingly gave the order.
     Just then Sir Redvers came tramping up the steps and gazed
intently at the vessel. The camera was focussed on the General. The
General tried to shove the Captain in the way, taking him by the
shoulders to do so. When I had secured three or four [shots] he
called out to me: 'That'll do; if you take any more I'll throw you
overboard.'

It was presumably a joke, but after what he had seen in the boat at
Madeira, Dickson did what he was told. In his book he publishes a still
photograph from this episode, showing Buller glowering and grab-
bing the Captain and trying to push him in front of the camera to block
the shot.

Despite his appearance, Buller was an intelligent general, and popular with ordinary soldiers, with whom he was always happy to mingle. His blimpish appearance and abrupt manner covered a sharp mind and a considerable degree of shyness. He was experienced, having fought in China, Canada, the Ashanti campaign, the Zulu War, and the first Boer War. He was fiercely aggressive, and personally brave; he was awarded the Victoria Cross while fighting the Zulus. But, under pressure in South Africa, he had a tendency to make hasty decisions, and sometimes even to show signs of panic.

Buller disliked the press intensely, and made no secret of it. In this, he followed the views of his mentor, Sir Garnet Wolseley, who had hand-picked Buller to be one of his officers in the Ashanti War of 1873. That made him a member of the Wolseley Ring, which was to dominate the British army for the rest of the century. In 1869 Wolseley had famously if ungrammatically described war correspondents in *The Soldier's Pocketbook* as 'those newly invented curse to armies who eat the rations of the fighting man and do no work at all'.

Wolseley was too arrogant to worry that journalists might observe his mistakes and report on them; he merely thought they had no worthwhile function to perform on his campaigns, since his own official despatches were clearly going to be better informed and more valuable than the comments of a group of amateur onlookers. Let the newspapers print his own accounts in preference to the report of their correspondents; people at home would be much better informed if they did.

Field Marshal Roberts, who would soon take command when Buller's campaign stalled, preferred the opposite strategy. More subtle and less openly arrogant, he realized that by taking the war correspondents into his confidence and explaining his strategy to them, he could mould public opinion at home, influence government thinking, and help win his arguments with other commanders in the field. At times, too, the press could be valuable in floating suggestions which could confuse the enemy. There were useful career advantages as well. Because of the way Roberts had treated journalists over the years, the press looked on him favourably. As a result, he had become far and away the most popular military commander Britain had. This popularity had fed through to his own soldiers, who came to believe he was invincible.

Before hostilities began, no one – from the soldiers who were to fight the war, to the journalists who would report it, to the politicians who provoked it – seemed to understand that it would be different from everything that had gone before. It was not simply imperial hubris which led most people in Britain to expect that the war would be over by Christmas; it was the experience of dozens of military actions around the world. Even if, as in Zululand or Afghanistan, these wars began with a defeat for the British forces, they invariably ended with a resounding success in battle, a victory parade in the capital, and the awarding of medals and titles.

The international view was that the British army was as good as any in the world, with the possible exception of the German army. Its equipment was impressive: the soldiers' Lee–Metford and Lee–Enfield Mark II rifles might not have performed quite as well as the Mausers that the Boers used, but they were still accurate and fast-firing. The British had adequate numbers of Maxim guns which, though not new, were formidable weapons. Their field guns and howitzers were effective, and fired Lyddite shells which, though they proved to be less effective than the experts thought, were completely up to date. British artillerymen were thoroughly experienced as a result of the small wars they had fought in half a dozen countries. On paper, therefore, the British army was an impressive fighting force.

Yet the problem lay in the quality of the average British infantryman. He was inadequately paid, fed and clothed, and subjected to harsh discipline, so it had long proved difficult to recruit men of good quality. At this stage British soldiers were not encouraged to use their own initiative; instead, they were trained to follow parade-ground discipline in battle. Their tactics, developed in a dozen small wars, were to fire devastating, highly disciplined volleys to break the enemy's formation. As a result, there was no great emphasis on marksmanship. British commanders tended to rely on the old-fashioned tactics of advancing and attacking en masse. This was precisely the wrong way to fight what was essentially a fast-moving, individualistic force of men, well-armed, highly motivated, and accustomed from childhood to operating in the veld. As for the British forces which were based in South Africa, there were only 14,500 of them when the war broke out. Until that point South Africa had been regarded as relatively safe, so the garrisons scattered across the country were small and ineffective.

On board the *Dunottar Castle* there was an air of quiet confidence about the coming war – until, after fifteen days at sea, she passed a White

Star liner, the *Australasia*, heading for Southampton. Several people aboard the *Australasia* held up a huge blackboard which read 'BOERS DEFEATED – THREE BATTLES – PENN-SYMONS KILLED'. It was the first news the ship had had since leaving Madeira, and it came as a shock to everyone on board, from Buller and his staff to the journalists.

Major General Sir William Penn-Symons had met his death commanding his troops at the Battle of Dundee, in Natal. Aware of the shortcomings of his soldiers, he had ordered them to carry out a frontal attack, in full view of the enemy. Deliberately showing himself to the Boers in order to rally and encourage his men, he had been mortally wounded and died an agonizing but heroic death. To say that the Boers had suffered three defeats was hardly accurate; yet even from the seven words chalked in big letters on the blackboard and hung over the *Australasia*'s side, it was manifestly clear that the British had failed to achieve the easy successes they had expected. By the time the *Dunottar Castle* docked at Cape Town in a rainstorm on the evening of Monday 30 October, the basic pattern of the war's opening phase had been established: and it was not a comforting one.

The war correspondents made their way ashore as fast as they could, desperate to find out what had been happening; not a particularly easy thing to do on a wet Monday night at the Cape. General Buller and selected members of his staff stayed on board, waiting for the latest intelligence report from army headquarters. As they stood on deck in the pouring rain, the news was read out to them quietly, so that no one else would hear.

The three supposed defeats of the Boers had just been hit-and-run attacks in which both sides had lost a lot of men. But the latest news, just a few hours old, was far worse: 1,000 British troops had lost heavy casualties earlier that day at the Battle of Nicholson's Nek, and were likely to surrender in the next few hours. General Sir George White, commanding the main British force in South Africa, some 12,000 men, had managed to stop the Boers advancing to Durban but had then been forced to take refuge with his troops in Ladysmith, where they were now surrounded by a much larger force of Boers. Mafeking was also besieged.

It was a sobering arrival in Cape Town. When they finally managed to find out what had happened, the British press corps from the *Dunottar Castle* agreed among themselves to call it 'Mournful Monday'.

2

THE BOER WAR

No previous conflict, including the Franco-Prussian War of 1870, had attracted so many front-line correspondents. At the height of the Boer War there were at least seventy accredited journalists from Britain in South Africa. But after the collapse of formal Boer resistance, with the annexation of the Orange Free State on 28 May 1900, the occupation of Johannesburg on 31 May, and the flight of President Kruger and many of his officials on 5 June, the great majority of the journalists came home.

Histories of the Boer War, and of war reporting, have tended to regard the British correspondents essentially as cheerleaders who ignored the frequent failures of the officers and the occasional poor performance of the troops. There are, certainly, moments of unguarded enthusiasm which can be embarrassing a century later. The published diaries of William Dickson sometimes show an almost adolescent innocence.

> Sunday, February 4th [1900] – The battle was to have been fought today, but the General has promised that it shall take place to-morrow instead. All are jubilant. It makes me proud to hear the plucky chaps swearing, with flashing eyes, to 'raise hell with the brutes,' and to punish them for their lost comrades. Not a thought of self and the horrors with which they are about to deal.

It is Dickson's excitability, rather than his facts, which is hard to accept. Men like the soldiers he describes shared his values and world view. There is no reason to doubt that they behaved as he described.

More sophisticated writers sometimes strike a similar note. Bennet Burleigh's account of the Battle of Tugela River, published in the *Daily Telegraph* on 24 January 1900, is often quoted as an example of ludicrous jingoism:

> Our indomitable soldiers walked erect and straight onward. Not Rome in her palmiest days ever possessed more devoted sons. As the gladiators marched proud and beaming to meet death, so the British soldiers doomed to die saluted, and then, and with alacrity, stepped forward to do their duty – glory or the grave.

Yet, whenever this is quoted, the passage which follows immediately afterwards is invariably left out. Burleigh goes on to make it clear that he disapproves of frontal attacks like these:

> Perhaps there may be occasions when the sight of men coming on so steadily in the face of almost certain death, will try the nerves of their antagonists; but my own view is that, save where men have to get to within running distance of a few lines of trenches, the system of rushes from cover to cover by small squads is far less wasteful of life.

Bennet Burleigh was an interesting, if flawed, figure. Although he worked for the *Daily Telegraph*, the most Conservative of newspapers, he was a lifelong socialist, and never concealed his radical opinions. He stood unsuccessfully for Parliament three times, and he led a distinctly bohemian existence with his wife, Bertha, a sculptress. He was tall and heavily built, with fierce blue eyes, a walrus moustache, and (like so many foreign correspondents, then and later) a loud, assertive voice. Difficult, aggressive and often controversial, Burleigh was a strong supporter of the freedom of the press.

In his twenties (he was born around 1840) he went to the United States at the time of the American Civil War and served with the Confederate forces. He was twice captured and sentenced to death, and escaped both times. In 1878 he returned to London and once disguised himself as a gas fitter in order to get into the lobby of the House of Commons and report on one of the big stories of the day. His career as a war correspondent began in 1882, when he covered the Egyptian campaign and achieved at least one remarkable scoop – the fall of Cairo. On the strength of that, he was hired by the *Telegraph*, for which he reported for more than twenty wars.

Two years later, in the Sudan, Burleigh covered the Battle of Tamai when the Hadendowa (tribesmen from Kipling's poem 'Fuzzy-Wuzzy', as in 'So 'ere's to you, Fuzzy-Wuzzy, at your 'ome in the Soudan;/ You're a pore benighted 'eathen but a first-class fightin' man') broke a British infantry square. Burleigh turned instantly from reporting to fighting, and helped to rally the surviving British soldiers. His friends claimed that he deserved a Victoria Cross. But he was never a tame reporter, willing to write what the army wanted. The Boer War provided the high point of his career, but he continued to report wars and crises for another ten years; his last campaign was the 1912 Balkan War, when he was seventy-two. He died two years later.

§

The correspondents who covered the Boer War inevitably saw things from the British national perspective, and some, like Burleigh, were deeply nationalistic; this did not mean that they believed they had an obligation to cover up British disasters. After the defeat at the Battle of Magersfontein on 11 December 1899, where General Wauchope and 270 of his Highlanders were killed, the despatch written by the *Globe*'s correspondent, Gilbert Sackville, the eighth Earl De La Warr, was heavily censored. Nevertheless a good deal of what he wrote and thought was transmitted, and the passion still pours out from the yellowing pages in the files:

> It is useless to disguise the fact that a large percentage of our troops are beginning to lose heart in this campaign. Can you blame them? A close succession of frontal attacks on an invisible foe securely intrenched, where retaliation is almost impossible, will shake the nerve of the bravest. Our men have fought well; their conduct under most trying and adverse circumstances has been admirable. But they have been asked to perform miracles, and, being human, they have failed.

The censor did not allow De La Warr to say who was to blame, but the despatch is a clear indictment of General Lord Methuen's tactics. Magersfontein was one of the three defeats during 'Black Week', 10–15 December 1899, the others being Stormberg and Colenso. De La Warr was overwrought when he wrote his despatch. He was horrified at the pointless waste of life; Methuen had had no idea where the Boer defences were, and did not reconnoitre their positions properly.

The correspondents could be frank about the way ordinary soldiers behaved in defeat, too. This, for instance, is an account of the disaster at Spion Kop on 25 January 1900, with nothing much omitted:

> Men were staggering along alone, or supported by comrades, or crawling on hands and knees, or carried on stretchers. Corpses lay here and there. Many of the wounds were of a horrible nature. The splinters and fragments of the shell had torn and mutilated them in the most ghastly manner. I passed about two hundred while I was climbing up. There was, moreover, a small but steady leakage of unwounded men of all corps. Some of these cursed and swore. Others were utterly exhausted and fell on the hillside in stupor. Others again seemed drunk, though they had had no liquor.

The writer was Winston Churchill, published in the *Morning Post* on 17 February 1900. He was subject to military censorship, like everyone else, but this passage is a reminder that a great deal of what they wrote made it through to print. No one who read the *Post* that morning can have had any doubt at all of the unpleasant reality of the war.

A.G. Hales, an Australian journalist reporting for the *Daily News*, wrote with furious anger about the lack of proper cleanliness and medical care for wounded soldiers. After the airing of the scandal in the press, the army introduced the rudiments of better hygiene, but it took an effort reminiscent of William Howard Russell's reporting from the Crimea to bring any sort of change. Hales, as we shall see later, was an outright racist; but he was also a fierce defender of the interests of the ordinary soldier.

It has often been suggested that the British correspondents showed no interest in the poor state of medical care available to the army in South Africa. Yet William Burdett-Coutts, staff correspondent to *The Times* and a Unionist (i.e. Conservative) MP, wrote: 'The men are dying like flies for want of adequate medical attention.' A Royal Commission set up to investigate quickly found that his accusations were broadly correct. The Army Medical Services were subjected to a thorough shake-up, and better systems of care and hygiene introduced.

Even the more conventional war correspondents made no attempt to hide the disturbingly high level of British casualties. J.B. Atkins of the *Manchester Guardian* was less concerned with grand strategy and more interested in the experiences of the ordinary soldier. At the Battle of Colenso on 15 December 1899 he described

> men with waxen grey faces and clotted bandages swathed about them; men who smiled at their friends and instantly changed the smile for a gripping spasm; men who were clinched between life and death; men who had died on the way and were now carried hurriedly and jerkily, since it no longer mattered; men who bore a slight pain contentedly because they were glad that they would be tucked away safely in a hospital for the rest of the campaign; men of a different constitution who took it ill that so slight a pain should cause them so great an incapacity; men who were mere limp, covered-up bundles, carried on stretchers through which something dark oozed and dripped.

Atkins's sympathy extended to General Buller as well.

> Buller, having lost the Battle of Colenso, had decided to withdraw rather than continue fighting. A weaker man, a less heroic soldier, would have carried the position with an appalling loss of life. Buller's decision to retire was a proof of his bravery and good generalship.

Back in London, the government did not agree. Buller's role as commander-in-chief was stripped from him, and Lord Roberts appointed. Lord Kitchener joined him as his chief of staff. The steamroller, as the press called it, was about to start moving.

The correspondents at the front had hidden nothing about the disaster. The patriotic certainty with which many correspondents had approached the war quickly faded and the result was a remarkably honest account of what was really happening.

§

Morale in Britain was seriously shaken. Bertha Synge wrote to Sir Alfred Milner on 3 November 1899 about the way the news was received in London:

Picture the newsboys at the corners (I was going to the London Library) shouting 'Terrible Reverse of British Troops – Loss of 2,000.' Imagine the rush for papers as we all stood about the streets – regardless of all appearances, reading the telegrams with breathless anxiety. Carriages stopped at the corner for papers to be bought – bus conductors rushed with handfuls of pennies as deputation for their passengers . . . The War Office is besieged – no one goes to the theatres – concert rooms are empty – new books fall flat – nothing is spoken of save the war . . .

British public opinion needed some form of reassurance, and the press soon found it in the three big sieges of the war: Ladysmith, Kimberley, and, most sensational and interesting of all, Mafeking.

Were the sieges of the Boer War an attempt to divert attention from the defeats of Black Week and reassure public opinion that British determination and pluck were undiminished? That, certainly, was the effect, and the news from Ladysmith, Kimberley and Mafeking duly cheered up a nation which had suffered a serious blow to its self-esteem. But was it deliberate? That is to say, did the editors of *The Times*, the *Daily Mail* and the rest collude with the government in offering an alternative and more positive subject in order to distract the British people?

Not in any literal sense. At the end of the nineteenth century the British government had no effective system of influencing the press, and there was more independence among newspaper editors at the start of the twentieth century than at the start of the twenty-first. Yet newspaper editors do not have to speak to each other to find themselves devoting large amounts of attention to the same subjects. The effect can be the same, but it arises from competition more than from collusion. And there is no doubt that their readers wanted something more positive from South Africa.

The sieges were a godsend to editors desperate to keep the public attention on a war which had entered a dour and depressing phase. When written up in the newspapers, they provided a winning combination: bulldog courage, a particularly British sense of humour, and a few leading celebrities. When the facts got in the way of the story, they were sometimes brushed away.

None of the British newspapers had a correspondent in Kimberley when the siege there began. *The Times* drew on accounts from Reuter's of skirmishes near Kimberley, but carried no reports from the town itself. The only journalists actually inside it during the siege worked for the local *Diamond Fields Advertiser*. This was significant, since the most prominent person bottled up in Kimberley was Cecil John Rhodes; and he owned and controlled the *Advertiser*. Ever since the Jameson Raid, Rhodes was no longer the political force he had been, but he was still a potent symbol of imperialism.

From his point of view, the lack of independent reporting was a considerable relief, since no word reached the outside world of Rhodes's appalling behaviour during the siege. The presumption was that the atmosphere inside Kimberley was one of gallantry and steadiness under fire, inspired by Rhodes's own behaviour. This was not true. Rhodes carried on a series of sometimes hysterical rows with the long-suffering Colonel Robert Kekewich, who commanded the Kimberley garrison. Partly, no doubt, the military censorship was to blame. Probably the correspondents themselves felt that it would be disloyal and unpatriotic to report the divisions between the two key men in Kimberley. After the siege was over, *The Times* carried one or two brief reports which touch lightly on the fierce disagreements; but given the well-known links between Rhodes and the paper's colonial editor, Flora Shaw, it is not surprising that nothing of the true flavour comes out:

> Mr Rhodes . . . felt that, in view of the uncertain duration of the siege, it was necessary to get rid of as many mouths as possible. This idea had been at first opposed by the military authorities, but they gave way eventually, and he managed to get rid of some 8,000 out of the 10,000 natives in the compounds.

The result was, predictably, starvation, disease and death on a shocking scale. The Africans who were ejected by the British were predictably refused help by the Boers, and, unable to leave the area, sickened and died in large numbers. There was no mention of any of this in *The Times*.

Nor did it report the fact, well known in Kimberley, that Rhodes started to believe that Kimberley was about to fall. He panicked and, without telling Colonel Kekewich, telegraphed General Buller to demand immediate help: something Buller could not provide. Later in the siege, Lord Roberts gave Kekewich the authority to arrest him if necessary;

though it never came to that. When the siege finally ended, Rhodes managed to get Kekewich dismissed. Some weeks later he was quoted as saying: 'Kekewich? Who's he? You don't remember the man who cleans your boots.'

Afterwards, *The Times* continued to cover up for Rhodes by serializing the siege diary of the Hon. Mrs Rochfort Maguire, which was full of sugary praise for him. If tough, self-confident correspondents like Angus Hamilton or Bennet Burleigh had been in Kimberley, it is hard to think that these things would have gone unreported. The journalists of the *Diamond Fields Advertiser* chose not to anger their proprietor, and kept quiet.

Several top journalists were caught up in the siege of Ladysmith, but it was a gloomy affair, boring and largely without incident. The garrison commander; General Sir George White, failed to provide much leadership or initiative. The Boers seemed to have no desire to take on the defenders in an all-out attack, and chose to pepper Ladysmith with artillery shells instead. The occasional assaults were fierce enough, but they were never successful.

The most famous of the correspondents was George Warrington Steevens. He represented an important development in the history of 'the new journalism'. Alfred Harmsworth, keen to give the *Daily Mail* a touch of intellectual distinction, had recruited Steevens from Pembroke College, Oxford, where he was a young classics don with a splendid record of intellectual achievement. He was amusing and charming, but Harmsworth spotted another quality in him: a boyish, slightly wayward willingness to take risks, to sacrifice himself, which was so much a part of the ethos of late Victorian imperialism. Later, on 22 January 1900, the *Mail* described him as 'Modest, almost shy, alert, amazingly industrious, most amiable, and true as steel, of a curious and original humour in speech and literary style.'

Steevens proved to be an adventurer, as well as a quick and vivid writer. He took naturally to danger and discomfort, and to the making of fast and not always well-based judgements; all things, in other words, that an Oxford don might have been expected to avoid. One of his old university friends, Anton Bertram, plainly jealous of the glamorous life Steevens now led, wrote to the leading academic Oscar Browning on 26 December 1898: 'He has made himself the hero of the British clerk & shopkeeper . . . [H]is most prominent qualities seem to me those of the jingo, the cynic, & the philistine.'

Steevens's writing style was wiry, tough and conversational with a biting wit lying concealed in it. He followed Kitchener's Sudan campaign in 1898, and described him in his book *With Kitchener to Khartoum* in deeply unflattering terms.

> His precision is so inhumanly unerring, he is more like a machine than a man. You feel that he ought to be patented and shown with pride at the Paris International Exhibition. British Empire: Exhibit No. 1, hors concours, the Sudan Machine.
>
> It was aptly said of him by one who had closely watched him in his office, and in the field, and at mess, that he is the sort of feller that ought to be made manager of the Army and Navy Stores.

No wonder Kitchener detested him even more than he hated most journalists. He would surely never have been able to forget that last savage taunt. From a twenty-eight-year-old whose job was to bring him into regular contact with Kitchener, not a forgiving man, the whole passage shows an immense self-assurance. His books on the Sudanese and South African campaigns sold phenomenally well, and are a familiar presence on second-hand bookstalls to this day.

Everyone forecast the most brilliant future for Steevens. But in Ladysmith, besieged with the rest, with inadequate sanitation, he caught typhoid fever. He died on 15 January 1900 and was buried in the rapidly growing cemetery. His talent, charm and wit died with him.

§

On 23 March 1900, the *Daily Mail* gave pride of place on its front page to an article which had been smuggled out of the third besieged town, Mafeking. Everything about it was sensational, including the name of its author.

OUR LIFE IN MAFEKING
SOME CURIOSITIES OF THE SIEGE
(By LADY SARAH WILSON)

> Three lunar months to-day (I write on January 4 and despatch this by a trusty native through Rhodesia, in the faint hope that it may escape the Boers and reach the 'Daily

Mail') since this town was invested, and we are still cut off from all communication with the outside world, except what can be carried on by the uncertain means of native runners . . .

I think it may interest friends at home to hear how a handful of Englishmen and Englishwomen have passed the last three months in this little town on the bare veldt, closely invested by a force which at first outnumbered the besieged by about ten to one.

It did indeed interest them, not least because Lady Sarah Wilson was the daughter of the Duke of Marlborough, and therefore (though she was only thirty-five) Winston Churchill's aunt. Beautiful, adventurous and brave, she had gallantly managed to reach Mafeking in order to join her husband, Captain Gordon Wilson of the Royal Horse Guards, and experienced with him the often difficult conditions of the siege. Once she was captured by the Boers, and was indignant at being exchanged for 'a common horse thief'. After she had arrived in Mafeking, the *Daily Mail* made contact with her and recruited her to be its correspondent. Her despatches caused a sensation whenever they arrived in London.

More than Ladysmith or Kimberley, Mafeking ensured that the mass of newspaper readers regarded the war as part of the nation's imperial adventure, rather than something questionable and potentially disastrous. Yet the sieges were not merely an exercise in British damage-limitation: they had a certain military value. They prevented the Boers from winning a stunning early victory, before British reinforcements could arrive to bolster the small garrisons. By sitting down in front of Mafeking, the Boers allowed themselves to be diverted from moving in force into the Cape Colony. Similarly, the siege of Ladysmith blocked them from capturing Durban.

It was a period which wanted, and perhaps needed, heroes. Late Victorian Britain had at least a dozen weekly magazines for men and boys which extolled the spirit of manly adventure. The leading titles were the *Boy's Own Paper*, which contained writing by people such as Arthur Conan Doyle and G.A. Henty, and the *Wide World Magazine*.

Robert Baden-Powell, who wrote for the *BOP*, stressed the importance of living 'clean, manly and Christian lives'; Cecil Rhodes continued to read the magazine enthusiastically when he was in his forties. Boyish adventurousness was a peculiarly imperial quality; it was one of the things that distinguished the British, with their public school ethos and their emphasis on team sports, from other European nations. And in the last quarter of the nineteenth century adventurousness seemed to centre particularly on Africa, through the novels of Rider Haggard, Bertram Mitford, Grant Allen and others, and the real-life adventures of men like Alfred Beit, Barney Barnato and Rhodes himself.

And so when war broke out in South Africa British newspaper readers wanted stories that were exciting and uplifting. Mafeking seemed to offer them.

At the heart of it all was the curious, entertaining figure of Baden-Powell himself. He was a successful cavalry officer, as good at polo as he was at drawing or singing; he could make audiences weep with laughter with his comic songs, and he was the centre of attention at any party. As early as July 1899, realizing that war was probable, Lord Wolseley ordered him to South Africa. He was given the title 'Commander-in-Chief, North-West Frontier Forces'; the frontiers in question being those of the Transvaal, Cape Colony and Bechuanaland. In the local Tswana language the word 'mafikeng' meant 'the place of stones'. With its population of 1,200 whites and 7,000 blacks, it was the only town of any size for hundreds of miles around.

After it was all over, an irritable captain in the relieving force, H.P. de Montmorency, wrote:

> To me the whole affair of the siege was at the time, and always has been, an enigma: what in the world was the use of defending this wretched railway-siding and these tin shanties? To burrow underground on the very first shot being fired in a campaign, and to commence eating his horses, seemed to me the strangest role ever played by a cavalry leader with his regiment of mounted men . . .

This is true, if uncharitable, and it became the standard judgement on Baden-Powell by his fellow soldiers. To his credit, the man himself agreed. Over the years he made a number of disarmingly self-deprecating comments about his efforts at Mafeking. In his book *Sketches in Mafeking and East Africa*, published in 1907, he wrote: '[T]he so-called siege has from various causes been given an exaggerated reputation when it was in reality an investment – of rather a domestic kind at that.' Twenty-seven years later, in *Adventures and Accidents*, he went further: 'Mafeking was, as an actual feat of arms, a very minor operation which was given an exaggerated importance.'

In many ways, it was not much of a siege. The Boer forces under General Piet Cronje numbered 8,000 at first, though the number dropped sharply later. A concerted effort to capture the town might eventually have succeeded, given the small numbers and lack of experience of Baden-Powell's defence force, but it never happened; the Boers seemed too lethargic. As a result the siege lasted 217 days. Yet it was not without its dangers. The *Daily Chronicle* man, E.G. Parslow, was lucky to escape with his life when a shell landed on the Mafeking Hotel, just feet from where he was standing. He was hurled into a woodpile and was unharmed. But his luck ran out a few days later. During an argument in the bar of Dixon's Hotel he told an artillery lieutenant called Murchison that he was no gentleman. Murchison pulled out a gun and killed him.

Correspondents in the town sent back long reports about the way the British were holding up under siege. They made no effort to pretend the siege was anything more than an often boring, uneventful waiting game. Baden-Powell himself, in his official despatches which were reprinted in the British press, often set the tone.

> One or two small field guns shelling the town.
> Nobody cares.

Or:

> Four hours' bombardment. One dog killed.

The reaction in Britain (and around the world, since the interest in Mafeking was vast and international) was one of enjoyment at Baden-Powell's efforts to make light of the whole business. His chirpiness was one of the things people most admired him for.

And he could be quite funny. He would get his signallers to send endless messages to non-existent reinforcements. He wrote thoroughly misleading letters about the high morale of the defenders to his close friend, Kenneth McLaren, who was held prisoner by the besieging Boers. He ordered civilians of all ages and states of health to stand-to and give the impression that the defending forces were much larger than they really were. Best of all, from the journalists' point of view, he organized games of cricket on Sundays because he knew it infuriated the puritanical Boer commander in the besieging trenches.

At times the Boer bombardment could be distinctly unpleasant. Angus Hamilton described what it was like to be under fire in *The Times* of 25 October 1899:

> With a terrific impact the shell struck some structures near the railway, and the flying fragments of steel spread over the town, burying themselves in buildings, striking the veldt two miles distant, creating a dust, a horrible confusion, and an instant terror throughout the town.

Yet Hamilton did not deliberately exaggerate the nature of the siege. Emerson Neilly, of the *Pall Mall Gazette*, said quite clearly in the book he wrote immediately after the end of the siege: 'Frankly, our defenders' pluck did not save Mafeking, great and heroic though that pluck was. The cowardice of the enemy saved us.'

Baden-Powell censored the Mafeking correspondents' despatches himself. Hamilton and the others must have had a disturbing feeling that there were very clear limits it was unwise to cross. If the press corps had issued regular critiques, Baden-Powell could have thrown them out of the town, and their newspapers would have terminated their contracts.

For the modern reader, the worst aspect of the siege was Baden-Powell's treatment of the Africans. Offhand racism was displayed in much reporting of the Boer War, and even though it was regarded by both sides as exclusively a white man's conflict, the casualties among the black population were disturbingly large.

A.G. Hales, the Australian correspondent for the *Daily News* who exposed the poor state of hygiene among the British forces, wrote an account of his experiences called *Campaign Pictures: Letters from the Front* (1900). He was obsessively hostile to Africans, and his book makes unpleasant reading:

> Every Division was accompanied by swarms of niggers, who drew from Government £4.10s. per month and their food. These niggers had a gentleman's life. They waxed fat, lazy, and cheeky. Four-fifths of them rode all day on transport waggons, and never earned a

fourth of the wages they drew from a sweetly paternal Government
... [T]he saucy niggers led the lives of fighting-cocks ...

Yet in Mafeking itself, the suffering of the black population was not ignored by the journalists. Angus Hamilton, like most other British people at the time, probably regarded the Africans as being of a lower order than Europeans. But his reports for *The Times* show a genuine awareness of their plight:

> We have had many more natives killed than whites ... They lie about under tarpaulins, behind zinc palings, wooden boxes, and flimsy sheds ... and perhaps for days their shelter may escape the line of fire; but there comes a moment made hideous by the scream of a shell as it bursts in some little gathering of dozing, half-listless natives. At such a moment their bravery is extraordinary – is indeed the most fearful thing in the world. The native with his arm blown off, with his thigh shot away, or with his body disembowelled, is endowed with extreme fortitude and most stoical resolution.

Baden-Powell harboured strong feelings of European racial superiority which were characteristic of the era, and placed a far higher value on the lives of whites than on those of blacks. He tried to force the African population out of Mafeking, with the exception of those he had recruited for the town's defence. He cut down savagely on their rations, and made them pay threepence each for a pint of soup made from horsemeat: money which few of them possessed. Large numbers of Africans died of hunger.

Some of the defenders sympathized strongly with them, and demanded that rations set aside for the white population should be shared with the Africans. Baden-Powell called these people 'grousers', and announced he would be grateful if anyone who heard them expressing their views would 'apply the toe of the boot'. Angus Hamilton wrote angrily in *The Times*:

> There can be no doubt that the drastic principles of economy which Colonel Baden-Powell has been practising in these later days are opposed to and altogether at variance with the dignity and liberalism which we profess ...

This was passed by Baden-Powell himself, in his capacity as censor. By contrast, Lady Sarah Wilson scarcely mentioned the subject when writing for the *Daily Mail*. Nor did F.D. Baillie, Churchill's colleague on the *Morning Post*. As a former professional soldier he tended to see things from a strictly military point of view, and no doubt felt that the *Post*'s readers would not be interested in the plight of the Africans. Yet other members of the Mafeking press corps spoke out as strongly as Angus Hamilton. Vere Stent of Reuter's reported that the medical teams in Mafeking were treating Africans badly, and he accused a Doctor Hayes of operating on them without the use of anaesthetics.

The picture that has sometimes been presented, that timidity on the part of the correspondents, censorship in Mafeking, and self-censorship by newspaper editors combined to keep the British public in the dark about the realities of the siege, is incorrect. Instead, several of the Mafeking correspondents were prepared to write about some of the worst aspects of Baden-Powell's conduct of the siege.

At the time, Emerson Neilly's reporting for the *Pall Mall Gazette* was more guarded. But when, only a few months later, he published a book about his Mafeking experiences (*Besieged with B.-P.*) he held nothing back.

> [W]ords could not portray the scene of misery; five or six hundred human frameworks of both sexes and all ages, from tender infant upwards . . . standing in lines, awaiting turn to crawl painfully up to the soup kitchen where the food was distributed. Having obtained the horse soup, fancy them tottering off a few yards and sitting down to wolf up the life-fastening mass . . .

Within a few months of the ending of the siege, the darkest side of what had happened at Mafeking was fully exposed. If there was no public outcry it was because the great majority of people in Britain did not care.

On 11 May 1900, in the last days of the siege, there was a full-scale battle at Mafeking involving around three hundred attackers. They crept into Mafeking through the 'native' village and captured Game Tree Fort. Among their prisoners was Angus Hamilton. Colonel Baden-Powell counter-attacked, and eventually the invaders were overwhelmed and their prisoners freed. At least thirty-six men on the Boer side were killed or wounded.

Lady Sarah Wilson had been awakened by shooting on the far side of the town:

> To this awe-inspiring tune I dressed, by the light of a carefully shaded candle to avoid giving any mark to our foes ... I had a sort of idea that any moment a Dutchman would look in at the door, for one could not tell from which side the real attack might be. In various stages of deshabille people were running around the house looking for rifles, fowling pieces, and even sticks, as weapons of defence ... The Cockney waiter, who was such a fund of amusement to me, had dashed off with his rifle to his redoubt, taking the keys of the house in his pocket, so no one could get into the dining-room to have coffee except through the kitchen window.

The *Mail*'s readers loved this kind of nonchalance, and they always enjoyed Lady Sarah's habit of describing what she and everyone else was wearing.

Thanks in part to the efforts of the Canadians and Australians in Colonel Herbert Plumer's relief column, the siege came to an end six days later, on 17 May 1900. Inside the town a total of 71 Europeans and 329 Africans had been killed.

Angus Hamilton, Emerson Neilly and Vere Stent had been frank about the sometimes disturbing behaviour of Baden-Powell, and open about the sufferings of the Africans. Given the exaggerated status of Baden-Powell, and the extraordinary passions which the relief of Mafeking gave rise to when it was reported in Britain, this is not a bad record.

§

Winston Churchill and Bennet Burleigh could have joined the others in Ladysmith, but they decided to continue reporting the war as a whole. Churchill caused a sensation by being taken prisoner. (The Boer officer who captured him was Louis Botha, who later became a firm friend of Churchill's during the First World War when he was South Africa's prime minister.) Churchill soon escaped from a prisoner-of-war camp which was established in a school building in Pretoria. There was always a suggestion that Churchill had let his fellow prisoners down by carrying on with their plan to get out, when they had taken the decision not to go that night. But his escape made him a hero in Britain.

By the middle of 1900, the entire course of the war had changed. Field Marshal Lord Roberts, with a cleverly executed feint, had destroyed the last big Boer army in the field at Paardeberg. The Union Jack was raised over Pretoria, and President Kruger fled to Europe. In traditional fashion, the war was declared over. Most of the newspapers brought their correspondents home, glad to be free of the cost of keeping them in the field; and the correspondents were delighted to go. Soon Lord Roberts handed over to Kitchener, and sailed back to Britain to accept the plaudits of his country.

Yet the war wasn't over, after all. Some of the Boer generals reappeared at the head of guerrilla bands and waged a renewed campaign against the British. The newspapers in Britain were inclined to leave the reporting of this second phase to the news agencies. As a result, they missed one of the most discreditable episodes in modern British military history.

Reuter's correspondent was H.A. Gwynne who became Kitchener's preferred channel for disseminating information. Every newspaper was now dependent on Reuter's for breaking news. Since the remaining correspondents were heavily censored, this gave Kitchener considerable control over newspaper copy.

The war had always had its savage side. The Boers did not play the game according to the rules, and were inclined to ignore the niceties of white flags and red crosses. The books, letters and interviews of British soldiers abound with stories of Boer treachery. The newspaper correspondents – this is from a *Times* correspondent on an incident at the Battle of Belmont on 25 November 1900 – reported these things, but were usually more restrained than the soldiers:

> One of the saddest incidents of the fight was the death of Lieutenant Blundell, of the Grenadier Guards. Seeing his men firing at a man above him whose foot had been broken by a bullet, he called out to them to cease firing and went forward to help the Boer. The latter's only answer was to raise his rifle and shoot him through the body.

Edward Knight of the *Morning Post*, a talented and likeable journalist, was injured when a Boer officer raised the white flag. Knight stood up to get a better view, and someone shot him. He survived, but his arm was amputated.

Entire Boer families would take the oath of allegiance to their new British overlords and be given permission to stay on their farms as a result. Then, directly the British soldiers left, they would break their oath by continuing to supply and shelter the guerrillas, and help them in their attacks on the army. The British saw all this as treachery of the worst kind. Their armed forces were trained to follow the rules more closely than any other Western army did. For them, playing the game and doing the right thing were of immense importance.

Aside from Bennet Burleigh of the *Telegraph* most of the journalists who reported this new stage of the war were South Africans. Edgar Wallace, for instance, was a twenty-five-year-old working-class boy who had escaped his illegitimate background by becoming a soldier. He started to write professionally at the same time and bought himself out of the army in 1899, joining Reuter's and then moving on to become a *Daily Mail* correspondent in 1900. He was clever, sharp, prickly, and not over-burdened with principles. And his time in South Africa had given him an intense dislike of those Boers who refused to cooperate with the British after the surrender.

His despatches were heavily influenced by Kipling's *Soldiers Three* stories, which were written in Cockney, Northern English or Irish dialect; though Wallace's ear for the spoken word was nowhere near as accurate as Kipling's. His articles would start off as reports of battles or advances, but then turn into tales by the soldiers involved; though Wallace may have made some of them up. That, certainly, is what many journalists and soldiers believed.

One story told to Wallace was about a Boer who was allowed to live on his farm provided he gave in his arms. The British camp commander, 'not the fool his eyeglass and his drawl led you to believe', realized that the Boer farmer was laying land-mines in a nearby culvert so British explosives experts set up a counter-trap for him. That night, while the farmer was going round setting up another land-mine, he tripped on the wire the British had laid for him. And: 'Well, this blank blank Boer was found in a dozen different places the next morning.'

It is hard to read Wallace's despatches with much enjoyment. Yet they were highly popular at home: the readers of the *Daily Mail* enjoyed the feeling of angry retribution which characterizes them.

His most virulent article was in the *Mail* on 13 August 1901. It was called 'Woman – The Enemy', and was about the Boer women who helped their husbands fight on. The best answer, he maintained, was to shoot them.

> There have been many occasions since the war started when I have wished most earnestly that . . . the exact status of woman had been made equal to that of man. I have often wished her all the rights and privileges of her opposite fellow. The right to wear his clothes, and adopt his freedoms, to earn money, smoke cut cavendish, and wear a ring on her little finger. Also to share a man's trials and hardships and responsibilities. To lead men into action, to be always eligible for the Victoria Cross, to be honoured for her gallantry – and shot for her treachery. Especially shot for her treachery.

The liberal press in Britain was outraged. The *Daily News*, which had been bought by Lloyd George's anti-war syndicate, wrote:

> That chivalrous, and humane product of the twentieth-century civilisation, Mr Edgar Wallace, surpassed himself in the *Daily Mail* yesterday morning . . . Mr Wallace supports his villainous proposal by a medley of those unverified second-hand stories in which this gentleman revels. Perhaps if Mr Edgar Wallace would manage to see a battle and describe it at first hand – though we admit there are certain risks to be run in the process – he would be doing better work than by writing this ruffianly stuff from the safe retreat of Johannesburg.

For rather different reasons, Lord Kitchener also hated Edgar Wallace. He thought he was a counter-jumper, and he was stung by Wallace's fierce attacks on the censorship system he had set up. He also shared the *Daily News*' contempt for Wallace's way of working. Other war correspondents went to the front line and shared the risks the soldiers experienced; Wallace did not. But in the second phase of the war there were far fewer front lines, and Wallace roamed around, picking up stories from 'Tommy Atkins' and passing them off as fact.

In the summer of 1901 Wallace was in Pietersburg in the Northern Transvaal, when he heard that there had been a battle at Vlakfontein, 200 miles away. The British wounded were being taken by train to Krugersdorp, and Wallace headed off to talk to them. One of them told him that the Boers had been shooting the British wounded wholesale at Vlakfontein.

Wallace wrote it up without seeking further confirmation, and took it to the censor's office in Johannesburg. It was, as he had expected, virtually obliterated. In the normal way, that would have been that. Journalists had to sign a form promising not to evade the censorship procedures. But Wallace sent a copy to London by post. This was strictly forbidden.

The despatch took a month to reach the *Mail*'s offices, but it caused a sensation. It was vintage Wallace:

> Abandoning the old methods of dropping the butt end of a rifle on the wounded soldier's face, when there was none to see the villainy, the Boer has done his bloody work in the light of day, within sight of a dozen eyewitnesses, and the stories we have hardly dared to hint, lest you thought we have grown hysterical, we can now tell without fear of ridicule. The Boers murder wounded men.

There was uproar in Parliament, and the Secretary of State for War cabled Kitchener, asking for his opinion. Kitchener, enraged, cabled back without bothering to investigate that the entire story was a lie. The British army had found from experience that although the Boers were sometimes inclined to break the rules of war, and often looted the bodies of the dead, they were usually generous and helpful to the British wounded, caring for them as well as they cared for their own casualties.

But this time there was something more to Wallace's story than poorly sourced rumour and his own imagination. Four days later, Kitchener was obliged to cable the War Office again in some embarrassment: a Lieutenant Hern had come forward to say that he had seen a Boer soldier shooting the wounded at Vlakfontein. But since the British command had taken the side of the Boers against the British press, the War Office decided to sit on Kitchener's retraction.

It seems likely that Wallace's story was partly true, and partly exaggerated. *The Times History of the War*, published in 1907, investigated and concluded: 'The evidence, when sifted, proves that a man called Van Zyl, who was wounded himself, crawled about and shot at least three wounded men before he could be stopped. Otherwise the behaviour of the Boers was good.'

§

Yet the British themselves were committing very real atrocities at this time; not intentionally, but through overwork and poor administration and lack of proper concern. The terrible death-rates from disease among Boer women and children in the concentration camps proved to be one of the most disturbing aspects of the war.

The correspondents who remained in South Africa were often furiously partisan and unwilling to find out what was really going on. And back in London, pro-war newspapers like *The Times*, the *Morning Post*, and the *Daily Mail* simply swept the reports about the concentration camps under the carpet or tried to discredit them. Bennet Burleigh, the lifelong socialist, made no effort to investigate the scandal, and poured scorn on those who wrote about it. It was British journalism's greatest single failure of the war, and a lasting national reproach.

There had often been a tendency on the part of the British war correspondents to turn a blind eye. When they burned the farms of Boers who were on commando, for instance, and took away the families' animals and even their furniture, there was a tendency to be forgiving. The cult of 'Tommy Atkins', the much-suffering foot-soldier with a heart of gold, had taken over. In the *Daily Mail* on 1 January 1901, Edgar Wallace, the man who advocated executing women for treachery, wrote about '. . . brave, good-hearted Tommy – the man who would gladly lay down his life to protect any woman in the world, whether she were Dutch or English or Japanese'.

The gap between sentimental romanticism and ugly fact was a wide one, and no British journalist wanted to draw attention to it. A Central News Agency correspondent, Alfred Kinnear, who was invalided back to Britain early in the war, wrote with apparent approval in his book

To Modder River With Methuen, published in 1900, of the behaviour of soldiers when they descended on the Boer homesteads of women and children who were supposedly protected by the laws of civilized warfare:

> After the battle of Modder River, 'Tommy' would a-looting go, and many were the odd prizes that he brought into camp. A fat turkey and a good capon dangling from the sporran of an Argyll presented an appetising picture to the men of his company. But anon you would meet a Northumbrian carrying a birdcage and a Scot wheeling a perambulator 'lifted' in one of the Boer houses on the river bank. A Lancer was making heroic efforts to reconcile his charger to a squealing sucking-pig hanging from his holster. But what that young soldier meant to do with a child's bassinet, or that other with a toilet table, who shall say?

It was a politician, Lloyd George, and not a journalist, who informed the nation that General Bruce Hamilton had burned down the town of Ventersburg and then posted up a notice saying that the women and children of the town should go and ask the Boer commandos for food.

The decision to set up concentration camps where the wives, families and servants of Boers who had refused to surrender would be interned, was Kitchener's. It was a typically forthright, unsentimental approach to the problem of guerrilla warfare, where the enemy crept back constantly to his home for supplies and comfort. Burn the farms, imprison the families, and the guerrillas would starve: eventually his policy succeeded in putting an end to the guerrilla campaign – but at a high cost.

Soldiers are rarely good at looking after civilians. The British army in South Africa did not set out to be brutal, but that was the result. For officers and men deluged with administrative problems, the families of their enemy did not receive priority. And so hundreds, sometimes thousands, of men, women and children, black and white, in open trucks, would be left in railway sidings for days and nights at a time, without food, water or shelter, because the main lines were required for military traffic. When they finally reached their destination, they would be housed in tents with no clean water, no way of washing the bed-sheets after someone had died of dysentery, no sanitary facilities other than a single pail per tent, and often no trenches for the disposal of human waste; and this in temperatures which were sometimes as high as 90 degrees Fahrenheit.

This was how the British army had run its own camps, until the campaign in *The Times*. But for the Boers the results of this new system were indistinguishable from a policy of genocide. Kitchener kept sending back reassuring accounts of the camps, without actually investigating them. Each month the death toll rose, until in October 1901, the worst month of all, the deaths numbered 3,156 out of the camp population of 111,619. Fortunately, the weather later cooled down and the figures began to drop; but it was no thanks to the British military.

Kitchener refused to allow any journalists to visit the camps. Leo Amery, the *Times* correspondent, of whom better might have been expected given that he was personally friendly with many Boers and spoke reasonable Afrikaans, played the army's game by reporting that new camps were helping and the death rate was rapidly decreasing. In fact it would continue to rise for another four months.

At this time someone who actually knew the truth was doing the rounds in London, telling everybody what the real situation was. Emily Hobhouse, a short, plump Cornishwoman of forty-one, with a pleasant but determined face, had earlier pulled all sorts of strings to travel to South Africa with twelve tons of supplies donated by concerned anti-war groups in Britain.

When she returned to London in May 1901 her story shocked everyone who was prepared to listen. After meeting her, the Liberal leader, Sir Henry Campbell-Bannerman, asked his famous riddle, 'When is a war not a war? When it is carried on by methods of barbarism in South Africa.' C.P. Scott, the editor of the *Manchester Guardian*, had already devised the phrase 'concentration camps'. It was not a neutral expression, as is often suggested; Scott took it from the terrible *reconcentrado* camps which the Spanish had created in their recent war in Cuba. The British concentration camps were at least as bad, said Emily Hobhouse:

> When the 8, 10 or 12 persons who occupied a bell-tent were all packed into it, either to escape from the fierceness of the sun or dust or rain storms, there was no room to move, and the atmosphere was indescribable, even with duly lifted flaps. There was no soap provided. The water supplied would not go round . . .

No wonder when dysentery and enteric fever struck, people died like flies. The interviews Emily Hobhouse gave, and her articles in the *Guardian*, were dismissed by the pro-war press as Boer propaganda. Bennet Burleigh continued to deny in the *Daily Telegraph* that any problem existed. So did Edgar Wallace in the *Daily Mail*. *The Times* tried to counter Emily Hobhouse's reports by commissioning articles from women who claimed to know South Africa. Mrs Sarah Heckford, for instance, who had lived on a farm in the Transvaal for many years, wrote:

> When ... Miss Hobhouse harrows her own feelings and endeavours to harrow the feelings of others by describing what she imagines to be hardships to Boer women and children in the concentration camps, she provokes a smile from those who know the habits of the Boers. Overcrowding is habitual among them to a shocking extent; so is indifference to what would strike Miss Hobhouse as the elements of comfort, and even decency, among rich as well as poor Boers.

But Emily Hobhouse was too aggressive in her approach to be really effective. Even her friend, General Jan Christian Smuts, wrote that she had a 'strong and vivid personality which at times made her difficult to work with'. She was entirely right about the concentration camps, but she could not persuade her political opponents to believe her.

It took a group of formidable women to investigate the situation. The Fawcett Commission, self-appointed, was six in number, and there was a distinctly feminist air about it; Mrs Millicent Fawcett was the head of the women's suffrage movement in Britain. In the second half of 1901 the commission travelled widely through South Africa, visiting camp after camp. When they saw the reality of the measures Kitchener had introduced, they were horrified.

At Heilbron, for instance, they found that a group of women and children infected with measles had been sent to the camp there. The report later read: 'There is barely language too strong to express our opinion of the sending of a mass of disease to a healthy camp; but the cemetery at Heilbron tells the price paid in lives for the terrible mistake.'

At Mafeking things were worse still. The Commission had warned the superintendent of the camp that his neglect of hygiene would cause problems. He took no notice. When the members came back in November, people in the camp were dying at the rate of thirteen a day. 'Grossly culpable neglect', the commission called it.

The women of the Fawcett Commission succeeded, as Emily Hobhouse had not, in forcing the British government, the army, and the civilian administration in South Africa, to realize that something had to be done. Basic, sensible measures the commission proposed were put into practice. In February, during the southern hemisphere summer, the annual death-rate fell to 6.9 per cent. Soon it had dropped to a figure lower than that of many big British cities.

Perhaps 26,000 whites and 12,000 black people died. Many Afrikaners still refuse to believe that this was not a deliberate policy, and the deaths played the biggest part in keeping an angry, embittered Boer nationalism going. One day, when Jan Smuts finally fell from power in 1948, it would lead to the victory of the National Party, which would, over a period of forty years, introduce the repressive structure of apartheid, which would cost even greater misery. In the long run Kitchener's quick, easy and cheap solution to the guerrilla war was neither quick, easy nor cheap.

The correspondents in South Africa who could have stopped all this failed to do so. It remains one of the worst lapses of decent, honourable journalism in the entire twentieth century.

§

It was Edgar Wallace who scored the last victory of the Boer War.

Peace negotiations started in earnest in April 1902, after the disasters of the concentration camps and the destruction of thousands of Boer farms by the British army. Kitchener set up a camp for the Boers, and another for the British. Barbed-wire fences guarded by armed soldiers surrounded them, and the world's press corps were kept, complaining and angry, in another compound, some way away.

The final phase of the negotiations lasted fifteen days. The Boers were still demanding independence for their republic, and the British were still refusing to agree. At this moment, the *Daily Mail* splashed across its front page that a peace agreement could be expected within days. No one could work out how the news, which was broadly correct, could have leaked out.

Kitchener suspected Edgar Wallace, whom he now regarded as a personal enemy. But Wallace wasn't even in the journalists' camp; he was sometimes seen in the area, but mostly seemed to be travelling back and forth to Pretoria by train. Kitchener sent him a warning: if he were found to have been involved, he would be punished severely. Blandly, Wallace pointed out that he had been visiting Pretoria, looking after his investments.

And then, on 31 May 1902, the Boer delegation finally agreed to accept the British terms. They went to see Kitchener in total secrecy to tell him. In London that afternoon, only a couple of hours after Kitchener had been told the Boers' decision, the *Daily Mail* produced the biggest scoop in the newspaper's short history. 'PEACE IS SIGNED' it trumpeted, and it hit the streets at the very moment when the delegates were putting their names to the agreement in Pretoria.

The British press, as much in the dark as ever, condemned the *Mail* for pretending that its completely unfounded speculation was fact. An editorial in the *Daily Telegraph* said witheringly 'All the pretended revelations which have been given to the world are the veriest guesswork of speculation.'

But they weren't. The next day the government announced the peace agreement in the House of Commons, and the *Mail*'s scoop was shown to have been entirely true.

There were accusations in some papers that the *Mail* had bribed a civil servant in London. A few days later, in order to end these suspicions the *Mail* decided to come clean. Wallace, it said, had a contact within the camp, a soldier. This man – unnamed – had been a sentry at the camp, and had agreed to let Wallace know by a series of signals how the talks were going. If he brandished a red handkerchief, that meant that the talks were stalling. A blue one indicated that they were making progress, and a white one that the treaty was definitely going to be signed. The train from Pretoria to the Vaal River passed close by the camp and Wallace made the journey several times a day. When the sentry came off duty he would walk down to the barbed-wire fence beside the railways tracks, wait for the train, and blow his nose – using the appropriate handkerchief. Wallace then contacted a Johannesburg stockbroker called Caesar Cohen. Using another code based on the buying of stocks, he would telegraph a message to the *Mail* in London, thereby avoiding the military censor.

It was Wallace's final revenge on Kitchener, and on the journalists who had always disapproved of his work. Altogether, it was a fine example of journalistic enterprise. Officialdom was deeply offended, and Wallace received this letter.

Censor's Office, Johannesburg
July 1, 1902

Dear Sir,

I have been instructed to write and inform you that in consequence of your having evaded the rules of censorship subsequent to the warning you received, you will not in future be allowed to act as war correspondent: and further, that you will not be recommended for the medal.

Wallace didn't care. He was soon to be made editor of the brand-new *Rand Daily Mail*.

How much of an achievement was it to have scooped the rest of the world's press by twenty-four hours? Not much, in the context of a terrible war that had seen hundreds of thousands killed, wounded or made homeless, and in which Britain had abandoned some of the key principles which its citizens thought were basic to its existence. Edgar Wallace, like the other journalists, could have had a far greater and more admirable scoop if they had uncovered the scandal of the concentration camps; but they chose not to.

British journalism changed radically as a result. The potential of the mass market, the opportunity to speak directly to ordinary people and enlist their support for causes the editors and proprietors believed in, the chance of making big profits, the opportunity to force governments to alter their policies: all these things now became more possible than before. But would the basic reporting become more honest and open? On the evidence of the latter stages of the Boer War, it seemed depressingly unlikely.

3

ALIENS

At the start of the twentieth century British newspapers rarely spoke openly of the country's decline, any more than American newspapers would a century later. Yet it is impossible not to notice the signs of gloom and nervousness which had settled over the country. Comparisons with the way other countries did things abounded.

> In his speech at New York on Tuesday, Mr Hay uttered words which British statesmen would do well to lay to heart. The attitude of American diplomacy, he said, is diligence and 'attention to business' ... This is a rule the importance of which was long since understood in Germany ... In England, however, the importance of knowledge has never been unequivocally recognised ...
>
> (*Daily Mail*, 21 November 1901)

> The building of the German Dreadnoughts is a menace to our country. The German nation thirty years ago was a boy; today it is a man; tomorrow it will be a giant. The revival of the Holy Roman Empire, if the Pan-Germans have their way, is at hand. (*Daily Mirror*, 16 August 1906)

The Times of Wednesday 25 November 1908 quotes with anxiety an editorial in the Paris newspaper *Le Temps*:

> For England to be sure of the morrow, for her to be qualified to become an ally, it is necessary and it is sufficient for her to equip herself with the army she does not now possess. It is necessary and it is sufficient that she should remember that that army, in comparison with other European armies, was better a century ago than it is today ...

These are merely random quotations from the press over a period of seven years, but they represent a constant undertone of insecurity: that Britain has been far too careless about itself and its security, and that trouble is building up both at home and abroad. The mood is a new one: the editorials of the last quarter of the nineteenth century, when the British Empire reached its zenith, were very different in tone. The Boer War had shown up big failings in the British military system. Germany and the United States had both overtaken Britain in terms of gross domestic product during the 1890s. Disturbing new threats were appearing, both at home and abroad. The gloom was often justified, as the next couple of decades were to show. But the perception of the world as a more dangerous place owed a good deal to 'the new journalism'. The press, appealing now to a much broader audience, played up the dangers: sometimes responsibly, sometimes not.

The term 'yellow press' was borrowed from America to describe the attention-grabbing, scandal-mongering, rabble-rousing, exaggerated, often misleading but always lively form of journalism pioneered by Joseph Pulitzer and William Randolph Hearst in America, and C. Arthur Pearson and Cecil Harmsworth in Britain. The phrase was coined by the New York Press, and came from a comic strip called 'The Yellow Kids', which appeared in both of the Press's down-market rivals, Hearst's *New York Journal* and Pulitzer's *New York World*. It managed to emphasize both the childishness of much of the popular press, and the fact that the newspapers which belonged to it often seemed like carbon copies of each other.

In the first decade of the twentieth century the *Mail*, the *Express* and the *Mirror* appealed to different levels of the same broad social grouping: conservative-minded members of the upper working class and the lower middle class, better educated than their parents and with greater social ambitions. Not surprisingly, therefore, the three papers competed in presenting very much the same news agenda. And high on that agenda was the perceived threat from immigrants.

The British tabloid press a hundred years later displays much the same agenda. Harmsworth's *Daily Mail* had shown the way, and a new, much livelier press emerged in the years immediately after the Boer War. Harmsworth himself founded the *Daily Mirror* in November 1903. 'I intend it,' he wrote in its first issue, 'to be really a mirror of feminine life as well on its grave as on its lighter sides . . . to be entertaining without being frivolous, and serious without being dull.'

But it had a hard time getting established. It gave up its emphasis on women's matters, and a year later it dropped the traditional, advertisement-covered, front page in favour of a big headline and a single large engraving, with photographs inside. A year later its circulation was close to half a million.

The *Daily Express* was already in existence, having been founded in 1900 by Arthur Pearson. It had pioneered the idea of printing the most important news on its front page. Its articles were eye-catching, often remarkably trivial, and seemingly obsessed with sudden death.

MURDER BY REQUEST
TWO SISTERS KILLED IN A TRAGIC MANNER

BEATEN TO DEATH
KILLS SEVEN NAVVIES IN A FEW MINUTES

MAD BULL HAMSTRUNG
KILLS ITS KEEPER AND INJURES FOUR OTHER PERSONS

A closer look at these sensational stories, which appeared on 22 March 1906, shows that the sisters were murdered in Germany, the murderous foreman was in New York, and the mad bull rampaged in Paris. The intention was to attract readers, not necessarily to keep them informed. (This, after all, was the newspaper which sent the explorer Hesketh Hesketh-Prichard to Patagonia at great expense in 1900 to investigate reports that a giant hairy mammal had been spotted there. The reports turned out to be wrong.)

But another front-page story in the *Express* that day was home grown, and altogether more serious.

OVERRUN BY ALIENS
FOREIGN AREA IN EAST LONDON STEADILY EXTENDING

BRITONS OUSTED

Although the Jews were certainly the most distinctive group of immigrants, the 1901 census indicates there were over 630,000 Irish immigrants in England, Scotland and Wales, many of whom faced ethnic and religious prejudices. The presence of Irish people in Britain had fomented anxieties about aliens on a much smaller scale as far back as the 1820s and 1830s.

The Jewish population of Britain rose from something like 60,000 in 1880 to something like 300,000 by 1900. These figures are inevitably vague, since census figures are unreliable in indicating ethnic groupings and religion, particularly with Jews; many Poles and Russians were assumed to be Jews, even if they were not. Colin Holmes, in *John Bull's Island: Immigration and British Society 1871–1971*, estimates that in 1875 the British Jewish community numbered 51,250. The 1901 census indicates that there were around 250,000 to 300,000 Jews in the UK, and over 100,000 of these had recently arrived from Eastern Europe.

Particular influxes were linked to savage waves of repression by the imperial Russian government, which also controlled Poland. These culminated in the pogroms of 1903–6, when an estimated 2,000 people were murdered. The British press scarcely reported the attacks. But the inevitable aftermath, a massive inflow of immigrants, attracted great attention in the newspapers, most of it deeply hostile. The press, and particularly the yellow press, was starting to create a national ideology defensive in character, feeding on and disseminating an obsession with race and fears about the decline of the racial stock. The pattern, much discussed in Britain then and in later decades, was that the best and most self-reliant Britons were emigrating to the white, English-speaking dominions, and to a lesser extent to the United States, and their places were being taken by people of physically and mentally inferior types; in this case, from Eastern Europe: the *Daily Express* of 25 November 1901 fulminated:

> Nobody has a word to say for the unrestricted admission of this rubbish, except a few amiable people who have no knowledge of the modern immigrant alien, and whose ideas upon the subject are based on vague recollections of respectable Huguenot refugees or exiled Italian patriots of the Garibaldian days . . .
>
> The East End of London and other crowded districts

are filled with people who naturally have no British patriotism, and who only feel contempt instead of gratitude towards the country that admits them. A vast proportion of the foreign immigrants to this country could never be of the slightest use to us. On the contrary, they have become an intolerable nuisance.

The Times of 28 January 1903 printed an article 'from our special correspondent' straying into open anti-Semitism:

It is the invasion of foreign Jews, because of their habit of congregating in the East-end of London, which attracts most attention. They are not, in many respects, a pleasant community. They have a way of squeezing Christians out of houses and districts in which they obtain a foothold; and there is some ground for complaint that the laws against overcrowding are not enforced against them. They are at the onset the victims of the 'sweater', and the more active among them become 'sweaters' in their turn.

Robert H. Sherard, writing in the *Daily Mirror* of 14 December 1903, explained how well British Jews had integrated into Britain, how clean they were, and how well they brought up their children. But – articles like these always contain a 'but' – the influx of foreign Jews was causing immense problems. He quotes 'an officer with twenty-five years' experience of the East End slums' as saying:

... [A]fter a period of life in this country, the alien develops into a good citizen. But his presence prevents our English children from developing. When he first lands in this country he brings nothing with him but vermin and vice. He has no cleanliness. He has no sense of morality ...

The *Express* was almost comically virulent, looking for every possible way of stirring up feeling against the immigrants. On 1 August 1903 it ran a set of front-page headlines that made startling reading:

NATION MADDER.
CAUSES OF INCREASING INSANITY.
MENACED BY ALIENS

> As a nation, we are growing madder and madder. This
> unfortunately is proved beyond a doubt by the appalling
> figures of the new annual report of the Lunacy Commis-
> sioners . . .
>
> Whereas in 1859 there was one insane person for
> every 536 sane, there is now one to every 293 . . .
>
> What is the cause? What is the remedy?

The *Express*, naturally, knows. It has consulted Dr Ernest W. White,
professor of psychological medicine at King's College London, who
thinks it is the result of immigration.

> With the increase of population the best kind of aliens
> have not been encouraged to settle in London, to inter-
> marry with our people, and to infuse new blood into the
> race. On the other hand, we have received unlimited
> numbers of the worst kind of aliens – needy town-
> dwellers, with poor bodies and poorer minds, sapped
> often by disease; of the criminal type, and in many cases
> with neurotic inheritances. If no stop is put to this, the
> stability of the race, mental as well as physical, will be
> undermined.

The editorial staff of the *Express* were clearly under instruction to get the
word 'Alien' on the front page as often as possible, in as alarming a
context as possible. Some examples:

English Expelled.
East-End Captured By Foreigners.
'Alien Insolence'

–12 December 1902

The Alien Peril
'World's Riff-Raff'

–13 January 1903

Alien Horde for Great Britain
80,000 Foreigners Ready To Land This Year

–5 April 1906

Alien Horde Coming
7,000 Outcasts To Be Imported From Germany

–16 May 1906

The *Daily Mail* carried a regular feature entitled 'Our Foreigners Day By Day', with sub-headings like 'Remarkable Facts About The Criminal Alien'. The *Mail* drew a connection between the immigrants and the rise in burglaries and attacks in London, though the link with the recent Jewish arrivals and crime was undercut by the fact that most of the criminals who were named in court had German surnames, rather than Polish or Russian Jewish ones.

The newspapers of 'the new journalism' competed with one another to put pressure on the government to come up with a bill to curb immigration; but ministers talked louder than they acted, and the Alien Immigration Bill of 1904 was mild enough. The criteria for allowing foreigners to enter were largely unchanged; if they could show that they had money to support themselves, and an address to go to, or that their lives were in danger in their homeland, they were usually allowed in. While the pogroms continued, therefore, so did the wave of immigration; as the *Daily Mirror* reported on 29 December 1904.

MORE ALIEN HORDES.
Fresh Army of Russian Jews Descending on England.
ORGANISED INVASION

It was usually the subeditors rather than the reporters who wrote about foreign immigrants, even though the East End was, as one newspaper pointed out, only fifteen minutes by hansom cab from Fleet Street. This was an issue on which the newspapers of 'the new journalism' chose to editorialize, rather than to seek out information which might prove to be inconvenient. A century later, the *Sun*, the *Mirror*, the *Daily Express* and the *Daily Mail* were doing exactly the same about the issues they felt strongly about; one of which, of course, was the immigration of foreigners (into the same areas of the East End, among others) who, they said, brought disease, crime, poverty and dangerous political and religious beliefs with them.

A front-page article in the *Daily Express* on 22 March 1906 ('Overrun by Aliens') describing how local people are being forced out by Jewish immigrants, contains many statements ('Among the British residents of the East End there is growing anger at what they consider their betrayal by the Government') but no quotations from these residents, no account of how their lives have changed, nothing in fact except a long interview given to 'an "Express" representative' with a member of the Immigration Board, which existed to limit immigration. The cross-heads separating the article into sections are even more inflammatory than the text: 'Strangled!' (though in fact it is the Immigration Act which is described as having been strangled) and 'No Room For Englishmen'.

> From Whitechapel to Bow Bridge, along Mile End Road – about a couple of miles – there is now scarcely an English shopkeeper left. Even the Jewish shopkeepers of old standing are being ruined by the newcomers, who get their clothes, boots and furniture made by their fellow workmen instead of going to the shops.

Yet on the few occasions when ordinary, non-polemical journalism was given its head, it was quite favourable to the immigrants. For the edition of 11 April 1904, for instance, the *Express* actually decided to send a reporter on the cab drive to the East End. Perhaps the news editor thought the reporter would uncover more evidence of hideous poverty and racial threat; but, when the article appeared, even the front-page headline indicated a milder approach.

ALIENS ON STRIKE.

JEWISH BAKERS' CRUSADE IN THE EAST END.

PICTURESQUE SCENES

And the scenes were picturesque indeed. A bevy of dark-eyed Jewish tailoresses, bearing banners inscribed with Hebrew characters; a red-coated band of Jews playing the 'Marseillaise'; a small banner covered with Russian letters; a long, fantastic crowd of short, pale aliens singing snatches of something to the air of the great French hymn in strong guttural staccato – these were the chief features of the strange and striking demonstrations.

The reporter for the *Express* did not trouble to find someone who could translate the Hebrew or Russian. One speaker addressed the audience in English. It was the novelty of the demonstration. Yet there was no account of what he said. Still, the reporter's interest was engaged, and the colour of the occasion drove out the desire to make a judgement:

> Hebrew patriarchs with white and flowing beards; precocious children; women in gaudy sky-blue and red; pretty faces, framed in high attic windows; squat men, suffering victims of European oppression, lounging in doorways or joining in the long procession – all added to the interest and force of the crusade.

'Crusade' might not have been the *mot juste*, but although the scene must have seemed deeply foreign to readers of the *Express*, it was not quite the dirt-riddled, diseased vision which the *Express*'s habitual reporting would have led them to expect. And the strikers' demands, a twelve-hour day with a minimum wage of one pound, six shillings a week and one day off in seven, were scarcely revolutionary. They were roughly similar to most industrial demands at the time.

A curiously hybrid article was published in the *Daily Mirror* on 10 December 1904, containing some first-hand reporting and at the same time a lot of contrasting material inserted by a subeditor who was following the newspaper's editorial line. The headlines were the usual ones:

ALIEN INVADERS.
Russian Reservists Swarm Into London
STRIKING FIGURES

Yet in complete contradiction to this, the reporter has stumbled on an interesting news story: the number of young Russian Jewish men coming to England to escape serving in the Tsar's army is actually dropping. The article starts like this:

> Russia-in-England is full to overflowing, but the rush of reservists from the country of the Tsar is diminishing.
>
> A long time was spent yesterday by The Daily Mirror among the refugees with a view to investigating the alien side of the question.
>
> For the most part they are able-bodied men who have run away from their homes to avoid service . . .
>
> There they were yesterday, crowding the sawdust-strewn floors of the Jewish shelter in Leman-street, vociferously stating their views of life in little groups of five or six, bursting into tears as they remembered their wives and families, then, as the sun went down and Sabbath approached, turning their faces to the wall and saying their prayers as good Jews should.
>
> The secretary of the shelter said that no questions were asked. If a deserving Jew, immigrant or transmigrant, knocked at the door he was admitted.
>
> The whole cost was borne, he continued, by the Jews, whose endeavour was to pass the people on to their destination.
>
> The reason, he declared, that they came through London was that it was the cheapest route. The Jews were as anxious they should not stay as the English. The cost was very heavy and they had enough to do to support and find work for their community already.
>
> The Russian rush would soon be over, and hundreds of those here sailed away two or three times a week, and everyone who came was booked through another country.

Having painted a radically different and much less excitable picture from the one the newspapers usually presented, the article then changes tack abruptly. A cross-head reading 'Figures Which Speak' follows, together with the words 'So much for the alien side of the question, but what is the other?'

The other is the argument, familiar from the normal editorial line of the press, that large numbers of immigrants are allowed in because they claimed to be in transit to another country, but in fact remained in Britain. And having given rational, inquiring journalism its head at the beginning of the article, the *Mirror* then subsides into the usual unsupported statements, without figures or quotes from anyone who might be an authority on the subject: 'In the boot-making, cabinet-making, and wholesale clothing trades the alien has reduced the rate of wages in the East End to a sum impossible for any but himself.'

This may well have been the case; it is, after all, a familiar pattern. But the *Mirror*, having at last found itself some interesting copy by sending a reporter to find out what was really going on, quickly retreats to the kind of journalism of assertion which it feels safer with. The other newspapers, bright and challenging though they claimed to be, scarcely troubled with eye-witness reporting of the immigration story at all. It got in the way of their editorial line.

§

The Alien Invasion had some positive attractions for the popular press, all the same. The cheap, sensational novels of Guy Boothby, William Le Queux, Max Pemberton and others had habituated British readers to the themes of anarchism, bombs in the street, romantic young women revolutionaries, and free love, all of which emanated from late nineteenth-century Russia. Now, it seemed, these things were appearing in London.

An editorial in the *Daily Mirror* of 5 January 1911 shows how the ethos of the sixpenny novel had seeped into journalism:

> ... [N]ot many years ago we remember, returning from a visit to an East End 'settlement', to have passed a certain very mean street with dark arches and glimmering greasy windows, and there to have seen a half-opened door through which divers bedraggled persons were passing, of

the sallow black-haired haggard type that affects soft hats
and carries pamphlets in portfolios or coat pockets. There
was a rather bored policeman at the door obviously on
duty; there was another policeman at the end of the street.
We asked the second policeman what was going on in the
hall, behind that door. 'Them's Anarchists,' he said curtly;
and that was all.

In the years before the Russian Revolution of 1917, the British press was
rarely much good at distinguishing the complex gradations of far left-
wing politics. Anarchists, nihilists, communists, socialists, and 'labourites'
(the word, with adapted spelling, is still in use a century later by American
journalists to describe supporters of the British Labour Party) were labels
used seemingly indiscriminately by the newspapers.

Anarchists or otherwise, the immigrants who came to late Victorian
and early Edwardian London brought their own crime and their own
feuds with them. In the East End the main gangs all came from the
Russian Empire: the Odessans, the Bessarabians, and the so-called
'Aldgate Mob', who were controlled by a Jewish gangster called, though
perhaps not to his face, 'Darkie the Coon'.

In 1911 Londoners lived in one of the safest cities in the world, but
they were easily worried. And the Conservative press, in particular, gave
them the feeling that they were being swamped by foreigners who
brought violent crime with them.

On 7 January 1911 the *Telegraph* printed a remarkable article which
purported to show that immigration had more than tripled in seven years:

The foreign population of London has grown from one of
41,000 in 1904 to an estimated total of 150,000 at the present
day, as shown by the following table:

Year	Aliens living in London
1904	41,000
1905	55,000
1906	60,250
1907	95,000
1908	136,000
1909 (estimated)	140,000
1910 (estimated)	150,000

These figures had been picked up in exactly the same form from the previous day's *Daily Mail*. On the day the *Telegraph* article came out, the *Express* also printed them – again, exactly as they had appeared in the *Mail*. It seems to have been part of a concerted campaign by some organization or individual.

By Monday, the liberal *Daily News* had had a chance to check the story. It found that the figures which the *Mail*, the *Telegraph* and the *Express* had all printed were entirely false. The year in which London had had an alien population of 41,000 was not 1904 but 1861; and the other figures related to previous decades too, so that there were 55,000 aliens in London in 1871, not 1905; 60,250 in 1881, not 1906; 95,000 in 1891, not 1907; and 136,000 in 1901, not 1908. In other words, the alien population of London had not risen from 41,000 to 136,000 in four years, but in forty years. None of the newspapers concerned printed a correction.

These articles appeared at a particularly significant moment, when the subject of aliens and crime was obsessing the nation. The week before, on 2 January 1911, according to an excited special correspondent of the *Telegraph*, 'a scene unparalleled in the history of English civilisation was witnessed in the very heart of one of the most congested parts of the East-end of London'. The headlines unfold the story graphically:

**BATTLE WITH ANARCHISTS IN THE
EAST END OF LONDON**

DESPERATE MURDERERS AT BAY

**SEVERAL HOURS' FIGHTING WITH THE
SCOTS GUARDS AND POLICE**

MAXIM AND FIELD GUNS READY FOR ACTION

HOUSE SET ON FIRE

ASSASSINS RESIST TO THE DEATH

KILLED IN THE BLAZING RUINS

SCENES OF THE FIGHT

BULLETS AND FLAMES

The siege of Sidney Street is one of the most memorable events of the years immediately before the First World War. A small group of criminals had carried out a botched burglary in nearby Houndsditch two days earlier, and had murdered three policemen in the process. The members of the gang were all immigrants from Latvia.

It has been plausibly suggested by Donald Rumbelow in his book *The Houndsditch Murders and the Siege of Sidney Street* that some members of the gang had been involved in planning the so-called 'Tottenham Outrage' of Saturday 23 January 1909, when two armed Latvian refugees from the East End had tried to snatch the wages for a rubber factory in Tottenham. They opened fire, and two people were killed and more than twenty injured. But the Latvians were caught after a six-mile chase by a group of unarmed policemen.

Then on 16 December 1910 another group of Latvians tried to rob a jeweller's shop in Houndsditch. The police tried to stop them, but one policeman was shot dead and two died of bullet-wounds in hospital. One of the gang, George Gardstein, was later found dead at a flat which had been occupied by two other Latvians, Peter Piatkow and Fritz Svaars. On 2 January 1911 the police had a tip-off that Svaars and other members of the gang were hiding at a house at 100 Sidney Street.

At dawn the following morning, 200 policemen cordoned off the area and the siege began. The people inside the house opened fire and seriously injured a policeman. Winston Churchill, whom we last saw as an inexperienced young journalist in South Africa, was now Home Secretary. He characteristically ordered in a detachment of Scots Guards from the Tower of London, and arrived himself in the early afternoon to direct the operation. Late that night the house caught fire. The next day two bodies were recovered. The press supposed them to be those of Fritz Svaars and Peter Piatkow, whom they had dubbed 'Peter the Painter'.

Inevitably, the story was written up in lurid yellow-press style. The *Mail*'s main story, which reads almost like a caricature, was by William Maxwell:

Never has London seen such a dramatic spectacle

There had, of course, been little matters such as the execution of Charles I, the Fire of London, the Gordon Riots of 1780 and the parade to mark Queen Victoria's Diamond Jubilee; but William Maxwell, in his excitement, his haste, and his desire to grab the reader's attention, has forgotten about those. It sounds as though he was still breathless when he dictated his account:

> A midnight investment by armed police: a raid followed by an active siege: Scots Guards in action: a Maxim and two guns ready for battle: bullet-swept streets: men wounded in an assault: a house blazing while firemen looked on: two charred bodies taken from the funeral pyre of criminals who for six hours had fought against desperate odds with the certainty of death before them.

The Times, inevitably, sounds less out of breath:

> A house in Stepney, to which the Houndsditch murderers had been traced, was surrounded yesterday by a large detachment of police and military. The criminals were fully armed and well supplied with ammunition. Shots were exchanged for nearly seven hours until the building caught fire and the men within either shot themselves or were burnt to death.

Yet not even *The Times* could escape the 'never before . . .' contagion.

> The scene when the Home Secretary arrived was possibly the most curious that has ever been witnessed in London. Cordons of police kept dense crowds away from the approaches to Sidney-street. Sidney-street itself was bare for the whole length of the front of Martin's-buildings. At the Mile-end-road end a detachment of Scots Guards, with their rifles at 'the ready', and several policemen armed with sporting shot guns were lined up, while at the head of Lindley-street stood a medley of 'plain-clothes men', some looking like respectable clerks, others disguised as wharf hands . . .
>
> At intervals the sharp cracks of the service rifles were punctuated by the savage snaps of the automatic pistols that returned the fire, and it was possible to see the dust of

> the striking bullets as they chipped the masonry of the
> windows behind which the police and soldiers were
> ensconced.

The reader is reminded that, like the great majority of London's citizens, most British reporters had never heard a shot fired in anger before. Not so Winston Churchill, who was still only thirty-six. The thought excited even *The Times*.

> It is some time since the Home Secretary was under fire,
> but his old military capacity had not deserted him. He was
> full of resourceful suggestion. His first idea was that metal
> shields should be improvised to enable the police to
> approach the building. Then the astounding suggestion was
> made that a cannon should be brought to blow in the front
> of the building. Just think of it! A field-gun in action in a
> London street!

Not to mention the use of exclamation marks twice in two lines in *The Times*.

It was left to the *Manchester Guardian*, separated both politically and geographically from most of the London press, to inject a little calm and reflection. There is, the *Guardian* says, no evidence whatever for newspaper claims that the gang was plotting against foreign diplomats or preparing to stage an attack at the time of the coming coronation of George V. And it poured cold water on some other absurdities:

> In yesterday's 'Daily Telegraph' and 'Daily Mail' great
> prominence was given to the discovery of bombs in the
> Sidney-street ruins. They are described in the 'Telegraph'
> as five cylinders, made of gunmetal, on each of which was
> a projection which 'it may be assumed was intended for the
> percussion cap which was to ignite the explosives on
> impact'.

The truth, according to the *Guardian*, was rather less exciting. The cylinders were used for stamping cheap metal buttons – the trade of one of the respectable lodgers at 100 Sidney Street.

Finally, the *Guardian* warns of the dangers of lynch-mob journalism.

> The assumption that dangerous criminal tendencies exist among the poorer foreign Jews in London is unwarranted by anything in the Houndsditch affair, for neither of the two dead men were Jewish either by race or faith, and in any case, as the Chief Rabbi observed on Saturday, Anarchism and lawlessness are opposed to the letter and spirit of Judaism.

A hundred years later, the *Guardian* would find itself using very similar terms to warn against the assumption that there was a natural link between Islam and terrorism.

The reporting of the Siege of Sidney Street did not show the British press in an attractive light. If some of the reporting bordered on the hysterical, it was because these things – armed gangs of foreign desperadoes, shoot-outs with the police, artillery in the streets – were unprecedented. With the basis of normal, everyday existence disrupted, the earlier calm of Edwardian Britain crumbled quickly. Change was happening all round. There was rebellion in the House of Lords. Women were behaving with previously unthinkable militancy in demanding the vote. Unionists in Northern Ireland were starting to threaten treason. There were strikes in industries which had always been quiescent. Hyperbole and excitability were starting to seem perfectly normal. After almost a century when Britain was at peace with its neighbours, the outside world was starting to look distinctly threatening.

This national mood was guided, rather than followed, by the yellow press. The new journalism reported in racy and excitable ways on militant actions by women or by Irish nationalists, and greatly magnified the result. Breaking windows, chaining themselves to railings or setting off bombs attracted the kind of attention they would never have received before the arrival of newspapers like the *Daily Mail* and the *Daily Mirror* on the scene. Now, gesture politics became instantly valuable, in a way they were not before 1897. What people read, they thought; and what they thought, they soon spoke out loud. It was a form of contagion. If *The Times* could catch it from the yellow press, then soon the politicians would catch it themselves.

4

ALL-HIGHEST

In the House of Lords on 10 July 1905, Field Marshal Lord Roberts, frail, elderly and hunched, rose from the red leather benches on the government side, and in a reedy voice read out a speech full of warning. Having won the Boer War six years earlier, after taking over when defeat seemed a real possibility, he believed that Britain was once again thoroughly unprepared to meet its military commitments. He was sure it would soon be necessary to fight again. 'The lessons of the late war appear to have been completely forgotten,' he intoned. 'I sometimes despair of the country ever becoming alive to the danger of the unpreparedness of our present position until too late to prevent some fatal catastrophe.'

A few months later, the journalist and thriller writer William Le Queux put the finishing touches to a book for which Lord Roberts had written an introduction. Le Queux, unlike Roberts, was very full of himself, and boasted a good deal about the quality of his inside information. He called his autobiography, published in 1923, *Things I Know*. In it he says, 'I think I can claim to be the first person to warn Great Britain that the Kaiser was plotting a war against us.'

His thrillers were slapdash and usually rather empty, though they were very popular; Gladstone and Queen Alexandra, both rather serious-minded people, were fans of his. In 1903 he wrote a good series of linked short stories, published as *Secrets of the Foreign Office*. The hero is a spy called Duckworth Drew, who travels around Europe as the 'chief confidential agent of the British government'. Most of the stories contain plots against Britain by the French, German and Russian governments.

Le Queux believed that neither the outgoing Conservative government of Arthur Balfour nor the incoming Liberal government of Sir Henry Campbell-Bannerman, which took power in an electoral landslide in 1906, were spending enough on defence. Europe had become a dangerous place, Le Queux argued, and Britain needed a strong army as well as a strong navy. Eight years later, he and Lord Roberts were vindicated.

Le Queux's 1906 book with an introduction by Roberts was called *The Invasion of 1910: With a Full Account of the Siege of London*. It was impressive-looking, and its red cover was stamped with the imperial German eagle to show who, precisely, was going to do the invading. This was necessary, because twelve years earlier Le Queux had written another book called *The Great War in England in 1897*, also with an approving note by Lord Roberts, only then it was the French and the Russians who were the invaders. They, like the Germans in *The Invasion of 1910*, were eventually beaten in Le Queux's book, but in both cases it was a very close-run thing, and Britain's lack of military preparedness was responsible for the original weakness.

Characteristically, Le Queux showed no signs of embarrassment at having selected different enemies a decade earlier. In 1894, when he wrote his previous invasion book, France and its ally Russia seemed much more likely to wage war on Britain than Germany. But Germany's industrial and military growth since then, and its emperor's obsessive envy of Britain, ensured that by 1906 it constituted a perfectly credible threat. Two years earlier, in April 1904, Britain and France had signed the Entente Cordiale, an understanding directed at the threat which both countries felt Germany posed.

Alfred Harmsworth, the *Daily Mail*'s founder, was another big supporter of Le Queux. They shared a delight in motoring, and Harmsworth invited him on many of his early expeditions by car ('I was one of the first to make the trip by road across France to Monte Carlo,' Le Queux writes). They were very different men, but both had an impatience with the quiet self-satisfaction of Edwardian England, and both were inclined to jingoism. And so, on 16 March 1906, a half-page advertisement appeared in the *Mail*:

THE INVASION OF 1910

WITH A FULL ACCOUNT OF THE SIEGE OF LONDON

WHAT LORD ROBERTS SAYS TO YOU:

Speaking in the House of Lords on the 10th July, 1905, I said:
'It is to the people of the country I appeal to take up the question of the Army in sensible, practical manner. For the

sake of all they hold dear, let them bring home to themselves what would be the condition of Great Britain if it
were to lose its wealth, its power, its position.'

The catastrophe that may happen if we still remain in
our present state of unpreparedness is vividly and forcibly
illustrated in Mr. Le Queux's new book, which I recommend
to the perusal of everyone who has the welfare of the
British Empire at heart.   – ROBERTS, F.M.

Beneath this is a map of Britain, reproduced from the book, which shows
the scene of two big sea-battles off the north-east coast, the fictional
advance of German troops from their landing-zones in Essex, Norfolk
and Yorkshire, the fighting around London, and the words underneath,
which must have seemed quite shocking to the peaceable readers of the
Mail that morning,

INVESTED, BOMBARDED & SACKED.

'Keep this Map for Reference', advises the *Mail*; 'It will be Valuable'. It
was an example of clever public relations. Le Queux had worked out the
routes the Germans would be most likely to take when invading Britain;
the *Mail*, which was much less interested in verisimilitude than in making
money, changed the line of the German advance to take in towns and
cities where the *Mail* already had a high readership, in order to increase
its sales. Le Queux didn't mind: it was a work of fiction anyway, and this
would simply ensure it was a more profitable work of fiction.

The text of the advertisement continues:

This Intensely Interesting Narrative by Mr. Wm. Le Queux begins in the LONDON 'DAILY MAIL' To-Morrow.

Order the 'Daily Mail' TO-DAY.
Order the 'Daily Mail' TO-DAY.

The attention the *Mail* gave to the book was a distinct embarrassment to
the new Liberal government. Sir Henry Campbell-Bannerman and his
ministers were less enthusiastic about spending money on defence even
than the Conservatives had been. Lloyd George and other radical Liberals

(now including Winston Churchill who in 1904 had crossed the floor of the House of Commons and had become Lloyd George's ally and personal friend) were planning measures such as the introduction of pensions for the poor and elderly. The previous government had negotiated the new treaty with France two years earlier to counter the threat from Germany, but the Foreign Office believed it was a bad idea to stir up the unpredictable German emperor unnecessarily.

The following Wednesday, 14 March, the *Mail*, in its campaign to promote Le Queux and his book, printed a front-page report on the previous day's questions to the prime minister at the House of Commons. It was nothing more than a straightforward puff for both the book and the newspaper, and scarcely reads like a news item at all:

THE INVASION OF 1910

MR. LE QUEUX'S NEW NOVEL IN THE 'DAILY MAIL'

QUESTION IN PARLIAMENT

Literary circles were a good deal surprised yesterday by the asking of a question with regard to a new novel in the House of Commons, and at the reply of the Prime Minister, Sir Henry Campbell-Bannerman. The question and answer are reported by our Parliamentary correspondent as follows:

The widespread interest with which the publication of the 'Daily Mail's' great war story – which commences today – has been anticipated was illustrated by a question put to the Prime Minister in the House of Commons yesterday by Mr Rudolph C. Lehmann.

'I beg to ask the First Lord of the Treasury,' he said, 'a question of which I have given him private notice – viz., whether his attention has been called to an advertisement appearing in the morning papers entitled "The Invasion of 1910", and whether the Government can take any step or express any opinion which would discourage the publication of matter of this sort, calculated to prejudice our relations with other Powers.'

Ministerialists [supporters of the Government] raised a cheer, and a few Unionists [i.e. the opposition Conservatives] laughed derisively.

'I was greatly surprised,' replied Sir Henry Campbell-Bannerman, 'to see the publication to which my hon. friend referred, appearing in some newspapers of which but a few years ago which we were all proud. I do not know what step the Government will take. I am afraid they can do nothing; but we can safely leave it, I think, to be judged by the good sense and good taste of the British people.'

And then – because a hundred years ago, as now, to make any kind of public attack on a yellow-press newspaper risked being treated as an enemy and held up to ridicule – the *Mail* added a gratuitous little paragraph: 'Mr Rudolph C. Lehmann, who put this interrogatory, is a humorist. He has written much for "Punch", and for a brief period edited "The Daily News". His contributions to permanent literature include the "Adventures of Picklock Holes".'

William Le Queux enjoyed the attention, and the *Mail*, which had a vested interest in the success of his book, ensured that he got as much of it as possible. Immediately underneath this front-page news item was another, couched in ingratiating terms. Again, the yellow press behaved very much as the tabloid press would behave a century later: any friend of the proprietor's could expect an easy ride.

THE PRIME MINISTER AND THE NEW NOVEL
THE AUTHOR INTERVIEWED

If the public in general were surprised [by the Commons exchange], the author himself, Mr. William Le Queux, was astounded. 'The attention,' he observed, at his charming flat at Queen Anne's-gate, 'drawn to my new book is, I am bound to say, not unpleasing, but I am a little surprised that the Prime Minister should have given utterance to an unfair and unjust criticism of it, before he has read it. He is not, I believe, the only critic who deals with us novelists in that way.

'I am afraid I do not know exactly on what grounds he bases his objection to my work . . . If it is to be on the score that a novel can arouse international feeling, I can only say that my works are at least as popular in Germany as in this country . . . I am not the least afraid that my German readers – who number some millions – will be foolish enough to get angry about my work . . .'

Seventeen years later, in his autobiography, Le Queux gave a rather more exaggerated version of the exchange in the House of Commons. He claims that Campbell-Bannerman, 'denouncing me as a mere scare-monger, declared that such work was pernicious literature, "calculated to inflame public opinion abroad and alarm the more ignorant public at home"'.

The next day, he wrote, the prime minister wrote him a personal letter apologizing for what he had said in the Commons. It is a notable feature of *Things I Know* that all sorts of famous people attack Le Queux, then realize that they are wrong and he is right, and write to say they are sorry; though the letters never seem to survive. Campbell-Bannerman, who was long dead, was unlikely to challenge his version of events.

The Invasion of 1910, and Le Queux's earlier story of invasion, were by no means the first predictive books of their kind. As far back as 1871, immediately after the sweeping victory of the Prussians in France, George Chesney had written a book called *The Battle of Dorking*, about the ease with which the Prussians could invade Britain next. In 1893 a varied group of authors, including a rear admiral, a colonel and the war correspondent Archibald Forbes, collaborated on a book called *The Great War of 189-*, which forecast a British war with Germany, and included a German advance on Paris not unlike the one that happened twenty-one years later. And in 1903 Erskine Childers published his excellent and highly successful novel *The Riddle of the Sands*, which dealt with German preparations for war against Britain and the efforts of a couple of amateur sailors to thwart the agents who were planning for a coming invasion.

The enthusiastic backing of the *Daily Mail* took *The Invasion of 1910* out of the realm of ordinary publishing, and placed it firmly on the public agenda: 'Everyone congratulated me on it. At the Savage Club, at the Devonshire, at Boodles, at the Reform, at the houses I visited, I was hailed as the man-who-dared-to-tell-the-truth.'

But the truth about what? By this stage, few people in Britain could have failed to realize that if their country fought a war, it would be with the Germans. Le Queux had no revelations to make there.

Germany's huge scheme to build up its navy in competition with Britain's had worried the government and the newspapers since the start of the decade. Back in 1901 the *Daily Mail* had aggressively supported the campaign by Lord Charles Beresford to improve the British Mediterranean fleet, and soon it and its Harmsworth stablemate the *Mirror* were clamouring for a build-up of the Royal Navy generally.

At the time when Le Queux's book was serialized in the *Mail*, though, the military correspondent of *The Times*, Charles à Court Repington, was arguing strongly in his column that too strong a concentration on naval power was a bad idea. It gave people the feeling that Britain was immune from invasion, he argued, and made them reluctant to bolster the army. The *Mail*, by promoting Le Queux's book, now found itself campaigning for a bigger army, too. As long as their readers supported them by buying the newspapers, the Harmsworth group's editors didn't worry about the accusation that they were inconsistent.

Much of Le Queux's book was designed to show how weak the British army was; which was why Lord Roberts and many others gave him their support. Its intention was to act as a wake-up call to the British people, and to a certain degree it was successful – especially since it had the effect of combining with other, less publicized campaigns and merging them into one. But as the author of an improbably large number of spy novels, Le Queux had another concern: he believed that German spies were in place all over the country, and were working for the moment when Germany would attack Britain. His autobiography *Things I Know* was much more outspoken about this alleged threat than he had been at the time.

> I discovered, as far back as 1905, a great network of German espionage spread over the United Kingdom. I found out the secret through a friend in Berlin, who was at the time under-director of the Kaiser's Spy Bureau, and who had married an Englishwoman who was believed by all, except her husband, to be German. As is usual in Germany, his master [the Kaiser] did not exactly 'play the game' with him, and, therefore, in 1905, he told me frankly what was in progress.

I came back from Germany and endeavoured to awaken public
opinion concerning the peril, but my voice was, alas! that of one
crying in the wilderness. Spies! What on earth did Germany want
to spy on us for? Were we not good friends with Germany? . . . Did
not the great War Lord in his golden helmet come to Buckingham
Palace . . . ?

William Le Queux claims that this highly placed source of his gave him
the transcript of a speech by the Kaiser, made at a secret conference in
Potsdam in 1905. According to this, the Kaiser told his audience – top
government figures, generals, admirals and so forth – that he intended
to attack Britain. He reminded them of something Field Marshal Blücher
had supposedly said a century earlier, when he looked out at London
from the dome of St Paul's Cathedral: 'What a splendid city to sack!'

He went on to tell the assembled politicians and generals of the need
to find a just cause for starting a war with Britain.

'My army of spies scattered over Great Britain and France, as it is
over North and South America, as well as all the other parts of the
world where German interests may come to a clash with a foreign
power, will take good care of that . . . I have issued already, some
time since, secret orders that will, at the proper moment, accom-
plish what we desire!'

In spite of Le Queux's willingness to embroider the truth, it is not
absolutely out of the question that this transcript, or at least some part of
it, was genuine. The Kaiser often ranted excitably about the threat to
Germany, its encirclement by Britain, France and Russia, and the
inevitability – even the desirability – of war; and in the end, of course, his
theories were put into practice. The transcript convinced Le Queux, but
he found it impossible to persuade any newspaper editors or politicians
to take it seriously. The irony is, of course, that the self-obsessed, rather
ludicrous spy novelist turned out to be more correct in some respects
about the Kaiser's intentions than the better-informed, moderate
establishment he tried to convince.

Yet there is no serious evidence that Germany had planted large
numbers of spies in Britain, of the quiet, humble kind Le Queux
imagined. For the most part, the spying which took place was done in the

traditional way, by army and navy officers attached in one form or another to official institutions – chief of which was of course the imperial German embassy in London. No doubt they received information from time to time from German citizens living legally in Britain, but efforts by Le Queux and the yellow press to whip up feeling against ordinary Germans were mostly unsuccessful. Rightly, British people tended to assume that the Germans were pretty much like themselves, and would not want a war. But they tended to forget that it would be what Kaiser Wilhelm and his advisers wanted that mattered, and not ordinary Germans.

§

Kaiser Wilhelm II was an odd man, awkward, fiercely impatient and unstable, subject to childish outbursts. He was physically damaged by the after-effects of a badly conducted breech birth which left his arm withered. Emotionally, he was damaged by his relationship with his parents, who were cold and distant. There was insanity on his father's side, and it is not impossible that it affected him. He could be absurdly vain, and loved parading in the immense variety of uniforms which he created for himself. To this day, German cameramen use the expression 'Kaiserfilming' to mean going through the motions of filming someone without actually bothering to switch the camera on. The story goes that cameramen whose job was to film the Kaiser knew their editors would never use all the material he wanted them to gather of him, so after a while they simply pretended to be filming him.

Wilhelm was only twenty-nine when he came to the throne in 1888, and he showed signs of a liberal temperament. This brought him into conflict with the chancellor he had inherited, Count Otto von Bismarck, who actively wanted to crush socialism and trade union activism. The Kaiser forced Bismarck to resign over this issue in 1890.

Towards the British, Wilhelm's attitude was complex and often deeply irrational. On one level he adored Britain. He dressed like an English country gentleman, he used English shaving products and English lotions, he decorated his private yacht with pictures of great British naval victories, and there were few things he enjoyed more than a nice cup of tea. He loved his grandmother Queen Victoria, though she found him deeply irritating, and when she was on her deathbed he kept watch beside her. In her last moments he elbowed his way through the others and she died in his arms. Whether she would have chosen to do this is unclear.

Yet he never understood Britain or the British; especially not the essential thread of moderation which ran through its social and political life, and made it what it was. Nor could he rid himself of the suspicion that Britain's unflappable politicians, together with his elderly, lazy, pleasure-loving, openly Francophile uncle, Edward VII, were planning Germany's downfall by weaving a hostile alliance around her.

In 1900 he appointed a new chancellor, Bernhard von Bülow. Von Bülow was more inclined than his predecessors to let the Kaiser have his head in foreign affairs, while he himself dealt with domestic policy.

This suited Wilhelm: he increasingly preferred foreign affairs, about which he had strong and often ill-founded views. Since he was related to most of the monarchs of Europe, he believed that personal diplomacy among his cousins was what counted, forgetting that Britain and France, as well as others, were democracies. It was this network of relationships which gave German diplomacy before the First World War its curious soap-opera feel: for the Kaiser and the Tsar, and to a lesser extent for Queen Victoria, Edward VII and George V, the politics of Europe were all in the family.

The Kaiser's worst and most dangerous habit was making policy without forethought, theorizing without practical evidence, thinking the inappropriate out loud. He sometimes used the silliest and most irresponsible language: in July 1900, for instance, he told his troops as they were about to leave for China where the German ambassador had been killed in the Boxer Rebellion:

> Just as the Huns under their king, Etzel, created for themselves a thousand years ago a name which men still respect, you should give the name of German similar cause to be remembered in China for a thousand years . . .

This was a gift to his enemies, and fourteen years later, when the First World War broke out, Allied propaganda made full use of his concept of the Germans as 'Huns'.

Earlier, in January 1896, the Kaiser had enraged British public opinion by sending a telegram of congratulation to President Kruger of the Transvaal for having captured the 600 irregulars involved in the Jameson Raid:

> I express to you my sincere congratulations that you and your people, without appealing to the help of friendly powers, have succeeded, by your own energetic action against the armed bands which invaded your country as disturbers of the peace, in restoring peace and in maintaining the independence of the country against attack from without.

This might seem like a reasonable description of the Jameson Raid; but at the time the Raid's failure was greeted in Britain as a serious blow to national pride, and it was a mistake to taunt the British over it. It was perhaps even more foolish to hint that Germany was one of the 'friendly powers' to which Kruger could apply for help. The telegram achieved nothing of value; instead, it did great harm to Germany's relations with Britain.

By 1908, goaded by the years of attacks by the *Mail*, the *Express* and the *Mirror* on Germany's ambitions, and on himself, the Kaiser's ability to get himself into trouble created yet another serious crisis. That October the staid, unadventurous *Daily Telegraph* achieved a scoop of major international importance: an interview with Wilhelm II, in which he said a variety of unwise and incautious things. The interview was another step down the path which led to the First World War.

The *Daily Telegraph*, like all the serious newspapers of the time in Britain, still published advertisements on its front page. The main news of the day appeared inside, opposite the editorial page. In the edition of 28 October 1908 the Kaiser's interview was carried relatively prominently, but in two single columns at the top of the page.

Alongside it is an article about the heavy sales of Queen Alexandra's Christmas Gift Book; other articles around it are headlined 'Unrest in Constantinople', 'Missing Nurse Found', and 'Ladies Before The Lords', which describes how two women graduates of Edinburgh University will shortly argue before the House of Lords (an 'unusual spectacle') that they should be allowed to vote in the election for the University's Member of Parliament.

The presentation of the Kaiser's interview is odd and distinctly clumsy. No effort is made to show its peculiar significance. The conventional manner of displaying the news in the mainstream press did not lend itself to any form of sensationalism, so the reader has to work through the text for some way before understanding what the article is about. The only hint of its true importance is the number of headlines – four, instead of the three devoted to Queen Alexandra's book. The *Mail* would have presented it very differently. Nevertheless, it was one of the greatest journalistic coups of the twentieth century.

THE GERMAN EMPEROR AND ENGLAND.

PERSONAL INTERVIEW.
FRANK STATEMENT OF WORLD POLICY.
PROOFS OF FRIENDSHIP

The article starts with a brief word about the origins of the interview, without explaining for several paragraphs what it was actually about.

> We have received the following communication from a source of such unimpeachable authority that we can without hesitation commend the obvious message which it conveys to the attention of the public.

Then, without even a different format or type-face to introduce a change of voice, we are pitched into a series of comments by the writer, whose name or status we are never given. It is, altogether, a clumsy effort; almost as if the *Telegraph* were embarrassed at having to run it:

> Discretion is the first and last quality requisite in a diplomatist, and should still be observed by those who, like myself, have long passed from public into private life. Yet moments sometimes occur in the history of nations when a calculated indiscretion proves of the highest public service, and it is for that reason that I have decided to make known the substance of a lengthy conversation which it was my recent privilege to have with his Majesty the German Emperor.

> I do so in the hope that it may help to remove that obstinate misconception of the character of the Kaiser's feelings towards England which, I fear, is deeply rooted in the ordinary Englishman's breast. It is the Emperor's dearest wish that it should be eradicated.

Yet the passage that follows next was destined to ensure that nothing of the sort would happen.

> As I have said, his Majesty honoured me with a long conversation, and spoke with impulsive and unusual frankness. 'You English,' he said, 'are mad, mad, mad as March hares. What has come over you that you are so completely given over to suspicions quite unworthy of a great nation? What more can I do than I have done?
>
> '. . . [I]t is one of my dearest wishes to live on the best of terms with England. Have I ever been false to my word? Falsehood and prevarication are alien to my nature. My actions ought to speak for themselves, but you listen not to them but to those who misinterpret and distort them. That is a personal insult which I feel and resent. To be forever misjudged, to have my repeated offers of friendship weighed and scrutinised with jealous, mistrustful eyes, taxes my patience severely.'

If the aim was to establish a new relationship with Britain, the tone was all wrong; and it quickly became even worse.

> . . . 'The prevailing sentiment among large sections of the middle and lower classes of my own people is not friendly to England. I am, therefore so to speak, in a minority in my own land, but it is a minority of the best elements as it is in England with respect to Germany.
>
> 'That is another reason why I resent your refusal to accept my pledged word that I am the friend of England. I strive without ceasing to improve relations, and you retort that I am your arch-enemy. You make it hard for me. Why is it?. . .'

Then the interview, which was really more of a collection of remembered monologues, went on to infuriate France and Russia, which had previously been Britain's enemies, as William Le Queux had envisaged back in 1894, but were now her allies.

> [W]hen the struggle [the Boer War] was at its height, the German government was invited by the governments of France and Russia to join with them in calling upon England to put an end to the war. The moment had come, they said, not only to save the Boer Republics, but also to humiliate England to the dust. The Kaiser says he refused this by now embarrassing proposal. More than that, he claims that at the time of Black Week, in December 1899, Queen Victoria wrote to him in sorrowful terms about it. He wrote back in sympathetic terms, he said.
>
> 'Nay, I did more. I bade one of my officers procure for me as exact an account as he could obtain of the number of combatants in South Africa on both sides and of the actual position of the opposing forces. With the figures before me, I worked out what I considered the best plan of campaign under the circumstances, and submitted it to my General Staff for their criticism. Then, I dispatched it to England.'

His plan, he says, turned out to be very similar to the one Lord Roberts drew up.

> Was that, I repeat, an act of one who wished England ill ?

The tone of all this is somehow familiar, yet it takes the modern reader a little time to recall why. It is very much the way in which hostile dictators have tended to address us in our own time: Ahmadinejad of Iran, Saddam Hussein of Iraq, Colonel Gaddafi of Libya, Robert Mugabe of Zimbabwe, and, further back in time, Idi Amin of Uganda: the half-mocking, half-complaining, self-obsessed tone of a man who has felt himself belittled and now believes he can hit back without any sense of restraint.

> But, you will say, what of the German navy? Surely, that is a menace to England! Against whom but England are my

squadrons being prepared? If England is not in the minds of those Germans who are bent on creating a powerful fleet, why is Germany asked to consent to such new and heavy burdens of taxation?

My answer is clear. Germany is a young and growing empire. She has a worldwide commerce which is rapidly expanding . . . Germany must have a powerful fleet to protect that commerce and her manifold interests in even the most distant seas . . .

She must be prepared for any eventualities in the Far East. Who can foresee what may take place in the Pacific in the days to come . . . ?

Look at the rise of Japan; think of the possible national awakening of China . . .

So that was it. The real target for Germany's fleet wasn't Britain after all: it was Japan. Having angered the British, the French and the Russians, the Kaiser gratuitously chose to threaten a fourth power. The whole thing was disturbingly maladroit for the leader of a great power who liked to do his own diplomacy. It reads like the work of an adolescent. Perhaps there was indeed a touch of insanity about the imperial warlord. At first the British press wondered whether it could possibly be genuine. The *Express* wrote:

> The now famous interview with the Kaiser was so bewildering that it was generally accepted that a prompt denial would come from Berlin. No disavowal has, however, been issued, and it must therefore be assumed that the Kaiser has been correctly reported . . .

The first reaction in Germany was also one of disbelief, according to the *Telegraph*'s man in Berlin on Thursday 29 October.

> So far the papers, always more reserved in their judgements than their British counterparts, have not yet expressed more of an opinion on the monarch's remarks than a few exclamatory or unbelieving sentences at the close of their despatches. Some of these . . . are both

interesting and instructive. For instance, the naval chauvinistic *Berliner Neueste Nachrichten* says: 'We have reproduced this announcement because the *Daily Telegraph* is one of the most serious of the English papers. We are compelled, however, from every conceivable point of view to pronounce the conversation not so much a misunderstanding as an invention.'

The German press was inclined to be ponderous, taking significantly longer to digest the news than the press in the rest of the Western world; it is that way still. It took two days before the German newspapers reacted in earnest. Then, the *Telegraph* correspondent reported, the interview 'has acted here like an explosion'. The right-wing newspapers, usually deeply hostile to Britain, were incensed. According to the correspondent, 'What seems to cause them most annoyance is the thought that the Emperor should have prepared a campaign to be used against the Boers.' The correspondent quotes the Kaiser's favourite newspaper, the *Tägliche Rundschau*, as saying:

Seldom, indeed, has a pronouncement of the German Emperor been received by the German people with more mixed feelings, with more disquietude, and dismay, than the message to the English people . . .

If the announcement should be confirmed, then we must confess that we not only no longer understand our Emperor, but that we most deeply condemn and regret his manner of action.

Such things were not written lightly by the German press. The emperor hated criticism, and had the legal power to imprison journalists who insulted him; though it was usually cartoonists who suffered. The *Daily Express* correspondent in Berlin, perhaps under pressure from his news desk to produce something exclusive himself, announced portentously on Friday 30 October: 'I am in a position to state that the Kaiser's feelings are deeply hurt, and that he is keenly disappointed by the unfavourable reception of his protestation of warm friendship for the British people.' No one else, British or German, managed to get any reaction from the imperial court. Maybe the *Express* man had a friendly source close to the emperor who could tell him this sort of thing with authority; but given the emperor's dislike of the British newspapers, and the lowly status of the *Express*, that seems unlikely. Nowadays when tabloid newspapers talk about the feelings of the great, it often comes under the heading of what is sometimes called in the business a 'stands to reason' story: as though the journalist is saying 'Well, that's what they would think, isn't it?'

Perhaps the *Express* correspondent in St Petersburg was using the same technique when he wrote his despatch for the paper. In this case, though, there is no doubt that he was justified: 'The Kaiser's conversation published in London is attributed in St. Petersburg to his imperious temperament. As a piece of statesmanship it has provoked amusement in official circles.'

In France the interview was described as 'the confessions of the Emperor'. But according to the *Daily Mirror* there was immense embarrassment in Paris about the Kaiser's revelation during the Boer War of the plot to humiliate France's new best friend, Britain.

> The whole of the French Press denies with great heat the statement made by the Emperor that but for him Russia and France, helped by Germany, would have interfered and 'humbled England to the dust' during the anxious days of the Boer War . . .
>
> To this France declares that Germany twice proposed to intervene, but that the conditions were such as to make it impossible for France to accept the proposal.

France, the *Mirror* man went on, was astounded at the disclosures. But, he added shrewdly,

> one fact emerges, clear and uncontradicted. There was actually a proposal that the three Powers should combine to take Britain at a disadvantage, and 'humiliate' her . . . [I]n all French comments on the disclosures there is no denial that such a scheme of intervention was proposed and fell through.

By the weekend, even the German newspapers had had enough time to make an editorial judgement on the previous Wednesday's thunderbolt. The leader in the *Tägliche Rundschau* was headed 'Catastrophe'. In words neither it nor any other German newspaper had dared to use about the Kaiser's actions before, it announced bleakly:

> It is difficult to find words in the presence of this proof of our art of governing, which cannot be matched even in our days of decadence . . . [T]he Emperor, in his impulsive way, appears to rule the field of our foreign policy alone, and . . . constitutionally responsible persons are degraded to be the chorus which has to follow and shield and palliate him and disentangle the twisted threads.

Predictably, there were soon accusations that the whole thing had been deliberately engineered by the British to cause trouble. Forgetting that the *Daily Telegraph* was the only remotely pro-German newspaper in Britain, *Germania*, the leading voice of the political centre, fell into the familiar trap of assuming that the whole thing was a political manoeuvre: 'The real object of the *Daily Telegraph* is to set Russia, France and Japan against Germany.' *Tageblatt* agreed:

> The unnamed diplomatist who publishes the Emperor's words pretends to be our friend, but the subtlest enemy of Germany and the German Emperor could not have conceived any more effective plan of inflicting injury.

By this time, the chancellor, Prince Bernhard von Bülow, offered his resignation, with effect from Saturday 31 October. The Kaiser refused to accept it.

In Britain, the hunt for the identity of the Kaiser's anonymous interviewer was on. The *Daily Mirror* wrote on Friday 30 October, 'Official circles deprecate the random guessing at the identity of the Daily Telegraph's informant, but it is stated that neither Sir Frank Lascelles, Sir Horace Rumbold, nor Lord Weardale were concerned. Three days later, on Monday 2 November, the *Mirror* is still playing the same game.

> The authorship of the interview, as printed in the Daily Telegraph last Wednesday, has been attributed to Mr Sidney Whitman, a well-known writer on German affairs and author of 'Imperial Germany', but The Daily Mirror is informed that he absolutely denies the responsibility.

Gradually, over the next few days and weeks, the story emerged of how the interview was conducted, and why it slipped through the official system in Berlin. It proved to be very different from the speculation of the press in both Britain and Germany. The origins of the affair dated back to the end of the previous year. In December 1907, Wilhelm II had paid an official visit to Britain, and had been given the usual hostile reception by the British press. Afterwards he had stayed on for a fortnight as a private guest at Highcliffe Castle, the country house of a personal friend, Colonel Edward Stuart-Wortley, in the New Forest. Stuart-Wortley was extremely well connected. Edward VII had asked him personally to help lay the groundwork for the Entente Cordiale between Britain and France. That was his only real experience as a diplomat, even though this was how he later presented himself in the *Daily Telegraph*. In reality, he was something of an innocent in international affairs.

As the Kaiser's host, Stuart-Wortley had to listen for two long weeks to the Kaiser's constant complaints about the reaction of the British press and the British people. Finally he suggested that the Kaiser should consider countering the bad press by giving an interview to a leading British journalist: W.T. Stead, for instance. This would enable him to explain how much he loved all things British. It should be done for the *Daily Telegraph*, Stuart-Wortley said, because it took a calmer and less aggressive line towards Germany.

But the Kaiser rejected the idea; he had an intense dislike of journalists, especially British ones. Still, Stuart-Wortley refused to give up. He was convinced, rather naively, that if the British public could only understand the Kaiser's real feelings, the mood towards him would change radically.

He consulted Harry Lawson, who was the son of the *Telegraph*'s owner, and decided that it would be better if he himself wrote an account of the Kaiser's conversations with him at Highcliffe, together with remarks the Kaiser had made to him when he was his guest at the army manoeuvres in Germany, earlier in the year. Stuart-Wortley put the proposal to the Kaiser before he left Highcliffe, and this time the Kaiser agreed. A senior journalist was sent down from the *Telegraph*, and Stuart-Wortley dictated the entire article to him from notes and from memory. By this stage the Kaiser had left Highcliffe Castle and was back in Germany.

The journalist made some suggestions about the content and form of it, and wrote it up. No doubt we can detect his hand in the typically journalistic way the interview begins with the line 'You English are mad, mad, mad as March hares.' The article is unexpectedly well organized, given the rambling way the Kaiser must have delivered his ideas. The man from the *Telegraph* must have bitten his lip when he heard Stuart-Wortley's account of what the Kaiser had said; if Stuart-Wortley was too unworldly to understand the likely effect of the interview, the *Telegraph* man was not. If he had given any indication from him of the explosive nature of the interview, Stuart-Wortley would have toned it down at once.

One hurdle remained: the Kaiser himself would have to vet the article. The *Telegraph* man must have been on tenterhooks, assuming that it would be rejected when it reached Berlin. But Wilhelm was always unlucky. Although Stuart-Wortley sent the finished article to him, he seems not to have read it himself. Instead, he passed it on to his chancellor, von Bülow. Von Bülow, it was later said, was too busy to read it. He sent it on to the foreign ministry, with instructions that someone should go through it carefully and return it to him. It ended up on the desk of a long-serving counsellor in the political department, Reinhold Klehmet.

Klehmet was a plodder, an elderly man whose chief concern was to keep his nose clean. He believed (or later said he believed) that he had been ordered merely to tidy up the article for the press, not to vet the opinions it contained. Correcting the ramblings of the All-Highest was too intimidating a job for a civil servant who was starting to think about his pension.

He sent the finished article, duly checked for factual inaccuracies, back to von Bülow's office. Once again, von Bülow was too busy to look at it. Should we be a little suspicious of all this buck-passing? After all, von Bülow knew the Kaiser extremely well, and must have been all too aware of his master's proven ability to dig himself into trouble. Did he think it would strengthen his own hold over foreign affairs if the Kaiser made a mess of things in the interview? Possibly; but if so, the article had such a bad effect that any such ploy failed completely. When the storm broke, von Bülow's position was badly undermined, even though the Kaiser refused to accept his resignation. Nine months later, when his budget proposals broke up the coalition on which he depended in the Reichstag, he offered his resignation again. This time it was accepted.

In England, meanwhile, Stuart-Wortley proved to be no better than the German officials at spotting the many land-mines which his article contained. There seems to be no question that he deliberately allowed the Kaiser to dig a grave for himself. Stuart-Wortley was a decent, honourable, not particularly bright man who took his responsibility as the Kaiser's host and friend far too seriously to have conjured any trap.

Directly he received the article back from Berlin, duly approved, he sent it on to the *Telegraph*; and the senior figures there, despite their stuffiness, their black morning coats and their high starched collars, must have found it difficult to believe their good luck. They were, after all, journalists first and foremost; and an exclusive is to a journalist what a victory in the field is to a general.

As for Colonel Stuart-Wortley, he was deeply shocked by the international reaction aroused by his proposal to help the Kaiser improve his image. Like his friend the Kaiser, he was an unlucky man. Eight years later, at the Battle of Loos in October 1915, when he was in command of the 46th Division, he lost 3,800 officers and men in an attack he had argued against. The following July, on the first day of the Somme, he was ordered to stage an attack which he could see had no possible chance of success. He held his men back, and was sacked for lacking the necessary offensive spirit – in effect, a scapegoat for the failures that day. He saved a large number of lives, but his military career was finished.

The Kaiser never fully recovered from the publication of his remarks to Stuart-Wortley. The reaction sent him into a depression for several weeks, and he stayed out of the public eye for months. The unprecedented degree of criticism levelled at him at home meant that the German press had broken through an unseen barrier: he lost the reputation of being untouchable. In future the German press mocked him more often, even if they had to be careful about the way they did it.

In Britain and France he seemed more and more of an enemy, unstable and unreliable. The accusations of a man like William Le Queux no longer seemed quite as absurd as they once had. Le Queux found it easier to get his alarmist articles published in the press, and the old, ineffective system of internal security was reformed in order to guard against German spies. In 1909, MI5 was created, in recognizably the same form that exists today. More men and women joined the increasing number of volunteer organizations which were being formed in order to prepare the country for the inevitable war with Germany.

It was the *Daily Express*, not usually one of the more thoughtful newspapers, that got it exactly right, two days after the publication of the *Telegraph* interview: 'The Kaiser intends to show us the absurdity of our suspicions of his country. Inadvertently he has offered us the strongest proof of the reality of our fears.'

5

WRONG TURN

Around midday on 28 June 1914, the normal Sunday morning calm in the newsrooms of the British press was broken by a telegraphed message from Reuter's news agency:

TWO REVOLVER SHOTS

(Reuter's correspondent.)

Sarayevo [sic], Sunday.
As the Archduke Francis Ferdinand and his wife, the Countess of Hohenberg, were driving through the streets here today, a young man, stated to be a student, fired two revolver shots at their motor-car.

Both were mortally wounded and died from their injuries within a few minutes.

The details of the assassination remained confused. A few hours later, another message appeared:

3 p.m.
It now appears that two attempts were made on the lives of the Archduke Francis Ferdinand and his wife. The first took place as they were driving to the Town Hall, when a bomb was thrown at their motor-car. Both the Archduke and his consort then escaped unhurt, though several other persons were injured.

Slowly, hour by hour, the details came through. The basic reason for the continuing confusion is clear. Even though the Archduke and his wife had run a very considerable risk in going to Sarajevo, none of the Vienna correspondents of the British press had troubled to go there to cover the visit. As a result, the newspapers had to depend on Reuter's news agency. But Reuter's correspondent had decided not to go to Sarajevo either. Instead, he relied on a 'stringer', probably a local journalist working for a Sarajevo newspaper, for coverage of the visit.

The problems of communication, the fact that the stringer was inexperienced and busy with the demands of his own newspaper, together with the sheer chaos that always surrounds a major incident, all made it harder for the outside world to understand exactly what had taken place in Sarajevo. There was much the same confusion when President Kennedy was assassinated in 1963 in Dallas: another visit which, despite the warnings of violence against him, scarcely any of the main news organizations, American or foreign, sent their leading correspondents to cover.

Despite the confusion, the lead in *The Times* the following morning, 29 June 1914, was a model of clarity.

AUSTRIAN HEIR AND HIS WIFE MURDERED.

SHOT IN BOSNIAN TOWN.
A STUDENT'S POLITICAL CRIME.
BOMB THROWN EARLIER IN THE DAY.
THE EMPEROR'S GRIEF.

The Austro-Hungarian Heir-Presumptive, the Archduke Francis Ferdinand, and his wife, the Duchess of Hohenberg, were assassinated yesterday morning at Serajevo [sic], the capital of Bosnia. The actual assassin is described as a high school student, who fired bullets at his victims with fatal effect from an automatic pistol as they were returning from a reception at the Town Hall.

The outrage was evidently the fruit of a carefully-laid plot. On their way to the Town Hall the Archduke and his Consort had narrowly escaped death. An individual, described as a compositor from Trebinje, a garrison town in

the extreme south of Herzegovina, had thrown a bomb at
their motor-car. Few details of this first outrage have been
received.

It was a deliberately provocative day for the heir to the Austro-Hungarian
Empire to have chosen to visit Sarajevo. Sunday 28 June was the 525th
anniversary of the battle of Kosovo, when a Serbian army threw away its
nation's independence in a carelessly planned battle against the Turks. It
has remained a special day of mourning to Serbian nationalists ever since.
In Sarajevo, the Bosnian capital, a resentful and embittered group of
ethnic Serbian students decided to stage a blow for Serbian pride by
murdering the Archduke Franz Ferdinand during his visit. Their plan is
thought to have had the backing of the Black Hand, a shadowy extremist
organisation which was controlled by the head of military intelligence in
neighbouring Serbia.

Given the risk, it was brave of the Archduke and his Duchess Sophie
to go ahead with their plan. During the previous days there had been
intelligence warnings of a plot to kill him, and three years earlier someone
had tried to murder the Emperor Franz Josef when he went to Sarajevo.
But the Archduke was irascible and aggressive, and was keen to show the
Serbian nationalists that he had no fear of them.

With hindsight, a terrible inevitability seemed to hang over the entire
events of that day. Seven conspirators were stationed along what was then
called Appel Quay, which runs along the river in the old heart of Sarajevo.
Each of them was armed with a bomb or a revolver.

The first man lost his nerve as the Archduke's open car passed, and
did nothing. The second had a hand-grenade ready, and threw it at the
car; but the driver, spotting the grenade in the air, jammed his foot down
on the accelerator, and the car shot forward at speed. The grenade
bounced off, and the ten-second fuse meant that it exploded under the
following car, injuring two of its occupants and a number of spectators.

After that the other conspirators decided they had no chance of
carrying out their attacks, and drifted away. The Archduke went on to
the City Hall, where he protested furiously to the Lord Mayor about the
outrage. Then he announced he would cancel his official programme and
head off instead with the Duchess to visit Sarajevo Hospital, where the
injured had been taken. The couple went down the front steps of the City
Hall and climbed into their car again.

But no one had remembered to tell the driver where they were going.

Assuming that they were keeping to the original plan, he turned right off Appel Quay into Franz Josef Street, heading for the next scheduled destination. Then someone called out to him that he had taken the wrong turning. Flustered, he put the gear lever into reverse in order to back down the street to the Quay; and in doing so he managed to stall the engine.

One of the conspirators, the weak and slightly built Gavrilo Princip, who was a month short of his twentieth birthday, had agreed with the others that there was no point in continuing with the assassination plan. As a result, he had gone to a café in Franz Josef Street to get a coffee and a sandwich. As he sat there, he watched the Archduke's car as it passed almost directly outside the café after taking the wrong turn. He ran out, just at the precise moment when the car stalled. The Archduke and his wife were sitting ducks, right in front of him. Princip pulled out his revolver and shot them from a range of six feet, hitting the Archduke in the neck and chest, and the Duchess in the stomach.

Count Franz von Harrach, a senior member of the Archduke's entourage, was standing on the running-board on the far side of the open limousine from Princip. He described afterwards how he was splashed by the Archduke's blood. The Duchess cried out, 'For God's sake! What's happened to you?' Then she slid off the seat and lay on the floor of the car. Von Harrach thought she had fainted, until he heard the Archduke say, 'Sophie, Sophie, don't die. Stay alive for the children!' Von Harrach asked if he was in pain. The Archduke answered, 'It's nothing.' He said the words again several times until he lost consciousness. By the time the car arrived at the governor's residence both he and his wife were dead.

The murders led, not just to the start of the First World War five weeks later, but directly or indirectly to many of the most important events of the twentieth century: the Russian revolution, the rise of Stalin's Communism and Hitler's Nazism, the Second World War, the Holocaust, the atomic bomb, the decline of Europe and its colonial empires, the Cold War, the seemingly endless conflict in the Middle East, the growth of militant Islam. If the Archduke's car had not taken a wrong turn and stalled, would any of these things have happened? Perhaps; but they would have happened differently. The balance of Europe could well have been maintained indefinitely, had it not been for one particular chain of events. There was no absolute inevitability about the First World

War; and if someone had remembered to tell the Archduke's chauffeur where to go, it might never have happened.

For many years the place where Princip stood as he fired his pistol was marked by a couple of footprints set in concrete on the pavement. The café on the corner where he sat was turned into a museum to Serbian nationalism. At the start of the Bosnian War in 1992 these things were destroyed by an angry anti-Serbian crowd. Later, someone set up a wooden memorial in several languages. The English words on it read 'May Peace Prevail On Earth'.

No British newspaper at the time regarded the murders as anything more than a terrible but purely localized act of terrorism. There is not a single suggestion in any British newspaper or magazine that the incident might start a war, or that Britain could conceivably become embroiled in it. The overriding danger to Britain's peace and stability seemed to come instead from Ireland. In 1912 the Liberal government had put forward a bill to give Home Rule to Ireland, and by the summer of 1914 the bill was nearing a final vote.

Ulster Protestants had formed a large and well-armed paramilitary organization to fight any attempt to force them to accept rule from predominantly Catholic Dublin, and a nationalist militia in the south had been formed to counter it. Civil war seemed likely, and three months earlier it had become clear that the British government could not automatically call on the loyalty of the British army in Ireland, whose officers' sympathies were mostly Unionist.

At the Curragh, the main British army base near Dublin, fifty-seven out of seventy army officers said in March that they would resign their commissions rather than march northwards to deal with any possible resistance from the Ulster Volunteers. It did not quite constitute a mutiny, because the officers had not been given any specific order; but faced with its inability to rely on the army, the government was obliged to back down.

It was a serious blow to democracy in Britain, and in June 1914 there was still no certainty that civil war in Ireland could be avoided. By comparison, the murder of a foreign dignitary in a part of Europe which the British still called the Near East seemed a great deal less important. Yet the path which would lead directly to war within a matter of days was already being mapped out in Vienna, Belgrade, and – on Sunday 5 July – in Berlin. There, a senior Austrian official met the Kaiser, who assured him that Germany would support Austria in dealing with Serbia even if Russia became involved on Serbia's side, and even if it led to war. This was not just another of the Kaiser's sudden fantasies; the following day, when the Austrian official met the German Chancellor, Dr Theobald von Bethmann-Hollweg, he was given the same message.

The plans for provoking a war with Serbia took some days to mature; yet a sense of unease was starting through the region. The Austro-Hungarian ambassador in Belgrade announced that Serbian terrorists were planning to blow up his embassy and attack Austro-Hungarian citizens living in Belgrade. It came to nothing; yet on Tuesday 14 July, twenty-one days before war broke out, *The Times* correspondent in Vienna wrote a report for the next day's paper which gave the first faint hint in the British press that something disturbing was going on.

> The feeling of uncertainty which has taken hold of the public is affecting the Vienna Bourse most adversely. Very heavy falls of prices were noted all round yesterday, and although during the early part of today a recovery took place, since the panic in Belgrade has not been justified by events, it is apprehended that it will not prove lasting.

That monitory paragraph from Vienna appeared in *The Times* on Wednesday 15 July. There were many more immediately pressing news items, and the lead story had an ominous headline:

NEARING THE END.

The reference was to the bill on Irish Home Rule, which was worrying enough in Britain and Ireland. Various other news items that day had a disturbing air to them: a treason trial in Berlin which implicated the Russian military attaché, a naval scandal in Japan with a former Reuter's correspondent sentenced to two years' imprisonment, trouble in Albania, and the headlines

RASPUTIN STILL ALIVE.
STABBED BY A FOLLOWER OF HELIODORUS.

In fact, Rasputin still had another two and a half years to live.

By the following week, on Wednesday 22 July, the crisis had taken on a new seriousness. According to the *Times* correspondent in Vienna, 'There is a general feeling today that the end of the period of uncertainty as to what Austria-Hungary will officially demand of Servia [sic] is approaching, if not impending.' Yet to British readers the story must still have had a distinctly Ruritanian feeling to it.

> The principal ground of this assumption is the fact that Count Berchtold travelled to Ischl last night, where he was received by the Emperor Franz Joseph this morning, and that yesterday evening what is believed to have been an important meeting of the Hungarian Cabinet dealing with the situation was held in Budapest.

Like Germany, Austria-Hungary was an autocracy in which the press was allowed a certain amount of freedom, but was rarely taken into the government's confidence; so a British correspondent could glean little insight from the local press. And of course foreign correspondents themselves were unlikely to be given any briefing by the German or Austro-Hungarian governments about their intentions. British journalists in both countries were reporting largely in the dark: another reason why no one foresaw where events were leading.

That day, with thirteen days to go before war broke out, the headlines were becoming more disturbing. *The Times* ran as its fifth story:

THE AUSTRO-SERVIAN CONFLICT.
VIENNESE THREATS OF WAR.
RESENTMENT IN RUSSIA.

The *Manchester Guardian*'s correspondent, determined not to get excited, ended by getting the story badly wrong.

> Vienna is notoriously the most jumpy capital in Europe, and the talk about war between Austria and Servia is surely not to be taken very seriously.

Two days later, on Saturday 25 July, *The Times* sounds a new note of alarm, though its writers still assume that whatever happens will be restricted to the continent. And now, at last, the story has become the paper's lead.

GRAVE DECISIONS IMPENDING.
THE RISK TO EUROPE.

A grave international crisis has been precipitated by the Austro-Hungarian ultimatum to Servia. The Austro-Hungarian Note, of which the full text was published in the late editions of The Times of yesterday, is in substance a violent indictment of Servia.

At St Petersburg the impression is profound. A Council of Ministers sat for several hours and is stated to have taken grave resolutions.

A message has been received from Servia imploring Russian help.

In France considerable irritation and much anxiety is shown. The Austro-Hungarian Note is described as unprecedented in its arrogance and in the extravagance of its demands. Doubt is expressed as to the possibility of localising the dispute.

In competent diplomatic circles in London the situation is regarded as graver than those which existed during the annexation crisis of 1908–9 or during the Balkan wars of 1912–13.

You have the impression that the diplomats in London and Paris are feeling their way forward through a fog day by day, and that the correspondents, habituated to receiving nothing but official statements, are suddenly having to find out what their contacts really think, rather than what they are prepared to announce in public. The line from Paris about the difficulty of localizing the dispute must have been the first inkling that the great majority of *The Times*'s readers had had that France, Germany and Russia might become involved; though the correspondent who wrote those words did not spell it out. Britain was still not mentioned.

In its main editorial on the morning of Sunday 26 July, the *Observer*, edited by the tough-minded J.L. Garvin, was stark and accurate. The war was now only nine days away.

EUROPEAN PEACE IN DANGER.

> Experienced critics of foreign affairs have long been convinced that the Great War, if it ever came at all, would come with utter unexpectedness. Suddenly in the Near East a cloud that seemed no bigger than a man's hand threatens the blackness of tempest that overwhelms nations.

Yet that afternoon it seems clear that the British government itself had no real expectation that Britain would inevitably be involved in the coming war. Sir John Simon, the Attorney General, spoke to a gathering in Manchester of the Altrincham Liberal Club.

> We have been so filled with our own political developments that some of us may not have noticed how serious a situation is threatening on the Continent of Europe . . . [L]et us all resolve that, whatever may be the difficulties and dangers which threaten the peaceful relations in Europe, the part which this country plays shall from beginning to end be the part of a mediator simply desirous of promoting better and more peaceful relations.

This is not the speech of a Cabinet minister who has been instructed to prepare the nation for war. Nor does it sound like the speech of someone who thinks that Britain will be dragged into war, but prefers not to say so publicly. The Liberal government under Herbert Asquith still believed it could stay on the sidelines if – or rather when – war broke out.

Even so, *The Times* was beginning to think the unthinkable. The next day, Monday 27 July, its headlines were increasingly disturbing.

IN THE BALANCE.
AUSTRIAN MINISTER LEAVES BELGRADE.
THE SERVIAN REPLY.

REMOVAL OF THE SEAT OF GOVERNMENT.
HURRIED MOBILIZATIONS.
A MOVEMENT FOR MEDIATION.

Elsewhere on the main news page that day, the headlines tell the story neatly and skilfully:

WAR FEVER IN VIENNA
Demonstrations Before German Embassy
No Decision Yet Taken In Russia
French Pessimism
Germany The Key To The Situation
British Naval Manoeuvres
Orders To First And Second Fleet

Now, at last, Britain is being mentioned – not as a participant, but as a concerned and anxious onlooker. And there is a hint from the editorial writers, after having a weekend to reflect on it, that Britain might become involved after all. It is clear that now, eight days before the outbreak of war, *The Times* believed it would be necessary for Britain to enter the war on the French side, if France herself became involved.

> Should there arise in any quarter a desire to test our adhesion to the principles that inform our friendships and that thereby guarantee the balance of power in Europe, we shall be found no less ready and determined to vindicate them with the whole strength of the Empire, as we have been found ready whenever they have been tried in the past.
> That, we conceive, interest, duty, and honour demand from us. England will not hesitate to answer their call.

The language is convoluted, but the last eight words show what it really means. Right across the continent governments believed that *The Times* was the voice of the British ruling class, and that it reflected, in particular, the views of the Foreign Office. So when this editorial announced that England would not hesitate to answer the call of honour, it was taken by diplomats everywhere as meaning that the British government had spoken.

But it had not. Most informed people in Britain itself would have been aware that *The Times* was no longer what it had been. Since 1908 it had been owned by Alfred Harmsworth, now ennobled as Lord Northcliffe: the man who had single-handedly invented yellow journalism in Britain, and had made the *Daily Mail* and the *Daily Mirror* the loudest and most aggressive newspapers in Fleet Street. Northcliffe disliked the prime minister, Herbert Asquith, and had little time for the Liberal Party, which had been in power since 1906. For its part, the government did not regard the increasingly right-wing *Times* as a useful conduit for its views.

The author of this editorial must have been the editor of *The Times*, Geoffrey Dawson. He would certainly have consulted his proprietor, Northcliffe: the man who had appointed him to the job two years earlier, at the age of only thirty-eight. When Northcliffe bought *The Times* in 1908, he gave all sorts of assurances that its journalistic independence would remain total, much as Rupert Murdoch did when he bought the paper in 1981. But a newspaper proprietor does not have to pick up the phone to his editor to order him to take a particular line; an editor who wants to hold on to his job will do as much of his master's bidding as his conscience will allow. J.L. Garvin, who was chosen by Northcliffe to edit the *Observer* when he bought it in the same year, had such angry disagreements with him that Northcliffe got rid of the paper to William Waldorf Astor two years later.

Geoffrey Dawson, too, would eventually have enough of Northcliffe's interference. He stayed at his post on *The Times* throughout the First World War, but once it was over he resigned in 1919 because he felt Northcliffe was using the paper for his own personal ends. (He came back when *The Times* changed hands in 1923, and eventually turned it into the leading voice of appeasement to Hitler and Nazi Germany.) But in 1914, having taken over the most prestigious job in British journalism less than two years earlier, Dawson was still feeling his way. He was not going to ignore what Northcliffe wanted.

And the following morning, Tuesday 28 July, it was clear from the *Daily Mail*, stablemate of *The Times*, what Northcliffe believed. His anti-

German feelings had certainly not abated, as the paper's main leader showed.

A PISTOL AT ENGLAND'S HEAD.

In the light of Napoleon's famous saying that 'Antwerp in the hands of a great naval Power was a pistol presented at the head of England', extreme significance attaches to the acquisition by the German Vulcan Company of the right to construct 'a private harbour' near Rotterdam.

The point for the British public to consider is the close proximity of the new port to the British coast. Whereas Antwerp is 135 miles from Harwich, the site of the new German harbour is only 115 miles distant . . .

The *Manchester Guardian*, by contrast, was still determinedly calm and neutral.

We have no . . . commitments. War between Austria and Servia would be very regrettable; still it would not be a European calamity . . .

That day, with the outbreak of hostilities now only a week away, the *Guardian* published several letters deploring the rush to war signed by various authority figures on the left. There was one from a number of leading academics, with the name of the master of Magdalene College, Cambridge, the charming, clubbable A.C. Benson, at its head.

By Wednesday the 29th *The Times* was even more outspoken than before. The balance of power in Europe must be maintained, it said.

It is for that object that we entered into the Entente with France, and into the enlarged Entente with France and her ally [Russia, whose repressive policies made even *The Times* unwilling to mention its name]. To that Entente we shall remain faithful in the future, come what may. We trust that our fidelity to it is not going to be tried by the most terrible of all tests . . . But . . .

> England will be found as ready to stand by her friends
> today as ever she was to stand by them when she was
> aiding Europe to fling off the despotism of NAPOLEON.

In the last days of peace, references to Napoleon crop up regularly in the columns of Northcliffe's newspapers; presumably he told his editors to put them in. On Friday 31 July the *Mail* was certain that war was on its way.

> Whatever the suffering, whatever the loss in store for us,
> we shall meet it, not indeed 'with a light heart', but with
> that same sober and fixed resolution with which in
> another age we confronted such a danger to our exis-
> tence when the armies of Napoleon swept the Continent.

By contrast, the *Manchester Guardian* doggedly wrote: 'We have been specifically assured that there is no contract between us and France which impairs our freedom of action in the event of a war.'

In the strictest terms, this was right; yet it was the Napoleon complex of the Northcliffe press, rather than the more peaceable view of the *Manchester Guardian* which would shortly prove more accurate.

Later that Friday Russia announced a general mobilization; Germany declared martial law. The London Stock Exchange was closed, 'an event without precedent' according to the *Daily News*. Interest rates in Britain shot up from 4 to 8 per cent, and for the first time the prime minister, Mr Asquith, made it clear that Britain might have to be involved in the coming war.

The head of a leading private bank (presumably, from what follows, German-Jewish by origin) contacted the financial editor of *The Times*, Hugh Chisholm, and asked him to beg Lord Northcliffe, on behalf of the City, to stop printing editorials urging Britain to join in the coming war on the side of France. The only way to avoid economic catastrophe, the financier said, was for Britain to maintain a strict neutrality. Chisholm was angry, but agreed to put this viewpoint to Lord Northcliffe, who would be presiding at that afternoon's editorial conference at Printing House Square, the offices of *The Times*.

The paper's long-serving foreign editor, Henry Wickham Steed, was a powerful figure in his own right. He had written that morning's editorial urging British involvement alongside France. Steed was as pushy and self-promoting in his way as William Le Queux, and he betrayed various other unpleasant characteristics as well. He writes about the editorial meeting in his memoirs:

> Lord Northcliffe, who presided, said, 'I think Mr Chisholm has something to say.' Chisholm then repeated his interview with the financial magnate. He was still white with rage. When he had finished, Lord Northcliffe asked my opinion.
>
> 'It is a dirty German-Jewish international financial attempt to bully us into advocating neutrality,' I said, 'and the proper answer would be a still stiffer leading article tomorrow.'
>
> 'I agree with you,' said Lord Northcliffe. 'Let us go ahead.'

That afternoon Steed duly wrote the stiffer leading article.

> We dare not stand aside with folded arms and placidly watch our friends placed in peril of destruction. Should we remain passive, should the fortune of war go against those whose interests march with our own, we know full well that it would be our turn next.

Saturday 1 August, when Steed's editorial appeared in the morning's *Times*, was the start of a Bank Holiday weekend. The social pages of the newspapers were full of the doings of the great, as though everything were going on as usual:

> Queen Alexandra, the Empress Marie, and Princess Victoria leave London next week for Sandringham.
>
> Prince Henry of Prussia is to be the guest of Lady Ormonde at Solent Lodge, Cowes, for Cowes Week.
>
> Mr and Mrs Harold Pearson have left 6, Richmond-terrace, Whitehall, for Capron House, their place at Mid-hurst, where they will entertain a party for Goodwood Races . . .

Paris, according to the *Daily News* correspondent on Saturday morning, 'after a quiet night on the boulevards, sombre enough now that the chairs that stretched halfway across the pavement are removed, woke up in a decidedly cheerful frame of mind'.

But there was no matching cheerfulness on the news pages. The Liberal and left-wing press were angry at the way Lord Northcliffe's papers, in particular, were urging the need for Britain to side with France in the coming war. The lobby correspondent of the radical *Daily News* is almost incoherent in his annoyance.

MISCHIEF-MAKING IN TORY PRESS.

> There is indignation in the Liberal Party at the articles in one or two of the Tory journals egging this country on to war, irrespective of the merits of any hypothetical situation which may arise ... The antiquated 'balance of power', which has been revived as an argument, will be idle stuff to offer the people in this country when bread riots break out in the industrial centres in a few weeks' time.

'A.G.G.', in an article entitled 'Why We Must Not Fight', made the point more coherently elsewhere in the *Daily News* that morning. He called *The Times*, the *Mail*, the *Mirror* and the *London Evening News*

> the patriotic gramophones of Lord Northcliffe shouting for war – as they always shout for war. Let the public remember that, with all its affectation of gravity, the voice of 'The Times' is the same voice as that which speaks in the 'Daily Mail', the 'Evening News' and all the rest of the rabble of Jingo journalism. It is only the accent which is a little more polite.

The opposition by the *Daily News* to Britain taking part in the coming war was matched that morning in C.P. Scott's *Manchester Guardian*. Scott, like the banker who tried to influence *The Times*, had also decided it was was all Lord Northcliffe's fault.

> We advise Englishmen that they have no sympathy to spare for Europe. Let them keep it for themselves, and think

first of all for England, for English honour and English interests. For there is in our midst an organised conspiracy to drag us into the war should the attempts of the peace-makers fail.

The *Daily Herald*, the Labour Party newspaper, was characteristically louder. Under the headlines

WORKERS MUST STOP THE WAR!
THE GREATEST CRIME OF THE CENTURY

the lead article reads:

> We are all agreed . . . that war only benefits the Capitalist and exploiting classes. We also know that the workers have nothing to quarrel about, and that there is no reason why they should be at each others' throats, no reason why they should slaughter each other, except that it sometimes brings profit and glory to other people.

But that Saturday the fuse leading to the explosives which would destroy the peace of Europe was finally lit. Austria had gone ahead with its ultimatum to Serbia; Germany supported Austria; Russia, which backed Serbia, now began its lumbering preparations for war. This automatically triggered Germany's Schlieffen–von Moltke plan to attack both France and Russia.

Henry Wickham Steed, watching it all from the vantage point of the *Times* foreign desk, later called it the most terrible day of his life. He wrote: 'It was known that Germany was about to declare war on Russia, and that war between Germany and France would follow immediately. The one question was whether England would stand firm.'

At a special editorial meeting that afternoon, Northcliffe said he had information that the British government was going to 'rat'. What, he asked, did Steed think *The Times* should do? Steed replied, 'We have no choice. If the Government "rat" we must pull off our wigs and go bald-headed against the Government.'

As he listened to this, the editor of another newspaper owned by

Northcliffe (Steed doesn't name him, but it was Thomas Marlowe of the *Daily Mail*) was shocked. 'Attack the Government in a moment of national crisis? Impossible! The country would never forgive us.'

There was a fourth person at the meeting, who can only have been Geoffrey Dawson, *The Times*'s editor. He pointed out diplomatically that there was no need to make a hurried decision. '. . . [W]e do not appear until Monday morning. Between now and tomorrow night much may happen.' Steed writes in his memoirs that he left Printing House Square more miserable than he had ever felt, before or afterwards, and spent a wretched night.

That Saturday there were still efforts to limit the scope of the war. The Kaiser tried to persuade Austria to restrict its war aims to capturing Belgrade, and the British Foreign Office finally sent a warning to Germany that Britain would join in any war in Western Europe. Sir Edward Grey, the Foreign Secretary, did this on his own authority, without the knowledge or agreement of his Cabinet colleagues; they would almost certainly have instructed him not to do any such thing.

The German Chancellor, Bethmann-Hollweg, was deeply shocked when he received the message, but by now it was too late: the machinery of war was already turning. If Grey had sent his message a day earlier, it might have persuaded the Germans to put more pressure on Austria.

But he didn't. Ever since the moment when the Archduke Franz Ferdinand's driver stalled his engine in Franz Joseph Street in Sarajevo, there had been a variety of chances to avoid catastrophe.

They had all come to nothing, by sheer bad luck. And if Britain had not decided finally to support the French, then Germany would probably have knocked out both France and Russia in a matter of weeks. The war really might have been over by Christmas.

Even as late as Saturday 1 August there was no certainty that Britain would join in. The main argument between the members of the Cabinet had narrowed down to the significance of the Entente with France and Russia. Sir Edward Grey felt he was the guardian of the agreement, having negotiated it in its final form, and he maintained strongly that Britain was morally obliged to come to France's aid if Germany attacked.

The majority feeling within the Cabinet was still against Grey, and most Liberal MPs would probably not have supported him either. The Labour MPs and Irish Nationalists, on whom the Liberals depended for a majority in the House of Commons, would certainly have been against any such move. If, at that point, the Cabinet had decided in favour of war, its majority in the House of Commons would have evaporated, and the Asquith government would have collapsed. Later that afternoon, when Grey saw the French ambassador, Paul Cambon, he was forced to warn him that he could not promise Britain's support for France.

It was only the following day, Sunday 2 August, that the Cabinet changed its collective mind. The Schlieffen–Moltke plan for invading France and capturing Paris involved marching through Belgium and breaching its neutrality; and it was now far too late for Germany to change the plan. If the Germans had only clipped the south-eastern part of Belgium, Britain might well have closed its eyes to it. But no British government, of whatever political make-up, could ignore the all-out invasion of Belgium, given that Britain was one of the main guarantors of Belgium's territorial integrity. When, on Sunday morning, Germany demanded that Belgium should allow its forces to pass through, King Albert I appealed to Britain and France for help.

The British Cabinet met three times on Sunday, but the Belgian issue had clinched things. It had ceased to be a strategic question, and become a moral one: protecting a small, partially dependent country from invasion. Asquith, Grey, Winston Churchill and Lloyd George had all been strongly in favour of sending the British army to support France. Now that Belgium had become the main issue, they found it suddenly easy to convince almost everyone else in the Cabinet. Two ministers who still could not agree both resigned. British involvement in the coming war was certain.

That Sunday, according to Wickham Steed, an attempt by German intelligence to pass large amounts of intelligence about Britain to the military High Command in Berlin was thwarted. Several German-speaking postal officials were, as usual, on duty at the post office in London where letters to Germany were collected before being sent on. One of them noticed that an unusually large number of letters from all over Britain had been addressed to Charlottenburg, a suburb of Berlin. Strictly against all the rules, he decided to open some of them, and found they were full of secret information. The British security service was called, and allowed many of the letters to go through, in order to persuade the addressees that nothing had been intercepted. The people who had sent them were later arrested. That, at any rate, is Steed's story; it sounds like one of Le Queux's.

What strikes any journalist about the crisis which led up to Britain's declaration of war on 4 August was how little the newspapers seemed to know about what was going on behind the scenes. During the second half of the twentieth century governments habitually briefed the media about the key issues, in order to win their support. Individual ministers who disagreed with the government line learned how to bend the ear of friendly journalists, in order to get their viewpoints out in public and perhaps influence the argument in Cabinet. From the 1960s on, their divisions would be argued out by ministers or their supporters on radio and television. Nothing as serious as the question of war and peace could possibly have been permitted to go on entirely behind closed doors, without the public's knowledge.

Yet in 1914, although the business of Parliament was reported with great thoroughness, that of the Cabinet was usually not reported at all. Ministers demanded, and got, the freedom to hold their discussions away from public scrutiny. There were occasional off-the-record briefings about the practical results of Cabinet decisions, but journalists, like the public, had to wait for the government to tell Parliament about its decisions before they could find out what was being done in their name. Often they never found out at all.

A century later, speculation and endless discussion, much of it empty and not particularly well-informed, fills our airwaves and the columns of our newspapers. It can be intensely irritating, but it does mean that people understand better what is being done in their name; and governments know they cannot survive if they do not explain the issues to the public and try to win their approval. If there had been a similar culture of comment and discussion in 1914 it is hard to think that a world war could have crept up on Europe virtually without being noticed.

Instead, the British Cabinet plunged the entire nation – indeed, the entire British Empire – into the worst war in human history after a decision-making process which had been entirely secret and extraordinarily fast. Every minister knew how momentous the decision was; and many of them understood Lord Kitchener's view that the war could last as long as three years or more. 'All over by Christmas' was something people said to cheer themselves up; but those who understood the realities of modern warfare realized it could last far longer than expected, just as the Boer War had.

Some people, though, had a premonition about those realities. Three days earlier, the *Daily Herald* ran an article entitled 'An Open Letter To Bill Smith', the typical British worker.

> War is hell, Bill Smith. Make no mistake about that. Here is a glimpse of an eye-witness's account of the Battle of Sedan.
>
> 'Let your readers fancy masses of coloured rags glued together with blood and brains, pinned into strange shapes by fragments of bones. Let them conceive men's bodies without legs, and legs without bodies, heaps of human entrails attached to red and blue cloth . . .'

The *Herald*'s article continues:

> They won't tell you that in the patriotic press; the war correspondents dare not cable the truth . . . No! You won't be told the truth about war by the patriots who are going to get their share of glory by staying at home, while you and yours are out collaring all the gore.

It would all turn out to be disturbingly prescient; except that the horrors of the Western Front would far exceed anything seen at the Battle of Sedan. And they would last four years, instead of a single day.

6

DEFENCE OF THE REALM

'We had a door to our dugout, near Beaumont-Hamel, on the Somme, which was made of corrugated iron. It shook and made a racket every time there was an explosion. Someone had nailed a page out of the *Daily Mail* on it, I remember.'

The old man who was being interviewed for the BBC was in his eighties by this stage, and had fought on the first day of the Somme. Later, at the Battle of Passchendaele, he was badly injured and spent the rest of his life with a pronounced limp.

The page from the *Mail* fixed on the door of the dugout contained what appeared to be an eyewitness description of an attack by British soldiers. It was full of references to the gallantry of the men and their keenness to get at the enemy. In reality, the majority of the officers and men who had taken part in the attack were dead, wounded or captured, and the 'eyewitness' had seen none of it. One of the survivors had fixed the newspaper to the door. He had written across it in red pencil, 'If the bastard comes here, kill him.'

It was not a joke. It was not always safe for newspaper correspondents, especially those from the *Daily Mail*, to visit the front line. The danger was not from the shelling or the constant sniping; it was from the soldiers whose efforts the correspondents were always praising to the heavens. The term 'yellow press' now took on another meaning: the journalists were too cowardly to run the risks that the soldiers ran every minute.

British troops often hated the way the press wrote about them, but not because they felt themselves to be victims who longed for their sufferings to be reported. On the contrary, their morale was usually surprisingly high under the atrocious conditions of the trenches. With a couple of mild exceptions, the British army, reinforced by the troops from the Empire, did not mutiny, even in 1917 when revolution was in the air in Russia, and the French army could no longer be relied on to obey orders. The British grumbled endlessly about everything, they hated some of their generals and all of the staff officers, they detested the civilians who sat comfortably at home and kept saying how proud they were of the sacrifice the soldiers were making; but the men at the front carried on doing what they were told, even when that meant charging directly at the machine guns and the barbed wire opposite.

They were proud of themselves and of their ability to put up with the worst conditions imaginable. They joked about their shortcomings. They sang, to the tune of the Anglican hymn 'The Church's One Foundation':

> We are Fred Karno's Army, the ragtime infantry.
> We cannot fight, we cannot shoot – what ruddy use are we?
> But when we get to Berlin, the Kaiser he will say,
> 'Hoch, hoch, mein Gott, vot a jolly rotten lot
> Are the ragtime infantry!'

It was inverted pride, since they clearly never doubted that they would eventually win and get to Berlin. They certainly did not look for pity; but equally they did not want to be lied about, and that was what many of the newspapers seemed to do.

Long after the First World War was over, A.J. Cummings, the editor of the *News Chronicle*, a thoughtful, lively, middle-brow London newspaper, wrote a book about the British press. As a working journalist himself, he was naturally concerned to put the profession in a good light. But even he felt nothing but contempt for the work of the correspondents who had covered the First World War. He stopped thinking as a journalist, and reverted to the mindset of the front-line infantry officer he had been twenty years earlier: 'To men fighting for their lives day by day in the foulest of physical conditions it was nauseating to read, day after day, the lying official communiqués in the Press.'

It was more nauseating still, he went on, to read the endless drivel written by the war correspondents who struck 'a loud and continuous note of light-hearted optimism to cheer the spirits of the troops at the front and to stimulate the morale of the civilians at home'. In other words, he and soldiers like him wanted the correspondents to write honestly. And they almost never did. When some completely pointless raid resulted in large numbers of killed or wounded, it would be written up as a daring, purposeful achievement.

Some correspondents liked the drama of what they wrote, and the prominence it gave them. The most famous of these was William Beach Thomas, who has been described by an editor of *The Times* in our own days, Sir Peter Stothard, as 'a quietly successful countryside columnist and literary gent who became a calamitous *Daily Mail* war correspondent'; Stothard suggests him as the original for Evelyn Waugh's William Boot in *Scoop*.

Tall and athletic, Beach Thomas had read classics at Oxford. He had considerable charm; Philip Gibbs, a much more thoughtful and sensitive front-line correspondent, said he was 'a Peter Pan figure' who would sometimes go bird's-nesting in no-man's-land. Yet Thomas's prose, supposedly written on the battlefield, was over-written, self-advertising, and infuriated many soldiers by making out that the war was an enjoyable game.

MID-BATTLE RELIEF

WHY 'THE DAILY MAIL' WAS BROUGHT UP PRIVATE'S EXPLOITS IN 24 HOURS

From W. BEACH THOMAS.

WAR CORRESPONDENTS' HEADQUARTERS, FRANCE, Monday

The Australian unit who sat down at their second and third objectives on Thursday and quietly in the open read The Daily Mail, smoked cigarettes, and ate sandwiches were at the very centre of the battle, and have a moving tale of fighting to tell; and it deserves to be retold.

Some of the men themselves and their officers imparted bits of it to me this morning while they sat in the sun at the edge of a snug French orchard, cleaning machine-guns, Verey-light pistols, and kit . . .

. . . [O]rders were issued in one unit that every officer's batman or servant was to carry up to 25 sandbags loaded with newspapers, chiefly The Daily Mail and The Daily Mirror [Beach Thomas was correspondent for both papers], and cigarettes and sandwiches . . . [T]rivial as the incident may seem, it helped the men a good deal. Old hands laughed and most nervous youngsters felt that if this could be done everything must be all right. Indeed, it became a point of honour and a sign of coolness to be seen sitting and reading amid the shells and shell-holes of this old Flanders playing-ground.

Beach Thomas was the most hated of the correspondents, both for painting the soldiers in false colours and for pretending that he spent his whole time sharing their dangers. He was parodied several times by the wonderful *Wipers Times*, a comic newspaper written by front-line soldiers for front-line soldiers. It was the *Private Eye* of the Western Front, anarchic, mocking everything and everybody, and doing so with a surprisingly gentle grace. Here, for instance, is a spoof article which catches precisely Thomas's naive, awkward style with its pomposity, its self-obsession and its strange non-sequiturs.

A MESSAGE FROM MR. TEECH BOMAS

BY OUR SPECIAL CORRESPONDENT MR TEECH BOMAS
MR TEECH BOMAS SPEAKS
No Man's Land, 20/7/16

I write from the middle of the battlefield. There are a lot of bullets but I don't mind that. Also the air is thick with shells. That also I don't mind . . . Let me tell you of the gallant dash of the Umpshires: Into the pick of the Prussian Guard they dashed. The few of the Guard who remained cried 'Kamerad' and surrendered. That rush was epic . . . I then walked over the German lines to have a look at them. There were a lot more bullets but what would you? . . . Tomorrow I will tell you more. I return now to the battle.

H. TEECH BOMAS

In the autobiography he published in 1925, *A Traveller in News*, Beach Thomas maintained that he did not realize how much of the information that was fed to him by the military authorities was misleading. This did not explain, however, how he came to give the impression that he had seen the action he described, when much of his time was spent at Headquarters. After the first day at the Battle of the Somme, which he reported cheerfully and positively, he later said that he was 'deeply ashamed of what I had written, for the very good reason that it was untrue. Almost all the official information was wrong. The vulgarity of enormous headlines and the enormity [sic] of one's own name did not lessen the shame.'

Yet all the evidence is that the headlines and the byline were the reason why he wrote as he did. The front-line soldiers might have the greatest contempt for him, but the readers back home loved it all and thought Beach Thomas was wonderful. He treasured a letter from a factory manager who wrote: 'Without your despatches we could never have persuaded the men to work through the bank holiday.'

It is from this period of the war that a habitual scepticism about the press properly begins in Britain. Before that, newspapers had enjoyed a good deal of credibility, and correspondents and editors were authority figures. But when the soldiers, millions of them, saw for themselves what was really happening on the Western Front, and read the newspapers' accounts, that credibility vanished at once. Occasionally the British papers were available in France the same day, though usually they arrived one or two days later. The front line was a frightening, alien world, utterly different from anything the soldiers had experienced before; and yet it was just a few hours away from home.

§

The Defence of the Realm Act, known without affection as DORA, passed into law on 8 August 1914, the fourth day of the war. It was a hurried, disturbingly broad piece of legislation (Stephen Koss, in *The Rise and Fall of the Political Press in Britain*, calls it 'vacuous') and it affected mostly newspapers. It now became an offence to gather or publish any information about the numbers or deployment of British soldiers, ships or aircraft, to publish any information which might be of use to an enemy, to spread false reports or make false statements likely to cause disaffection in the forces or to prejudice recruitment. For anyone trying to write accurately and impartially about the war, this covered a very great deal of ground.

DORA created conditions where facts were hard to discover, and truth for its own sake became a rare commodity. Rumour, as a result, tended to gain the upper hand over provable reality. Not surprisingly, perhaps, the British press, as a result, reported the First World War with more conscious falsity than it reported any other major international event of the twentieth century. The North American, the Australasian, and the French press were no better, and the German press was usually worse; but the British press had always congratulated itself on maintaining higher standards.

The British are, in their own self-assessment and the assessment of other countries, rational, calm, and slow to get excited. Yet the suddenness with which the First World War erupted, the difficulty (as a result of DORA) of discovering what was really going on, and the great fear of what the war might bring, helped to create a febrile atmosphere in which all sorts of unlikely things were believed. The deliberate scare-mongering of the yellow press, and particularly the *Daily Mail*, the *Daily Express* and the *Daily Mirror*, tended to condition people to believe what they read. In 1909, for instance, there was a rash of reports about Zeppelins being spotted over Britain, and there were often stories about German waiters congregating in coastal towns in order to spy on the movement of ships. Once the war began, rumour took on a new force, because censorship meant that ordinary people were more inclined to believe the stories they heard from others, and to pass them on.

One of the myths shared by almost everyone, from politicians and diplomats to the man in the street, was that of 'the Russian steamroller'. Russia's vast population, and its proportionately vast army, was felt to be an important element in the balance of forces. Once the steamroller began to move, the sheer weight of numbers would crush the Central Powers, Germany and Austro-Hungary. The Russian commander, General Vladimir Sukhomlinov, wrote after the war that in 1914 the British ambassador in St Petersburg, Sir George Buchanan, had begged the Russians to send a complete army corps to Britain. Sukhomlinov, knowing how stretched the Russian forces really were, thought he had gone mad.

But the desire to believe in the weight of Russian numbers was so strong that it quickly turned from a wish to a hard fact. Stories spread amazingly fast. Russian troops were seen on station platforms stamping the snow off their boots; no one seems to have stopped to ask themselves how the snow could have remained unmelted on their boots for days or perhaps weeks. They were heard calling in hoarse voices for vodka at Carlisle and Berwick-on-Tweed. At Durham, one of them jammed a penny-in-the-slot machine with a rouble.

On 8 September 1914 a news agency report from Rome (why Rome?) said that 250,000 Russians were being deployed in France. When the British newspapers put this to the Official Press Bureau they were told that there was no confirmation of the story, but that they were free to publish it: a clear sign that the military authorities thought it would be useful propaganda. The following day's *Daily News*, instead, decided that this must mean the story was true.

> The official sanction to the publication of [the Rome telegram] removes the newspaper reserve with regard to the rumours which for the last fortnight have coursed with such astonishing persistency through the length and breadth of England ... [T]he rumours ... are almost more amazing if they are false than if they are true.

For once the *Daily Mail* was more cautious than many papers, and suggested that the original story might have had its origins in a statement by a Russian official that 5,000 Russian reservists had received permission to serve with the Allies.

On the other hand, by Monday 14 September a special correspondent reporting from Belgium for the *Daily News*, P.J. Philip, actually found the Russians – or so he said: 'For two days I have been on a long trek looking for the Russians, and now I have found them – where and how it would not be discreet to tell.'

Not possible either, since P.J. Philip had invented the story. He had found a reference in a Belgian evening paper to Russian troops fighting with the Belgian army, assumed it must be true, and wrote it up for his newspaper. That journalists believe other journalists' reports when they know how dubious their own can be is always surprising. On 18 November an MP asked the Undersecretary of State for War in the House of Commons if any Russian troops had passed through Britain on their way to the Western Front. He answered: 'I am uncertain whether it will gratify or displease my hon. friend to learn that no Russian troops have been conveyed through Great Britain to the Western area of the European War.'

So one story that people drew comfort from had come to nothing. There were others. On 29 September 1914 the *Evening News*, another Harmsworth paper, published an article called 'The Bowmen', by the writer Arthur Machen, who often ventured into short stories of fantasy and the occult. His article was not labelled as fiction, and there was a separate short story in the paper that night. 'The Bowmen' was not Machen's best work, by any means, but it demonstrated his ability to write convincingly. He described how a British soldier in the retreat from Mons had called on the name of St George, who duly appeared and summoned up an army of ghostly archers from the Battle of Agincourt to attack the Germans pursuing them. The Germans were duly destroyed by volleys of phantom arrows. Afterwards the newspaper forwarded a number of readers' letters to Machen, asking for more information. Since he had not claimed that the story was anything more than fiction, he wrote back in each case to say it had been entirely imaginary.

But things started getting out of hand. Soon clergymen and Catholic priests were asking for permission to reprint his story in their parish magazines. In April 1915 a clergyman asked him for the sources of the story; and when Machen said it had been purely fictional, the clergyman told him he must be mistaken: it had clearly happened. Machen decided to scotch the whole story by publishing 'The Bowmen' in book form, and added a preface making it clear it was entirely a work of the imagination. Yet many people insisted on believing it all the more; they had developed a powerful emotional need for the reassurance that heavenly intervention gave them.

By early 1915 there was even a dirge-like song, sung by Foster Richardson, called 'The Angels of Mons', which proved remarkably successful. Opening with the sound of church bells to give it the requisite religious flavour, it began:

Have you heard the solemn story of the Angels of Mons?
That tale of love and glory of the Angels of Mons?
How our soldiers, pained and weary, were pressed on every side?
How the boys were mad and fearful in the thund'ring battle tide?
When suddenly before their eyes appeared a wondrous light.
A force of angels floated through the darkness of the night . . .

And so on for several verses. It is easy to feel superior about all this credulity. Yet the story of the ghostly bowmen, now usually presented as angels, continues to attract believers today, particularly in the United States, where such forms of belief are on the rise again. At a time when people were frightened for the future of their country, for the lives of their sons and grandsons at the front, it is not surprising that comforting fictions like the Angels of Mons should find plenty of supporters.

Such fantasies as Russians with snow on their boots and angels shooting arrows at the Germans were harmless. But many of the stories which appeared in the British press were more disturbing. The newspapers, encouraged by army intelligence, achieved remarkable success in demonizing the enemy. Like all the most effective propaganda, the stories had a certain plausibility to them. Older people in Britain remembered how public opinion had swung round in the Franco-Prussian War of 1870. Most people had initially sympathized with the Prussians, who were Protestants and generally regarded as being decent and upright. More importantly, perhaps, they seemed to pose no threat to the British. France, by contrast, was run by the corrupt, immoral regime of Emperor Napoleon III, and had been the national enemy for centuries. But the Prussians behaved so brutally when they invaded France, executing people for being *franc-tireurs* or guerrilla fighters, and enforcing the cruel and unnecessary siege of Paris, that British opinion swung against Prussia and in favour of France; and it had never swung back. From then on, the British tended to think of Prussia as brutal and militaristic; and the unpredictable antics of Kaiser Wilhelm II reinforced this view.

The fear of the *franc-tireurs* was strong among the invaders of 1870, and played an important part in the minds of the German army in 1914. In reality they were responsible for fewer than 1,000 casualties during the Franco-Prussian War, but, contrary to the laws of war, the Prussians took ferocious reprisals against places from which they had been fired on.

Few armies respond well to being fired at by guerrillas, but the Germans developed a psychosis about it which did serious damage to their reputation. The US forces in Vietnam and Iraq reacted to attack in rather similar ways, often opening fire randomly on civilians in areas where they had been ambushed. The German response was made in cold blood, to teach the local population a lesson. So, with the memory of 1870 still strongly present, there was an expectation that when the Germans invaded Belgium and France they would behave savagely. It was this expectation which the British wartime propaganda services took advantage of.

After the war, there was a tendency in Britain to assume that there had been no truth whatever in the atrocity stories. This has continued until our own day. It would mean, of course, that the German occupying forces of 1914–18 behaved completely differently from those of 1870 and 1940–4: by no means impossible, certainly, but perhaps unlikely. Official inquiries once the war was over indicated that something like 5,500 Belgian civilians had been executed by the German invaders, and about 900 French civilians. By the standards of the Second World War, or of later conflicts like Vietnam, Bangladesh, Rwanda, and Iraq, these are tiny losses; but they came after long years of peace in Europe, where war crimes, especially against women and children, were greeted with genuine horror.

Regular soldiers who are frustrated by guerrilla tactics, as happened with the British in the Boer War, often behave brutally; and there is no real reason why German soldiers who deliberately killed children – and there were various attested cases of this in Belgium – were not also capable of mutilating men and women they suspected of carrying out or supporting acts of resistance. But the overall result of these stories, accurate or otherwise, was to make it far easier for people who might normally be sceptical of such things to accept deliberately falsified stories. As a rule, British people, like Americans, have to be worked up to a level of moral outrage to support a war. Stories of German atrocities provided the required incentive.

As the Germans swept through Belgium, burning towns and villages and killing civilians as they went, people in Britain were attuned to the idea that their enemy was committing atrocities, and wanted evidence of it. Editors, aware of this pressure and believing that atrocities were being committed, demanded stories from their reporters. The reporters did their best to find them. It would have taken a good deal of moral courage to tell the foreign editor of, say, the *Daily Mail* or *The Times* that stories going the rounds, and being reported in other newspapers, could not be substantiated. There was a collective will to exaggerate, to believe, and to pass the stories on with extra exaggeration.

There was, for instance, the case of the crucified Canadian. Several variants of this existed in the early days of the war. Sometimes the victim was a young girl (there was a strongly sexual edge to some of the imaginings); sometimes it was an American who had been caught up in the fighting; but the story eventually coalesced around the idea that it was a Canadian officer. These stories were not, as far as one can tell, invented out of nothing by the British propaganda service or by journalists. They were rumours, passed on from soldier to soldier until one of them reached the ears of a war correspondent. In this hectic climate the correspondent would have been grateful to supply his desk with the kind of thing it was demanding. Therefore he would have passed on the details without checking them too much. Every journalist for a century and a half has been aware of the concept of the story that is too good to check – in case it turns out to be false.

This is how the Paris correspondent of *The Times* wrote up one such story for 10 May 1915. He was honest enough about the lack of a firm source, but neither he nor his newspaper checked it out. Perhaps, in wartime, that would have been too difficult anyway.

> Last week a large number of Canadian soldiers, wounded in the fighting round Ypres, arrived at the base hospital at Versculles. They all told a story of how one of their officers had been crucified by the Germans. He had been pinned to a wall by bayonets thrust through his hands and feet, another bayonet had been driven through his throat, and, finally, he was riddled with bullets. The wounded Canadians said the Dublin Fusiliers had seen this done with their own eyes, and they had heard the officers of the Dublin Fusiliers talking about it.

If Irish soldiers saw it, why didn't the Canadians, who were presumably closer to the incident? Like so many of these stories, the source is never quite an eyewitness himself – just someone who has heard it from an eyewitness.

Five days later, a correspondent for *The Times* confirmed his colleague's story. The story was current where he was, he wrote, but since there was no absolute proof, men were unwilling to believe 'that a civilised foe could be guilty of an act so cruel and savage'. In fact, he said, the victim was a Canadian sergeant, though he admits he hasn't heard that 'any of our men' actually saw the crime committed. But he had reason to believe that written depositions about the discovery of the Canadian's body had been handed to staff at Headquarters.

It sounded like confirmation, yet it wasn't. Rather, it was another example of the entirely human tendency to weigh in on the side of a colleague who had only supplied what was asked of him: the details of an atrocity. It helped that the correspondent had heard that eyewitness evidence had been sent to Headquarters; this must have made him feel more confident about writing up his story. An open-minded reader might wonder whether all that happened was that a bayoneted body had been discovered, and that the wounds had been imaginatively interpreted as being from a crucifixion. The correspondent clearly did not know that on 12 May 1915, three days before he filed his confirmatory report, an MP had asked the Undersecretary of State for War in the House of Commons if he had any information about three Canadians (the figure had gone up) who had been crucified. Hansard reads: 'MR. TENNANT: No, sir; no information of such an atrocity having been perpetrated has yet reached the War Office.'

After that, the story of the crucified Canadian no longer appears in the news pages, but it continued to be believed by vast numbers of people.

In 1928, when anti-war revisionism was at its height, the left-wing MP Arthur Ponsonby produced a book called *Falsehood in War-Time*, which examined a number of atrocity stories and found no truth in any of them. New editions of the book continued to be published until 1940. There was the case of the young nurse from Dumfries, Grace Hume, as reported in lip-smacking detail by the *Star* on 16 September 1914. She was working at a hospital at Vilvorde when the Germans arrived; her breasts were cut off and she died in agony. Before she died she wrote a note, which the *Star* quoted, and which was smuggled to her sister in Dumfries.

The *Evening Standard* printed the letter, and quoted the official censors as saying they had no objection to its being published, but that they took no responsibility for the correctness of the statement. Two days later, *The Times* reported that the martyred nurse was actually safe in Huddersfield, and had never even been to Belgium. Her seventeen-year-old sister Kate was charged with having forged both the letters, and was later found guilty.

There were plenty of other stories: the stamp which, when it was steamed off the envelope containing a cheery letter from a prisoner of war, revealed a message to say that the Germans had cut out his tongue.

Since letters from prisoners of war did not carry stamps – they were delivered by the International Red Cross – this was scarcely very convincing, and never reached the papers. *The Times* and the *Manchester Guardian* investigated stories about the vicious tattooing of men's faces with German symbols, and found them improbable too. On the other hand, the story about the factory which rendered down human bodies into soap was published, and was widely believed. The source seems to have been a mistranslation of an article referring to the rendering down of animal bodies.

In the years immediately after the war, the feeling grew that the army, the government and the press had deliberately encouraged people to believe that the Germans had a diabolical propensity for cruelty and must be stopped at any cost: thereby justifying the terrible losses on the battlefield. The reality is, as usual, more complicated. The army and the censors merely refused to deny them outright if they seemed to be useful. The government, which had a tradition of avoiding outright lies in Parliament, often denied them. But it scarcely mattered, because at a time when information was so tightly controlled, rumour came into its own; and the press competed to reinforce the rumours.

The journalists could and should have been more careful about what they reported, of course – though it would not have been very easy to check the details of stories. But journalism, like the writing of history, can be a careless trade. When deadlines are close, it is difficult to check everything. The author of *Falsehood in War-Time*, for instance, quotes an account by a *Daily Mail* correspondent, Captain F.W. Wilson, who jauntily described to the *New York Evening Post* three years after the war how he had invented the story of a little girl saved from a village near Brussels, burned by the Germans in August 1914.

There is no doubt that the Germans burned the village, Courbeck-Loo, and killed many of the inhabitants. The little girl though was Wilson's invention; he didn't even go to the village, he confessed. But he ran into a problem: large numbers of *Mail* readers, including Queen Alexandra, wanted to help the little girl or even adopt her. Vast quantities of baby clothes were donated. Captain Wilson had to think fast. He announced that the little girl had died of a highly contagious disease, which was why she couldn't be given a public burial. 'We got Lady Northcliffe to start a creche with all the baby-clothes,' he joked.

It is a depressingly plausible story, and illustrates how easy it was for the yellow press to invent atrocity stories. Captain Wilson's confession was picked up by a pacifist journal, the *Crusader*, and published on 24 February 1922. The *Crusader* had a Christian, pacifist and sometimes socialist perspective. When it published what it maintained was the truth about Captain Wilson's story of the little girl of Courbeck-Loo, a backlash to false reporting was well under way, and people were starting to realize how they had been duped.

In 1975 it was republished in the excellently researched study of war reporting, Phillip Knightley's *The First Casualty*. Like many histories produced in the 1970s, it has a distinctly anti-establishment tone to it. Nowadays the story of how Captain Wilson invented the Courbeck-Loo atrocity appears on the Internet: further evidence of how journalists either make up horror stories or use them without checking.

The trouble is, the true facts of the story have proven curiously difficult to check. Captain F.W. Wilson certainly worked as a correspondent for the *Daily Mail*, but there is no record of any interview with him in the archives of the *New York Evening Post*. Nor does any appear in the archives of the *New York Times*, sometimes mentioned as the source. A careful, detailed search in Wilson's paper, the *Daily Mail*, has failed to turn up any news item in 1914 about a little girl being saved from the well-reported German atrocity at Courbeck-Loo. Queen Alexandra didn't send any baby clothes for her, because she never heard about her in the first place. Nor is there any evidence that readers sent in money or clothes for the little girl – though they may well have responded to the original atrocity. The *Crusader*, with its Christian principles, is unlikely to have invented it, and would have laid itself open to a libel action if it did. Perhaps Captain Wilson, who seems to have been a fairly cynical character, made up the story of how he made up the story. The only safe conclusion is that, in spite of the preoccupation after the war with the way the newspapers had lied about what happened, not all accusations about atrocity stories are necessarily true.

§

In the first three weeks, two of the war's greatest battles were fought, and both were calamitous defeats for the Allies. The Battle of the Frontiers, which began on 14 August and lasted until 25 August, cost France a third of a million men; the Battle of Tannenberg, which began on 22 August, resulted in the almost total destruction of the Russian Second Army. The British public was told about neither of these disasters at the time.

On Tuesday 18 August, for instance, when it was already clear that the French were losing the Battle of the Frontiers, *The Times*' military correspondent was reporting: 'All the news from the land frontiers is good. It is true that there has been no collision between the main armies as yet . . . but this is no reason why we should not be very fairly confident about the position of the land forces of the Allies.'

And then he turned his attention to the Eastern Front: 'The Russian avalanche begins . . . Germany has gained nothing, absolutely nothing, from her superior readiness in the east.'

As he wrote that, the Battle of Tannenberg was just about to begin. It was a Russian catastrophe, in which unknown hundreds of thousands died. *The Times* did not mention the outcome of the battle until Monday 12 October, and then only in a throwaway reference in the middle of a review of the German press. The *Daily Express* first mentioned it in a single line a year later, on 1 September 1915. It was not until the war was over that the British press printed any real account of the seriousness of the Russian defeat.

Was it censorship that blanked out of the Battle of Tannenberg and the Battle of the Frontiers? Probably not; the system was hardly functioning at that stage. Was it ignorance and the fog of war? Perhaps to some extent, certainly with Tannenberg. There were no British correspondents with the Russian armies, and the Russian censors in St Petersburg did their best to stop all word of the defeat getting out. But the same was not true of the Battle of the Frontiers. Reporting from the battlefield was difficult, but word soon leaked out to Paris about the scale of the defeat.

It looks as though the military correspondent of *The Times*, Colonel Charles Repington (who had been forced to resign from the army before the war after having an affair with the wife of a fellow officer), may have decided to ignore whatever news had seeped through from Tannenberg and the Battle of the Frontiers, and produced a string of outright lies in order to maintain the British public's faith in the Russian steamroller and French military prowess.

§

In the first days of the war, the Conservative barrister F.E. Smith was appointed to set up a Press Bureau in order to control news from the front. It was an extraordinary appointment. Smith (who was later to be created Lord Birkenhead) was a clever, witty risk-taker, impatient with bureaucracy, and not at all sympathetic to the interests of army men like Lord Kitchener. His *bons mots* in court were famous. ('What do you suppose I am on the Bench for, Mr Smith?' 'It is not for me, Your Honour, to attempt to fathom the inscrutable workings of Providence.') He was the complete opposite of the plodding, unimaginative men who would soon be given the job of telling journalists what they must not say. F.E. Smith was not destined to last long in the job.

For the first two or three weeks of the war, his Official Press Bureau was fairly disorganized. The newspapers assumed it would be like the Boer War, where journalists had to be accredited by the War Office, but could travel round and dig out stories. At the start, therefore, the journalists fell into two categories: those who headed off immediately for the front, and those who waited for accreditation.

The more cautious, law-abiding journalists applied to the War Office in Whitehall. There they were treated with contempt by staff officers half their age, who knew what their boss, Lord Kitchener, felt about the press. Nothing happened for ten months. It was the summer of 1915 before Kitchener allowed five correspondents to be based at General Head-quarters in France.

A century and a half of war journalism has demonstrated that the correct way to deal with a breaking news story is to leap before you look. You must never worry how you will get in or how you will get out again afterwards: you must head off straight away. Philip Gibbs, who had one of the better records as a correspondent in the First World War, had never been anyone's poodle. Given a plum job by Lord Northcliffe on the *Daily Mail*, he fell out with him very fast and resigned.

The *Daily Chronicle* hired him to go to Germany in 1913, hoping to show that the jingoistic British newspapers were wrong in believing that Germany wanted war. His trip was less than successful: Germany, he found, was actually rather keen on war. Gibbs said so, and the *Chronicle* disapproved. From there he went to Ireland and infiltrated a group of gunrunners preparing for what at that stage looked like the coming civil war between Unionists and Nationalists.

At midnight on 4–5 August, he and a few correspondents like him hurried off to France with no accreditation and no help from officialdom, British or French. All he took, he wrote immediately after the war in his book *Realities of War*, 'were bags of money which might be necessary for the hire of motor-cars, hotel life, and the bribery of door-keepers in the ante-chambers of war . . .'

The motor cars look different, the hotels have more facilities to offer, but the door-keepers of war are no less demanding now than they were almost a century ago. Philip Gibbs is one of those correspondents who, you feel, could slot into today's journalism with no more than a half-hour's explanation about how things have changed during the intervening years. Gibbs was not strong physically, and he was a deeply sensitive man; yet in spite of the horrors he endured on the Western Front, he consistently showed real courage and determination.

In just a week, he and his colleagues had an extraordinary time. They were, he writes, arrested, gaoled, let out, caught again in forbidden places, re-arrested, and expelled from France. They had seen terrible things: hundreds of thousands of refugees, towns destroyed, mangled bodies, and the endless parade of wounded from the hopeless early battles in which the Germans were always victorious, and the French and British were always on the retreat. Then, finally, he was sent back to his office in London.

'Had a good time?' asked a colleague along the corridor, hardly waiting for an answer.

'A good time!' . . . God! . . . Did people think it was amusing to be an onlooker of world-tragedy? . . .

I had not changed the clothes which were smeared with blood of French and Belgian soldiers whom I had helped, in a week of strange adventure, to carry to the surgeons. As an onlooker of war I hated the people who had not seen, because they could not understand.

During the Battle of Mons in late August, the BEF, outgunned, outnumbered and outmanoeuvred by the Germans, was forced to retreat: a disorganized, completely unplanned affair, though the soldiers – even without the help of the archers of Agincourt – never lost their sense of discipline and their morale.

By chance Arthur Moore of *The Times* and Henry Hamilton Fyfe of the *Daily Mail* were wandering around northern France, trying to find stories and evade the British and French military authorities. Like Philip Gibbs, they had crossed the Channel in the first days of the war. When Kitchener found out that Fyfe was still there, he threatened to have him shot – though he would not have had the powers to do it. The Germans, however, had warned that they would execute any British or French journalists they captured, and they certainly meant it. But this did not deter the two correspondents. Long after the war, Hamilton Fyfe wrote in his book *My Seven Lives*: 'Moore and I went on getting as near as we could and sending all the news that we could pick up (it was given to the pursers of steamers and met by special messengers on the other side).'

The first they heard about the battle at Mons, and the retreat from it, was when they came across a British army lorry by the side of the road.'Come from Amiens,' the driver told them. 'All the rest went on, we got something wrong with our engine. Rare old turn-out it was, all of a sudden.'

Other soldiers then told them how all the British troops in the area of Amiens had been forced to retreat, and no one had any idea where they were supposed to be going. The intrepid pair then headed to Amiens, where they began to grasp the full extent of the disaster. They could hear the German guns, and spoke to dozens of fugitive soldiers who had lost their units and were completely disorientated. The men had thrown away their equipment, yet they did not seem depressed or anxious, merely puzzled. Fyfe noticed how most of them emphasized the funny side of their experiences. That Friday night, 28 August, he and Moore found somewhere to rest and write their despatches. Then they set out to drive to Dieppe, in order to get on a boat leaving for England.

The despatches arrived in London on Saturday evening. At that stage *The Times* had a Sunday edition, though the *Mail* did not. Wickham Steed and George Freeman, the acting editor of *The Times*, were alerted, and they read Moore's article directly it arrived. A story like this, which might even be the precursor to Britain's defeat in the war, would obviously make a powerful impact on public opinion.

This was a scoop of major proportions. The two editors were shocked by Moore's despatch, but it does not seem to have occurred to them to suppress it. Instead, they went to work on it, softening some of its details and implications so it would stand a better chance of being passed by the censor. Then they sent it round to the chief censor, F.E. Smith. Smith was a heavy drinker, and the article did not reach him until after dinner that evening. Nevertheless he saw the immense significance of what he read, and decided that it had to be published. It would, he thought, awaken the country to the danger it was in, and encourage more men to enlist. He cut out entire sentences and replaced them with dots, having the effect of making things seem even worse than they actually were. And he reinstated some passages that Steed and Freeman had crossed out. Two hours later, the article came back with a handwritten note from Smith:

> I am sorry to have censored this most able and interesting message so freely, but the reasons are obvious. Forgive my clumsy journalistic suggestions, but I beg you to use the the parts of this article which I have passed to enforce the lesson – reinforcements and reinforcements at once.

Moore's despatch, published in *The Times* of Sunday 30 August, was the work of an exhausted, emotionally overwrought man. To modern eyes, it reads less like a news report announcing a major defeat in battle than a feature article or even an open letter to the censors. But the extraordinary nature of the story it told made up for all its imperfections: one of which is the strange, offhand and personal way it is written.

> Amiens, 29 August
>
> I read this afternoon in Amiens this morning's Paris papers. To me, knowing some portion of the truth, it seems incredible that a great people should be so kept in ignorance of the situation which it has to face. The papers read like children's prattle, gleanings from the war talk of their parents a week ago . . .
>
> This is not well. I would plead with the English censor to let my message pass . . . [I]t is important that the nation should know and realise certain things. Bitter truths, but we can face them. We have to cut our losses, to take stock of the situation, to set our teeth . . .
>
> Our losses are very great. I have seen the broken bits of many regiments . . . [But] there is no failure in discipline, no panic, no throwing up the sponge . . . The men are battered

with marching, and ought to be weak with hunger, . . . but they are steady and cheerful, and whenever they arrive make straight for the proper authority, report themselves, and seek news of their regiment.

To sum up, the first great German effort has succeeded. We have to face the fact that the British Expeditionary Force, which bore the great weight of the blow, has suffered terrible losses and requires immediate and immense reinforcement. The British Expeditionary Force has indeed won imperishable glory, but it needs men, men, and yet more men.

The last sentence was put in by F.E. Smith, who was distinctly tired and emotional at the time. The main headline on Moore's despatch that August Sunday morning had a powerful effect on everyone who read it.

BROKEN BRITISH REGIMENTS BATTLING AGAINST ODDS.

Alongside, *The Times* reprinted the article by Moore's colleague, Hamilton Fyfe, which (because his own paper, the *Mail*, did not appear on Sundays) was also used as the lead that morning in the *Weekly Dispatch*, another Northcliffe paper. Its headline was equally alarming:

GERMAN TIDAL WAVE – OUR SOLDIERS OVERWHELMED BY NUMBERS.

After so much optimism in the British press, this came as a savage blow. The next day, F.E. Smith kept quiet about his part in approving the article. In the absence of any word from him, the bureaucrats at the Official Press Bureau put out a disapproving statement:

These messages ... should be treated with extreme caution. No correspondents are at the front, and their information, however honestly sent, is therefore derived second or third-hand from persons often in no condition to tell coherent stories ...

This bears the perennial stamp of Whitehall. It is deliberately and consciously untrue – Kitchener might have given orders that there should be no correspondents at the front, but that did not mean that there were none – and it is a characteristically sly attempt to undermine the credibility of the message. Moore and Fyfe had seen with their own eyes the broken remnants of regiments, and the soldiers they interviewed had told them the clearest of stories. Of course those stories were second-hand; what else is a journalist's interview? At no stage did the Press Bureau deny the facts in the two despatches. It did not need to: the subtle casting of doubt on someone's accuracy and professionalism does the job far more effectively than open falsehood.

The rivals of *The Times*, having failed to obtain the story themselves, lined up behind the authorities in condemning the despatches; newspaper behaviour rarely changes. Perhaps the other papers felt they had to, since most of them had been publishing positive, optimistic reports from France. The rest of Fleet Street found itself in an awkward position. The editorial team at the *Daily News*, a Liberal newspaper which had been strongly against entering the war, seems to have turned hastily to the War Office for a story to counter the one in *The Times*, and as a result produced a set of headlines which read like the worst kind of jingoism:

TRUTH ABOUT OUR ARMY IN FRANCE.

Official News of Glorious Achievements.

CASUALTIES 6,000.

Four Days of Battle Against Overwhelming Odds.
Routed Germans Speared By Lancers and Scots Greys.

The following day, Monday 1 September, the *Daily News* gloated openly. *The Times*, said the lead editorial in the *News*, had suggested that the British army had been broken into fragments and reduced to something hardly better than a mob. '[T]he article . . . was *calculated* [my italics] to disturb and distress the public mind.'

By contrast, *The Times* said nothing that morning. It did not add to its coverage from Amiens, and instead waited for F.E. Smith to pronounce on it. He stood up in the Commons that afternoon and announced – to gasps of surprise from both sides of the House – that he had passed the despatches himself. He believed, he said, that it had been right to do so. Next day *The Times* wrote grandly, '[W]e assume that written apologies will reach us in due course.'

But the thought that Northcliffe, the vulgar, crowd-pleasing ultra-belligerent, should have been right about something as important as this, was particularly hard for some newspapers to swallow. The *Manchester Guardian*, for example, did not apologize; on the contrary, it continued to disapprove of the original scoop. Referring to Moore's despatch, it wrote: 'The misleading telegram was rather poor, rhetorical stuff. It was not what a war correspondent of the "Times" in its greatest days would probably have thought of sending to it.'

The perennial motto of the British press has always been *homo homini lupus*: man behaves like a wolf to his fellow man. Just as it was about to become impossible to report with freedom and honesty from the front, one of the few genuinely first-class journalistic scoops of the First World War was dismissed as badly written and unworthy, simply because it was an exclusive.

§

Kitchener was predictably furious about the two Amiens despatches, and organized it so that Hamilton Fyfe of the *Daily Mail*, as the author of one of them, was sent to Russia to report. This was the start of Lord Northcliffe's feud with Kitchener; you didn't mistreat his men and escape without paying a price. Journalists on both the *Mail* and *The Times* were instructed to criticize him whenever possible; and the last two years of his life were made more difficult accordingly.

By late 1914 it was still possible for journalists to travel to France, and pick up news from the edges of the war zone; but the authorities, British and French, were on the lookout for them. When Philip Gibbs went to investigate conditions in Red Cross hospitals he was arrested – even though the value to the enemy of any reports he might have written would have been negligible – and Kitchener threatened to have him shot. Kitchener appointed a serving officer, Colonel Ernest Swinton, to describe the action on the Western Front. These reports were then handed out to the newspapers for publication. Editors who had grown up in the cut-throat atmosphere of Fleet Street were appalled. Swinton wrote more than a hundred reports under the pen name 'Eyewitness', which covered all the early battles of 1915. Their tone was almost invariably upbeat, and they bore very little relationship to the ugly reality of the war at that stage. The public soon became aware of the contempt the press had for Swinton's reporting, and the joke everywhere was that it wasn't so much Eyewitness as Eyewash.

Yet Swinton was no hidebound military dullard. He is credited with playing an important part in the development of the tank (the idea for an armoured, tracked vehicle came to him while his car was slipping in the mud near the front line in October 1914). He wrote a military manual about the tactics of small units, half-humorously entitled 'The Defence of Duffer's Drift', which remained in official use until the Second World War. Back in 1907 he had given official encouragement to the American showman and inventor 'Colonel' Samuel Franklin Cody for man-carrying kites, which could be used at the front for observation purposes. And when Cody made the first man-powered flight in Britain in October of the following year, Swinton took an interest in the early development and use of aeroplanes.

His other claim to fame was inventing the expression 'no-man's-land'. He was keen to tell the truth, and was as angry as any of the professionals when his copy was mangled by the censors – for he, like everyone else, had to submit it for vetting. But he saw things exclusively as a soldier, and was willing to write his reports the way the military wanted. And so, when he came to write on the disastrous Battle of Neuve Chapelle, his despatches on 13 May 1915 managed to present it as a victory.

EPIC OF NEUVE CHAPELLE.
BRITISH ARTILLERY OVERWHELMING.
VIVID ACCOUNT BY 'EYE-WITNESS'.

On the morning of the 12th the German counter-attacks were renewed along the whole front round the village and to the north of it. These again resulted only in great losses to the enemy, who also left many prisoners in our hands. By this time the Germans were beginning to show signs of great exhaustion, and on more than one occasion the men of the attacking line lay down and held up their hands when we opened fire.

No doubt all of these things happened, and Swinton may well have seen them. But as an account of what had really happened across the Neuve Chapelle front it was the purest fantasy. The British under General French started with an intense artillery barrage, which was intended to destroy everything in the German trenches. But as happened many more times in the next couple of years, the British shells often failed to explode, and the German trenches were too deep and well-protected for the shells to penetrate.

The barrage acted instead as a warning that an attack was coming. The moment the barrage ended, the Germans set up their machine guns and mowed down the advancing British troops. More than 11,000 of them were killed or wounded that day, and by the time the fighting petered out, the following month, the British had suffered 100,000 losses. Far from being a victory, it was a disaster bringing about the downfall of General French.

'Eyewitness' was discredited as a result. Even Kitchener began to realize that he had to allow journalists into France; though he was determined that they would report only what he wanted.

F.E. Smith had resigned as head of the Official Press Bureau soon after the publication of the Amiens despatches, and had been replaced by a two-man directorate consisting of Sir Edward Cook, a pleasant and amusing former editor of the *Daily News*, and a former colonial administrator, Sir Frank Swettenham. The new system remained in place until the end of the war. Both Cook and Swettenham were liked and generally respected, but the system they ran was much criticized in Fleet Street.

Modern accounts of the reporting of the First World War sometimes give the unlikely impression that editors and correspondents welcomed the censorship of their work for patriotic reasons. This was never true; and although there was a great deal of self-censorship, no one liked submitting their reports to the suspicious officers and civil servants whose job it was, effectively, to ensure that nothing of value got past them.

The novelist H.M. Tomlinson, who had worked for two radical newspapers and became the war correspondent of the *Daily News*, regarded the censorship with a loathing that made him almost incomprehensible when he came to write about it afterwards. At first, he said, the censor merely cut out news and opinions which might be of use to the enemy; but later:

it became necessary to turn into enemies of the State those who . . . denounced generals for wasting the lives of boys in purposeless actions . . . and those who asked whether the war was to go on till all were dead, or whether it might be stopped profitably at any time by using a little common sense.

Virtually every journalist shared Tomlinson's disgust. Even the genial Sir Edward Cook was embarrassed by it. He drew up the materials for a book on the Bureau's wartime record, *The Press in Wartime*, which was published posthumously in 1920. As a former editor himself, he put up only a lukewarm case for censorship; one example of its value, he said, was that the British Expeditionary Force was transported safely to France because no one was allowed to write anything about the subject. Another example he gave was the mobilization of the Royal Navy in complete secrecy. It would not have been enough, he wrote, to have left the decision to publish or not to publish these things to the newspaper editors themselves; a third party, with full legal powers, had to do that. He seemed unable to find any more cases where censorship had been of any value.

Cook clearly felt he had betrayed one of the most basic instincts of the profession. Once, he wrote, a journalist of a big American news agency asked to interview him. Cook agreed, on one condition. The journalist assumed he was going to say that the interview must be submitted to the censor; but Cook assured him it was a rule of the department that they never censored articles or telegrams which criticized censorship. The condition he wanted to make was that the journalist must not speak too well of their work.

'So do not give us any flowers,' I said. 'It really would be a terrible blow if you did . . .'

It was a characteristically quixotic thing to say, and no doubt it eased Cook's conscience a little. But he did nothing to stop the pettifogging interference of the officials who often wielded their blue pencils without regard to common sense or meaning.

After Henry Hamilton Fyfe of the *Daily Mail* was banished from northern France on Kitchener's orders, he moved on from Russia to Spain, Portugal and Italy: not exactly areas where he was likely to score any great reporting successes. He wrote scathingly about censorship and the censors, but insisted he bore them no malice. 'One can't be angry with people who make one laugh,' he wrote later. He described how he had wanted on one occasion to report that an Allied army had been forced to retreat, but the censor cut it out.

> 'That can't tell the Germans anything,' Fyfe complained. 'They know how far they have advanced.'
> 'Are you sure of that?' the censor replied; 'perhaps they may not.'

Another time Fyfe wrote about the shrapnel 'bursting in the blue sky'. The censor cut out the last four words.

> 'That would show where this incident took place,' he explained. 'It would indicate the south too clearly. In the north the sky is never blue.'

By June 1915 there were five accredited correspondents in place in northern France: Philip Gibbs for the *Daily Chronicle* and the *Daily Telegraph*, William Beach Thomas (*Daily Mail* and *Daily Mirror*), Percival Phillips (*Daily Express* and *Morning Post*), Henry Perry Robinson (*The Times*) and Herbert Russell (Reuter's). The censor appointed to vet their copy was a former leader writer of the *Manchester Guardian*, C.E. Montague.

The correspondents could go pretty much where they wanted, but they always had to be accompanied by an escorting press officer. John Buchan, who worked for the War Propaganda Bureau and also worked sometimes as a correspondent in France for *The Times*, writes amusingly of the relationship between the two in his novel *Greenmantle*, published in 1916. The book's hero, Richard Hannay, asks his fellow-convalescent Sandy Arbuthnot, who had fought alongside him at Loos in 1915, if he is willing to do some special war work.

> 'O my sainted aunt!' said Sandy. 'What is it? For Heaven's sake put me out of pain. Have we to . . . take the shivering journalist in a motorcar where he can imagine he sees a Boche?'

Sometimes the journalist and escort became friends, as Philip Gibbs bore witness.

> [W]henever we go under shell-fire or into unpleasant places the
> Press Officers must come with us. They do it with excellent grace
> and more zest than one might expect from those who have to risk
> their lives to appease another man's curiosity. The chauffeur we
> can leave a mile behind us on the road (where he sometimes has a
> more dangerous time than we), but the Press Officer must tread the
> shell- holes and slimy trenches with us to the bitter end and back.

During the occupation of Iraq, the US army operated almost exactly the
system that was put into place by the British army in 1915.

A conscientious and brave man like Philip Gibbs often risked his life
more than most men in the front line. They, after all, spent a fortnight at
a time in the trenches and were marched back to the rear, a system which
kept their morale high; but correspondents like Gibbs spent their whole
time within range of enemy artillery and snipers. Though the officers
were often disdainful towards them, the ordinary soldiers usually enjoyed
their company. By 1917, Henry Perry Robinson of *The Times* wrote in
the anachronistically named magazine *The Nineteenth Century* that
although relations with the military had greatly improved by then,

> the Army has still some little way to travel in the directions, first,
> of understanding that nothing can ever be as powerful as the truth
> and, second, of trusting further to the discretion of Correspondents
> who know the use of the weapons which they wield much better
> than the Army can ever teach them.

This is an argument which generations of journalists have used, with,
almost always, the same result: that is, no result at all. Some military
people doubt the patriotism of journalists; some doubt their understanding of what is going on, or their discretion, or their intelligence.
But they all know that the safe way out of any difficulty is simply to
say no.

Frustration was the war correspondent's companion: he knew that
much of his best material would never make it past the censor. He was
obliged to make whatever the censor passed available to the other war
correspondents: the material was regarded as 'pool', to be used by all. At
first it was difficult to persuade people to cooperate in this way. At last it
worked, and the five permanent correspondents, plus those like John

Buchan who came in from time to time, got on well; except, as Philip Gibbs describes, when deadlines drew closer and they each had to read out their notes on the day's events for the rest to hear:

> Time was short while the world waited for our tales of tragedy or victory . . . and tempers were frayed, and nerves on edge, among five men who hated one another, sometimes, with a murderous hatred (though, otherwise, good comrades) and desired one another's deaths by slow torture or poison-gas when they fumbled over notes written in a jolting car, or on a battlefield walk, and went into past history to explain present happenings, or became tangled in the numbers of battalions and divisions.

§

The horrors of front-line warfare were so great that if the newspapers had been free to describe them honestly, it would certainly have been harder to persuade men to come forward and join up in sufficient numbers. Better, the politicians and the generals believed, to hide the truth from the British public, so that they would continue to support the war and encourage their sons to join the forces. Many people who did have some idea what conditions at the front were like allowed their sons to volunteer; Rudyard Kipling, for instance, who reluctantly helped his seventeen-year-old son to enlist, only for him to be killed at the Battle of Loos in 1915; the poem which Kipling wrote about his death makes hard reading.

'Have You News of My Boy Jack'?

'Have you news of my boy Jack?'
Not this tide.
'When d'you think that he'll come back?'
Not with this wind blowing, and this tide.
'Has any one else had word of him?'
Not this tide.
For what is sunk will hardly swim,
Not with this wind blowing, and this tide.

'Oh, dear, what comfort can I find?'
None this tide,
Nor any tide,
Except he did not shame his kind –
Not even with that wind blowing, and that tide.

Then hold your head up all the more,
This tide,
And every tide;
Because he was the son you bore,
And gave to that wind blowing and that tide.

Compare that with the insider-trading smugness of another father, David Lloyd George, whose son Raymond volunteered and was killed on the Somme that year. For all his early pacifism Lloyd George swung fully behind the war, and in its early days used his magnificent oratory to encourage young men to join up. At the very same time he wrote privately to his wife:

I am dead against carrying on a war of conquest to crush Germany for the benefit of Russia . . . I am not going to sacrifice my nice boy [Gwilym, or Wil] for that purpose. You must write Wil telling him he must on no account be bullied into volunteering abroad.

But Gwilym Lloyd George had a mind of his own. He joined up, commanded a battery of artillery at the Somme and Passchendaele, and was mentioned in despatches. He managed, against the odds, to survive the war.

§

Censorship did not prevent British newspapers printing full accounts of the Christmas truce of 1914, even though GHQ disapproved of soldiers fraternizing with the enemy. The 'Eyewitness' system, by which the despatches of Colonel Ernest Swinton were issued to all newspapers, was still in force. But in the days after Christmas all the main newspapers published letters from front-line soldiers to their families at home, describing the truce. The censors failed to stop them. On 2 January 1915 a *Daily Mirror* editorial reads:

> The papers have been full of stories about this Christmas in the trenches. Either from those returned on leave from the front, or from letters, we hear and read the same report of perfect friendliness between individuals, officers and men, of the opposing sides.

Two days later the *Manchester Guardian* printed a letter from Gunner Herbert Smart, with the Royal Field Artillery, who had played football for Aston Villa before joining up. The Germans, he says, had a Christmas tree in their front-line trench and hung Chinese lanterns along the top of a parapet.

> 'Come over,' said one German soldier; 'I want to speak to you.' We didn't know how to take it at first, but one of the nuts went over, and as no harm befell him others followed. But our commanding officer would not let more than three at a time go. I went out myself on Christmas Day and ex-changed some cigarettes for cigars. The German I met had been a waiter in London, and could use our language a little. He says they do not want to fight.
>
> Fancy a German shaking your flapper as though he was trying to smash your fingers, and then a few days later trying to plug you!

And on 6 January the *Guardian* ran a letter from an officer to friends:

> [T]here was perfect peace, and we could hear the Germans singing in their trenches. Later on in the afternoon my attention was called to a large group of men standing up half-way between our trenches and the enemy's, on the right of my trench. So I went out with my sergeant major to investigate, and actually found a large party of Germans and our people hob-nobbing together, although an armis-tice was strictly against our regulations. The men had taken it upon themselves. I went forward and asked in German

what it was all about and if they had an officer there, and I was taken to their officer, who offered me a cigar. I talked for a short time, and then both sides returned to the trenches. It was the strangest sight I have ever seen. The officer and I saluted each another gravely, shook hands, and then went back to shoot at each other again. He gave me two cigars, one of which I smoked, and the other I sent home as a souvenir. If only I had had a camera I could have sent you an interesting picture.

7

THIS BLOODY BUSINESS

On Friday 28 December 1917 C. P. Scott, the editor of the *Manchester Guardian*, had breakfast with Lloyd George. Lloyd George warned him he was 'in a very pacifist temper' that morning. The night before, he said, he had been at a dinner given for Philip Gibbs, the war correspondent, who was just back from the Western front. He gave, Lloyd George said,

> the most impressive and moving description . . . of what the war in the West really means that I have heard. Even an audience of hardened politicians and journalists was strongly affected. The thing is horrible and beyond human nature to bear, and I feel I can't go on with this bloody business: I would rather resign. The generals are absolutely callous as to the gigantic casualties and order men to certain death like cattle to the slaughter.

By the time the assembly of politicians and journalists sat there at the dinner table listening to Gibbs telling them what conditions at the front were like, the war had been going on for 1,605 days. We find it almost impossible to believe that they did not know what a couple of million of their fellow countrymen had been experiencing only a few hundred miles away; yet it is true. A twofold vow of silence hid what was really going on.

One vow was maintained by the soldiers themselves. They found it was easier to keep quiet about the reality of the trenches than to tell people what they were really like. Soldiers who came back on leave or were invalided home realized that their friends and families simply had no understanding of conditions on the Western Front; so why bother to try to tell them? A veteran of the Battle of Passchendaele told the BBC in the 1970s:

It wasn't that people back home didn't sympathise with us, it was just that they couldn't grasp how dreadful it all was: the terrible racket the guns made, the sights you saw, men being blown into pulp, the bits of bodies, and that awful mud, and the fear you felt, all the time, day and night, when you were up in the forward lines. So when you got back home you didn't even try to tell anyone. It would have shocked them too much. And maybe they wouldn't have believed you. You see, they weren't told about it in the newspapers, and they believed what the newspapers told them.

In March 1917 the journalist Michael McDonagh noticed a newspaper poster which read:

BATTLE RAGING AT YPRES
GATWICK RACING – LATE WIRE

Philip Gibbs recorded a fierce reaction to this lack of awareness from soldiers who went home on leave: 'They prayed God to get the Germans to send Zeppelins to England – to make the people know what war meant.'

When Siegfried Sassoon was invalided back to England in 1917 after taking part in the Battle of Passchendaele, he planned to make a public statement about the horrors of the Western Front and the need to end the war. Instead, he allowed himself to be persuaded by his friend and fellow-poet Robert Graves to undergo treatment for shell shock and keep quiet. Graves believed that Sassoon would only damage himself and his reputation if he campaigned for an end to the war. Given the state of public opinion, Graves was probably right; but it was a surrender to the fierce control which the War Office had imposed on news from the front.

A different vow of silence was observed by the small number of correspondents who reported on the war at the front. They too knew what the reality was like. Sometimes they had experienced it for themselves; more often they had listened to soldiers describing it, and had seen the aftermath. It was not merely that they could not get the truth past the censors, they felt a genuine reluctance to damage the national interest. If politicians and journalists could be so shocked by Philip Gibbs's account of the true state of things, what effect might it have on a war-weary country?

In any case the censors would never have allowed it. And if the newspapers had defied the censors, editors, subeditors, reporters, perhaps even printers, would have been liable to imprisonment under DORA, the Defence of the Realm Act. Although some journalists certainly considered it, they would never have persuaded their colleagues to go along with such a massive defiance of the law, and of public opinion; since, in spite of all the immense sacrifices the British people had made – indeed, largely because of those sacrifices – it is clear that the country wanted to defeat Germany.

§

By the time of the Battle of the Somme, which began on Saturday 1 July 1916, the early leaders of the war on the British side were all going or gone: Asquith, the prime minister, would soon be replaced by Lloyd George; Sir John French, the commander-in-chief, had been ordered to resign in December 1915, after the failure at the Battle of Loos; while on 5 June 1916, Lord Kitchener, the minister of war, had drowned when HMS *Hampshire* – he was on a diplomatic mission to Russia – hit a mine.

In French's place had come Sir Douglas Haig, who had successfully intrigued against him. Haig disliked war correspondents but knew that he needed them to keep public opinion on his side. He saw them as rarely as he could, and for the most part avoided giving interviews; but he kept on good terms with many of the owners and editors of the newspapers. A few days before Kitchener's death, Haig gathered the accredited correspondents together at GHQ and briefed them on the battle which would begin on the Somme a month later. It was full of the over-optimism and iron-bound self-confidence which characterized his entire approach to fighting the war. He persuaded them that the great breakthrough would take place, and outlined his tactics: an unprecedentedly massive artillery bombardment in depth, which would destroy not only the front lines but the entire German defensive system. This would make it possible for the infantry to punch their way through, and allow the cavalry, at last, to overrun the enemy. The correspondents were clearly flattered at being taken into Haig's confidence. One of the unchanging features of journalists over the years is their pleasure in hobnobbing with the great ones of the earth, and a distinct inclination to fawn. As the great ones sometimes find, this tendency can last only as far as the door; but more often it has its effect on what is written afterwards. The more confidential the briefing, the more likely it is to bind journalist and briefer in an unbreakable confederacy.

Haig was both inspiring and convincing. This would be the first large-scale battle to be fought under his overall command, and they believed him when he told them that it was certain to be successful. So when, having shared with them the most important secret in the world at that moment, he turned to the part they would play in raising the confidence of the nation and of the men at the front, they found it irresistible.

Over the decades since 1916, the correspondents who attended that briefing at GHQ have been roundly condemned. By agreeing to take Haig's line, they became dupes and liars, betraying the readers, and encouraging them to support the continued wastage of hundreds of thousands of lives. Yet in wartime, when their country's future is at stake, journalists will always feel the pull of patriotism. Even those who do not work for the more jingoistic media cannot automatically report things as openly as they might otherwise do. Their position is a difficult one, and these are not easy issues on which to judge men like the accredited correspondents of 1916.

All the same, any journalist worth his or her salt will feel another pull. While the circumstances may rule out complete honesty, as they did in 1916, it is reasonable to expect that some hint of reality will come through the despatches – some sign that, whatever the official version, the facts on the ground are different. The year 1916 was probably the hardest in twentieth-century British history for journalists to do their job properly. The correspondents were kept away from the front line and fed a diet of information rich in lies.

Marooned at GHQ, they would have no alternative sources to check official statements. They would not see the progress of the battle for themselves and would feel the need to bolster public confidence at home. And, of course, they knew that everything they wrote would be subjected to rigorous checks by military censors.

None of this makes their actions seem any more excusable; but it does perhaps explain them. We should not see these men as willing deceivers, not even William Beach Thomas, who loved the attention his stories gained. They were, mostly, able men who wanted to be honest and to do their duty as patriots. Unfortunately for them the Battle of the Somme would make their failure be seen as the failure of journalism in general.

The first day of the battle was an almost entirely unmitigated disaster. The initial bombardment was spread much too thinly along the front line, and reached far too deep into German-held territory. The guns pounded away for seven days altogether, and fired 1.5 million shells. But the shells were still too few.

There was, at Kitchener's insistence, a high proportion of shrapnel shells; he had found them to be highly effective in the Boer War. But this was a very different kind of war. Shrapnel was far less effective than high explosive for cutting barbed wire, and it was useless against men sheltering deep below the ground in concrete-lined positions. The barrage, terrible though it was, failed to destroy even the front line of the German defences. The effect of the bombardment seemed impressive enough; captured Germans were bemused and terrified, and the guns could be heard as far away as Hampstead Heath in London. But great stretches of the German barbed wire remained uncut, and the shells often did not explode. The deep German positions were mostly impervious to the shelling.

The moment the bombardment lifted, just before 7.30 a.m., the German machine-gunners had about a minute and a half to scramble up to their positions and begin firing before many of the British troops had even got as far as their own wire. Some commanders had anticipated this; General Plumer, for instance, ordered his men to creep into no-man's-land while the artillery was still firing, and they were able to dash forward and capture the first lines of trenches. The 36th (Ulster) Division did the same, and got as far as the German second line, which they held for most of the day until they had to withdraw. The Glasgow Commercials, a 'Pals' battalion of the new Kitchener Army, also waited close to the German front line during the artillery barrage. They captured the Leipzig Salient and held it – one of the few real successes of the day.

§

The men of the Newfoundland Regiment were bottled up in the reserve lines because the communications trenches were blocked. When the whistle blew for the attack they 'hopped the bags' and walked, laden down with equipment, for about a hundred yards to the British wire. When they got there they had to queue up to get through the relatively few gaps; and they were shot down there in their hundreds. Of the 780 men who went forward, 684 were killed or wounded: a casualty rate of 87 per cent. Only 68 appeared for roll call the following day. The Newfoundland Regiment had effectively been wiped out as a fighting unit.

The system of medical care was disastrous. Casualty clearing stations could only deal with 9,500 cases; the injuries were more than six times higher than that. Yet because of poor communications, by the evening of the 1st, the British thought their losses amounted to 16,000: not at all excessive, given the attrition rate on the Western Front. Partly for this reason, spirits at GHQ were quite high, even though the battle had not gone the way Haig had anticipated. But over the following days the true scale of casualties grew. It was not until 6 July that the figures for the first day had all come in. At 60,000, they were the worst losses the British army had suffered in a single day in its history.

The Battle of the Somme continued, for want of any alternative plan, until 16 November. By that stage British casualties had risen to 400,000, and for the most part the objectives set for the first day of the battle had still not been achieved, 139 days later. The battle was stopped then because it became obvious that the British army would not have enough men to fight on into 1917 if the losses continued at the same rate.

In this most brutal and wasteful of wars, it is true that the Battle of the Somme was the first of the hammer blows which would eventually destroy the German army. It is also true that Haig was reasonably good at learning from his mistakes, though there were plenty more to come. The German army had been badly shaken and had suffered heavy losses, and the Second Army chief of staff, General Grünert, was sacked for agreeing to a partial withdrawal in the southern sector. Yet it is hard to think of the early part of the battle as anything but a serious British setback – a defeat, even.

This is not how the newspapers presented it. On the contrary, all the main correspondents who covered the start of the battle – Philip Gibbs for the *Morning Chronicle*, Henry Perry Robinson for *The Times*, William Beach Thomas for the *Daily Mail*, John D. Irvine for the *Daily Express* and H.M. Tomlinson for the *Daily News* – saw it in the terms that Haig had explained in his briefing a month before. They had decided, or had perhaps been ordered by Haig's staff, to stay at GHQ to cover the early stages; not because of the danger, but because they assumed they would get the best picture of what was happening. They were in competition with one another, and the best way to be first with the news of the expected massive victory was to be where all the information was gathered.

In reading their despatches now, we should remember that the correspondents had been primed to expect something very different from what unfolded. Their editors back in London were also expecting news of a victory. An editorial in the *Daily News* on Monday 3 July – the first day of publication for the British dailies after the battle – shows a sense of relief:

> The emotion caused by the news of the British advance on Saturday is unlike anything else experienced since the war began. For nearly two years we, in common with our Allies, have had to keep a stiff upper lip under the blows of an enemy who had all the advantages of the choice of moment, of specific preparation, of interior lines, and of an overwhelmingly superior machine.

Now, the papers assumed, we were hitting back so hard that there was a good chance the war would soon be over. To puncture those hopes would be a very serious thing indeed for the correspondents.

But anyway they were reliant on information from staff at GHQ; and the staff too were trying to make sense of confused reports. In the immense confusion of battle it was hard to get a clear picture. Radio didn't exist for ground troops (though it did for the British aircraft which circled over the battlefield), and field telephones were highly unreliable because shellfire destroyed the cables.

The only effective method of getting information back to headquarters was by runner; and the life expectancy of a runner in the Battle of the Somme was often just an hour or so. But by the evening of 1 July, it must have become clear that scarcely any of the first day's objectives had been attained.

However many allowances one makes for the correspondents at GHQ, it is plain they added their own lavish gilding to falsely optimistic information fed to them. They wrote what they wanted to be true, and they do not seem to have exercised any serious measure of scepticism. So while British soldiers were being mown down in their thousands the correspondents were still writing about ultimate victory.

William Beach Thomas, focused as usual on himself, wrote in the *Mail*:

> In the first battle, which I saw open with incredible artillery fury at six o'clock this morning, we have beaten the Germans by greater dash in the infantry and vastly superior weight in munitions. I may, perhaps, claim to be in some position to estimate methods and results. I watched the night bombardments, both German and British. I saw at close quarters the hurricane of the morning bombardment, which heralded that first gay, impetuous and irresistible leap from the trenches, many of which I had visited earlier, knowing what was to come . . .
>
> That inhuman, oscillating bullet of the German rifle and machine-gun and round bullets of the shrapnel, some of them sprinkled with phosphorous, threaded the woof of the cloud, but it was blind shooting. The cloud played its part, and many a man who left his trench behind its cover owes his life to the beneficent obscurity. Nevertheless, I believe many of the men would have liked to charge in full daylight for sheer pride of manhood and zest of clean sight. The 'up and at 'em' spirit was strong in our army this summer morning.

No wonder the front-line troops detested Beach Thomas so much, and mocked his often almost incoherent embroidery of the few facts he can actually assemble. While deliberately giving the false impression that he has seen the attack himself, he provides an entirely sanitized account of it.

In the *Daily Mail* of Wednesday 5 July, his reporting reached a climax. So did the *Mail*'s showcasing of it. Even the appearance of the print gives the impression of excitement, perhaps almost a sense of hysteria.

MR. BEACH THOMAS'S FINEST DESPATCH.
GOMMECOURT.

BRITISH FAILURE THAT WON THE DAY.
MARCH THROUGH A DEATH ZONE.
MAIN GERMAN FORCE PINNED DOWN.
MR BEACH THOMAS IN FRICOURT.

Mr Beach Thomas describes below first his visit to Fricourt and then the most glorious feat of the battle, the British attack at Gommecourt against the Germans' heaviest mass, an attack that failed at the spot but made possible success elsewhere.

From W. Beach Thomas.
Press Camp, France, Monday.

This morning, the third day of the battle, I was able to penetrate into Fricourt village itself and move up close to the edge of the wood some 500 yards behind our infantry, just at the time when they completed their brilliant attack across the base of the German wedge left at this place by the fighting of the first day . . .

Our attack at Gommecourt, the northern end of the frantic battle, was as heroic as anything in the war. I know the trenches there well and happen to have intimate personal acquaintances with some of those engaged. I had played cricket with them, and football . . .

At 7.30 a.m. and earlier on July 1 their [the Germans'] guns, closely concentrated and full of calibre, set up a triple barrage (five curtains). Through all of these barrages of intense fire our men marched quite steadily, as if nothing was in their way, as if they were under review. At every step men fell, and the trenches here are very far apart from the Germans . . . When these steady, steadfast soldiers, true to the death, paraded in more than decimated numbers through and across the third barrage, the enemy – in their

turn heroic – left their trenches, erected machine guns on
the parapets, and the two parties fought one another in the
open.

I have not the hardihood to write more. Heroism could
no further go. Our men died, and in dying held in front of
them enough German guns to leave altered the fate of our
principal and our most successful advance in the south.

They died defeated, but won a greater victory, in spirit
and in fact as English history or any other history will ever
chronicle.

Beach Thomas, for all the incoherent emotion of this – you can feel him
breaking down when he writes the phrase 'these steady, steadfast soldiers'
– is correct in two things. Firstly, Gommecourt was a feint, intended to
distract the Germans from the main thrust of the fighting further along
the front; and it was indeed a defeat. Secondly, the courage of the British
troops (and, as he rightly says, of the Germans too) was remarkable. It
remained so even at the worst times of the battle.

But we have to remember that although this sounds like an eyewitness
account, it wasn't. On 1 July, when it happened, he was back at base. And
even when he was allowed to see the captured village of Fricourt he was
still a good quarter of a mile behind the front line. Beach Thomas is
attempting to do three things. Firstly, as always, his despatch is an
advertisement for himself. What does it matter that he played cricket and
football with the soldiers? The reader would much rather know what
happened to the individuals he played alongside.

Secondly, he is attempting to turn Gommecourt, which is just a
sideshow compared with the main battle, into an important and glorious
event in its own right, for the sole reason that this is where he decided to
go after the fighting had moved on. The *Daily Mail*'s habit, for purely
commercial reasons, of building up Beach Thomas's reporting gave him,
and his editors, the feeling that his presence there was something of
significance in itself. If he had chosen to go somewhere else that Monday
morning, that would then have been represented as a key battleground
where history was made.

Thirdly, he is easing his readers into the reality of the fighting,
without telling them the dreadful details. According to his report, the
advancing British soldiers slog it out in the open with the German

machine-gunners. The fact is, as we have seen, that in many parts of the battlefield large numbers of British soldiers fell a long way from the German lines, sometimes as they queued bravely and patiently to get through their own wire. Beach Thomas must surely have found out at least a little of this by the time he wrote his despatch two days afterwards. But by skilfully giving the impression that he has seen the action for himself, he turns it from the slaughter it was into a hand-to-hand fight, of a kind his readers could understand and admire. If they had known what had really happened, it would have created immense anger and revulsion; and none of the correspondents wanted to be responsible for that.

The first day on the Somme played an essential part in Philip Gibbs's transition from enthusiastic adventurer to the burdened, angry figure he became when he made his speech to the dinner in his honour in December 1917. Unlike Beach Thomas, Gibbs never told his readers what he had done himself; he judged that they were more interested in the terrible things of the war.

After the first day of the battle it is clear that he began to understand something of the slaughter which had taken place. In the years that followed, he admitted that he failed to write the full truth about it, on the grounds that it might weaken the will of the British people to continue with the war. In a later period it might have sounded almost megalomaniacal to claim that a journalist would have such power; but on the Western Front there was a certain truth in it. Besides, Gibbs knew that the censors would cut out anything unacceptable to the military.

As a result he went round gathering the survivors' stories, without attempting to varnish them. He found the courage of the soldiers deeply moving; his accounts reinforce the sense of their dogged self-sacrifice. He too believed that the British army had registered what he called 'one of the most splendid achievements of British arms ever written down in history'; and he reminded his readers that most of the British soldiers at the battle were volunteers who had been civilians less than two years earlier. He writes far more about the cost of the battle than about its glory.

> The officer who came round the village with me had a
> lonely look. After a battle, such a battle as this, it is difficult
> to keep the sadness out of one's eye. So many good fellows
> have gone . . .

There were a lot of Yorkshire men among them who fought at Fricourt, and it was those I saw today . . . Some of them were still shaken. When they spoke to me their words faltered now and then, and a queer look came into their eyes. But, on the whole they were astoundingly calm, and had not lost their sense of humour.

In the first advance over No Man's Land, which is 150 yards across to the enemy's front line trench, some of these men could remember nothing. 'It was just a dreadful blank . . . I was just mad at the time,' said one of them. 'The first thing I know is that I found myself scrambling over the German parapets with a bomb in my hand. The dead were lying all around me.'

But a sergeant there remembered all. He kept his wits about him, strangely clear at such a time. He saw that his men were being swept with machine-gun fire, so that they all lay down to escape its deadly scythe. But he saw also that the bullets were first washing the ground so that the prostrate men were being struck in great numbers. He stood up straight and called upon the others to stand, thinking it would be better to be hit in the feet than in the head. Then he walked on and came without a scratch to the German front line.

[T]he men who have told me these things are young men who do not like the things they have seen. But, because it is war, they go through to the last goal with a courage that does not equal.

In the year 1920 Philip Gibbs published three different books about his experiences – almost as though he was trying to exorcize the guilt and horror he still felt. In *Now it Can be Told* he described his discovery that the first day on the Somme had in fact gained a very small advance, paid for at a catastrophically high cost. It reads like a confession:

There was the illusion of victory on that first day of the Somme battles, on the right of the line by Fricourt, and it was not until a day or two later that certain awful rumours I had heard from wounded men and officers who had attacked on the left up by

Gommecourt, Thiepval, and Serre were confirmed by certain knowledge of tragic disaster on that side of the battle-line.

It looked like victory, in those days, as war correspondents, we were not so expert in balancing the profit and loss as afterward we became . . .

Victory? Well, we had gained some ground, and many prisoners, and here and there some guns. But as I stood by Montauban I saw that our line was a sharp salient looped round Mametz village and then dipping sharply southward to Fricourt. O God! had we only made another salient after all that monstrous effort? . . .

§

Yet away from the Western Front it was sometimes possible for a correspondent to speak out, and thereby affect the entire course of the war. Ellis Ashmead-Bartlett was a tough, aggressive adventurer of thirty-four hired by the *Daily Telegraph* and other papers to report on the Gallipoli landings in April 1915. He sent back the first eyewitness accounts of the battle.

He was lavish in his praise of the ANZAC troops, and contributed very largely to the legend of their part in the Gallipoli campaign. 'These colonials are extraordinarily cool under fire,' he wrote in the *Telegraph* two days later, and though this sounds patronizing, that was certainly not his intention, 'often exposing themselves [to it] rather than taking the trouble to keep under the shelter of the cliff.'

As the fighting developed, it reached a similar stalemate as existed on the Western Front (which the Gallipoli landings had been designed to circumvent). On both sides the losses grew. In June, by the end of the third battle of Krithia, casualties were running at around 25 per cent. The Naval Brigade, originally 1,600 strong, lost half its strength. In August the Wellington Battalion holding the heights at Chunuk Bair, lost 110 of its 150 men.

Ashmead-Bartlett soon found himself clashing with the Allied commander, General Sir Ian Hamilton: elegant, charming, brave, intelligent but essentially unlucky and unsuccessful. Ashmead-Bartlett got on rather well with him at first. Hamilton, who had twice been recommended for the Victoria Cross, liked his style and his courage. In May, on board a ship anchored off Cape Helles, Ashmead-Bartlett realized it was going to be attacked by a German U-boat operating in the area, and proceeded to drink the last of the ship's champagne just before the torpedo struck.

Soon, though, Ashmead-Bartlett's despatches took on a critical tone. Hamilton was angry, and threatened him with serious consequences. Ashmead-Bartlett went back to London and briefed several members of the Cabinet about the real situation there. Then he returned, armed with a brand-new film camera; with it, he took the only moving pictures of the campaign known to exist. By August he was reporting for the *Telegraph*, the *Mail*, the *Express*, and the *Mirror*. This gave him even greater authority and his style became more acidic than ever: 'Chaos reigned supreme. No-one seemed to know where the headquarters of the different brigades and divisions were to be found. The troops were hunting for water, the staffs were hunting for their troops, and the Turkish snipers were hunting for their prey.'

The following month the Australian journalist Keith Murdoch joined him briefly, and the two formed an alliance. Murdoch would later be the father of Rupert, the modern-day equivalent of Lord Northcliffe, owning a range of newspapers from the *Sun* to *The Times* and television stations, and using the powers this gave him in ways which were just as controversial.

Ashmead-Bartlett wrote a long letter to Asquith, the prime minister, listing all the things that were going wrong with the Gallipoli campaign. Murdoch took the letter to France for him. It has been suggested that the *Guardian* correspondent H.W. Nevinson, who was a friend of Hamilton, found out and told the military authorities. Nevinson's biographer, Angela John, is among those who have dismissed this rumour. It would have been deeply uncharacteristic of Nevinson, who was a campaigner against slavery in Africa and the mistreatment of suffragettes in Britain. He was daring and brave as well as compassionate, and cannot have approved of the slaughter at the Dardanelles, where he was himself injured. But however it came about, Murdoch was arrested by the military authorities at Marseilles, and the letter was confiscated.

Hamilton ordered Ashmead-Bartlett out of Gallipoli, and he headed straight back to London. With a fine disdain for the rules, he persuaded the *Sunday Times* to interview him, which meant that the resulting article did not have to be submitted to the censors. The effect on public opinion and on the government was immediate. Hamilton was recalled, and soon the Allied troops were evacuated from Gallipoli in the only really well-planned operation of the entire campaign. Churchill, one of the Gallipoli campaign's strongest advocates, did the honourable thing and resigned from the Cabinet, going to fight on the Western Front, where he was lucky to survive. And – although Gallipoli was far from being the only reason – it led to the downfall of Asquith as prime minister, and his replacement by Lloyd George.

It was easier for Ashmead-Bartlett to make a fuss about the disaster of Gallipoli, than for someone like Philip Gibbs on the Western Front. Any major change in tactics or strategy on the Western Front might well have led to Britain's defeat. Perhaps, too, if Gibbs had come back to London during the Battle of the Somme and used the same ruse as Ashmead-Bartlett, the government would have used all its powers under the Defence of the Realm Act to silence him.

Still, it is hard to avoid the feeling that Gibbs would never really have wanted to try. In the end, the difference between the two correspondents was that Ashmead-Bartlett was tough, self-assured and fearless, while Gibbs was much less certain of himself. What, though, might have happened if Ashmead-Bartlett had found himself reporting on the battles of the Somme and Passchendaele?

§

The Third Battle of Ypres, which became known as Passchendaele, began at 3.50 on the morning of 31 July 1917, after ten days of the heaviest bombardment ever endured at that time. The unusually heavy rains which gave the battle its terrible quality, had already begun; but it proved too late to call it off. After the initial push, which had gained little ground, the attack was halted until the end of September, when it was renewed. The weather continued to be appalling, and the use of mustard gas by the Germans pushed the casualties of the British and their Allies even higher.

In the gladiatorial context of the First World War, where success was possible only by the sacrifice of hundreds of thousands of human lives, Passchendaele can be regarded as a British victory, unlike the Somme the previous year. By the time the battle ended, after the capture of the little village of Passchendaele by the British and Canadian infantry on 6 November, around 66,000 Allied soldiers had been killed and 180,000 injured: unthinkably high figures for later wars, but significantly lower losses than were suffered by the British at the Somme, or the French at Verdun. The Germans, by contrast, lost more than 400,000 men: almost twice as many. The damage done to Germany's manpower and its will to go on fighting was immense, and the battle played a major part in the final victory of the Allies a year later.

Yet to see Passchendaele with this sort of detachment is to ignore the sheer horror faced by the men on the ground. At Passchendaele a serious wound often meant a slow death by sinking into the mud and drowning. Men were so exhausted, and so frightened of the mud themselves that they were sometimes reluctant to help them out. A soldier who had been at Passchendaele told the BBC in an interview that he watched a horse fall down in a shell hole close to his position and slowly, over a period of three days, dig itself deeper into the mud until it drowned. Why didn't he and his men do anything to help it? 'There was so much death all round us, there didn't seem to be any point,' he answered.

Philip Gibbs, in his book *Now it Can be Told*, quotes Sir Douglas Haig as saying that some of the descriptions of Passchendaele were exaggerated; it was often said that Haig didn't visit the battlefield, on the grounds that if he saw these things for himself he might not be able to order his men to keep fighting. This was Gibbs's reply, free of the restraints of censorship:

> [N]othing that has been written is more than the pale image of the abomination of those battlefields, and no pen or brush has yet achieved the picture of that Armageddon in which so many of our men perished . . .
>
> They . . . advanced through slime into slime, under the slash of machine-gun bullets, shrapnel, and high explosives, wet to the skin, chilled to the bone, plastered up to the eyes in mud, with a dreadful way back for walking wounded, but little chance sometimes for wounded who could not walk. The losses in many of these battles amounted almost to annihilation for many battalions, and whole divisions lost as much as 50 per cent of their strength after a few days in action, before they were 'relieved'.

During the battle one general, Sir George Montague Harper of the 51st (Highland) Division, took Gibbs aside and criticized him and his colleagues for their refusal to write openly about the conditions at

Passchendaele. Harper was an attractive figure with a deep regard for his men; in return, their affectionate nickname for him was 'Uncle'. 'We tell the public that an enemy division has been "shattered",' he told Gibbs. 'That is true. But so is mine. One of my brigades has lost eighty-seven officers and two thousand men since the spring.' He could not, he said, blame his fighting officers for hating the staff at GHQ.

Yet Gibbs's own reporting (he was now working for the *Daily Telegraph*) was criticized both at headquarters and at home for being too bleak and pessimistic.

> The weather is still abominable. Heavy rain storms have waterlogged the battlefields and there are dense mists all over the countryside.
>
> Generally the situation is exactly the same as it stood at the end of the first day of battle . . .
>
> The ground is all of a swamp and the shell holes are ponds. The army lies wet, and the foulness of Flemish weather in winter is upon them in August . . . War is not a blithe business, even when the sun is shining. In this gloom and filth it seems more miserable.

There are times, reading Philip Gibbs's reports, that you feel this emotionally frail man is close to breaking down under the strain of the things he has to witness. Yet he is never blind to the spirit of the soldiers. Here, for instance, he is with a north-country regiment:

> The men who went over today swore that, with any luck, or even without luck, they would plant their flag high, and among those men there was a grim smouldering fire of some purpose which bode ill for the enemy they should find against them. These are not words of rhetoric to give a little colour to the dark picture of war, but the sober truth of what was in those men's minds yesterday when they made ready for this new battle.

Was Gibbs worried, when he wrote that last sentence, that people would think he was sounding too much like Beach Thomas? Perhaps. In the early stages of Passchendaele, Beach Thomas himself was as upbeat as ever, yet by October, the third month of the battle, even Beach Thomas was starting to report things as they really were.

> It seemed impossible to attack with success. Men were exhausted by the mere walk to this or that point behind the line; gunners toiling with shovels in the midst of incredible mud the day before the battle laugh sardonically as you pass them. 'This is supposed to be going to be a battery position,' they said, 'and believe me if you can.'
>
> To those of us who have seen and walked in the mud of the battlefield it seems incredible that the British and French soldiers nevertheless walked through to the objectives ...
>
> Men fell into foul shell holes and were pulled out by their friends. They stumbled and caught their feet in the infinite tangles of this sinister country.

Beach Thomas cannot manage for long, however, without dropping into the enthusiastic tone of 'Teech Bomas', his alter ego in the *Wipers Times*:

> I am writing this preface to my dispatch where the battle is no more than a tumult of noise and a mad scramble for a dark dawn, but this may be said: that every man fighting today has his feet on the higher and drier soil, and that the whole plan of today's battle is made possible by the heroism of troops from the Yorks and Lancashire's and Midlanders and others, who defied bodily exhaustion as they defied the enemy four days ago.

Men who had fought at the Somme felt that Passchendaele was far worse. Yet they too regarded it as a victory, even though the Germans did not collapse as hoped. It was only in November that the Allies managed to reach their original objectives. Still, the French army was saved after the disastrous failure of its ill-planned and wasteful Nivelle offensive; if the Germans had been able to follow up their success there, the French army would probably have mutinied and fallen apart, and the Germans would have won the war.

Morale was not good in the British army, all the same. Nigel Steel and

Peter Hart, in their book *Passchendaele*, quote a letter home from
Corporal Laurie Rowlands of the Durham Light Infantry:

> [E]very man Jack is fed up almost past bearing, and not a single man
> has an ounce of what we call patriotism left in him. No-one cares a
> rap whether Germany has Alsace, Belgium or France too for that
> matter. All that every man desires now is to get done with it and go
> home ... I may add that I too have lost pretty nearly all the
> patriotism that I had left, it's just that thought of you all over there,
> you who love me and trust me to do my share in the job that is
> necessary for your safety and freedom. It's just that that keeps me
> going and enables me to 'stick it'.

By 'patriotism' Rowlands seems to mean the jingoistic overconfidence
which journalists like Beach Thomas and newspapers like the *Mail*,
Express and *Mirror* tried to encourage. Yet his determination to finish
the job in spite of all the horrors, is the spirit which Philip Gibbs cele-
brates in his despatches; and it was the spirit which, a year later, would
win the war.

§

The year 1917 was one of mutiny and revolution. In Russia, after the
abdication of Tsar Nicholas II, the new democratic government decided
to continue fighting. But the so-called Kerensky Offensive in Galicia
against the Austro-Hungarian forces in July was a disaster. The Russian
army was increasingly unwilling to obey orders, and the failure of the
offensive led directly to the Bolshevik coup d'état in November. Yet
sections of the German army were becoming mutinous and unreliable,
influenced by events in Russia and to a lesser extent by the hammer-blow
struck by the British at Passchendaele. Any hint of mutiny on the German
side was anxiously picked up by the British press, but the results were
always disappointing.

The French army, too, was in a highly volatile and unreliable state.
The abject failure of the offensive in April 1917, which General Robert
Nivelle had promised would end the war in forty-eight hours, led to
widespread mutinies among the French troops. There was no mention
of the mutiny whatever in the British press, and as usual the French

offensive was reported predominantly as a success. *The Times*, on 16 May 1917, reported that Nivelle had been replaced by Pétain, but there was no explanation and of course no speculation.

Early in September, while the Battle of Passchendaele was in full swing, there was even trouble among Allied forces at the big Etaples base. A New Zealand gunner was arrested wrongly for desertion by the highly unpopular military police and held in gaol. A large crowd of mostly ANZAC troops protested outside the gaol, and a military policeman fired at them, killing a Scottish NCO. Then the military police fled. Over the next couple of days the demonstrations grew bigger, and although the men were ordered to stay in camp they disobeyed and marched through Etaples.

Then a detachment of 400 men of the Honourable Artillery Company arrived. They were armed with wooden staves, and had been carefully chosen to ensure there were no working-class men among them. They were supported by a small number of cavalry and a detachment of machine-gunners. Three hundred mutineers disobeyed their orders to stay in camp, and were arrested. The rest caved in, and the mutiny was over. One of the ringleaders, Corporal Jesse Short of the Northumberland Fusiliers, was court-martialled and executed.

The War Cabinet in London sent the South African prime minister, General Smuts, to investigate the mood of the front-line troops. After talking to large numbers of men he found that their grouses were mostly easily remedied, and he reported back that the troops were basically in good heart and reliable. The next few months showed that his judgement was right.

None of this was reported in the British newspapers. The censors would have cut out any hint of the events at Etaples if presented. The army was aware that there was a strong class element to the unrest. Fear of the influence of left-wing ideas led the army to ban the moderately socialist, anti-war *Daily Herald* from France.

On 9 October 1917 there was an interesting editorial about labour relations from an unexpected quarter: the *Daily Mail*. It can only have been written with the knowledge of, or perhaps on the orders of, the volatile Lord Northcliffe himself. Was he getting nervous about what he saw as the coming revolution, and trying to position himself differently? Or was he genuinely sympathetic (if only briefly) to the cause of the working class?

> A country where the power is in the hands of the working man is proof against the revolution by bullet. A Labour Ministry [i.e. government] such as we are fairly certain to have in the distant future will be regarded by many as 'revolutionary'. In reality it is quite likely to be as hard-working and hard-headed as any of our modern governments. In any event it would not be a government which would look kindly on 'conscientious' objectors.

Conscientious objectors were particular hate-figures for the *Mail*. On the same day it ran an article with the headline

THE REVOLTING 'CONCHY'.
TOO UNPOPULAR TO BE DANGEROUS.

A few days earlier, the *Mail* took a tone it would scarcely ever repeat for the rest of the twentieth century.

> If the splendid patriotism and endurance which the British working men and women have shown in this war have sometimes been clouded over by 'unrest', if strikes have occurred apparently without just cause, it has been nine times out of ten because officialdom and authority has been lacking in frankness, in the human touch, and in responsiveness to the new conditions.

That this was a policy decision by Northcliffe is shown by the fact that *The Times* was starting to complain about war-profiteering and heavy-handed government control as causes of industrial unrest.

But the *Mail* could not allow itself to take this line for very long. Now it was becoming obsessed with something rather less rational: the Bolo hunt. The word 'Bolo' seems to have originated as a short form of 'Bolshevik' though later the letters BOLO were used to mean 'Be on the look-out'.

In 1918 William Le Queux, ever active when it came to witch-hunting, wrote a pulp thriller called *Bolo the Super-Spy*. The *Daily Mail* would no longer have considered serializing the book, as it had once serialized *The Invasion of 1910*. Nevertheless on 4 December 1917 it ran a prominent article headlined

THE BOLO HUNT.
A POWERFUL NETWORK OF INTRIGUE.

written by someone bylined only as 'B'. Possibly it was Le Queux himself.

> At no time since the war began have German agents been so busy in England as at the present time. Events are hurrying to a crisis in all belligerent countries. It is now or never with the German agents. If they wish to justify their existence and their pay they must act.

> I want to make a strong plea for more publicity and more energy in the government's hunt for 'Bolo' – the military and naval spy, the poisonous 'agent', the soft voiced pacifists, the amateur Lenin, and the Hun trader.

Most British newspapers believed that Lenin and the Bolsheviks were nothing more than the creatures of German intelligence. It is true that, in order to destabilize the Tsar, the Germans arranged and paid for the 'sealed train' which took Lenin and thirty or so leading Bolsheviks across Europe from Zurich. Yet there was a noticeable reluctance in most of the British press to take Lenin and the Bolsheviks seriously. On the day of the revolution, 7 November 1917 (which, in the Julian Calendar was 25 October); the *Daily Mail* carried a big story from its Petrograd correspondent, A.M. Thompson, which manages both to be patronizing and to miss the real story. His report is headlined:

AMAZING PETROGRAD.
DREAMERS BEGINNING TO ACT.

There is no sense of the urgency of the moment. This would be one of the days that shook the world; the American John Reed, whose phrase this was, was also reporting from there, but managed to understand a great deal more about what was going on. Thompson's despatch begins:

The Nevsky Prospekt in these whirling days is a perpetual roundabout of political hobby-horses. From noon to night the crowd surges densely, swelling into a pack outside a newspaper office where telegrams are displayed, but mostly caracoling in vertiginous circles of theoretical debate. Bankers discuss the situation with unemployed ratcatchers; captains with disgruntled privates; excited women with everybody. In my widest dreams of a democratic millennium I never envisaged such a comic levelling of rank and class as is daily displayed under the beaming sun of Petrograd, and the worst of it is that nobody laughs.

What most attracts Thompson's attention is, predictably, the sight of women soldiers parading through the streets. They are led by Commandant Botchkareva, a butcher's widow, who has fought in the trenches and been wounded. Her aide-de-camp is 'a pretty girl of 21 – a colonel's daughter, delicately nurtured, highly educated, who has told me that she joined the movement in order to shame the recalcitrant soldiery'. While Thompson is chatting up 'delicately nurtured' young women in uniform, the Bolsheviks are preparing their coup d'état, which will change history. His only reference to the Bolsheviks is to 'certain Leninites' who had been arrested that day without resisting. 'I gather', he says, 'that their valour was of that better kind which does not waste itself.'

He could quite easily have found out what the Bolsheviks were doing that day by talking to Western journalists staying at the Astoria Hotel. The hotel guests, apart from Thompson, included John Reed, Arthur Ransome of the *Daily News*, and Morgan Philips Price of the *Manchester Guardian*. All three had established good relationships with Lenin and Trotsky. But Thompson lacked any great interest in politics, and regarded all these politicos – 'dreamers' – with a patronizing eye.

The correspondent of the *Daily Telegraph*, E.H. Wilcox, was more serious and understood the situation. Yet even he managed not to grasp the significance of the Bolshevik takeover. Thursday's *Telegraph* carried the headline:

EXTREMIST RISING IN PETROGRAD.
STATE BUILDINGS SEIZED.

Underneath is a confusing series of despatches and reports by Reuter's and by Wilcox, all jumbled together, some dated Tuesday 6th and some Wednesday 7th. Events were extremely difficult to follow at that stage, and by noon on Wednesday Reuter's correspondent reported that 'An armed naval detachment, acting under the orders of the Maximalist [i.e. Bolshevik] Revolutionary Committee, has occupied the offices of the official Petrograd Telegraph Agency.' In other words, getting reports out of Petrograd would now be a great deal harder.

Wilcox's despatch, as printed on the morning of Thursday 8th, is already out of date; he was working under difficult conditions. '[I]t would appear that a real trial of strength between the Russian Provisional Government and the Maximalists has become inevitable.'

His story appeared twenty-four hours after the 'trial of strength' had taken place. His analysis of the Party, for the benefit of the *Telegraph*'s readers, is fairly muddled too.

> To begin with, there is the small body of convinced fanatics, many of them cultured and self-oblivious men and women, who sincerely believe that the regeneration of humanity can only be brought about by the complete destruction of all existing political, industrial, and social forms ... Then there are the adherents of the old régime, who realise very clearly that their best chance lies in the failure of the revolution, and that this is inevitable if once the Bolsheviki get things into their own hands. Next there is the large number of Germany's agents and sympathisers, who see in Maximalism the force most likely to complete the ruin of the Russian army. Finally, there is the rabble who think only of loot.

Only two elements of this are in any way recognizable as reality: the fanatical ideologues and the would-be looters. Followers of the old regime joined the Bolsheviks later, chiefly out of self-preservation; and the German agents are mostly creations of Wilcox's imagination. There were plenty of German agents in Petrograd, but it seems doubtful that many would have infiltrated the Bolsheviks. No doubt Wilcox's editor was demanding analysis from him on a subject he knew relatively little about, and he had to come up with something.

The worst forecast was made in that Friday's *Daily Mail*. Under the headlines

ANOTHER UPSET IN RUSSIA.
ZEDERBLUM, ALIAS LENIN, CLAIMS POWER.

The editorial writer continues:

> At the head of this new super-revolution is apparently M. Lenin (alias Zederblum), who not long since was wanted by the Russian police as a German-paid agent and Bolo in Russia. His right-hand man is M. Trotsky (alias Braunstein), an Anarchist who has made most countries too hot for him.

The use of aliases seems intended to play up the Jewishness of the Bolsheviks, though Lenin himself was not a Jew.

Then comes the real misjudgement. 'Russia's part in the war has been a small one for the last eight months, and it can hardly be said that this coup d'état makes very much difference to the other Allies.'

The *Mail*'s editorial writer has forgotten that the crumbling remnants of the Russian army are holding several hundred thousand German and Austrian troops in place on the Eastern Front. Directly the Russians drop out of the war, those troops can be used on the Western Front to enable the big German offensive in the spring of 1918, which will come very close indeed to ending the war in Germany's favour.

§

On an evening in mid-November 1917, Morgan Philips Price of the *Manchester Guardian*, public school- and Cambridge-educated but now a firm convert to the Russian revolution, left his room at the Astoria and headed in the bitter cold to the Smolny Institute, a former girls' school taken over as the Bolshevik seat of government. He was going to Trotsky's office in the hope of getting a briefing.

When he got there, Trotsky's attractive secretary Yevgeniya Petrovna Shelepina told him that Trotsky was too busy to see him but had suggested to her that Price might like to see the untidy bundle of papers on her desk. (Afterwards Shelepina married Arthur Ransome, the *Daily News* correspondent, who sympathized with the Bolsheviks even though he was secretly working for MI6; he told MI6 as much. Later, he would write the *Swallows and Amazons* books for children.) Philips Price realized he had stumbled across a story of major international proportions. The papers were the texts of the secret treaties between the various Allies in the war.

Philips Price took the papers back to the Astoria and stayed up all night transcribing the treaties. He then sent a series of articles to the *Manchester Guardian*, which published them from November to February 1918. They caused an international sensation. It had always been assumed that there were secret agreements between the Allies. President Woodrow Wilson of the United States had inveighed against the concept of secret diplomacy, which he maintained was the main cause of the war. Instead, he famously called for 'open covenants of peace openly arrived at', and wanted diplomacy to proceed 'always frankly and in the public view'; an admirable ambition, but one that is perennially difficult to achieve.

These were some of the key passages in the treaties which Russia had signed with Britain, France, Romania, and Japan. They contain the concessions required to keep Russia and the most reluctant ally, Italy, in the war.

Constantinople, the Straits, and Persia, 20 March 1915:

Britain consents to the annexation by Russia of the Straits and Constantinople, in return for a similar benevolent attitude on Russia's part towards the political aspiration of Britain in other parts. The neutral zone in Persia to be included in the British sphere of influence. The districts adjoining Ispahan and Yezd to be included in the Russian sphere, in which Russia is to be granted 'full liberty of action'.

The Treaty with Italy, 26 April 1915.

Italy to receive the Trentino, the Southern Tyrol, Trieste, the county of Gorizia and Grdisca, Istria, Northern Dalmatia, numerous islands off the Dalmatian coast, Valona (in Albania), twelve islands off the coast of Asia Minor, a prospective addition to her colonial territory in Africa, and a share in the war indemnity.

The Partition of Asiatic Turkey, Spring 1916.
Agreement between Britain, France and Russia as to their 'zones of influence and territorial acquisitions' in Asiatic Turkey. Britain to obtain Southern Mesopotamia, with Baghdad, and two ports in Syria. France to obtain Syria, the Adana vilayet, and Western Kurdistan. Russia to obtain Trebizond, Erzerum, Bitlis, Van, and territory in Southern Kurdistan. An Arab State or confederation of States to be formed. Palestine to be subject to a special regime.

Agreement between France and Russia, 11 March 1917.
Russia to support France in her demands for Alsace-Lorraine, and the Saar Valley; the rest of the German territories on the left bank of the Rhine to constitute a neutral State. France, in return, 'recognises Russia's complete liberty in establishing her Western frontiers'.

When these sensational details were published, it was found that some of the agreements cut across others made with different countries, or (in the case of Arabia) contradicted clear promises made by the British to the leaders of the Arab revolt, in which T.E. Lawrence had played a major part. Lloyd George moved immediately to smooth things over. Since 'new circumstances' had changed the conditions under which these arrangements had been made, he said, Britain was perfectly ready to discuss them with her Allies.

The response at home and abroad was inevitable: the treaties showed Britain and France in a distinctly bad light. They had meddled secretly in the affairs of many other countries in order to satisfy their own greed or that of the Allies. From now on, it would be much harder to insist that the war was being fought on the basis of principle.

§

At a couple of minutes before eleven o'clock on the morning of Monday, 11 November 1918, Henry Major Tomlinson, the *Daily News* correspondent, was standing on the roof of a building near the Embankment in London, looking out over the river at the ugly iron structure of Hungerford Bridge.

Tomlinson was forty-five. A childhood accident and his exposure to the noise of so much artillery in the war had left him deaf and rather withdrawn. He came from a lower-middle-class family in the East End of London, and after spending some time at sea he had turned to journalism. His writing in France had always been thoughtful, and was marked by a deep sympathy for the people caught up in the unthinkably great tragedy of the war. Now he was left with a great hatred of war in general, which never left him.

A short man, described by the writer John Middleton Murry as 'quiet, weary, sad, with his unforgettable face, carved and weatherbeaten like the figureheads of the sailing ships under whose bowsprits he walked and dreamed as a boy', Tomlinson stood looking at the Thames as the seconds ticked away before eleven o'clock. Even at this moment, when the war was virtually over, a few men were still dying on the Western Front in France: the last lives were being sacrificed with even greater pointlessness than before.

In a moment or two, the church bells would start to ring out across Britain. Just as they were sounding there would be a knock at the front door of the house belonging to the parents of Wilfred Owen, arguably the best poet the war had produced. In that supreme moment of relief and happiness a delivery boy would hand them an official War Office telegram to tell them that their son had been killed a few days earlier.

Tomlinson had his eyes fixed on Hungerford Bridge, which carried the trains from Charing Cross station down to the coast, from where the passengers sailed to France.

More than four years ago I crossed it on a memorable journey to France. It seemed no different today. It was still a Via Dolorosa projecting straight and black over a chasm. While I gazed at it, my mind in the past, a rocket exploded over it. Yes, I saw a burst of black smoke. The guns had ceased?

A tug passing under the bridge began a continuous hooting. Locomotives began to answer the tug deliriously. I could hear a low muttering, the beginning of a tempest, the distant but increasing shouting of a great storm . . .

Out in the street a stream of men and women poured from every door, and went to swell the main cataract which had risen suddenly in full flood in the Strand. The donkey-barrow of a costermonger passed me, loaded with a bluejacket, a flower-girl, several soldiers, and a Staff captain whose spurred boots wagged joyously over the stern of the barrow. A motor cab followed, two Australian troopers on the roof of that, with a hospital nurse, her cap awry, sitting across the knees of one of them . . .

A private car, a beautiful little saloon in which a lady was solitary, stopped near me, and the lady beckoned with a smile to a Canadian soldier who was close. He first stared in surprise at this fashionable stranger, and then got in beside her with obviously genuine alacrity . . .

I returned soon to the empty room of an office where I was likely to be alone, because, now the War was over, while listening to the jollity of Peace which had just arrived, I could not get my thoughts home from France . . .

It still seemed too good for many people to believe. The suddenness of the Allied breakthrough after the years of stalemate was hard to grasp. Early in the year, when the Central Powers were reinforced by troops from the Russian front, Germany seemed within a hair's-breadth of victory. General Haig, usually so calm and confident, issued an order of the day which talked about Allied soldiers having their backs to the wall. And then the German effort, made at huge cost, was halted, and the Allies found the strength for one last offensive. It was enough: Germany was defeated.

The *Manchester Guardian*, which had been against the war at the start, and then supported it for patriotic reasons, was disposed to be generous to the enemy at the moment of celebration. On 12 November 1918 its editor, the redoubtable C.P. Scott, wrote:

> This is the great day – the great day of Peace, hoped for, longed for, at times appearing remote, almost unattainable, yet never despaired of, resolutely pursued, at last conquered. Now it is ours, and not ours only: it is the world's, it is for our enemies no less than for ourselves . . .

Scott was worried, with good reason, about the arrival back in Germany of so many angry, defeated, poverty-stricken soldiers with no jobs to go to. The outcome of the war would not be happy if they should find themselves foodless as well as workless.

> In the interests of order, in the interests of humanity, we must see to it that the German people, whose fate is now largely in our hands, shall not starve. That is a first duty which we owe to a conquered enemy. Let it be handsomely performed.

The Northcliffe press, it goes without saying, disagreed. *The Times* was dignified but disapproving.

> [T]he inexpiable brutalities which she [Germany] perpetrated so long as she had the power, and against which no classes of her people dared to protest, have filled us with a loathing and a righteous indignation which will not readily pass away. She has been false and cruel. She must bear the penalty in our mistrust and in our abhorrence.

Three months earlier, *The Times* recalled, the colonial secretary of the Imperial German government had demanded the return of Germany's colonies, conquered by the Allies. Now he was warning that the tough conditions of the Armistice would cause starvation in Germany. Even at this eleventh hour, *The Times* demanded that the Germans should show evidence of their good faith.

Down at the far end of the Northcliffe stable, the *Daily Mirror* was little short of savage that Tuesday morning. Its front page was excellent, with interesting and well-selected pictures illustrating the headline 'How London Hailed The End Of The War'. But with it came a pictorial section which displayed the uglier features of the yellow press: the exaggeration, the tight focus on individuals as objects of hate, the whipping-up of the lynch mob. The front page of the special section, broadsheet-sized, carries seven large, oddly selected photographs. Under the words

THE HUN ARCH-CRIMINALS' HURRIED FLIGHT FROM JUSTICE

the Kaiser, wearing his hussar's cap with its large skull and crossbones, glares out defiantly. Underneath is the caption

> The ex-Emperor William II., to whose personal account must in the last resort be debited all the horror and waste of the war which has devastated Europe, slain millions of men and women, and thrown the whole world into mourning. He must answer for his work.

Alongside him, a military cap perched jauntily on the side of his head, is his son.

> The ex-Crown Prince of Germany, who has personally committed some of the worst outrages to be laid to the charge of blood-mad Hun barbarians. Murderer, incendiary and thief, he richly deserves the worst punishment that can be awarded him.

In the centre is a painting of an angel hovering over the body of a woman, with the caption

> 'Shot at dawn!' Floods of innocent blood cry out for justice on the murderers.

This is Edith Cavell, whom the Germans shot in Belgium for helping wounded British prisoners escape. A photograph of her appears alongside, and underneath the caption reads: 'Nurse Edith Cavell, assassinated by the Germans in defiance of every law, divine and human. The Kaiser could have prevented the crime, but chose to permit it, and is chiefly responsible.'

On the right is the photograph of a captain in the British Merchant Navy, captured by the German navy for having helped in the sinking of a German ship, and executed. It reads: 'Captain Charles Fryatt, commander of the G.E.R. steamer Brussels, deliberately done to death by the Huns. The Kaiser, by refusing to interfere, made himself the principal assassin.'

The bottom half of the page shows the chateau at Middachten, in the Netherlands, 'in which the ex-Kaiser has found a temporary hiding-place from the vengeance of his late subjects and the judgement of the Allies'. A photograph of his host, Count William von Bentinck, appears on the left, and, on the right, another impressively moustachioed figure with the caption: 'Field-Marshal von Hindenburg, one of his infamous master's chief organisers of atrocity and frightfulness. His callous cruelty was notorious even among the Huns, who made him their idol.'

Perhaps it is too much to expect that any newspaper would, after four years of the fiercest warfare, recall that not long before the war broke out, the Northcliffe press were praising the Kaiser as a man of moderation and a trustworthy figure. But the *Mirror* supplement is an ugly production on a day of national rejoicing, and looks ahead to the kind of pressures which created the Versailles Treaty, leading to another world war.

Not surprisingly, there were plenty of returning soldiers who disapproved strongly of this kind of screaming from the sidelines by journalists who had sacrificed nothing in the war, and had indeed profited from it. 'The yellow press' was always a term of abuse, but for the soldiers immediately after the armistice it came to mean some of the things that were worst about civilian behaviour during the war.

Siegfried Sassoon, who had tried to campaign for an early end to the war, summed up the soldiers' hatred for the politicians and journalists.

'Fight to a Finish'

> The boys came back. Bands played and flags were flying,
> And Yellow-Pressmen thronged the sunlit street
> To cheer the soldiers who'd refrained from dying,
> And hear the music of returning feet.
> 'Of all the thrills and ardours War has brought,
> This moment is the finest.' (So they thought.)
>
> Snapping their bayonets on to charge the mob,
> Grim Fusiliers broke ranks with glint of steel.
> At last the boys had found a cushy job.
> . . .
> I heard the Yellow-Pressmen grunt and squeal;
> And with my trusty bombers turned and went
> To clear those Junkers out of Parliament.

The hatred of the press gradually faded as the returning soldiers got used to civilian life once again. But the mistrust of what the press wrote never entirely faded. It remains to this day.

8

BLACK AND TANS

The experience of the First World War had been so intense and had intruded so deeply into the life of almost everyone, that it was followed by a powerful reaction: a determination that things must be different in future. The concept that this must be a war to end all wars was shared by vast numbers of people. There were signs of a new idealism and high-mindedness. There was, for instance, a growing sense that governments should be judged on different and tougher criteria from those which applied to individuals. The state, in other words, should be expected to behave better than those who set out to challenge it. Such an attitude had always existed, of course, but now it seemed to be much more widespread; especially in the press.

Ireland after the Easter Rising of April 1916 proved to be a test bed for this approach. The reporting of the Rising itself followed the traditional pattern: most British newspapers supported the way the army responded, and so did the press of the Allied countries. The United States was not even involved in the war yet, but its mainstream newspapers (though not the smaller ones which catered for the Irish population) largely agreed that the Rising was a German-funded stab in the back.

This changed in the aftermath of the Rising. Conservative newspapers in Britain continued to support the actions of the army, but even they showed unease at the actions of the Black and Tans and other auxiliary groups. The result was the start of a perceived imbalance which remains to this day: journalists tended to be harsher on the misdeeds of govern-ments and the forces of law and order than on the actions of insurgent groups. In his book *The News from Ireland: Foreign Correspondents and the Irish Revolution* the Irish writer Maurice Walsh has pointed out that the murder of more than 200 people in Belfast during Ireland's war of independence went virtually unreported, while the original Bloody

Sunday, when British troops fired on a Gaelic football crowd in Dublin, killing 14, became an international cause célèbre.

Much the same was true in the Northern Ireland troubles that began in 1969. IRA murders, for instance, of a Belfast Catholic woman who cradled the head of a dying British soldier out of common humanity, received far less coverage around the world than the deaths of civilians at the hands of British soldiers or the Royal Ulster Constabulary.

For at least sixty years, left-wing guerrilla groups have found it easier to get the interest and support of foreign journalists than right-wing governments or right-wing guerrillas. Yet the Provisional IRA was an exception to this. Throughout its campaign of violence it was un-repentantly Catholic and deeply conservative in social and religious matters; yet that did not seem to matter to journalists from left-wing newspapers in France, Germany and Italy.

British journalists, too, were often inclined to accept the IRA's version of events rather than the British army's; and they sometimes found afterwards that they had been right to do so.

After the First World War the old, instinctive alliance between journalists and authority was weakened. As a result of the lies and fierce controls of the war, journalists began to show a more questioning approach. In future not everything British officialdom did would be accepted without question. And it was in Ireland that the first real signs of this change in attitudes began to show.

§

It was not until 12.45 on the morning of 29 April 1916 that the first in-dependent reports of the Easter Rising in Dublin reached the offices of the *Daily Mail* in Carmelite House, just off Fleet Street. The rising had started at 10.15 on Easter Monday, the 24th, but for the next five days the only news of it were official statements from the British military authorities who had blocked off all lines of communication between Dublin and London. The *Mail* was so angry about this that it devoted the opening of its story that Saturday morning to a homily against censorship.

DETAILED ACCOUNTS OF THE DUBLIN RISING.
FIRST NARRATIVES AFTER SIX DAYS OF SECRECY.

REBELS SHELLED BY A GUNBOAT.
BIG FIRE BLAZING IN SACKVILLE STREET.
NEWS OF THE COUNTRY OUTBREAKS

> It has been suggested that the newspapers should be
> taken over and controlled by the Government. This
> week's suppression of news is a lesson to the public of
> what that would mean. Whatever news the Cabinet have
> had from Dublin there are countless other people with
> relatives in the centre of rebellion who have had no
> intelligence for almost a week of anxiety.

To rub in the message, the *Mail* carried two brief reports in the next
column which showed that Irish Nationalists in America were told about
the rising directly it started, and that documents about its planning had
been found when the secretary to the German military attaché was
arrested in Washington. If they knew, the implication was, why shouldn't
the British people?

Now that communications had been re-established, the newspapers
could start providing the kind of detail the authorities in Ireland had
blocked. Much of it seemed absurdly small-time; perhaps the patronizing
tone the British habitually took towards Ireland and the Irish made it
harder to strike a note of real drama. The first eyewitness account of the
rising that *The Times* published as its second lead – after the official
communiqués, that is – was a rambling story from one of its Irish correspondents which began, chattily,

> Shortly after 10 o'clock on Easter Monday morning I had
> occasion to ring up, from Dublin, a personal friend in
> Dundalk. This friend first of all asked me what the
> weather was like in Dublin, and then said, with a
> significance which I afterwards understood, 'How are
> things in the City?'

The *Times* correspondent replied that the only bit of excitement he had
seen was the people going to the races. His report has an unmistakably
Somerville-and-Ross feel to it.

The British authorities, based in Dublin Castle, showed a distinct disregard for events in Ireland in the early years of the First World War. Augustine Birrell, the Chief Secretary for Ireland, was a charming, cultivated, highly intelligent lawyer and belletrist who had achieved some remarkable things for Ireland in previous years. From 1912 onwards, though, he had been sidelined by the politicians in London. Worse, he and his advisers had failed to notice that while the mass of Irish people followed John Redmond, the leader of the main Nationalist party, in backing Britain in the First World War, other groups were turning to extremism. After the Rising broke out, on 1 May 1916, the *Daily Mail* ran an editorial attacking Birrell under the headline 'Dublin Is No Place For A Feeble Farceur'.

As a result of Birrell's weak grip, the Royal Irish Constabulary received no orders from Dublin Castle to prevent Sinn Fein and other groups from parading around the city. The rebels were able to march with loaded weapons, unchallenged, to the buildings they had planned to capture. It was emblematic of the sleepwalking fashion with which the Dublin authorities had governed Ireland since the start of the war.

The *Times* correspondent who had been tipped off by his friend in Dundalk also seemed to be sleepwalking.

> Shortly before noon I was walking down O'Connell-street, with the intention of going to Stephen's Green, when I noticed a body of Sinn Feiners, about a hundred strong; but there was nothing particular about them to attract attention. Dublin is used to such sights. They were, however, marching with fixed bayonets.

There was a general sense of disbelief, of the absurdity of what was happening. Another special correspondent writes to *The Times*: '. . . [S]hooting was proceeding irregularly both in the direction of Sackville-street and the Liffey. It was, to say the least, a disquieting reception, quite unlike what one is accustomed to receive in the Irish capital.'

The *Daily Mail*, by contrast, was stressing an alternative view of Ireland in Britain: that it was a country of rogues, thieves and drunks. The *Mail* correspondent, filing his report from Belfast, says that the centre of Dublin 'was given up to a wild orgy of drink and loot, and for three days pandemonium reigned'. His report has clearly been worked up from a mixture of a few interviews with eyewitnesses who had escaped to Belfast, a great many assumptions, and plenty of imagination.

> The crackle of rifle shots could be heard, and now and again a shriek of pain above the wild hurly-burly of the shouting, swearing mob . . . The dregs of the city had been drawn to the spot. Loot was the uppermost thought. Half the shops in Sackville-street were sacked.

Next, there is a wonderful exculpatory passage: 'Respectable citizens, holiday-makers from Belfast, and people of the most unimpeachable loyalty and probity, to save their skins, were compelled to take part in the thievery.'

After we have been introduced to the respectable Protestants forced against their will to loot the shops of Dublin, we are back in the realm of imaginative re-creation, on the I'm-sure-it-must-have-been-pretty-much-like-this pattern.

> Sealskin coats and silk blouses were soon to be seen on women with bare feet and ragged petticoats reeking strongly of porter; children who had never possessed two-pence of their own were imitating 'Charlie Chaplin' with stolen silk hats in the middle of the turmoil and the murder.

A special correspondent for the *Mail*, in a story written from 'Near Dublin' at midnight on Thursday, but not published until Saturday, is encouraging:

> There is every indication to-night of an all-round check to the Dublin maelstrom.
>
> My news from the city is more than reassuring, more than hopeful; and there is abundant promise of the Sinn Fein raiders scuttling back to their burrows before the trained soldiery.

He too gives us an impression of what has gone on, while signalling in the first few words that he has not actually witnessed it himself, though he is half-inclined to give us the impression that he has:

> ... [T]here will ever be a picture in the mind's eye of Sackville-street torn up and ramparted with overturned vehicles of every kind; of the Four Courts (The Irish Law Courts) invested and turned, so to speak, inside out with the rebels entrenching themselves behind great piles of ancient and historic tomes and records, and of machine-guns whirring from the front windows of the aristocratic and elegant Shelbourne Hotel. And all through the popular shopping centre, loot, loot, and once again – loot!

The use of the word 'whirring' to describe the sound of machine guns, indicates that the correspondent has never heard a machine gun fired, in Dublin or anywhere else.

The first reports of the uprising, based solely on official statements, had appeared in the London papers the previous Wednesday, 26 April. The *Daily Express*, also working on the basis of traditional British prejudice, headlines its story

CRAZY REBELLION IN IRELAND.

The leading editorial in that day's *Times* agrees about the craziness of the uprising, but blames it on Germany.

> The Germans have always counted on armed insurrection in Ireland.
>
> They have striven to provoke it from the outbreak of the war, and at last they have succeeded in getting their dupes to indulge in an insane rising . . .

The Times continues: 'There has not been the slightest sign of alarm in any quarter, and we shall be greatly surprised if the general population even in Dublin take the "insurrection" very seriously.'

This assumption would have far-reaching consequences both for Ireland and for Britain.

§

During the Rising, Harold Ashton, a *Mail* correspondent, went to Cork and visited Sinn Fein's headquarters there. In an article appearing on 3 May 1916 he wrote:

> There was nothing remarkable about their door except that the knob had been removed and the hole of it enlarged. I had not been in Cork an hour before I had discovered the Sinn Fein 'password' – it was easy enough.
>
> I whispered it through the hole. The door immediately swung open and I walked in, to be instantly confronted by a wild-eyed, ragged-haired slip of a youth who jabbed at me with a bayonet and sent me staggering backwards. Behind him in the narrow passage were a dozen more equally wild-looking and similarly armed youths. They pressed forward, flashing their bayonets and demanding to know by what traitorous methods I had gained admission to their stronghold.
>
> I said I represented The Daily Mail and had two simple questions to ask – whether it was true that the police had ordered them to give up their arms and ammunition within a certain time this afternoon, and whether – today, tomorrow or at any other time – they had decided to hold up Cork after the manner of their brethren in Dublin . . .

In Cork, writes Harold Ashton, you ask these questions as if you were asking about the weather. He was referred to their leader, who reminded him of Byron, 'slightly soiled'. This man was holding a slim volume of the plays of Sophocles in his 'white, ladylike fingers' and spoke in a soft, cultured voice. "'If they come to demand our arms," he said a trifle wearily, as if he were tired of discussing the obvious, "we shall shoot them."'

But he and his men would not be taking over the centre of Cork. Something, he said, had gone wrong with the arrangements; the military had got to the Post Office in force.

The British press looked at Ireland through its own patronizing lens, seeing only absurdity, the occasional mindless criminality, and a basic lack of importance. Even the revolutionaries have ladylike hands and read Greek plays when they are not planning their ultimately abortive acts of violence.

§

Lord Northcliffe, who was himself from a Protestant, Anglo-Irish family, owned a newspaper empire which spoke to every group in Britain: *The Times* to the upper and upper-middle class, the *Daily Mail* to the middle and lower-middle class, and the *Daily Mirror* to the working class. It was an unprecedented spread of influence by a single individual which would not be equalled until Rupert Murdoch's day.

The close result in the 1910 election, during which the Northcliffe press campaigned loudly for the Conservative cause, meant that Asquith had to depend on Irish Nationalist MPs to stay in power; and their price was Home Rule. Opposition to this in Ulster, which was also supported strongly by the Northcliffe press, took on an increasingly violent tone. Soon, some Ulster Protestants who talked loudly of their willingness to die for the total union of Ulster with Britain were threatening that they would make approaches to the Kaiser for German help.

The Northcliffe newspapers made no attempt to condemn this kind of open disloyalty. On the contrary, they took the line that it was the fault of the Liberal government. The *Daily Express* competed with the *Mail* to provide a megaphone for angry Ulstermen. Most of the rest of the press was instinctively pro-Unionist. Only two newspapers regularly put the case for Home Rule: the *Daily News* and the *Manchester Guardian*. Together they had a circulation of less than 250,000.

The *Mail*, echoing the tactic of the Ulster Unionists, hinted more and more crudely that if their demands were not met there would be violence and rebellion – though such words were never quite used. On 7 July 1914, for instance, the *Mail* proclaimed: 'Ulster must be given the security she demands. There can be no question of surrender on her part, and those who expect any weakening of her attitude must be prepared for a rude awakening.'

And on Friday 10 July, when a world war with Germany was less than a month away, the *Mail* warned:

> [Ulster] is prepared to stake her very existence in battle
> rather than submit to Home Rule in any form or in any part
> of her area. To carry out her resolve she has today, as
> Ministers have admitted in the House of Commons, 85,000
> Volunteers, armed, organised, and equipped for the field,
> with reserves behind them.

Negotiation while pointing a loaded gun at your adversary is a tactic
which, over the decades, the *Mail* had deplored and would continue to
deplore. But not in the case of Ulster; that, the *Mail* believed, was an
issue of principle. On Monday 13 July the *Mail* criticized the Liberal
newspapers for reporting so few of the threats from the Ulster volunteers.

> A very grave feature of the Ulster crisis is the continued
> suppression of news concerning it in the Liberal Press . . .
>   The fact is that the Radical newspapers, having so long
> practised the policy of hushing-up, are afraid to reveal
> the full truth now that affairs are marching fast to the
> denouement.

The *Guardian*, for its part, argued that the Ulster Volunteer Force had
been 'worked up to such a pitch' that they would be 'seriously disappointed should they not be called upon to fight'. Very soon now they
would indeed be called upon to fight, but not for an Ulster free from the
threat of rule from predominantly Catholic Dublin.

John Redmond, the Irish Nationalist MP who had managed to ensure
that the demand for Home Rule would remain a constitutional and not
a violent one, offered his volunteers to fight Germany; and the Ulster
Volunteer Force did the same. For almost two years the idea of Home
Rule seemed to have been put on the shelf. But the Irish Republican
Brotherhood continued to work for total independence, and went ahead
with planning the Easter Rising.

At first, after it had taken place and been put down, it seemed that
the Rising had been a complete failure. Sir Roger Casement, who had
tried to recruit Irish prisoners of war in Germany to fight for Ireland's
independence, had returned to Ireland the week before the Rising in a
German ship with a cargo of weapons. The ship was captured and

1. Aboard the *Dunottar Castle* (*Illustrated London News*, 11 November 1899). General Buller is in the left foreground with his ADC. Churchill is behind them in a dark cap, perhaps being discreetly briefed. The man sitting on the deck in the dark suit is Earl de la Warr of the *Globe*, who later reported angrily about British losses at Magersfontein. The middle-class correspondents are not featured.

2. Dame Flora Shaw (1852–1929): the first woman on the permanent staff of *The Times*. As its colonial editor she had a powerful influence on British policy towards the Boers. Later she invented the name 'Nigeria' and helped found Hong Kong University.

3. Charles Prestwick Scott (1846–1932) edited the *Manchester Guardian* for fifty-seven years. His moderation and commonsense made him perhaps the greatest newspaper editor in British history.

4. Lady Sarah Wilson (1865–1929), Winston Churchill's aunt, was hired by the *Daily Mail* to write an eyewitness account of the siege of Mafeking. Her reporting annoyed the established correspondents in the town and ignored many of the key incidents, but the readers adored her.

5. Bennet Burleigh (c.1840–1914) was a correspondent of the old school. A bohemian and lifelong Socialist, he nevertheless ignored the tragedy of the British concentration camps during the Boer War and assured his readers the reports about them were exaggerated.

6. Edgar Wallace (1875–1932). As the *Mail*'s Boer War correspondent he avoided the front-line but wrote tellingly about ordinary soldiers. He scooped the world with the news of the peace treaty with the Boers and was rewarded with the editorship of the *Rand Daily Mail*.

7. The *Daily Telegraph* takes the opportunity to boast that it had the world's largest circulation and now contained no fewer than fourteen pages.

8. Celebrating the siege of Mafeking. The siege was given huge attention at home, and Colonel Robert Baden-Powell became a national hero; yet little actually happened there.

NORTH BRITISH AND MERCANTILE
INSURANCE COMPANY.
ESTABLISHED 1809.
FIRE, LIFE, ANNUITIES, BURGLARY.
TOTAL FUNDS
£17,100,000.
ANNUAL INCOME
£3,600,000.
For full particulars apply to
Chief Offices { 61, Threadneedle-street, London, E.C.
{ 64, Princes-street, Edinburgh.

Daily

NO. 1,851.   LONDON, T

TO-DAY'S STORY.

THURSDAY MORNING.

The weather forecast for to-day is :—
Changeable, with some snow or sleet
showers ; north-easterly winds, moderate
or light at most places inland, generally
fresh or strong on coast ; cold.

Lighting-up time, 7.13 p.m.

The alien invasion of East London is ex-
tending rapidly, and many British shopkeepers have been obliged to close their
establishments in consequence.—(Page 1.)

An anti-British campaign is being engineered by the Cape Bond. (Page 1.)

Mr. Chamberlain made a great speech in
defence of Lord Milner, and the vote of
censure was negatived without a division.—
(Page 1.)

In a powerful speech Mr. Chamberlain
reviewed the causes that compelled the last
Government to sanction Chinese labour, and
predicted that the policy of the present
Government would lead to irretrievable disaster in South Africa. The Government refused his proposal to send out a Royal
Commission.—(Page 1.)

Additional troops have been sent to Lens,
owing to the menacing attitude of the
strikers. A strike is also threatened in
the mining centres of the Loire.—(Page 5.)

THE MILNER "CENSURE."

MR. BYLES BRINGS IN HIS "PATRIOTIC" MOTION.

NO DIVISION.

GOVERNMENT STEPS IN TO SAVE ITS FACE.

A SORRY AFFAIR.

BRILLIANT DEFENCE BY MR. CHAMBERLAIN.

a servant. If that were the charge, well, it
could not be met by a mere censure of the
House.

"Nothing short of an impeachment would
justify a charge of that kind."

Mr. Chamberlain then recounted all the
facts of the case. A Mr. Evans reported
to Lord Milner that he had found it necessary to give permission to inflict a limited
amount of corporal punishment. Lord
Milner did not dissent.

"I deeply regret," said Mr. Chamber,
lain, "that any public servant should have
given this illegal permission, which was
given by Mr. Evans, and I think it is very
much to be regretted. In common fairness
it must be admitted that Lord Milner
would have been less on his guard in listening to this counsel, coming, as it did, from
a known protector of the Chinese.

"I would further remind the House that
Mr. Lyttelton, when the matter was brought
to his notice, expressed his profound regret
that anything of the kind had taken place.

"I shall be greatly interested to know
what view the Government are going to
take. It is only this morning we learned
the particular way the Government propose
to deal with the matter. They have put
down an amendment.

Sir, it is a cowardly amendment. I in-
finitely prefer the resolution. What
—(speaking with a gesture of contempt)
—an amendment! An amendment which
insults Lord Milner—(Opposition cheers)
—and at the same time accepts the sub-
stantial part of the resolution!

WEAK CONCLUSION.

"SLAVERY THE MIL

NO COMMISS INQUIRY T APPOINTE

POLICY OF

By Our Parliamentary

HOUSE OF COMMONS
The debate was Chinese
as well as in the evening.
In the first sitting the Go
fiantly resisted all the efforts
tion to get them to send o
of inquiry into all the cha
slavery.

Mr. Chamberlain raked
fore and aft with his chaf
the Ministerialists were st
mannered at times—in their
"Pretty defenders of the
Transvaal!" said Mr. Char
ing an almost ribald throng
It was a rebuke extorted fr
disposition of the packe

Express

DELICIOUS COFFEE.
RED
WHITE
& BLUE
For Breakfast & after Dinner.

‌H 22, 1906. ONE HALFPENNY.

DEATH IS
...LIKE.

...BLE SERMON BY
...BISHOP OF
...ONDON.

London delivered a re-
‌...at St. Pancras Church
‌...ich he gave a forecast of
‌when dying.
‌...nderwent an operation a
‌...nd it was while under the
‌...æsthetic that he had what
‌...experience of what death

‌...on," he said, "when you
‌...it is that makes you for
‌...unseable, you seem to be
‌...moment out of the body
‌...out of the body—the body
‌...nad.

‌...your mind, is perfectly
‌y it is the experience of
‌...at you seem to be swept
‌...stars towards your God.
‌...ou are out of the body,
‌...only for a few moments,
‌...death will be,
‌...and I am perfectly cer-
‌...that when that moment
‌...only one thing that will
‌...only one thing that will
‌...being under the power of
‌...d that is unrepented and

MURDER BY
REQUEST.

TWO SISTERS KILLED
IN A TRAGIC
MANNER.

STORY OF FAILURE.

"*Express*" *Correspondent.*

BERLIN, Wednesday, March 21.
Karl Brunke, a bank clerk, nineteen years
of age, was sentenced in the Brunswick
Criminal Court to-day to eight years' penal
servitude for murdering two sisters, Martha
and Alma Haare, at their own request.

The German criminal code differentiates
between ordinary murder and murder committed at a victim's request. Paragraph
216 of the code provides for punishment of
at least three years' imprisonment for murder committed at the serious and plainly
expressed desire of the victim.

Brunke, in replying to questions addressed
to him by the judge, said he was keenly
interested in literature, and had read Kant,
Schopenhauer, and other philosophers. He

TWELVE "QUEENS"
IN PARIS.

MARKET ROYALTIES WHO
ARE HOLDING A
JOINT COURT.

"*Express*" *Correspondent.*

PARIS, Wednesday, March 21.
Twelve market "queens" were giving a
royal reception as they drove through Paris
to-day as a preliminary to the Mi-Carême
procession to-morrow.

Six of the queens rule the Paris markets, and the others are the representatives
of workers in Rome, Madrid, Vevey, Calais,
and St. Malo. The Committee of Fêtes
have been busy yesterday and to-day receiving them with the requisite respect and
ceremonial.

The Queen of Rome, a statuesque beauty
who styles herself a "Roman of the Hills,"
because she was born in sight of the Seven
Hills, arrived in Paris yesterday afternoon
with a distinguished suite.

At 4.30 this morning the tired committeemen were at the Gare d'Orsay to meet the
Queen of Madrid, who in private life is
Senorita Concepcion Ledesma, an embroiderer. When "her Majesty" stepped
from the train, the committeemen forgot
that they were fatigued. She is a dark-
eyed girl of sixteen, and the enthusiastic
officials voted her the prettiest queen who
has visited Paris for years.

CHOICE OF ARTISTS.

The Queen of Madrid was accompanied
by half a dozen typically Spanish maids of
honour, all embroiderers. The queen and
her maids were chosen by a committee of
Spanish artists.

The next arrival was the "Goddess" of
Vevey, Mlle. Hermione Tavernay, accompanied by two maids of honour and seven
"delegates" from the vineyards of Vevey.
Mlle. Tavernay is styled a "goddess" because democratic Switzerland does not re-
cognise queens.

Two Queens of Calais were received at
the Gare du Nord with equal ceremony.
One queen represented the fishwives, the
other the Calais lacemakers. The Queen
of the Lacemakers wore a wonderful lace
hat, which is at once the envy and despair
of the fashionable milliners.

A belated arrival was the Queen of St.
Malo, likewise a representative of the fish-
ing industry.

Accompanied by the five Queens of the
Paris markets and the Queen of Queens of
Paris, the visiting queens were driven
through the city to-day, wearing their
national costumes. Afterwards they were
entertained at luncheon. To-night they
were the guests of honour at the Folies-
Bergère.

BEATEN TO DEATH.

FOREMAN KILLS SEVEN NAVVIES
IN A FEW MINUTES.

"*Express*" *Correspondent.*

NEW YORK, Wednesday, March 21.
A sensational fight between a railway
foreman and a gang of navvies is reported
from North Carolina.

The navvies, who were Hungarians and
Italians, were dissatisfied with their treatment, and made an organised attack on
the foreman during the dinner hour.

Seizing an iron bar, the foreman threatened to brain the first man who approached
him. The navvies made a rush to over-
power him, but he wielded the bar with
such effect that in a few minutes he had
beaten seven of the men to death. The
rest of the navvies fled.

MAD BULL HAMSTRUNG.

KILLS ITS KEEPER AND INJURES
FOUR OTHER PERSONS.

"*Express*" *Correspondent.*

PARIS, Wednesday, March 21.
A prize bull, which was being led from
the National Agricultural Show, went mad
in the street to-day, and in two minutes

OVERRUN BY
ALIENS.

FOREIGN AREA IN EAST
LONDON STEADILY
EXTENDING.

BRITONS OUSTED.

The announcement in the "Express" that
of 1,000 aliens who have landed in London
within the past week not one has been de-
tained or rejected, has opened the eyes of
those who imagined that the alien invasion
had been stopped by the new Act.

The flock of pauper immigrants gathered
on the shores of the Continent has been
quick to take advantage of the practical
destruction of the Act by the Home
Secretary, and now that the whole purpose
of the Act has been nullified by the new
regulations, the influx of aliens is bound
to increase by leaps and bounds.

Among the British residents of the East
End there is growing anger at what they
consider their betrayal by the Government.
The news that the Home Secretary, in
raising the number of aliens constituting
an immigrant ship from twelve to twenty,
acted in flat opposition to the views of the
Immigration Board, has roused the keenest
indignation.

STRANGLED!

"The fact that no meeting of the board
has had to be held for ten days conclusively shows that the Act has been
strangled," a member of the Board said to
an "Express" representative yesterday.

"It is preposterous to suppose that
among the 1,000 aliens landed during that
time there was not a single undesirable.
There must have been any number of cases
unfit for admission. The explanation, of
course, is that Mr. Gladstone's instructions to the immigration officers have made
it practically impossible to object to any
case.

"If the alien is a pauper, he can only
has to say he is a refugee.

"If he is medically unfit, he only has
to say that he would be caused suffering
by being sent back.

"If he wants to stay in London, he only
has to say that he is on his way to America.

"If by any strange chance under the
new rules he should be sent back, he only
has to come again on a ship bringing fewer
than twenty steerage passengers, as most
of the Dutch vessels do.

To all such cases his plea is now a pass-
port into London, and once he is here he is
at liberty to remain.

"People in the East End take with a
grain of salt the statement that the transmigrants all go out of London again. We
know that many so-called transmigrants remain. The proof is to be seen in the
rapidly increasing area occupied by the
aliens."

NO ROOM FOR ENGLISHMEN.

"From Whitechapel to Bow Bridge, along
Mile End-road—about a couple of miles—
there is now scarcely an English shopkeeper
left. Even the Jewish shopkeepers of old
standing are being ruined by the newcomers, who get their clothes, boots, and
furniture made by their fellow-workmen instead of going to the shops.

"Having absorbed Whitechapel and Stepney and captured a large part of Mile End,
the aliens are now moving on Manor Park,
further east. Those who have been in Stepney and Mile End a few years are being
ousted in their turn by newcomers, and are
moving into the outer districts.

"A large part of London Fields is now
occupied by the alien bootmakers, and the
invasion is advancing on Hackney Downs.
A Hackney shopkeeper told me a few days
ago that he is being hemmed in by aliens,
and that his trade is being ruined.

"People who have not experienced the
alien invasion may be unable to understand
the anger of the East End at the strangling
of the Act, but people who have had to leave
their houses and close their shops on account of the aliens are in no mood to see
the Act killed without protest."

SLIPPING THROUGH AT GRIMSBY.

There can be little doubt, the "Express"
Grimsby correspondent telegraphs, that the
recent departmental instructions regarding

---

9. The front page of the *Express* in 1906. The last column on the right betrays an approach to immigration that would become a staple of tabloid coverage a century later.

10. *Far left.* King and Kaiser. Edward VII cordially disliked his cousin, Wilhelm II, and Wilhelm was certain Edward was plotting Germany's downfall. The Kaiser habitually tried to disguise the fact that his left arm was withered, by resting his hand on his sword-hilt.

11. *Left.* The prolific, self-congratulatory thriller-writer William Le Queux (1864–1927), whose campaign about the German threat in the *Daily Mail* led to the establishment of MI5 and a great many sales.

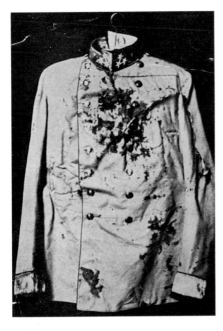

12. The jacket worn by Archduke Franz Ferdinand on 28 June 1914 when he was murdered in Sarajevo.

13. Philip Gibbs (1877–1962) was in many ways the best and most conscientious of the British correspondents on the Western Front. He did his best to evade Army censorship when the war began, and was reluctant merely to reproduce the official line about the fighting.

14. Ellis Ashmead-Bartlett (1881–1931), the *Daily Telegraph*'s man at the Dardanelles. His reporting created the ANZAC legend and (with a little help from Rupert Murdoch's father) brought about the Allied withdrawal.

And Gladys never draws QUITE bare—
   because we think its bad for you's.
Poor lonely you's who write to me, I tell
   you's stories, frilly ones—
Half French, half English, double-paged,
   my pretty-pretty pattern runs.
I write about my woman friends as
   PETITES AMIES—you's, confess
How much that MOT-A-PROPOS lends to
   your Phrynette of naughtiness !
Did I tell you's of Dolly, who's fiancée
   to a brace of you's ;
And how that MECHANTE Margot lost a
   pair of ROSE DU BARRY shoes ?)
What would you's do, poor lonely you's,
   without my letters to peruse,
I seem to hear you's voices shout a
   hundred thousand loud NA POO's !

GILBERT FRANKAU.

31/7/16.

A MESSAGE FROM MR. TEECH BOMAS.

BY OUR SPECIAL CORRESPONDENT
MR TEECH BOMAS.
—:o:—
MR TEECH BOMAS SPEAKS.
—:o:—

No Mar's Lard, 20/7/16.
I write from the middle of the battlefield. There are a lot of bullets but I
don't mind that. Also the air is thick
with shells. That also I don't mind. Let
me tell you all about it while I can
think clearly. Before the battle com-
menced I took up a favourable position
in No Man's Land, the little larks were
larking and the morning was fine. Ther
Hell broke loose and as things got
really hot I climbed up the rope of a
sausage and joined two A.S.C.'s who
were also watching the proceedings.
Let me tell you of the gallant dash of the
Umpshires: Into the pick of the Prussian
Guard they dashed. The few of the
Guard who remained cried " Kamerad "
and surrendered. That rush was epic. I then
walked over the German lines to have a
look at them. There were a lot more
bullets but what would you ? Now I
thrill with an ecstacy. Here they come,
the wood is ours. Strange associations,
here we see the submarine co-operating
with the cavalry and shells falling thickly.
Then—the peasants—I witnessed the
thrilling scenes of the last peasants
leaving their happy farms in No Man's
Land, harnessing their mongrel dogs
into their little carts and driving off
when the battle got a bit hot. It was
epic. Taking a place is one thing but
putting it back is another. Profound
but true, and so the wood was won. A
correspondent must always see to write.
This may appear unnecessary to the
cognoscenti, but it is so. To-morrow I
will tell you more. I return now to the
battle.

H. TEECH BOMAS.

TRENCH CONVERSATIONS.
—o—o—o—
NO II.
—:o:—

SUB.(To man wearing cardigan over
shirt on blazing hot day)—' What the
deuce are you wearing your cardigan for
on a day like this ? "
   MAN.—To keep my shirt clean, sir !

The Kaiser once said at Peronne
That the Army we'd got was " no bon,"
   But between you and me
   He didn't " compris "
The size of the job he had on

15. The *Wipers Times* lampoons William Beach Thomas, the *Daily Mail* war correspondent much disliked by the troops. Edited by Captain F. J. Roberts and Lt. F. H. Pearson and produced on a looted printing-press, it was the trench equivalent of *Private Eye*.

16. Dressed to kill: the upper-class IRA volunteer Countess Markievicz, née Constance Gore-Booth (1868–1927). During the Easter Rising she fought in a fetching green outfit, but no one doubted her courage.

17. The *Dublin Evening Herald* of 22 November 1920 reports on the vicious murders carried out by the British forces and the IRA.

Casement was arrested. The Rising itself petered out with the death or surrender of everyone involved.

More than 500 people had died, 318 of them ordinary civilians. The British army lost 116 dead, the police 16, and the rebels 64. On Monday 1 May, a week after the Rising began, *The Times* ran as a footnote to its main coverage an account from a doctor who said:

> The rebels fired on all traffic regardless of consequences and tram after tram was riddled with shot. Some men who saw this scene, although limping along on crutches [they were apparently soldiers convalescing from the Western Front], approached the rebels. 'For God's sake don't shoot innocent people' cried one, while another called out, 'You are killing your own mothers and sisters.' But the rebels were heartless. The men advanced, and I regret to say that the miscreants fired on the helpless fellows, each of whom was incapable of defence. Red Cross nurses went to the assistance of the Tommies.

Interestingly, none of the London newspapers seems to make anything much of reports like this, of which there were quite a number. In other circumstances they might well have been treated as useful propaganda, but perhaps the news editors felt there was no need to play up such details because readers would have regarded the Rising as outrageous anyway; there was no point in trying to propagandize those who were already convinced.

Mainstream opinion in Ireland was appalled. In Dublin the *Irish Independent*, strongly nationalist, called the Rising 'a miserable fiasco, leaving behind its trail of woe and horror'. Under the headline 'Criminal Madness', its main editorial on 4 May 1916 read:

> No terms of denunciation that pen could indite would be too strong to apply to those responsible for the insane and criminal rising of last week. Around us in the centre of Ireland's capital, is a scene of ruin which it is heartrending to behold. Some of the proudest structures in what was one of the finest streets in Europe are now reduced to shapeless heaps of smouldering ashes.

Scarcely anyone except the most extreme Nationalists disagreed. Later it became axiomatic that as the captured rebels were marched through the streets, they were spat on and insulted by working-class women whose husbands were at the front. There is doubt about this entire episode, which is not supported by contemporary reporting. Some writers have suggested that if the incident were true, it could have occurred in a Protestant working-class area near the barracks.

A Canadian, Frederick Arthur McKenzie, travelled back to Ireland after the Rising had begun with Augustine Birrell, the Chief Secretary whose laxness allowed the Rising to happen. In a book published later in the year, *The Irish Rebellion: What Happened and Why*, McKenzie wrote:

> I have read many accounts of public feeling in Dublin in these days. They are all agreed that the open and strong sympathy of the mass of the population was with the British troops. That this was in the better parts of the city, I have no doubt, but certainly what I myself saw in the poorer districts did not confirm this. It rather indicated that there was a vast amount of sympathy with the rebels, particularly after the rebels were defeated.

McKenzie may well have been right; yet the notion that there were large numbers of reports in the British press about local anger against the rebels does not seem to be correct. The only exception came in stories about Countess Markievicz, who was booed and jeered as she was taken away after surrendering at St Stephen's Green; perhaps the crowd disliked her for being Anglo-Irish and an aristocrat – or a woman. Perhaps many people, British and Irish, wanted the stories to be true; and perhaps, given that Dublin newspapers like the *Irish Independent* came out strongly against the Rising, people assumed that they were true. Yet the suggestion that the British press, for propaganda purposes, was full of stories about working-class rejection of the rebels is as much of a myth as, it seems, the story itself.

The rejection was however almost universal among middle-class Irish people; and the British response to the Rising squandered that advantage. On Friday 28 April, General Sir John Maxwell, a big-boned, affable, rather lazy man without a great deal of imagination, was sent to take over the administration of martial law in Dublin. For a fortnight he was the sole ruler of Ireland, and many of the decisions he made were disastrous.

Maxwell ordered that those responsible for the Rising should be tried secretly by court martial. It has been argued that the real blame for this lay with the British government, which should never have allowed him such latitude; in particular, he should not have been given charge over the fate of the prisoners. He himself felt it to be a terrible burden, and (according to his daughter) could not sleep when he had to make the final decisions about them. The prime minister, Henry Asquith, might have prevented the executions which followed, but characteristically he decided not to intervene.

Maxwell himself commuted all but fifteen of the death sentences which the court passed. But the execution of James Connolly, in particular, was seen as an act of vindictiveness. Connolly, a brilliant, charismatic labour leader and one of the chief figures in the Rising, had been badly injured in the leg and could not walk to the execution wall. Instead, he was tied to a chair and shot.

The Northcliffe papers by and large welcomed the executions. The *Mail* wrote on Thursday 11 May: 'There is no code of ethics which permits the slaughter of policemen and British soldiers in cold blood and forbids the execution of men caught in arms and in treasonable alliance with the enemy of the nation.'

Yet even the *Mail* felt a certain unease about the secret nature of the courts martial.

Why Hide The Truth?

it asked:

Publish The Dublin Evidence.

The Times said very much the same thing the following morning, in much more stilted language.

> Everybody will learn with relief that the necessity for further executions of a summary kind is now over, but a certain number of these executions were [sic] absolutely necessary to teach the traitors who take German money that they cannot cover Dublin with blood and ashes without forfeiting their lives. We think, however, that the Government have been foolish in not stating plainly why

these men were shot, and we welcome MR. ASQUITH's promise that any further trials for murder shall be held with open doors.

In the same edition *The Times*' special correspondent in Dublin sounds a faintly uneasy note, which he then corrects with a familiar assumption of assurance. This is a very British despatch about an Irish problem:

On the question of the executions public sentiment is more elusive. The consensus of opinion seems to be that the executions, including those announced today, should be sufficient. On all hands it is recognized that the rising was engineered and financed by Germany, but that the rank and file were the dupes of the leaders, who were themselves duped, and now that the leaders have suffered the penalty they deserved there is a widespread disposition to take a more lenient view of the offence of their followers.

But it was not nearly as simple as he supposed. By contrast, on 22 May, under the excitable headline

For God's Sake, An Olive Branch!

the *Manchester Guardian* quoted a letter from an anonymous but apparently well-known Irish writer. He said he was proud that both his sons were serving in the British army, but was appalled by the death sentences against Connolly and the rest: 'Why, in the Fenian rising [of 1867] no one was executed. The leaders got twenty years, of which they served but five . . . We thought we had been advancing since then.'

The contrast between Irish leniency and a British determination to let the law take its course is stark.

The *Guardian* went on to quote a New York paper, the *Nation*, as saying with considerable foresight that, while the British government had ample justification for executing the leaders of the Rising, 'time would show the executions to have been a blunder in public policy'. There could, the *Nation* said, have been 'a more magnanimous, a wider, a less impulsive and more far-sighted method than placing the Irish rebels before a firing-squad'. The *Guardian* clearly agreed.

The situation was made worse by occasional acts of brutality by British soldiers. There was the case of the pacifist Francis Sheehy-Skeffington. On Tuesday 25 April he had called a meeting near his home in the suburb of Rathmines to protest against looting, and was handing out leaflets when a group of British soldiers arrived. They arrested him and two other men, one of whom was a Scotsman, thinking they were Sinn Fein supporters. They took them to Portobello Barracks, where they were handed over to Captain Bowen-Colthurst, an Irishman who was attached to the 3rd Royal Irish Rifles. Bowen-Colthurst had experienced heavy fighting on the Western Front, and was clearly unhinged: he apparently believed that Portobello Barracks was likely to be attacked at any moment. Afterwards it was very much in the interests of the British army to emphasize his insanity; though if this was true, it is unclear why he would have been placed in a position of authority.

Bowen-Colthurst ordered Sheehy-Skeffington to say his prayers, and when he refused Bowen-Colthurst said some for him. Then he ordered his hands to be tied behind his back. At that moment a young man called Coade was brought in, together with another man, after being caught in an alley behind the barracks. Coade called Bowen-Colthurst a fool, and tried to run away; Bowen-Colthurst shot him and fatally injured him, while Sheehy-Skeffington looked on.

Bowen-Colthurst told Sheehy-Skeffington he would be held as a hostage, and that if anything happened to a detachment of soldiers who were being sent out on a raid, he would be shot. Early the following morning Sheehy-Skeffington and the two other innocent men, Dickson and MacIntyre, were taken out and executed.

A Royal Commission was set up to investigate the three deaths. Even today the dry details of the court proceedings have a real power.

You have heard the suggestion about prayers. The night before did they know they were going to their deaths? – Not to my knowledge. They were shot in front, but they did not say anything.

Do you mean to say that when the guns were pointed at them they did not ask for a priest? – Not to my knowledge. They did not utter a cry.

Not when they stood there and the barrels of the guns were pointed at them?

> At this stage Mrs MacIntyre, the mother of one of the [murdered] men, sobbed hysterically, and cried, 'I can't listen to it any longer. Oh, my poor son! Take me out of here.' She was escorted by attendants from the court, crying.

Bowen-Colthurst had been arrested and taken to Broadmoor in England. He escaped execution.

It has often been suggested in Ireland that the British press blackened Sheehy-Skeffington's name. On Monday 8 May the *Daily Express* reported: 'There is no longer any doubt that Mr Sheehy-Skeffington, one of the chief leaders of the rebellion, was shot in St Stephen's Green last week.'

But the passage occurs towards the end of an article mostly concerned with the fate of Countess Markievicz, and has clearly been put together by a subeditor in London. It does not seem to be a deliberate attempt to besmirch Sheehy-Skeffington; if it were, it is unlikely to have been slipped into the latter part of a report. Rather, it looks as though the writer based his accusation on the assumption that Sheehy-Skeffington could not possibly have been shot if he had not been a rebel leader. The article adds that a brother of Sheehy-Skeffington's wife was one of the soldiers who helped to suppress the Rising.

On Friday 12 May the *Daily Mirror* carried a statement by Mrs Sheehy-Skeffington, which put an end to any suggestion that he had been a rebel leader:

> On Monday afternoon outside Dublin Castle an officer was reported bleeding to death in the street, and the crowd being afraid, owing to the firing, to go to his assistance, my husband himself went, at imminent danger to his life, to drag away the wounded man to a place of safety to find, however, that by that time the body had been rescued by some soldiers.

The previous day the *Express* had been obliged to accept that Sheehy-Skeffington was not a violent Nationalist. Instead, though the *Express* did not say so, he had paid a high price for being a good citizen.

Countess Constance Markievicz, by contrast, did not pay a high price at all. She was very much a New Woman, who came from a famous

Anglo-Irish family, the Gore-Booths. In Paris as an art student she met and later married a Polish count, though they soon split up. She rode in horse races, and was an ardent feminist, though she also had a high social life. She went to her first Sinn Fein meeting direct from a grand occasion at Dublin Castle, still wearing a silk gown and elaborate head-dress. She was given a hostile reception at the meeting, which obscurely pleased her.

According to the *Daily Express* a printing press was found at her house in Rathmines, on which pro-German literature had been printed. The police confiscated it, but true to Augustine Birrell's easygoing approach no action was taken.

When the Rising broke out, she was part of the group which took over St Stephen's Green. Journalists from the British yellow press wrote articles about her as she pranced around with a revolver in her hand, dressed like a man, entirely in green: green trousers, green jacket, and green hat with an errant green feather. The countess was an absurd figure in many ways, but no one could doubt her courage. She and her comrades held out for six days, longer than almost anyone else, and gave up only when they were shown Padraig Pearse's order to surrender. She kissed her revolver as she handed it to the officer who arrested her.

At her court martial she was sentenced to death, but General Sir John Maxwell commuted this to penal servitude for life. In an editorial on 8 May 1916 the *Daily Mirror*, like other yellow press newspapers, approved of the application of mercy – but only because the Germans, who executed Edith Cavell, would not be able to claim a propaganda advantage.

> ... [T]he German War Staff knows quite well that where Britain errs is on the side of humanity in warfare. Even the Hun has at last realised how his name stinks in the nostrils of humanity ...
>
> That is why he will be disappointed at the fate of the Countess Markievicz. He would like to wipe out a little of the stain of his brutal murder of that noble woman, Miss Cavell, who gave her life in her labours to save others, by holding us up to execration for carrying out a well-deserved sentence of death upon a rebel and a traitor.

The following year, 1917, all prisoners serving sentences for their part in the Easter Rising, including Constance Markievicz, were released. But by then it was probably already too late; and soon the break between Britain and Ireland would become irreparable.

§

In January 1920 posters began to appear on the walls of several cities in Britain calling for volunteers to help the Royal Irish Constabulary. It would be, the poster said, 'a rough and dangerous task'. Returning to civilian life had not been easy for many of the men demobilized from the army. Jobs were still relatively few, and a civilian existence often seemed boring for men who had grown used to risking their lives constantly.

Altogether, over a period of two years, nearly 10,000 men came forward. In both Britain and Ireland they were familiarly known as the Black and Tans, because initially they often wore mismatched uniforms of dark tunics and khaki-brown army trousers. Even when they received their new uniforms, similar to those of the regular RIC, the nickname continued.

In May, Winston Churchill, Secretary of State for War, proposed that a second group should be formed to help the RIC. They were called Auxiliaries (soon to be known in Ireland as 'Auxies') and commanded by Major General Henry Tudor. Both groups were well paid by the standard of the time, and the Auxiliaries, in particular, attracted some good quality men, including three who had won the VC in the recent war. The situation in Ireland was by now completely out of the British government's control: there were strikes, massive intimidation, the burning of police barracks and constant attacks on the families or girlfriends of policemen. At the same time, Sinn Fein was beginning to establish itself in many parts of Ireland.

While his political colleagues at Dublin Castle were urging for Home Rule, Tudor wanted to use strong measures to restore law and order. Churchill and Lloyd George agreed to let him try. On 9 August 1920, Parliament passed the Restoration of Order in Ireland Act, giving the British authorities in Ireland sweeping powers.

At first, most of the British press went along with this. The *Daily News* and the *Manchester Guardian*, both liberal papers, had serious doubts, but Ireland had become so lawless that opinion in Britain was usually behind any attempt to restore law and order. Yet there had been changes even in those newspapers which might have been expected to support the new, tough policy wholeheartedly. The *Daily Mail*, though it unsurprisingly backed the government line, had appointed a socialist sympathizer, Alexander M. Thompson, as its correspondent in Ireland as early as 1917.

The *Mail* even published, on 30 September 1920, a long list of places where reprisals had been carried out by the Black and Tans in the previous nine days, recording precisely why the attack had been made: for instance, 'reprisal for the shooting of Inspector Burke, RIC; reprisal for the murder of five policemen in an ambush on September 22; reprisal for Sinn Fein attack on Trim barracks'. The *Mail* did not particularly condemn these attacks, but the fact that they listed them at all meant that there was no serious doubt that a policy of reprisals was in operation.

The most outspoken British correspondent was Hugh Martin of the *Daily News*. He was remarkably even-handed: he was honest about Republican atrocities, but equally frank about the murders and revenge attacks carried out by the Crown forces. According to Martin, the Black and Tans and Auxies were among the best soldiers who had fought in the Great War, but they were completely out of their element in Ireland. He wrote: 'They believe that the Irish "let the British down", and they are not averse from getting their own back in their own way.'

He traced a series of revenge attacks in Limerick in 1920 to the murder of a Black and Tan in July. If anything of the sort happened again, the dead man's comrades swore, they would give the town 'gip'.

Next, two Black and Tans were attacked in a park in Limerick, robbed, and tied to a tree. Their comrades decided to sack the city centre in revenge, doing £30,000-worth of damage in 1920 values. Hugh Martin went around the city examining the damage and describing it for his paper. He was regarded as an enemy by the RIC and the Black and Tans, who threatened to kill him several times. He carried on reporting, but slept in a different place every night.

Thirty or forty Black and Tans set fire to houses in the city centre, clapping and cheering and firing their guns. They killed one of their own comrades by mistake, and murdered others, including a veteran of the Boer War and the Great War. Martin wrote: 'There are men in authority in Dublin who, knowing that they themselves can do nothing, are glad that the Black and Tans could so easily be made to see red.'

In a memorandum of 12 November 1920, General Tudor ordered his men to show the highest discipline, but said they would have the fullest support even if they took 'the most drastic action against that band of assassins, the so-called IRA'. The men under him drew the obvious conclusion: their commander would back them up, no matter what they did.

At nine o'clock on the morning of Sunday 21 November, an IRA death squad staged a series of well-planned murders of British intelligence officers in various parts of Dublin. That afternoon, as a crowd assembled at Croke Park a group of Auxiliaries opened fire on the crowd, killing ten people outright. Four others died later, creating by chance the same number of murders as that of the intelligence officers: fourteen.

The *Daily Mirror*'s report the next morning was typical of the way the London papers handled the story. It clearly suspected that there was some connection between the events, but was not prepared to say so. Nor did its correspondents try to investigate further; instead, they relied on official statements.

12 BRITISH OFFICERS KILLED IN DUBLIN MURDER RAID

Trapped in Their Rooms by Gun-men Gang and Shot at Sight – Four Arrests

10 KILLED AND 70 WOUNDED AT MATCH

Twelve British officers and ex-officers and two 'Black and Tans' were the victims yesterday of a deliberately planned campaign of assassination in Dublin.

The officers were trapped in their private quarters outside barracks, and some of them shot dead in their beds. The two R.I.C. Auxiliary Force victims were killed while on their way for reinforcements. Four men were arrested.

Ten persons were killed and seventy injured at a match in Dublin yesterday after-noon attended by 15,000 people. Troops arrived and shots were fired by them and Sinn Fein sentries.

No trains were allowed to leave after one o'clock.

CAPTAIN'S WIFE SEES HUSBAND SHOT DEAD
Fate of Two 'Black and Tans' Who Went For Help.
BLOW AT SECRET SERVICE

It is perhaps inevitable that a British newspaper would put the murder of fourteen British soldiers first, and the killings at the sports ground second, especially if the circumstances of the second incident were less certain.

Yet if any basic groundwork had been done by the *Mirror* people in Dublin, it would have revealed that the second round of killings was the result of the first. Indeed, it was clear that the *Mirror* suspected that the official version of the Croke Park murders was highly questionable; yet the *Mirror* had been content to rely on a not very accurate news agency report for the Croke Park massacre, and on official army statements for the intelligence murders.

Captain Maclean, Mr Smith (civilian) and Mr Caldown (civilian) were attacked by a band of twelve men at 117, Morehampton-road, and taken from their bedrooms to the top storey of the house, where they were shot.

Lieutenant Bennett and Lieutenant Aimes were at 38, Upper Mount-street, when they were suddenly attacked by twenty men. The same gang proceeded to 22, Lower Mount-street, and seized Lieutenant Mahon.

All three were then taken to a room at the back of the house and killed.

When the party knocked at the door of Captain Newbury's sitting-room Mrs Newbury opened it, but seeing several men, at once slammed and locked it.

The raiders burst in the door and started to beat in the door of the bedroom adjoining. Captain Newbury, on the other side, struggled to keep it shut. Mrs Newbury was standing by.

When the door gave way the captain, already wounded and bleeding, tried to escape through a window, but as he was halfway through, several men fired. He was hit by seven shots and killed.

In some cases the death squads panicked, or had wrong information. One group went round to murder a Captain Crawford, who, instead of being a spy, had the unromantic but necessary job of commanding a motor-repair depot of the Army Service Corps. When a gang of armed men went round to his house in Fitzwilliam Square he remained remarkably calm.

> Mrs Crawford was in bed at the time, and Captain Crawford was in his dressing-room, when a knock came at the door.
>
> Opening the door, he found three Webley revolvers thrust in his face and was told to put up his hands.
>
> He refused to do so and asked, 'Is this a joke?' The armed men replied, 'It is no joke,' and a fourth man poked a gun into his stomach.
>
> With two men standing over him, Captain Crawford was questioned. On his telling them that he was in charge of the motor repair department they asked him: 'Why did you come here? Why don't you stay and mind your own business in England?' ...
>
> Captain Crawford said, 'My wife is not very well, and if you are going to shoot me please take me downstairs.'
>
> Signs of haste became apparent, and the party left, the leader calling out, 'You clear out of the country in twenty hours.'

The stoical Captain Crawford and his wife decided to stay on in Dublin.

The *Mirror*'s report on the murders at Croke Park is much briefer, and appears alongside this. The account is confused, and because it follows the text of a Press Association story closely it repeats a foolish spelling mistake in the PA original. Altogether, it is a sloppy piece of work. Yet the use of the word 'Tale' in the second headline seems like a hint that there is something more to the story than appears on the surface.

SCENES OF BLOODSHED AT BIG DUBLIN MATCH.

Shots Fired Among Crowd of 15,000 – Armoured Car Tale.

10 KILLED, 70 WOUNDED

When upwards of 15,000 people had been watching a challenge match between Dublin and Tipperary at Croke Park, Dublin, yesterday, for a quarter of an hour, armed forces entered the ground.

Wild confusion ensued, shots flying in all directions. Ten persons were killed and between sixty and seventy wounded.

According to the Central News, the firing took place at a Gaelic football match at Croke Park, after armoured cars mounted with machine guns had entered the field.

The crowd tried to get away and were seized with panic.

The name of the park is given as Crow Park in a Press Association message, which says that a hurling match was in progress.

The authorities, it is stated, had reason to believe that Sinn Fein 'gunmen' went to Dublin under the pretence of attending a hurling match, but really to carry out the murders . . .

A mixed force of troops and police surrounded the ground at Crow Park.

They were fired on by Sinn Fein pickets when they were seen approaching and returned the fire, killing and wounding a number.

The *Mirror* has, perhaps deliberately, taken shelter behind a sloppily written account written by a Press Association reporter who is perhaps new to Ireland; no one who had lived there long would surely write about 'Crow Park'. The official statements the article is based on are clearly flimsy. The murder squads may well have travelled to Dublin under the pretext of going to the match, which was either Gaelic football or hurling, but hardly both. (It was in fact a Gaelic football match.) But they are hardly likely to have gone to the match after carrying out their killings. Nor is it plausible that armed Sinn Fein pickets were there, willing to fire from the cover of a large crowd onto soldiers arriving in armoured cars. The story is precisely the kind that soldiers the world over tend to invent when they have committed some act of revenge against the local population.

In the House of Commons that Monday a fight broke out when an

Irish Nationalist MP tried to ask the Chief Secretary for Ireland, Sir Hamar Greenwood, why he had recited the horrors of the deaths of the British soldiers and said nothing about the deaths at Croke Park. A Conservative MP punched him, the Nationalist hit back, and the Speaker suspended the sitting. Winston Churchill went over with a colleague to calm the Irish MP down. A few minutes later the Conservative apologized, and the Irishman repeated his question at greater length, making the precise link between the two sets of killings. 'You're a liar,' someone else shouted.

On 23 November 1920, two days after the murder of the intelligence officers and the massacre at Croke Park, the *Times* correspondent in Dublin, Philip Graves, an Anglo-Irishman and wartime army officer, wrote a despatch linking the murders of the British officers and the massacre at Croke Park, without quite saying that the one happened because of the other. It was a skilful and determined piece of writing, which not even the fiercest patriot at *The Times* would have been justified in cutting. The reader is left in no doubt that the Croke Park incident was a direct revenge for the earlier murders.

> No section of the Irish Press conceals its horror at the murders [of the British officers], or its despair at the social and political outlook; but the Nationalist newspapers hold strongly that reprisals are largely responsible for the state of complete chaos into which the country is drifting. They denounce the shootings at Croke Park yesterday, in which 10 or 12 spectators of a football match lost their lives.

Alongside is an article giving the official explanation from Dublin Castle for the Croke Park shooting. According to this, an officer with a megaphone was sent with the Auxiliaries to Croke Park. His task was to tell the crowd that several men with guns were thought to be among them, and that there would be a search. If everyone stood still, he was supposed to tell them, no one would be hurt. But (according to the statement) before the Auxiliaries even arrived at the ground they were fired at by pickets. There was also firing within the ground, with the intention of creating a stampede so the suspects could escape.

This is the kind of accusation that officialdom often makes, to put its own people in the right. Sometimes, no doubt, it is correct. In this case,

Philip Graves does not seem to think so. He quotes various eyewitnesses who spoke of the horror of screaming women and children who were crushed in the stampede, and says that the Crown forces searched thousands of people in the crowd; presumably without finding anything, since the official statement makes no mention of any weapons being discovered. Finally, Graves reports at the very end of the article comments which wholly contradict the official version:

> The Gaelic Athletic Association describes as being 'too ridiculous' the official statements that there were pickets posted at the approaches to the field and that they fired on the troops, and eye-witnesses declare that they heard no firing until the Crown forces were inside the ground.

The Gaelic Athletic Association was strongly nationalistic, and might be expected to say something of the sort; but Graves has given it virtually the last word: a strong indication that he thought the GAA and the eye-witnesses were right.

Even the *Daily Express*, usually far more likely to defend the British forces belligerently, made it clear it on Monday 22 November that it was disturbed. It spoke of

> a wholesale slaughter of servants of the Crown, followed inevitably by confused shootings by troops. This way lie anarchy and ruin, not only for Ireland, but, by repercussion, for a civilisation shaken profoundly by war and the aftermath of war.

A week later, on Tuesday 30 November, *The Times* published an article by Philip Graves, under the bold headline

Two Terrors In Ireland

> If only the people in England knew ... Everywhere in Ireland today you hear this cry. Men and women of every shade of political opinion and religious faith – Catholics, Protestants, Unionists, Nationalists, even large numbers of Sinn Feiners – are united in that inarticulate appeal. They

are not in the mood to put any trust in Governments and statesmen. But they feel that if the people in the sister isle knew what is happening in the country they would inevitably take steps to put an end to the intolerable suffering, the nightmare of terror, by which they are now cowed and tortured.

Thousands of people, Graves writes, are sleeping out in the open because they are too afraid to sleep at home. There is no doubt whatever about the terror he is referring to. It cannot be the terrorism of Sinn Fein, since the British have shown they cannot end that. There are now, he emphasizes, two terrors in Ireland. He speaks of the dangers to the forces of the Crown, but continues: '[B]ecause of the cruelty and brutality and treachery of their assailants, some of them have themselves committed acts of terrorism and violence of which no disciplined force should be guilty . . .'

Now other newspapers found the courage to write about it. A wide range of people in Britain were appalled by the accounts. King George V, Church of England bishops, Conservatives, Liberals, Labour Party politicians, General Jan Smuts, and many others made their views felt, privately or publicly. Greater control began to be exercised over the Auxiliaries and the Black and Tans. Soon, negotiations began for the Treaty of 7 January 1922, which gave Ireland the status of a Dominion Free State.

It had been a disturbing display of weak and culpable government by Britain, but it had helped the British press to see itself in a different light. From now on newspapers would be a little less inclined to feel it was their duty to act as the voice of the established order. As for individual journalists, they had had a clear lesson in thinking for themselves. It was part of a slow process of change which was starting to manifest itself in the British press.

9

THE COMING MAN

The first time any sizeable number of people in Britain came across the name 'Hitler' was on the morning of Monday 18 October 1920, when *The Times* ran a brief paragraph on its second international news page.

This story came well down the page, in between other brief items: a telegram to George V from King Faisal of Iraq congratulating him on the conclusion of the Iraq Treaty; delays in the reparation plan which Germany was expected to pay; a new air speed record (232 miles per hour); a fatal accident to a well-dressed British woman called Mrs Bowen who fell from a train in France; a new egg-laying record in the United States; and, completely divorced from the rest of the German news, more riots in Berlin. Then comes this easily overlooked report:

GERMAN FASCISTI
(FROM OUR CORRESPONDENT.)
COLOGNE, OCT. 17.

According to an Augsburg message, the National-Socialists of Bavaria are emulating the Italian Fascisti.

Under the command of a Herr Hitler, an armed body of some 180 men recently bivouacked in Rosenheim and travelled in lorries to Allach, where there was trouble between them and some workmen. Herr Hitler's agents are stated to be purchasing quantities of arms throughout the Bavarian Oberland.

It seems a strange, random set of sentences. Why would the readers of *The Times* be interested in knowing that an obscure political extremist had camped out in one little-known German town and gone to another, where he and his followers had had a fight with some presumably left-wing workmen? Or that he was laying in a stock of weapons?

The typical foreign correspondent, then as now, is a jackdaw. He or she (though at this time it was almost invariably 'he') will make a note of all sorts of potentially significant people and events, with the intention of writing about them at some more relevant moment. It looks as though this rather perceptive correspondent guessed at Hitler's possible future importance, but could not find a way of getting something about him into the paper until now.

There was plainly a shortage of more important news that Monday; *The Times* of 1920 would not usually have given space to stories about egg-laying records in America. If news was indeed in short supply, that would have meant that the Cologne correspondent could slip in a column inch or two about Hitler and know that he had, at last, got the name of someone who might well come to matter soon onto the pages of his newspaper – the British paper of record. In that case, the correspondent was abundantly right. Other serious British newspapers, for instance the *Manchester Guardian*, would not mention Hitler for more than a year to come.

Perhaps it was the mention of Rosenheim that caught the *Times* man's eye. Three months earlier, on 21 July 1920, Hitler had made an important speech there. Up to that time he had tended to restrict his political agitation and his speech-making to Munich, where his support was growing; according to Ian Kershaw's biography *Hitler* the NSDAP, the National Socialist German Workers' Party, had begun 1920 with a membership of 190 and ended it with 2,000. *The Times* had a correspondent in Munich, but he was not particularly active and showed little interest in the activities of the far right. As his support increased in the second half of 1920, Hitler started to speak to meetings outside the city. Now, in October, he was back in Rosenheim.

His speech there was significant in his development as a politician of the far right. He had spoken in the past about the disastrous state of Russia under Bolshevik rule, and had pointed out that many of the Bolshevik leaders were Jewish; but this was the first time he had made the theory of Marxism itself his target. And at Rosenheim, as at virtually every speech he had made so far that year, he attacked the Jews with savage obsession. This was something relatively new for him; before 1919 he seems never to have mentioned the Jews in any serious way in his speeches. So, whether by chance or good judgement, *The Times* had drawn its readers' attention to Adolf Hitler at precisely the time his political views were hardening into a clear doctrine.

For the British newspapers over the next few years, Hitler, if they noticed him at all, was just a small-time rabble-rouser. At first, small paragraphs noted his progress from one street-battle to another; there was no serious account of what he believed, and no one quoted his speeches. Gradually, though, he attracted more attention; and the *Times* correspondent, H.G. Daniels, made the journey to Munich and described for *The Times* of 22 May 1923 what was happening there.

> A stranger arriving in the city on a Hitler field-day might well imagine that the town was occupied by a foreign Power. On these occasions bands of storm-troops march about in strictly military formation ... Many of these 'storm-troops' are lads of from 17 to 20, but professional and business men, ex-officers, students, and farmers can be seen in the ranks. Recently Hitler's men have been equipped with steel helmets of the regulation Government pattern – presumably surplus war material ...

Daniels was the main *Times* correspondent in Berlin until 1927. Educated at Cambridge, he had previously reported for the *Express* and the *Guardian*, and had worked in the censors' office during the First World War. He had a lively time in Germany. During the Kapp Putsch he had to dodge the bullets of both sides, and at various stages during his years there he was apparently threatened with assassination several times. His editor had to send him a letter of support which gave him a certain confidence in resisting intimidation. He was the author of several books about Germany between the wars; they show a balance between left and right which is unusual for the time

Daniels was inclined at first to be mildly patronizing about Hitler: the 'silly little man' approach which was adopted by many of Hitler's instinctive enemies until it was too late.

> Adolf Hitler has been described as one of the three most dangerous men in Germany. This is probably a rather flattering estimate of the little Austrian sign-painter, who

less than three years ago was earning a precarious living
by charging a small admission fee for the meetings he
addressed in obscure beer-halls.

But Daniels was correct in his analysis of Hitler's attraction. He was
starting to draw plenty of middle-class people, many of whom had
fought in the war, as well as unemployed, angry, purposeless youths. He
presented himself as the one man who could save a nation which was
frightened of abject poverty and sick of the unfulfilled promises of
politicians.

Morgan Philips Price, who had been the *Manchester Guardian*'s man
in Russia throughout the Bolshevik revolution and beyond, had now
based himself in Germany and was working for the Labour Party
newspaper, the *Daily Herald*. He was a thoughtful, sympathetic, slightly
humourless man, who spoke fluent Russian and had made excellent
contacts with the Soviet leadership. But the editor of the *Guardian*, C.P.
Scott, felt he had become too close to the Bolsheviks. Scott believed it 'did
not do' for a correspondent to identify quite so completely with the
government on which he was reporting. Philips Price left Russia and
based himself in Germany towards the end of 1918.

At first he carried on working for the *Guardian* as a freelance, but
soon he was approached by George Lansbury, the editor of the *Daily
Herald*. Because the *Herald* had a great deal less money than the
Guardian, his articles had to be shorter; telegraphic costs were high. And
since he was writing for a different readership he had to adopt a much
punchier, more effective style than he had used for the *Guardian*. He had
been slower than others – and certainly than *The Times* – in identifying
Adolf Hitler as a key figure, but his despatches have real force; this was
his account of Hitler's Munich in the *Herald* of 5 April 1923:

> Iron crosses. Armed Reichswehr troops wearing steel
> helmets and with a hint of the goose-step in their marching
> gait. A cluster of young Hakenkreuzler [Swastika-wearers]
> roaring 'To Hell with the French beasts!' 'Down with the
> Jews!', 'Deutschland über Alles!' Flaming placards on every
> street corner announcing another Fascist meeting at which
> Hitler, Mussolini's mimic, will speak on Germany's Hour of
> Revenge . . .

> Bavaria is seething with hatred – hatred of Protestant
> North Germany, of the French, Jews, Republicans, Liberals
> and, above all, Socialists. All are anathema. All will get
> short shrift when the hour of reckoning strikes.

Philips Price was a first-rate correspondent, but sometimes his political views got in the way of his reporting. As a convinced Marxist, he had had no problems whatever in getting close to the Bolsheviks in Petrograd in 1917. His instinct was right in heading for Munich in 1918, because it was one of the most interesting places in the world at that moment, and his experience in Russia had shown him how societies in turmoil behave. But he had no sympathy whatever for the doctrine of National Socialism, and this prevented him from getting under the surface of the NSDAP and understanding how they thought.

Perhaps it was Philips Price's Marxism, too, which prevented him from understanding the significance of Hitler as a man. Philips Price believed passionately that history and politics were shaped by economic forces, not by personalities. As a result his reports are far more concerned with the effects of unemployment and poverty on people in Bavaria than on the rise of Hitler. His work is full of sharp insights. In the *Daily Herald* of 22 January 1923 he writes: 'Fascism here is of a peculiar northern, Teutonic kind, not flashy and dramatic, as in Italy, but thorough, quiet and efficient.'

Philips Price describes in the same despatch how, after the first big inflation had ebbed, the foreign speculators were no longer spending time in Munich, taking advantage of Germany's financial collapse, and as a result the banks were empty. He writes how he went to cash a cheque, the first time he had been in a bank for three months. 'The bank clerks were standing idly behind the counter and looked very pleased to see someone come in . . .'

Again and again, as you read his articles, you hope to find the same clear observation directed at Hitler and the strange collection of thugs and misfits around him; only to be disappointed. They would have been deeply hostile to him, as a Briton and a Communist; and he would have hated them. He mostly watched them from a distance, and never seems to have tried to meet Hitler.

Philips Price was not deceived by the anti-capitalist rhetoric Hitler often used at this stage, to draw in left-wing and working-class supporters. He understood that it was not the real thing. But when he came to describe the man himself, he even managed to get his facts wrong – a rarity for him. Adolf Hitler, he wrote in the *Herald* of Thursday 5 April,

> a native Austrian and a locksmith by trade, has pushed his way to the leadership of the Bavarian counter-revolutionary movement. A skilful demagogue, who wins converts to Fascism by drinking beer with the common people, he has mastered the routine of whipping up popular passions.

He attended one of Hitler's meetings, and quotes some of the things he said.

> How can we help the Fatherland? I'll tell you how. By hanging the criminals of 1918 [he means the Socialists who took over power in Berlin and surrendered to the Allies]. By punishing the worthies of the [German Socialist] Republic we shall gain the respect of foreign nations.

Yet he gives us no word-picture of Hitler, no description of the crowd, nothing about the place where the meeting was held or the atmosphere. Coming from such a sharp, lively writer, it seems remarkably inadequate. The fact is, he isn't really interested. He had succeeded in Russia because his emotions had been heavily engaged. In Munich his hostility to National Socialism, however much we as his readers agree with it, prevents him from giving us a proper account of what was going on there. Germany left him cold. For us, his readers, that is a real loss.

§

During 1922 and the start of 1923, opinion in Munich had changed noticeably towards Hitler. There was much about him that was ludicrous. Good news would make him shout and jump up and down, grimacing with joy: it was a habit he could never quite stifle, right up to the fall of France in 1940. These unguarded extremes of behaviour, and his Charlie

Chaplin appearance (often commented on by his enemies) encouraged many people to regard him as a joke; yet, as 1923 wore on, Hitler began to be thought of much more seriously. He was increasingly taken at his own assessment of himself: as a man of destiny. The *Daily Mail*, whose new proprietor Lord Rothermere would become one of his fervent admirers, sent a correspondent to interview him for the edition of 2 October 1923. The interview is brief, but contained the following prophetic thought from Hitler: 'If a German Mussolini is given to Germany . . . people would fall down on their knees and worship him more than Mussolini has ever been worshipped.'

A month later, on the evening of Thursday 8 November, Hitler decided to forestall the plans of his political rivals and stage a coup. All the top leaders in Munich were gathered at the Bürgerbräukeller to celebrate the fifth anniversary of the revolution which had overthrown the Kaiser. Half an hour into an interminable speech by Gustav Ritter von Kahr, the general state commissar, a group of Hitler's storm troopers arrived, bringing a heavy machine gun with them. No one had any doubt what was happening, and most of them thought they were going to be murdered. To make himself heard, Hitler jumped on a chair and fired his revolver into the ceiling.

He made a clever, short speech that brought everyone in the hall round to his side – though no doubt the machine gun helped – and for a moment things seemed to be going his way. He announced, with his usual melodramatics, 'Either the German revolution begins tonight or we will all be dead by dawn!' As it turned out, neither eventuality happened. Hitler's ally Ernst Röhm, who had been sent to take over the local army base, forgot to cut the telephone lines. Army reinforcements swept into Munich. After a march through the city the next day in which a man who had linked arms with Hitler was shot dead beside him, Hitler and the ancient General Erich Ludendorff, Germany's First World War hero, were arrested.

In his report for *The Times* on 10 November 1923 Daniels was scathing.

> As usual the Putsch seems to have been extraordinarily ill-prepared. Neither General Ludendorff nor Herr Hitler seems to have taken the trouble to find out what would be the attitude of the Reichswehr [national army] under General

von Lossow, or of the Bavarian National police. As might
have been expected, these followed their officers, who
followed their chief.

Daniels clearly believed that Hitler would now be consigned to the
dustbin of history. Hitler himself seems to have thought the same thing.
The psychologist in the prison at Landsberg am Lech, forty miles west of
Munich, claimed many years later that he had to dissuade Hitler from
committing suicide. All the same, as the *Mail*'s correspondent noticed, a
groundswell of support for Hitler remained in Munich. '[T]he people still
seem to be under the spell of this patriotic orator. Picture postcards of
him and his "general staff" are prominently displayed in the shop windows.'

When Hitler appeared in court with Ludendorff and their eight co-
defendants, he suddenly found an audience again. The *Times* correspondent, who had gone to Munich for the trial, reported that a small
number of onlookers had gathered around the barbed-wire barricades
outside the Army School, which Hitler had previously designated as his
headquarters. Now it was where his trial would take place. The spectators
ventured only a subdued cheer as General Ludendorff, in a closed car,
drove up to the entrance. But Hitler realized two things: firstly, that
Ludendorff, no orator and perhaps a little bemused at finding himself in
court, would be taking a back seat at this trial, while Hitler could have
the limelight he throve on; secondly, that no one was going to stop him
speaking for as long as he wanted. Daniels described what happened in
his report for *The Times* on 27 February 1924:

> Beginning almost nervously, the little Austrian sign painter
> soon recovered himself, and his speech was reminiscent of
> many that he had made in the beer-halls of Munich. There
> was no applause, but it was evident that the sympathies of
> a very large proportion of those who were in the Court were
> with the speaker.

Hitler was allowed to speak for four hours. It was unwise of his judges
not to cut him short. By the end of that first day, Hitler could see that he
was back in business.

The trial dragged on for a month, becoming more and more of a platform from which Hitler could denounce the Socialist government in Berlin with complete impunity. At the end of the defence case a month later, on Thursday 27 March, the correspondent of the *Daily Express* wrote, 'Ludendorff and Hitler were surrounded by excited men and women, who sobbed and laughed hysterically, and showered both flowers and good wishes upon them.'

While the British correspondents reporting from Munich had started to realize Hitler's growing importance, their editors back in London had not. The report in the *Daily Express* from which this quotation comes was headlined 'Flowers For "Hero Ludendorff"'. The editors at the *Express* still saw Germany in terms of the recent war, in which Ludendorff had been a major figure. Now he was little more than a useful front-man for Hitler. At least one of the British correspondents in the courtroom admitted to feeling sorry for him. 'In my journalistic life,' wrote H.J. Greenwall of the *Express*, 'I have heard nothing more pathetic than the speech the ex-general made . . .'

The *Mail*'s correspondent agreed.

> It is for them [i.e. 'the great majority of Germans'] un-
> utterably painful to see the once idolised general arraigned
> on the terrible charge of high treason, along with Adolf
> Hitler, a political adventurer and demagogue of the worst
> sort.

Hitler was found guilty and sentenced to five years in prison, of which he served eight months. Ludendorff was acquitted.

One evening while the trial was on, H.J. Greenwall went to a Weinstube, 'Die Fledermaus', near the central railway station in Munich, to pick up a little local colour. It was there, he said, that the leaders of the small far right-wing secret and semi-secret associations of former students and soldiers gather, to plot their 'abortive revolutions'. Greenwall, after talking to them, comes up with some fairly unlikely prophecies: for instance that Prince Rupprecht, who had been a leading general in the First World War, would become President of Bavaria, and perhaps the leader of Germany.

As for Hitler, Greenwall reveals that he was gassed by the British during the war. The readers of the *Express* were starting to learn things that had not been reported in Britain before. 'Previously he had been badly wounded, but after he recovered from the gas attack he stated that he had seen a vision and received a message. He had been summoned as the saviour of Germany.'

You can sense Greenwall's amusement at this. Yet he is beginning to understand a little of Hitler's significance. 'Hitler, the tub-thumping patriot, may be heard from again some day.'

Perhaps Greenwall felt he should keep his forecast muted, for fear of being criticized by his colleagues back in London. Then, as now, the criticism that was often made of foreign correspondents was that they had 'gone native' – that is, that they saw things more from the perspective of the country where they were based, than from that of their readers at home. Being too impressed by the future chances of the little Austrian tub-thumper with his patriotic visions might well have been regarded in London as evidence that Greenwall was 'going native'.

§

Six years later, in 1930, no one had any doubt that Hitler was the coming man. His time in Landsberg am Lech prison, where he wrote *Mein Kampf*, had been put to good use. The book was not at first the best-seller he had hoped, partly because of its turgid contents and high price of twelve Reichsmarks. Volume One sold 23,000 copies, and Volume Two only 13,000. But as his political fortunes picked up, so did his sales. By 1933 his royalties had made him a rich man.

Yet despite his inadequacies as an author, people throughout Germany and Austria, and not just Bavaria, were beginning to see him as a saviour. In Britain there was a touch of real nervousness. For the first time it became possible to envisage the kind of country Germany might become if Hitler were in power. Although the British press had scarcely mentioned it, Hitler's attitude to the Jews was becoming known to increasing numbers of people. So was the treatment he advocated for political prisoners. When, therefore, on 14 September, Hitler's Nazi Party suddenly became the second largest party in the Reichstag, there was distinct anxiety. Hitler was no longer just another slightly ludicrous nationalist; he was beginning to look like a threat.

During the previous decade, the face of the British press had changed completely. Lord Northcliffe had died in 1922, and his brother Harold Harmsworth, now Lord Rothermere, had taken over the newspaper empire. One of his earliest decisions was to sell off *The Times* to John Jacob Astor. At a stroke this made the empire more prosperous, since it no longer had to bear *The Times*' habitual losses, and less of an incipient monopoly, which had disturbed governments and public opinion alike. By 1931 he also sold off the *Daily Mirror*, which meant that the *Mail* and the immensely profitable *Evening News* alone formed the central core of his empire. By 1926 the *Mail* was achieving sales of 2 million a day. As a result, Rothermere's personal wealth had reached £25 million, which made him the third richest man in Britain.

By now, though, he had a rival. Max Aitken was born in Canada in 1879, and came to Britain in 1910 – possibly to escape the consequences of a business scandal. He bought the *Evening Standard*, and in 1916 he went on to buy a controlling interest in the *Daily Express*, which he had been helping to bail out for the previous five years. In 1917, he was created Lord Beaverbrook, a name which hinted at his Canadian background, and soon afterwards became minister of information, though his time in office was not happy and his officials resigned in large numbers. Beaverbrook turned the *Express* into a clever and imaginative newspaper, which people felt they had to read if they wanted to be properly informed and entertained. Whereas the *Mail* was usually bought by the women in middle- and upper-middle-class homes, the *Express* appealed strongly to men. Beaverbrook's swashbuckling character ensured that it developed a distinctive voice of its own: bold, with a wide reach and an appeal to a younger readership. By 1934 it had a circulation of 1.75 million, and after the Second World War it became the highest-selling newspaper in the world.

Beaverbrook's foreign correspondents were the best in Fleet Street; they were also among the best paid. And although the paper was instinctively Conservative, it was only moderately so. Beaverbrook enjoyed hiring people for their quality, rather than their political views. His staff included several journalists who described themselves as Communists. He was a personal friend of the Prince of Wales, later the Duke of Windsor, but this did not stop the *Express* from leading the way in publishing the full details of the interest the Duke and Duchess showed in Nazism. Beaverbrook liked his journalists to be fearless, and he always insisted he could never interfere with their reporting. It wasn't true, but it helped to make the *Express* the most interesting newspaper in Fleet Street.

All this helped to distinguish the *Express* from the *Mail* at the start of the 1930s. Lord Northcliffe had worked as a journalist at the start of his career, and had the journalist's interest in facts as facts, even if he often wanted his newspapers to twist them. Lord Rothermere was different. He used his newspapers to promote his more grandiose political ideas, much as William Randolph Hearst did in the United States. By 1929 Rothermere's power and political influence were as great as his brother's had once been, and he joined with Lord Beaverbrook, with whom he had moderately friendly relations, in order to create a new right-of-centre political grouping, the United Empire Party, which concentrated on free trade. Yet in spite of having the two liveliest and best-selling newspapers in the country behind it, the party soon faded: clear evidence that newspaper propaganda was not enough on its own to mould people's political opinions. After ten years the party faded away.

Within a year, Rothermere had shifted much farther to the right. He had always liked Mussolini, and had used the *Daily Mail* to support him. Now he began to back Hitler, and in Britain Sir Oswald Mosley's British Union of Fascists. Fascism, Rothermere believed, was essential to pump new life and discipline into the soft, effeminate youth of Europe. He went to Munich in September 1930 to watch the Nazis win more than a hundred seats in the parliamentary elections, and for five years after 1933 (when Hitler became Chancellor of Germany) he kept up a warm and admiring correspondence with him. Hitler thanked him more than once for the backing which the *Daily Mail* gave him.

If Rothermere was an archetype of the domineering press baron, instructing his editors and correspondents precisely what line to take on events and not permitting them to publish anything which clashed with his own views, Beaverbrook was the archetype of the enabler, no less domineering and intrusive but willing to allow the writers and editors he appointed to put forward their own views. He had a strong sense of mischief, and got considerable pleasure from watching his correspondents' despatches irritate the establishment. Unlike Rothermere, he had no overriding political principles which he wanted to force onto the British public, beyond a general conservatism.

And so the *Express* correspondent in Berlin was allowed to have his head, neither under orders to write positively about Hitler nor to attack him. After the Nazis' shocking success in the elections of 1930, the *Express* of Friday 16 September chose to point out the dangers of Hitler's character and attitudes. But most of all it emphasized the ironies of the situation:

> A paradox of the German elections is that Herr Hitler, the despotic leader of the Fascist Party, whose unprecedented 800 per cent increase has caused a sensation throughout the world, will himself be unable to enter the Reichstag, for this super-Nationalist is himself a man without a nation.

Some of the *Express* correspondent's judgements read so oddly that you wonder if he can have seen Hitler, who in the flesh was 5 feet 8 inches in height and had strangely pale greenish eyes:

> This tall, English-looking man with fanatical blue eyes and clipped English moustache under an energetic nose, has, ever since he lost his Austrian nationality by volunteering for the German army in 1914, been a man without a country of his own . . .

Beaverbrook liked to see challenging, lively articles in his newspapers; he had no interest in plodding accuracy. Reading carefully through the paper, as he did every morning, he probably enjoyed this slightly wild report – even if he knew how tall Hitler really was, and the true colour of his eyes.

Ten days later, the correspondent was in court in Leipzig to hear Hitler defending three army officers who were supporters of his, and were on trial for treason as a result of their opposition to the coalition government. He gave, the *Express* said, an astounding speech to the court. Beaverbrook liked words like 'astounding' and 'dramatic', and encouraged his correspondents to use them; with the result that, eighty years later, journalists still use them to describe quite ordinary, mundane occurrences. He liked to read colourful, aggressive phrases too, as his editors and correspondents knew.

The key phrase in Hitler's speech, 'Heads will roll in the sand', was used three times on the front page of the *Express* of Friday 26 September: once in the headline, once as text over a rather dull picture of Hitler standing in court, and once in the body of the despatch itself:

'After two or three more elections,' [Hitler] declared, 'our party will be in a majority. If we are victorious then we certainly shall establish a new State tribunal whose duty it will be to deal with the criminals of November 1918. Then heads will certainly roll in the sand.'

The fact that Hitler was dangerous and potentially violent was no reason for Lord Beaverbrook to shun him; and, in the self-advertising fashion pioneered thirty years early in the *Daily Mail*, the report ends with a paragraph in heavy type: 'How Hitler proposes "to free Germany from enslavement" will be revealed in an article which he has written exclusively for the next issue of the "Sunday Express".'

Beaverbrook loved nothing more than a good scoop; and he must have enjoyed beating Lord Rothermere thoroughly by getting Rothermere's hero to write a personal article for the Beaverbrook press.

Nevertheless, when it was published in the *Sunday Express* on 28 September 1930, it turned out to be rather bland. For Hitler to write a 1,500-word article without mentioning the Jews or talking about his social policies ensured that it would be little more than a rant about Germany's wrongs and the need to stop Bolshevism. A face-to-face interview would probably have gleaned a good deal more. The most important news point in it was that, following the Nazis' remarkable success in the elections a fortnight before, he had no intention of carrying out a coup d'état; he realized now that he could come to power by means of the ballot-box.

Yet there were some interesting and characteristic passages, even if the real fire was almost entirely absent. Entitled

MY TERMS TO THE WORLD
By
ADOLF HITLER
Germany's New 'Iron Man'

it has the authentic tone of the man himself.

The election was a signal of the approaching revolt of the German soul. The shock and surprise felt abroad, and also in those political and Press circles here in Germany which

have little contact with the working people, were great . . .
Our aim, our purpose, is to free Germany from political and
economic conditions that mean slavery.

Gradually, as he would work himself up in his speeches, he works himself
up in this article, culminating in an immense, oratorical passage; it sounds
as though it could have been dictated by him, rather than written down.

France says I am a danger and that Germany means war.

When we speak of the outrageous injustice of the Polish
corridor . . . which is like a strip of flesh cut from our
body . . . France and Poland say we are getting ready to
make war . . .

When Germany protests against the grossest injustice,
when it demands its rights, when it refuses to submit to
further humiliation, when it points out how its former
enemies have broken their solemn promises, when it
points out that the economic ruin and Bolshevisation
of Germany cannot possibly be helpful to the world in
the present great economic crisis, then the world is
immediately told that 'we are getting ready for war'.

Interestingly, although he counters or explains away the other accusations
against him – that he plans to take power by force, that he is against
private property, that he is an atheist – he never actually deals with the
accusation that his Germany is getting ready for war.

Two days later, on 30 September 1930, the *Daily Mirror*, still a
Rothermere paper but only for a few more months, carried a prominent
article which may possibly have been intended as some kind of riposte
to the *Sunday Express* scoop. Written by a wartime hero and right-wing
Conservative MP, Oliver Locker-Lampson, it is a hymn of praise to
Hitler. Locker-Lampson was a ludicrous figure who, the following
year, founded a group of blue-shirted vigilantes called the 'Sentinels of
Empire'; their mission statement, complete with split infinitive, was 'to
peacefully fight Bolshevism', and their motto was 'Fear God! Fear
Naught!' Like Beaverbrook's and Rothermere's United Empire Party, it
quickly faded away.

In the *Mirror* article, Locker-Lampson makes a risible revelation about Hitler, clearly intended to endear him to the British: Hitler had not only played cricket and raised a cricket team, but had then come up with several proposals for changing the laws of the game. According to Locker-Lampson, some British officers told him that in 1918 they had been prisoners-of-war in a camp near the hospital where Hitler was recovering from the injuries he received in the front line. He came round to see them, and asked if he could watch a cricket match; he apparently thought it might be good if German soldiers were encouraged to play it.

Hitler sat on the edge of the field and watched them. Then he came back a few days later with a full German eleven and asked if they could have a match. This apparently took place, though Locker-Lampson does not answer the one question that occurs immediately to everyone: who won? Presumably the British team, since Hitler later told the British officers that, having thought it over, he had decided to make some changes. Cricket was not tough enough for Germans; he would not allow them to wear pads when they batted or kept wicket, and he wanted a larger and harder ball.

In the remainder of the article, Locker-Lampson strives hard to give the impression that he has met him, but never quite says so: '[A]fter a few hours in his company any honest observer must admit that folk become electrified. The temperature of the room rises in his presence. He enhances the value of life. He makes his humblest follower feel twice the man.'

Locker-Lampson, like the *Mirror*'s proprietor, is a true believer.

> [H]e means to ride off on the patriotic ticket, and play for a tear-up of the treaties and a rip-up of reparations ... And his motto might be the one he suggested years ago to those English cricketing friends when reforming the old game's rules: 'Ohne Hast, ohne Rast' (unhasting, unresting).

§

Not all British observers who saw Hitler either from a distance or from close-up were happy about his rise to power, even if they wrote for Lord Rothermere. In January 1933 the *Daily Mail*'s man in Berlin, Rothay Reynolds, reported with apparent unease on the results of the recent political manoeuvring there. Franz von Papen, the conservative leader, believing he could tie Hitler down and control him, had asked the aged President Hindenburg to appoint Hitler chancellor and himself vice chancellor. Reluctantly, Hindenburg agreed; and twelve catastrophic years of Nazi domination followed.

If, as seems clear from his early reporting on Hitler, Reynolds thought he was dangerous, it was difficult for him to say so openly. Rothermere's sympathies were abundantly clear to his staff, and the editors and correspondents, whatever their personal views, could not be too critical of Hitler. They had to take into account three different forms of pressure: the insistence from Rothermere, not always explicit yet always felt, that Hitler should be presented in a favourable light; the feeling that Reynolds and, it seems, several leading figures in the *Mail*'s newsroom shared, that Hitler's arrival in power was extremely dangerous for the outside world, and the need to address the facts as openly as possible. The result, as the *Mail*'s headlines on 31 January 1933 show, was a studied neutrality.

HITLER AT HEAD OF GERMAN NATION

FORMER FOES RALLY TO HIS BANNER
STORM TROOPS IN NIGHT MARCH OF TRIUMPH
HINDENBURG TAKES THEIR SALUTE
PEACE TREATY THREATENED

The opening of the story is taken from news agency reports, written up in the *Mail*'s newsroom. The first three paragraphs show a variety of responses, none of which Lord Rothermere could take exception to. Herr Adolf Hitler, the former lance corporal in the German Army, has achieved his life's ambition.

> He was yesterday created Chancellor of Germany, and is at the head of a National Government in which he will work side by side with powerful German industrialists, skilled diplomatists, and men of high military rank.
>
> Last night tens of thousands of Nazi Storm Troops and 'Steel Helmets' paraded in Berlin to honour the new Chancellor.

Rothay Reynolds's despatch, which follows the introduction, is also a delicately judged performance. A journalist who works for an intrusive, opinionated proprietor always has a hard job when writing stories which the proprietor is interested in. The only workable defence is the truth, so it is reasonably safe for Reynolds to refer to Hitler, mildly slightingly, as 'the son of an Austrian tax-collector'. His triumph has been so dazzling, Reynolds writes with care, 'that it may easily divert attention from the historic importance of today for Germany and the world'. It is a carefully worded warning, from a man who has seen at first hand how Hitler and his thugs operate. His editors put the next paragraph into heavy type, emphasizing his real meaning.

> All the forces of Germany which are determined to tear up the Peace Treaty and make Germany a Power capable of imposing her will on Europe are now united.

There is nothing there about Fascism energizing the young people of Europe – Rothermere's obsession. Reynolds understands the danger that Hitler's Germany will from now on pose to Europe; but because the shadow of the proprietor lies across his typewriter, he cannot quite say so.

Yet he gets it wrong. Like most of the people who dislike Hitler, and are scared by him, he underestimates him.

> That the Nazis will be disappointed is certain, for Herr Hitler can work no miracle. Here lies the danger for him and his party. As an agitator and inspirer he has been supreme. But he has yet to show that he has the qualities of a statesman.

Reynolds was mistaken. Hitler may not have had the traditional qualities of a statesman, in the sense that he understood the breaking-point of others, and was able to make the kind of compromises which would save the face of his opponents. Instead, right from the start he demonstrated his ferocious vision, which would trump the effete efforts of the kind of men Europe regarded as statesmen. Furthermore, Reynolds was wrong to suggest that Hitler could not work miracles. Germans had become used to weakness and failure ever since 1918, and Hitler was just about to start working miracles of precisely the kind that Germans longed for most.

The *Daily Express*, whose proprietor did not have the same belief in Hitler, did not lead on his assumption of power; though this was because Lord Beaverbrook himself wrote the main story, about his campaign to stop wage cuts. As with the *Mail*, the owner's wishes and obsessions had to be taken carefully into account. And so the main headline reads

Every One Can Help To Stem Tide Of Panic Pay Reductions

Hitler came second, with a strange hotchpotch of stories, headed by 'a startling disclosure' (though who disclosed it is not clear) that a military plot had propelled 'Adolf Hitler, ex-labourer', to the chancellorship.

The retiring chancellor, General von Schleicher, 'was said to have planned for Potsdam troops to march on Berlin'. Hitler, according to the *Express* correspondent, Philip Pembroke Stephens, had joined his old enemy von Papen, 'the autocratic Junker', to defeat the plot. There seems to have been no truth in this story whatever. The *Express*'s main editorial was evasive. 'Mountebank or hero? There have been many who have called Hitler either name. Events will decide now which of them history will fix on him.'

The Times, under its editor Geoffrey Dawson, would later press for greater appeasement of Hitler. But at the moment of his rise to power, the main editorial had little more to say than the *Express*, though it said it at far greater length and with more information at its disposal. But the information concerned the technicalities of politics and the relative positions of the various parties in the Reichstag. There was no examination of Hitler's real motives, or of the forces that had brought him into government.

There is a wonderful suggestion at the end of the *Times* editorial that if the Nazis could gain some experience of government, then they could be drawn into becoming a constitutional party; and it ends with the equally out-of-touch suggestion that the future of what it calls 'German parliamentarism' would depend mainly on Hitler's ability to exercise power with responsibility. Reading the British newspapers of the time, you have the sense that most of them are staffed by decent, comfortable journalists who believe, in spite of everything, that 'Herr Hitler' would also be fundamentally decent and comfortable, if only things could be made a little easier for him.

Nor was this true only of *Times* journalists. The *Daily Mail* reported elsewhere in that day's paper from Washington that a Republican senator, William Borah, chairman of the Senate foreign relations committee, had spoken approvingly of Hitler's appointment as chancellor: 'I am impressed with Hitler, who speaks more and more with the voice of the German people in reference to matters arising from the War and the Versailles Treaty, which will have to be revised in the interests of peace.'

Like many Conservatives in Britain, including Lord Rothermere, Borah supported the new chancellor because, after an early flirtation with anti-capitalist rhetoric, he had settled down as a firm defender of capitalism against Marxism-Leninism. When Hitler and his supporters used brutal methods to suppress German Communism, sympathizers in Britain and the United States were inclined to look away.

On the night of 27 February 1933, four weeks after Hitler became chancellor, fire broke out at the Reichstag. It was a thorough, carefully planned provocation by agents of the Nazi Party, but several Communist deputies in the Reichstag were accused of planning it, while a Dutch Marxist, Marinus van der Lubbe, who was known to be mentally disturbed, had carried it out. The supposed plot gave Hitler the excuse to suspend many basic constitutional rights, and introduce rule by decree. It was a disturbing moment for Germany and for the rest of Europe. Several British papers were forthright in their reporting of the affair; especially *The Times*, whose stand-in correspondent in Berlin, Donald McLachlan, was clear that the whole affair was deliberately arranged by the group around Hitler.

The *Mail*, by contrast, printed the accusations of Hitler's officials as though they were facts. Again, its writers tried to remain neutral, but in this case their apparent balance failed to give any understanding of the basic realities.

PRESIDENT VON HINDENBURG LAST NIGHT SIGNED A SENSATIONAL DECREE AIMED AT THE TOTAL DESTRUCTION OF COMMUNISM IN GERMANY.

This is the German Government's crushing reply to the destruction by fire of the greater part of the Reichstag

building on Monday night, for which Communists are held
to blame.

The country has been placed under a system of martial
law in which armed police are in supreme command, and
has declared the death penalty on all who foment revolt
against the Government, or take part in any disturbances
in which arms are used.

The police are given the right to raid every home in
Germany, the postal and telephone services are no longer
secret, and scores of other public rights are withdrawn.

Berlin police yesterday exposed an elaborate Communist
plot to wreck the elections on Sunday.

They state that the Reds had planned to murder police
and other officials in the streets by disguising themselves
in police and Nazi uniforms, and to wipe out their foes by
poisoning food and water supplies.

The government's sweeping new powers are reported in full, but there is
not a hint of scepticism about the accusations or the likely reason why
Hitler and his supporters should have made them. The *Mail*'s special
correspondent, Rothay Reynolds, now seems to endorse the official
version. The fact that Hindenburg had signed the decree 'shows his sense
of the danger in which Germany stands', Reynolds wrote. In fact,
Hindenburg was now merely a figurehead. Hitler was the master of
Germany, and nothing he demanded would be denied.

Even the dubious details of the Communist plot are accepted entirely
at face value in a side-bar story by Reynolds:

PLOT TO WRECK ELECTIONS
STREET SLAUGHTER AND POISONING
BERLIN UNDER ARMS

From Our Own Correspondent
BERLIN, TUESDAY.

The police announced tonight that in the cellars of
Karl Liebknecht House, the Berlin headquarters of the

Communists, they had found documents showing that revolution and civil war throughout Germany were planned to begin on Saturday, the eve of the general election.

They state that the Communists intended to assassinate a number of prominent men and had plans for poisoning large quantities of food and for killing people wholesale.

The interior minister, whose photograph appeared at the top of the page, was Captain Hermann Goering.

Comparisons between the *Daily Mail* and the *Daily Express* are instructive, because they competed for roughly the same readers and had very much the same lively, if manipulative, approach to the news. Yet the *Express* presented a far more realistic picture of the Nazis than the *Mail* did, because it was less cluttered with its proprietor's preconceptions.

On 23 March 1933, three weeks after Hitler had started his clampdown on Communists, the bill that in effect gave him dictatorial powers for four years came before the Reichstag. The next day's *Express* caught the atmosphere skilfully. 'Chancellor Makes Listeners Tremble', said the main headline, 'While Storm Troops Shout Threats Through Windows'. Pembroke Stephens, the special correspondent of the *Express*, described how thousands of storm troopers marched past the Kroll Opera House in Berlin, where the Reichstag deputies were meeting, and shouted warnings through the windows. The Socialists ignored them and voted against the bill; their opposition to it had been strengthened by the fact that two of their number had been arrested as they arrived at the Opera house. The *Express* has caught the menace of the Nazi regime, while the *Mail* has deliberately chosen to ignore it.

There was clearly a concerted campaign to quieten fears abroad about Nazi policy towards the Jews. On 27 March 1933 the *Mail* carried a report by Rothay Reynolds headlined 'Hitler And The Jews', based on an interview with a leading Nazi.

Dr. Hansstaengel, one of Herr Hitler's closest co-operators, told me today: 'The Chancellor has authorised me to say that all the reports of the mishandling of Jews are barefaced lies.'

> I asked him why many Jews are being discharged from
> public offices, and he replied: 'Speaking for myself, I must
> say that the Jews have abused their power in Germany,
> politically, morally, and financially. They are being dis-
> charged from office because they are not national and
> because they have failed to protect the people from Marxist
> infection and from atheism.'

The *Mail* has opted once again for an uneasy balance. Hansstaengel's words are presented to us at their face value, without being challenged. Perhaps Reynolds, the correspondent, told himself that the Nazis' true aim was clear from the quotations he gives us; but the reality must have been that he knew his proprietor would not allow him to put the true position.

A few hours earlier, Hermann Goering, the Prussian interior minister, had invited the representatives of the foreign press to his house to give them his version of the same message: 'The Government is shocked, indignant, and indeed speechless at the reports which have been written abroad about Jews in Germany.'

It is hard to decide whether Goering is being cynical, or whether he was already showing signs of his later weirdness. Sadly, Reynolds does not help us. He merely quotes Goering as saying:

> [A]part from a few regrettable executions, nobody in
> Germany had been done any harm [sic], at any rate, far
> fewer than in 1918.
> 'There is not a man in Germany,' he said, 'whose finger
> nail has been hacked off or who has had the lobe of his ear
> pinched off, and all have kept their sight . . .

Again, no comment from Reynolds. The reader is left to wonder why Goering should be so precise about injuries which might have been inflicted and yet supposedly weren't.

A separate group of foreign correspondents was taken to a Berlin prison and shown three political prisoners who, according to left-wing reports, had been badly beaten up. They were, the group said reassuringly, in good condition. Reuter's, meanwhile, reported a comforting announcement from the US State Department: 'Whereas there was for a short time considerable physical mistreatment of the Jews, this phase may be considered to have virtually terminated.'

§

Only three days later, on 30 March 1933, the *Daily Mail* reported a new phase in the persecution of the Jews.

HITLER AND A JEWISH 'WAR'

'WOULD ONLY HIT JEWS'
BOYCOTT BEGUN
SHOPS SHUT IN MANY GERMAN TOWNS

At first glance, the article itself seems reasonably thorough and factual, but it plainly accepts the basic premise of Germany's anti-Jewish campaign: that it is a response to the boycott in America and Britain of German goods, generated by pro-Jewish feeling there. There is no hint in the article of the real position: that the Nazi regime was using the boycott as an excuse to launch a campaign against Jews in general. It begins: 'The Chancellor, Herr Hitler, explained to the Cabinet today the counter-measures taken in reply to Jewish propaganda abroad alleging anti-Semitic "atrocities".'

It is the word 'atrocities' rather than 'propaganda' which the paper puts in inverted commas. For journalists, inverted commas tend to indicate something they do not believe or accept; so the *Mail* seems to show that it regards the international campaign against Germany as propaganda, and does not accept that atrocities are necessarily being committed at all. Hermann Goering, after all, had assured the *Mail* personally that no one had lost a fingernail.

Any doubts Rothay Reynolds may once have had about Hitler and the Nazis now seem to have been thrown aside. He quotes, without any hint of scepticism, Hitler's statement that if the Nazi Party does not act against the Jews, then ordinary Germans might take 'independent action' – difficult, one would have thought, given the draconian powers the government had awarded itself over people's lives – and that this could have 'undesirable consequences'. Then there is another strange sentence, which one is reluctant to take at face value, and yet which seems like a personal comment by Reynolds himself: 'The boycott of the Jews is to begin in every town and village in Germany on Saturday "at 10 a.m. sharp". In some cases the racial ardour of true Germans is such that they have already begun the boycott . . .'

Can this possibly be meant seriously? There is nothing else in the article to suggest that it might be an attempt at irony. The rest of what Reynolds writes is a painstaking account of various anti-Semitic actions being taken in a range of towns and cities:

> EBERSWALDER: National Socialist pickets demanded the closing of Jewish shops. During the night windows of Jewish shops were smeared with tar.

> GÖTTINGEN: Last night there was spontaneous action against the foreign boycott propaganda, and windows of Jewish shops were smashed.

Again, the word 'propaganda' seems to be taken at the value the Nazis themselves placed on it.

By contrast, the *Daily Mirror*, no longer under the control of Lord Rothermere, writes much more frankly about the assault on the Jews. It headlines a report from Reuter's news agency that in the Saxon town of Annaberg Nazi pickets used rubber stamps to mark the faces of customers at Jewish-owned shops with the words 'We are traitors'. It also repeats on its front page a photograph it has already used some days earlier, showing a Jewish man walking barefoot through the centre of Munich, carrying a placard apologizing for the fact that he had complained of being beaten up.

The *Mirror* prints a telegram to Hitler from the Tory MP, Commander Oliver Locker-Lampson, whom we last heard of praising Hitler and revealing his interest in, of all things, cricket. Now, even Locker-Lampson has had second thoughts:

> The decision to discriminate against the German Jews has had a most damaging effect upon the good feeling for Germany which was growing stronger . . . This action against the Jews is making the work of myself and other friends of Germany almost impossible.

Meanwhile *The Times*, which had previously been part of the Northcliffe group and would soon become the main mouthpiece for the appeasement of Hitler, was becoming strongly critical of him. And although it maintained a certain decorum, its use of inverted commas in its account on 11 May 1933 of the first Nazi book-burning is as revealing as the *Mail*'s:

'UN-GERMAN' BOOKS DESTROYED
A BERLIN BONFIRE

FROM OUR OWN CORRESPONDENT BERLIN, May 10

About 20,000 'Marxist', pacifist, Jewish, or other 'un-German' books, 'collected' by the Nazi-led students of Berlin University during recent days from public libraries and private owners, were burned tonight in the Opera Place in Berlin in the presence of Dr. Goebbels, the Minister for Propaganda.

The *Times* man describes how books by anti-war authors, especially Remarque's *All Quiet On the Western Front*, works critical of Mussolini, all Marxist publications, anything by Jewish authors, the works of Thomas Mann, Stephan Zweig, Arthur Schnitzler, Ernest Hemingway, Jack London and others, were burned in a ludicrous ritual devised by Goebbels himself. (The *Times* correspondent cannot help himself, however, from adding a harrumphing note of his own: 'The destruction of books on sex by Dr Magnus Hirschfeld and other books classified as "obscene" or "trash" will cause no regret to the great majority of Germans.')

He reports that a dozen students, each carrying one book, were summoned to the microphone, 'where each recited an appropriate couplet, ending with the words, "I consign to the flames the writer Emil Ludwig," or whoever the writer was.'

Then Dr Goebbels stepped into the glare of the searchlights and the bonfire, and declaimed against the 'filth' of the Jewish 'asphalt-literati'.

On 16 May 1934 *The Times* ran an outspoken article 'from a Correspondent lately in Germany' attacking Julius Streicher, the savage Gauleiter of Franconia who edited and often largely wrote *Der Stürmer*. The article was markedly stronger than the editorials carried by *The*

Times itself on the subject. *Der Stürmer*, the correspondent writes, carries 'the grossest libelling of individual Jews', and even 'an unfavourable conversational comment on Streicher's anti-Semitic policy is enough to get a man into a concentration camp'. As for the newspaper itself, it is 'devoted from first to last to the most crude and violent type of anti-Semitic propaganda tainted with prurient and pornographic elements which render it attractive to a certain kind of depraved mind . . .'

In case the readers of *The Times* should feel this is a little strong, there are several quotations from *Der Stürmer*; this, for instance: 'Our knowledge of the Jewish question has led us to the opinion that all Jews, in fact, should be castrated.'

The *Manchester Guardian* was consistently better informed about German realities than any other British newspaper. On 4 October 1933, for instance, an article signed merely 'From a Correspondent' reveals how Ernst Röhm's SA, or Stormtroopers, soon to be dismantled during the 'Night of the Long Knives', are being superseded by Hitler's private guard, the SS. It describes how the SA's methods of taking prisoners to their barracks, giving them a beating, then allowing them home, is giving way to the newer methods of the SS and the Gestapo.

Their purpose, the article says, is to get confessions or information through the use of torture. The Gestapo go out at night, usually between 3 a.m. and 4 a.m., visit a particular street, and search a certain number of people. Most of the information they work on comes from private denunciations.

The unnamed reporter, who was possibly J.G. Hawkins, the *Guardian*'s Berlin correspondent, quotes the case of a man who has recently been arrested by the Gestapo. They came to his door at 4 a.m., beat him up, searched the flat, and took him off to the Columbiahaus on the Tempelhof and questioned him about forbidden publications. He said he had none. His captors took him to the cellar, stripped him, laid him on a table, and four men flogged him with horsewhips. Then he was questioned again, and gave the same answers; on which he was taken to the cellar and horsewhipped again. The whole procedure was repeated the following morning, so he had been whipped three times in eleven hours. Presumably the Gestapo believed him eventually, because they stopped beating him and he was released. He had to sign a form undertaking to say nothing about his treatment. But he told the *Guardian*'s correspondent, and showed him his injuries. 'I saw my informant's back about a fortnight after he was flogged, and it was even then in a terrible state.'

The Berlin correspondent of the *Daily Express*, Pembroke Stephens, was arguably the most effective British journalist based in Germany in the first years of Hitler's power. Unlike many of the others, he liked to go and see things for himself whenever possible. In May 1934 he visited Hamburg to find out what effect the international action against German goods had had. His despatch on Wednesday 16 May was headlined

World Boycott Strangles Germany's Greatest Port

> A graveyard among cities – that is the picture presented by Hamburg, Germany's doorway to world trade.

> No town has suffered more from Hitler than this once wealthy city of commerce. The Jewish boycott has robbed Hamburg of her export business.

The Nazi authorities might have approved of this article, since it provided a kind of justification for their revenge on German Jews. By reporting from Hamburg Stephens seems to have been trying to show them that he was prepared to see the question from both sides: something foreign correspondents often feel obliged to do, in order to protect themselves from being expelled. Much of the rest of his reporting was far more hostile in tone. After his trip to Hamburg he was arrested by the Gestapo near Magdeburg, where he had been asking questions about a new chemical factory, but he was released after a short stay in gaol. This did not deter him, and he continued travelling round. On Friday 25 May, the *Express* ran a long article from him on its front page. This changed his future, and the future policy of the paper as well.

NEW HITLER BLOW AT THE JEWS
PLAN TO SEIZE ALL THEY POSSESS?
VIVID DESPATCH BY PEMBROKE STEPHENS
'BEST THING YOU CAN DO IS DIE'

Datelined Arnswalde, Stephens's despatch begins, 'What is happening to the Jews left in Germany? . . . I have spent the past few days visiting districts where the Jews are reported to be suffering most keenly, to answer the question which so fascinates the world.'

He estimates that there are half a million Jews still remaining in Germany. A hundred thousand had emigrated in the sixteen months since Hitler took power.

The article continues on page 2, where it has a new set of headlines stretching over seven columns:

GERMAN JEWS ARE FACING THEIR DARKEST DAYS

DENIED A LIVING – SAVINGS GONE

FRIENDS DARE NOT GREET THEM; THEIR CHILDREN PLAY ALONE

Stephens reports that Breslau and Nuremberg are the worst areas for anti-Semitism.

> Cases of reported murder of Jews are exceedingly difficult to prove. People are afraid to reveal what they know, and emphatic denials are invariably furnished by the secret police.
>
> I heard of cases of brutality in Stettin and Hamburg, but visited both places without being able to confirm the news.

He describes the town of Arnswalde in Pomerania, from where he sends his despatch, as being typical of German anti-Semitism.

> Friends of fifty years' standing do not greet their old Jewish friends when they meet them in the village: they look the other way.
>
> Jewish children are boycotted by former playmates as if they had the plague; farmers willing to borrow money from the small Jewish trader in democratic days do not take their

> debts seriously; customers prefer not to buy in Jewish shops, and storm troopers stand outside the doors of Jewish cinemas warning visitors away . . .
>
> Robbed of work, denied civic privileges in a country which despises them, what is the German Jew to do but follow the brutal advice of officials: 'The best thing you can do is to die.'

Will things get better, as Jewish leaders hope? Stephens correctly predicts that the Nazis will not moderate their policy. Yet at this early stage in Nazi Germany's development, he cannot foresee the outright genocide of the Jews. Like everyone else, he seems to assume that the purpose of Nazi policy is to drive out as many Jews as possible, and intimidate the rest.

The *Express* was starting to realize that Pembroke Stephens was a valuable commodity. His reports stirred people's emotions, and attracted interest. As a result of his enterprise and courage, Stephens gave his readers a better picture of Jewish suffering in 1934 than any other British newspaper managed to do. The paper's proprietor, Lord Beaverbrook, and its remarkable editor Arthur Christiansen understood something else: in Stephens they had a man who made news as well as reported it.

Six days after his story from Arnswalde appeared on the front page of the *Express*, the Gestapo arrested Stephens and, eventually, threw him out of the country. This time, on Saturday 2 June, his article led the paper.

MY EXPULSION BY THE NAZIS

VIVID STORY TOLD BY PEMBROKE STEPHENS
ARTICLE ABOUT JEWS THAT ANGERED HITLER
'DAILY EXPRESS' TO PROVE ITS TRUTH

By PEMBROKE STEPHENS.

Berlin correspondent of the 'Daily Express', who arrived in London last night by air from Amsterdam, following his arrest and expulsion from Germany.

> I was arrested by two secret service men at 3 p.m. on
> Thursday in front of my servants and taken in a closed car
> to police headquarters, where I was locked up in a pen
> like a beast in a cage behind high wire netting. I was not
> allowed to telephone my wife.

Like most journalists who find themselves in this kind of position, Stephens remains keenly aware of the absurdity of it all. His Gestapo captors did not know exactly where they were supposed to take him, so they drove around Berlin for more than an hour trying to find the right prison. He spent the time trying to get on better terms with them, and thereby escape a beating.

When they eventually found it, the prison was a frightening place.

> I heard the moans of a woman prisoner in pain, and saw a
> youth handcuffed to a detective being led away to his cell.
>   Grim photographs of murdered men with blood-stained
> faces distorted in death grinned at me from the walls.

These, it seems, were pictures of prisoners who had been beheaded. Stephens had to look at them for an hour before he was taken into another room and given a piece of paper informing him that he was going to be expelled from Germany. Soon afterwards another document was read out to him: 'You are hereby expelled from Prussia, because you have conducted yourself in a manner hostile to the State. Expulsion will be followed by forcible ejection from the German border.'

He was taken by train to the Belgian frontier, and released there. His escort tried to be pleasant, and he left Germany almost with regret. Yet he had known all along that he ran the risk of being thrown out. Nine months earlier, in September 1933, he had written an article for the *Express* in which he had said he was determined to tell the truth about Germany whatever the consequences: '[E]vents have proved my belief that it is impossible to tell the truth, the real truth, about Germany, and remain an accredited correspondent in Berlin.'

News organizations dislike it when their correspondents are thrown out of a country, for whatever reason. It costs money, it does not always look good (though Germany was probably an exception to this), and it is hard to persuade the local government to accept another correspondent as a replacement. Often the journalist who has been expelled suffers an obscure punishment back home, finding it difficult to get a decent posting again. But the *Express*, with its buccaneering proprietor and its shrewd editor, understood that this was something different – something that could be turned to the *Express*'s advantage.

As a result, it used Stephens to spearhead its new campaign. From now on, the *Express* would be Britain's leading anti-Nazi newspaper. Over the next few weeks article after article condemning Germany appeared: 'The Evil Genius of Germany – Goebbels The Jew-Baiter'; 'Menace To Europe' (which begins with a quotation from a French official: 'Germany is the mad dog of Europe. She must be kept on a strong chain.'); 'Austria's New Leader – He Believes Hitler Is "Crazed"'; and a long article on Julius Streicher called 'Jew-Baiter No. 1'.

But this intensity of coverage could not be maintained in a daily newspaper, and slowly Pembroke Stephens turned his attention to other things. So did the *Express*, though it remained staunchly anti-Nazi and supported Winston Churchill's campaign for rearmament. As for Stephens, he continued to crusade against the violence of far right-wing regimes, and later went to China to report on the atrocities which were being committed there by the Japanese. He was shot in the head and killed on the last day of the Chinese army's stand against the Japanese outside Shanghai in 1937. His friend, a rowdy, apparently indestructible *Daily Mail* correspondent called O'Dowd Gallagher, was there when it happened. Gallagher wrote the story of Stephens's death and sent it, not to his own paper, but to Stephens's. 'I couldn't', he explained, 'scoop him on his own obituary.'

No one has written a life of Philip Pembroke Stephens, and he has not been thought worthy of inclusion in the Dictionary of National Biography; yet he was one of the heroes of British journalism in the 1930s. It took courage to write openly about the behaviour of the Nazis in the streets. Most of the foreign correspondents in Berlin chose to ignore this as much as possible, and concentrated instead on the safer business of reporting political and diplomatic issues. Stephens was not that kind of journalist. He preferred to go and see things for himself, and that always gave him plenty of controversial things to write about. And he was fortunate to have the support of Lord Beaverbrook, who liked to encourage crusading journalism.

Stephens was not a particularly gifted writer, but he was a man of considerable principle, and thoroughly prepared to take risks. As a result he gave the *Daily Express*, which could easily have chosen to take the *Daily Mail* approach to Hitler, a creditable cause to support. Wayward and sometimes foolish though Beaverbrook and the *Express* would often be over the coming decades, the campaign on behalf of Germany's Jews would always be counted in their favour.

10

THE CAUSE

For Martha Gellhorn, one of the greatest writers on war and social unrest in the English language during the entire twentieth century, which her long life almost spanned, it was quite simply *la Causa* – the Cause. 'We would have done anything for it, short of actually lying,' she would say. Hundreds, perhaps thousands, of other journalists around the world felt the same way about the Republican side in the Spanish Civil War, though they did not always stop short at lying. Some journalists felt the same about Vietnam, or the wars against Saddam Hussein; others found their Causa in the Bosnian War. But Spain was the template, a war in which the supporters of both sides regarded it as the ultimate clash between right and wrong.

Tensions in Spain between left and right had been growing for decades, but the civil war began as a botched coup d'état on 17 July 1936, when General Emilio Mola tried to overthrow the Popular Front government. Although Mola failed, he was supported by General Francisco Franco, the commander of the Spanish colonial army in Morocco. The Popular Front was weak because the Socialist leader, Francisco Largo Caballero, had refused to join it, confident that, with support from the working class and the peasants, he could deal with any uprising from the right and eventually form a government of his own without having to depend on the Popular Front.

Outside Spain, the Popular Front's only potential friends were Britain, France and the Soviet Union, but the first two were too nervous about domestic opinion to help, and although Stalin supplied the Front with weapons, he had a different agenda altogether. The Front's natural enemies, Germany and Italy, were under no restraints and did everything they could to destroy it. The Front was strong in the industrial areas of the country, in the Basque region, and in Catalonia, both of which wanted independence from the Madrid government.

The heartland of the right-wing rebels was the main agricultural areas.

Franco and his army, airlifted from Morocco to the mainland by German and Italian planes, carved their way northwards towards Madrid, carrying out massacre after massacre. If the journalists who travelled with them had tried to report these things, and most of them did not, their despatches would have been cut or stopped altogether by Franco's censors. As a result there was minimal reporting on the villages destroyed, the men shot out of hand, the children killed, the women and girls raped by the forces of the right.

The Republican government, by contrast, saw its only real salvation in the backing of people and governments in Europe and beyond. As a result it encouraged foreign journalists to come to the areas it controlled, and imposed little in the way of censorship on them, even when they wrote for right-wing newspapers deeply opposed to the government. This might have been honourable, but in the circumstances it was less than practical. As a result the outside world, which heard next to nothing about the crimes carried out by the right, heard a great deal about the crimes of the left: the murder of priests committed in revenge for the killings carried out by the ultra-Catholic rebels, the savage sentences of ad hoc revolutionary courts, and the breakdown of law and order which often happened directly the traditionally right-wing police were chased out by supporters of the left. In Barcelona the anarchists began what was portrayed in much of the European and North American press as an orgy of violence and terror.

From the start, then, people in Britain were provided with what looked like a clear picture: Spain was in the hands of the violent, uncontrollable left, and the right had been goaded into taking action in order to restore some kind of proper control. Reuter's news agency, usually calm and understated, carried a report datelined Barcelona on 21 July 1936 which claimed that anarchists, Communists and Socialists, all apparently acting together (unlikely, one would have thought), had destroyed almost every church in the city, and had paraded through the streets in looted clerical robes. This was picked up and used by most British newspapers, with or without a byline crediting Reuter's but always with the dateline 'Barcelona'.

At this stage, as now, news agencies habitually dateline their material from the place where their information comes from, rather than where the correspondents writing the despatch happen to find themselves. In this case the Reuter's correspondent does not seem to have been in Barcelona, but was merely passing on reports he was getting from there. There is no intention to deceive in this practice, yet readers will always assume that news agency correspondents are in the place mentioned in the dateline, even when they aren't.

The *Daily Express* had taken a stand against Hitler, but it knew that its comfortable middle-class readers always had an appetite for stories of cruelty and destruction carried out by the bloodthirsty left. Sefton Delmer was the most prominent, though not the most senior, of the correspondents on the *Express*. He was a German specialist, having been born in Berlin in 1905, the son of a British academic, and had been a colleague of Pembroke Stephens. But whereas Stephens had set out to expose Nazi atrocities, Delmer had decided to concentrate on getting close to Hitler and other leading Nazis, with such success that at one stage the British embassy in Berlin reported to the Foreign Office its suspicions that Delmer was a Nazi sympathizer. He wasn't; he was merely interested in getting stories he thought the *Express* would appreciate. His colleagues believed he had no qualms about embellishing them or even making them up if required.

Delmer was large, friendly, boisterous, and highly competitive. In Spain, the *Express* wanted atrocity stories, and Delmer, like other *Express* correspondents, provided them: 'Priests are being dragged with a prayer on their lips from their monasteries to be shot – in the backs – by firing squads. Some of them have had their heads and arms hacked off after death as a final vindictive act.'

There is a tabloid ferocity about this which suggests embellishment. The parenthetic phrase 'in the backs' sounds like an intensifier, as though shooting someone in the back is somehow worse than shooting them from the front; though if we had a choice most of us would probably prefer not to see our killers' faces. As for the cutting off of heads and arms after death, executioners usually seem sated or even sickened by what they have done; the thought of taking axes and chopping up the bodies rarely seems to occur to them. The fact that none of these stories are ever predicated with phrases which make it clear that Delmer or his colleagues were there in person shows that they are either hearsay or outright inventions.

Sefton Delmer was scarcely much of an authority on the violence in Barcelona at this stage. His first reporting trip to Spain lasted for little more than a single night: he drove down from France with his brand-new wife (plus her Siamese cat in a basket) on their honeymoon. He blagged his way through the border, using his League of Nations press card, issued in Geneva, and they managed to reach a village just north of Barcelona. But the new Mrs Delmer was getting understandably worried by the sound of gunfire from what might or might not have been firing squads (her husband was sure they were), and the two of them hurried back to France, with their cat, the following morning. They stopped off in Perpignan so that Delmer could file a despatch which the *Express* printed on 21 July 1936 under the headline 'Armed Reds Bar Way To City Of Terror'. It relayed the wild rumour that thousands of people had been massacred inside Barcelona.

The *Express* particularly liked stories about excess and near-insanity too. Six days later it carried this report about (but not actually from) Barcelona:

> ... [O]n the firing line are city clerks who have let their beards grow and are heavy eyed with free liquor and days without sleep. The Robespierre of Barcelona sits on a pedestal fashioned like a throne on the balcony of a magnificent house in the Ramblas, the famous thoroughfare between the Plaza Cataluña and the port ... On either side of the throne the leader's lieutenants sit on chairs with rifles over their knees and blood red silk scarves round head and waist. But for their menacing and unkempt appearance they would be like fancy-dress pirates.

There were murders in Barcelona, certainly, and there was a great deal of looting. There were also, inevitably, gangs and gang-leaders; but wildness and violence on the scale that the *Express* and Reuter's suggested seems to have been a mere intensification of the rumours that were going around. Yet reports like these establish a standard which other journalists are then required (or feel obliged) to match; so that a more honest correspondent, visiting Barcelona, might well find a certain scepticism, even irritation, from his news editor back home if his reports did not emphasize the theme of crazed left-wing bloodletting.

Editors like to have material which matches what their rivals are reporting; if one correspondent describes inflamed crowds racing through the streets in priests' robes, looking for nuns to rape, other newspapers are going to feel unsatisfied by quieter, less violent accounts – even if they half-suspect their man may be right and their rivals are exaggerating. In later decades, once television news cameras started recording the actuality of events, it became harder for the more imaginative newspaper correspondents to embroider the big events in quite the same way, since they knew their readers and their editors were watching and that a reality check existed. During the Spanish Civil War, however, there was no reality check; exaggeration and outright invention set the tone, right from the start.

Yet too much of the wrong kind of violence was not always appreciated by editors back home either. Cedric Salter, who freelanced from Spain for various London newspapers, sent in a powerful and entirely true story to one of them about an old man who was caught trying to smuggle potatoes into Barcelona for his starving family. A fight ensued, and the old man and a policeman were killed. The paper, which he prudently didn't identify, rejected his story, explaining:

> Newspapers are mostly read at breakfast, and there is nothing better calculated to put a man off his second egg and rasher of bacon than reading a story forcing him to realise that not so very far away there are people dying for a handful of potatoes. If one newspaper puts him off his breakfast, he takes pains to buy another one. That we naturally wish to avoid.

Spain during the Civil War was a place which some British editors and correspondents often seemed to regard as a fantasy land, where the reporting had to match their readers' demands rather than be pegged to the acts.

It seems to have become accepted that, overall, the British press strongly supported the Nationalist side in the war. The truth is more complicated than that. It also tends to run counter to the pattern which had emerged in the first third of the twentieth century so far. Usually, as we have seen, the reporting from the journalists on the spot has tended to be more nuanced and less biased, while the editorial line back home at the newspaper has been more prejudiced, or at any rate more clearly defined. In Spain, because the war was a cause for journalists on both the left and the right, it is they who are often fiercely partisan, while their foreign desks and editors tend to be relatively more neutral.

We have seen how Sefton Delmer and some of his colleagues on the *Express* played up the chaos and violence they claimed happened in Barcelona; yet in a number of leaders Arthur Christiansen, the editor of the *Express*, made it clear that the newspaper itself wanted to remain neutral. He must have realized that it would be deeply illogical to condemn the Nazis in Germany for their brutality, and then support Franco in Spain.

Delmer himself contrived to maintain a kind of balance in his reporting between the Republicans and the Nationalists, by reporting the atrocity stories put out by both sides. In the *Express* of 30 July 1936, at the start of the war, he reported that Franco's soldiers had been going into prisons and killing the prisoners they found there. On 10 March 1937 his report on the bombing campaign of Franco's air force was headlined 'War Planes Swoop On British Hospital'. In between, on 11 August 1936, he sent the *Express* a typical Nationalist propaganda story about the discovery of the charred body of a bishop who had been burned alive by the 'Reds'. Delmer was not partisan in his horror stories: he merely wanted them to be vivid. And the *Express*, knowing that vividness was popular with its readership, was happy to publish them.

British Conservatives were divided, often in their own minds. When Winston Churchill was introduced to the new, Republican Spanish ambassador, Pablo de Azcárate, at a party in London in September 1936, he refused to shake his hand, murmuring, 'Blood, blood.' Nineteen months later, in April 1938, Churchill expressed his sympathy for the now hard-pressed Republic to Azcárate. Soon afterwards he told a Buenos Aires newspaper that although Franco had 'all the right' on his side, he himself, being English, preferred the triumph of the 'wrong cause', because a victory for Franco would mean victory for Mussolini's Italy and Hitler's Germany. Even the *Daily Telegraph*, which might have been expected to take the Nationalist line, tried not to be overly partisan.

Lord Rothermere never had the slightest doubt whom he supported, and he made the *Daily Mail* Franco's loudest supporter in Fleet Street. As early as 22 March 1933, more than three years before the civil war broke out, the *Mail* reported that Spain's troubles lay with the anarchists, socialists and 'Reds', but that the coming together of right-wing and

moderate parties was a 'bright spot on the horizon'. The editorial staff
and the correspondents in the field knew that they were expected to
emphasize stories which supported the Nationalists and discredited the
Republicans. Many of the *Mail*'s staff then, as throughout the newspaper's
history, were instinctively liberal-minded; journalists often tend to be.
But Rothermere paid better than just about any other proprietor, though
Beaverbrook competed enthusiastically with him, and people who
worked for the *Mail* and its sister papers knew what they had to do for
the money.

There was nothing liberal about Randolph Churchill, Winston's
turbulent son. (Later in his short life, when he was operated on for a
growth which proved to be benign, his equally difficult friend Evelyn
Waugh remarked that it was typical of modern medicine that it would
take Randolph Churchill and extract the only benign thing about him.)
Randolph, unlike his father, openly wanted a Nationalist victory and did
everything he could through his reporting to make it happen. On 3
February 1937, Randolph, who seems to have been in Spain at the time,
wrote an article about the next day's parliamentary by-election in St
Pancras, in central London. Everything, from the central-casting names
of the candidates to the carelessly partisan tone of Churchill's article,
makes it hard to take it seriously; it could be a passage from an Evelyn
Waugh novel, with Randolph Churchill as Basil Seale.

Keep the Socialist Out at St. Pancras

HIS COMMUNIST ALLIES

The Candidates:
Mr. R. Grant-Ferris (Con.).
Mr. H. M. Tibbles (Soc.).

By RANDOLPH CHURCHILL

St. Pancras polls tomorrow; and every elector should
remember that a vote for Mr. Grant-Ferris is a vote for
national defence and peace, and that a vote for his
Socialist opponent is regarded by the Communist Party
as a vote to save Madrid for the Spanish Reds . . .

The local Communist Party secretary had apparently revealed that around fifty of its members were working for Mr Tibbles. The *Mail* must have told Churchill about this. 'In addition to his undesirable political associates, the views advanced by Mr. Tibbles on the two burning questions of the hour have lost him the support of most reasonably minded people in the division . . .'

These questions, according to Churchill, were 'the provision of adequate national defence', his father's big cause at the time, with some reason, and 'a meddlesome and aggressive foreign policy which would aggravate half the nations of the earth' – by which Randolph Churchill means Germany and Italy. He had not grasped his father's understanding that countering the right-wing dictatorships was essential for Britain. Then this remarkable article continues:

> The polling booths will be open between the hours of 7 a.m. and 9 p.m. All who wish to assist the Conservative candidate, particularly those who can lend a car, should communicate with the Conservative election agent, Mr. Heather, at 302, Kentish Town-road. Telephone Gulliver 3244.

These homely details can only have been added in London; impossible to think of the volcanically irritable Churchill having to bother with the Conservative agent's phone number. Between them, Churchill and the *Mail* were successful: Grant-Ferris, the Conservative, just squeaked in. The effect of the by-election on the siege of Madrid was not recorded, even by Randolph Churchill.

At this stage, anyway, the assault on Madrid was in its very early stages; though the readers of the *Daily Mail* might not have realized it. On the contrary, Churchill and his colleague in Spain, Harold G. Cardozo, were predicting the speedy fall of Madrid to the Nationalists from the start of 1937. Cardozo wrote a story headlined 'Decisive Battle For Madrid' on 12 March 1937. Eleven days earlier, the *Mail* had published Churchill's account of an interview with General Franco, carried out in Salamanca. He had assiduously invoked his father's name to get it. The article is wholly free of any kind of scepticism, or even of any obviously balanced questioning.

Franco On His Policy To Spaniards
STATEMENT TO RANDOLPH CHURCHILL
Mercy for Red Rank and File
'IN MADRID SOON'

'A humane and equitable clemency is a policy which can ensure a reconciled and united Spain.'

This was the keynote of the statement made to me today by General Franco at his headquarters here.

'Our Red opponents have committed innumerable crimes and atrocities which cry out to Heaven for a just retribution. This they will assuredly receive.

'For the ringleaders and those who are guilty of murder, death must be the penalty. But to the ordinary rank and file of our opponents we shall continue to show leniency and mercy . . .'

Randolph Churchill fails to give his readers even the faintest reminder that Franco's troops, with his full knowledge, had carried out atrocities of their own. Franco had a perfect right to score political points in an interview like this. But Churchill presents us with Franco's assertions as though they are unchallenged facts: Madrid will fall soon, the enemy will be treated with mercy.

Like Rothermere, Randolph Churchill was in the business of telling people what to think – not of providing them with the information to make up their own minds. In fact, Madrid would not fall for almost exactly two more years of fierce fighting, on 27 March 1939. As for leniency and mercy, there was none. In the end Franco had 150,000 people executed, and at least 500,000 imprisoned; many of them in labour camps which owed much in their design and organization to Buchenwald and Dachau.

Another *Mail* correspondent, Cecil Gerahty, often reported the alleged atrocities of the 'Reds'. His 1938 memoir, *The Road to Madrid*, went into some detail about them; yet he is honest enough to admit that he never actually witnessed any atrocities himself; he relies on eyewitness accounts and interviewed various 'Reds' before they were executed for their crimes, and treats all this evidence as though it were unquestionably true. No doubt some, and perhaps many, of the stories were. Journalists have to work fast, and their reliance on the quality of their sources often has to be instinctive. But there is a world of difference between journalists who weigh their sources carefully and are honest about the strength of what they report, and those who put out stories which they only half-believe themselves, to get a good showing in the paper, and please a biased editor or proprietor.

John Langdon-Davies of the *News Chronicle*, strongly liberal in its views, was meticulous in his reporting about atrocity stories from either side. On 4 September 1936 the *Chronicle* printed an article by him, apparently written from London, which was headlined:

Truth About Barcelona
TERROR STORIES EXPOSED

> The contempt that one feels for the lies and calumnies against the Spanish people which have disgraced a certain section of the Press must not blind one to the very serious problem of public order facing the [Spanish] government ...
>
> In Barcelona and elsewhere people are being taken from their beds every night and shot by anonymous political gangsters. This is true.
>
> The absurd stories of bodies thrown out in the streets for the dustmen to take away, or piled in public gardens to rot, may be left to thrill a certain type of reader, but those who realise how serious events in Spain are for the future of European civilisation will want to know the truth.

Almost every morning, Langdon-Davies wrote, bodies would be discovered on the road from Barcelona to San Cugat known as La Rabassada. They were those of capitalists and wealthy bourgeois who were suspected of Fascist sympathies, or had incurred the enmity of criminal gangs. There had, he estimated, been 200 murders a month – not the 2,000 which right-wingers in Barcelona claimed, and certainly not the 'cartloads' which some journalists had written about in the British press. Two hundred killings in a single city in one month is serious enough, Langdon-Davies implies; there is no need to exaggerate the number for the sake of propaganda.

He too wrote a book in 1938, *Behind the Spanish Barricades*, in which he addressed the question of atrocities with honesty and care.

> I am sure in my own mind that no nun has been raped or made to dance naked to the red mob. I know that priests have been killed, and ... I am prepared to doubt the stories on the other side of Moors cutting off children's hands because they raised them in a communist salute ...
>
> People who gloat over atrocities can never begin to understand the true tragedy; those who see terror in terms of blood and bestiality cannot understand the silent unobtrusive Terror, quite unsensational, quite without sex-appeal, that really exists.

The *Daily Mail* did not agree. On 5 March 1937 it ran the following brief story – one of many completely unsupported, almost casual accusations over the months.

Reds' 'Rock Of Slaughter'

From A Special Correspondent
Burgos, Thursday.

> Prisoners captured during the Basque reds' attack on Oviedo report that Santander is in the grip of a ferocious terror, the number of executions being counted in hundreds. Most of them take place at the foot of the lighthouse rock. The lighthouse keeper has gone mad from seeing the daily orgy of slaughter and hearing the victims' cries.

There seems to have been no truth in this at all. It doesn't even sound true. The *Mail* has restricted it to three sentences and tucked it away at the foot of a column, as though it had no great faith in the story. It was the kind of thing, presumably, which kept Lord Rothermere happy. The first few months of 1937 saw an intensive effort by the *Mail*'s correspondents in Spain to persuade people in Britain that the war in Spain was won and lost.

Tanks Rout Madrid Reds

– Monday 8 February

and the variant, just over a month later,

Reds Routed By Tanks

(The conclusive battle for Madrid is now being fought ...)

– Friday 12 March

Duped Britons Desert Reds

– Monday 1 March

'We Want Bread, Not War' Says Madrid Walls Chalked With Peace Pleas

– Friday 5 March

Spain's Reds Losing Heart

– Friday 12 March

Deadly Accuracy of Franco's Bombers

– Monday 12 April

Most, and perhaps all of this, is propaganda, pure and simple. The reason why these stories weren't true was that the supporters of the Republican cause were so afraid of the ferocity of the Nationalists that they fought on much harder and longer.

But when the *Mail*'s version of the war in Spain was challenged, it could respond savagely – and in a way familiar to its readers seven decades later.

Menace of Red Bias on Radio
PROTESTS BY THE PUBLIC ABOUT B.B.C.

On Wednesday 13 January 1937, the whimsically named F. W. Memory wrote:

> 'The Daily Mail' has again to call attention to the mischievous use being made of the B.B.C. for the dissemination of left-wing propaganda.
>
> This is being done in a subtle but wholesale manner, and has now reached such a pitch that grave concern is caused not only in this country but also throughout the Empire.
>
> A group of M.P.s is determined to raise the matter in Parliament. They will insist that the Government exercise its authority over the corporation to ensure that millions of listeners shall no longer be offended by the broadcasting of 'pink Bolshevism'.
>
> Hardly anything broadcast is free from suspicion – left-wingism is prevalent in the B.B.C. interpretation of news, it is common in 'talks', and raises its head in addresses to school children. It has been known to obtrude in 'entertainment'.

People had, apparently, been writing to the *Mail* in scores (a perennially useful word for journalists, since it sounds immense, but can mean as little as forty, which is two score) to complain about the left-wing bias of the BBC. The precise cause of complaint was a BBC radio commentary by F.A. Voigt on the civil war in Spain a few days earlier. The *Mail* immediately makes it personal:

> Mr Frederick Augustus Voigt is a journalist who contributes to the Manchester Guardian, the pacifist and Radical journal. In no way is it suggested that he himself is a Communist, but he has moved in circles in which Red influence has been pronounced . . .

In fact, Voigt was described by his tutor at King's College London, as 'a first-rate and rather old-fashioned liberal'. He had been the *Guardian*'s correspondent in Berlin from 1920 to 1933, and by 1937 he was a highly trusted member of the 'Z Organisation', which was a parallel intelligence system set up by the Secret Intelligence Service, MI6, to provide information to the British government. Voigt had certainly moved in circles where 'Red influence' was prevalent, but it was for professional and patriotic reasons. He had drawn attention many times to the growing dangers of Nazism. After Hitler's rise to power he went back to London as the *Guardian*'s diplomatic correspondent, and was often invited by the BBC to give talks about current affairs.

In 1938, the year after the *Mail* attacked him, he wrote a book called *Unto Caesar*, in which he put Nazi Germany and the Soviet Union on a par with each other as dangerous totalitarian states. Ten years later, after the Second World War, Voigt irritated George Orwell by publishing a book called *Pax Britannica*. This suggested that the British Empire should be supported because it was a bastion against Communism in Asia and Africa; Orwell called this 'neo-toryism'. Altogether, Voigt scarcely resembled the picture that F.W. Memory had painted of him in the *Daily Mail*: a left-wing firebrand who was trying to propagandize the British people by means of a worryingly pliant BBC. The unnamed MPs who were supposed to be raising the issue in the House of Commons do not appear to have done so.

A couple of days later the *Mail* had another bite at the cherry, quoting among others the Revd D.S. Buchanan-Allen, from South Devon: 'Permit me to welcome your loyal and courageous attack upon the menace of the Red bias on the radio. The propaganda of its pink Bolshevism has attained the persistency and wide distribution of a grave public scandal.'

After that, the *Mail* went quiet on the subject for a while. Why did it raise it in the first place? No doubt it did indeed receive plenty of letters of complaint; but newspapers receive angry mail all the time, and usually ignore it. In this case, though, it is hard to ignore the possibility that Lord Rothermere himself, or someone close to him, heard Voigt's broadcast, was as enraged by it as the Revd Buchanan-Allen, and insisted that the *Mail* should run an across-the-board attack on the BBC as a result. Rothermere was known for his outbursts, but they usually faded after a while; this was probably one of them. What did not fade was his settled support for Hitler, Mussolini and Franco.

Yet if the *Mail*, and everyone else, had only known it, there was indeed an active, dedicated Communist who was working away in Spain for the British press: not for the *Guardian* or the BBC, but for *The Times*. Its correspondent there was Kim Philby.

Philby, son of the domineering explorer and Arabist Henry St John Philby, was already a Communist sympathizer by the time he reached Trinity College, Cambridge, in 1930. One of the dons there, Maurice Dobb, helped him to serve his chosen cause by putting him in touch with a crypto-Communist organization. He worked for a section of the Comintern in Austria, and was recruited by Soviet intelligence. By 1936, after working for a while on a small liberal magazine, the *Review of Reviews*, which was intended to draw a line under his Communist past and give him a neutral political persona, he was instructed to infiltrate a pro-Nazi organization in Britain, the Anglo-German Fellowship. It numbered various socialites, businessmen and politicians in its membership; Winston Churchill nicknamed it 'the Heil Hitler Brigade'. Some months later, in February 1937, Philby's controller ordered him to go to Spain under the cover of being a freelance journalist. The London *Evening Standard* took him on as a stringer, and so did a German magazine called *Geopolitics*: not pro-Nazi, but conservative in tone.

Franco's agents in London gave him introductions to various figures on the Nationalist side, and the plan was that he should infiltrate Franco's headquarters. It has never entirely been established whether his Communist controllers were trying him out to see if he had the toughness of mind to assassinate Franco himself, or whether they simply wanted him to send back information so that someone else could do the job. Philby could be remarkably cool in a crisis. He carried his Soviet code on a piece of ricepaper in his pocket, and in April 1937 was arrested by the Civil Guards in Córdoba. Three men searched his bags with the greatest care, then turned to search him. He threw his wallet on the table in such a way that it fell on the floor, and all three men bent to pick it up. As they did, Philby screwed up the ricepaper and swallowed it.

When he returned to London the following month, his Soviet handlers decided he was not the sort of person to entrust with carrying out an assassination. Instead, they ordered him to join a leading British newspaper, in the hope that this would make him more attractive to British intelligence as a recruit. His father helped him to get a job on *The Times*, covering the war in Spain, and he was soon back there.

Philby's reporting was intelligent and insightful – the more so, since his sympathies were wholly different from those his readers might have imagined. Like a novelist, he was creating a character, 'Our Madrid Correspondent': uncommitted, unemotional, unexceptional, even while he was reporting things that privately gave him real pain. (When he drove into Barcelona, which had just been captured by Franco's forces, he described it later as 'the worst time of my life'.) He was not a gifted writer, and his style was heavy and clumping. This, for instance, is the opening paragraph of a despatch published as a page lead in *The Times* of 21 September 1936:

> Señor Casares Quiroga and his Cabinet, who were in office at the time the new Spanish revolt broke out, were walking a tight-rope suspended over a cauldron of unrest, into which increasingly violent blasts of opposition and controversy threatened to precipitate them.

The desire to taunt his true ideological enemies, even if only surreptitiously, was strong. Perhaps his NKVD handlers, as they read this paragraph, felt a twinge of anxiety:

> Prisoner of its Marxist associates, the Quiroga Cabinet was not free to defend a truly Parliamentary regime, although it did all in its power to maintain the appearances; and gradually there formed the 'political confusion' which Lenin indicated as the propitious moment for a supreme effort by the masses. It remains to be seen what the masses will do with it.

It was dangerous to quote knowledgeably from Lenin's writings, but Philby, throughout his clandestine life, enjoyed taking risks. During the course of his career as a double agent, Philby enjoyed throwing out subtle, easily deniable hints about his true allegiance. After the Second World War, in his office at MI6, he displayed a framed photograph of Mount Ararat, straddling the border between Turkey, on the Western side, and Soviet Armenia; the photograph was taken from the Soviet side.

But the risks Philby liked to take were intellectual rather than physical. He always preferred to sit in an office and write about policy and trends, rather than go and see what was happening on the ground.

Nevertheless he scored some remarkable successes as a correspondent: not least during the battle for Teruel.

The city is noted for its harsh climate. At the end of 1936, Vicente Rojo, one of the Republican government's most effective generals, staged an offensive there to relieve the pressure by Franco on Madrid. It turned out to be one of the worst winters Spain had ever suffered, and many soldiers simply died of cold. Unusually for him, Philby drove down to Aragon on 31 December 1936 to see the scene of the battle, together with several other journalists, two American and one British: Richard Sheepshanks, one of Reuter's best correspondents, Edward J. Neil of the Associated Press, and Bradish Johnson, the young and newly arrived correspondent of *Newsweek*. They were in a convoy with several other press cars, and had stopped soon after noon in the main square of the village of Caude, a few miles from Teruel, to wait for another car to catch up with them.

The group were sitting in their car, smoking, when a stray long-range shell fired from the Republican side landed right in front of them. Shrapnel was sprayed everywhere. The other three were killed or seriously injured, yet such are the strange ways of high explosive that Philby suffered nothing worse than a minor head-wound.

In a clear and dignified report on the battle, written in Saragossa on the afternoon of 2 January 1937, and published the following morning, Philby wrote first about the battle he had witnessed.

> The combatants are fighting under terrible conditions. Friday and Saturday were days of snowstorms and of bitter winds sweeping the plains. At night shelter is scarce, and most of the troops are sleeping in the open air under greatcoats and rugs. In spite of such hardships the Nationalists appear cheerful, which speaks very highly for their moral [sic] and discipline.

The Times carries three other brief reports from other correspondents in Spain after this, and then runs Philby's account of what had happened after the shell landed.

> Your Correspondent was able to leave the car and cross the square to a wall where a group of soldiers was sheltering.

Thence he was taken to a first-aid station, where light head injuries were speedily dressed.

Meanwhile Spanish Press officers worked gallantly in an attempt to rescue the other occupants of the car regardless of falling shells.

Johnson, in the driver's seat, was already dead. Sheepshanks was still breathing, but was so badly injured in the face and head that he died a few hours later.

Mr Neil was fully conscious when taken to a first-aid station at Caude on a stretcher, and showed concern about the fate of his typewriter. His leg was fractured in two places, and later 35 pieces of shrapnel were removed from it. He was taken to Saragossa and operated on. Gangrene had set in and he died at midday today.

Is this just the calm, stiff-upper-lip account of a man who for his own reasons has to watch his words and emotions with the greatest care? Or is there a faint touch of callousness to it – in the line about the typewriter, for instance? Later in his life Philby seemed to have no conscience about dispatching dozens of men to their deaths at the hands of Stalin's agents. Perhaps even in the square at Caude he felt that all this was part of the grand Marxist sweep of history. Because of his injury, Philby was decorated by Franco in March 1938, and treated with respect and interest. It was all very useful in building up his 'legend' as a conservative-minded journalist. Afterwards he wrote, 'My wounding in Spain helped my work, both journalism and intelligence, no end – all sorts of doors opened for me.' The dispassion is total.

§

In August 1937 the Nazi government in Germany expelled the *Times* correspondent, Norman Ebbutt. It was something the paper's editor, Geoffrey Dawson, had long striven to avoid. In his official history of *The Times*, published between 1935 and 1952, Stanley Morison, a conscientious objector and gifted typographer whose criticisms of the old-fashioned appearance of *The Times* resulted in his being commissioned to recast its entire look in 1932, claimed that Dawson had censored Ebbutt's reports to avoid trouble with the Nazi regime. Yet the chief foreign subeditor at the time, G.L. Pearson, who was personally opposed to appeasement, maintained that this was not true: he said that Ebbutt's reports were printed exactly as he wrote them, and others on the staff agreed.

Whatever the precise truth, it is a fact that the Nazis were intensely angry with *The Times*. In the spring and summer of 1937 the German press and radio were full of virulent attacks on Britain and British journalism, particularly that of *The Times*.

But the Nazis' fury against *The Times* was not due to anything Norman Ebbutt or anyone else had reported from Germany. Instead, it stemmed entirely from a report from Spain in April 1937, four months earlier, by another *Times* journalist, George Lowther Steer, about the bombing of Guernica. The American journalist and historian Herbert Southworth, who was the leading authority on Spain at the time, described it as probably the most important piece of reporting during the entire war.

Dawson had published Steer's despatch, even though he must have known it would infuriate the Hitler regime. In a letter to H.G. Daniels he wrote: 'No doubt they [the Nazi authorities] were annoyed by Steer's first story of the bombing of Guernica, but its essential accuracy has never been disputed, and there has been no attempt here to rub it in or harp upon it.'

Dawson supported the Nationalist forces of General Franco, like most conservative-minded people in Britain and the rest of the world. But he certainly did not question the accuracy of the report by his correspondent with the Republican forces in Bilbao, George Lowther Steer, about the bombing of Guernica. Nor did he try to stop it being published. Dawson might have been one of the loudest voices of appeasement, but he knew a good news story when he saw one, even if it was likely to offend Adolf Hitler. He ran the best newspaper in the world, not a propaganda sheet.

Steer was born in South Africa in 1909, and was sent to Britain for a classic upper-middle-class education at Winchester and Christ Church, Oxford. After working for the *Cape Argus* and the *Yorkshire Post* he applied to *The Times*, which sent him to Abyssinia in 1935 to cover the expected invasion by Mussolini's forces. There he met and worked with Evelyn Waugh, a correspondent for the *Daily Mail*. Waugh was six years older than Steer, and already a well-known and highly successful novelist ('about as good a novelist as one can be while holding untenable opinions,' George Orwell said of him, with his usual precision) but, in the complex scale of British snobbishness, Waugh was inferior to Steer in a number of ways. Waugh had been educated at Lancing School and Hertford College, Oxford: neither of them regarded then as good as Steer's school and college. Waugh's reporting was louche and second-rate compared with Steer's; and although the *Mail* was a great deal livelier than *The Times*, no one would have thought it a better paper.

But Waugh was British, while Steer was merely South African. Waugh had an unconcealed contempt for Abyssinians and a patronizing sympathy for Mussolini's Fascists; Steer took up the cause of Abyssinia and Haile Selassie, and revealed that the Italian air force were using poison gas against the local population. Waugh resented all this, and when he came to write *Scoop*, his magnificent satire on journalism, Steer has a spitefully drawn, walk-on part. He is immature, over-educated and has a ludicrous, faintly Afrikaans-sounding name:

> Mr Pappenhacker of The Twopence, was playing with a toy train – a relic of College at Winchester, with which he invariably travelled. In his youth he had delighted to address it in Latin Alcaics and to derive Greek names for each part of the mechanism. Now it acted as a sedative to his restless mind.

Waugh did not want to run the risk that the identification would not be made. There was no mistaking the newspaper Mr Pappenhacker wrote for. *The Times* cost twopence: more than any other London newspaper.

In reality there was nothing of Pappenhacker about Steer; instead, he was the romantic ideal of the foreign correspondent. Just before he was thrown out of Abyssinia by the Italians, Steer married the beautiful and sensuous daughter of a Spanish father and an English mother, Margarita de Herrero y Hassett, who was in her late thirties, ten years older than he was; less than nine months later she died giving premature birth to a stillborn baby. (Curiously, Steer's second wife, Esme Barton, who fell in love with him at Margarita's funeral, had also been lampooned by Waugh in his earlier comic novel *Black Mischief*; she was 'Prudence Courteney', the carelessly promiscuous daughter of the foolish British ambassador in what was clearly Abyssinia. After the book was published Esme Barton flung a glass of champagne at Waugh in an Addis Ababa nightclub.)

Just as Steer had adopted the cause of Haile Selassie in Abyssinia, so he adopted the cause of the Basques in Spain. They responded in kind, giving him a minesweeper to take him to France when he was told the news of his first wife's death. He buried her at Biarritz, on the Spanish border, then returned immediately to work. Now he was more committed than ever to the Basque cause, and, with no interest now in his own safety, he spent long hours in the most dangerous sections of the front line, with the soldiers he increasingly identified with and liked. 'A journalist is not a simple purveyor of news,' he wrote; and indeed, his work would soon turn into the journalism of advocacy and commitment.

Nevertheless, his most important despatch was a model of calm and objective writing. On 27 April 1937 he and Christopher Holme, a Reuter's correspondent, were driving to Guernica and had reached the nearby village of Ambacegui when six German Heinkel planes attacked it. Steer and Holme lay in a bomb crater while some of the Heinkels flew over repeatedly machine-gunning them. Back in Bilbao that evening they had dinner with a group of other correspondents, including Noel Monks of the *Daily Express* and Mathieu Corman, a Belgian journalist who worked for a pro-Republican newspaper in Paris.

A Basque official, visibly upset, came in and told them that Guernica was on fire. Some of the journalists round the table decided to wait till morning, but Steer and the other three, though they were all tired, decided to make the fifteen-mile car journey back to Guernica. From fifteen miles away the night sky was lit up by the fires. They arrived at eleven o'clock, to find the local people and Basque soldiers still trying to dig out the bodies of the dead. Steer immediately started interviewing survivors, who told him in detail what had happened. He found the tubes from three German incendiary bombs, and having got his story took them back to Bilbao.

Holme's despatch for Reuter's, sent that night, was picked up by several British newspapers the following day, Wednesday 28th; but an agency report, crisply worded, precise and factual, rarely has the same impact as a much longer and more detailed despatch of a newspaper's own experienced correspondent; especially if, like George Steer, he is writing with passion about the things he has seen. Holme had an entire day's advantage over Steer, but afterwards had the grace to accept that Steer's report was much better than his own. Back in Bilbao, Steer had a decent night's sleep, then turned to write an article which remains one of the classics of twentieth-century reportage.

He himself maintained later that *The Times* was unhappy with his story, and several writers, taking their cue from him, have said that Dawson, the editor, ran it only reluctantly. That may well have been the case, though as we have seen Dawson had no doubts about its truth. Nor about its significance: it was displayed prominently, on the editorial page rather than the main foreign news one. It begins as the last column on the right and turns over to a later page. It certainly was not hidden away in any sense, and that day's second editorial, strongly and sympathetically worded, was devoted to Steer's revelations. Dawson may have been nervous about offending German opinion, and he may have taken a line over the Munich Agreement which has been justly and almost universally condemned; but on 28 April 1937 he seems to have done Steer justice in presenting his story.

THE TRAGEDY OF GUERNICA

TOWN DESTROYED IN AIR ATTACK
EYE-WITNESS'S ACCOUNT

From Our Special Correspondent
BILBAO, April 27

Guernica, the most ancient town of the Basques and the centre of their cultural tradition, was completely destroyed yesterday by insurgent air raiders. The bombardment of this open town far behind the lines occupied precisely three hours and a quarter, during which a powerful fleet of aeroplanes consisting of three German types, Junker and Heinkel bombers and Heinkel fighters, did not cease unloading on the town bombs weighing from 1,000lb. downwards and, it is calculated, more than 3,000 two-pounder aluminium incendiary projectiles. The fighters, meanwhile, plunged low from above the centre of the town to machine-gun those of the civilian population who had taken refuge in the fields . . .

At 2 a.m. to-day when I visited the town the whole of it was a horrible sight, flaming from end to end. The

> reflection of the flames could be seen in the clouds of
> smoke above the mountains from 10 miles away . . .

By the early years of the twenty-first century, the deliberate destruction of purely civilian targets has become commonplace. Sometimes, it seems, civilian targets are the only ones selected. But in 1937 this particular refinement had the power to shock civilized people in a way that is hard for us now to grasp.

In the form of its execution and the scale of the destruction it wrought, no less than in the selection of its objective, the raid on Guernica is unparalleled in military history. It was not a military objective. A factory producing war material lay outside Guernica and was untouched. So were two barracks some distance away. The town lay far behind the lines. The object of the bombardment was seemingly the demoralization of the civil population and the destruction of the cradle of the Basque race.

The writer of the editorial which appeared on the same page agreed. He clearly sympathized completely with George Steer's viewpoint.

> In a neighbouring column a Special Correspondent with the
> Basque forces describes the destruction of Guernica by
> GENERAL MOLA'S German aircraft. It is a tragic story – the
> pitiless bombardment of a country town, the centre of
> Basque tradition and culture, by an air fleet which en-
> countered no resistance and did practically no damage to
> the scanty military objectives beneath it. The planning of
> the attack was murderously logical and efficient. Its aim
> was unquestionably to terrorize the Basque Government
> into surrender by showing them what Bilbao may soon
> expect.

The response was immediate. The head of Franco's foreign press bureau, Luis Bolín, declared that Basque activists had dynamited the town themselves. Set out in black and white, the claim seems absurd; and yet under similar circumstances it has been a first instinctive reaction by pressure groups and governments down the years, from the Algerian war to Northern Ireland, from Sarajevo to the invasion of Iraq, and from the invasion of Lebanon to the invasion of Gaza: the victims did it to themselves, in order to gain international sympathy. The second instinct, which again is habitual, is to try to damage the character and professional abilities of the journalist involved; this is by no means something invented by modern politicians. Right-wing British literary figures like the quarrelsome, difficult Douglas Jerrold, ultra-Catholic and ultra-Conservative, attacked Steer. So did Arnold Lunn, a Catholic who opposed Hitler but supported Franco.

On the morning of 28 April Steer received a cable from *The Times*:

VIEW OTHER SIDE'S DISMISSAL YOUR GUERNICA STORY
FURTHER JUDICIOUS STATEMENT DESIRABLE.

Grand organizations like *The Times* of the 1930s, which seem so forbidding and monolithic from the outside, are usually prey to deep anxieties. They are constantly afraid that their high reputation for accuracy and reliability will be undercut by a moment's inaccuracy and unreliability. As a result, however robustly they seem to respond to external criticism, they are timorous and uncertain. They do not altogether welcome exclusive reports like Steer's Guernica despatch; on the contrary, such things make them nervous. Why haven't other organizations got the same story? How can we be certain we are right? Might it not have been better for us to have waited until others reported it as well?

The text of *The Times*' foreign desk's cable has the faint reek of all this, like a nervous sweat. The fact that the Reuter's correspondent had witnessed what Steer did, and reported very much the same thing, should have been enough for the anxious editors at Printing House Square. By cabling Steer they were merely advertising their own lack of confidence. Yet to a practised eye it is clear that they are not themselves in any real doubt about Steer's exclusive. The word 'judicious' is meant as an oldmaidish joke. They are merely covering their own backs.

Steer, at twenty-seven, probably didn't understand any of this. He dashed off an angry statement which *The Times* published on 29 April. It gave detailed evidence for the Germans' guilt, and ended: 'That they bombed and destroyed Gernika [sic] is the considered judgement of your correspondent and what is more the certain knowledge if that is possible of every wretched Basque civilian who was forced to suffer it.'

Steer was worried that *The Times* might be too scared to publish this, and sent a copy to his friend, the Labour MP and Basque supporter Philip

Noel-Baker, urging him to make use of it. Yet it duly appeared the following day in *The Times*, in a prominent position. A week or so later Steer had to write another rebuttal of the Franco camp's denials, but on 15 May he was able to quote the logbook of a German pilot who had just been shot down near Bilbao to demonstrate that he had taken part in the bombing of Guernica.

Throughout the episode *The Times* had behaved nervously but not particularly badly. By this stage, though, Steer had had enough of its timorousness, and wanted to be much more outspoken in his support for the Basques than *The Times*, with its anxieties about the reactions of the Francoists, the Germans and their British fellow-travellers, would allow. He also wanted to write a book about Guernica and its destruction, and needed to get it done quickly. He was neither sacked, as some right-wingers suggested at the time, nor 'let go', as has often been suggested since. He and *The Times* no longer felt entirely comfortable with each other, and it was probably a relief to both of them when he left.

A leading *Times* journalist, Thomas Cadett (later a distinguished BBC correspondent), took him into his apartment in Paris, and Steer began the writing of *The Tree of Gernika*, which sold extremely well and was praised by a range of people including Martha Gellhorn, who advised her friend Eleanor Roosevelt to read it. Not everyone approved of it. George Orwell, in reviewing it, wrote: 'Mr Steer writes entirely from the Basque standpoint, and he has, very strongly, the English standpoint of being unable to praise one race without damning another. Being pro-Basque, he finds it necessary to be anti-Spanish . . .'

Orwell was certainly correct about his writing from a pro-Basque standpoint; Steer even used the words 'we', 'us' and 'our' when talking about the Basque forces. He was an exemplar of what a famous war correspondent later in the century, Martin Bell, called approvingly 'the journalism of attachment'.

As war with Germany came closer and finally arrived, George Steer was able to exercise the journalism of attachment without worrying about his editors back home. He reported on the Russo-Finnish War and the behaviour of the Italians in North Africa, and Haile Selassie, from his first great enthusiasm over Abyssinia, attended his marriage to Esme Barton and was godfather to their son. Steer was effective in getting the British to support Haile Selassie with a successful campaign to drive the Italians out of East Africa, and played an important part in it himself. Steer, now in the Intelligence Corps, drove in a loudspeaker van at the head of the emperor's victorious column as it entered Addis Ababa.

He was a successful soldier, and rose to the rank of lieutenant colonel, leading a psychological warfare campaign in Burma against the Japanese. And then, on Christmas Day, as he was driving some of his men to a sports ground after lunch, he turned his jeep over and was killed at the age of thirty-four. *The Times* published an affectionate obituary of its wayward son, while his good friend Thomas Cadett, writing in the *New Statesman* on 3 February 1945, called him 'an adventurer who was never out for himself, only for a cause'.

His reporting of the atrocity at Guernica was a fine example of accurate, passionate journalism, which drew the attention of the entire world. Soon, it had another, wholly unpredictable result. It was reprinted in full in the French Communist Party's daily newspaper, *L'Humanité*, on 29 April 1937, and Pablo Picasso read it. He was working at the time on a mural commissioned by the Republican government in Madrid for the Spanish display at the 1937 World's Fair in Paris, and had been making preliminary sketches of a model for it. But he was transfixed by Steer's article, and changed his entire concept. Eleven feet tall and twenty-five feet wide, his painting shrieked his anger at the atrocity at Guernica. It is, perhaps, his most famous painting.

Steer's report was a first-class piece of journalism, but so many towns and cities would be deliberately destroyed from the air in the decades to come that the bombing of Guernica might well not have been remembered. Picasso's painting ensured that it would never be forgotten.

11

ABDICATION

It was on 10 January 1931 that the dashing but curiously weak and inadequate Prince of Wales, whom his friends and family called David, walked into the drawing room of a country house at Melton Mowbray, as the guest of Lady Thelma Furness, an American with whom he had a brief affair, and met another member of the American colony in London: Mrs Wallis Simpson. Her friends called her Bessie.

She was thirty-four, he was almost exactly two years older, and it seems to have been love at first sight. She had been married twice; her first husband was a drunk, and in breaking up with him she had a much-noted affair with an Argentine diplomat and was finally divorced in 1927. Her second husband, Ernest Aldrich Simpson, was the son of an English father and an American mother, and the following year she came to London, where he managed his family shipping business, to marry him. Less than three years after, she met the Prince of Wales and would later start an affair with him.

By 1935 he had become wholly dependent on her, and could not bear to be away from her. Members of his household staff, even those who were fond of him, found it deeply embarrassing. As the health of his father, George V, deteriorated, he decided that Mrs Simpson must be his queen – even though she herself would almost certainly have settled for a morganatic marriage, and perhaps even for no marriage at all as long as she could remain with him. From the moment when his father died on 20 January 1936 and he succeeded him as King Edward VIII, it became his only real concern.

Until that point, only the new king's immediate social circle knew of the intensity of his affair with Mrs Simpson. Beyond that, plenty of people knew what was going on but assumed that Mrs Simpson was nothing more than what would have been called at one time a *maîtresse en titre*: his main, but not necessarily sole, mistress. Her presence wasn't hidden; on the contrary, many of the Court Circular columns in *The Times* and the *Daily Telegraph* mentioned her name and that of her complacent husband when they reported the activities of the Prince of Wales. But no newspaper, in Britain or in America, where the fascination with the story was intense, reported that there was anything between the pair. But the hints were there from the start, for those who knew what lay behind the stories.

As early as 11 March 1935, *Time*, which reported obsessively on the Prince of Wales with a particularly grating tweeness, published a reference to her:

> To get busy with . . . the Silver Jubilee, Edward of Wales was recalled last week from Vienna and Budapest where he has been sporting with a mixed party of twelve gay friends featuring charming, horsy, Baltimore-born Mrs. Simpson and her aunt.
>
> In Budapest graceful Mrs. Simpson startled Hungarians with a dinner coat of multi-colored woven and spun glass, [and] danced the Gypsy Czardas with H. R. H., a single enormous diamond sparkling in her hair.

Yet at this stage there was no indication to outsiders that his affair with her was any different from all the semi-public affairs he had had over the years with other women, many of them older than he was.

By 8 June 1936, the Prince of Wales had become king and *Time* was enthusing pointedly again:

> For socialite gossips, the event of the week was a formal dinner given by Edward VIII in his rooms in St. James's Palace. Guests listed in the Court Circular included:
>
> Mrs. Ernest Simpson, the former Wallis Warfield of Baltimore, Md., known to the world press as King Edward's favorite dancing partner, his companion on numerous holiday excursions.

A week later, *Time* reported that someone at the *Daily Mirror* had decided to break the story in Britain about the king's female guests. According to *Time*, it appeared in the first edition, but before the 3 a.m. edition – when the intention was to accompany it with a photograph of Mrs Simpson

holding a little dog – but the decision was taken to kill it. There is no
mention of this in the semi-official history of the *Mirror*, written by the
Labour MP and author Maurice Edelman; but *The Mirror: A Political
History* is distinctly obsequious, and always puts the best construction on
everything the *Mirror* did.

Newspapers on the Continent were also starting to report the
relationship between the king and Mrs Simpson, after they took a cruising
holiday off the coast of Croatia in mid-August. From time to time they
would disembark and go shopping. Mrs Simpson would speak to the
shopkeepers in German, which some of them understood. On 31 August
Time reported:

> The King on his Balkan holiday last week went about with
> Mrs. Simpson and his other guests taking pictures with a
> small German camera. Once when a police-man seized a
> camera from a press photographer who was snapping King
> Edward, His Majesty intervened. Taking the camera away
> from the policeman, Edward VIII handed it to the camera-
> man, saying with a grin, 'Here, take your camera back.'
> Trunks belonging to His Majesty were labeled inconspicu-
> ously with his incognito 'Duke of Lancaster' but great
> capitals fully six inches high proclaimed the trunks of MRS.
> ERNEST SIMPSON.

Stanley Baldwin, who was planning to retire as prime minister after the
king's projected coronation, had already tried to tell the king that sailing
down the Yugoslav coast so openly with Mrs Simpson would be a mistake; but at the end of August the American press quoted a British
journalist, Robert Seeds, whose father was an ambassador (this seems to
have given it more credibility), as reporting that the king had said, 'Look
here, if you don't stop it, Baldwin, I won't attend your beastly old
Coronation.'

No mention of any of this appeared in the British press. There was a
rigid self-denying ordinance, brokered by Lord Rothermere and Lord
Beaverbrook, and agreed to by the owners or editors of every other
newspaper in the country, not to refer to the affair with Mrs Simpson in
any way. Eight years later, on 7 July 1944, George Orwell wrote about it
in the left-wing magazine *Tribune:*

No bribes, no threats, no penalties – just a nod and a wink and the thing is done . . . Weeks before the scandal officially broke, tens or hundreds of thousands of people had heard all about Mrs Simpson, and yet not a word got into the press, not even into the [Communist] Daily Worker, although the American and European papers were having the time of their lives with the story. Yet I believe there was no definite official ban: just an official 'request' and a general agreement that to break the news prematurely 'would not do'.

In reality there was not even an 'official' request: none was necessary. Beaverbrook and Rothermere thought it up between them, and every other newspaper was so tame, so scared of breaking ranks, that it kept to the pact long after it should have been necessary.

Beaverbrook was a strong supporter of the king, as was Winston Churchill. The staff of the *Express* were ordered on pain of dismissal not to write or print anything that would alert the British public to what was going on. The paper published a photograph of the king standing on the deck of the royal yacht. In the original, Mrs Simpson was standing close beside him; but the picture was doctored so that she did not appear.

Because the Press Association and Reuter's news agency were part of the circle of silence, the BBC, which could only report what the news agencies told it, said nothing either; though it is wholly unthinkable that the BBC would have broken the story at that stage, even if it had not been shackled by controls over its news reporting which the newspapers had insisted on. The BBC was, as ever, more nervous even than the press, especially when dealing with the royal family.

Thomas Jones, familiarly known as 'T.J.', who had been deputy secretary to the Cabinet under four prime ministers including Baldwin, and was once described as 'one of the six most important men in Europe', wrote to an American friend of his on 12 December, after the news had broken: 'There was "a gentleman's agreement" which kept the affair out of our Press while it was raging with you and elsewhere . . . Even the *Daily Worker* was behaving properly.'

An agreement that could keep the main Communist newspaper in Britain silent about a scandal which could potentially wreck the monarchy was a very powerful one indeed.

W.H. Smith's and other retail newsagents at first sold copies of American newspapers and magazines with the offending paragraphs carefully cut out with scissors. By October, however, that became impossible. *Time* concentrated heavily on the story and was therefore more affected by the censorship than most, and retaliated on 9 November with its now habitual snideness:

> Newsstand sales in the British Isles are the virtual monopoly of a Pickwickian middle-class firm on the walls of whose offices hang life-size portraits of members of the family who died for Queen (Victoria) & Country. It was not a matter of direct government censorship last week but of Pickwickian family pride that for the first time all sales of U. S. newspapers and magazines which mentioned King Edward and Mrs. Simpson abruptly ceased in England.

By that stage it was clear to everybody who knew about it that this was not simply another affair of the king's, but something that would affect both the constitution and his own position. In early October the New York magazine *Town and Country*, which was read by the kind of wealthy people who knew or identified with Mrs Simpson, commented: 'The King is proud of her. Anyone bold enough to object to her being at the royal table would be quickly disgraced.'

It claimed, though without citing any evidence, that the king had given her jewellery worth a million dollars, and added:

> In shipping $50,000 worth of this year's finest U. S. silver fox pelts to a 'royal purchaser' in London last week, the Manhattan fur export firm's owner Julius Green hinted: 'Some people take it for granted these silver foxes are a gift to Mrs. Simpson.'

This was quite a hint.

By 12 October *Time* and others were reporting that Ernest Simpson, originally the complacent but now increasingly wronged husband, had transferred his clothes from the flat he had shared with Wallis, and moved them to the Guards' Club, while she was due to move into a house in Cumberland Terrace, a Nash building on the eastern side of Regent's Park in London. There was scarcely anything, in other words, which newspaper readers in Canada, the United States and the leading countries of Europe did not know about the private life of Edward VIII; and yet millions of people in Britain were still not allowed to know anything whatever about their king, his mistress, and the constitutional crisis that lay just ahead.

It seems at first sight to be a straightforward clash of cultures: Britain, stodgy and more than a little repressive, seeing nothing wrong with keeping its people in the dark, while America, brash and free-spirited, insists on the right to tell absolutely everything. Yet it wasn't like that. In its attitude to the story, the American press was strictly divided along class lines, with the newspapers and magazines which reflected the views of the upper class showing a marked reluctance to say anything about it. The first clear reference in the *New York Times* to Mrs Simpson as the king's lover came only in October, when it carried an article based on a briefing from a senior British official – no doubt the ambassador in Washington. The *New York Times* wrote it up as follows:

> There is nothing furtive in His Majesty's relationships with his friends. He considers his private life a thing apart from his kingship. This attitude, unusual in a King, has been so distorted by mystery and ill-founded rumor that it has placed these three persons [Edward VIII, Mrs Simpson, and her husband Ernest] in an invidious position.

After the news finally broke in Britain, one of the most famous journalists in America, Walter Lippman, congratulated the British press in his column in the *New York Herald Tribune* for the fact that nowhere in the British Isles had any newspaper or magazine yet coupled the names of the king and Mrs Simpson:

> The reticence of the British press cannot be put down to an effort of the King to suppress knowledge of his regard for Mrs. Simpson. The true explanation is that the British press is forbidden by a recently enacted law to make a public spectacle out of any divorce case. It may print only the bare facts of the legal proceedings.

There was no truth in this whatever; Lippman simply made it up. But it reflected his sense that it was much better to keep the country's dirty laundry out of sight, rather than show it to the world.

Someone he would probably have regarded as being neither his equal socially nor journalistically, Westbrook Pegler of the *New York World-Telegram*, several levels below the *Herald Tribune* in class terms, quickly put him right:

> They do have their laws in England, but if a story is big enough an English paper can go ahead and print it – and get away with it . . . The present case is the greatest divorce story in the history of journalism . . . Moreover, the English are thorough masters if not the inventors of the 'I hear' and 'they say' school of journalism, the questioning innuendo and the sly hint which get the story across without laying it on the line, and they could handle this one in that familiar technique . . . One can only decide that in the present case the press of England has lifted its cap to a fast grounder and let it roll to the outfield to cool off.

Even for those who don't speak baseball, the meaning is clear enough.

There were rumours that the leading banker J.P. Morgan had asked American newspaper and magazine editors on behalf of the king's brother and sister-in-law, the Duke and Duchess of York, to keep quiet about the news. (The duke would soon become King George VI as a result of Edward's abdication.) The great banker's sister, Anne Morgan, who obviously belonged to America's upper class, told the editor of the magazine *New York Woman* that she was resigning from the magazine's editorial advisory board because an article in it had described the king as being 'infatuated' with Mrs Simpson; even though that was a statement of fact, and she as a friend of the king and Mrs Simpson must have known it.

The twenty-eight titles in the newspaper empire of William Randolph Hearst, which together had a readership of more than 20 million, also played the story down or openly censored it, but for a very different reason. In October 1936 Hearst arrived at St Donat's Castle in the Vale of Glamorgan, which he had bought after seeing a photograph of it in *Country Life*. (When George Bernard Shaw was invited there, he famously commented, 'This is what God would have built, if He had had the money.')

Hearst's plan was to stay there for at least a month and crack the story of the king's relationship with Mrs Simpson himself. In order to position himself properly for this, he had already instructed his newspapers to ignore all news items about the king and Mrs Simpson to the best of their ability. As a result, his various correspondents, working away in London, found to their frustration that their reports were cut down or failed to appear altogether.

Hearst had decided that the one important question was whether Edward actually intended to marry Mrs Simpson, or simply regarded it as a meaningful affair which could never be officially acknowledged. This is a question which hindsight shows to have been unnecessary, and if Hearst's links with the monarchy were as strong as he sometimes implied, he would have known the answer already.

Eventually, his efforts achieved a result of sorts. The king would not discuss the matter with him, but his assistant private secretary, Sir Godfrey Thomas, was allowed to give him a lengthy briefing; and on the basis of this Hearst chose to believe that the king had personally authorized him to reveal the truth about his feelings towards Mrs Simpson. Hearst wrote the story himself at St Donat's in early November, and it was dictated to New York with instructions that it should be printed on the front page of all his daily newspapers. There is something both elephantine and slightly ludicrous about his writing style – an affliction which newspaper barons often seem to suffer from:

> Within a few days Mrs. Ernest Simpson, of Baltimore, Md., U. S. A., will obtain her divorce decree in England, and some eight months thereafter she will be married to Edward VIII, King of England.
>
> King Edward's most intimate friends state with the utmost positiveness that he is very deeply and sincerely enamored of Mrs. Simpson, that his love is a righteous affection, and that almost immediately after the Coronation he will take her as his consort.
>
> It is stated definitely that King Edward is convinced that this is both the right thing to do and the wise thing to do.
>
> He believes that it would be an actual mistake for a King

of England to marry into any of the royal houses of the
Continent of Europe, and so involve himself and his empire
in the complications and disasters of these royal houses.

Hearst's further insights were completely off the mark:

King Edward will marry Mrs. Simpson in the private chapel
of Buckingham Palace. The marriage, which will take place
several weeks after the King's coronation next May, will be
performed by one of the chaplains to the King.
    Before the marriage takes place Mrs. Simpson will be
made a peeress in her own right. After her marriage to His
Britannic Majesty she will also take one of his ducal titles,
becoming the Duchess of Lancaster or the Duchess of
Cornwall, probably the former.

Yet he was not the only American to get it all profoundly wrong. The
New York Times was if anything worse:

The King is known to be strongly attached to Mrs. Simpson,
to whom he admits he owes much. She has given him new
confidence in himself, and it is said he now no longer views
with aversion the idea of matrimony. But informed circles
stress that if he does marry, the bride will not be Mrs.
Simpson, although he will remain Mrs. Simpson's friend.

The informed circles of the New York *Daily News* agreed.

King Edward VIII will marry a hand-picked Princess and not
Mrs Wallis Simpson, after all. The King and Commoner
interlude has ended, and London believes that Edward was
breaking the news tonight to his American sweetheart at a
rustic rendezvous far from Buckingham Palace. Any of six
princesses whom he might have married, but ignored, will
be chosen as the next Queen of England.

There is something reminiscent in all this of Evelyn Waugh's eternally
accurate 'novel about journalists' *Scoop*, which was published two years

later, in 1938. Wenlock Jakes, the great American journalist, is working on his book *Under the Ermine*, about political and social life in Britain: "'I shall never forget", he typed, "the evening of King Edward's abdication. I was dining at the Savoy Grill as the guest of Silas Shock of the *New York Guardian*. His guests were well chosen, six of the most influential men and women in England . . .'"

They are of course nothing of the sort: the wife of a publisher, a boring journalist from the *News Chronicle*, an insurance agent, and a woman described as 'the Mary Selena Wilmark of Britain'. Not one of them voices any opinion about the abdication. "'There, in a nutshell, you have *England*, her greatness – and her littleness." Jakes was to be paid an advance of 20,000 dollars for this book.'

October was a particularly difficult month in Britain. MPs were starting to complain privately about the number of letters they were getting from their constituents, complaining about the news they were hearing from abroad about the king and Mrs Simpson. British journalists who wanted to do their job properly found it particularly hard. Although Mrs Simpson sued her husband for divorce on Tuesday 27 October, it was still impossible to write anything about it – or about the wider issues.

An American cartoonist, John Tinney McCutcheon, published a drawing in his paper, the *Chicago Tribune*, showing Edward VIII as Prince Charming kneeling in front of Mrs Simpson as Cinderella, and finding that her foot fits his jewelled slipper. In the background John Bull is telling a man representing British journalism to keep quiet. The journalist is tearing his hair and saying: 'Ye gods! The biggest news story in the world – and I've got to sh-h-h.'

The *Evening Standard*'s cartoonist David Low was equally frustrated, and went off on a tour of North and South America. Beaverbrook had issued specific orders that he should not draw anything about the subject. On 9 December, after the news of the affair had broken and the king had abdicated, Low gave vent to some of his frustration by drawing a cartoon for the *Standard*, captioned 'Difficult Days For Low', in which he showed himself being locked into a steam-bath by Beaverbrook. A headline on a newspaper in the corner reads 'Restraint Is Absolutely Necessary'.

A particularly fierce cartoon which he drew the previous week, captioned 'The Wallace Collection' and showing paintings of Mrs Simpson's first two husbands, with another of the king hanging beside them, was intended to appear on Friday 4 December. It didn't. Even though the scandal of the king's relationship with Mrs Simpson had been revealed by that point, Beaverbrook would not allow anything critical of Mrs Simpson or the king to appear.

Journalists showed their frustration in other ways. The *Daily Telegraph*, for instance, angered by the way American newspapers condemned the British press for its silence, hit back rather gratuitously by pointing out that the press in America almost never told the people that their president was confined to a wheelchair. 'Actual view of the President's disability never fails to surprise the public,' the *Telegraph*'s man in Washington wrote. He went on,

> Neither the reporters nor the photographers have prepared them for it. The crowd invariably falls silent when Mr. Roosevelt moves down the ramp, and gives an enthusiastic cheer of relief when he reaches the bottom. Secret Service men will seize any camera that shows this incident or the President getting into a motor car, and will tear out the film. Their right to do so appears doubtful, but nobody so far has ever questioned it.

From 20 October onwards journalists and photographers from the *New York Times* and virtually every other American newspaper began arriving in Ipswich for the hearing of Mrs Simpson's divorce action against her husband. The town's two leading hotels were completely booked out. The smallest details were recorded, in this case by the *New York Times*:

KING'S FRIEND IS GUARDED
Edward's Personal Protector, A 200-Pound Detective, Keeps Watch on Mrs Simpson

The divorce action was heard a week later, but there was still no mention of its relevance to the king in the news pages of the British press, even though more and more people in Britain were starting to hear about it on the grapevine. Yet they did not, for the most part, hear how well Wallis Simpson was behaving under these difficult circumstances, offering again and again to leave him, and coming close to doing so by November. Nor did they hear of the anonymous death-threats which she often received.

Claud Cockburn, the brilliant, wayward, dedicated Communist who had founded and edited the gossip-sheet the *Week*, later described this period in his memoirs with precision:

> The newspapers were victims of a more than usually painful attack of discretional lock-jaw. They were determined to show responsibility, delicacy, restraint and the Best Possible Taste if it was the last thing they did before total paralysis gripped them. In the suffocating silence the trend was running strongly against the King.

The *Week* consisted of nothing more than a few typed and mimeographed sheets, written and produced by Cockburn himself, whose range of friends and acquaintances was as legendary as his wit. Cockburn was able to boast by 1936 that eleven foreign ministries, Buckingham Palace, and virtually all the embassies in London subscribed to it. Based originally on *Le Canard enchaîné*, the French satirical magazine, and started with a capital of £50, the *Week* shone with Cockburn's wit and knowledge of European and American politics.

It has often been suggested that the *Week* broke the news in Britain of the king's relationship with Mrs Simpson. It almost did, but not quite. The left-wing politician and writer John Strachey was the friend of a friend of Lord Louis Mountbatten, who was an avid reader of the *Week* and an adviser to King Edward. Mountbatten believed that if the story of the king's love for Wallis Simpson were made public, it would bring about a big upsurge in support for the king; in the last few days of November he asked Cockburn through Strachey if he were prepared to publish the facts.

> I was rather far from being a passionate champion of the monarchy, but the atmosphere of pompous discretion was almost unbreathable, and anyway it looked as though whatever happened we should have a lot of fun . . . I accepted, of course.

Cockburn prepared to print a special edition of the *Week* to accommodate the announcement. To make sure that the police couldn't interfere with the delivery of the copies through the post, he asked twenty or so friends to be ready to pick them up from his tiny office in Victoria Street, and deliver them personally. A couple of typists were on stand-by, the duplicator was serviced, two friends waited to put the finished copies into envelopes. All that was needed now was the information from Mountbatten via Strachey. At eleven that night Cockburn received a phone call to say there was a delay, but that the material would arrive before midnight.

Shortly before one, a despatch rider brought round a small envelope containing a single sheet of paper. On it was typed these words: 'The situation has developed too fast.'

Strachey had also passed the same question from Mountbatten to Kingsley Martin, the editor of the left-leaning literary magazine the *New Statesman*, and like Cockburn Martin was enthusiastic. The king even asked to see a draft of the article Martin would write; but in the end, as happened with Cockburn, the king cried off.

It is difficult to understand why the *Week* or the *New Statesman* wrote nothing about it, independently of the king. Neither the government nor the police had imposed the ban on reporting about the king's affair; the 'discretional lock-jaw' which Cockburn attacked so wittily was entirely self-induced. So why should a gossip-sheet which was completely outside the pale of conventional journalism share the general silence? Perhaps it was just a failure of nerve on Cockburn's part. His memoirs say nothing of his reasons for failing to break the story; only this: 'But for a good many months I could devote very little time to it. The Spanish War had broken out.'

It sounds a distinctly feeble excuse. The brilliant gadfly of British political and social life seems to have suffered just as much from the general lock-jaw as everyone else.

In the end it was someone altogether removed from public affairs and high society who broke the silence, without any idea of what he was doing. At fifty-seven, Dr Alfred Blunt was the serious-minded yet rather innocent High Church Bishop of Bradford. He held strong views about the evils of unemployment and the need for the rich to help the poor, which got him into trouble with Conservative MPs. Unusually for a bishop, he believed that the Church of England should be disestablished.

At the start of November, a well-known Anglican maverick, the Bishop of Birmingham, had argued that the coronation of the new king should no longer be a Communion service, and should be turned into a secular ceremony. Bishop Blunt took strong exception to this view, and started to write a speech condemning it, which he planned to make at his annual diocesan conference at the start of December. Two weeks before, on the afternoon of Tuesday 17 November, the Archbishop of Canterbury, Dr Cosmo Lang, invited all the Anglican bishops in the British Isles to a secret meeting at Lambeth Palace. There he broke the news to them that it would not be suitable to prepare for a religious coronation, since the king was spending a great deal of time in the company of an American woman who was twice divorced, and whom the American press openly called 'the Queen-designate of England'.

This came as a great shock to the less worldly, more retiring bishops at the meeting; men like Dr Blunt of Bradford. By contrast, the better-connected Bishop of St Albans had gathered together an album of cuttings about the king and his mistress from the American press, and showed it to Blunt, who was duly scandalized. Blunt then rewrote his speech for the diocesan conference. Most of it was still about the need for the coronation to be a Communion service, but he couldn't resist adding that the religious effectiveness of the coronation would depend

> on the faith, prayer and self-dedication of the King himself; and on that it would be improper for me to say anything except to commend him ... to God's grace ... We hope that he is aware of his need. Some of us wish that he gave more positive signs of such awareness.

Blunt began speaking soon after the conference opened. A local reporter, Ronald Harker from the Bradford *Telegraph and Argus*, was covering what must at first have seemed like a very dull event. Suddenly he pricked up his ears: it was unheard-of for anyone, especially a churchman, to criticize a reigning monarch. Harker took careful notes, and back at the office he went over them carefully with a colleague. Together they decided that this was a story which would interest the Press Association in London, and put it on the wire.

At five that afternoon, the charming, far-sighted (if occasionally irritable) Duff Cooper, Secretary of State for War, caught a train back to London from Leeds, where he had been talking to students at the University about the need to start training for the coming war. He had bought a couple of local evening papers at the platform newsagent's, and idly turned to them during the journey. They both carried the Press

Association story prominently, but left out the key passage about the king. Cooper knew all about the scandal, naturally, but was stunned that it should have become public in this odd way. 'I suppose,' he later wrote in his autobiography, *Old Men Forget*, 'it was the first time in the century that the Sovereign of Great Britain had been openly rebuked.'

Yet at this point, on the afternoon of Tuesday the 1st, the bishop's attack was limited to the news pages of a couple of provincial papers, and there was still no hint of what the king was supposed to have done. This became public by another route. Bishop Blunt had thoughtfully sent an advance copy of his speech to the Bradford office of the *Yorkshire Post*. That day, Arthur Mann, the *Post*'s editor, was down in London to discuss the scandal with Geoffrey Dawson, the editor of *The Times*. His deputy back in Leeds sent the text of the speech to him, and Mann read it that afternoon. He immediately assumed that someone in authority, probably the Archbishop of Canterbury, had put the bishop up to making the speech. 'I thought the time had come for the silence to be broken and the issue squarely faced,' he said later. Like other leading journalists at the time, he managed to turn his previous silence and sudden nervous decision to go with the story into an act of journalistic principle. Instead, it seems clear he did it only because he felt it would be safe to do so, since one of the nation's most important figures was in favour.

So Mann settled down and wrote an editorial for the next morning's *Post*:

> Dr Blunt must have good reason for so pointed a remark. Most people, by this time, are aware that a great deal of rumour regarding the King has been published of late in the more sensational American newspapers ... But certain statements which have appeared in reputable United States journals, and even, we believe, in some Dominion newspapers, cannot be treated with quite so much indifference: they are too circumstantial and have plainly a foundation in fact.

The *Post* had the story to itself at this point; it was too late by this time for the London dailies to comment on it. But by the morning of Thursday the 3rd the story was finally out in the open. Harold Nicolson, then an MP, wrote that day in his diary, 'The storm breaks.' The serious papers were against the king, and most of the popular ones, including the Beaverbrook titles, supported him.

The *Daily Mirror* was to become the loudest of all in his favour, but in the early hours of that morning this was not obvious. The first two editions were printed with no reference at all to a story which was now clearly in the public domain; it seems that the chairman of the group, John Cowley, who disliked the paper's increasing tabloid excesses, had told the staff that the *Mirror* should avoid it for the time being. But the editorial director, Harry Bartholomew, with whom he had a mutual rivalry, turned up in the office in his pyjamas and took control. Bartholomew was an aggressive, highly competitive man, who had deliberately driven the paper down-market and raised its sales accordingly.

The third edition of the *Mirror* during that long night revealed that the prime minister, Stanley Baldwin, had had an audience with the king the previous day, discussing 'urgent and political matters not connected with foreign affairs'.

There was even a mention of 'grave issues', though that told no one anything. It was only at 3.53 in the morning, too late for the edition to reach large parts of the country, that the *Mirror* finally ran the story, together with a photograph of Mrs Simpson, under the awkwardly printed headline

THE KING WANTS TO MARRY MRS. SIMPSON: CABINET ADVISES 'NO'

THE KING, THE 'DAILY MIRROR' UNDERSTANDS, HAS
TOLD THE CABINET OF HIS WISH TO MARRY MRS. SIMPSON,
AMERICAN-BORN SOCIETY WOMAN NOW LIVING IN
LONDON. THE CABINET HAS ADVISED AGAINST IT.

Far from revealing anything about the nature of the relationship, or the background to it, the *Mirror*'s front-page report describes how Baldwin had driven to Buckingham Palace ('by car', it adds helpfully) and had been shown in to see the king for a meeting lasting an hour and forty minutes. So although the *Mirror*, like the rest of Fleet Street, had built up large amounts of information about the king's relationship with Mrs Simpson, it still held back from telling its readers most of what it knew. Nevertheless, by Saturday 5 December it had swung powerfully

behind him, putting GOD SAVE THE KING! on its front page and
bellowing

TELL US THE FACTS, MR. BALDWIN!

In fact, Baldwin had told the House of Commons the basic facts the
previous day: that there was no legal possibility under English law for
Mrs Simpson to become a 'morganatic' wife for the king, as some people
had suggested as a way out of the problem. If the king married her,
Baldwin said, she would automatically have the full status of queen, in
spite of the fact that she would be twice divorced. To prevent her being
queen, a law would have to be passed; and neither the Commons nor the
governments of the Dominions would allow that to happen. If the king
went ahead and married Mrs Simpson, the implication was, the
government would fall and there would be a full-scale constitutional
crisis. It is hard to see what more Baldwin could say than he had already
said: the position was completely clear.

Perhaps the noise the *Mirror* was making was intended to distract
attention from its total silence up to the point when someone else
accidentally revealed the truth. It was no more courageous, no more on
the side of the people against the establishment, than *The Times*, which
had been just as slow to tell its readers what was happening, and now
condemned the king publicly for his actions. The *Mirror*'s leading
columnist Cassandra (William Connor) wrote what was, even for him, a
particularly violent and largely fact-free attack on just about everyone
except the king himself:

> I ACCUSE!
>
> I am writing about what I regard as the biggest put-up
> job of all time. I accuse leaders of the Church of England of
> putting our King in a position from which it was almost
> impossible to retreat. I accuse the Prime Minister and his
> Government of manoeuvring, with smooth and matchless
> guile, to a desperate situation where humiliation is the only
> answer.

But in spite of the support his cause received from the *Mirror*, the *Mail*
and the *Express*, the king abdicated only eight days after the story of his

relationship with Mrs Simpson had reached the public. It had happened as a result of an odd combination: an unworldly churchman, a reporter from the Bradford *Telegraph and Argus*, and the editor of the *Yorkshire Post*, all of whom had misunderstood some part of what they were setting out to do.

Mrs Simpson left the country almost as soon as the news broke, and went to Cannes. Edward was finally persuaded that he could not marry her and remain king; and on the last day of his reign, Friday 11 December, Edward made a live radio broadcast for the BBC from Windsor Castle. He was introduced by the director general, Sir John Reith, as 'His Royal Highness, Prince Edward'. In order to read his very brief introduction, Reith had to sit in the chair in front of the microphone, then stand up and allow Edward to sit down in his place. As he did so, Edward kicked the table leg, and the noise was picked up by the microphone. Long afterwards, in a famous interview with Malcolm Muggeridge, Reith said that several journalists, hearing this over their radios, reported that Reith had gone out and slammed the door in disgust.

The broadcast was brief and dignified; Edward's script had been checked and improved by his supporter and friend, Winston Churchill. Many of those who heard him in Britain and around the world found it impossible to forget the unaffected way in which he spoke of his inability to do his job without the support of the woman he loved. His reign had lasted 327 days, and was the briefest of any English monarch since that of his namesake, Edward V, in 1483.

Seventeen years later, in 1953, the fiery Hugh Cudlipp, a Welshman whose two elder brothers were both editors of national newspapers, and who had edited the *Mirror*'s Sunday equivalent before becoming the group's editorial director, published a history of the *Mirror*; he gave it the characteristically buccaneering title *Publish and Be Damned!* Even though he had seen the reality of the *Mirror*'s approach to the Abdication Crisis from the heart of the *Mirror* group, he managed to give the impression that it was the *Mirror* which had broken the story of the king's affair with Mrs Simpson, deliberately crashing through the psychological barriers set up by timid editors and staff in the rest of Fleet Street. He spoke of '[t]he *Mirror*'s decision to end the secrecy and publish the facts' when in fact the *Mirror* had been just as reluctant to do these things as the rest of the press were: and not just the stodgy, old-fashioned, conservative papers, but also the *Daily Worker* and even the innovative, lively and supposedly subversive journal the *Week*. In the preface to *Publish and Be Damned!*, Cudlipp writes '[T]his is the exciting story as one man has seen it, told so far as he is aware without prejudice or rancour, and above all he hopes without humbug.'

Yet the notion that the *Daily Mirror* somehow behaved in a braver and more honest fashion than the other British newspapers during the build-up to the Abdication Crisis was completely false. This was one of the most dispiriting episodes for good reporting in the entire twentieth century. Every single British newspaper abrogated its duty to tell people what was really going on, because its editor thought it would be intrusive, distasteful, disloyal, or damaging to do so.

Even the brashest of newspapers experienced an excess of politeness and good manners during those months of silence, and in doing so they managed to epitomize the hypocritical, mealy-mouthed, head-in-the-sand approach which characterized so much about Britain in the 1930s. In the long run, keeping quiet about the king's affair and pretending it wasn't happening did nobody any good: the country least of all.

And afterwards, to maintain that they had done the right thing when they knew they hadn't was, to use Hugh Cudlipp's expression, humbug.

12

APPEASEMENT

The attempt to control and intimidate the British media, rather than simply influence it, began not with Tony Blair, nor with Margaret Thatcher, nor even with Harold Wilson, though each of these three introduced new and increasingly aggressive approaches. The first British prime minister to use the techniques of outright press manipulation was Neville Chamberlain. This does not, of course, fit the view that posterity has of Chamberlain; we think of those hawklike yet somehow foolish features, the morning-coat and high wing-collar, the ever-present umbrella, and he seems to us like an elderly Edwardian innocent who has wandered out and got lost.

The reality was different. He was fiercely cold and autocratic, and ran his government by sheer toughness of character. Yet he did not begin like this. James Margach, a lobby correspondent for half a century, said that when he first knew Chamberlain, 'he was the most shy, kindly, generous-minded and warm-hearted of men, always friendly and understanding although by nature cold, indrawn and lonely.'

Chamberlain, as the son of Joseph Chamberlain, was not a natural Conservative; on the contrary, he was strongly influenced by the essentially radical political opinions of his father. He was a born social reformer. Health care for all, slum clearance, pensions for the old and sick – these were the issues which mattered most to him. But chance and politics had led Joseph to the Conservative Party, and his son stayed there. Like so many men just too old to fight in the First World War, Neville Chamberlain hated war (his cousin, to whom he was as close as a brother, died on the Western Front).

He first learned the techniques of news management when he was Chancellor of the Exchequer under the relaxed, rather lazy Stanley Baldwin. Baldwin allowed him to brief the political correspondents.

When Baldwin resigned in 1936 Chamberlain took over; yet he carried on briefing the press himself.

It seemed to him that with the great powers rearming and at each others' throats, the essential questions of social reform at home were being ignored. What was needed, he believed, was something the Foreign Office was too set in its ways to achieve: a deal that would answer Hitler's territorial demands and allow Britain to get back to raising the living standards of its own people.

Chamberlain was impatient, tough-minded and sudden-tempered: an old man in a hurry, who understood that neither time nor public opinion was on his side. He was not remotely attracted by Hitler or Mussolini, as many leading people in British public life were. Figures from Lloyd George to Sir Nevile Henderson, the British ambassador in Berlin, had stars in their eyes when they met Hitler, but neither Chamberlain nor his close ally, the Earl of Halifax, had any time for him at all. (It was mutual; according to Christopher Andrew's history of MI5, *The Defence of the Realm*, Lord Halifax was shown an MI5 report which revealed that Hitler had referred to Chamberlain as *ein Arschloch* – an arsehole. Halifax underlined this three times in red and is thought to have shown it to Chamberlain himself.) Chamberlain and Halifax saw Hitler simply as the man they had to come to an arrangement with, if a second and even more devastating world war were to be avoided. By the last few weeks of 1937, their strategy was beginning to come to fruition.

§

On the afternoon of 10 November 1937, in the London streets, the placards advertising the *Evening Standard* carried details of an important scoop:

LORD HALIFAX FOR GERMANY

The story wasn't the lead: that was devoted to the sudden death of the former prime minister, Ramsay MacDonald, on a voyage to South America. But there was no doubting the significance of the second lead.

> The 'Evening Standard' understands that plans are being
> made for Lord Halifax, the Lord President of the Council, to

visit Germany in the near future. He will have an interview
with Herr Hitler. It is proposed that Anglo-German relations
should be discussed.

Anthony Eden, the Foreign Secretary, thought it would look as though
Halifax was running after Hitler. The Foreign Office was thoroughly
against doing deals with the dictators. Chamberlain took no notice. That
evening, at a dinner for the 1922 Committee of Conservative back-
benchers at the Savoy, there were loud cheers when he confirmed that
Halifax was going to Germany.

Who had leaked the story to the *Standard*? The natural assumption
was that someone senior in the Foreign Office had tipped off the paper,
perhaps in the hope of stirring up feeling against the trip; it could well
have been Rex Leeper, the head of the News Department.

Chamberlain addressed the Lord Mayor's banquet at the Guildhall
in London and dropped a very broad hint that future agreements would
be better pursued by informal discussion rather than public declaration.
He would, he said, abstain from saying anything further. It may be that
the *Standard*'s correspondent asked Rex Leeper of the Foreign Office
News Department what Chamberlain had meant, and that Leeper told
him, off the record, knowing that it would help the Foreign Office's
approach if it were made public.

Nowadays such leaks happen every day of the week, and are not
usually worth discussing in detail. But in November 1937 factions within
the government were learning to conduct their debates on the most
important issues of the day through the press. As Eden and his associates
saw it, Chamberlain's domineering, undiplomatic methods obliged them
to operate in new ways. Lloyd George and Baldwin had both used the
press to leak details of their plans and even to discredit members of their
governments; but this was the first time anyone had, as the phrase would
one day have it, 'leaked back'.

On 12 November, the *Standard*'s senior stablemate, the *Daily Express*,
printed another story that may well have come from the Foreign Office;
most likely from Rex Leeper. The decision to send Halifax to Germany
had, the *Express* said, 'been made without consulting the Foreign
Secretary, who knew nothing of the proposal until he saw it in the
newspapers' – that is, presumably, in the leaked report from his own
official in the *Standard*.

The next day, Saturday 13 November, the *Standard* came up with another exclusive. At first sight it seemed to justify the decision for Halifax to visit Germany.

HITLER READY FOR TRUCE
NO COLONIES DEMAND FOR TEN YEARS

The British Government have information from Berlin that Herr Hitler is ready, if he receives the slightest encouragement, to offer to Great Britain a ten-years' 'truce' on the Colonial issue. During the 'truce' the question of Colonies for Germany would not be raised. In return for this agreement Herr Hitler would expect the British Government to leave him a free hand in Central Europe.

This was clearly wrong. Hitler never hinted at any such thing, and had probably already guessed, with his sharp nose for political weakness, that the Chamberlain government would eventually let him do what he wanted in Europe.

It was possible, of course, that Chamberlain's advisers thought that a deal along these lines was feasible, and that this suspicion had been hardened up a touch, either by the briefer or by the correspondent who wrote the story. But the most likely explanation is also the most Machiavellian: that the briefing came from Leeper or someone else at the Foreign Office who knew the Germans would be infuriated by such a suggestion, and might refuse to receive Halifax as a result.

The response from Germany was certainly angry. A statement from the official Nazi Party press agency, the NSPK, called it 'the height of sensation-mongering' and said it was deliberately intended to poison the atmosphere – which it may have been. Perhaps, the statement said, it might be better to postpone any visit by Halifax. The British ambassador, Sir Nevile Henderson, who had been accused by British politicians of being too supportive of Hitler, believed the *Standard* had got the story from a Foreign Office contact, and told Eden so. He also said he believed Hitler himself had drafted the statement attacking the story. Eden wrote back denying that anyone in the Foreign Office was against Halifax's visit. Leaking stories to the press was not the FO's way of doing things, he said. Neither statement was true.

Chamberlain was furious, and hit back in kind. His chief press secretary, George Steward, spoke to senior journalists on the *Daily Telegraph* and *The Times*, stressing the damage the *Standard* had done to Halifax's mission. On Tuesday 16 November both newspapers did what was expected of them. The *Telegraph* called the *Standard* article 'an inexcusable indiscretion . . . ill-timed and mischievous . . .' The diplomatic correspondent of *The Times*, who also used the word 'mischief', said the story was 'quite unfounded speculation'; which it was.

In spite of Berlin's anger an excuse had been found for Halifax to visit Germany: an international exhibition organized by the German hunting association and patronized by Goering, the Reichsjägermeister, or 'Reich hunting master' of Nazi Germany. Halifax, despite his withered arm, was an enthusiastic foxhunter. He arrived in Berlin on Wednesday 17 November, and was shown round the exhibition with great respect. When the visit ended, on Friday, the *Evening Standard* seemed anxious to make up for its much-criticized exclusive three days earlier with a pious vote of confidence for Halifax's trip: 'The idea that Britain will play a merely passive and defensive part in discussions with the German government is a preposterous misunderstanding of the position.'

But the *Standard*'s cartoonist, David Low, took an altogether different and more scathing view on the same page. Hitler, looking (as usual in Low's work) absurd and pompous at the same time, has linked arms with an even more absurd Halifax in baggy tweeds with a mangy lion sheltering behind him. He is showing him his hunting trophies on the walls – animal heads with 'Weimar', 'Versailles' and 'Locarno' on them. But Halifax, his legs shaking, is looking round at three more plaques on the walls which are empty – and presumably reserved for Austria, Czechoslovakia and Poland. 'Nazi Hunting Exhibition', reads the caption.

David Low was a New Zealander, a broadcaster and writer as well as a draughtsman. Lord Beaverbrook persuaded him to join the *Standard* in 1927, and gave him nearly half a page for his cartoons. Low's price, apart from a sizeable amount of money, was set out in his contract: he would have 'complete freedom in the selection and treatment of subject-matter for your cartoons and in the expression therein of the policies in which you believe'.

Beaverbrook stuck by the agreement, even when Low caricatured him as a grinning mannikin of a Pilgrim Father, travelling to America in the foolish hope of getting help for Britain in the war with Germany. British politicians learned to put up with his shrewd assaults: the looming, awkward Halifax, the decorative but spineless Anthony Eden, the smug and almost invariably wrong-headed Chamberlain, portrayed with an umbrella as his head and a beaky nose as the handle.

But his savage cartoons of Mussolini and Hitler caused the most trouble. Low never lost an opportunity to remind readers of the reality behind Fascism. The paper was banned in Italy and Germany. During his visit to Berlin, Halifax had to endure complaint after complaint about Low. Goebbels even had an album of the most offensive of them, and brandished it at him.

Back in London, Halifax told Beaverbrook about the problem. On the roof terrace of his flat, with Hyde Park stretching out before them, Halifax explained that every Low cartoon about Hitler was shown to the Führer himself. 'Do I understand you to say', Low asked, 'that you would find it easier to promote peace if my cartoons did not irritate the Nazi leaders personally?' Halifax said he would.

For a while, Low avoided drawing Hitler and Mussolini ('Hit and Muss', as he called them) individually. He amalgamated them into a character called 'Muzzler', with Mussolini's round face and blue chin and Hitler's quiff and toothbrush moustache. Later, after the collapse of Halifax's and Chamberlain's efforts, Hitler and Mussolini returned in their full glory. Low's name was on the list of people in British public life the Gestapo had orders to arrest after the German invasion of Britain. The British government offered him a knighthood as early as the 1930s, but he turned it down. It was only when the offer was renewed in 1962, a year before his death, that he finally accepted.

In the *Standard* of 19 November 1937, the day Halifax left Berlin after the International Hunting Exhibition, Low's cartoon showing Hitler displaying the empty plaques for further heads caused a serious problem. The editor, Percy Cudlipp, chose to distance the paper from its cartoonist; the editorial alongside read:

> Low is a great cartoonist to whom the 'Evening Standard' allows independence of expression. And, as our readers know, the political opinions of Low often differ drastically from those of the 'Evening Standard', as expressed in its leading articles . . . The foreign policy of Mr Chamberlain . . . is based not upon fear or upon weakness, but upon realism.

It was the ferocity of Chamberlain's Downing Street machine that had obliged the *Standard* to undercut its own cartoonist. This ferocity arose, not from a sense of power, but from a sense of weakness. Chamberlain and Halifax knew how little support they had in the country for their policy of appeasing Hitler. They were determined to force the policy through by pressurizing the newspapers. When Eden resigned as Foreign Secretary in February 1938, unable to take any more of Chamberlain's negotiations behind his back, and was replaced by Halifax, it was a particularly dangerous moment for the prime minister.

The Institute of Public Opinion carried out three polls showing how tenuous the government's support really was. In February, in reply to the question 'Do you believe Mr Eden was right in resigning?', 71 per cent said yes, 19 per cent no, and 10 per cent didn't know. In answer to the question 'Do you favour Mr Chamberlain's foreign policy?', 26 per cent said yes, 58 per cent said no, and there were 16 per cent don't knows.

In March, the question was: 'Should Great Britain promise assistance to Czechoslovakia if Germany acts towards her as she did to Austria?' 33 per cent said yes, 43 per cent said no, and 24 per cent (an extraordinarily large percentage, which in itself indicated anxiety) didn't know.

No previous prime minister had ever tried to manage the news in such a way, even in wartime. Chamberlain grasped the inner weaknesses of the lobby system, of the newspapers, and of the BBC with a ruthlessness only paralleled in the past thirty years. He understood that many editors and lobby journalists were flattered by his attentions, and would forgo their objectivity in exchange for membership of an inner circle to which he confided his views and plans. In reply, they would repeat these things in their articles.

Chamberlain appointed a career civil servant from the Forestry Commission, George Steward, as press officer. Steward knew his place, and never answered any questions at all if he could help it. James Margach from the *Sunday Times* once asked him when Chamberlain was going on a trip to the North of England. 'Don't ask me that,' Steward snapped. 'It's a state secret.'

Chamberlain used two close friends as his enforcers, to make warning calls to journalists and their employers. One was Sir Horace Wilson, who was nominally a Downing Street adviser on industrial relations. The other was Sir Joseph Ball, a former policeman and MI5 official who had been appointed head of the Conservative Research Department and had planted agents at Labour Party headquarters. Chamberlain targeted political correspondents of the Conservative press, and converted them to his views. Journalists are by instinct outsiders, onlookers, yet many have a hunger for approval which can make them obedient and pliant.

The lobby correspondents of all the newspapers received their briefings twice a day from George Steward. For a select few there were regular, sometimes weekly, briefings from Chamberlain himself. These took place over lunch in an upstairs room at St Stephen's Club, across from the Houses of Parliament.

Geoffrey Dawson, the editor of *The Times*, was particularly close to Chamberlain. Yet this was more because he shared Chamberlain's view that it was necessary not to irritate Hitler overmuch, than because he was under Chamberlain's thrall. The day before the Munich conference, in September 1938, Duff Cooper resigned as First Lord of the Admiralty, and gave his reasons in an impressive and moving speech which made a big impact on the House. *The Times'* parliamentary correspondent, Anthony Winn, reported it and described its effect on other MPs. Dawson spiked his report, and replaced it with one he wrote himself, by-lined 'From Our Lobby Correspondent'. He called Duff Cooper's speech 'a damp squib', and went on: 'Emotional gourmets had expected a tasty morsel but it had proved rather unappetising.'

The Times is nowadays seen as one of the chief engines of the British appeasement of Hitler in the 1930s. In each of the main crises of the decade, from the march into the Rhineland to the dismemberment of Czechoslovakia and even the crisis in Poland, *The Times* argued that peace in Europe could only be assured if Germany's resentment over its crushing punishment after the First World War were reversed.

Yet Dawson, whom Churchill's close ally Robert Boothby called 'the Secretary General of the Establishment, the fervent advocate of Appeasement', had not always believed that the European dictators should be appeased. *The Times* was fiercely opposed to Mussolini's invasion of Abyssinia in 1935, and attacked Chamberlain's willingness to give way to Mussolini's demands in remarkably savage terms. After the attacks in *The Times* the Foreign Secretary, Samuel Hoare, was forced to resign.

On the core issues, Dawson was a single-minded appeaser. He believed it would be a serious mistake to go to war with Germany over Czechoslovakia in 1938, and gave Chamberlain the full backing of *The Times* at Munich. This caused a crisis within the newspaper, since many of its staff disagreed profoundly. Yet by the end of 1939 and the beginning of 1940, Dawson had become one of Chamberlain's strongest critics, blaming him for not prosecuting the war with Germany more aggressively. In October 1939 he sacked Basil Liddell-Hart, the chief military commentator of *The Times*, on the grounds that he was too defeatist.

There was one editor who was even more favoured: a small, neatly dressed man of seventy, working-class by origin, who would slip into Downing Street, scarcely noticed, at 3.30 every Friday afternoon, for half an hour or more of private conversation with Chamberlain. William Waite Hadley, editor of the *Sunday Times*, was quiet, calm, and deferential, and was a personal friend.

Hadley was an unlikely person to edit a great national newspaper. He left his little village school at East Haddon, in Northamptonshire, at the age of twelve to work as a labourer. At night school he learned shorthand and joined the *Northampton Mercury*, where he showed a talent as a reporter. In 1887 he went to the *Rochdale Observer* as editor, and then, crucially, to the *Merthyr Times*, where he became firm friends with John Mathias Berry, a local estate agent and Liberal alderman. Hadley gave one of Berry's sons, William, a job on the *Merthyr Times*.

At the advanced age of fifty-eight Hadley was invited to London to be the parliamentary correspondent of the *Daily Chronicle*. It was then that he came to know Neville Chamberlain, who was still working his way up in politics. Six years later the paper merged with another, the *Daily News*, and Hadley, now sixty-four, was out of a job. It was then that his kindness to William Berry all those years earlier paid off. By now William Berry, as Lord Camrose, was editor-in-chief of the *Sunday Times*, and in 1931 he offered Hadley the post of assistant editor. A year later he was promoted to editor.

Hadley was passive and calm, not at all inclined to challenge Chamberlain. Week after week, the thoughts of Neville Chamberlain were faithfully transcribed and presented to the paper's readership by Hadley. Even though Lord Camrose was a staunch opponent of appeasement he allowed Hadley to back appeasement all the way.

§

By the end of 1937, Chamberlain was facing serious problems in his dealings with Hitler. He and Halifax had miscalculated: Hitler had no definite, clear-cut price in exchange for peace. Instead, he used the grievances dating back to Versailles to generate momentum for greater territorial claims. Chamberlain seems not to have understood Hitler's search for Lebensraum. He was frustrated by the lack of precision in his demands, without realizing that this was merely part of his negotiating technique.

The congenial little gatherings in St Stephen's Club were becoming less pleasant. Chamberlain had never liked taking impromptu questions, and the arrangements were becoming more rigid. He would now refuse to answer any question not sent to him at least four hours in advance. This meant no follow-up questions, no discussion, no exchange of views. Worse, the tone of the meetings was becoming sharper. Chamberlain had always been imperious, but now he could be short-tempered, even spiteful.

He began to hector the correspondents. James Margach, who attended the meetings, wrote that if someone asked about Hitler's treatment of the Jews or his record of broken promises, Chamberlain would express surprise 'that such an experienced journalist was susceptible to Jewish-Communist propaganda'.

> [W]hen asked a question which he resented he would attempt to snub a correspondent with frozen silence; after an eloquent pause, staring contemptuously at the questioner without saying a word in reply, he would turn aside, look in a different direction, and snap: 'Next question, please.'

If a journalist persisted, Chamberlain would ask him pointedly which newspaper he belonged to. It was an almost undisguised threat, as though Chamberlain were hinting that he could take the matter up with the journalist's editor if he felt like it.

There was one political correspondent at these briefings, from the *Yorkshire Post*, who could not be bullied in this way. The *Post* was solidly Conservative, but its editor, Arthur Mann, was strongly anti-appeasement. He himself was no great scholar, rarely wrote for the paper, and had only been abroad a few times in his entire life. But he was shrewd and well informed, and his chief leader writer, Charles Tower, was an expert on German affairs. Soon, Mann did what few others dared to do, and told Chamberlain that he was much too willing to go along with what Hitler wanted. Chamberlain was furious; but the *Yorkshire Post* was still represented at the lobby briefings.

There were no correspondents from the BBC at the meetings. At that stage the BBC had only a small news-gathering staff, and was still largely dependent on the news agencies. Right from the start, newspapers had been worried about how news broadcasting would affect their sales, and had persuaded successive governments to limit the BBC's freedom of action. Until 1928 it was not allowed to discuss any subject deemed controversial. John Reith, as director general, fought hard to break down these restrictions, but when he suggested broadcasting the proceedings of Parliament Lord Riddell, owner of the *News of the World*, told him, 'You are trying to take the bread out of our mouths.'

The BBC had had a bruising time during the General Strike of 1926, with Winston Churchill as Chancellor of the Exchequer in favour of taking the BBC over and obliging it to take government propaganda, and unions and Labour Party supporters angry that their views were not properly represented. During the crisis the BBC was allowed briefly to broadcast its own news (read by John Reith himself) and even to do its own news gathering. In the following year, 1927, a News Section was set up and began to edit its own bulletins when it was finally allowed to install a news agency tape-machine. By 1933 it had its first foreign correspondent, Vernon Bartlett, who provoked a flurry of complaints. Bartlett was strongly anti-Fascist, but he nevertheless argued that Hitler had the right to walk out of the disarmament talks in Geneva. Among the angry listeners who wrote in was Ramsay MacDonald: the first of a long list of British prime ministers who would take exception to some BBC news report and complain about it.

In theory, the BBC was free of government control. In reality, right from the start, it was subject to all sorts of pressures, and only managed to create a free space around itself by winning many key battles with successive governments, and by appealing to public opinion. But there were always problems. During the delicate negotiations with dictatorships like Germany and Italy, the BBC's reports by outside experts were often a source of anxiety. Nazi officials never believed – or at any rate claimed that they did not believe – that the BBC could speak about any significant subject without the British government's full knowledge and sanction.

As a result, even well-intentioned people at Westminster felt they had to make sure the BBC did not say things that would be interpreted in Berlin as representing British government policy. Rex Leeper, head of the Foreign Office News Department, was one. As early as February 1935 he minuted, 'We really must find some way of guiding the BBC's foreign comment more than we do.' When, early in 1936, it began planning a series of broadcasts on European affairs, a special Cabinet committee was convened on 30 March to discuss it. The minutes recorded blandly: 'It was decided to ask the BBC to refrain from arranging for independent expressions of views on the situation.'

The wording was accurate. The government could only ask the BBC; it had no power to order it not to broadcast the series, and in later decades the BBC learned that it could get away with refusing. But at this early moment in its existence, it acquiesced. Its charter was coming up for renewal, and if the government were angry enough it could perhaps have changed the rules so that the BBC was damaged.

In April 1937, with the situation deteriorating, the BBC wrote a memorandum to the government saying that it should be free to arrange discussions 'on all questions regarding foreign affairs which are freely discussed in the press'. It recalled a speech of Stanley Baldwin's in November 1936, which said that it took a democratic country two years to grasp an international situation properly; this, the BBC argued, seemed to imply 'a desire on the part of His Majesty's Government that the electorate should be better informed in regard to foreign affairs'. The BBC statement continued: '[T]he public – there is some evidence to show – suspect the existence of an official "censorship", and regret it.'

The memorandum achieved nothing; Chamberlain was more determined than ever to stifle alternative views. The public was right: an official censorship of a kind had been effectively imposed on the BBC. It was not total: the news was usually (though not always) untouched by it, and there were talks exposing the reality of Nazism and Fascism, as well as the methods and tactics of Franco's forces in Spain. But individual politicians and commentators who opposed Chamberlain's strategy, from Winston Churchill to Sir Oswald Mosley, found it very hard to get on the air. In January 1937, for instance, Winston Churchill told Lord Davies, who was urging him to start a campaign of speeches in favour of the League of Nations Union(a body set up to promote the aims of the League of Nations): 'If we could get access to the broadcast some progress could be made. All that is very carefully sewn up over here.'

The method of control over the BBC was simple enough: senior government officials would write or telephone a warning about some aspect of its coverage. This was usually successful, and there was rarely any need to specify any kind of sanction or punishment. In future decades, under Margaret Thatcher and Tony Blair, it came to be known inside the BBC as 'heavy breathing'.

In July 1938 Chamberlain's close associate, Sir Horace Wilson, who was notionally the government's chief industrial adviser, told the BBC to look at the opinions being aired in a series of thirteen talks called *The Past Week*. They were given by the writer and former diplomat Harold Nicolson, and had started out fairly light-heartedly. But as Hitler's threats towards Czechoslovakia over the Sudetenland became heavier, Nicolson's talks began to concentrate on the issue, and his tone became more serious. The series was popular, and attracted a good deal of positive comment, but soon the Foreign Office, too, started to object. In August someone from the BBC contacted Nicolson and asked him not to alarm the public. He wrote back: 'I feel strongly that the public at this juncture has got to be alarmed.'

By noon on Monday 5 September, when Nicolson had finished writing his script for that evening's edition, the BBC was so nervous that it was sent to the Foreign Office News Department for approval. Rex Leeper sent it to his boss, the Permanent Undersecretary, Sir Alexander Cadogan. Put in at the head of the Foreign Office in order to get rid of Sir Robert Vansittart, who was openly against Nazism, Cadogan went along with the policy of appeasement, though only up to a certain point.

He told the BBC that the Foreign Office would prefer that no talk at all should be given. The time was 3.30 in the afternoon. The executive asked if this was an instruction. The official who passed on the message said, 'The Foreign Office cannot instruct the BBC on a matter like this, but the recommendation is very strong.'

Nicolson was furious, but agreed to rewrite his script. When he showed it to his producer, it proved to be about how Nazi thugs had beaten up the Protestant Bishop of Rothenburg in front of his altar. The programme editor was thoroughly alarmed, and said this would be much too difficult to broadcast. Nicolson asked angrily what he should talk about that evening. Snatching at the first ideas that came into his head, the executive feebly suggested two things: either the Persian railway system, which Nicolson knew well, or Lord Halifax's recent speech about accommodation for foreign students in Britain.

By now time was getting alarmingly short; the talk had to be broadcast at five past ten that evening. Nicolson agreed to write one last script, but said he would walk out if this were rejected. The BBC must have been hugely nervous by now; but when the sheets of paper were handed over, it turned out that he had written about the rise in the price of milk to sevenpence a quart; as a gentleman farmer, he knew enough about it to talk for ten minutes on the subject.

Three days before, on 2 September, and eleven days later, on 16 September, two talks which the foreign correspondent Vernon Bartlett was supposed to have given on world affairs for *Children's Hour* were cancelled at the request of the Foreign Office. With the meeting at Munich very close now, no one wanted to take any chances; and the subject of Bartlett's talks, though the scripts are not to be found in the BBC's files, was almost certainly the Nazi threat to Czechoslovakia.

On 12 March 1938, the day of the Anschluss, when German troops marched into Austria, the BBC's reporting of it was brief and sounded as though it had been censored. There was a good deal of complaint about this within the BBC. The following week there was the usual programme review meeting, where the output of the previous seven days was discussed:

> In the light of evidence supplied by appropriate officials the BBC's general treatment of the Austrian crisis was examined and discussed ... Though Home Service News Department had supplemented the agency news in various ways, output had been limited ... partly owing to a 'ban' apparently imposed by the Foreign Office. Neither H.S.N.E. [Home Service News Editor] nor DT [Director of Talks] had been aware of the existence of this 'ban' ...
>
> Various members of Programme Board expressed curiosity as to the nature of the Foreign Office 'ban'; C(P) [Controller of Programmes] was not able to tell them whether the 'ban' had been directly imposed by the Government, or whether the BBC, acting on a hint from the Foreign Office, had not in fact imposed a 'ban' on itself. The vagueness of the arrangement was commented on.

The ban had indeed been imposed on itself. As an organization the BBC had become so spineless that it was scarcely necessary for the Foreign

Office to send a warning; it was an early example of what the political writer and BBC reporter Michael Cockerell has called the Corporation's 'pre-emptive cringe'.

No one seems to have instructed the BBC to keep Winston Churchill off the air; it did so of its own accord, knowing that his views were regarded by the government as dangerous. Many of these views were certainly reactionary; for much of the time his obsession was with India rather than the Nazi threat, and he called for a fiercer approach to the Congress Party and Mahatma Gandhi than any British government of the time would have adopted. It is easy to forget, after his triumphs in 1940 and later, how extreme Churchill could appear. He was yesterday's man, having played his part in worsening the British depression by insisting on a return to the gold standard when Chancellor. His aggressive approach to the General Strike had made him seem divisive, and he was still a hate figure to many people in the labour movement.

It was not only the BBC which wanted to silence him. Twice a week, from 1936 onwards, Churchill had written a column in Beaverbrook's *Evening Standard*. It was his most useful outlet, and although his views about the danger of Hitler in Europe were opposed to Beaverbrook's own, it was part of the ethos of the *Standard* and its sister-paper the *Daily Express* to allow contrary views in their pages. Yet it was impossible not to notice that Churchill's ideas clashed with those of the paper. When Joachim von Ribbentrop, handsome, aristocratic and moderate-sounding, was picked by Hitler to be his ambassador in London, the *Standard* wrote a gushing paragraph in Londoner's Diary of 27 October 1936:

> Herr von Ribbentrop brings many qualities to the task. He is an excellent host. He has a frank and genial manner. He speaks English both fluently and accurately.
>
> But he has one virtue which commends him especially to English people. He is sincere in his goodwill to this country.

In March 1938 the Beaverbook papers started putting a strapline on its front page which read 'There will be no European war'. Sometimes, when there was room, the words 'The Daily Express declares that Britain will not be involved in a European war this year, or next year either' would be added. Churchill believed there was bound to be a European war soon; he was certain that even with Chamberlain as prime minister it would not be possible for Britain to coexist with Hitler indefinitely.

Beaverbrook backed two horses at the same time. He believed that Britain needed far better defences than it possessed, and used his newspapers to campaign for more planes, ships and guns. Yet he enjoyed the society of Joachim von Ribbentrop and went to the 1936 Olympic Games in Berlin as his guest. He wrote articles for his own papers which supported the appeasement of German demands: 'What concern is it of ours whether the Germans in Czecho-Slovakia are governed from Prague or have their home rule?'

In private he had stronger and more reprehensible views. On 9 December 1938 he wrote to an American newspaper owner and a personal friend, Frank Gannett:

> The Jews have got a big position in the press here. I estimate that one third of the circulation of the Daily Telegraph is Jewish. The Daily Mirror may be owned by Jews. The Daily Herald is owned by Jews. And the News Chronicle should really be the Jews Chronicle. Not because of ownership but because of sympathy.

None of these assertions was true. It was simply that each of the newspapers Beaverbrook named was critical of Hitler. By the time he wrote this letter, he had got rid of Winston Churchill's *Standard* column. Nearly a year before, in February 1938, the *Daily Express* had attacked Churchill's support for Czechoslovak independence in the column, and his opposition to Hitler's threats in support of the Sudeten Germans. After that, in order to make sure his column would not be axed, Churchill muted the opinions he expressed in it. But as the crisis deepened, he began appealing to the *Standard*'s readers to support the Czech people. Eventually the editor, R.J. Thompson, wrote to tell him that the paper no longer wanted him to write for it: 'It has been evident that your views on foreign affairs and the part which this country should play are entirely opposed to those held by us.'

Churchill wrote back in great irritation to point out that David Low's cartoons were usually much more opinionated than his column: 'I rather thought that Lord Beaverbrook prided himself in forming a platform in the *Evening Standard* for various opinions including of course his own.'

Beaverbrook had an affection for Churchill; but it seems likely that Chamberlain had warned Beaverbrook that Churchill was damaging the chances of peace. It was a difficult argument to counter in 1938. Nevertheless, the *Daily Telegraph*, which was strongly anti-appeasement, took him on and gave him a better platform than he had had in the *Standard*. Churchill, characteristically, forgave his old friend Beaverbrook and, after coming to power, made him first Minister of Aircraft Production and later Minister of Supply.

Lord Rothermere, by comparison, was effectively a Nazi supporter, and although he never quite ordered his newspapers to follow the full range of his own opinions, the *Daily Mail* in particular came disturbingly close.

In July 1933, six months after Hitler came to power, Rothermere himself wrote an editorial for the *Mail* headlined 'Youth Triumphant': 'The minor misdeeds of individual Nazis would be submerged by the immense benefits the new regime is already bestowing upon Germany.'

These minor misdeeds already included the setting up of concentration camps at Dachau and Oranienburg, where prisoners started arriving on 31 March 1933. Probably, though, Rothermere means the beating up of Jews and Communists in the streets, and the smashing of Jewish-owned shops.

It was during 1933 that he began a correspondence with Hitler, which was fawning on Rothermere's side and cooler on Hitler's. They first met at the end of 1934, and Rothermere went back to Germany again and again. He appointed George Ward Price as the *Mail*'s correspondent in Berlin. Ward Price was careful that his reporting was exactly what the Nazi leadership would have wanted. He first wrote for the paper in 1906, when he was a student at Cambridge, and was appointed a foreign correspondent a year later. He wrote a strangely cold autobiography called, self-revealingly, *Extra-special Correspondent*, and another book called *I Know These Dictators*. This was no exaggeration. He interviewed Hitler and Mussolini several times, never apparently asking a single question to trouble them.

When German troops entered Vienna in March 1938 to a huge outpouring of support from Austrians, Ward Price went with them as a special guest. In the black and white newsreel film of the occasion, he can be glimpsed on the balcony of the Hofburg Palace, not far from Hitler himself. Ward Price never apologized for his attitudes, and from the book he wrote about the period of appeasement in July 1939 (it was called, neutrally enough, *The Year of Reckoning*) it is difficult to get any sense that he realized appeasement had even failed. A dull, dry, solitary man, as even his *Times* obituary in 1961 indicated, he remained a strong anti-Communist all his life, and never seems to have renounced his pro-Nazi opinions.

Rothermere encouraged Ward Price's articles, though during the Second World War, when he spent part of the time as a correspondent in North Africa, he never again achieved the kind of prominence he had enjoyed as the *Mail*'s correspondent in Berlin. Perhaps, privately, he was a reminder to Rothermere of his own former closeness to Hitler and Mussolini, whom of course the *Mail* now lashed daily.

In the early 1930s, Ward Price was Rothermere's chosen reporter for stories about the far right. On 7 June 1934, for instance, he covered a big rally by Sir Oswald Mosley and the British Union of Fascists.

15,000 AT BLACKSHIRT MEETING
SIR OSWALD MOSLEY'S CALL FOR ACTION

Amid rousing scenes of enthusiasm, 15,000 people heard Sir Oswald Mosley address the great Blackshirt meeting at Olympia, Kensington, last night.

Although Communists made repeated attempts to create disorder, they were effectively dealt with by Blackshirt stewards. Between 500 and 600 police were on duty, and 12 arrests were made.

REDS' FUTILE PROTESTS
By G. WARD PRICE

If the Blackshirt Movement had any need of justification the Red hooligans who savagely and systematically tried to wreck Sir Oswald Mosley's huge and magnificently successful meeting at Olympia last night would have supplied it. They got what they deserved.

This is nothing more nor less than propaganda. A crowd of 15,000 in a big auditorium like Olympia is neither huge nor does it necessarily represent magnificent success. The last line – 'They got what they deserved' – echoes the street savagery of the Nazi papers which Ward Price would have read in Germany.

At this stage, Rothermere was totally behind Mosley. Six months earlier, in the *Daily Mail* of 15 January 1934, he had written a full-page feature called 'Hurrah for the Blackshirts!':

> The Blackshirt movement is the organised effort of the younger generation to break this stranglehold which senile politicians have so long maintained on our public affairs.
>
> We must keep up with the spirit of the age. That spirit is one of national discipline and organisation.
>
> The Blackshirts are the only political force in Britain that is working for these ends . . .
>
> That is why I say, Hurrah for the Blackshirts! They are a sign that something is stirring among the youth of Britain.

Rothermere himself was sixty-five at the time. The article lasts more than 1,000 words, but there is no mention of Hitler, and no reference to the Jews, though the British Union of Fascists was obsessed with the subject. At the end a brief notice reads: 'Young men may join the British Union of Fascists by writing to the British Union of Fascists, King's-road, Chelsea, London, S.W.'

At the June meeting in Olympia, a journalist from the *Manchester Guardian* reported that forty or so Blackshirts would gather round anyone who had the temerity to ask a question. According to the Guardian's editorial:

> The plain fact is that to the average non-Communist Englishman (and there seem to have been many such in the Olympia crowd) the methods and pretensions of this semi-military organisation are an intolerable provocation.

The *Daily Express*, still printing articles about Nazi atrocities, did not support Mosley or the Blackshirts; even though a public meeting addressed by Lord Beaverbrook had been violently disrupted by

Communists. Its coverage on 15 June of a discussion of the Olympia meeting in Parliament was finally balanced between the two extremes, as the headlines showed:

'BRUTAL' BLACKSHIRT METHODS ATTACKED BY M.P.s

SIR OSWALD MOSLEY AS THE 'AL CAPONE' OF POLITICS

SPIKED RAILING SHOWN AS A 'RED' MEANS OF ATTACK

The *Daily Mail*, however, insisted on defending the Blackshirts. On 12 June it carried an editorial, either written by or heavily influenced by Lord Rothermere, which seemed to justify their use of force. The editorial was called 'Protecting Free Speech' – which had apparently been what Mosley's men had done when they beat up hecklers.

Eight days later, in the *Daily Mail* of 20 June 1934, on a page otherwise dedicated to pictures of Ladies' Day at Ascot ('Left, Lady Inchcape in a plaid taffeta frock with square neck, puff sleeves, and black velvet sash'), the large centre photograph was a film star-like study of Mosley in a black turtle-neck sweater, looking self-consciously handsome, with his right eyebrow cocked as though he were defying someone off camera. The caption reads:

> A new and striking portrait of Sir Oswald Mosley, the most outstanding figure in English public life today. Even those who dissent most strongly from his aims will concede that he possesses in a marked degree the rare gift of political courage – a quality lamentably lacking in most of his contemporaries.

That, however, was the high-water mark of Rothermere's support for Mosley. The violence at Olympia had tarnished the Blackshirts badly in the public mind, and Rothermere no longer found it politic to support them so publicly.

He continued to court Hitler, however. In January 1937 he and the ineluctable Ward Price went to the Berghof as Hitler's guests. Goebbels jotted in his diary, 'Rothermere pays me great compliments . . . Strongly anti-Jewish . . . He is a strong supporter of the Führer.' MI5 files released in 2005 show that Rothermere wrote to Adolf Hitler congratulating him on annexing Czechoslovakia in 1939, and encouraging him to march into Romania as well. It was only when war became inevitable that Rothermere quietly cut his links with the Nazis; yet it is hard to find any hint in the *Daily Mail* that he personally, or the *Mail* itself, conceded that he had been wrong to support Hitler so strongly. The *Mail* scarcely missed a beat as it changed from strident backing for Nazism to equally strident patriotism.

In September 1939, just as war broke out, Rothermere produced a book (ghost-written by his long-suffering associate Collin Brooks) called *Warnings and Predictions*; but in a panic lest it should now seem too pro-Nazi, he made a series of sweeping changes to it. It was a rather satisfying irony: the man who had lectured the British public on the need to bow to Hitler's demands ended up desperately trying to follow public opinion in resisting him.

§

Chamberlain's grip on the British press continued firm through the spring of 1938 and into the summer. Anthony Eden had resigned as Foreign Secretary on 21 February 1938 because of serious differences with Chamberlain over policy towards Mussolini, and a peace offer by President Roosevelt, but the public knew nothing of his reasons. Downing Street rang several newspapers, together with the BBC, to ask them not to mention the reasons for his going. The Paramount newsreel company interviewed the Labour Party leader, Clement Attlee, about the resignation. He said he was worried that it had happened because Eden could not accept further concessions to Hitler and Mussolini. A few hours later, Downing Street approached Paramount and asked that the item should be cut in the national interest. It was.

Eden himself said nothing about his reasons for resigning. It was not until May, three months later, when Chamberlain had lunch with several American and Canadian journalists and let the information slip out, that the public discovered what had happened. The warning that newspaper reporting could make the international situation worse was usually effective; no one wanted to be responsible for bringing about a war. Hugh Dalton, the Labour Party's spokesman on foreign affairs, wrote in his diary on 5 June 1938:

> [Lord] Southwood [the proprietor of the Daily Herald] has been sent for several times by Halifax and flattering appeals made to him as a great Press magnate. There has been some reflection of this in pressure to prevent too critical a line on foreign policy.

Yet very soon these tactics would cease to work. The public may not have been receiving proper information, but it was turning against Chamberlain. Appeasement had never commanded majority support in the country. When the issue was one of abandoning Czechoslovakia to Hitler, support for the policy began to collapse.

All the same, people were understandably nervous. As early as November 1932, before Hitler had even come to power, the then prime minister, Stanley Baldwin, told the House of Commons:

> I think it is well also for the man in the street to realise that there is no power on earth that can protect him from being bombed. Whatever people may tell him, the bomber will always get through . . . The only defence is in offence, which means that you will have to kill more women and children more quickly than the enemy if you want to save yourselves.

The previous war, the greatest that had ever been fought, had ended only twenty years before. It remained strongly in the minds of most adults, and now the expectation was that another war would be fought over towns and cities, and that even more people would die. In his memoirs, written thirty years later after he had resigned as prime minister, Harold Macmillan wrote, 'We thought of air warfare in 1938 rather as people think of nuclear warfare today.'

The Spanish Civil War, which was still going on, demonstrated that this was not true, since neither Madrid nor Barcelona, both of which had been heavily bombed by Italian and German planes, had suffered huge loss of civilian life. Yet the Committee of Imperial Defence, containing top military commanders, warned Chamberlain early in 1938 that if war broke out with Germany there could be 150,000 civilian deaths in the first week. As it turned out, that was nearly the number of civilians who died in the entire six years of the war: terrible losses, but nothing remotely like the scale of destruction that the British high command had expected.

§

On the afternoon of Thursday 25 August, the deputy editor of *The Times*, the gentle and slightly other-worldly Robert Barrington-Ward, strolled into the Foreign Office and was shown up the grand marble staircase into the magnificent office where Halifax was working at his desk. Halifax gloomily showed him documents about Germany's military build-up and the increasingly noisy demands of ethnic Germans in the Sudetenland, inside Czechoslovakia's southern borders, who had been encouraged by Hitler to seek reunion with Germany.

Halifax was starting now to have doubts about appeasement, and in less than four weeks would give up the policy altogether. By contrast, Barrington-Ward's confidence in Hitler's intentions was still so great that he seemed not to notice Halifax's anxieties. Instead, he wrote a note to his editor, Geoffrey Dawson: 'I continue to doubt, as I think you do, whether Hitler will really be ready to take all the risks implicit in forcible action.'

For Barrington-Ward it was a matter of faith. He had been a brave soldier, and was awarded both the MC and the DSO in the First World War. But he believed passionately that the Allies had been wrong to treat Germany so vindictively afterwards, and was certain that, even now, more understanding of Germany's demands would solve the problem. On 31 August the diplomatic correspondent of *The Times*, the confirmed appeaser Leo Kennedy, wrote a short article based in part on Barrington-Ward's misinterpretation of the briefing from Halifax. It said that official sources 'had no reason to doubt Herr Hitler's own declarations of peaceful aims'.

This was so wildly untrue that Halifax himself rang Barrington-Ward that afternoon to complain. Dawson was at his country house in Yorkshire, leaving Barrington-Ward in charge of the paper. The next day Leo Kennedy came into the office. He had recently spent time reporting for *The Times* from Czechoslovakia, and managed to take a dislike to it and to the government of Dr Beneš. Now he wrote a bland editorial for the next morning's paper, and then began drafting another leader he thought might come in useful in the next few days. The subject was, essentially, how to deal with the Sudeten problem. He had not properly finished it by the time he went home.

On the afternoon of Tuesday 6 September, Dawson came back from holiday and went through his in-tray. Kennedy's draft for the leader was lying there. Dawson rewrote it and, at 11.45 at night, showed it to the only senior editorial figure left in the office, William Casey. (Casey had been part of a delegation of senior staff members who had gone to Dawson in 1936 to complain about his support for appeasement. Nothing came of this attempted revolution.)

Casey was a pleasant, easy-going, rather lazy man, but his views on appeasement had not changed. When he read the editorial he was appalled, and tried to get Dawson to tone it down. For the most part he failed. Time was short, and at 12.05 a.m. it had to be sent down to the printers.

The Times, in publishing it, had committed itself to a policy which not even Chamberlain had fully advocated at this stage: forcing Czechoslovakia to give up the entire Sudetenland. Rewritten in Dawson's tortured late Victorian English, the key passage read:

> [I]t might be worthwhile for the Czechoslovak Government to consider whether they should exclude altogether the project, which has found favour in some quarters, of making Czechoslovakia a more homogeneous State by the secession of that fringe of alien populations who are contiguous to the nation with which they are united by race.

In other words, Czechoslovakia might actually be better off if it got rid of its turbulent ethnic Germans. It was the first suggestion anywhere that Czechoslovakia should be carved up, and it was made even before Hitler had come up publicly with the proposal himself.

There was an immediate outcry about it, and Sir Robert Vansittart, the chief anti-appeaser in the Foreign Office, was only one of many to warn that Hitler, assuming someone in the British government had suggested this to *The Times*, would feel certain he had Chamberlain on the run. That was exactly what Hitler did think when he read it; and although Chamberlain would have been forced down this road at some stage, Dawson's thoughtless, hurried editorial meant that the whole process was speeded up. Dawson himself professed not to understand what all the fuss was about. But for the Czechs, Dawson's hurried editorial was the start of a national catastrophe which would last, altogether, for fifty-one years.

§

At an emergency Cabinet meeting held on Saturday 24 September, after his return from seeing Hitler at Bad Godesberg, Chamberlain described his thoughts on the flight back.

> That morning he had flown up the river over London. He had imagined a German bomber flying the same course. He had asked himself what degree of protection we could offer to the thousands of homes which he had seen stretched out below him and he had felt that we were in no position to justify waging a war today in order to prevent a war thereafter.

It was about as good a defence of last-ditch appeasement as he could have made. But the supporters of appeasement were fading away, and the country as a whole was getting used to the idea, with some incredulity, that war might be just around the corner. The newspapers were full of photographs of barrage balloons going up and reports about army manoeuvres and other preparations for war. Two days earlier, on the evening of Monday 22 September, while Chamberlain was deep in negotiation with Hitler about the dismemberment of Czechoslovakia, the Ministry of Health in London issued a statement on the BBC:

> Thirty-four hospitals in the London area have been allotted as clearing stations for air raid casualties, and detailed plans have been prepared for removing between three and four thousand patients by ambulance trains to towns over fifty miles from London.

Yet in spite of the fears which official announcements like these provoked, British public opinion was shifting even more strongly against Chamberlain's policy. A Mass Observation poll taken at this time indicated that only 18 per cent of people supported Chamberlain, while 44 per cent of all respondents described their feelings about appeasement as 'indignant'; among men only, the proportion who said they were indignant was 67 per cent. Thousands of people demonstrated in White-hall that evening, chanting 'Stand by the Czechs!' and calling for Chamberlain's resignation. Even though criticism in the press and on radio, newsreels and the newly emerging medium of television had been muted, and it was hard even to read anti-appeasement views in all but a handful of national newspapers, the majority of people were not in favour of appeasement.

During the Cabinet meeting which began with Chamberlain des-cribing his feelings about flying over London, most of the ministers present turned against him. Even Halifax finally listened to the arguments of Cadogan and decided that Hitler's demands for taking over the Sudetenland were unacceptably high. Chamberlain had now had two meetings with Hitler, one at Berchtesgaden and one at Bad Godesberg, and he had failed to extract any serious concessions from him.

At 8.00 on the evening of Tuesday 27 September, Chamberlain broad-cast to the nation. In a reedy voice which emphasized the unrelenting pressure he had been under, he began in his polite, old-fashioned way by thanking the people who had written to thank him for his efforts: mostly women, he said, and there had been many from France, Belgium and Italy, and even from Germany. Reading these letters, he said, had been overwhelming; and he began to speak the passage which has been quoted against him ever since: 'How horrible, fantastic, incredible it is that we should be digging trenches and trying on gas-masks here because of a quarrel in a faraway country between people of whom we know nothing.' The following day, at 3.30 in the afternoon, he rose in the House of Commons to make a statement. For a man who hated drama, it was to be an extraordinarily dramatic occasion; the parliamentary sketch writer of the *News Chronicle* wrote that there had been nothing comparable with it in history.

> When he came into the House – after prayers were over and the special Collect had been said – he was as quiet and lonely as a ghost; and as pallid. I never saw as solitary a man than that thin figure in black who moved so quietly and then, on his way to his seat, was stopped,

suddenly, by a wave of cheering the warmth of which
came as a surprise to him.

In the galleries above sat Baldwin and 'pale Halifax',
and the American and Italian ambassadors; and not
far away from Chamberlain was Churchill, angry and
brooding, 'foreboding written on his face'. Chamberlain
droned on, with all attention focussed on him. And then,
up in the Peers' Gallery, someone handed Halifax a piece
of paper; and when he read it, I saw him smile for the
first time I have ever seen him smile. He showed it to the
plain, blunt Baldwin at his side . . . and he too smiled.

A minute later the news was in the Prime Minister's
hands; and it seemed to us, in the gallery above, that he
could not understand it; for [Sir John] Simon pointed to
it as he might point to the alphabet of a child who must
learn to read.

After staring at the note carefully, Chamberlain looked up. 'I have now
been informed by Herr Hitler that he has invited me to meet him at
Munich tomorrow morning.'

The House rose to its feet, cheering and waving; the relief was
palpable. Churchill, whom the *News Chronicle* sketch writer calls 'the
grim conscience of the people', stayed in his seat for a while, but the
emotion of the moment meant that even he stood up in the end. 'Then
he sat again, and presently got up and disappeared into the chaotic crowd
beneath the clapping peers and ambassadors above, his back bent and his
purpose and beliefs unchanged.'

Why did Hitler, who had seemed fixed on war, offer Chamberlain a
last attempt at peace? We know now, what many people at the time
suspected: that it was purely a tactical gesture. Hitler was still determined
to take over the whole of Czechoslovakia, but he was prepared to put it off
for a few weeks. No British newspaper or commentator suggested this at
the time: the feeling of reprieve was too great. Most people, including many
of those who were wholly against Chamberlain's efforts at appeasement,
allowed themselves to hope that peace might still be possible.

One or two newspapers temporarily lost all grip on reality. The *Daily
Mirror* explained the next day why Hitler had blinked, with an exclusive
which was the purest fantasy.

> A WARNING FROM THE GERMAN MILITARY CHIEFS
> THAT WAR AGAINST BRITAIN, FRANCE AND RUSSIA
> WOULD BE 'MOST UNPOPULAR' IN THE ARMY LED
> HITLER TO ACCEPT MR. CHAMBERLAIN'S 'LAST, LAST'
> APPEAL FOR A FURTHER TALK ...

'Our political correspondent' tells us that even Hitler's ambitions in Czechoslovakia are moderate. 'Hitler, I am told, is likely to agree to a token occupation by German troops of a small strip of the Sudeten areas.'

Alongside is a fiery but equally delusional leader. The *Mirror* had been staunchly anti-appeasement, but now, in the excitement of the offer of talks at Munich, it had got the wrong end of the stick. 'We have called the criminal bluff of the Third Reich. And their Leader knows it. Let them remember that this time the Nazi Whip can be cracked no more.'

In fact, as Chamberlain made his arrangements to fly to Germany for the third time in less than a month to join Hitler, Mussolini and the French prime minister, Edouard Daladier, the whip was just about to be cracked more fiercely than ever.

§

PEACE!

The headline on the front of the *Daily Express* three days later, on 30 September 1938 was said to have been the biggest type ever used on a British newspaper. The single huge word was flanked by two boxes, one of which read:

Ultimatum withdrawn at Munich

and the other

Cession less than Hitler plan.

None of the three statements turned out to be true or lasting, but for the moment the national mood was one of overwhelming gratitude and relief. And it was not just limited to Britain. The *Mail* headlined a story from New York:

WALL-ST. GOES MAD – FOR JOY

Wild-eyed traders, almost overcome with elation as new
peace hopes were born, were swamped with buying orders.
Strangers clapped each other on the back.

Yet the shameful reality of the Munich agreement was clear from the start.
The following morning, only thirty hours after the deal was signed,
German troops would begin crossing into the Sudetenland, taking it over
gradually. Hitler's long-planned but secret timetable for annexing
Czechoslovakia had always been 1 October. As for the rest of the Munich
agreement – the slow takeover of the Sudetenland, the fact that the
German soldiers would wear forage caps instead of helmets, the international commission determining the new frontiers of Czechoslovakia,
and the international force which would police the areas surrendered to
Germany – these were merely fig leaves for Chamberlain and Daladier,
and would anyway depend entirely on Hitler's goodwill. There would be
no international force to oversee the German takeover.

Vernon Bartlett, formerly of the BBC and now of the liberal, anti-
appeasement *News Chronicle*, was at Munich for the meeting and called
it the day he disliked most in his life. He could never forget, he wrote
thirty-six years later, the expressions on the faces of the two Czechoslovak
representatives when they came out of Chamberlain's sitting-room at the
Petersberg Hotel in Munich, after being told the terms of the deal Britain
and France had done in their name. Bartlett wrote a bleak account of the
deal Chamberlain had agreed:

> Two days ago, the British and French governments
> were prepared to help Czechoslovakia if she were
> attacked; the same governments are now pledged to
> hold themselves responsible for the fulfilment of the
> plan for German occupation.

The chairman of the *News Chronicle*, Lord Layton, was deeply involved
in the running of the paper. He had helped to found it in 1930, as an
amalgamation of two pro-Liberal newspapers, the *Daily News* and the
Daily Chronicle, and spent four or five hours each day in the paper's
offices in Bouverie Street, looking through the copy. He and the paper's

editor, Gerald Barry (who was later to become the director general of the Festival of Britain) had many disagreements; Barry found Layton too cautious, and wanted to take the paper further to the left.

On the day of the Munich Agreement Layton read Bartlett's report. He thought it was overly depressing, and probably thought it would contrast too strongly with the delight and relief of the rest of Fleet Street. He told Barry that he thought Bartlett's despatch should be spiked. There was an immediate revolt among the entire senior staff. Barry told him they would not bring the paper out that night if the despatch were dropped. Layton backed down, and the despatch was the centrepiece of the paper.

Layton, though a liberal, was too much in awe of Chamberlain as a person, and of the office of prime minister. Seven months later, in April 1939, the *Chronicle* ran a story that Chamberlain was privately trying to do a deal with Mussolini that would weaken the links between Italy and Nazi Germany. Chamberlain summoned Layton to Downing Street and gave him a dressing-down as though he were a guilty schoolboy.

> The Prime Minister said he had sent for the Chairman of the News Chronicle and had protested in the strongest possible terms as to the attitude which his paper had adopted in this matter. The Chairman had apologised.

Chamberlain had got into the habit of treating the newspapers and the BBC as though they were branches of government. And editors and proprietors were too inclined to behave as though they were. If the *News Chronicle* had been wrong about the story – and it seems to have been right – then the proper thing for Chamberlain to have done would have been to put out a statement about it. And the proper thing for Layton to have done would have been to undertake to print it.

§

On Friday 29 September, the *Evening News*, under the headline 'LONDON GOES TO HESTON', gave details of how people could get to London's airport, close to the present Heathrow, to welcome Chamberlain home from Munich. Large numbers of extra buses and Tube staff had been laid on.

The following day, Saturday the 30th, thousands of people turned up, and the roads to Heston were jammed with traffic. Chamberlain, tired after his long journey but exhilarated by the sight of the huge crowd, appeared at the door of the plane, waving his hat. Then he spotted Halifax and shouted, 'I've got it! I've got it!'

In the crowd of journalists and photographers who engulfed Chamberlain at the foot of the plane was a tubby, pleasant-faced, enthusiastic figure in a dark suit who was in the process of transforming the BBC's news reporting. Richard Dimbleby had recently returned from making a series of ground-breaking reports from the Spanish–French border about the masses of refugees escaping Franco's war. These had been of such a high order that he had become the BBC's top reporter.

Now he strained forward like the others to hear what Chamberlain had to say.

> I want to say that the settlement of the Czechoslovak problem which has now been achieved is, in my view, only a prelude to a larger settlement in which all Europe may find peace.

He paused, and took a sheet of paper out of the breast pocket of his jacket. Unfolding it, he held it over his head for the cameras and the crowd to see.

> This morning I had another talk with the German Chancellor, Herr Hitler, and here is a paper which bears his name upon it as well as mine. Some of you perhaps have already heard what it contains, but I would just like to read it to you . . . 'We regard the agreement signed last night . . . as symbolic of the desire of our two peoples never to go to war again.'

'Huh!' Dimbleby, a strong anti-appeaser, whispered to the man next to him. 'I wish that were true.'

The crowd cheered and sang 'For he's a jolly good fellow', and Chamberlain was driven off with Halifax sitting beside him in the back of a limousine, as people crowded forward to congratulate him, sometimes jumping on the running-boards and beating the windows in their pleasure at everything he had achieved. He presented himself with his wife and the king and queen on the balcony at Buckingham Palace – a sign of the king's own political feelings – and eventually went on to Downing Street, where a further large crowd had gathered. Inside, someone said, 'Neville, go up to the window and say "Peace in our time".' Chamberlain was annoyed. 'No, I don't do that sort of thing.' But he did. With his wife beside him, he leaned out of the big window over the front door of No. 10 and said, 'I believe it is peace for our time. We thank you from the bottom of our hearts.' He paused, and the crowd roared. 'Now I recommend you to go home and sleep quietly in your beds.'

On 15 March 1939, less than twenty-four weeks later, Hitler sent his troops into Prague in total disregard of everything he had promised Chamberlain. Munich did not mean peace in our time; it simply gave everyone a year's respite. And by then even the *Daily Mail* was turning away from its old attitudes. Its reporter, Ralph Izzard, wrote a fine description of the last train out of Bratislava. Most of the refugees were Jewish:

> A number of women who apparently did not dare to remain in Slovakia had their jewellery unfastened from their dresses, their rings taken from their fingers, and their necklaces taken from their throats. This was done by Hlinka Guards [Slovak stormtroopers]. There were no wardresses in the room.

The *Mail* was finally facing reality. It announced the following day on Hitler's invasion of Czechoslovakia, 'Britain has no cause for self-reproach.' But it ended: 'One thing, and one thing only, will serve Britain – her own armed might.'

Not even the *Daily Mail* thought war could long be avoided now.

13

FIRST BLOOD

The first news the British government had that German troops had ignored its ultimatum and invaded Poland on Friday 1 September 1939 came from a young woman of twenty-seven who had been a journalist for only five days. Clare Hollingworth was to become one of the most celebrated defence and foreign correspondents. She worked for the *Daily Telegraph* from 1939 to 1949, for the *Guardian* from 1950 to 1967, for the *Telegraph* again until 1984, and for the *Sunday Telegraph* from 1984.

In later years, Clare Hollingworth, with her thick glasses, poor eyesight and aunty-ish manner, was famous for her unmatchable instinct for a story, and for her extraordinary exclusives; on one occasion she beguiled a Soviet admiral into taking her on board the latest Warsaw Pact nuclear submarine, even though he knew she was a Western defence correspondent. But he had taken a fancy to her (many men did) and wanted to impress her by telling her its most secret capabilities. It was the lead in the next day's paper.

The man who had hired Clare Hollingworth was the *Telegraph*'s correspondent in Berlin, Hugh Greene; the brother of the novelist Graham Greene, he later became one of the BBC's best directors general. He sent her to the German–Polish border to investigate the build-up of tension there. On Thursday 31 August she saw huge quantities of German armour assembling, and rang Greene to tell him. He seems to have felt she was getting overexcited.

She took a room at a hotel right on the border, overlooking the main road. At 4.45 the following morning she was awakened by the grinding sound of tanks rolling past her window. When she could get a call through to Greene, he would not believe her until she held the phone out of the window so he could hear the tanks for himself. He advised her to ring the British embassy in Warsaw, and she had to do the same thing to convince them that Germany had invaded without first declaring war.

As the news reached London that Friday, a carefully prepared series of organizational changes went into effect, and Britain went onto a war footing. At around 5.35 p.m., the postmaster general's office warned the BBC director general's office that senior managers and engineers should open their sealed instructions. An announcement on the *Six O'Clock News* said that the national and regional radio networks of the BBC would be merged with immediate effect. At 8.15 p.m. a voice said for the first time, 'This is the BBC Home Service.'

On Sunday 3 September, the Home Service announced that Neville Chamberlain would address the nation at 11.15 a.m. His words, in the harsh, tired accents which perhaps already showed the stress of the bowel cancer which killed him a year later, were some of the most famous ever spoken by a British prime minister:

> This morning the British ambassador in Berlin handed the German government a final note stating that, unless the British government heard from them by eleven o'clock that they were prepared at once to withdraw their troops from Poland, a state of war would exist between us. I have to tell you now that no such undertaking has been received and that consequently this country is at war with Germany.

'God Save the King' was played. In the BBC newsroom, everybody stood to attention; all over the country, even in their own homes, people were doing the same thing. There was a peal of bells, and then, only six minutes or so later, the first air-raid siren of the war began to wail. People behaved with remarkable calm, given that many of them must have thought that the vast, hugely destructive raids forecast by Baldwin, Lord Rothermere and Chamberlain were already on their way.

Most of the BBC news staff filed downstairs in orderly fashion into the bomb-shelters in the basement. 'My God,' someone said to Godfrey Talbot, then a subeditor but soon to be one of the BBC's most famous war correspondents, 'my wife's out in the street.' A smaller group, which included the announcer John Snagge, grabbed their gas masks and helmets and ran up to their rooftop position, five storeys above. After ten minutes everyone gathered in the newsroom again, with embarrassed smiles: it had been a false alarm. An unidentified aircraft had been seen approaching the south coast, and the alarm had been sounded. The plane turned out to be British.

That afternoon the editor of BBC News, R.T. Clark, a tall, pleasant, rather shy man, called his staff together. Many of them scarcely knew him; the television news service, based at Alexandra Palace, had closed down for the duration, and its staff had been amalgamated with radio news at Broadcasting House. With so many faces turned expectantly to him, Clark was abrupt and gruff: 'It's war now. Tell the truth, that's our job. Thanks very much and good luck.'

Later he amplified his thoughts in a memo: 'It seems to me that the only way to strengthen the morale of the people whose morale is worth strengthening, is to tell them the truth, and nothing but the truth, even if the truth is horrible.'

It was thoroughly characteristic of the BBC: high-minded, more than a little vague, and entirely open to individual interpretation. Further, it was decided that the BBC would report the same news to everyone: to its domestic audience, to the Empire, to occupied Europe, and to Germany itself. The truth would not be adapted for propaganda purposes.

The BBC governors set out the tone the various foreign language services should adopt: 'We should address even individual Germans . . . as an Englishman or Frenchman would speak to them if they could meet in a neutral café . . . Above all, there must be no room for ranting.'

The BBC would infuriate many people over the next six years, and certainly wouldn't always live up to its unspecific principles. But for the voice of a liberal democracy with its back against the wall, this was an immensely valuable and successful set of rules.

§

In 1939 the grand art deco tower of the London University Senate House, designed by Charles Holden and completed only two years earlier, was the second tallest building in London after St Paul's Cathedral. It had a distinct attraction for dictators, real and imaginary: Oswald Mosley planned to install Parliament there if he took power, and it has often been suggested that Hitler would have established the centre of Nazi power there if the invasion of Britain had been successful. For George Orwell, it was the natural headquarters for Big Brother's Ministry of Truth in *Nineteen Eighty-Four*.

In September 1939 the Chamberlain government turned it over to the brand-new Ministry of Information. It was to become famously creative across a range of artistic fields; but for British and foreign journalists its primary function was almost entirely negative, since it was here that the censors were based. Libertarians, anarchists and conservatives hated the Ministry and the building in equal measure; Basil Seale, a highly disreputable character in Evelyn Waugh's novel of the Phony War, *Put Out More Flags*, manages to penetrate its doors and finds the Ministry ramshackle and hopelessly disorganized.

> 'What is your work, Geoffrey?'
> 'Well mostly it consists of sending people who want to see me on to someone they don't want to see.'
> They came to the door of what had once been a chemical laboratory, and entered. There was a white porcelain sink in the corner into which a tap dripped monotonously. In the centre of the oilcloth floor stood a card table and two folding chairs.

Yet in spite of its manifest confusion, the Ministry of Information, even more than the BBC, succeeded in establishing the sense that we still have today of a not particularly well-prepared, not very efficient, instinctively peaceable society nevertheless finding within itself the determination not to cave in to despotism and overwhelming force. When we think about the Second World War, we see it through the words of J.B. Priestley and the film documentaries which Humphrey Jennings made for the Ministry of Information: little boats setting out across the Channel, Dame Myra Hess giving piano concerts in the National Gallery, firemen battling infernos, Underground stations packed with decent, gutsy people defying Hitler night after night – people who made endless cups of tea and kept calm and carried on.

These things all existed, of course, and they represented most people's view of themselves then, just as they do today. But this view of a courageous nation united as never before in the face of tyranny conveniently leaves out some less attractive features: the strikes by miners and factory workers for more money or greater safety, which enraged large numbers of soldiers on active duty at the time; the looting and petty theft that happened after many bombing raids; the criminal activities of widespread gangs of deserters; the habitual blackmarketeering of many well-to-do people, and the flight of their families to safety overseas. The fact that these things are emphatically not our images of the war is a measure of the Ministry of Information's success.

The Ministry's six-year history is also the record of its victory over itself. The very name seems like an example of George Orwell's 'Newspeak' *avant la lettre*, and the Ministry of Information was set up in the expectation that its first and perhaps only major task would be to help control public opinion before, during and after a devastating aerial assault. It therefore had its origins in the belief, fostered by Lord Rothermere and other appeasers, that the war would be brief and hideously destructive, and that the side which attacked first – presumably Germany – would certainly win. Yet from the very start the Ministry represented far more than just an agency for dealing with the emergencies of war.

Planned originally by the senior military men and civil servants of the Committee for Imperial Defence, starting in 1935, it was a remarkable example of the British mind at work: it ranged from the rambling, ad hoc and almost absurd to the insightful and inspirational. People across the country expected it to become totalitarian, or at least prescriptive; it didn't. Instead, it turned itself into a mirror of the nation. Under the immensely difficult conditions of wartime, when for a long period of time the very existence of Britain was at stake, it became the greatest patron of the arts that the country had ever known, with a budget of more than £4 million (the equivalent of something like £150 million in 2010) at a time of the greatest austerity.

The MOI could be infuriating, but it never attempted to be dictatorial; quite the contrary. The range of talent it employed was remarkable, from writers and poets – Dylan Thomas and W.H. Auden wrote scripts for some of the best factual films ever made – to actors including Noël Coward and Laurence Olivier, and war artists like Eric Kennington, Paul Nash and William Rothenstein.

The Ministry was called many things: 'misbegotten', 'the apotheosis of muddle', 'The Ministry of Aggravation'. In less than two years after its launch on 4 September 1939, it had four ministers in fewer than two years, including Sir John Reith and Duff Cooper. But the fourth, Churchill's former adviser Brendan Bracken, seemed to understand the Ministry's faintly disorganized and wilful nature, and had the right contacts in Fleet Street to win over the support of the press. Bracken's background helped. Decades later it emerged that he had come from Republican Irish stock, but had managed to hide his past completely. With his shock of red hair, thick glasses and bad teeth, he nevertheless always dressed superbly, and because of the lack of orthodoxy in his own life he must have had an instinctive sympathy for the raffish people under his control. In spite of the very limited ideas of the men who had originally planned it, the Ministry of Information was one of the main British successes of the entire war.

Its central task was to oversee the war reporting of the newspapers and radio, but its earliest efforts ranged from the ineffectual to the disastrous. Few people with any experience of Fleet Street or broadcasting were brought in to man the relevant departments at the Ministry. Of the total of 999 employees of the Ministry ('the 999' became one of its nicknames), only 43 new recruits were actually journalists.

Its first head was Lord Macmillan, an able lawyer but one with a reputation for putting far too many irons in the fire. In the past he had headed inquiries into lunacy (it was a standing joke in the Ministry that this was his sole useful qualification for the job), coal-mining, street offences, shipbuilding, and income tax law.

He was on the political honours committee, the Pilgrim Trust, the court of London University, the BBC advisory council, the British Museum, the Soane Museum, the Carnegie Trust for the Universities of Scotland, the National Trust, King George's Jubilee Trust, and the Society for the Promotion of Nature Reserves, and several more. And yet, for reasons that are not entirely clear, he seemed to have plenty of time on his hands. When a staff deputation went to complain to him about the long hours they had to work, they found him reading a novel. He lasted only a few months.

The first and most important thing the Ministry had to do was organize an efficient and equitable system of press censorship, and it failed almost immediately. The chief censor was Vice Admiral C.V. Usborne, who like everyone else in the topmost positions at the Ministry had no experience whatever of the job. He had spent all his adult life in the navy, and had probably never spoken to a journalist.

The first crisis of the war was erupting just as he arrived at his office in Senate House on the morning of Monday 4 September. Reports were coming in of the sinking of a British liner, the *Athenia*, 250 miles off the coast of Ireland. She had been torpedoed at 7.40 p.m. on Saturday evening while carrying 1,400 passengers, three-quarters of them women and children, who were heading for the safety of Canada; 311 were American. A large proportion of the 112 people who died were women and children.

The captain of the U-boat that sank her, U-30, Oberleutnant Fritz-Julius Lemp, said after the war that he thought she was an armed merchant cruiser or a troopship. But he must have seen the passengers on her decks and in the water, because he falsified his logbook that night and swore his crew to secrecy about what they had done; though not before he had come to the surface and fired on the lifeboats and the ship's superstructure to put her radios out of action.

In the very first hours of the Second World War, then, there was an atrocity of the kind which the British government and British press had accused Germany of committing many times during the First. Yet now the newspapers were surprisingly careful in their treatment of the story. This, for instance, was the *Daily Mail*'s report:

CHILDREN WERE BEING PUT TO BED AS ATHENIA WAS TORPEDOED

Mothers in Evening Gowns Raced to Save Them

This is the truth about the sinking of the British Atlantic liner Athenia, told by the first survivors of the 1,418 passengers and crew to land at Greenock in the Firth of Clyde and at Galway, Eire, yesterday. Nothing has been added to, or taken from their statements.

Here, in the words of the people who SAW what happened, from the moment of the disaster to the time of rescue, is the whole tragic story of the Athenia disaster.

Why should the journalist who wrote this spend so much time establishing the accuracy of his story? Perhaps because he and his editor remembered the bad reputation the newspapers, and the *Mail* in particular, had created for themselves a quarter of a century before.

The sinking of the *Athenia* was a shocking story, as the crossheads showed: 'Nearly Drowned in Swamped Boat'; 'Saved Her Child, Water Up To Neck'; 'Children, Women, Dead in the Sea'; 'Sailor Gave Woman His Lifebelt' ('He had one round him, but he took it off and said: "There you are, madam, you need it more than I."'). The war which had only just started would generate so many terrible atrocity stories that there would soon be no need to use exaggerated language about them, and very little doubt in the minds of readers that they were likely to be true. Still, the *Daily Mirror* kept the old yellow press tradition going.

NAZIS SHELLED LITTLE CHILDREN
IN LINER HORROR

The Nazi U-boat which sank the British liner Athenia was itself sunk later by a British destroyer, said survivors who landed at Greenock yesterday.

All the survivors told the same grim story of murder on the high seas; of killing and sinking without warning; of children killed and maimed as the torpedo burst.

It is a poorly written story, based on nothing very much. The supposed sinking of the U-boat was not mentioned again in the article, and no other British newspaper suggested that it might have happened. Yet even this story, invented though it probably was, is different in kind from the sort of story the *Mirror* often printed during the First World War. It is not open propaganda, trumpeting non-existent hate-crimes; it is simply a low-quality story. To that limited extent we could perhaps say that it is slightly better. British journalism has moved on.

Yet even if the *Mirror* had tried to check whether a British destroyer had sunk the U-30, which it probably didn't, it would have found it impossible to get an answer. Within hours of opening its doors, the Ministry of Information was overwhelmed with phone calls and demands for information. The transatlantic cables were jammed with traffic, as American and Canadian reporters tried to send their stories home. The censors battled to read through the immensely long reports which were being written, and soon gave up in despair. Newspaper editors decided to go ahead and publish what they wanted anyway.

But the Ministry did manage to put out a reasonably good statement about the torpedoing of the *Athenia*, though the repetitious phrasing betrays the haste with which it was composed:

Such action is in direct contravention of the rules regarding submarine warfare by which Germany is bound. These rules, to which Germany agreed to adhere, laid down clearly that no merchant ship may be sunk without warning, and that in any case no

merchant ship is to be sunk until the safety of all passengers and
crew has been assured.

The confusion at the Ministry of Information was as nothing compared
with the outright panic which took over in the Leopold Palace opposite
Hitler's Reich Chancellery, in Berlin, where Goebbels's Reichsminis-
terium für Volksaufklärung und Propaganda, the Ministry of Public
Enlightenment and Propaganda, was based. Hitler had given orders at
the very start of the war that U-boat commanders should stick to the
Hague Convention, and not launch attacks without warning. Oberleutnant Lemp had falsified his logbook and sworn his crew to secrecy
not, presumably, because he was worried about having committed a war
crime, but because he had mistakenly disobeyed the direct orders of his
Führer.

Late that morning Berlin issued a statement saying the *Athenia* had
hit a mine. From Senate House the Ministry of Information countered,
quoting the Admiralty as saying that no mines had been laid anywhere
near the area where the *Athenia* had gone down. Leopold Palace then
accused Churchill, as First Lord of the Admiralty, of ordering the sinking
of the *Athenia* in order to turn American opinion against Germany. That
sounded even weaker. Britain had won the first round in a long propaganda war.

Ten days after the war started, a genial, witty retired rear admiral, Sir
George Pirie Thomson, came back from holiday in the South of France
to find himself called to the Admiralty. He was summoned to the First
Lord's office and met Churchill himself, who told him, 'Go at once to the
Ministry of Information and give Admiral Usborne a hand with press
censorship. He appears to be hard pressed.' Thomson later confessed that
his experience of journalism had been 'limited to reading my newspaper
at the breakfast table,' but unusually for a senior naval officer, he
discovered a liking for, and even a camaraderie with, the people whose
reporting he had to censor. Early on in his time at the Ministry of
Information he told an *Evening Standard* reporter, 'I should be awfully
grateful if you wouldn't address me as "sir".' Journalists usually found to
their surprise that they liked him; and he was to stay in his job at the
Ministry for the rest of the war. In 1947 he published a volume of shrewd
and pleasant memoirs, called *Blue Pencil Admiral*.

He arrived just in time. Twice during the day on 12 September a

Paris radio station, not bound by the same security constraints as British news organizations, reported that the first contingent of the British Expeditionary Force had landed in France. Up to that moment the British press had been meticulous about observing the news blackout; patriotism was regarded as much more important than exclusives in a war where the future of the country was in question. But both the newspapers and the BBC had prepared large amounts of material for the moment the Ministry of Information told them they could use it. Now editors bombarded Usborne and Thomson for permission to go ahead. By the early evening the two admirals appealed to the War Office, and the War Office agreed. Thomson passed the message on, and went home.

His officials began the long task of going through every article and broadcast script, often ringing the War Office to check whether some point of detail could be used. The Scottish, North and West of England editions and the Irish editions, north and south, were printed and sent off to the main railway stations for distribution. But the War Office was growing more and more nervous about the amount of information that was being passed for publication. Just before 11.30 p.m. someone's nerve snapped. The Ministry of Information was told that there must after all be no news of any kind in the next morning's papers about the BEF's landing.

The police were sent in to raid the editorial and production departments of every daily newspaper. They stopped the trains from leaving and took charge of the bundles of newspapers on board. They stopped private cars to check that no one had bought or kept a copy. By this stage the newspaper proprietors were complaining to everyone in government they could find. That began to work, and after two and a half hours, the War Office changed its mind again. At 2.30 in the morning the papers were told they could publish after all.

The *Daily Mirror* columnist 'Cassandra', William Connor, wrote:

> The muck-up the other night on the release of the news that British troops were in France was an absolute disgrace. Scotland Yard excelled itself, and newspaper offices were alive with coppers grabbing bundles of contraband newspapers and generally chucking their weight about. Primarily the responsibility for this blunder lies on Lord Macmillan. I

am told by an apologist for his lordship that he is a brilliant
lawyer and that he can claim journalistic experience since
he was editor of the 'Juridical Review' from 1900 to 1907. If
that's journalistic experience then I'm an expert on law, for
I was once fined for riding a bicycle without a bell in 1922.

Usborne, who could not cope with this sort of thing any more than Lord
Macmillan could, was gone within a few weeks. But Rear Admiral
Thomson, who took over as chief censor at the end of 1940, found he was
rather enjoying it all. He understood that the journalists had a job to do,
and could be trusted not to report sensitive facts if they could be shown
good reason why they shouldn't. He was also prepared to fight the
journalists' cause with the War Office if they could persuade him that
something was important. After the war was over, one of his censors told
him his nickname among them had been 'Stet' Thomson, because he so
often jotted 'stet' ('let it stand') beside things they had crossed out of the
journalists' copy. Thomson made sure there was enough give and take in
the system to ensure that it worked reasonably well. And so for five years
Thomson had to decide, day by day, hour by hour, just how much war
news your favourite newspaper and the BBC could give you without at
the same time telling the enemy what he wanted to know.

When the system was originally planned, in 1935, it was decided that
the British press should not be forced to submit its material for
censorship. It should be enough, the government thought, that like every
other British citizen, journalists were prohibited by Defence Regulation
No. 3 from 'obtaining, recording, communicating to any other person or
publishing information which might be useful to an enemy'. But since
the press had a duty to keep people informed, 'Defence Notices' (in effect,
the same D-Notice system we have today) were issued, giving journalists
and their editors a list of subjects about which they had to have prior
censorship advice if they wanted to publish anything. There were more
than 400,000 separate newspaper editions during the war, and 650,000
news items were submitted to censorship; in other words, only an average
of one and a half news items were put to the censors per edition. There
was much irritation on both sides, but no one was actually prosecuted
for breaking the law.

On 8 November, Bernard Gray, a *Mirror* correspondent with the BEF,
wrote from France,

I approve of censorship ... It's necessary. And so long as it's reasonable, neither you nor I should have an objection. But I can picture you, anxious to hear all you can about the British troops in France, wondering if the news you get from me is accurate, or whether it is propaganda imposed on war correspondents by the censorship system.

Gray clearly remembered the doubts that were cast on the reporting of the First World War, and felt he had to defend himself against the accusation that he was simply a tool of the authorities.

Though the censors do sometimes cut things out of my despatches, they never tell me what to put in.

And the knocking-out process is limited to the elimination of anything that might either directly or indirectly be of advantage to the enemy.

George Orwell, writing in 1943 in his essay 'The Freedom of the Press', agreed:

Any fair-minded person with journalistic experience will admit that during this war official censorship has not been particularly irksome. We have not been subjected to the kind of totalitarian 'co-ordination' that it might have been reasonable to expect. The press has some justified grievances, but on the whole the Government has behaved well and has been surprisingly tolerant of minority opinions.

Submitting to censorship goes against the instincts of every journalist, even the supine and the timid. But because of the serious existential threat to the country and the willingness of organizations and individual journalists to obey the rules, it worked surprisingly well.

For American and Empire journalists, who were left outside the cosy relationship, it was less attractive. Some Americans, not concerned about the dangers that loose information posed for Britain, did their best to get round the censorship. In November 1939, as the cruiser HMS *Belfast* left the Firth of Forth, she hit a magnetic mine laid by the German submarine U-21 and was seriously damaged. The War Office put an immediate block on any reporting of the incident, but a *New York Times* correspondent sent a series of telegrams to his office which contained the news; it was reported on the front page of the newspaper two days later. His first telegram read, in part, 'Remember it's the last word that counts', and it was followed by seven others, sent through different cable companies:

> We are sending story about submarines. Please tell Harvard I want my son entered. As ordered, am setting forth. Government was not attacked. If you persist someone's reputation may be damaged. Smith covers Dublin not Belfast. Untrue that any prisoners escaped.

When put together, the last words of these telegrams read 'Submarines entered Forth, attacked, damaged *Belfast*, escaped.' There was a huge fuss in the War Office and the Ministry of Information; publishing the news was useful to the Germans, who found out about the success of their U-boat's mine-laying exercise. But Rear Admiral Thomson was characteristically relaxed about the episode. Realizing that conserving the paper's goodwill was of more value to Britain than keeping a military secret, he used his influence with the War Office to ensure that the *New York Times* was not punished. Its correspondents did not break the rules again.

There was a certain level of common sense about the censorship system, which ensured it had a grudging acceptance. It was even turned into a joke. The *Mirror* of 27 November 1939 quotes a poem called 'Epitaph to a Censor', which one of its correspondents found pinned on the wall of an RAF censor's office in France:

> Here at length in sweet repose
> A censor lies: but who, God knows.
> When raving Pressmen shot him dead,
> Filled, like his pencil, full of lead,
> E'en in the graveyard he was game –
> Arose and blackened out his name.

From the early days of the war, the *Daily Mirror* started hinting that Chamberlain should go. The *Mirror* was not taken particularly seriously by the government, but there was a recognition that it represented, and had a considerable influence on, working-class views; and even the autocratic Chamberlain could not ignore that. On 13 September, ten days after the war began, the *Mirror* ran an editorial which read: 'In 1939 we cannot endure fools in high places as we did after 1914. The self-revealed blunderers must go. We endured muddlers too long in the last bitter struggle.'

It was a warning. The *Mirror* regarded itself, to the irritation of the other newspapers, the politicians and the Ministry of Information, as the voice of the people, commonsensical, straightforward, and impossible to bamboozle. It soon became annoyed with Churchill, whose appointment as First Lord of the Admiralty it had strongly supported, because he claimed to want 'complete silence' about naval operations, while in fact he hogged the limelight by making all the announcements about the navy himself. These revelations meant that more people listened to his broadcasts on the BBC, and he was able to get better and better time-slots for them. On Tuesday 19 December, the *Mirror*, frustrated by his habit of making speeches which broke important items of news that the censors had banned the newspapers from reporting, decided to challenge the system.

THE CANADIANS ARE HERE

Alongside this headline the *Mirror* put a little block of text:

> We are telling this news – although the War Office and the Censor had banned it until tomorrow.
>
> For, in spite of that ban, the First Lord of the Admiralty, Mr Churchill, chose to steal the limelight of other Government departments and made the story public last night. And when the world knew – then the Censor released it.

Datelined from 'A Western Port', as though to emphasize its willingness to go along with every other aspect of censorship, a *Mirror* correspondent wrote:

> A wild skirl of bagpipes shrilled from the great grey transport across the waters to the watchers on the quay. Then, drowning the pipes, drowning the roar of the aircraft

on their beat around the ship, we heard the shrill cry
coming over the waves: 'Yahoo.'

The Canadians had come to Britain.

Another box of text, headed 'Why Has This News Been Held?', ends:

> The nation should be told the news at once. It should not
> be saved up to colour Mr Churchill's speeches ... This
> senseless suppression of news that can be of no value to
> the enemy, and that you have the right to know, will have
> to stop. After all, we are fighting one form of dictatorship.
> WE DON'T WANT TO ACQUIRE ANOTHER.

After this it was noticeable that the censorship ceased to be arranged quite
so clearly to suit Churchill's personal advantage.

The press was honest about reporting German successes in sinking
the merchant ships on which Britain depended for its existence, and the
censors made no attempt to stop this. The headlines become depressingly
monotonous: 'Five More Ships Sunk', 'Blown in Two, Sinks in Three
Minutes', 'Another British Ship Sunk'. As the weeks went by, stories like
these shrank in length, their headlines became smaller and smaller, and
they no longer appeared on the front pages; not because they did not
matter, but because they had become so frequent.

§

Early on, war news was distinctly thin, except in Poland. But the fierce
fighting there in early September was notably under-reported by the British
press. *The Times* had a correspondent in Warsaw, but scarcely a very
inspired one; he stayed in the capital, then left in a hurry when the Germans
came closer. His analysis of the enemy's strategy was distinctly flimsy.

> The German invasion, as far as can be observed at present
> – reports are scanty and hard to confirm – seems to have
> two separate aims, apart from terror. Towns and villages of
> strategic importance for communications are being
> bombed, and military offensives are being directed so as to
> pinch off certain cities commanding wide areas.

The obviousness of all this, the passive voice, the vague terms ('certain cities', 'wide areas') are signs that the *Times* man had nothing much to go on but felt obliged to send in a report anyway. The Polish authorities were looking defeat in the face, and had no time to brief him; the British embassy clearly had no information from the front and knew no more than he did. He buries the only real story which he might have told in a quotation from an official communiqué: the Germans suggested to the Poles that neither side should attack civilian targets, but although the Poles hastily agreed German planes immediately started bombing twenty-one 'open' towns and cities.

The *Daily Mirror* had no foreign staff to speak of, and certainly no correspondent in Poland; but a week later, on Monday 11 September, it used agency reports (though without acknowledging them) to create a dramatic and fairly accurate picture of what was happening in the capital.

> PARTS OF WARSAW ARE IN FLAMES. THE CITY FIGHTS
> ON. AS HEAVY GERMAN BOMBERS DROP INCENDIARY
> BOMBS ON THE CAPITAL THE MEN, WOMEN AND
> EVEN THE CHILDREN OF WARSAW HAVE SPRUNG TO
> THE DEFENCE OF THEIR HOMES.
>
> Women are fighting beside their men. They are throwing
> grenades as the Germans advance; they are picking up
> rifles and machine-guns from the hands of fallen troops . . .
> [I]n one suburb where street fighting took place for a few
> hours, children poured scalding water on to the heads of
> the Germans.

Much of this has been written up by the subeditor on the basis of a Warsaw Radio broadcast the previous night, which had promised melodramatically that 'Hand-in-hand, Polish soldiers and women will destroy Hitler', and a German radio report which complained that contrary to the rules of warfare civilians were firing on German soldiers. The response of German soldiers to this was usually ferocious and ill-disciplined, as happened in Belgium in 1914, and earlier in France in 1870; though in the Second World War the Nazi authorities encouraged their soldiers to behave with a cruelty that would not have been permitted in earlier wars.

The British press was also reacting true to type. Nothing, as we saw in the First World War, in Ireland in 1916, and in Spain from 1936 onwards, fascinated British journalists and (presumably) their readers quite like stories of women joining in the fighting. Perhaps this is just the inevitable response from a settled country where the civilians had not been faced with invading troops; but even in 1939 it seems to say something about British reactions to the changing position of women.

The *Daily Mail*, for its part, was recycling some of its familiar correspondents in slightly different roles. Harold Cardozo, whom we last saw exaggerating Franco's successes in Spain, was now doing the same thing in France.

FRENCH ARMY POURING OVER GERMAN BORDER

Fighting All Along Line; Advance Against Shell and Machine-gun Hail

HEAVY BOMBING

by HAROLD CARDOZO, Daily Mail Correspondent

PARIS, Wednesday.

French troops are tonight pouring over the frontier between the Maginot and Siegfried Lines, penetrating into German territory. In all sectors they have been faced with resistance. Artillery men have shelled them. Machine-gunners have poured a rain of fire on them. But according to the Paris radio they have captured many fortified positions with tanks. Their morale is excellent.

Perhaps it was; but as an account of what was really going on this is woeful – and not just in terms of writing style, though 'Artillery men have shelled them' must be one of the weakest lines in the reporting of the entire Second World War. This French attack (unlike some of Cardozo's accounts of offensives in Spain) did genuinely take place. The French enjoyed what should have been a decisive advantage in terms of numbers, since most of the German army was involved in attacking Poland.

The Wehrmacht withdrew from a couple of dozen German villages near Saarbrücken, which the French then occupied. But after they had taken Warndt Forest the French offensive came to a halt. On 12 September, with British agreement, it was decided not to attack any further. The aim of the strategy was to draw off German forces from the attack on Poland, but Hitler and the German High Command had read the situation correctly: the French army, like the British Expeditionary Force, lacked the will to press the offensive home. Not a single German soldier was diverted to the Western front to counter it. When the French and British decided to call it off, no one troubled to tell the Poles. The Western democracies had shown themselves to be as feeble and soft as Hitler had always said they were.

Another of the *Mail*'s star correspondents from the previous few years was given a makeover. Hitler's admirer, the personal friend of Goering and Ribbentrop, George Ward Price was now described in the paper as 'Britain's Best-Informed Writer on Hitler and Modern Germany'; which was accurate, given that he, like his proprietor Lord Rothermere, had been so close and so sympathetic to the Nazi Party. Not that it was easy to guess any of this from his articles now: Ward Price was now as full of fighting talk and anti-Nazism as anyone.

On 5 September the *Mail* ran a prominent article by him called 'Germany's Weakness'. This weakness, apparently, was that ordinary Germans, whose 'fundamental inclination is towards Communism', would eventually stop supporting Hitler.

> I do not expect anything to happen until the hardships of war have broken the superficial crust of German solidarity, but it was perhaps significant that as Hitler drove away from the Chancellery to assume command on the Eastern Front, four of his bodyguard were standing on the running-boards of his car.
>
> I have seen Hitler moving about Germany scores of times, but never before has he needed such protection.

It seems an absurdly trivial observation on which to base such a wide-ranging judgement.

By 8 October, Ward Price had changed his mind. It wouldn't now be the German people who would pose the real threat to Hitler, but the

Soviet Union. He wrote a feature article called 'Hitler's Last Ride', which dealt with the problems Hitler would face after his victory over Poland.

> [W]hen the cheering dies down and he finds himself alone, or with a few of those of his subordinates who are not totally subservient in mind as well as word, grim doubt must creep into his mind.
>
> As he looks eastward across the Vistula he will remember with apprehension that but a few miles distant are the outposts of the great Red Army . . .

Britain's best-informed writer on Hitler seemed to have surprisingly little insight into the mind of the man he had once so admired; vulnerability to 'grim doubt' was scarcely one of Hitler's characteristic weaknesses. Hitler had nothing but contempt for Stalin and the Red Army, whose officer corps had been decimated in the Moscow treason trials as a result of cleverly planted but false information leaked to the Russians by Hitler's military intelligence.

Perhaps, though, it didn't matter why Ward Price was suggesting that Hitler could not last much longer; the important thing was that he should do it at all. The *Mail*'s readers would not easily have forgotten his sudden transformation from sympathizer to bitter critic. It looks as though he, or perhaps the *Mail*'s owner, thought he had to write fiercer and fiercer stuff, in order to forestall any doubts about his true beliefs now that war had broken out: 'Never was the outlook so sombre for Nazi Germany as at the moment when, having succeeded in her bandit-stroke against Poland, she faces the Nemesis that the arrogance of her own demigod has aroused.'

This was the intensity of language which Ward Price and Rothermere had previously reserved for the enemies of appeasement. They and the *Mail* clearly wanted to wipe out any memories of their views in the recent past.

§

After the first few months of war, the initial excitement had faded. It was clear that the real test of strength was still some way off. 'Big Scale Battle May Not Be Fought This Year', reported David Scott of the *News*

Chronicle on Thursday 5 October, quoting some prescient staff officers he had spoken to in Northern France. The sense of lassitude which had been evident before Hitler's attack on Poland began to return. Yet at the same time so did a feeling that the old ex-appeasers in government weren't really interested in prosecuting the war with any enthusiasm. Chamberlain kept his bowel cancer a complete secret from his colleagues and from the press, but it must have affected his professional energy and perhaps his judgement. People began to sense this. A cartoon by Zec in the *Daily Mirror* at this time showed a row of empty seats in an empty Cabinet room. The meaning was clear: no one was in charge.

But one chair in the Cabinet room was unquestionably occupied: Winston Churchill's. His return as First Lord of the Admiralty had brought a liveliness to Chamberlain's government which (except for Leslie Hore-Belisha, the Secretary of State for War who was much disliked by the generals for his 'showmanship', and was sacked by Chamberlain in January 1940) was otherwise completely lacking. Of the three services, the Royal Navy under Churchill was by far the most aggressive. He misused the intelligence reports he received to give the impression that more U-boats were being sunk than was actually the case, but this helped him to put Chamberlain in the shade. The *Daily Mirror* wrote on 3 October 1939: 'It is hardly premature to say that in popular imagination Churchill has already ousted Chamberlain as the dominant war figure.'

In the early months of the war, when only nine out of around sixty German submarines had been confirmed sunk, Churchill claimed that half of the entire U-boat fleet had been destroyed. On 27 September 1939, the *Manchester Guardian* reported: 'Mr Churchill, First Lord of the Admiralty, described in the House of Commons yesterday how great a measure of success Britain has already won in the war against the menace of the German U-boat.'

The press, which was in no position in wartime to question his figures, and would anyway not have wanted to do it for reasons of national morale, reported his claims as fact.

But this willingness on the newspapers' part to accept what they were told was becoming dangerous. The invasion of Norway in April 1940, and Britain's woeful response to it, was the turning point for the Chamberlain government. Yet the British press played a scarcely discernible part in the unfolding events. They were spectators.

Norway, a neutral country with an immensely long seaboard, useful ports and large supplies of wood and iron ore, was an obvious German target. Hitler had made it clear in 1939 that Germany must take control of it before the British could get there. Churchill understood that cutting Germany's supplies of iron ore through the port of Narvik would seriously hamper Hitler's production of military equipment for the rest of 1940. But Chamberlain and others in the Cabinet opposed Churchill's demands for vigorous action in Norway. It was not until Monday 8 April that the Royal Navy laid mines in neutral waters off the Norwegian coast. The previous Thursday, Chamberlain, using one of the slang phrases which he occasionally slipped into his speeches when he wanted a head-line, said that Hitler had 'missed the bus' with his plans to invade Norway. It was the old Chamberlain speaking, with all his former smugness. It was just as self-delusional.

Within twelve terrible hours on Tuesday 9 April, German forces invaded Denmark and Norway, and took control of Oslo and the main Norwegian ports. It was a textbook example of Blitzkrieg, one of the fastest and most effective actions of the entire war. Churchill quickly sent in a task force headed by HMS *Warspite*, and the British took control of part of the coast, destroying thirty German naval ships; but the cost to the British was also high.

For the most part Churchill escaped without blame, either in the press or from public opinion. The *Daily Mirror*, which despite its left-wing, populist self-image had been less critical of the Chamberlain government than it might have been, was now full of Churchill's praises. On Monday 15 April its main editorial read: '"We shall sink every German ship," said Mr Winston Churchill on Thursday, and by heaven, these brave words are coming true . . . On Saturday night the public learned that the enemy had been "socked" again, another seven of their destroyers having been sunk at Narvik.'

The previous Friday, 12 April, a hastily assembled expeditionary force of British, French and Polish soldiers was sent to Norway. Many of the British troops were Territorials who had never seen action before. They lacked proper equipment; although spring had not yet started, they were given no snowshoes or skis, and no white camouflage for use in the snow. They were woefully under-supplied with weapons, ammunition, com-munications equipment and even maps. Troops earmarked for one sector would be suddenly diverted to another at the last moment. It took two whole days for the War Office to give permission to RAF pilots to attack

Norwegian airfields held by German troops. The various service chiefs in London disagreed continually about what should be done. Churchill, who had taken over as head of the Cabinet's military coordinating committee a few days earlier, had no power to take decisions on his own.

It was an object lesson in how to lose a war; and yet every element of this disaster, from the shambles on the ground to the utter confusion in Whitehall, was kept hidden from the British public. The newspapers themselves knew scarcely anything about it. Because of the confusion with which the task force for Norway had been put together, there was no system for war correspondents to go with the troops. Censorship was one of the few things which worked effectively. All the British people were told about the fighting was that it was going well. 'Herr Hitler has committed a grave strategic error,' Churchill told the House of Commons. '[W]e have greatly gained by what has happened in Scandinavia.'

The BBC, reliant solely on the news agencies, which had no more to go on than the statements concocted by the War Office, was serenely, absurdly optimistic. 'British expeditionary forces are pressing steadily forward from all points where they have landed in Norway. Resistance has been shattered along the railways. In the Namsos sector, the British and French are advancing successfully towards Trondheim.'

The *Mail* was trumpeting much the same sort of thing, with a noisier patriotic accompaniment: 'The Royal Navy has embarked on a glorious enterprise. Hitler is shaken by the hammer-blows of our sailors and airmen.'

In the end, the British acquitted themselves rather well in Norway. On 28 May the expeditionary force, together with the Norwegians, captured Narvik and thereby achieved the first Allied infantry victory of the Second World War. But it was soon meaningless. Germany had begun its Blitzkrieg in France, and the British forces were needed there. Narvik was abandoned soon afterwards, and Norway was left to its fate.

At the beginning of the brief Norwegian campaign the only note of questioning came from the *Daily Herald*, the official newspaper of the Labour Party. The *Herald* boasted one of the largest circulations of any newspaper in the world; in 1933 it had had certified net sales of two million. Yet as far as advertisers were concerned, it was the wrong 2 million. Most people who bought the *Herald* were by definition predominantly working class and socialist: therefore not likely to be big consumers. Although the Trades Union Congress had oversight of its editorial policy the *Herald*'s publisher, Julius Elias (created Lord Southwood by Chamberlain in 1937), had insisted that it should support appeasement, in the hope that potential advertisers would not be offended.

Was it Southwood's continuing loyalty to Chamberlain that made the *Herald* criticize Churchill's Narvik operation? Or was it Labour's residual dislike of Churchill the maverick Conservative? Whatever the reason, the *Herald* was unconvinced by Churchill's strategy.

> In this unequal battle the British ships, because of the great bravery and skill of the men aboard them, won a brilliant victory.
>
> But one of the British destroyers was sunk, a second so severely injured that she had to be run ashore, a third seriously damaged, a fourth slightly damaged. Only the fifth was untouched . . .
>
> Why . . . were our men and ships risked in this uneven combat?

The *Herald* also complained that the Admiralty, under Churchill, had agreed to the publication of a Reuter's report which wrongly claimed that the cities of Bergen and Trondheim had been captured by the British. The Admiralty, said the *Herald*, must not allow this kind of thing to happen again, otherwise people around the world would soon assume that news passed by the British censor was no more reliable than Nazi propaganda. It is not impossible that the *Herald* had been given a private glimpse of the chaos in Norway, perhaps through the experiences of someone related to someone on the paper's staff. Perhaps; but it was not based on the observations of one of its correspondents.

It took an American journalist, and the letters of one or two officers, which were sent back to Britain, for the facts to come out. Leland Stowe of the *Chicago Daily News* managed to link up with a few survivors of a battle outside Namsos, where the British had suffered heavy losses. One of them, a lieutenant in the Territorial Army, told him excitedly:

> 'We've been massacred! Simply massacred! We've got no planes! The Jerries have been bombing us all after-noon . . . It's been bloody awful! . . . We've got no proper clothes for these mountains. We've got no white capes.

> The Jerries could see us everywhere in the snow. They
> just mowed our men down. I tell you, it's that bloody
> Chamberlain! I'm glad you're a reporter. For God's sake,
> tell them we've got to have aeroplanes and anti-aircraft
> guns! Tell them everything we've said!'

The *Chicago Daily News* reports caused a sensation in the United States, and were much reprinted. American opinion, never very enthusiastic about losers, turned further against Britain and became even more isolationist. According to the *New Republic*, a liberal political journal, 'even if it became desirable on other grounds to enter the conflict against Hitlerism, it would be fatal to enlist under this banner'.

A combination of censorship and self-censorship ensured that none of this, including Stowe's despatches, was reprinted in Britain; but the word quickly spread in newspaper offices and beyond. The Ministry of Information put out a statement by the War Office which called the American reports 'an obvious distortion of the facts': not an outright denial. As in the First World War, a noticeable gap was opening up between the official news and the news people heard in pubs and on the street. The CBS correspondent Edward R. Murrow, who, unlike many of the American correspondents in Britain, was a confirmed Anglophile, reported on this in a broadcast on Monday 22 April.

> There can be no question that the handling by the press and radio
> in this country of the news from Norway ... has undermined the
> confidence of a considerable section of the British public in the
> integrity and accuracy of its news sources.

The second source of information was letters from the front. Officers in Norway found ways of getting round the censorship, and sent their letters unedited to Britain. Some wrote to their MPs, or to other politicians. Then, on Thursday 2 May, Chamberlain told the Commons that British forces were evacuating two of their positions in Norway, Namsos and Andalsnes. He admitted, too, that the expeditionary force had not been properly equipped and had lacked air cover. It was a great shock to the country. The crime writer, Margery Allingham, wrote in her war diary that it was 'a sudden and paralysing revelation that Chamberlain was a vain old man who had nothing particular up his sleeve'.

At first it seemed possible that Churchill might be more damaged by it all than Chamberlain. To his enemies, it seemed like a repeat of the Dardanelles, which had brought him down in the First World War. When an internal political crisis erupts today, the newspapers are full of insinuations and leaks from supporters of the different sides. But in May 1940 the newspapers were less open to this kind of backstairs campaign. Chamberlain's supporters, especially Lord Dunglass who twenty-four years later would briefly become prime minister as Sir Alec Douglas-Home, passed around many stories designed to damage Churchill, but not to the press; they were intended for the ears of politicians. Churchill, by contrast, stayed remarkably loyal to Chamberlain right through the crisis, and instructed his followers not to undermine him.

The lobby correspondents of the newspapers knew what was going on, but gave the public no real hint during the first few days of May that a titanic battle for Britain's future was going on behind the scenes. The editorial writers did not intervene to influence the debate in the Conservative Party. Chamberlain should have been grateful for the newspapers' silence; but he had developed an intense anger against the press since the collapse of his efforts at appeasement. At the Cabinet meeting on 3 November 1939 he went into a long rant about the press and its hostility to his policies. It

> amounted to a mass-produced and artificial agitation which bore no relation to any spontaneous feeling of indignation in the country. The explanation of so unpatriotic a course of conduct on the part of newspaper proprietors lay in the degeneration of our Press . . . A free Press today meant a commercial Press out for money and not interested in principles or ideas.

The man who had bullied and controlled the press so successfully had no understanding of what motivated the men and women who wrote for it.

The debate on Norway, which was to change the course of the war, opened in the House of Commons shortly before four o'clock on the afternoon of Tuesday 7 May. Mistaken as ever, Chamberlain had written to one of his admiring sisters, 'I don't think my enemies will get me this time.' When he made his opening statement he argued that this was a time for closing ranks, not for 'quarrelling amongst ourselves'. It was weak and unconvincing, and one correspondent described it in the following morning's paper as 'his obituary notice'.

The *Daily Mail*, in its report of the opening day of the debate, showed how its approach had changed. Not long before, it would have relegated any criticism of Chamberlain to the end of its article. Not now. Percy Cater, the *Mail*'s parliamentary correspondent, opened his report like this:

> Two sensations followed swiftly in the Norway debate in the House of Commons last night. Admiral of the Fleet Sir Roger Keyes created the first with a devastating attack on 'ineptitude' and timidity in the use of the Fleet.
>
> Mr L.S. Amery, who followed, created the second. He attacked the Government strongly, and startled the House with this crushing conclusion:
>
> 'Cromwell said to the Long Parliament, when he thought it was no longer fit to conduct the affairs of the nation: "You have stayed too long here for any good you are doing. Depart, I say, let us have done with you. In the name of God, go."'

It was Leo Amery's attack which did the real damage. He was an interesting character who has appeared in this history briefly before; he was a *Times* correspondent in the Boer War, who worked alongside Churchill (who had once pushed him into a swimming pool at Harrow School), just avoided being taken prisoner with him, and was briefly accredited to the Boer forces and spoke Afrikaans. He made friendships easily and kept most of them his entire life. The Second World War would later see his promotion to the Cabinet and his son Julian's courage and success during his service with the Special Operations Executive; it also saw his other son John defect to the Nazis, and suffer execution as a traitor after Hitler's defeat.

Leo Amery's speech in the Commons, culminating in the quotation from Cromwell, played a significant part in Chamberlain's fall. Yet he was lucky. The Speaker, Sir Edward Fitzroy, a Chamberlain loyalist, knew he was planning to attack Chamberlain and seems to have ignored him deliberately each time he stood up in the hope of catching Fitzroy's eye. He finally called him at around eight o'clock, when most of the MPs had drifted out to have dinner and the House was almost empty. But Amery's friends went around calling MPs back to the chamber, and by spinning out his speech he managed to wait until it was almost full before launching into the devastating final section.

After he had wound up the debate and the division was called, Winston Churchill walked into the 'aye' lobby in support of Chamberlain. He had been punctilious about backing him during the debate. It was right both morally and tactically; his loyalty to Chamberlain now and later ensured that Chamberlain felt obliged to be equally loyal to Churchill in the vital Cabinet debates that would follow.

The teller read out the result of the vote in a harsh voice: 'The ayes to the right, 281. The noes to the left, 200.' There was bedlam. Although Chamberlain had won the vote easily, he would usually have had a majority of around 250. To have lost so much support from his own party was a resigning matter.

The following morning, the *Daily Herald*'s perceptive lobby correspondent, Maurice Webb, described the likely effect of the attacks:

GOVT. CHANGES COMING:
CHAMBERLAIN MAY GO

Sweeping reconstruction of the Government, involving the possible resignation of Mr Chamberlain, is now widely regarded as inevitable in the near future . . .

[T]he Prime Minister's speech yesterday was regarded in every responsible quarter as that of a losing man.

Webb was right. He had gauged the feelings of Conservative MPs correctly. It wasn't easy: those who were against Chamberlain were often nervous about challenging a prime minister who had so often crushed dissent ruthlessly in the past, while those who were in favour of his staying had been unsettled by the clear revelation of his unsuitability. Maurice Webb's was the only report that morning to make such a bold prophecy.

Yet Chamberlain did not resign immediately. That night, after the vote, he went to his office in the Palace of Westminster and asked Winston Churchill to see him. Once again, Churchill stayed loyal. He advised Chamberlain to stay on. Chamberlain decided that he would see if he could raise the necessary support the next day; but he soon realized he could remain only if the Labour Party joined his government: and he knew that was an impossibility. That morning the lead editorial in the *Herald*, Labour's newspaper, was headed 'Go! Go! Go!' And: 'He has worked hard and selflessly. He has done his best for us. But we have reached a stage at which, if we are to avoid defeat and slavery, his best will not do.'

So Chamberlain had to go. But who should succeed him? He wanted the Earl of Halifax, but Halifax himself knew this was impossible. He had no experience of military affairs, and would have to let Churchill control the key Cabinet committees; and since he was a peer he would not be able to sit in the House of Commons, where the real decisions were made. There too Churchill would be in control. By the evening it seemed clear that Churchill would get the job.

The next morning, Friday 10 May, the BBC reported that German troops were invading Belgium, Luxembourg and the Netherlands. Chamberlain tried to use this to stay on, but had to give way. The lobby correspondents knew all about these manoeuvrings, but there was no mention of them in the press. When it became clear that the Netherlands would fall that day to the Germans, Chamberlain went to see King George VI, who had been an enthusiastic appeaser (that was not reported in the press, either) and advised him to invite Churchill to be the next prime minister. Churchill went to Buckingham Palace that evening. He had got the job without stabbing either Chamberlain or Halifax in the back. But he was considerably relieved, all the same; with characteristic realism and a touch of humour he wrote later, 'Considering the prominent part I played in it [the disastrous Norway campaign] . . . it was a marvel I survived.'

Rarely has the British press greeted an incoming prime minister with such rapture. Newspapers which had sniped at Winston Churchill for decades now regarded him as the country's saviour.

> The new Prime Minister will be hailed by the people
> as the man called by Destiny to serve the nation at
> this grave hour.

That was the *Daily Mail* on the morning of Saturday 11 May, the very paper which in the past had called him 'reckless', 'unreliable' and 'careless of the country's interests'.

> He is one of those who have never been deceived by
> the character and purpose of our treacherous enemy
> . . . [H]e realises what he has to face, and what, under
> his leadership, we all have to face.

That was the *Daily Mirror* on the same day, praising a man it had once described as 'difficult to trust'. But the British press was anxious to put party divisions aside. In its editorial the *Mirror* itself chose to draw a line under its opposition to Chamberlain.

> [I]n the moment of his withdrawal, we salute him in
> silence and say not one word about or against his
> record as the nation's leader during the gravest crisis
> in our history.

The *Manchester Guardian* hoped that for the first time Britain now had bold leadership and a truly national government. The *Daily Herald* made it clear that the Labour Party, which had consistently refused to join a coalition with Chamberlain, would now do so with Churchill. Only *The Times*, which had also begun to criticize Chamberlain before his resignation, spoke wistfully of his 'courageous and distinctive service'.

14

DUNKIRK TO THE BLITZ

On Monday morning, 17 June 1940, Godfrey Talbot was the senior sub-editor on duty in the BBC newsroom in Broadcasting House. At around eleven o'clock the bells on the agency tape machines rang, and the messenger ran over with the piece of paper he had torn off the printer. Reuter's was reporting from France that Marshal Pétain, who had taken over as prime minister from Paul Reynaud the previous day, was asking Germany for armistice terms. Talbot read through the wires that were soon pouring out of the machines, and dictated his story for the *One O'Clock News* to a typist.

> The word got around Broadcasting House that this terrible thing had happened, the French had given up. I was conscious of people coming and standing behind my shoulder and you could hear the swift intake of breath as they read what I was dictating.

Although it had been half-expected, it was a terrible shock. After the invasions of Denmark, Norway, Luxembourg, Belgium and the Netherlands, it had seemed unlikely that the German Blitzkrieg could be stopped by the lacklustre French army and the small, inexperienced British Expeditionary Force. And yet the news during the previous couple of weeks had seemed so positive. The BBC, whose reports were still almost exclusively derived from the news agencies, was relentlessly optimistic. Its only war correspondent in the field was Richard Dimbleby, but in April he had unaccountably asked to be switched from the Western Front to Cairo, thus missing the fall of France. Only twenty-six and with a young man's enthusiasm for the job, Dimbleby had helped to set the prevailing tone when he reported on the BEF in France:

From the Colonel on the staff to the P.B.I. (if those of you who know it will forgive the expression) squatting over an open wood fire, cooking a great pile of sausage meat buns, with faces as solemn as owls, there is the same feeling. These people don't think they will win – they know it.

The newspaper correspondents took the same line. The initiated might have noticed that some things went unmentioned, that questions were raised but not answered, but most people did not. They probably preferred it that way.

§

A month earlier, on 10 May 1940 – the day Churchill took office as prime minister – the German Blitzkrieg had begun. The *Daily Herald*'s front-page account is based exclusively on news agency reports, which are in turn entirely dependent on statements from the various war ministries of the countries involved. People reading the *Herald* or any other British newspaper that morning would not have guessed that the greatest onslaught in military history was being unleashed across a dozen fronts. For the *Herald*, as for the rest of the press, the most important element in the story was the BEF's advance into Belgium: in fact, one of the least significant elements in the entire situation.

The *Herald*'s report is worth quoting at length, to demonstrate how little the British press understood about the situation. It is intended to be factual, though the flavour of propaganda is unmistakable. You have the feeling that the aim is to soothe as much as to inform.

BRITISH MARCH INTO BELGIUM

The British Expeditionary Force is marching into Belgium. This morning, with its French Allies, it is pushing forward on a 200-mile line. The first great battle of the Western Front is raging in the tiny state of Luxembourg.

French and German advance guards are in contact there, and what are described as 'considerable engagements' are taking place on both sides of the River Moselle.

Hitler is estimated to have sent an armada of at least

1,000 planes over Holland, Belgium, Luxembourg and France during the past 24 hours. More than 150 people, including newly-born babies, have been killed by his bombers.

The French have brought down 44 enemy planes; the Dutch claim 70 and the destruction of four armoured trains.

This was the position on the various fronts at three o'clock this morning: –

Luxembourg: The Germans have overcome the resistance of the Luxembourg customs guards and advanced towards the French frontier. French and German units are in contact and fierce fighting is going on.

Belgium: The Belgians have fallen back to their main line of defence in accordance with a pre-arranged plan. All aerodromes are still in Belgian hands. A terrific air battle has been going on near Mons. Fighting is reported from Aachen, the German frontier town.

Holland: Dutch troops are making a stand along the River Ysel and have successfully flooded part of the country. In the extreme south the Germans claim to have captured the town and fort of Maastricht, taking 3,000 prisoners, to have crossed the River Maas and seized prisoners. Parachute troops are in control of one or two aerodromes. Part of Rotterdam is in Nazi hands.

A communique issued by the War Office in London last night stated: –

'Leading elements of the B.E.F., in co-operation with the French Army, entered Belgium today. They were accorded a great welcome by the Belgian population.'

There is plenty more, but it is all in the same bald, unanalysed form: and there is no mention of the word Blitzkrieg, nor of Stuka dive-bombers, or even tanks. You could read through the whole article and feel that although things weren't going too well in Rotterdam or Maastricht and the customs guards of Luxembourg had taken a knock, the rest of it seemed to be pretty much level-pegging. The *Herald*'s own correspondent

F.G.H. Salusbury had a cheery tale to tell as he crossed the Belgian border with the British troops. The headline on his article read 'Belgium Greets The B.E.F. With Flowers, Cheers'. What had really happened was rather different. The Germans had launched Operation Gelb, Hitler's big offensive in the west. Army Group A under General von Rundstedt staged the main attack through the Ardennes; Army Group B under General Bock advanced through Belgium and Holland in order to draw the main British and French forces north. Three armoured corps from Group A headed for Sedan and Dinant, and brushed aside the resistance of small detachments of French forces. To the north, meanwhile, Group B carried out parachute landings deep inside Holland, while German units crossed the Maas River near Arnhem. A German airborne force landed its gliders on top of the Belgian fort at Eben Emael, which was meant to guard against any force crossing the Albert Canal. Here and elsewhere the Luftwaffe attacked its objectives with bombers and Stukas. By evening, the German advance had gone almost precisely to plan.

Was there was some deliberately propagandist purpose behind the *Daily Herald*'s optimistic coverage? No; the *Herald*, as the Labour Party's paper, had no interest in deceiving its readers about the progress of the war effort. Labour would soon be strongly represented in Winston Churchill's government, but it had not joined it yet. It, and therefore the *Herald*, were still free agents.

The reasons were less sinister, but the result was no less misleading. The British press had little serious culture of independent military analysis in wartime. The First World War and the Spanish Civil War had shown the need for it, but in a war of national survival people actively wanted to believe what their government told them; and the War Office, even if it had been prepared to be frank about the situation, had little real information beyond the position of its own forces.

As a result, the readers of the British press and the listeners to the BBC had little understanding of the fact that Hitler's lightning war against them had begun, and no expectation whatever that within ten days the Dutch army would surrender, Brussels would be captured, and German troops would reach the English Channel; nor that within thirty-eight days France herself would fall, and Britain would be left facing the victorious Germans alone.

It took days for the seriousness of the situation to sink in. But on

Thursday 14 May the *Daily Mail*, whose coverage had usually shown a distracting cheerfulness, carried a sombre set of headlines.

FRENCH LINES PIERCED
Tanks Through at Three Points

ATTEMPT TO CUT ALLIED ARMIES
Belgium: Race for Positions

'BEF Now Fully Engaged'
Serious Attacks Held All Day

Dawn to Dusk RAF Battle

The *Mail* had a correspondent with the BEF, Paul Bewsher, who saw some of the fighting for himself. He described how groups of refugees were being attacked by German planes, but in conditions like these, with fighting going on over a wide area, it was impossible for any individual correspondent to know the overall picture. The British troops Bewsher saw behaved well and defended stubbornly; but they were in the wrong place and had nothing like the Germans' equipment or ferocity.

By the following day, though, the *Mail* was printing stories which were almost indistinguishable from propaganda – mostly based on official British and French communiqués.

R.A.F. TURN THE SCALES
Bombs Shatter Tanks that Pierced the Line

By contrast, historians remember 14 May as the day when German tanks, following up on their successes the previous day, crossed the Meuse in large numbers at Sedan and Dinant. There were no effective counter-attacks by the French. The German armour then forced its way west, making a huge gap between the French 2nd and 9th Armies. Relying on official handouts in Paris, the *Mail*'s correspondent Walter Farr writes a short account of the crossing of the Meuse:

Light enemy units reached the opposite bank, and then,
under terrific fire from pill-boxes, dug in behind machine-
guns, to prepare a way for heavier motorised detachments.
Eventually 30-ton tanks were lumbering into France.

So far, so accurate; but the French official spin, unquestioned, seems to
counter it again.

The latest news from this area is that the Allied troops are
holding the enemy column, and are closing in on it . . .
   In Paris the official opinion on the operations of the past
24 hours is that the situation has been re-established.

By this stage the French 2nd and 9th Armies had been carved up by the
German advance, and did not even have orders about which way they
should retreat.

It was not just the *Mail*. The *Daily Herald* was almost indistinguishable:

BEF DRIVES ENEMY FROM 'MARTYR TOWN'

The martyr town is Louvain, or Leuven, which was sacked and partly
destroyed by German troops in 1914. The *Herald* correspondent, Richard
McMillan, had witnessed some of the fighting himself, and vouched for
the fact that German 'shock detachments' captured the railway station,
and were then driven out of it by the British forces ('among whom was
an Irish regiment'). Paul Bewsher of the *Mail* wrote a vivid account of
the fighting:

It is like a battle inside the Crystal Palace. The Germans are
in houses on an embankment 30 foot above the station.
Hand grenades are being flung by them through the roof
and machine guns fire out from above. Broken glass rained
down continuously on the platforms and subways where
our troops are holding positions.

It is exciting stuff, especially for correspondents who, like the British
soldiers involved, had probably never seen real action before, and the
sudden shift in tenses shows that it was probably dictated fast and

nervously. Bewsher's despatch has the nervy immediacy of a good front-line television news report. But it gets its strength, as television news does, from the fact that it is looking at an action close up; reports like this are no guide whatever to how the war in general is going. Two or three years later, when both soldiers and correspondents were more experienced, a brief firefight on this scale would never have attracted such notice.

Although McMillan, Bewsher and the other correspondents with the BEF would have known nothing about it at this stage, the British and French forces were getting ready to evacuate Belgium and retreat back to France, after just a few days. The British press had simply no idea of the scale of the disaster. In a smaller article alongside its coverage of the fighting at Louvain railway station, the *Daily Herald* is talking about '"MARKED IMPROVEMENT" at SEDAN'. In fact, the situation was already desperate.

For a short while, even at this late stage in the fighting, there was still space in the papers for the occasional act of derring-do by a correspondent. All too soon the dreadfulness of the war would take over, as it did in the First World War, and people at home would no longer be so accepting of that kind of thing when they themselves, and countless millions around the world, were suffering. But the *Mail*'s Ralph Izzard, a good writer and an intelligent and courageous observer, wrote a couple of highly readable articles about a lunch he had with a 'fifth columnist' in Amsterdam, and about his escape from the city just before it fell to the Germans; he describes the constant air raids, the flight of women and children, and the problems of his fellow journalists (including a lugubrious American, who lost his trousers in the bombing). Izzard was one of the *Mail*'s best writers, and when he died years later in 1992 Jan Morris wrote in the *Independent*:

> Ralph Izzard was most people's beau idéal of the old-school foreign correspondent, in that he was not only brave and resourceful, but also gentlemanly, widely read, kind, a bit raffish, excellent to drink with, fun to travel with, handsome but louche, honourable but thoroughly disrespectful.

It was not just an obituary for an individual, but for an entire calling.

§

In spite of its extraordinary significance there were no newspaper or agency correspondents at Dunkirk, no photographers, and only one newsreel cameramen. The newsmen accredited to the BEF were evacuated from Boulogne on 24 May, before the Dunkirk operation began. Some of the other British correspondents on the Continent had escaped, like Ralph Izzard; others, to the south of the invading German forces, had headed for Paris, where the French were still holding on. There were six accredited British newspaper correspondents who were temporarily based in the city, plus a man from the BBC, a couple of photographers and two newsreel cameramen. The main press hotel was, agreeably enough, the Crillon. When it became clear that Paris would soon fall (it finally happened on 14 June) they joined the long trek southwards, where they hoped to reach a port from which they could get home. These correspondents often had important and terrible stories to tell, but it proved impossible to get their material back to London. Like the rest of them, Noel Monks, a *Daily Mail* correspondent who had been accredited to the RAF in France and covered the last hopeless days as the Germans closed in and the French themselves turned hostile, was completely out of contact with his office in London. 'A whole world was collapsing around us, but there were no means of getting a line about it to our newspapers, simply because there were no more communications and no censors.'

The army and the RAF had enough to do to look after their own people. The journalists were left to look after themselves; they were obliged to band together into small groups, pool their resources, and do what they could. Monks had a good story – the French had refused to allow the remaining RAF planes to use their airfields in the latter stages of the withdrawal – but after he had struggled back to Britain via Bordeaux a month later, no one was very interested. France had fallen, Britain faced Hitler alone, the world had moved on.

On the evening of Sunday 26 May the War Cabinet ordered the Royal Navy to commence Operation Dynamo, the evacuation of as many British, French and other Allied troops from Dunkirk as possible, and the operation continued throughout the week. But for days the censors requested the newspapers to keep quiet about it. There are no references in the press to the extraordinary events on the Dunkirk beaches until the morning of Friday 31 May; and even then, because of the skewed nature of their coverage, based solely on official statements, the newspapers clearly thought that the last-ditch stand of the Allies was more significant than the operation to rescue the troops.

When King Leopold of Belgium surrendered on 28 May, Britain and France, which had risked their armies to help Belgium, found that they were suddenly exposed to even greater danger. Fortunately much of the Belgian army decided to ignore the king's orders, and continued to protect the British and French flanks, but the British commander, Lord Gort, had only an hour to decide what to do and issue his orders.

That morning, before the news of the king's actions had come through, the *Daily Herald*'s diplomatic correspondent, the level-headed and usually well-informed W.N. Ewer, summed up the situation in a lead story headlined:

SITUATION GRAVER THIS MORNING

> The military position in Flanders this morning is one of the utmost gravity.
>
> The British front indeed 'remains intact', as last night's GHQ communique puts it. The Germans are paying a terrible toll of lives for every attack they make.
>
> But for all that the fact remains that the British, French and Belgian forces to the north of the 'gap' are in grave danger of being cut off not only from the French army south of the Somme, but also from their own chief bases and sources of supply.

Ewer was a tough and clever man. He once rebuked Mussolini publicly for making an anti-British remark – not something many people would have dared to do – and silenced Andrei Vyshinsky, formerly the ferocious, bullying prosecutor in Stalin's show trials, at a news conference in Moscow. He was universally known as 'Trilby', because, like the eponymous heroine of du Maurier's novel, he used to walk around (even apparently at his club, the Savage) with his feet bare.

Ewer's articles contained none of the mindless optimism that many newspapers were printing during the fighting which led up to Dunkirk. Alexander Werth, the Russian-born correspondent for the *Manchester Guardian*, later described in his book about the fall of France how guilty he felt for the kind of 'soft soap' he had written about that aspect of the war. Ewer, in fact, did not go in for soft soap; he was too shrewd, and too well informed. Yet his article quoted above does not contain the slightest hint that British troops are being evacuated from Dunkirk. He stuck strictly to the terms of the D-Notice which Rear Admiral Thomson had issued, and did not permit himself the most indirect allusion to the major change in the situation.

Neither was there any reference to it in any of the papers the next day, but on Thursday 30 May, Walter Farr, the *Mail*'s man in Paris, struck a remarkable note of optimism, given the desperate situation. It sounds at first like the vacuous stuff that many of the papers, and the *Mail* especially, had been putting out on the basis of official communiqués. This time, though, it turned out to be justified.

B.E.F. MAY YET WIN OUT: FRENCH HOPES

The B.E.F., with the French Allies in Northern France, continuing their withdrawal to a defence line covering the coast, are fighting the greatest rearguard battle in history.

But tonight there is hope in official circles in Paris that the situation may yet be saved. There are indications that the German assault, by its very ferocity, is tiring.

For once the official statements on which everyone – newspapers, radio and the general public – was obliged to depend were not completely untruthful, even though they sounded as blandly reassuring as ever: 'The B.E.F. and the French armies in the north are still intact, it was authoritatively stated in London last night.'

Later that day, the decision was taken to allow the press to reveal something of the nature of the evacuation, four full days after it had started. There were even a few hundred feet of film, though there could have been more. A cameraman for Pathé News, Charles Martin, had got permission to go on board one of the naval destroyers which sailed for Dunkirk from Harwich. They arrived at dawn and he filmed the long, patient lines of soldiers wading out to the ship, some of them up to their necks in the water. He decided that the real priority was to help them on board, so he put his camera down and joined the sailors in pulling the men up the side.

It had turned from the frailest of hopes into a surprising success. The original plan was for the operation to last for two days in the hope of getting 45,000 men out of Dunkirk and back to Britain. On Monday the 27th, the first full day of Operation Dynamo, only 7,699 men were taken off. On Tuesday 28th the figure was 17,804. On Wednesday 29th, 47,310; on Thursday 30th, 53,823; on Friday 31st, the most successful day of all, 68,014, and on Saturday 1 June 64,429.

But by now the Germans were getting dangerously close to the port, and would soon be within two miles. The accuracy of their artillery and the constant attacks of their Stuka dive-bombers convinced the British and French to evacuate the men by night only. As a result the figure for Sunday 2nd was down to 26,256 and for Monday 3rd it was 26,746. On the final day, Tuesday 4 June, 26,175 soldiers, almost all of them French, got away. The last British soldiers left on Sunday, but among the French who were left there was a good deal of confusion. Many of them had gone into hiding and appeared only at the last moment; so, although there would have been sufficient capacity to take them as well, nearly 40,000 men were captured when the Germans finally took Dunkirk.

The total number of soldiers brought back to Britain has sometimes varied a little in the telling, but it comes properly to 338,256, of whom a little over 150,000 were French. During the battle on the beaches, the Germans outnumbered the Allies – there were Dutch and Poles as well as British, French and Belgians – by two to one: 800,000 to 400,000. The Allies lost 30,000 killed or wounded, the Germans more than 52,000. The British had also abandoned almost all their equipment, including nearly 1,000 pieces of heavy artillery. Raymond Daniell of the *New York Times* tried to report this, but the censor firmly struck it out.

When journalists are present at some important event, it does not, as we know, necessarily lead to greater accuracy of understanding. But it often helps to fix a single interpretation of the event in people's minds; and that, in the long run, tends to become the core around which both popular myth and formal history can coalesce and start to form the accepted version. The shorthand form of this is the old cliché that journalism is the first draft of history. Without the reporter's input, an accepted version becomes harder to achieve. Because there were no correspondents at Dunkirk, the popular version – plucky soldiers, the rescuers in the little boats, the constant bombing and shelling, the V-signs, the happy return – not only took over, it became tiresomely exaggerated.

Not surprisingly, it was only twenty years before this version was challenged. Richard Collier's book *The Sands of Dunkirk* is based on interviews with survivors who talked about drunkenness, robbery, murder and utter cowardice on the beaches of Dunkirk. Of course such things occurred. Given that so many officers and NCOs had been killed, and so many men had become separated from their units, there were plenty of breakdowns in discipline.

Yet this is no more the whole picture than the games of cricket, the Guards drilling on the sands, and the despatch riders' spectaculars to divert the troops even when the shells were landing. Both existed side-by-side, with the disciplined behaviour far outweighing the bad; but because there were no newspaper accounts from experienced correspondents (the censors were also missing at Dunkirk, so it might have been easier to have got more honest stories through the system) the right balance was never quite struck. But it never would have been, anyway. Journalists' stories usually combine elements that are broadly positive with others that are negative; and in wartime the censors usually cut out the negative things, with the result that the reporting tends to glow with unalloyed optimism.

It is just possible that if there had been journalists at Dunkirk some of the inaccuracies about the evacuation might have been disposed of: that the French were hostile and obstructive, for instance, or that the RAF left the soldiers unprotected against the Luftwaffe. It was the French rearguard action, tying up several German divisions, which bought enough time for the evacuation to take place, and the French navy lost seven destroyers to the Royal Navy's six as they tried to ferry the men to England. Tens of thousands made the journey back on French and Dutch ships. As for the RAF, it tended to attack the Luftwaffe some time before its planes reached Dunkirk, so the men on the ground were unaware of the air battles that were going on. As the Luftwaffe itself acknowledged more than once, it lost its air superiority for the first time in the war at Dunkirk, and it may well have lost more planes than the Allies as well.

It is hard to imagine why, knowing something at least of what was going on at Dunkirk, no enterprising journalist managed to get a small boat to take him across the Channel to see what was happening there. For the little boats were almost as much of 'the story' – journalists see everything in terms of 'stories' – as the evacuation itself. Somehow, they summed up everything the British felt they stood for: a decent amateurism, a willingness to sacrifice everything in order to help, the defiance of a free people against the worst dictatorship imaginable, and all bound up with the messing around in boats which British people often feel is something peculiarly their own.

The Royal Navy's own careful records show that only a few thousand soldiers were brought back to Britain in small boats, and this has sometimes led to suggestions that this too was just another romantic legend. In fact the boats were used chiefly to ferry the soldiers from the beaches and the port to the big ships standing out away from the shallow waters of the coast, which then transported them to England. At least 100,000 were taken off like this: almost a third of the total.

Yet even on Friday 31 May, five days after Operation Dynamo began, the newspapers seem divided as to which was the more important story: the fighting or the evacuation. The *Daily Herald*, uncertain which to concentrate on, tried to balance the two.

> THIS MORNING, WHILE THOUSANDS MORE B.E.F.
> HEROES ARE BEING FERRIED SAFELY HOME ACROSS
> THE CHANNEL, THE BRITISH, FRENCH AND BELGIAN
> REARGUARD IS LOCKED IN A LAST DESPERATE
> STRUGGLE ON THE FLANDERS COAST.

Below the headlines, Reginald Foster broke the news of the evacuation for the first time.

> Many thousands of men from the B.E.F. have been brought
> safely out of Northern France and Belgium.
>   They have been landing daily at ports on the South
> Coast.
>   Until now no hint could be given of this – one of the
> most glorious feats of British arms.

The BBC's *Six O'Clock News* that night followed the same line: 'Men of the undefeated British Expeditionary Force have been coming home from France . . . Their morale is as high as ever. They are anxious only to be back soon – "to have a real crack at Jerry".'

It was nothing more than propaganda. They had had their chance to 'have a real crack at Jerry'; how was it, if they were 'undefeated', that they needed another opportunity? But the BBC, like the newspapers, was anxious not to frighten people by being too frank about what had happened. It was easier to take refuge in patriotic blithering.

By the following day, Saturday 1 June, all the papers had decided that the evacuation was a more important and interesting story than the battle on the Flanders coast; even though the 51st Highland Division, which had protected the Dunkirk area, was about to be overwhelmed by the advancing Germans. And so the *Daily Mail*'s lead that morning, by the ineffable George Ward Thomas, now no longer introduced as 'the man who knows the Nazi leaders', concentrates on the returning soldiers.

> For hours yesterday I stood in the streets of an English Channel port and watched them streaming ashore, weary, heavy-eyed, but indomitable . . .
>
> It is a picture of staggering heroism, fighting spirit, and a determination that never weakened in the least degree in the face of overwhelming odds in men and material.

This of course is precisely the kind of tone that made the *Mail* so loathed by soldiers in the First World War: the vocabulary of praise is on autopilot, yet nothing could induce the purveyor of it to go and see for himself what he was talking about. In reality, though, the situation was very different. This would not be a war where civilians sat at home, understanding nothing of the sufferings of the soldiers. Soon life would be as dangerous for many civilians as it was for the troops, and everyone knew that the bombs would not be long in coming.

During the operation to repatriate them from Dunkirk, many of the soldiers talked about the reception they were likely to get at home. Large numbers seemed to expect that they would be shouted at or perhaps physically attacked for having been defeated. When they found they were treated like heroes, and that reporters like Ward Price were praising them to the skies, they were glad, not resentful. They fitted in with what they knew everybody wanted to hear, and with what they knew they ought to feel, even if they didn't, and they spoke in jokey but defiant terms about getting a rematch with the Germans. Like everyone else in Britain, they felt they would not have long to wait.

The press was overjoyed by the success of the evacuation. For the moment, there is no note of anxiety or questioning; just relief. The newspapers and the BBC had been happy to cover up the truth in what they thought was the national interest. It was left to Winston Churchill himself to decide that the national interest was better served by warning the British people that Dunkirk had been the culmination of a serious defeat. He was unwilling to join in the huge upsurge of sentiment that washed over the nation, and called Dunkirk 'a colossal military disaster'. In the House of Commons he warned gruffly that 'wars are not won by evacuations'. Yet even though they reported his words, the press and the BBC preferred to stress the glorious nature of what had happened. It was safer, and it did not offend their readers and listeners.

§

It was in the five-minute Postscript to the *Nine O'Clock News* on the BBC Home Service on Wednesday 5 June, the day after the last troops had been brought back from the beaches of Dunkirk, that the lasting image of the evacuation was fixed permanently in the British mind.

John Boynton Priestley, at forty-five a successful novelist and play-wright from a working-class background who had nevertheless been educated at Cambridge, was selected to make the first broadcast of the brand-new Postscript series that night. He had already made his mark as a commentator by writing topical articles for the *News Chronicle* from the beginning of the war. They were pungent and sharply observed and the BBC decided he would make a good broadcaster.

During the previous ten days the audience for the *Nine O'Clock News* was huge: perhaps 10 million. Most people stayed tuned in afterwards, because Priestley was a familiar if not yet a household name. His talk, in his rounded, gruff Yorkshire accent, as full-bodied as he was, showed signs perhaps of being a little too polished, its apparent simplicity the result of careful artifice. All the same, it had a sensational effect. He knew much better than to talk in high-flown terms about glory and honour. Instead he talked in an ordinary, down-to-earth way about things everyone could understand: and in particular about the little pleasure-boats which had made the crossing to Dunkirk and had been sunk there.

Among those paddle steamers that will never return was one that I knew well, for it was the pride of our ferry service to the Isle of Wight – none other than the good ship *Gracie Fields*. I tell you, we were proud of the *Gracie Fields*, for she was the glittering queen of our local line . . . But now – look – this little steamer, like all her brave and battered sisters, is immortal. She'll go sailing proudly down the years in the epic of Dunkirk. And our great grandchildren, when they learn how we began this war by snatching glory out of defeat, and then swept on to victory, may also learn how the little holiday steamers made an excursion to hell and came back glorious.

Only the British, you might think, could get this sentimental over a boat; yet there is no denying that it is highly effective stuff. The tone of his talk was much copied, and five days later, when the little boats came back to English waters, a *Daily Mirror* reporter tried his hand at the same thing: 'The Pandora was there, and the Rapid, the Elizabeth Green and the Lady Kay, and the others of that gay little Armada which plucked an Army from the jaws of death on the beaches of Dunkirk.'

On the strength of his clever, emotional broadcast Priestley became one of the most famous people in the country. His series of talks, running from June to October 1940, was a national and an international institution, seemingly encapsulating the best and calmest and most thoughtful qualities of the British. Yet not everyone liked him. Winston Churchill, for one, felt that the talks were too left wing in tone. After an intervention by his ally Brendan Bracken, the BBC dropped Priestley, even though listeners' letters were running at a level of three hundred to one in his favour. It was a familiar example of the BBC's quiet subservience to political pressure over the years.

§

The Battle of Britain, like Dunkirk, is encrusted with legend, much of it self-congratulatory. From the late 1960s on, it became a settled habit for the writers of history – not all of them historians, of course – to pull the legends to pieces; then, from the late 1980s onwards, more and more writers have tried to put them back together again. That is the way of history, both popular and academic. On a subject like this, the day-by-day reporting of newspapers is often of slight value; the correspondents had as little idea of what was happening as the rest of the population, and the essential statistics – how many planes were being shot down, how many pilots killed, how many of each were left – were of course top secret.

Dunkirk was at least an event; the Battle of Britain was just a name for a long drawn-out process, supplied by Churchill on 18 June 1940: 'The Battle of France is over. I expect the Battle of Britain is about to begin'. But it was vague and shapeless, and for some time neither the press nor ordinary well-informed people even realized that something as precise as a battle was going on. The British official histories later regarded the battle as taking place between 10 July and 31 October 1940 (itself a suspiciously neat cut-off date). German historians are vaguer: they see it as taking place between mid-August 1940 and mid-May 1941. In reality it was shorter than either of these estimates.

The first mention of the air war in George Orwell's diary, for instance, is on 9 August 1940, and it is impossible to get any sense from this that the future of the country is at stake:

> No real news for days past. Only air battles, in which, if the reports are true, the British always score heavily. I wish I could talk to some RAF officer and get some idea whether these reports are truthful.

They were not, of course; under the circumstances of a war being fought in three dimensions at 300 miles per hour, such a thing would be impossible. The RAF claimed to have shot down 2,698 German fighters and bombers, while the Luftwaffe claimed to have shot down 3,198 British aircraft, almost all of them fighters. The correct figures seem to have been 1,652 German planes lost, compared with 1,087 British ones; which means that the German claims were almost 300 per cent of the true number, while the British claims were 60 per cent too high.

In many ways a more important figure for the RAF was the number of pilots killed, since they were much less easily replaced than planes. According to the RAF's official Battle of Britain website, 2,353 British and 574 overseas pilots took part; 544 died. Apart from the British, who were naturally in a big majority, the RAF's pilots were drawn from twelve other nationalities: Poles, Canadians, Czechs and New Zealanders formed the biggest contingents, in that order. The highest proportion of deaths was among the Australians; there were 21 of them, and no fewer than 14 of those died. There were some from America, who had mostly enlisted with the Royal Canadian Air Force; but surprisingly few Americans seemed interested in fighting the Nazis at this stage in the war.

Orwell's instincts were, as ever, accurate. The newspapers were essentially fed the highest possible figures for German losses, and the lowest possible for British ones. As a result, the headlines always sounded suspicious, like this from the *Daily Sketch* on 13 July 1940:

> Eleven German 'planes were destroyed yesterday in daylight attacks on British coasts and shipping, the Air Ministry stated last night. Two of our fighters were lost. Yesterday's 'bag' brings the total German losses up to 75 lost or crippled in three days.

or this a month later:

Britannia's R.A.F. Rules the Air – New record
88 GERMANS DOWNED IN ALL-BRITAIN RAIDS

It has the ring of propaganda, and it ignored the very real dangers: irreplaceable British pilots killed, hard-to-replace Hurricanes and Spitfires being lost, airfields being bombed again and again. But German intelligence had greatly underestimated the number of fighters the RAF possessed and the efficiency of the British aircraft industry; and since German pilots were consistently tripling their real shoot-down rate, the Luftwaffe's credibility in Berlin was seriously damaged. Hitler had expected to strike a quick knock-out blow against the RAF, in spite of the fact that it constituted the only first-class air defence the Germans had come up against. The Luftwaffe had been given five weeks, from 8 August to 15 September, to destroy Fighter Command and make way for Operation Sea Lion, the amphibious and airborne invasion of Britain. When the RAF continued to put up sizeable forces of planes, even though their numbers were dangerously stretched, Hitler's belief in the Luftwaffe faded fast.

Nevertheless, RAF Fighter Command believed that two more weeks of attacks on its airfields would force it to move out of southern England for self-protection. This would have weakened Britain's air defences very considerably. The Luftwaffe, however, overconfident because of the inflated claims of the Luftwaffe pilots, believed it had virtually eliminated the RAF and its infrastructure. As a result it turned its attention to industrial and communications targets.

It was a serious strategic misjudgement, and on the night of Saturday 24 August it was compounded by a simple mistake. The details are still a matter of controversy, but it seems that a group of Heinkel bombers strayed off course and dropped their bombs over the East End and centre of London, killing large numbers of people. As an act of bravado, the RAF bombed Berlin the following night – something Goering, as the chief of the Luftwaffe, had promised would never happen.

The Luftwaffe's stock was falling even more sharply. By 14 September the rate of attrition which its pilots and planes were suffering had risen steeply, and every Luftwaffe unit was now well below its full strength. That day Hitler summoned a meeting at his headquarters. He insisted angrily that the Luftwaffe had not managed to establish air supremacy yet, and asked whether the invasion of Britain should be called off. It was decided to return to the discussion in three days' time. But the following day, 15 September, two massive attacks by German aircraft were decisively beaten off. Sixty German aircraft were shot down, compared with only twenty-six British. George Orwell watched one of the planes coming down.

> It fell slowly out of the clouds, nose foremost, just like a
> snipe that has been shot high overhead. Terrific jubilation
> among the people watching, punctuated every now and
> then by the question, 'Are you sure it's a German?'

When Hitler's follow-up conference was held on 17 September, the answer had become abundantly clear. He announced that Operation Sea Lion, the invasion of Britain, would be postponed indefinitely.

Ten days earlier, on Thursday 7 September, the RAF had realized it was off the hook. All that day and night 400 German bombers and more than 600 fighters attacked the London docks. The following morning Air Vice Marshal Keith Park, a New Zealander (who was once called 'the only man who could have lost the war in a day or even an afternoon' because he controlled the area over London and the south-east) flew over the area which had been bombed. 'It was a horrid sight,' he wrote. 'But I looked down and said, "Thank God for that", because I knew that the Nazis had switched their attack from the fighter stations thinking that they were knocked out.'

None of this was reflected in any way in the press or on the BBC. On the British side the details of the Battle of Britain were a close secret, and journalists could do no more than anyone else: look up at the sky at the vapour trails, and read the official statements issued by the Air Ministry. There was, of course, no hint from Berlin that the invasion of Britain had been called off.

For the journalists, it could be something of a game. Charles Gardner of the BBC made a much-quoted live commentary on the cliffs outside Dover on an aerial dogfight.

> Someone's hit a German ... and he's coming down ... he's completely out of control ... The pilot's bailed out by parachute ... He's going to slap into the sea and there he goes ... Smash! Oh boy! I've never seen anything as good as this ...

It was an excellent piece of live broadcasting, and it certainly chimed in with the feelings of a nation which was being attacked and might soon be invaded if the battle went the wrong way. But there were some doubts within the BBC about Gardner's open enthusiasm, and a few letters of complaint were received from listeners. Most people praised him for it, however.

It had proved surprisingly easy for the BBC to persuade the Ministry of Information to allow it to broadcast live on an air battle. Duff Cooper, the minister, understood that this kind of thing would go down remarkably well with British and overseas audiences. But the Air Ministry was worried about the effect on morale, and on the Germans, of the live broadcasting of a battle in which the RAF came off worse. As it turned out, luck was on Charles Gardner's – and the RAF's – side.

Newspapermen found time and again that precious details which they had uncovered about the progress of the battle and the men taking part in it would be cut out by the censor. It was deeply frustrating. In particular, a decision was taken that no individual pilots should be identified in the press. This was broken only after an American journalist, Dorothy Thompson (described by *Time* magazine in 1939 as one of the two most influential women in America, the other being the President's wife, Eleanor Roosevelt), managed to unearth the names and descriptions of three particular Battle of Britain aces, and published them in her column in America without going through the censor.

The three were Group Captain Douglas Bader, who had lost both his legs in a flying accident in 1931, but had been taken back by the RAF when he proved he could still fly almost as well with two false ones; Wing Commander Robert Stanford Tuck, who was famous for his elegant monogrammed silk handkerchiefs and his long cigarette holder; and an Afrikaans ex-seaman from South Africa, Group Captain Adolph 'Sailor' Malan, who shot down 27 German planes. All three were highly decorated. After the war Malan went back to South Africa and became a leading campaigner against apartheid. Douglas Bader, by contrast, became a notable right-winger after the war, and an aggressive supporter of white rule in Rhodesia. Tuck was a quieter man, in spite of his dress sense, and after a career in aircraft production retired to grow mushrooms.

Once their names had been published in America, the censors could not stop publication in Britain; so one of the basic requirements of popular journalism, having a hero to write about, became available and the Ministry of Information agreed that it was excellent propaganda.

Yet the Battle of Britain demonstrates more than most events in the twentieth century the shortcomings of journalism. As it happens, the thrust of much press reporting of the battle was broadly accurate. The RAF did shoot down more German planes than the Luftwaffe did British ones, as the newspapers said, and the battle was indeed won by the British. But the details of what really went on could only be established after the war was over; in particular, what a close-run thing it was. In such cases, it is impossible to think of journalism as being the first draft of history. It was simply the sum of what some not very well-informed people thought was happening at the time.

§

Since the 1970s a good deal of dedicated effort has gone into showing that the 'spirit of the Blitz' was little more than a propaganda effort got up by the Ministry of Information and obedient journalists, and that ordinary people believed it because they read about it or heard it on the radio. There is unquestionably some truth in this. If people were told that they were being stoic, they were more likely to stay that way. Stoicism made it much easier for the rescue services to do their job; it encouraged trust in the government; it made Britain look especially good in the eyes of the Americans, whose hoped-for entry into the war was a strategic objective second only to keeping Hitler's troops off British soil.

Desmond Hawkins, a script-writer who worked on a series for the BBC's North American service called *The Stones Cry Out*, had no doubt about what he was supposed to be doing. The series was about famous British buildings which had been damaged or destroyed in the Blitz Hawkins told Tom Hickman, the author of the BBC's own account of its wartime activities *What Did You Do in the War, Auntie: BBC at War, 1935–45*:

> [I]t was blatant propaganda. I mean, we had no doubt that we were writing propaganda to get America to stir itself and come in. But it wasn't propaganda writing, if you understand me. I would have enjoyed writing a documentary about St Clement Danes whether it had been knocked down or was still standing.

What he means is that the series had a clear purpose: to show that the Germans were deliberately committing a cultural war crime, of a kind intended to convince the Americans that Britain's cause was just. (German propaganda could, and did, do the same thing as a result of the RAF's bombing of Germany, of course.) But Hawkins was simply concerned with making the best programmes possible, on the grounds that intelligence and quality were likely to have a better propaganda effect than the generally cruder Nazi version. And no invention was needed; buildings a thousand years old were being damaged and destroyed by Hitler's war of aggression.

In a war of national survival, propaganda is a perfectly acceptable weapon to use. But Hawkins, like a great many journalists and politicians (including every minister of information), understood that it went further: that the best propaganda is the truth. During the Blitz, therefore, telling the truth about the usual stoicism of the British people, and ignoring the moments when they ceased to show it, was highly effective.

Sometimes, revisionist historians have given the impression that stoicism was a rarity during the Blitz – that people tended to behave badly rather than well, but that the propagandists covered up for them. This does not seem to have been true. Experience both in the 1940s and in more recent times has shown that this is how city-dwellers tend to react when they are being bombed. George Orwell described the same pattern of behaviour in Spain. The people of Berlin and Hamburg behaved with remarkable fortitude when they were bombed by the Allies.

In Belgrade in 1999, when NATO planes bombed the city on and off for seventy-seven days, people remained noticeably calm, though there was a great deal of anger, and the city came together in a remarkable show of solidarity against the enemy. In 1991 and 2003 the people of Baghdad, under attack by the Americans and British, behaved in very similar fashion. After the Blitz was over, George Orwell (who, we can be sure, would have been entirely honest about it if British people had behaved badly) wrote:

> It is a land of snobbery and privilege, ruled largely by the old and silly. But in any calculation about it one has got to take into account its emotional unity, the tendency of nearly all its inhabitants to feel alike and act together in moments of supreme crisis.

§

The first bombing raids on London occurred in August 1940, but on nothing like the scale that some had anticipated. From Saturday 7 September London endured fifty-eight consecutive days and nights of bombing, intended to destroy the morale of its citizens and soften them up for the delayed invasion. There was sporadic discussion inside the Cabinet and the Ministry of Information whether it was better to play down or play up the effects of the bombing, with both Churchill and the Information Minister Duff Cooper getting involved, but the clinching argument seemed to be that since everyone knew the raids were going on, they might as well be told about them in their newspapers and on the radio.

And so in the newspapers day after day, you can watch the myth of London in the Blitz being created. Sometimes, as in the *Daily Sketch* on 24 August 1940, after the first night-raid on the city, it seems deliberately propagandistic. A full page of carefully selected photographs is headed 'The Morning After – London Night Raid':

SUBURBS GIVE THE 'ALL CHEER' AGAIN

and a picture of two attractive women looking out of a shattered window is captioned: 'Smiling through – a shattered window. They won't worry if the worst they get is fresh air.'

Another photograph, of a group of disconsolate people going through the ruins left by a bomb, has a rather patronizing caption (the *Sketch* was a right-leaning paper aimed at a lower-middle-class readership): 'Residents salvaging their little treasures among the debris of their bombed homes.'

Then came a series of photographs inserted to cheer people up: a film starlet, Iris Meredith, wearing the 'latest in slacks – belted trousers topped with a spotted tuck-in shirt, and worn with a well-cut jacket'. Below her is a street-market bedecked with Union Jacks: 'Lambeth-walk, which gave the world a dance tune, is to give the R.A.F. a Spitfire. Many of its street traders display collecting-boxes as pictured here. And money is rolling in merrily.'

Beside these is a photograph of a German pilot after being captured, and the *Daily Sketch* Roll of Honour: three of the latest servicemen to be decorated with medals for bravery. The whole page has an unpleasantly manipulative feel to it.

The national newspapers and the BBC, being based in London, were largely London-centric. They all reported on the bombing of other cities, from Plymouth and Southampton to Coventry, Birmingham, Manchester, Liverpool, Glasgow and Belfast, yet the articles were often written in London from agency or stringer reports, and almost always lack the urgency and personal involvement of their reports about the bombing of London. They lack the emotion, too.

On 10 September 1940, after a great deal more damage had been caused and the large-scale day and night raids had been going on for three days, targeting the East End, the City and the West End, the *Daily Express* ran an article by one of its top women writers, Hilde Marchant, which contained the kind of emotion which Lord Beaverbrook and Arthur Christiansen both liked to see vented from time to time. During the previous day and night there had been a continuous air raid which had lasted with no serious pause for ten hours. Alongside the article are photographs of the aftermath: great clouds of smoke billowing up from the fires, crowds of women office-workers discussing how they are going to get to their jobs, and a flower vase completely untouched in a flat where everything else has been destroyed. The headlines over the article are curious, as though no one quite knew what to make of it:

Hilde Merchant looks at London – east and west – after the bombs

THE MEN GO OUT AGAIN TO WORK

£8-a-week flat tenants look for unbroken cups

At 5 a.m. I looked at London's distorted face and wept in her agony.

She was bleeding to the sky – flames and smoke rolled up to the heavens.

St. Paul's still threw a beautiful arc against the flowing red clouds.

The pinnacles and towers of our city still rose arrogantly.

Once again in the dark they had tried to flatten that working heart of our great town – the dockside, the East End, where the workmen live.

Again they had broken those small homes; and again the men came out, cleared the mess, went to work.

It is not a well-written article, but in it Marchant marvels at the stoicism of those whose homes had been bombed and it ends with a sudden personal outpouring of emotion which is quite painful, and must have struck a chord with almost everyone who read it:

And I thought, as I came away: –

'[H]ow useless to throw your bombs on this city.

'She may not preserve her pretty face, her carven stone, but she will preserve the spirit which built such a city.

'Though the bombs have dropped fifty yards from my own flat, I would rather stand here, in these streets, and die than see one strutting, heiling Nazi on this sweet soil.'

Different reporters seized on different things to keep the spirits of their readers up. Graham Stanford, in the *Daily Mail* of 11 October 1940, reported that Wren had built St Paul's Cathedral so well that a bomb which had destroyed the high altar had done very little damage otherwise – and the altar itself was only sixty years old. He quotes a group of people standing outside the cathedral:

> 'Well,' said one of them, 'St Paul's still stands.'
>   'Yes,' said another. 'It will be a long time before they destroy London this way.'

Somehow, these words don't ring entirely true. People rarely use expressions like 'St Paul's still stands' when they are simply speaking conversationally to friends. It is of course possible that this man said something rather more colloquial, and Graham Stanford tidied it up for his newspaper. All the same, these articles had the air of being written to a certain formula, neither entirely reportage nor feature articles, yet printed as though they were news reports. In other words, they were seen both by the writers and the editor as being propaganda of a kind, even though they described things that were presumably happening. Fact and near-fiction were chasing each other around, each drawing strength from the other. Next to the report on St Paul's, incidentally, is a court report which concerns a sixteen-year-old boy who has admitted being a Nazi sympathizer and confesses to having started fires during air raids to guide German bombers; so the basic function of a newspaper, to tell people honestly what is going on, has not necessarily been abandoned altogether.

Jane, the beautiful cartoon-strip heroine in the *Daily Mirror* who is always about to lose her clothes (though it wasn't until 1943 that, to encourage the troops and everyone else, she finally lost them altogether), was also a morale-booster. On 8 October 1940 she was on an airbase, cheering on the RAF bombers. 'Good luck boys! – Give 'em a pasting in Berlin!' Then she realizes that she's all alone in the blackout – until in the last picture in the strip a group of RAF ground crew gather round her, and one says: 'Can I take you back to your quarters, Miss?' It is remarkably innocent and cheery, and it underlines that the *Mirror* thought an important part of its function was to keep its readers' spirits up.

The *Daily Herald* saw things differently. It did not regard its function as being that of a cheerleader, but of a sympathetic critic, keeping an eye on the way the government ran things. When the Labour MP for Lambeth North, George Strauss, wrote an article about the suffering in

his constituency during the Blitz, he referred to 'the folly of the authorities' and described how the government's evacuation scheme had let
ordinary people down, particularly the elderly who could not stay with
relatives in the country because this would mean losing their supple-
mentary pensions.

If the *Mail* or the *Mirror* had followed this kind of line, it would have
become a campaign. Every edition of the paper would have carried some
attack on the authorities. The language would have been intemperate,
and the journalists who wrote the articles would have competed with one
another to attract the proprietor's or the editor's attention by finding
more and more suitable cases, and writing more and more extravagantly
about them. But the *Herald* was a different kind of newspaper: ideological
in tone, certainly, but not aggressively so. Above all, it had no single
owner who could enhance the careers of journalists that loyally parroted
his views. The *Herald* believed in holding authority to account, even when
it supported its work and purposes.

Peter Ritchie Calder, a committed socialist who later became a
leading authority on the sciences and served on a number of government
bodies, concentrated in particular on the way national and local authorities looked after the civilian population. He paid particular attention to
the way evacuation procedures and the welfare of the bombed-out and
homeless were managed: often not particularly exciting stuff, but
important and influential. Unlike a great many Fleet Street journalists,
he often visited provincial cities which had suffered in the Blitz and on
18 November 1940, for instance, the *Herald* ran a report he had written
on the aftermath of the bombing of Coventry:

> The whole of the Midlands has been organised to help the
> people of this stricken city. I have seen today the efforts
> which are being made. What has impressed me most is the
> way in which the authorities are applying, under diffi-
> culties, the lessons of London.

But the response of the ordinary people of the city impressed him as well:
'These incredible women of Coventry climbed over ruins to the fragments
of their houses. In the kitchens, among all the debris, they contrive to
cook their husbands' meals.'

In Liverpool and other cities Calder managed to remain honest in his accounts of the authorities' struggle to cope, without sounding too strident. On 18 October, writing about the numbers of women and children who had so far been evacuated, leaving behind their husbands and fathers, he made it plain that the total was 'not nearly good enough, but the difficulties are great. The steadfastness of the women and the devotion of the families is something which would be admirable if it were not asking for trouble.' Often entire families were refusing to go because it would mean that grandparents would have to be left behind.

He was also critical about the failure of the government and the local authorities to provide adequate places for people to live after they had been forced to leave their homes. In particular he attacked the way in which thousands of shocked and suddenly homeless people had been treated. The authorities had failed in particular to realize how important it was to get people feeding communally, instead of on their own. Women, he said, had been reluctant to take their children away from the danger zones because, with the men in the family gone, they had no idea where the family's next meal would come from. It said something for the Ministry of Information that it would allow this kind of criticism to be made in a daily newspaper at a time of great national uncertainty. But it says less for the rest of Fleet Street that scarcely any other journalists were prepared to criticize the inadequacies in the way the government dealt with ordinary people when they were at their most frightened and vulnerable.

Calder did not suffer as a result of his honesty; on the contrary, it was put to a controversial but valuable use in the interests of the war effort. In 1941 he was asked to join the top secret Political Warfare Executive, whose purpose was to undermine German morale through propaganda. Understanding that the best propaganda was the truth, it relayed back to Germany the reality of the damage Germany was suffering. The PWE was overseen by Anthony Eden, Hugh Dalton and Brendan Bracken, the minister of information, and its senior figures included at least one man we have come across before: Rex Leeper, the Foreign Office spokesman who had opposed Chamberlain's policy of appeasement.

There was always a certain amount of criticism in the papers and in talks on the BBC of the government's strategic approach to the war, though it tended to be muted. This was not so much because of the possibility of censorship, but because few editors wanted to annoy their readers or listeners by offending their sensibilities. To question the policy of bombing German cities in retaliation for the Blitz was liable to make any journalist or newspaper which criticized it very unpopular indeed. Cassandra (William Connor) in the *Daily Mirror* clearly felt a degree of unhappiness about it, but wrapped his feelings in the Union Jack:

> The air war is taking on its deadly rhythm.
>
> Munich is answered by Coventry.
>
> Coventry is answered by Hamburg.
>
> Tit for tat.
>
> A Roland for your Oliver.
>
> No one in this country welcomes this development. And there is ample evidence that it is not to Hitler's liking . . .
>
> The baptism of fire was Germany's own invention for her neighbours.
>
> But, unfortunately for her, we hold the recipe too, and the R.A.F. can be relied upon to cook it up blazingly hot and unspeakably strong.

It is a less than convincing endorsement, but it was obviously as far as Cassandra felt able to go. George Orwell recalled a conversation someone had had with an East Ender who joked that it might be better if the Germans bombed Germany and the RAF bombed Britain: it would save fuel, he said. Yet it is distinctly uncomfortable to read Orwell's own thoughts on the subject. Otherwise the essential voice of calm and decency during the Second World War, he nevertheless justified the all-out bombing of civilians in Germany; in an essay in his 'As I Please' column for *Tribune* on 19 May 1944 he argues that it is less damaging for a society to lose a cross-section of its population, including women and children, than it is to lose simply men of fighting age on the front lines; not an argument he would have put forward during the Spanish Civil War, for instance.

Surprisingly, perhaps, Churchill might have disagreed with him on the subject. In 1943, according to a conversation the author had with Churchill's private secretary John (later Sir John) Colville shortly before he died, Air Chief Marshal Arthur Harris (known as 'Bomber' or, within the RAF itself, as 'Butcher') got together a film to demonstrate to Churchill how successful the RAF was in destroying German cities. Harris was the leading advocate of strategic area bombing – essentially, that is, attacks aimed at civilian targets – as against the strategic precision targeting of strictly military objectives.

His film was shown in the tiny cinema in the Cabinet War Rooms, under Whitehall. After the seemingly unending parade of burning streets and smoking ruins, the lights went up and Harris sat there beaming with pride. Colville glanced at Churchill and saw tears running down his face. 'Are we beasts, that we should do these things?' Churchill muttered to him. But Churchill's private emotions made no difference: the bombing campaign continued to the bitter end. At this point in the war, there was no longer any real alternative to it, just as during the First World War there had been no real alternative to the war of the trenches. It had taken on a life of its own, as Siegfried Sassoon believed the war of the trenches did.

And regardless of the terrible cost, the campaign commanded powerful support from the media and from public opinion, precisely as the war in the trenches had done. Newspapers from the *Herald* to the *Mail* and *The Times* to the *Mirror* habitually used the pronoun 'we' when talking of the British forces. So did the BBC. The examples are almost endless:

70 Nazis Down in Week: We Lost 5

(*Daily Mirror*, Saturday 16 November 1940)

We Bomb Berlin, Skoda And New Sea Base

(*Daily Herald*, Thursday 21 November 1940)

Our fighters have today shot down four enemy bombers.

(BBC news bulletin, Monday 25 November 1940)

There was one solitary exception. The *Daily Worker*, deeply faithful to Moscow's line, treated Britain and Germany as though they were Tweedledum and Tweedledee, equally guilty and equally distasteful. Directly Hitler attacked Russia in June 1941, the *Daily Worker*'s line changed at once; but in the early part of the war Stalin was faithful to his pact with Hitler, and his supporters throughout the world were under the strongest instructions not to criticize Nazi Germany. The *Daily*

Worker, which was among the most unquestioningly loyal of Stalin's international mouthpieces, represented the war as being fought out in the interests of international capital, with working-class people as the victims. One of its main aims was to campaign for more and better shelters for civilians. On 11 September 1940 its headline read:

Another Nine-Hour Raid On London

OVER 3,000 DEAD AND WOUNDED IN TWO DAYS

Beside the lead article is a statement from the Communist Party's political bureau:

> The present barbaric air war on men, women and children in Britain and Germany is the crime of the ruling classes on both sides . . .
>
> The rulers who plunged the people into this war can neither stop the bombers nor protect the people from the bombs.
>
> The rich have provided themselves with luxury shelters. They have evacuated their children across the Atlantic. But they still refuse the shelters that can alone give protection to the people . . .

SHELTERS OF THE HALDANE TYPE MUST BE CONSTRUCTED EVERYWHERE.

These shelters, which were designed to be deep, had been designed by Professor J.B.S. Haldane, a chemist and geneticist from an upper-class background. He had become a committed Communist in the 1930s and was chairman of the *Daily Worker*'s editorial board. An idealistic and in some ways rather innocent man, he remained devoted to Stalin's memory long after his death. His shelters were regarded by the government, perhaps unfairly, as being too elaborate and expensive.

Suddenly, into the statement's text, which up to now has been about better methods of air-raid protection, erupts a sudden call to arms in heavy type:

TAKE OVER HOTELS, BIG HOUSES AND BLOCKS OF FLATS
TO PROVIDE NEW HOMES FOR THE HOMELESS.

This was precisely the kind of call which most alarmed the Cabinet, Labour members as well as Conservatives. It opened up the disturbing possibility that people who had lost their homes in the bombing might start commandeering empty or half-empty buildings and squatting in them. Yet it was the general tone of articles in the *Worker* which the government found unacceptable: its journalists adopted a sneering and at times defeatist tone, very different indeed from the one it would employ after Russia came into the war. On 21 September 1940, for instance, it launched into an attack on the way the other newspapers were reporting the war. A *Worker* columnist, William Rust, wrote an article headlined:

NEVER HAS THE PRESS BEEN
SO DEGRADED.

'Elsewhere I saw only a quiet calm that amazed me. Even the homeless chatted smilingly in the schoolroom in which they had been housed.' (Hannen Swaffer in the *Daily Herald*, September 9.)

The same night as this Swaffer slush appeared an East End schoolroom (called a rest centre) was bombed and over 200 refugees were killed. It may have been the one Swaffer visited. I don't know. It makes no difference to the fact that the *Herald* 'endurance' propaganda, as turned out by Swaffer, resulted in the deception of the public and concealed the Government neglect which led to the death of these workers and their children . . .

If Swaffer had told the truth it might never have happened. If the *Daily Herald* had reported the real feeling of the people, their anger and their fears, it might never have happened.

Hannen Swaffer was in fact a long-term socialist, with a particular interest in the poverty and vulnerability of the East End. A witty and generous man, he was inclined to pontificate on a wide range of issues, especially moral ones, and he attracted the nickname 'the Pope of Fleet Street'. Altogether he was an unlikely journalist to accuse of telling lies about the working class in order to please what William Rust called 'the millionaire Press'. But the *Daily Worker* wasn't interested in fairness or accuracy, so much as in making political points: the points that Stalin's Comintern, which insisted that Nazism and capitalism were two sides of the same coin, instructed it to make.

Stalin might be allied with Hitler, but it was in the Soviet Union's interests that the two belligerents should kill each other off. The *Worker's* policy, therefore, was one of revolutionary defeatism. It encouraged people in factories to demand more money, and by 20 December 1940 it was announcing on its front page that 'anger against the government and the scandals of its war policy' was spreading throughout the country.

A full six months earlier, in July 1940, it had received an official warning that it was contravening Defence Regulation 2D; this proclaimed that it was an offence 'systematically to publish matter calculated to foment opposition to the prosecution of the war to a successful conclusion'. That was clearly not only what the *Worker* was doing, it was also what it set out to do, on Moscow's orders. Again and again it infringed the regulation, but several government ministers, including the information minister, Duff Cooper, and the Home Secretary, Herbert Morrison, were minded to leave the *Worker* alone if at all possible, on the grounds that the British government must be careful to avoid any kind of comparison with the repression of the Nazis. There was a faint thought, too, that one day Stalin might be encouraged to join a coalition against Hitler, and that nothing should be done to make that harder.

Evidence that the *Worker* was actively organizing resistance to the way the government was waging the war settled the question. On 12 January 1941 a 'people's convention', supposedly 2,000 strong but probably numbering little more than a few hundred, gathered at the Royal Hotel, Woburn Place, London. The previous day Frank Pitcairn, the paper's diplomatic correspondent, described who would be coming:

> From Aberdeen, Dundee and Glasgow, from Newcastle
> and the Durham coalfields, from Liverpool and Mersey-
> side, from Manchester and the mills and mines of
> Lancashire, from Birmingham and all the industrial

> Midlands, from the valleys of South Wales, from Bristol
> and all the west country, from Portsmouth and South-
> ampton, the delegates are on their way to London.

But, Pitcairn warned, on the eve of the meeting the attacks of the millionaires upon these men and women of the people multiplied. 'The Times, mouthpiece of the wealthiest City interests, denounced the convention as a danger to the war aims of the rich, and seemed to appeal to Mr Ernest Bevin for redoubled vigilance in defence of their interests.'

By the afternoon of Tuesday 21 January Herbert Morrison contacted Scotland Yard and gave instructions that the Worker's offices should be raided and the presses stopped. He denied that he had launched an attack on the freedom of the press and of comment, arguing that the paper's 'slavish obedience to the Moscow line was a negation of the freedom of the printed word'.

The same evening the police raided the tiny office of the gadfly magazine the Week at 34 Victoria Street, and closed it down. This was an easier job for them, since the magazine consisted of a few cyclostyled sheets, written and produced by Claud Cockburn alone, known as a committed Communist.

But Cockburn moonlighted as well, working for the Daily Worker as its diplomatic correspondent – under the nom de plume of Frank Pitcairn, writer of the distinctly humourless article just quoted. He had joined the paper in 1935 and reported from Spain on the Civil War, his effectiveness shackled only by the need to stick unswervingly to Moscow's line. Later, perhaps partly as a result of an interview he did with General Charles de Gaulle, who explained to him that Communism was a form of romanticism, Cockburn lost his interest and his faith in it.

Did the Daily Worker and the Week pose a threat to Britain's war effort? With hindsight, certainly not. Herbert Morrison, who was instinctively inclined to let the newspapers say what they wanted, could easily have allowed them to continue. It's hard to avoid the feeling that he and his colleagues in Churchill's government were simply irritated by them to the point where they felt some action had to be taken. The Week closed down for good, and Cockburn found other outlets for his talent.

Once the Soviet Union was forced into the war by Hitler's surprise attack on 22 June 1941, there was pressure from the Labour Party to allow the Daily Worker to publish again. On 26 May 1942, against the advice and wishes of Herbert Morrison, the Labour Party voted to lift the ban, and the paper resumed publication on 7 September. But the political message was very different, and the tone of angry, spiteful defeatism had gone. The *Worker* still echoed the Soviet line with unswerving faithfulness, but inasmuch as that supported the Allied cause, so did the *Daily Worker*. But it rarely if ever found anything to praise in the policies or personality of Winston Churchill.

15

CENSORSHIP AND ENTERPRISE

In 1941 the Ministry of Information appointed Francis Williams, the former editor of the *Daily Herald*, to be the controller of its News, Censorship and Photograph divisions. His job was to set the policy for censoring the press, as well as to organize news releases and arrange the circumstances under which journalists operated. The rules made it clear that censorship could not be used to prevent journalists getting scoops, even if they were likely to cause embarrassment to British officials. The censors could intervene solely on grounds of military security.

Most British censorship dealt with relatively small, and sometimes very small, operational details. The Germans were known to be efficient at reading and listening to the British media with the greatest care. This helped William Joyce, 'Lord Haw-Haw', who on the basis of a line in a South London newspaper was able to announce on his programme for Britain on Radio Hamburg that Lewisham's town clock had stopped for a week now, and no one had done anything to get it started again. It gave his more credulous listeners the impression that he had informers everywhere, and such simple details added a veneer of truth to his much greater (and often false) claims, for instance that HMS *Ark Royal* had been sunk. She was finally sunk in November 1941.

On the night of 10 May 1941, Rear Admiral Thomson, the head of the censorship department, stayed late at his office in the Ministry of Information building. Outside a huge air raid, the biggest of the war so far, was raging. He was in a gloomy mood: the news from around the world was bad. Rommel had started a new offensive in North Africa, the Germans were attacking in Yugoslavia, Greece, Crete, and now Russia. One of his censors brought him a story from a morning paper that said that a Messerschmitt 110 had crashed not far from Glasgow, and a German officer had been found nearby, his parachute beside him.

Thomson told the censor not to pass the story; any report of a

German aircraft crash had to be confirmed by the Air Ministry before it could be published. He felt that there was something strange about the story, anyway. Why would a Messerschmitt fly as far as Scotland when it couldn't possibly carry enough fuel for the journey home? And some of the other details were distinctly odd: the pilot was wearing a gold watch on one wrist, and a gold compass on the other. His toenails were polished. According to the soldier who had arrested him, he said his name was Horn, and he wanted to see the Duke of Hamilton.

Soon more newspaper stories came in. They named the pilot as Hitler's deputy, Rudolf Hess, and said he had brought peace terms with him. Thomson refused to pass any of these stories, either. Editors began ringing him to protest, but he stood firm; suppose it was a hoax? Suppose Hess had a double, just as Hitler supposedly did? If Fleet Street announced that Hess had defected, and he were then put on public show in Berlin, Britain would be a laughing-stock; so Thomson reasoned.

The following morning, Sunday 11 May, Churchill was told but he refused to believe that the pilot could be Hess. By then, the newspapers had known for twenty-four hours that Hess had landed in Britain, but they were still not allowed to report anything more than the speculation from Berlin that he had either crashed or committed suicide. At 11.30 that night, almost too late for newspapers preparing to go to press, Downing Street issued a statement. Even then, they were not allowed to say that Hess had brought peace proposals with him, nor that he had landed near the Duke of Hamilton's estate.

The German press meanwhile ran a succession of stories revealing Hess's nervous symptoms and evidence of his insanity, while the British continued to say nothing about his health or mental condition at all. The Germans then changed their line, saying first that the British had led him into a trap and then that he had gone to persuade them that their cause was hopeless. Thomson believed that the lack of any claims from the British side had 'rattled the Germans and led them from contradiction to contradiction'. It probably did, though the newspapers were angry with Thomson and the government for not allowing them to say what they knew.

The result of the enforced reticence was, however, a propaganda coup for Britain: it gave people around the world the impression that Hess believed Germany was losing the war, and had defected in the hope of begging the British government to make peace on favourable terms. In fact, when the peace terms he had concocted were revealed some years later, they proved to be very tough indeed, and were accompanied by threats of German ferocity if they were rejected. But by then the war was nearly over, and Hess was almost forgotten.

The onus was on each newspaper to place everything it thought was questionable in front of the censors. But there was always the possibility that some unconsidered and seemingly routine trifle which might genuinely help the enemy could slip through. In some ways the censorship rules seem by today's standards to have been remarkably relaxed. The papers were free to publish the fact that Churchill was 'shortly' going to leave for a meeting with Roosevelt and Stalin, or with Roosevelt alone, as long as they kept quiet about the exact date and place of the meeting. The censors did not even try to stop the press reporting that the meeting would take place in the United States, Canada or North Africa.

Sometimes, though, censorship simply got in everyone's way, without achieving anything. In November 1943 a good deal of information started leaking out about the Cairo summit involving Churchill and Roosevelt, plus the leaders of other Allied countries: the Nationalist Chinese, the Czechs and others. By the middle of the month a French-language evening paper in Cairo reported that guests at the Mena House Hotel near the Pyramids had been asked to leave within three days because the hotel was wanted for official purposes. The story was sent out by telegraph before the Cairo censors, who were part of the British military structure in Egypt, received orders to put a block on it. As a result it was picked up in Britain and the United States.

By this time teams of British and American soldiers were building a perimeter fence round the hotel and laying extra telephone cables. People living nearby were told that their houses would be requisitioned for a month. Seventy British and American correspondents were flown in to cover the conference but were not allowed to send out any stories. Yet in neutral countries there were no such restrictions and on Monday 29 November the correspondent of the American news agency United Press International in Lisbon sent a message to New York via London which read: 'According to travellers, Churchill and Roosevelt have been in Cairo for several days and Stalin is en route to meet them at Teheran.'

UPI's British subsidiary, British United Press, submitted this message to the censors, who decided to send the newspapers a note which read: 'For reasons which will doubtless be fully appreciated it is hoped you will not publish this . . .'

The newspapers obliged, but by the following day the conference was over, and Roosevelt and Churchill had indeed moved on to Tehran to meet Stalin.

Rear Admiral Thomson, the chief censor, stepped in, calling the whole business 'a farce'. But before the seventy British and American correspondents in Cairo were allowed to file their reports about the conference, Reuter's news agency in London put together a fairly complete account of it, which was passed for transmission by the censors. NBC in New York picked up the story and splashed it right across America. The head of the US Office of War Information, Elmer Davis, accused Reuter's of breaking the agreed embargo; the correspondents in Cairo, who had been shackled by it, exploded in a frenzy of anger, and so did their offices in Britain and America; it was the worst such incident of the entire war.

In the end it turned out that one of Reuter's top correspondents, Douglas Brown, who had not been in Cairo, had spoken briefly to one of his colleagues, Tommy Chao. Chao was accredited to a Nationalist Chinese delegation passing through London, and the delegates had heard the news from the Chinese team in Cairo. Brown wrote up the story immediately. It was an entirely justified example of good journalistic initiative.

The rest of the world had known all about the conference for days. As for German military intelligence, the Abwehr, which had a widespread and effective espionage operation in Cairo, it probably heard all about the conference before almost everyone else.

§

There were times, too, when the military censorship might have worked against British interests. In the Far East in 1941, for instance, it was quite clear to many correspondents that despite the official statements there was a disturbing lack of will to resist the onslaught of the Japanese. Churchill himself had announced that Hong Kong would be defended 'with the utmost stubbornness', yet it fell on Christmas Day 1941. Martha Gellhorn and her new husband Ernest Hemingway had known it would when they passed through Hong Kong a few months earlier. She called Hong Kong 'a ticking time-bomb'; Hemingway forecast that 'the garrison would die like rats'.

Martha Gellhorn found Singapore even more disturbing. The deputy director of military intelligence told her, using the very formulation which helped to bring Chamberlain down a year earlier over Norway, 'Japan has definitely missed the bus.' She and just about every other correspondent based there knew that Singapore's impregnability, based on nothing more than sixty million pounds worth of concrete and six 15-inch naval guns which could only point out to sea, was a complete myth. She quoted the spokesmen at the Services' Public Relations Office (known as 'ASPRO') as repeating the phrase 'I am not at liberty to reveal . . .' again and again.

When, finally, war came, the unfortunate GOC Malaya, Lieutenant General Arthur Percival, proclaimed on Saturday 31 January 1942 that 'with firm resolve and fixed determination we shall win through'. Yet the very words hinted at a basic insecurity; and journalists like the slightly built, cheroot-smoking Ian Morrison, who was working for *The Times*, understood that the words were empty. He wrote later, in his memoirs *Malayan Postscript*: 'The world wanted to be sold Singapore. It wanted to believe that Singapore . . . was a bulwark against Japanese aggression in the Pacific.'

On 8 February, Morrison managed to get a berth on a freighter heading for the Dutch East Indies. Singapore fell a week after he left and, a month later on 8 March 1942, the Burmese capital Rangoon was the next to fall. Eve Curie, the daughter of Pierre and Marie Curie, was a war correspondent for the *New York Herald Tribune*, and reached the city on 14 February. She wrote of the 'ghastly odour of defeat, of retreat, of fear . . . the emptiness, the unforgettable silence of the large cities in danger'.

If the British press had foreseen these things six months earlier, as Martha Gellhorn had, Churchill might have done something about the weak, fatalistic leadership that was evident in Hong Kong, Singapore and Rangoon; but the British desperately wanted to believe that all would be well, and the correspondents there were not prepared to suggest anything to the contrary.

§

Between 1941 and 1943 the key fronts lay in Russia; indeed, the outcome of the Second World War was decided there. But Britain had no part to play on the Eastern Front. By contrast, Churchill had a fervent belief in the strategic significance of North Africa. In some ways he was right. Britain's position in Egypt protected the Suez Canal, and therefore access to India and much of the rest of the Empire. It also kept the Mediterranean open to the Royal Navy, and made possible the eventual invasion of Italy. But the real value of the North African campaign was to be predominantly psychological: after the flight from Belgium and France in 1940, and such disasters as the fall of Singapore and Rangoon, it showed their allies, their enemies and the British themselves that they could beat the Germans and win the war.

The North African campaign swung backwards and forwards, and the British press, accepting the significance of the campaign at the value Churchill placed on it, became absorbed with the fascination of what seemed, by contrast with so much of the rest of what was going on elsewhere, to be a gentlemen's war. Rommel was much admired by the British forces, and this admiration, passed on by the correspondents covering the North African campaign, was shared in Britain too.

The campaign was overseen by commanders who for the most part accepted that fighting in the desert was an individualistic business. Units such as the Long Range Desert Group, David Stirling's Special Air Service, and (most idiosyncratic of all) Popski's Private Army were encouraged to perform raiding and reconnaissance functions. They favoured unorthodox uniforms, insignia and rituals, and took a civilized, chivalrous approach to the enemy which the Germans largely reciprocated.

The British war correspondents in North Africa, too, were given far greater freedom than their colleagues in other theatres of war. Dressed in officers' uniforms with a 'C' on their caps (the first suggestion, 'WC' for 'war correspondent', was hastily dropped), they were placed under the supervision of Alexander Clifford, a *Daily Mail* correspondent whom the Ministry of Information had appointed as the official 'eyewitness'. For the journalists, the system worked extremely well, and was one of the reasons why there was so much interest in the Desert War at home as compared for instance with the so-called 'Forgotten War' against the Japanese in Burma and other parts of the Far East.

This was partly due to the sheer scale of the fighting in Egypt and Libya: it was impossible for the military to know what was happening right across the huge expanse of desert. The correspondents, who were usually free to travel out on their own to see for themselves what was going on, would often come across information which they would pass on to the generals and their intelligence staff. The military quickly realized that the journalists who were assigned to cover them had other uses too. The up-to-date if carefully selected information which the staff fed the journalists would usually appear the following morning in the newspapers or radio bulletins of Britain.

The North African campaign attracted some of the best writers in Fleet Street. Apart from Alexander Clifford, they included Clifford Webb of the *Daily Herald*, and the Australian correspondent Alan Moorehead, who worked for the *Daily Express*.

Alan McCrae Moorehead was twenty-nine when he came to North Africa in 1940, with a longing to become a high-powered war correspondent. Until this point he had mostly been on the sidelines. After a stint as a young reporter on the *Melbourne Herald* he went to London and got a job on the *Express* as a very junior member of the foreign staff, and was never in the right place at the right time. He worked as a stringer in Gibraltar during the Spanish Civil War, watching enviously from a distance as the stars of the *Express*'s reporting staff covered the real story. He moved to Paris for the *Express* in 1938, when the big events were happening in Berlin, and then on to Rome when Paris became the focus of world attention. But by this time he had honed his style and could turn out some highly effective copy. On 10 May 1940, with the world wondering whether Mussolini was going to enter the war, Moorehead wrote in the *Express*:

> [W]ar and glory marched through the capital . . . You didn't
> know the date, you didn't know how, but it was coming,
> boys, it was coming, and what the hell, it was going to be
> fine . . . Money, glory, medals, excitement, conquests . . .

Arthur Christiansen, the editor, must have spotted Moorehead's talent for infusing colour and excitement even into a story that resolutely refused to happen; yet he continued to miss the big story. A month after he had been moved on to Egypt, Mussolini finally declared war. Instead of being there, Moorehead found himself in another place where nothing much was happening – and this at a time when the Battle of Britain was as its height and news editors had no interest whatever in Egypt.

Another new arrival was Richard Dimbleby. He had left Western Europe at his own request, at the very moment that it was becoming the most important news story in the world. Few people had yet heard of him, but working for the BBC kept him separate from newspaper correspondents like Moorehead and Clifford: different professional requirements, different deadlines, and above all a different approach to the news. For Moorehead and Clifford it was all about descriptive ability ('colour') and the need to compete; Dimbleby had no professional competition, and the BBC disliked too much in the way of colour. As for emotion, of which he had plenty, they didn't want any of that at all. He was also sometimes criticized for being too enthusiastic: scarcely a negative quality, one would think, but journalists tend to be more spiteful towards their colleagues than other professional groups.

Nonetheless the correspondents were pleasant enough to each other when they met in the bar of Shepheard's Hotel, but Dimbleby, having no need to keep an eye on what the rest of the press corps was doing, lived completely separate from the others. Moorehead and Clifford, rivals and friends, lived in the distinctly downmarket Carlton Hotel, not being able to afford Shepheard's, where most of the press corps stayed. As a foreign correspondent Dimbleby was not particularly well paid by the BBC – some things never change – but he had money of his own, and used it to live in style on a houseboat on the Nile, with servants and a chauffeur for his elderly but glamorous motorcar. In their different ways, Dimbleby and Moorehead would become the most famous British correspondents of the entire war.

In Moorehead's case, it was for three main reasons. In the first place he enthusiastically sought out front-line positions from which he could see the action for himself. Secondly, he had a good analytical mind, and could sum up a whole battle in 1,500 words. And thirdly, his writing style was crisp and vivid. Once Moorehead finally had the kind of material to write about that he had been searching for ever since the Spanish Civil War, it was clear to Beaverbrook and Christiansen that he had the qualities they were looking for in a chief war correspondent; and after North Africa they made sure he was always at the heart of the action. And he always had the ability, as he had demonstrated in Rome, to take a routine incident and spot something more meaningful in it.

On the front page of the *Daily Express* on 25 November 1941, for instance, is a big news report assembled from news agency despatches under the revealing byline 'Express Staff Reporter' in Cairo about the second phase of an attack by British, New Zealand and South African infantry at Sidi Rezagh, not far from Tobruk. But the empty, unspecific headlines are a good deal more interesting than the story, which is clearly written from sources who themselves do not yet know what precisely is happening, nor what the outcome will be. The reader's eye soon wanders away to a sharply observed report by Moorehead, written two days earlier but held up by the fighting and the difficulty of getting his copy to a censor. He was, the dateline said, 'with the British tanks in Libya'.

> I have been watching prisoners come in. Four hundred Germans led one batch, with 300 Italians behind them. It was the same old story. A procession of men marching four abreast across the desert, a Bren-carrier in front, another behind, and a distraught British officer fussing around in a truck wondering what to do with them. Empty lorries are scarce up here. But the big surprise was this – the Italians looked better, marched better and had a better physique than the Germans. The Germans certainly had been in a tougher part of the line, but they were a long, long way from being panzers. They were thin-faced lads with flat chests, shaven fair heads. They looked hungry, tired, cold and disinterested.

It has the ring of clear-sighted observation, even though Moorehead had a strong belief in the need for wartime journalism to be patriotic, and believed in the need to give his readers something to believe in. He disliked reporting that smacked of gloom or defeatism. When Rommel's troops began seriously menacing Tobruk in June 1942, the BBC carried a talk by a commentator who suggested in passing that Tobruk was not after all vital, and might be lost without too much damage to the main thrust in North Africa.

It was nothing more than the briefest of mentions, and certainly not 'an announcement', as Moorehead later maintained, but he was as furious about it as the forces were, calling it 'disastrous and insane' in his book *African Trilogy*, published in 1944. Tobruk did fall soon afterwards, and it was not, as the commentator had rightly suggested, a disaster; five months later the Battle of El Alamein began the process of driving the Germans out of North Africa altogether. For Moorehead, the BBC, like his own newspaper and others, was primarily a propaganda tool in time of war; and for him the only audience which counted were the troops who tuned in when they came out of the front line.

But the BBC had taken an important strategic decision at the start of the war to broadcast the same news to everyone: not optimistic, heart-warming stuff directed towards the troops in the Western Desert, and more sombre, more accurate reports to people elsewhere. For Moorehead, the soldiers he was with were so important that he did not consider any other issues. And he believed that the journalist's chief duty in time of war was not so much to the truth, as to helping to ensure victory. Perhaps it would have been better if the BBC had not broadcast that particular viewpoint at the time it did; it was not, after all, an item of news. Hearing it, the defenders of Tobruk drew the certain conclusion that the BBC was reflecting the British government's view that they were finished, and that it didn't matter much anyway. It wasn't exactly an incentive to risk their lives further.

Like many newspaper correspondents then and later, Moorehead was no great admirer of the BBC. In *African Trilogy* he wrote, accurately, of the BBC's shortcomings in the North African campaign: as cautious and slow-moving as ever, it had failed to put even a single recording team into the region, and Richard Dimbleby found himself having to spend much of his time in Cairo trying to give the broader picture of the fighting, rather than seeing the action up close. Moorehead's analysis was a sharp one, but it was fair:

Through the delay in the transmission of cables [i.e. the reports from front-line correspondents like himself, delayed partly by the censors and partly by the problems of communication] and the absence of an adequate reporting staff in the front line the B.B.C. was as far behind the news as the world's newspapers were. The result was that when tired and dispirited men were coming out of battle they turned on their radios and heard a cheerful and glowing account of a victory that had occurred two or three days earlier. Understandably it infuriated them. They were irritated again when they had successfully gone forward to hear the B.B.C. broadcast a gloomy tale of some earlier setback. The old faith in the B.B.C. began to dissipate around this period and the soldiers began to ridicule the broadcasts.

The time would come when the BBC would get its unwieldy recording teams in place at the side of their star correspondents, and men like Richard Dimbleby would be able to broadcast from the front lines themselves; though there would be no possibility of any kind of live reporting from a war for decades to come. BBC correspondents at the front would still have to get their recordings, in the form of discs like 78 rpm records, back to a transmission area to be played over a radio link to London. This would take at least as much time as a newspaper correspondent like Moorehead needed to get a written despatch back to base, so the broadcasters had little advantage over the newspapers in that respect.

The build-up to the German attack on Tobruk was reported with remarkable honesty. Under the heading 'Battle not now on equal terms', Morley Richards, the military correspondent of the *Daily Express*, warned in a front-page article on 17 June 1942: 'Something has gone wrong in Libya. General Rommel has made dangerous gains, and last night's news [about Rommel's advance towards Tobruk] must be interpreted to mean that more reverses for the Eighth Army are inevitable.'

Four factors seem to account for the tide turning, temporarily at any rate, towards the Axis:

AIR SUPERIORITY WRESTED FROM THE R.A.F.

SUDDEN APPEARANCE IN THE DESERT OF LARGE NUMBERS OF 88MM. GUNS, HEAVIER THAN ANY FIELD PIECE WE POSSESS

ADAPTATION OF GERMAN A.A. GUNS FOR ANTI-TANK PURPOSES.

MORE HEAVY TANKS THAN AT GENERAL RITCHIE'S DISPOSAL

The following Sunday, 21 June, Tobruk fell. The *Express* gave the news and the reason for it in the headlines across its front page:

WHY TOBRUK FELL: OUTGUNNED AND OUTNUMBERED 3 to 1

It is news and excuse, all in one. There is no mention, of course, of the panic and despair inside Tobruk, since although they may have had their guesses about it, Moorehead and the *Express* staff in Cairo could have known nothing about that; and even if they had, it is almost certain that they would have had to keep quiet about it. 26,000 Allied troops, 2,000 vehicles and 5,000 tons of provisions were captured. Just before he was made a prisoner, a cameraman for Universal News, Ronnie Noble, was ordered by the military censors to destroy large numbers of reels of exclusive film of the defence of Tobruk and its fall. 'It was like having teeth drawn!' he said later.

There was only the faintest hint of the shock waves of fear and panic which the fall of Tobruk caused in Alexandria, only sixty miles along the coast. Underneath Moorehead's report, printed on Monday 22 June, there are just a few lines at the bottom of the front page under the heading:

ALEXANDRIA CIVILIANS QUIT

Evacuation from the danger zone, decided on weeks ago, began today. The evacuation commission said that it was moving to places in the interior 'the population of certain quarters of Alexandria more exposed than others to the danger of air-raids.'

Most of the evacuees live in or near the port districts which have borne the weight of Axis bombing.

Alexandria is well supplied with food and drink. The coastal defences maintain a constant watch. Gunners are able to put up one of the heaviest anti-aircraft barrages in the world.

The truth was rather different. The atmosphere in the city was one of hysteria. Crowds of account-holders mobbed Barclay's Bank in Alexandria, and withdrew a million pounds in a single day. The road south from Alexandria to Cairo was packed with precisely the sort of fearful, angry crowds who had fled from so many cities in Europe as the Germans approached. In Cairo, too, people were gathering everything up and preparing to leave. The British embassy signalled the approach of danger by burning thousands of documents; a cloud of black smoke hung over the building for the entire city to see. Yet the outside world heard nothing of any of this. The censors blocked all details of the panic in Egypt.

§

Churchill responded to the loss of Tobruk by sacking the commander-in-chief of the Middle East, Claude Auchinleck, and replacing him with General Alexander (later Field Marshal Earl Alexander of Tunis); while the field commander, General Neil Ritchie, was replaced by the brash and self-confident Lieutenant General Bernard Law Montgomery. There was, Churchill recognized, a clear need for a different style of leadership: the kind which the mood of the nation seemed to require. Montgomery understood this, and so did the Ministry of Information. What was wanted was someone with more democratic qualifications than the remote grandees who had so far led the British forces in their battle against an admired enemy like Rommel.

Yet Montgomery's utter certainty had a more attractive side: he paid no attention whatever to the conventions which other commanders insisted on. He lived a spartan life in his own small caravan, and insisted on wearing an ordinary infantryman's beret with a khaki sweater or a battledress tunic. Enthusiastically promoted by the Ministry of Information, these small and essentially irrelevant details were seized on by the press, and worked up into a legend which guaranteed his popularity. It took only a few more strokes to complete the sketch of the people's hero fighting the people's war: friendly and approachable when he visited his men, and although he was a censorious non-smoker and non-drinker in private he always armed himself with packets of cigarettes to hand out to them.

Stories about him abounded in the press: how, in his previous command, he had made his officers and men run six miles a week, or how he had invited a hundred officers to Christmas dinner, managed somehow to obtain enough turkeys for all of them, carved, served everyone there, and gave them a lecture on the meaning of Christmas. In the North African campaign the newspapers were delivered to him every morning at 5 a.m. He appeared at 8 a.m., worked all day and went to bed on the dot of 10 p.m. – even when someone came rushing to him with the news that Rommel had just launched a counter-attack. Having already made his arrangements to cope with that, he told the staff officer not to bother him. 'I'm going to bed,' he said.

The newspapers could not get enough of it. On 12 April 1943 the *Express* asked: 'Do you know a Montgomery story? . . . The *Daily Express* has been collecting anecdotes about the man the whole world is talking about.'

For its part, the *Daily Mirror* turned him into the hero of the ordinary fighting man and on 2 December ran a letter from one of Monty's 'Desert Rats' to his wife:

> Monty was passing our leaguer area and stopped to speak to one of the lads. Seeing one of the boys nearby, Monty asked him how he was off for cigarettes. 'B——y lousy. I haven't had a cig for a week.' With that, Monty went back to his car and handed him six packets of 20's, saying: 'Give a few to the other lads.'

The *Mirror* concluded: 'Yes, we can believe it. If there is one thing Monty knows it is how to lead men.'

It helped, of course, that Montgomery won battles. He had taken over after Auchinleck had laid the groundwork for victory at El Alamein. If Churchill had kept Auchinleck, Alamein would still have been a British victory. Yet Montgomery suited the popular press far more, and although that was not the reason Churchill made the change, it helped to keep up the confidence and enthusiasm of Fleet Street and of the newspaper readers for the rest of the war. Montgomery was not in any sense a man of the people; but a few small gestures could be magnified by the press into making him seem like one. That, together with his unbounded belief in himself, was responsible for a great deal of his success.

At the time of the fall of Tobruk, five months before the stunning victory at El Alamein in November 1942, five of the six *Daily Express* correspondents in the Middle East (the highest number of any newspaper) were openly pessimistic about the future there. Only Alan Moorehead believed as early as July that Egypt was safe and the British and their allies would be victorious in North Africa. Quoting himself later in one of his books, he used an expression which quickly became a cliché, once people saw that he was right: 'the turn of the tide'. By the end of 1942, unlikely as it had seemed a few months before, the tide had demonstrably turned.

§

By the spring of 1944 the tide was unequivocally with the Allies and plans to invade Europe began in earnest. As D-Day grew closer, the degree of control imposed on the movement of news and people was unprecedented in any free society.

So much was known by so many about some aspect of the build-up for the invasion that extraordinary measures were required to prevent the details coming out little by little, and adding up to something the Germans would certainly notice. By April 1944 many of the controls were already in place. Foreign diplomats and their staffs were forbidden to leave the country, and diplomatic messages could not be sent in code. All telephone calls and telegrams to and from the country were censored with special care.

No evening or provincial newspapers could be sent abroad, since by reporting even the smallest things – the attendance of soldiers at a show, for instance – they might show that something was happening. Mail was held up so that it could not be delivered until after D-Day. War correspondents had to be given special courses on digging foxholes, pitching tents and reading maps – yet because the absence of stories by leading war correspondents would be noticed, a variety of contrivances had to be thought up to make it seem as though they were working somewhere else.

Newspaper and radio editors were asked not to report any speculation whatever from neutral countries about the date of the invasion of Europe, since because they were well informed they might simply select the most likely ones and so tip off German intelligence. Military correspondents were not allowed to indulge in any kind of speculation about the landings, and all they could do was to suggest that the invasion could be anywhere from Norway to Bordeaux. One correspondent wrote about William the Conqueror's invasion of England in reverse; but because he settled on the beaches of Normandy as a likely place for the invasion, his article was banned.

Yet in spite of all this extraordinary care, the American news agency

Associated Press managed to give the Germans advance notice of the invasion. It had been scheduled to take place on Saturday 3 June, but bad weather in the Channel meant it had to be postponed. At 11 that evening AP telegraphed a flash to New York announcing that the Allies had landed in France. Within a minute, radio programmes across the United States were interrupted to give the news. From there it spread to Canada and to Central and South America. Huge crowds came out into the streets to celebrate.

It turned out that one of the telex operators in AP's London bureau, a young woman from Streatham in south-west London, had been passing the time by tapping out a trial message on the usual paper tape, just in case she was the one who might have to do it in earnest. 'FLASH EISENHOWERS HEADQUARTERS ANNOUNCE ALLIED LANDING', she wrote. Just at that moment someone came rushing over to her with a communiqué from Russia, and she typed that – on the same piece of tape. It was fed into the transmitting machine and was in New York seconds later.

The operator that end noticed after a few seconds that it did not carry the right number, or the letters PBC ('passed by censor'), and he tapped out 'BUST THAT FLASH' immediately. But it had already gone out all over America, and although AP killed it within two minutes it was too late. Some time afterwards, Allied military intelligence discovered that the Germans had thought it must be a deliberate act of misinformation, and that the invasion would not happen for some time; so in the end it did no harm whatever. As for the operator, she kept her job.

Seven hours later, at 6 a.m., all war correspondents were invited to attend a press conference at the Ministry of Information. They were handed a piece of paper which read:

UNDER THE COMMAND OF GENERAL EISENHOWER, ALLIED NAVAL FORCES, SUPPORTED BY STRONG AIR FORCES, BEGAN LANDING ALLIED ARMIES THIS MORNING ON THE NORTHERN COAST OF FRANCE.

The correspondents were locked into the conference room, and told they could start writing up their stories. Top British and American officers arrived to brief them. Some listened while they wrote, and added in the new information as it came to them; others kept their heads down and carried on hammering away at their typewriter keys. The censors sat waiting for the onslaught to begin, and got to work as fast as they could. By good luck and hard work, all the copy had been censored by the time the news came through from the Normandy beaches at 7.30 a.m. that the landings had taken place. At that moment the stories could be released around the world.

From the coast of France to the looming tower occupied by the Ministry of Information in central London, the biggest and most elaborate enterprise ever undertaken by human beings was working almost exactly as its planners had intended.

§

Aboard a destroyer off the beaches, Juno, Gold and Sword, a Reuter's correspondent, Desmond Tighe, had been keeping a running diary for later transmission to London:

> 5.37 a.m. The night bombing has ceased and the great naval bombardment begins.
> 5.45 a.m. The big assault ships start lowering their boats.
> 6.30 a.m. The whole invasion fleet is now waiting just seven miles offshore.
> 7.23 a.m. I [can] see the first wave of assault troops touching down . . . and fanning up the beach . . . Red tracers from close-range enemy weapons are searing across the beach. Men leap out of the craft and move forward. Tanks follow them. By now everything is an inferno.

But war is war, and things always go wrong. For the men whom Noel Monks of the *Daily Mail* was accompanying, the landing craft either didn't or couldn't go in quite close enough to the beach, and the men aboard her, weighed down with sixty-pound packs and needing to hold their rifles over their heads, found themselves jumping off into water that was too deep. They 'disappeared like plummets at the bottom of the ramp . . . Some managed to rid themselves of their heavy packs and come up. Some didn't.' Monks himself, six feet tall, felt himself treading on the submerged bodies of the drowned and the drowning as he made his way to shore.

Twelve years later, he would describe these things in his book *Eyewitness*, but at the time the censor cut them out of his copy. The people back home wanted heroics, not horror.

Both awaited Monks a short time later on Sword Beach, in the person of a sergeant in the Army Film Unit. The man came staggering towards him, his right arm shredded and drenched with blood, carrying in his left hand what was known in the trade as an onion-bag. It contained several cans of exposed film. '"Hey, War Correspondent," the sergeant shouted, holding out the onion-bag. "Could you see they get back for me? I've copped one."'

Monks realized he was far more worried about his film than he was about his terrible wound. Later Monks heard that the sergeant's arm had to be amputated. Once again, these were details which the censor refused to pass.

Reuter's sent fifteen men to cover D-Day. For them, getting material back fast was even more important than for correspondents like Monks, who had at best another ten hours or so to get their copy censored and despatched. News agencies depend on immediacy, and their reporters face a continual deadline. They put their trust in an older method: carrier pigeons. It was, if anything, worse than relying on the orthodox system. Charles Lynch, a Canadian whom Reuter's had assigned to the Canadian forces on Juno Beach, launched his pigeons into the air, but they all turned and headed inland, over the German positions. 'Traitors! Damned traitors!' Lynch shouted after them.

Robert Reuben, an American working for Reuter's, had slightly better luck, but only just: his pigeons reached the Isle of Wight, but only on the third afternoon after D-Day. Fortunately both Lynch and Reuben used more conventional means of sending their reports as well, which worked a good deal better. Still, Reuter's much smaller rival, International News Service, also used pigeons, and they worked perfectly: Joe Willicombe of INS launched four pigeons into the Normandy air, and they reached the Ministry of Information just a few hours later, carrying some of the first despatches to arrive in London from the beaches.

The BBC, which had begun the war so tentatively and had not even managed to get a correspondent in place for Dunkirk or the fall of France, had no fewer than forty-eight correspondents covering D-Day on the ground, at sea and back at headquarters: it was the largest number fielded by any news organization. The BBC had taken huge strides in the four intervening years. It had become the country's, and often the outside world's, most trusted source of news (even in the United States, its reports were regularly broadcast by 725 radio stations). This had given the BBC a confidence it had never previously shown where news broadcasting was concerned. The old rules about relying solely on news agencies for its reporting were set aside. Increasingly, it had sent its two- or three-man recording teams into the front line. Richard Dimbleby, for instance, made thirty reporting trips on missions with the RAF: more even than Ed Murrow of CBS. Most of them were over Germany, and he made his first flight with Wing Commander Guy Gibson as early as January 1943. On that occasion, he later confessed to his almost equally famous BBC colleague Wynford Vaughan-Thomas, he had 'achieved immortality in the ranks of the RAF by being the only man to be violently sick after a raid was over'.

On D-Day Dimbleby was in the air again, a passenger in a Wellington bomber with a BBC engineer, so low that they could see

> only long stretches of empty roads, shining with
> rain, deserted, dripping woods and . . . much nearer
> the battle area . . . a solitary peasant harrowing his
> field, up and down behind the horses, looking
> nowhere but before him and at the soil.

Like Alan Moorehead of the *Daily Express*, Dimbleby had the knack of investing ordinary, easily visualized detail with real meaning.

As the campaign progressed after D-Day, the problems of the correspondents grew harder. Now they had to scatter across the French landscape to hunt down their stories, write them up, then queue up with the rest to find a censor, most of whom ranged from being uninterested to obstructive or even downright hostile.

Famously, during Montgomery's disastrous Operation Market Garden, the ambitious attempt to hold the bridges (including Arnhem) across the Dutch waterways , a censor thrust a bundle of correspondents' despatches into his battledress and later claimed to have forgotten all about them. Cyril Ray of the BBC, who parachuted into Nijmegen with several other correspondents and witnessed some remarkable and dramatic scenes, never got a word on the air as a result. Given that 'the bridge too far', for all the brilliance of its conception and the courage displayed during its execution, was a badly muddled defeat, it cannot be ruled out that the officer wanted to censor all mention of what had happened.

After a despatch was subjected to censorship, and often arbitrarily and unreasonably hacked down in the process, the correspondent had to take it to an RAF centre from where it would be taken to an airfield to get it on board a notoriously unreliable light aircraft. If that were not possible, it had to be given to one of the heavily overworked military wireless operators to be transmitted to London together with all the rest of that day's traffic, important or trivial. Later, a cable was brought across to the Continent which made transmission quicker and easier, but in the early days all the correspondent could do was pray that the operator would send the message through in a reasonable space of time. All in all, it was a complete lottery whether a despatch reached London or not.

In 2004, to mark the sixtieth anniversary of D-Day, *The Times* excavated from its archives a range of material, including an exchange of service messages between Richard Deakin, its foreign editor, and one of its men in the field. John Prince was not a particularly successful correspondent, and he certainly wasn't a lucky one. But anyone who has done his job can understand and sympathize with his long litany of complaint and anguish. Here he is replying to a tactfully phrased message from Deakin to say they have only had one report from him in well over a week. At first Prince is economical with his words, but quickly, as the emotion takes over, he loses control. The exchange is worth quoting at length:

> Your message very disappointing – first word I've had of any sort since leaving. Apart from short wireless message filed in evening, which is rationed to 400 words and necessarily rather late since we don't get a briefing till 5.30, all my pieces have been sent by bag leaving at 10 a.m. and 2 p.m. to catch courier plane. I cannot control order in which this is censored in London, and all this delay must be at your end (occasionally the aircraft is cancelled for weather) ... [D]ifficulties are great. I'm out all day and night looking for material, the censorship is miles away from house where I've dug in, and given any lack of lumiere at night, there's little enough time for writing ... It's pitiful that British correspondents are still rationed to 400 words by wireless, which doesn't always work,

when Americans have direct transmission to New York by Press Wireless. B.B.C., of course, is getting favoured treatment for broadcasts by army channels. Could you please have a Times posted to me? I never see one. Regards.

In his reply Deakin demonstrates all the counselling skills of the experienced foreign editor:

YOUR SERVICE MEMO RECEIVED FULLSTOP REALIZE YOUR DIFFICULTIES TRYING HELP BY PRESSURE THIS SIDE FULL STOP FOR GUIDANCE OUR FIRST NEED IS FOR PROMPT HALF COLUMN DAILY ... FULLSTOP THANKS FOR EXCELLENT MAQUIS STORY RECEIVED 2045 HOURS FULLSTOP FAMILY SEND LOVE ALL WELL FULLSTOP SENDING PAPERS BEGINNING TOMORROW

§

A week after the transcendent excitement of D-Day and the relief at its success, attention swung abruptly back home. Prince and his fellow correspondents in Normandy found themselves facing serious competition for the lead story. On the night of Monday 12 to Tuesday 13 June 1944 the first of Hitler's vengeance weapons, the V-1, landed on London.

For the next eleven weeks, until mid-September, approximately a hundred V-1s were fired at London, destroying on average five hundred houses every day; altogether 6,000 people lost their lives. Many Londoners thought it was worse than the Blitz. When a war artist, John Groth of *Parade* magazine, left for Normandy at the end of June, his fellow-journalists based at the Ministry of Information jokingly called out 'Sissy!' Day after day, the V-1s fell on London and the south-east of England, each bearing a ton of Amatol in its warhead. The British Secret Intelligence Service had first received warnings from its agents in Germany as early as April 1943 that a new type of weapon was being developed for use against London.

By late summer 1943 air reconnaissance photographs from Peenemünde, an island in the Baltic, showed what looked like miniature aircraft on inclined ramps. At the same time the German press and radio were starting to report that a major new weapon, which would end the war quickly, would soon be available for use against Britain. These reports were picked up by the British press and the BBC, and given a great deal of prominence. Rear Admiral Thomson, the head of censorship, suggested to his boss, the information minister Brendan Bracken, that the government should brief editors about the whole subject. Bracken then advised Herbert Morrison, who was minister of home security, to invite a group of selected editors to come to the Ministry of Information, for a briefing on what would later, following American practice, be known as 'deep background'.

As always, Morrison believed in keeping good relations with the press. When the editors assembled at Senate House in October 1943, he told them that the government had heard from neutral sources that the Germans were experimenting either with a rocket or a pilotless plane – later it turned out that both weapons would be used – and that it was possible they would be successful. The government was, he said, making preparations for deep shelters and for mass evacuations, but that these should not be made public yet. Morrison had no objection, he said, to the reporting of stories from foreign sources about the secret German weapon, since this meant the British public would not be taken by surprise if it were used. According to Rear Admiral Thomson,

> [h]e asked however that undue prominence should not be given to the stories and that no indication should be given of the extent to which the Government were aware of, and were planning against, the possible use of such a weapon. Finally, he requested that all stories on the subject should be submitted to censorship.

In January 1944, when much more was known about the weapon, Morrison gathered the editors together again and told them it would be a winged plane-like missile with jet propulsion. It would not, fortunately, be able to carry a warhead containing more than one or two tons of explosive.

Nowadays the first V–1 is usually regarded as having struck Mile End, in the East End of London, on Tuesday 13 June 1944, killing eight people. But Admiral Thomson reveals in his memoirs that the previous night one was brought down, and fell in north-east London, but was not immediately recognized as being a rocket, since conventional manned bombers were also attacking London that night. The news agencies carried the report, officially approved, before the wreckage had been examined and proved to be one of the new weapons; as a result, the Germans knew from the start that their V-1s were getting through.

After that, with the full agreement of the editors on the Newspaper and Periodical Emergency Council, there was a blanket ban on reporting the V-1 attacks, on the grounds that the more information the Germans had, the more accurate the rockets would become. Slowly, though, this ban became intolerable, and in July Churchill himself gave the House of Commons a surprisingly frank account of the V-1s, including the numbers of casualties they had caused. And although it was still for the most part forbidden to be specific about the results of V-1 attacks, there were exceptions; the censors for instance allowed the papers and the BBC to report that 'a large number' of people had been killed when a V-1 hit the Guards Chapel, close to Buckingham Palace. As with conventional bombs, it was not possible to report a precise figure for deaths if a V-1 killed more than twelve people.

Gradually, though, the V-1s lost their effectiveness; later on British air defences were knocking three-quarters of them out of the sky, many over the Channel, and only 9 per cent were actually reaching London. By early September the Allied forces in France had overrun most of the V-1 firing sites. The Germans had to turn to something else.

On the evening of 8 September 1944 two unusually loud explosions were heard, one in Chiswick and the other in Epping Forest. The size of the craters showed that the Germans were using a new weapon. Yet the V-2 rocket turned out to be much less fearsome than the government had feared and only about 1,000 were ever fired, of which roughly half reached London.

The rule that there should be no specific reporting of the V-2s was even more unpopular with the press than the V-1 ban had been. According to Rear Admiral Thomson it was even unpopular with the censors themselves. Often the stories were so heavily edited that editors felt there was no point in printing them. The worst thing about censorship is that if newspapers and radio cease to tell them what they know is true, people lose their belief in anything they are told officially, and rumours, no matter how wild, take over. This happened now. The government still insisted that the Germans must be denied all information about where their rockets had landed; but after strong representations from editors it was decided to allow imprecise reports about explosions to appear in the paper a couple of days or so after they had happened.

The Ministry of War was convinced that this fooled the Germans and prevented them from improving the effectiveness of the V-2. It is certainly true that the V-2s were not upgraded significantly, and this may have been because of the news blackout. But the credibility of the newspapers and the BBC suffered, as hugely destructive explosions which people saw with their own eyes went unreported. Such feelings had no effect on the war itself, but they fostered a suspicion of officialdom and the press which the British government, to its credit, had tried to avoid for much of the previous five years.

§

The war was the making of the BBC's news service. Timid and submissive at the start, it had slowly outgrown the old restrictions about getting its information solely from agencies like the Press Association and Reuter's. The rules had to be rewritten to take account of the daily flood of news from across the world. Above all, the BBC had recruited an entire new department of correspondents whose names and voices became known throughout the country and far beyond: Richard Dimbleby, Wynford Vaughan-Thomas, Howard Marshall, Godfrey Talbot, the Canadian Stanley Maxted, Cyril Ray, Robert Barr and many others.

The BBC has always liked to believe that its fundamental reputation as a broadcaster of news was built on the reliable, measured, accurate service of its bulletins; and although that may be true, it was always a few specific moments which people remembered, and which gave the BBC a special importance in their lives: Bruce Belfrage pausing for a scarcely definable instant as a bomb landed on Broadcasting House while he was reading the *Nine O'Clock News*, and then continuing with the utmost calm; or the announcement that people should stay listening to their radios because important news – it was the victory at El Alamein – would shortly follow; or the excitement of hearing in great detail about the D-Day landings. These things brought the nation together in a way that nothing else could, and would never be forgotten.

One such incident occurred on Sunday 15 April 1945, after some of the best of the British war correspondents, Richard Dimbleby and Wynford Vaughan-Thomas among them, had reached the small town of Winsen in Lower Saxony with the advance forces of the British Second Army.

The military spokesman told them that the commander of a German camp close by had sent an emissary with an offer of surrender and an urgent request for help; typhus had broken out there. Wynford Vaughan-Thomas, a warm-hearted, generous-spirited man, wrote in 1967 in an appreciation after Richard Dimbleby's death: 'I couldn't see anything newsworthy in it, but Richard said, "I have a feeling this one's different," and took off in his jeep.'

He was not alone. Some of the most famous names in British journalism went too, including Alan Moorehead of the *Express*. The camp was Bergen-Belsen, the first of the Nazi death camps to be discovered. When the journalists came back some hours later, it was immediately clear to Vaughan-Thomas that they had seen unspeakable things. Dimbleby, almost too upset to speak, wrote out his despatch while the BBC's sound engineer, Harvey Sarney, fired up the miniature transmitting station in order to send it to London. 'You can't tell that on the air,' Vaughan-Thomas said, appalled. 'I must,' Dimbleby said. 'I must tell the exact truth, every detail of it, even if the people don't believe me, even if they feel these things should not be told.' He talked of the huge heaps of skeletons, the living trapped among the dead, the stench of excrement and death, the bodies left lying around with their livers, kidneys or hearts cut out and eaten by the starving survivors. Sixty thousand prisoners had lived and died like this. He said: 'I have seen many terrible sights in the last five years, but nothing, nothing, approaching the dreadful interior . . . of Belsen.'

Starting early on in the war, the BBC had a convention that it must accept the word of its correspondents. It was one of the reasons why their status within the organization was so high. But the calm voice of the 'Traffic' manager who took in the report came back a few seconds later to say that the duty editor could not put out Dimbleby's report unless it were confirmed by other sources. Dimbleby was rightly outraged. He at once got on the phone to the foreign editor and said that if his report did not go out he would never broadcast again in his entire life.

That must have frightened the duty editor, but the entire exchange was unnecessary. Dimbleby's broadcast had been passed quickly by the censor, and the BBC's technology was faster than anyone else's; before many minutes had passed the first news agency reports of the liberation of Belsen were starting to reach London. If anything, they showed that Dimbleby had held back some of the worst details.

In his despatch for the next morning's *Express* Alan Moorehead wrote: '[I]t was not always possible to distinguish men from women, or indeed to determine whether they were human at all.' Trying to avert his eyes from the 'livid straining faces and emaciated arms and legs under the filthy bedclothes', his handkerchief to his face in an attempt to protect himself from the stench, he told the British captain taking him round that he'd had enough. 'You've got to go through one of the men's huts yet,' he said grimly. 'That's what you're here for.'

The United Press correspondent Richard McMillan, a tough Glaswegian who had been through the Desert War and everything since, confessed that for much of the time he was in Belsen he was peering out between his fingers like a frightened child. Other horrors were awaiting the advancing Allies: Buchenwald, Dachau, Treblinka, Auschwitz among them. After Belsen, people like the comfortable BBC duty editor who couldn't believe Dimbleby's report no longer had their doubts.

Yet Dimbleby, like the other correspondents, failed to find anyone who admitted being a Nazi supporter among the Germans he came across. In one small town he went into a hotel kitchen to listen to the BBC's *Nine O'Clock News* on the radio. The news reader Freddy Grisewood read out a list of German towns which had been captured. The hotel owner and his family listened too, marking off each place on the map as it was announced. 'There was not one sound or sign of regret on their faces. No shock, no despair, no alarm . . . just as if they were a bunch of neutrals hearing all about somebody else.'

As the war in Europe came to an end, the correspondents who had spent the previous five years risking their lives to get to places first, to make sure their copy reached London before anyone else's, to head out in no-man's-land to check some small but essential fact, now suffered a sense of emptiness, even despair. Alan Moorehead and his friend Alex Clifford of the *Mail*, the strangely ill-assorted friends who had stuck together ever since the Desert War, turned down an offer from the Seventh Armoured Division to tour Berlin just after it had fallen. Moorehead wrote later, 'We could not bear to see another ruined city. We no longer possessed the necessary emotions for a victory parade.'

§

At 12.20 a.m. London time on Monday 6 August 1945, the Japanese city of Hiroshima, an important military and naval base, was largely destroyed by the most powerful weapon ever used in warfare. The following morning, under the words

THE BOMB THAT HAS CHANGED THE WORLD

the *Daily Express* carried two stories, side by side: one headline read 'Japs told "Now quit"' and described how Hiroshima

> was blotted out by a cloud of dust and smoke. Sixteen hours later pilots were still waiting for the cloud to lift to let them see what had happened.
>
> The bomb was a last warning. Now leaflets will tell the Japanese what to expect unless their Government surrenders.

Another headline read:

20,000 tons in golf ball

and explained:

> One atomic bomb has a destructive force equal to that of 20,000 tons of T.N.T., or five 1,000-plane raids. This terrific power is packed in a space of little more than golf ball size.
>
> Experts estimate that the bomb can destroy anything on the surface in an area of at least two square miles – twice the size of the City of London.

Much of the rest of the *Express*'s front page was given up to a statement prepared by Winston Churchill, who had been voted out of office two weeks earlier, and issued from Downing Street. It mostly dealt with the history of the project to create the atomic bomb, and the important part Britain had played in it. But the statement ended with a short moral reflection:

> This revelation of the secrets of Nature, long mercifully withheld from man, should arouse the most solemn reflections in the mind and conscience of every human being capable of comprehension.

Elsewhere on the front page was a quotation from, of all places, the Department of War in Washington, describing it as 'a revolutionary weapon destined to change war, or which may even be the instrumentality to end all wars'.

On Thursday 9 August the newspapers carried the text of a broadcast by President Truman the previous evening, warning that he was prepared to use it again. The same day, in the absence of any progress towards surrender, Nagasaki was attacked by a second and more powerful atomic bomb. On Monday 13 August *The Times* carried a report from Washington headlined

Nagasaki Like A 'Volcano'

> The results of the atomic bombing of Nagasaki are said to be beyond belief, but the most impressive fact yet disclosed concerning it is that the bomb dropped there has rendered obsolete the bomb used so effectively against Hiroshima . . .
>
> An American correspondent who flew over the Nagasaki area 12 hours after the bombing said the city was still a mass of flames and that it was 'like looking over the rim of a volcano in the process of eruption.'

But although the destructive capability of the atomic bomb was evident, it was not clear what precisely had happened to the people of Hiroshima and Nagasaki. The American commander, General MacArthur, had closed off the whole of southern Japan to journalists, in order to make sure they concentrated on the release of Allied prisoners of war from the Japanese camps. Many of them had suffered terribly. But a seasoned *Daily Express* correspondent, Wilfred Burchett, who used the name 'Peter Burchett' in his bylines for the paper, managed to reach Hiroshima. A tough, heavily set Australian with radical views, Burchett became an avowed Communist after the war. When the bomb was dropped, he was still in Okinawa, and heard about it while he was queuing for food at a US Marine Corps base. He decided at that moment that he was going to get to Hiroshima. He went without letting the *Express* know, and managed to slip on board a train from Tokyo. The journey took him twenty-one hours, and it wasn't easy: his compartment was filled with hostile Japanese officers.

Burchett reached Hiroshima on the morning of Tuesday 3 September. He had a letter of introduction to a Mr Nakamura, the local representative of the Domei news agency, and went to see the police chief of Hiroshima. Both men were delighted to see him, and together they drove him over the remains of a city which had ceased to exist. He visited the only surviving hospital, where the senior doctor, who had trained in the United States, showed him the wards where some of the worst cases were being cared for. '[H]ow can Christians do what you have done here?' the doctor asked him.

Profoundly shaken, Burchett settled down with his typewriter and wrote his story in duplicate, using the carbon paper he had brought with him. He gave one copy to the manager of Domei, who saw that it was tapped out by Morse code to Domei's headquarters in Tokyo, to be transmitted to London.

A few hours later, a group of American correspondents were flown in by the US Air Force on a facility trip. The USAF colonel in charge angrily refused to allow Burchett to take the plane back to Tokyo, and would not accept the other copy of his article. So Burchett had to make his way slowly back again, worried the entire time by the thought that he had been scooped by the Americans. Instead, when he reached Tokyo he found that his story had successfully reached the *Express*. On Wednesday 5 September, the day when the paper was boasting about its latest world record for sales – 3,320,173 – it dominated the front page.

HIROSHIMA, Tuesday.

In Hiroshima, 30 days after the first atomic bomb destroyed the city and shook the world, people are still dying, mysteriously and horribly – people who were uninjured in the cataclysm – from an unknown something which I can only describe as the atomic plague.

Hiroshima does not look like a bombed city. It looks as if a monster steamroller had passed over it and squashed it out of existence. I write these facts as dispassionately as I can in the hope that they will act as a warning to the world . . .

When you arrive in Hiroshima you can look around and for 25 and perhaps 30 square miles you can see hardly a building. It gives you an empty feeling in the stomach to see such man-made devastation.

Some 53,000 had died, he wrote, and another 30,000 were missing, 'which means "certainly dead"'. During the day he was there, a hundred people died from the after-effects of the bombing. Burchett describes the patients he saw in the hospitals where the police chief and the news agency manager took him:

> ... I found people who, when the bomb fell, suffered absolutely no injuries, but now are dying from the uncanny side-effects.
>
> For no apparent reason their health began to fail. They lost appetite. Their hair fell out. Bluish spots appeared on their bodies. And then bleeding began from the ears, nose and mouth.
>
> At first the doctors told me they thought these were the symptoms of general debility. They gave their patients Vitamin A injections. The results were horrifying. The flesh started rotting away from the hole caused by the injection of the needle. And in every case the victim died.
>
> That is one of the after-effects of the first atomic bomb man ever dropped and I do not want to see any more examples of it.

Inevitably, Burchett's description of radiation sickness created a sensation. With a fine dramatic flourish, Burchett arrived back in Tokyo just in time to attend a press conference given by the US army's chief spokesman about his report. As he walked in, he heard himself being accused of falling victim to Japanese propaganda; radiation sickness, the spokesman said, simply didn't exist.

But Wilfred Burchett relied not on official briefings but on sheer enterprise and the evidence of his own eyes. It was the last scoop of the war and it happened three weeks after it had ended.

16

SUEZ

At 11 a.m. and 3.45 p.m. each working day – the times have only occasionally changed for over a century – a select group of journalists has trooped into a side office at Downing Street or, more recently, the Lobby Room in the Palace of Westminster, to be briefed by the prime minister's spokesman.

The typical PMS has been a senior civil servant in his early fifties, self-effacing, able and often quietly amusing. The exceptions were felt by many of the journalists they dealt with to demonstrate the value of the archetype; there was relief when they went, even though life had been exciting while they were in charge. Their personal loyalty to the prime minister they worked for seemed to transcend almost everything else. None of them left the Lobby Room, where political manipulation and journalism interacted, a better place for having been there.

A Downing Street press secretary is not some kind of persuader. He is judged by the press in proportion to his closeness to his boss; his function is to make the journalists feel they are sampling (even if at second hand) the genuine views of the prime minister. As it happens, they are generally given short change, since the press secretary more often gets his briefings from the Cabinet secretary than from the prime minister.

The job has alternated between aggressive manipulators and quiet civil servants right from the start. The first Downing Street official to be given the specific task of briefing the press was the able and entirely cynical career civil servant William Sutherland.

Sutherland acquired the nickname 'Bronco Bill'; the connotations are those of circuses, of the Wild West, and of making horses – or newspaper correspondents – do what he wanted. It was not flattering, especially to the journalists. It is impossible to be certain which newspaper stories Sutherland was responsible for; but there was a great deal of poison in

British journalism during the Lloyd George years, and much of it emanated from Sutherland, at Lloyd George's behest. It was at this time that Humbert Wolfe, the Italian-born Jewish poet, author and civil servant, whom Sutherland knew well, wrote his famous but often misquoted squib:

> You cannot hope to bribe or twist,
> Thank God! the British journalist.
> But, seeing what the man will do
> Unbribed, there's no occasion to.

Uncharacteristically, Lloyd George put his relationship with the press on a proper footing immediately after Sutherland left. Geoffrey Shakespeare was a good example of the other type of official spokesman. Shakespeare quickly demonstrated a fair-mindedness, a clarity of thought, an unwillingness either to bully or be bullied, and a quiet sense of humour.

At twenty-eight, he was much younger than those who would do the job after him. But his father had known Lloyd George, and in March 1921 he was asked to take charge of press relations in Downing Street.

Shakespeare lasted in Downing Street for little more than a year; but although his tenure as the prime minister's official spokesman was so short, Shakespeare established a pattern for many future holders of the job.

Apart from interventionists like Neville Chamberlain, prime ministers have been content to give the job to men trained to present the current government's point of view in as favourable a light as possible, but who were not personally committed to it. Overall, it is probably fair to say that throughout the twentieth century the best and most honest relationships with the press were established by men like these; and the country was better informed as a result.

§

Lobby correspondents were, and still are, an odd subspecies of the journalistic genus. Unlike the top foreign or domestic correspondents, who all too often behave like grandees at best, and swaggerers at worst, the Lobby has traditionally been composed of quieter, less imaginative, less assertive characters. If the leading newspaper specialists are cockerels, crowing from the roof of the hen-house, the political correspondents are more like assiduous hens, pecking around for small items of news and turning out daily eggs of a remarkably similar smoothness and roundness. The Lobby is reliable, orderly, and surprisingly non-political. Its members cooperate more than they seem to compete, and after an important speech in the chamber or the arrival of a government statement they often go through the wording together, and agree between themselves on the significance and the main points.

As a result, political reporting tends to be rather similar across the spectrum of newspapers, television and radio. Newspaper reporting outside politics is much more of a collaborative business than most people realize, but it is always something of a shock for journalists who have previously worked in other fields to take up a job at Westminster – although there were always individual Lobby correspondents who ferreted out stories on their own fearlessly and aggressively. Ian Aitken, for instance, political editor of the *Guardian* from 1975 to 1990, told the authors of the 1984 study *Sources Close To The Prime Minister*:

> There is a terrible lot of nonsense talked about what Lobby journalists are. We are really general reporters in dirty raincoats. We just have a ticket to get us into the lobby, some of the bars or the corridors. The idea that we can be manipulated by forces unseen is simply nonsense.

That was true of Aitken himself, but not necessarily of much of the rest of the Lobby who felt more comfortable when they reported what everyone else was reporting.

By the end of the twentieth century the Lobby was run very differently from the way it had been even in the 1980s. Younger, less malleable journalists had come in with new demands for openness. The Lobby system, which had once been so secretive, was openly supported by government and reporters alike, and the old weasel phrases which once disguised the identity of the prime minister's official spokesmen and the origin of so much carefully massaged information had largely been dropped. By 2009 a group of young Turks maintained a website, updated every few hours, on which the latest briefings from Downing Street were set out.

As late as the 1980s, such an enterprise would have been disavowed by the government, and the Lobby itself would have insisted that it must be discontinued by the journalists involved, on pain of disbarment. Newspapers were still in the ascendant, and Lobby briefings were held to suit the deadlines of the written press, not of radio or television. Yet things changed very quickly, and by the 1990s television correspondents were reporting 'live' from the corridors of Parliament itself. By contrast, in 1980 the author, then the BBC's newly arrived political editor, was ordered out of Downing Street, together with his television crew, by Bernard Ingham, Margaret Thatcher's volcanic, florid-faced press spokesman.

Ingham was one of the last defenders of the newspaper tradition (he had himself been a labour correspondent for the *Guardian*) and supported the fundamentalists in their efforts to keep television at bay. By 1990, when Margaret Thatcher left office and Ingham went with her, this attitude was starting to seem overly quaint, even to the newspaper journalists themselves. Britain remains one of the less open democracies, though nowadays it is probably equal in terms of official reticence with America, which until it began its steady post-Vietnam retreat was the most open government in the world. Yet the differences with even the recent past are both sudden and impressive.

The Lobby was formalized in 1884, when a select few of the newspaper correspondents who had previously been obliged to wait outside the various entrances to Parliament, or else meet their selected sources in discreet corners of the Palace of Westminster itself by prearrangement, were given permission by the sergeant-at-arms to hang around in the lobbies. This gave them much greater access to MPs and ministers. Yet because of the personal nature of the permission – the sergeant-at-arms had to like you and approve of you – it was a jealously guarded secret. Slowly, it became more convenient for ministers or their officials to brief Lobby correspondents in groups rather than individually, though as always the correspondents tried to form their own private relationships with ministers.

The clandestine nature of arrangements like these was established to protect the flow of information; but very soon it had become part of the wholly unnecessary mystique of reporting a government, in a society which was deeply impressed by authority in any form. The radical MP Henry Labouchère proclaimed soon after the establishment of the Lobby,

'I am enabled on undoubted authority to state' ... 'I am in a position to inform' ... 'I learn from a private but official source' ...

18. (*Left*) Lord Northcliffe (1865–1922) and (*centre*) his brother Lord Rothermere (1868–1940), in the studio of the sculptor Courtenay Pollack. The Harmsworth brothers were the two most powerful, most innovative and arguably most dangerous figures in British press history; especially Rothermere, who supported Hitler and Oswald Mosley.

19. Morgan Philips Price (1885–1973). His reporting of the Russian revolution and its aftermath was excellent, but so partisan that C. P. Scott let him go as the *Guardian* correspondent for lacking objectivity. He went to Germany, but his reporting of Hitler's rise lacked his earlier edge.

20. Philip Pembroke Stephens (c.1894–1937), the Berlin correspondent of the *Daily Express*, whose courage in reporting the ugly reality of Nazi power awakened hundreds of thousands of British readers to the dangers of Nazism.

21. Tom Sefton Delmer (1904–79). He was Stephens' predecessor in Berlin for the *Express*, and had such good contacts in the Nazi leadership that he was wrongly regarded as a Nazi himself. A great embroiderer of stories, he was aptly recruited to write black propaganda during the war.

22. Guernica after the attack by German bombers, 26 April 1937.

23. Kim Philby (1912–88) with his head bandaged, in the Spanish village of Caude, immediately after his convoy had been shelled on 31 December 1937. Philby, a *Times* correspondent, was ordered by his Soviet controllers to cover his Communist links by pretending to be a Fascist sympathiser.

24. The consummate BBC war correspondent: Richard Dimbleby (1913–65) was charming, brave, hard-working, and perhaps a little innocent.

25. Comrades in the desert: Alan Moorehead (1910–83) of the *Express* and his close friend, colleague, and occasional rival Alex Clifford (1909–52) of the *Mail*.

26. Philip Zec's stark cartoon of March 1942 in the *Daily Mirror* was undercut by its ambiguous caption, suggested by the *Mirror* columnist Cassandra: '"The price of petrol has been increased by one penny." – Official.' Churchill and most of his ministers saw it, wrongly, as an attack on the oil companies.

— even Jane is doing her bit —

— to pep up production!

27. Norman Pett's 'Jane' cartoon strip in the *Mirror*, by contrast with Zec, cheered everyone up. She showed more and more flesh until 1943, when she bared all. On the day that edition reached North Africa, the British Eighth Army is said to have achieved an advance of five miles.

28. Rear-Admiral Sir George Pirie Thomson (1887–1965), chief censor during the Second World War. Sharp-witted and unstuffy, he trusted the British and American press and kept them on his side. He told one journalist, 'I should be awfully grateful if you wouldn't address me as "sir."'

29. James Cameron (1911–85). One of the most admired foreign correspondents of the century. Observing the atomic tests at Bikini made him a lifelong pacifist and a founder of the Campaign for Nuclear Disarmament.

30. (*Far right*) Wilfred Burchett (1911–83): Australian Communist sympathiser and *Express* correspondent, he was the first Westerner to reach Hiroshima after the atomic bomb was dropped. The Americans tried to discredit his story. Later he became a supporter of North Vietnam and even Pol Pot's Cambodia.

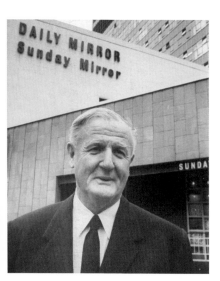

31. Cecil King (1901–87) was another offshoot of the Harmsworth family, with some of the same megalomaniac tendencies as his uncles Northcliffe and Rothermere. He turned the *Daily Mirror* into the world's bestselling paper, and later appeared to propose a coup against the British government.

32. Sir Harold Wilson (1916–95) and his political secretary Marcia Williams, later Lady Falkender (born 1932).

33. Nora Beloff (1919–97): one of the most distinguished women in twentieth-century British journalism, she provided the *Observer* with some of its best political writing. Yet her obsessiveness and weird behaviour made her a figure of fun to many male journalists.

34. Joe Haines (born 1928): Harold Wilson's press secretary was a spin-doctor before the term was invented. Later he continued as a 'teller of tall tales' (according to a review by Roy Hattersley), suggesting in a book that Wilson's doctor had offered to murder Lady Falkender. When this claim was repeated in a television play, the BBC had to settle out of court.

35. Bloody Sunday: a British soldier attacks a demonstrator, 30 January 1972.

36. The journalist as adventurer: Max Hastings of the *Daily Telegraph* prepares to enter Port Stanley ahead of the British forces at the end of the Falklands War.

37. Rupert Murdoch (born 1931) and his best and most aggressive editor, Kelvin MacKenzie (born 1946), with the first edition of the *Sun* to be printed at the union-breaking Wapping works.

38. John Major and his underpants, by the *Guardian*'s Steve Bell. Bell turned the underpants motif (which was first suggested by Alistair Campbell) into a powerful comic weapon which helped to do immense damage to Major's standing.

39. Tony Blair and Alistair Campbell. Their partnership lay at the heart of Blair's success; it also emboldened them to force through Britain's participation in the American-led invasion of Iraq, against the advice and wishes of most of the British establishment and a sizeable proportion of the population.

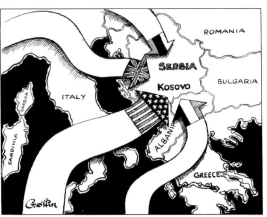

40. Griffin, in the *Sun*, tried to evoke the 'Finest Hour' spirit of 1940 during the 1999 NATO assault on Serbia by borrowing the image of the attacking arrows from the opening titles of the BBC television comedy series *Dad's Army*. But it was NATO which seemed like Dad's Army.

41. The BBC's director general, Greg Dyke, being mobbed by well-wishers among the Corporation's staff after announcing his resignation in January 2004, in the wake of the Hutton Report. The chairman, Gavyn Davies, also resigned. The Blair government's victory soon turned sour: public opinion strongly supported the BBC.

'the government thinks' ... All this sort of inventive trash, although disgusting to persons of good taste, has its effects with the millions.

Journalism, though conducted a century later with technology unimaginable in the 1880s and broadcast to unthinkably large audiences – the BBC alone now broadcasts to more people round the world than existed in 1880 – still speaks with much the same vocabulary that aroused Labouchère's contempt. And the information is usually gleaned in precisely the same way. In fact, the biggest part in the entire process, day after day, is played by chance: chance meetings, chance disclosures, chance timings, chance judgements, and just as frequently chance misjudgements.

For much of the twentieth century the Lobby was largely a passive organization, focusing on providing a conduit for government, and to a lesser extent opposition, policies and ideas to the public. Gallery reporters, meanwhile, offered daily reports and critiques of performances by speakers on the floor of the House. The business of judging the effectiveness and value of government policy was carried out by the editorial writers. The system was, in its way, admirable, but the effect was to encourage the mood of passivity. The Lobby journalist simply had to speak to a minister or a knowledgeable backbencher, find out what they thought or were planning to do, and write it up. It was not his job to challenge the views or worry whether the proposals were viable or even made sense. For forty-four years, beginning in the last years of Lloyd George and ending twelve prime ministers later with James Callaghan, James Margach was one of the most enduring and perceptive political correspondents at Westminster, ending his time as political editor of the *Sunday Times*. He had his share of famous exclusives, but was a peaceable, self-effacing man who got on well with most of the politicians he reported on. Even so, his account of his long years at Westminster, entitled *The Abuse of Power*, was a savage attack on the way successive prime ministers had manipulated the press.

Two objectives possessed them. First, to establish and fortify their personal power; and secondly to reinforce the conspiracy of secrecy, to preserve the sanctity of Government behind the walls of Whitehall's forbidden city.

All true, probably, though there must be some doubt about the extent of, say, Clement Attlee's lust for power; yet Margach's editors and his legions of readers might have been justified in asking why they had never heard anything about these twin prime ministerial obsessions when he was writing his weekly reports for the *Sunday Times*.

§

Clement Attlee was small in stature, and unimpressive – a public school traditionalist who loved cricket rather more than he loved politics. According to his press secretary Francis Williams he had an almost fanatical sense of duty.

Williams, an interesting and cultured man, who was brought up on a farm in Lancashire and left school at seventeen for a job as a journalist in Bootle, came to Downing Street after distinguished wartime service at the Ministry of Information. He was surprised to find that there was no news agency ticker-tape machine in the building to tip off the prime minister's staff about breaking news items. Knowing Attlee's intense dislike for anything to do with journalism, he persuaded him to allow a machine to be installed outside the Cabinet Room, on the grounds that it would enable him to keep track of the latest cricket scores. Williams later told how Attlee came rushing into his office soon afterwards.

> 'Francis, Francis, you know my cricket machine at the Cabinet door? When I checked it just now for the lunch-time score at Lord's it was ticking out the decisions and subjects discussed at the Cabinet meeting this morning. How can it do that? What's going on around here?'

Williams had to explain to him about his daily briefings with Lobby correspondents. Attlee still seemed bewildered, but he said, 'OK, Francis, I'll leave the show to you. Good work.'

Attlee's own meetings with journalists were brief, because he said so little at them. He had no interest in how he was portrayed in the newspapers, and when Francis Williams told him about some personal attack on him in the press he would reply, 'That so? Suppose they've got to say something. Circulation slipping, you think?' He would never ask to see a copy of the story. Perhaps this was wise; James Margach writes:

> Relations were never so poisonous, bad-tempered and embittered
> as during the years of the Attlee Government. To be frank, I have
> never known the Press so consistently and irresponsibly political,
> slanted and prejudiced.

It is not surprising. The majority of newspapers were pro-Conservative,
and by setting up the Welfare State the post-war Labour government
was challenging conservatism on every front. Each new battle, from the
nationalization of the coal mines to the establishment of the National
Health Service and even the independence of India was fought out even
more fiercely and with less restraint with the press than with the official
opposition.

Attlee, believing that his overwhelming majority in the House of
Commons was all that mattered, seemed oblivious to it all. But there can
be no doubt that the rapid decline in the popularity of his government
had a good deal to do with the constant noisy contempt shown by the
great majority of newspapers for what Labour was trying to do.

The Attorney General, Sir Hartley Shawcross, responded violently,
attacking 'the campaign of calumny and misrepresentation' carried out
by 'the Tory Party and the Tory stooge press'.

> [T]he truth is that there has never been a time when certain
> sections of the Press have more seriously abused the freedom which
> is accorded them under our constitution. Freedom of the Press does
> not mean freedom to tell lies.

Those Labour MPs who were members of the National Union of
Journalists were encouraged to campaign for a formal inquiry into the
whole question of press ownership and its effects on newspaper reporting,
which was championed in the Cabinet by a vociferous Aneurin Bevan.
Four weeks later, the Commons voted by a large majority to set up a Royal
Commission into the press. The results the following June were typical
of most Royal Commissions: it told people pretty much what they already
knew. There was no systematic distortion or suppression of the news, but
standards were lower than they should be and the distinction between
news and comment was not always properly observed.

The one tangible proposal was the establishment of a watchdog
intended to deal with these shortcomings. The newspapers, suspicious of

anything which might be used to control them, wrangled over the concept for years, and it was not until 1953 that the Press Council began its work. For many years the Council was an adequate, if not particularly energetic, defender of the rights of the ordinary citizen against the power of the press, but by the 1980s, and the arrival in force of the Murdoch empire, whatever teeth it had were thoroughly worn down. By the turn of the century it seemed to direct its chief energy at those who pointed this out.

§

Every big news organization in Britain regards its Lobby correspondents as the most important part of its news gathering operation. They produce more news than any other group, and the chances are that what they produce will provide greater interest than the rest of the news. There are times when politics takes a back seat – during the Second World War, for instance, the front pages were almost always dominated by war news. But when the war was finally over, and a new government pledged to change almost everything about the way Britain was run came to power, the Lobby correspondents came back into their own. Fleet Street's front pages during 1946 were overwhelmingly dominated by domestic political news.

Yet, just as the powerful debates within Cabinet in 1940 never made it to the front pages, many apparently important issues after the war were given the most cursory treatment or none at all.

One example is the circumstances surrounding the American loan of 1946. The war had devastated the British economy, but its aftermath around the globe meant that Britain, facing open conflict with Communists and nationalists in some parts of the world, had to go on spending huge amounts of money in order to keep going. But the previous year, the Truman administration had, virtually without warning, repudiated the Lend-Lease agreement, as soon as the Japanese surrendered. This went wholly unreported in the British press.

There was the same absence of comment in the press and on the BBC about the unexpected ferocity of British officials encountered in financial negotiations in Washington. The US was now determined to exact full repayment for every loan it had made to Britain during the Second World War, and the Attlee government was shocked by the unyielding attitude in Washington towards the negotiation of another loan. In the end, the British team, which included two of the most distinguished economists in Britain and the world, John Maynard Keynes and Lionel Robbins, managed to secure a dollar loan worth £1.23 billion; but it was at the cost of accepting, among other difficult conditions, a clause which made sterling freely convertible into dollars a year after the date of the loan agreement.

It seems to have been part of a deliberate American effort to destroy the Sterling Area and make the dollar the sole currency for international trade and business. When the clause came into effect, on 15 July 1947, sterling balances were sold right across the world, and an international panic ensued. Sterling's convertibility had to be suspended.

One of the main results for ordinary British people was that rationing had to be intensified, and the fact that it continued in one form or another until 1954 was the direct result of American demands. The remark that 'The Americans are hitting us worse than Hitler did' was frequently heard – and yet the British press rarely reciprocated; it is hard to find much open anti-Americanism, even in the *Daily Worker*, the Communist Party newspaper.

There is no evidence of any outright approach to the newspapers or the BBC by the government. Perhaps it was an instinctive response to the wave of anti-Americanism among the population at large, but for Fleet Street, and for the BBC, the entire emphasis seemed to be on trying to patch up the relationship with the Americans and get back to the sense of partnership which had existed during the war.

§

There were always some members of the Lobby with the penetrating minds and experience to be able to see through the briefings they were given, but they were few in number.

Occasionally, one would strike out on his own, but the results could be dangerous. During the complex and difficult negotiations on the Attlee government's plans to nationalize the steel industry, for example, the *Financial Times* Lobby correspondent Paul Einzig showed that he had good sources on both the government and the industrial sides. Einzig wrote a remarkably accurate and well-informed series of stories about the steel negotiations, leading Sir Norman Brook, the Cabinet secretary, to suggest that MI5 should put him under surveillance. Attlee agreed, and Einzig's phone was tapped and he was discreetly followed around – for no other reason than that he was doing his job rather too well for Whitehall's comfort.

But the coverage of Westminster and Whitehall during the Attlee years can only be described as patchy. Important issues such as the series of decisions that Britain should start making its own independent atomic bomb, went almost unnoticed.

The main research on nuclear fission had been done by a team composed of British scientists, together with some European refugees from the Nazis. But since the cost was well beyond Britain's means, the British agreed in 1941 to hand over all their research to the Americans, and sent a large team to work in New Mexico on the bomb's production. Yet despite this deep British involvement in the success of the programme, the United States Congress passed the McMahon Act in August 1946, making it illegal to share nuclear information with any foreign country, including Britain.

On 8 January 1947 a Cabinet committee secretly decided to develop a British atomic bomb. But so many people had to be drafted into the programme that officials, worried that some enterprising journalist might find out about it, suggested the following year that the government should issue a statement that work was going on to develop a number of weapons, including an atomic bomb. The Cabinet agreed, but it was decided that the news should slip out as quietly as possible.

Making a formal announcement in the House of Commons, the Minister of Defence, Albert Alexander, replied tersely to a bland question from a compliant backbencher:

> As was made clear in the Statement relating to Defence, 1948 (Command 7327), research and development continue to receive the highest priority in the defence field, and all types of modern weapons, including atomic weapons, are being developed.
>
> MR JEGER: Can the Minister give any further information on the development of atomic weapons?
>
> MR ALEXANDER: No. I do not think it would be in the public interest to do that.

It was an exchange worthy of the great tradition of governmental discretion, yet the press might have been expected to prick up their ears. But perhaps because of the existence of a D-Notice covering the issue, they said nothing of any interest the following day, even though the D-Notice certainly didn't warn against discussion of the ethics of making an atomic weapon, or the scientific problems, or the geopolitical issues.

The *Daily Express* gave it the most prominence, but only because it was tacked on to a story by the paper's rather sinister security correspondent, Chapman Pincher. This one was headlined

COMMUNIST MP SEES ATOM SECRETS

and described how the MP for Stepney, Phil Piratin, had visited the secret atomic power station at Didcot in Berkshire. The fact that he had been accompanied by twenty-one other MPs, and that they had all been selected by having their names pulled out of a hat, was less prominently presented. After a couple of paragraphs of this, the article continued

> In Parliament yesterday, Mr Alexander, Defence Minister, said that Britain is developing atomic weapons on the highest priority.
>
> He was asked to give more information but replied: 'I do not think it would be in the public interest.'

The rest of the newspapers gave the announcement of Britain's atomic warfare programme even less prominence. The *Manchester Guardian* had a few lines low down on an inside page; so did *The Times*. The *Daily Mail* and the *Daily Telegraph* put a bare report of the Commons exchange on the front page. The *Daily Herald* didn't even make it a news item; it put it in its parliamentary report section. As for the *Daily Mirror*, it didn't mention it at all. Nor did the BBC's news bulletins. Did the Lobby correspondents decide together that there was nothing much in it? It looks like it. And since the Lobby was and remains so strong, few editors are willing to question their political correspondents' judgement.

Much the same lack of interest and initiative was shown a year later, in late June 1949. The effects of the conditions attached to the American loan had turned out, as Keynes had warned, to be devastating to the weak British economy. There was strong speculation in the American press that Britain would be forced to devalue the pound. Some of this drifted into the newspapers in London, but not much. Perhaps editors felt it would increase the pressure on sterling, and felt it was their patriotic duty to prevent things becoming worse; it seems more likely, though, that they took their line from their political correspondents, who were being assured on a daily basis that nothing very serious was going on.

Little attention was paid when, on 13 June 1949, Sir Stafford Cripps circulated a paper warning that the outflow of dollars had become serious, and might soon be desperate. Two days later the Cabinet met, and agreed with Cripps's suggestion that he should use a speech the following evening to alert the nation to the danger. He warned his colleagues that within a year all Britain's reserves might have gone, leading to a complete collapse of sterling.

Only the *Financial Times* had mentioned any of this, and it was only Cripps's speech which jolted the newspapers out of their Lobby-induced slumber. On 23 June the BBC carried a report from Canberra of a speech by the Australian prime minister, Joe Chifley, warning of the effects of higher oil prices on sterling's gold and dollar reserves. But it was not until 27 June that the Economic Policy Committee of the Cabinet decided to tell the press what was really going on. 'Attention was drawn to the importance of giving adequate guidance to the Press, at the appropriate time . . . on the wider question of our dollar situation generally.'

It is the supercilious tone of the civil service mandarin: 'adequate' means 'as little as we can decently tell them', and 'the appropriate time' means 'when it suits our purposes'. But time was shorter even than the EPC's members thought, and the Lobby was briefed that evening, perhaps by Herbert Morrison. A report on the *Nine O'Clock News* announced: 'I understand that a meeting of ministers took place today to discuss the economy.'

The following evening the *Nine O'Clock News* used the word 'devaluation' for the first time. Over the next few days the extent of the encroaching disaster began to take shape. On 6 July an editorial in the *Financial Times* put the blame squarely on the government for keeping people in the dark: 'The British people are already far too dependent on outside sources for information vital to themselves. They are entitled, today at least, to an outline of the immediate steps the Government proposes.'

The following day, 7 July, Cripps told the Commons the government had no intention of devaluing the pound; on 19 September the pound was devalued by 30 per cent, from $4.03 to $2.80. The political shock was savage, and it was these months more than any others which destroyed the Labour government and ensured that within two years it would be out of office until 1964.

The crisis puts British journalism in the worst of lights: lazy, un-inquisitive, craven, obedient to authority, at a time when American, French and other newspapers seemed much better informed about the state of sterling. It is a depressing story; and it is hard to avoid the feeling that at the heart of it was the Lobby system.

§

On 25 October 1951, a month short of his seventy-seventh birthday, Winston Churchill was re-elected prime minister.

The newspapers politely chose to ignore his age, though the *Daily Mirror*, which was constantly at war with him, attacked him as a dangerous warmonger. It had quoted an off-the-record, unattributable statement by the French foreign minister, Robert Schumann, to the effect that Churchill had wanted a preventive war against Stalin's Russia. Churchill sued for defamation, and since the *Mirror* could not name Schumann or call him as a witness, it was bound to lose. The *Manchester Guardian*, by contrast, decided marginally in his favour. On 22 October it announced: '[T]he Labour Government has come to the end of its usefulness . . . [A] Churchill Government is . . . the lesser evil.'

The country, it seems, agreed. The Conservatives won by the narrow margin of sixteen seats, and the *Mirror*'s confused campaign seems to have done nothing to help Labour's cause.

The Lobby rules insisted that political correspondents must close their eyes to many things: fights between MPs, drunkenness, unsuitable behaviour of all kinds. They themselves extended the principle to cover Churchill's age and growing decrepitude, even though while he was leader of the opposition they had seen plenty of evidence of it. And because the political reporting in the press was entirely carried out by members of the Lobby, newspaper readers and the BBC's listeners were given no real indication of his physical decay. During his time in office Britain drifted aimlessly, getting stronger economically but lacking any sense of where it was going politically. Privately, Churchill had undertaken to stand aside for Anthony Eden after a year or so. When the time came, he changed his mind and his colleagues struggled to persuade him to retire.

Three different press barons, Lord Beaverbrook, Lord Camrose and his brother Lord Kemsley, were close personal friends of Churchill; as a result, the *Daily* and *Sunday Express*, *Evening Standard*, *Daily Telegraph*, *Daily Sketch*, *Sunday Times* and a slew of regional newspapers were all inclined to go easy on him (though it is fair to say that both during and after the war the *Telegraph* showed a consistent determination not to be slavish in its loyalty). As for the BBC, it did what the newspapers did, only more slowly and even more anxiously.

Nothing was questioned, nothing seriously critical was reported. A range of important debates was going on inside the Cabinet, on the future of steel, the decision to introduce commercial television, denationalizing the steel industry, developing Britain's nuclear deterrent, policy towards the United States, towards the Soviet Union, towards Egypt. Readers of the British press were given very little inkling of any of these issues. In part, it was the instinctive forelock-tugging of Lobby reporting, and now there was something else: a clear sense that the nation wanted a holiday from the stress and bitterness of political argument.

When he came into office Churchill allowed it to be known that he was returning to the older constitutional principle that the government's channel of information to the public passed through the Houses of Parliament, not directly to the newspapers. A press secretary, Fife Clarke, was eventually appointed, but he worked for the Chancellor of the Duchy of Lancaster, Lord Swinton, not for Downing Street, and his briefings lacked any intimate knowledge of Churchill's thoughts or plans. Swinton told James Margach how Churchill told him his relations with the press were good: he saw Beaverbrook, Camrose and Kemsley all the time, he said, and often saw the editors of *The Times* and the *Telegraph*. Swinton explained that this was no use at all; the men he should invite round for a quiet chat were the political correspondents. Churchill, then seventy-nine, answered: 'I'm too old, Philip, to learn these new tricks.'

When he went to America, Churchill always gave on-the-record briefings to the press, and after one particular trip, he was persuaded to give his own press the same opportunity. It was not a success. He kept everyone waiting for half an hour; then he announced that he could not talk about his American trip; then, when the journalists tried to ask him about it anyway, he replied: 'I'm very sorry, I can't say anything about that until I have reported to Parliament.' It was the first and last news conference he gave in Britain.

Three weeks after the Coronation, on the evening of Tuesday 23 June, Churchill suffered a stroke after a formal Downing Street dinner. He was able to walk back to his bedroom with assistance, but the next day his speech was slurred and his mouth was drooping. Two days later he was much worse, and lost the use of his left leg and left arm; Lord Moran thought he would not live through the weekend. Churchill ordered that nothing should be said about it; after a week he recovered remarkably well, though his attention span was very short. Soon afterwards he was a great deal better.

In 1983, an official Downing Street press statement, ostensibly by Churchill's doctors, was made public under the thirty-year rule. The first version, heavily amended, ran as follows:

> The Prime Minister has had no respite for a long time from his very arduous duties and there has developed a disturbance of the cerebral circulation which has result in attacks of giddiness. We therefore advised him to abandon his journey to Bermuda and to have a month's rest. Sir Winston Churchill had a similar though less serious attack in August 1949 when staying at Cap d'Ail.

This was clearly regarded as altogether too much information, and someone has gone through the statement in pen.

> The Prime Minister has had no respite for a long time from his very arduous duties and is in need of a complete rest. We therefore advised him to abandon his journey to Bermuda and to lighten duties for at least a month.

Both versions were intended to be wholly misleading; yet over the weeks that followed, rumours of the severity of Churchill's stroke slowly leaked out.

On 17 August 1953, under the headline 'What is the truth about Churchill's illness?' the *Daily Mirror* quoted an article in the *New York Herald Tribune* which reported that Churchill had suffered a stroke at the end of June. Although he had made an extraordinary recovery, it said, he was unlikely to be able to resume the active day-to-day leadership of the country.

The *Mirror* asked:

> Is there any reason why the British people should not be
> told the facts about the health of their Prime Minister?
>
> Is there any reason why they should always be the last
> to learn what is going on in their country?
>
> Must they always be driven to pick up their information
> at second hand from tittle-tattle abroad?

In 1953 it seemed probable that they always would. Churchill's health
never really improved, yet he remained prime minister for nearly two
more years.

§

The short, disastrous twenty-one months of Anthony Eden's premiership
marked a turning-point for British journalism. The old deference, the
sense of being passive, polite spectators, no longer seemed appropriate.
Even the BBC, the archetypically deferential onlooker, found its back-
bone. The experience of Suez changed the default tone which the press
and the broadcasters, now reinforced by the tougher, brighter, sharper
minds at the newly formed Independent Television News, would use
towards politicians.

Old attitudes were strikingly exemplified in a short clip of film which
a BBC cameraman shot outside 10 Downing Street as Eden was leaving
for the House of Commons. There he would announce the start of hostilities against Egypt: an action which would complete Britain's decline
from the status of world power. An ultra-polite BBC reporter can be seen
hovering on the pavement, reaching out with an unwieldy microphone
in his hand as Eden appears through the front door.

> BBC REPORTER: Excuse me, prime minister, do you
> have a word for the nation?
> EDEN: No, I don't think so, thank you very much.
> [Walks off.]

It was humiliating and funny in equal proportions, and the fact that it
was broadcast on the main news bulletin says a good deal about the BBC's

instinctive deference to political authority. Yet in future, political journalists would see themselves less and less as mute servants, human
microphones or notebooks for the convenience of their political masters.
From now on, helped by the greater intellectual toughness of ITN,
journalists would gradually come to feel that they had to challenge
politicians, not simply record their views. And increasingly a degree of
contempt would start to attach to those journalists, and there have
been plenty of them, who were willing to let themselves be used meekly
like this.

From the start Eden was indecisive, irritable, and often ill. Waiting
in Churchill's shadow for his chance to take over, he grew more difficult,
neurotic and thin-skinned than ever; and a badly conducted operation
on his gall bladder in 1953 meant that his health was actually worse than
Churchill's, even though he was twenty-two years younger. When the
Suez crisis erupted, he was physically and mentally weakened, and had
few friends, especially in the press, to whom he was condescending and
grand. He came to regard the newspapers, and even more the BBC, as
his enemy; and since he had never cultivated a good relationship with
the press, there was no one to defend him or present his views when the
moment came.

Within months of Eden's arrival in Downing Street, the sniping
began: less from the press than from within the Conservative Party. As
early as October 1955 the *Daily Telegraph* was calling for a reshuffle, and
soon an 'Eden Must Go' faction had appeared. By January 1956, when he
had been in the job for nine months, the deputy editor of the normally
supportive *Daily Telegraph*, Donald McLachlan, wrote a fierce attack on
him. It was a ferocious piece of work, under the headline

THE SMACK OF FIRM GOVERNMENT

and did not hesitate to stoop to the personal.

> There is a favourite gesture of the Prime Minister's . . . To
> emphasize a point he will clench one fist to smack the open
> palm of the other hand – but the smack is seldom heard.
> Most Conservatives, and almost certainly some of the wiser
> trade union leaders, are waiting to feel the smack of firm
> government . . .

Other newspapers, sensing weakness, followed with similar criticism. Within a year, Eden had been weighed and found wanting. From now on, it would be very hard to find an alternative view.

In any case, he had characteristically misunderstood the nature of British journalism, and thought the criticism was politically motivated. By recruiting a press secretary who was more to the left than he was – William Clark, who had worked for the British embassy in Washington, the World Bank, and the *Observer* newspaper – he hoped he could somehow shore up his left wing, while the right wing could be relied on to stand firm. He was wrong on both counts.

Clark was an honourable man. He was also an amusing one, and enjoyed telling the story of how he was called to a lecture about security in the Washington embassy in 1946. He was handed a copy of the Official Secrets Act to sign. Clark was dubious.

> 'Look, honestly, it's just a formality saying you must never pass information gained in the course of your work to unauthorized persons.'
>
> 'Are journalists unauthorized persons? Because if they are, I seem to have taken a Trappist vow of silence which would not suit my temperament.'
>
> 'Don't be frivolous, William. Of course you should talk to good journalists. It's not them we're after, it's people who might make use of the information . . .'

The head of chancery who offered that advice was Donald Maclean, who later defected to the Soviet Union with Guy Burgess.

But however much the Lobby respected and liked Clark as a man, they were unenthusiastic about him professionally, since it was clear to them that he was not close to Eden. Unsuccessful prime ministers always manage to convince themselves that with enough time they might turn their fortunes around. Instead, they grind on through gloom and greater unpopularity to the inevitable end. In Eden's case the pattern had already been clearly established by the time Clark arrived on 3 October 1955, six long months after Eden had taken over as prime minister. That night, Clark wrote in his diary: 'I do hope the PM is in control, but I'm not yet sure.'

§

Clark was to stay in Downing Street for less than seventeen months. He, like everybody else, was beginning to ask about Eden's grip, or lack of it, especially when Gallup polls showed his approval rating tumbling. The British press in full pursuit of a weakened politician is never an edifying sight but, like the hyenas they are often compared with, journalists sometimes perform an essential cleansing function.

Eden had never been popular on the right wing of his own party, with many Conservatives particularly hating the agreement he had negotiated with Egypt in 1954 to withdraw British troops. In response, Eden strove to present himself as tough and decisive – which was to contribute directly to the disaster in which he would soon find himself.

During the first months of 1956 the problems which accompanied the dissolution of empire were gathering thick and fast. In Egypt, the young Colonel Gamal Abdel Nasser had recently staged his coup and was looking for ways of humiliating the British who, after decades of interference and domination, seemed to be the natural enemy. The influential CIA station chief there, Kermit Roosevelt II, grandson of President Theodore Roosevelt, was doing his best to encourage this.

On the evening of Thursday 26 July 1956, in the broiling heat of Alexandria, Nasser appeared at a carefully choreographed rally to mark the fourth anniversary of his coup. It was one of the most important moments of the modern world, when Nasser emerged as one of the leaders of the anti-colonialist movement, determined to challenge the authority of Britain and France in the Middle East, and to get revenge on both Britain and America, who had withdrawn an earlier offer to finance his pet project, the Aswan High Dam. In his high, screeching yet remarkably effective voice Nasser shouted: 'The Suez Canal was dug by the efforts of the sons of Egypt; a hundred and twenty thousand Egyptians died in the process.'

In fact, the labour force which Ferdinand de Lesseps used to build the Canal was drawn from a number of countries and numbered 30,000 all told. Several thousand of them died. But Nasser was not writing history, he was stirring up an entire people. He went on:

> The Suez Canal Company, sitting in Paris, is a usurping company. It usurped our concessions. When he came here, de Lesseps acted in the same manner as do certain people who come to hold talks with me.

He meant, of course, the British and Americans; and he had given orders that when he mentioned de Lesseps's name the army should head out of barracks and take over the offices of the Suez Canal Company in Cairo, Port Said, Suez and Ismailia. Knowing this, he shouted: 'Today, O citizens, we declare that our property has been returned to us! We are realising our glory and our grandeur!' The huge crowd, tens of thousands strong, cheered and wept.

The instinctive hostility of the Fleet Street correspondents in Egypt – none of whom seem to have been in Alexandria – is clear from their reporting. There is no sense of occasion, no feeling that this was an important moment of change in the relationship between the Western powers and what was starting to be known as 'the Third World'. The *Daily Mail*'s correspondent, listening to the radio in Cairo was, unusually, a woman, Eileen Travis. Under the headline

NASSER GRABS SUEZ CANAL

she reported:

> Colonel Nasser today announced his revenge against the United States and Britain for withdrawing their offer to finance the Aswan High Dam. Egypt, he said, will use the revenue from the nationalised Suez Canal to build the dam.

Eileen Travis was one of a hundred or more journalists whose names appeared on the contacts list of a shadowy British propaganda organization, the Information Research Department. The IRD, founded by the Labour government in 1948 to counter Soviet propaganda around the world, and operating throughout its thirty-year existence in considerable secrecy, had a highly questionable reputation among journalists. It was particularly keen to get its version of events, and its hostile views of Soviet-bloc society, onto the BBC World Service, whose huge audiences around the world and high reputation made it an obvious target.

It would certainly have been pleased with Eileen Travis's reporting from Cairo that night. She labelled Nasser hysterical and vengeful, and hinted strongly that he had Communist leanings. Yet this is how most British journalists regarded him, without any help from the IRD. The headline of the *Daily Mail*'s 'Comment' column, printed alongside her despatch, made the point.

HITLER OF THE NILE

Hitler's name was invoked again and again throughout the crisis. Eden, who had often blamed himself for not resigning when Foreign Secretary in 1936, saw Suez as the way to show, finally, that he was indeed a man of decision.

The news broke in London just at the end of a formal dinner Eden was giving in honour of the Baghdad Pact, which included Iran, Iraq, Pakistan and Turkey, as well as the United Kingdom. As his guests left Downing Street, other people were arriving for an emergency meeting of ministers, senior civil servants and service chiefs. At this meeting, which was also attended by senior French and American officials, there was a long discussion of what action was open to Britain and France. But according to William Clark, who was there, the chiefs of staff warned him that they could not necessarily deal effectively with the challenge of invading Egypt.

As the early editions of Friday's newspapers arrived in Downing Street, it became clear there were strong divisions about the action Britain should take. The *Mail*, as we have seen, thought Nasser was a second Hitler who should be dealt with. The *Express* headlined its editorial

A TIME TO RESIST

but the tone was more querulous than aggressive:

Is Britain going to tolerate this new arrogance?

> With each act of surrender to Nasser the task of resistance has become harder, but the need for resistance has become more insistent.

The Times could not make up its mind at all: 'It is much too soon to work out all the implications of the act or to say what the counter-action of the British and other directly affected Governments should be.'

Yet Eden had uncharacteristically taken his decision already. At the

Downing Street meeting in the early hours of the morning, according to William Clark, 'Eden made it absolutely clear that military action would have to be taken, and that Nasser would have to go. Nasser could not be allowed, in Eden's phrase, "to have his hand on our windpipe."'

Later that morning Eden agreed to see the foreign editor of *The Times*, Iverach McDonald, whom he had known for twenty years. Long afterwards McDonald said that Eden was very calm and determined, and that he could not tolerate Egyptian control of the Suez Canal. *The Times*, cautiously, began to support Eden's line after that.

At first, the newspapers on the left backed Eden's line. The *Express*, like the other pro-war newspapers, stressed the need for Britain to stand up and assert her former strength. On 1 August 1956 its editorial said: 'If Britain allows a petty upstart dictator to push her around, she is finished.' Hugh Gaitskell, the Labour Party leader, concurred, denouncing Nasser's 'Hitlerian' behaviour in the House of Commons. The *Daily Mirror*, as loud as ever no matter which side it was on, followed Gaitskell's lead. Under the headline

DICTATOR NASSER

it hinted at very much the kind of solution Eden had in mind:

> [Nasser] may believe that by grabbing the Suez Canal and tearing up a solemn international agreement he inflates his own personal power. In fact, he merely brands Egypt as a liar, a cheat and a menace.

As an analysis of Nasser's motives, this was as wide of the mark as Eden's was. Nasser was not in any real sense a new Hitler. The seizure of the Canal was certainly an act of aggression which contravened international law; but it would have been possible to have negotiated a way round it. The greater danger was not, as Eden thought, Nasser's grip on Britain's and NATO's choke-point. It was the effect on two fading colonial powers of taking on the new force of Third World nationalism.

Even at that stage it might have been possible to come to terms with Egypt. Nasser had shown signs, shortly before the Americans withdrew the offer of money for the Aswan Dam, of opening up a little to Britain. But Eden, damned by the accusations of weakness and of left-wing sympathies from his own party, did not dare to take that line.

Gaitskell, however, understood the dangers of tackling this new force in the world without proper support, and he understood how unreliable the United States could be as an ally. He changed his approach, and advocated making sure that Britain had United Nations backing before taking action. The two most important figures on the *Mirror*'s board, Hugh Cudlipp and Cecil King, had close relations with Gaitskell at the time, and swung round instantly in his support. By Tuesday 14 August 1956 the headlines were bigger than ever (if not entirely correct in their use of apostrophes), but the tone was much more thoughtful.

The 'Mirror's' Message to Eden
NO WAR OVER EGYPT!

It was one of the biggest headlines the paper has ever employed, and took up almost half the front page. The story below was also in large type, and printed in bold.

> If [Eden] allows himself to be goaded into rash deeds by his own bold words, by the din from the sabre-rattlers and gun-boat diplomats, or by applause from France, he will find himself in a position that could be resolved in one way only – HIS OWN RESIGNATION AS PRIME MINISTER.

It turned out to be entirely accurate.

§

Suez transformed British journalism. It obliged journalists to face up to one of the most difficult issues in any democracy: where their duty should lie at a time of intense disagreement on a subject of the greatest national importance. Should they forget their individual reservations about a course of action some of them feel is profoundly wrong, and fall in behind the government and the armed forces? Reporting on military action in the three major wars Britain had fought during the first six decades of the century, journalists had been accustomed to using the pronoun 'we'. Now, suddenly, they found that the identification was no longer automatic.

There had always been conflicts between governments and journalists, of course, but newspapers had never challenged a British government over a decision to go to war. And the BBC had never broadcast attacks by politicians or intellectuals opposed to the government's action. For the BBC Suez was a painful and dangerous experience; but it came out of it transformed, and much more prepared to find itself under attack.

The world of television news had already changed. On 22 September 1955, a year before the Suez crisis, Independent Television News went on air for the first time. Its first editor-in-chief, the glamorous and highly intelligent former Labour MP Aidan Crawley, lasted only a year before resigning and being succeeded by Geoffrey Cox, but he created new expectations in the British public about the way television news should be presented. It was very different from the way the BBC had been doing things. One of the most popular journalists on ITN, Reginald Bosanquet, who became its chief newscaster in 1974, put the difference like this: 'The obsequiousness of BBC staffers no doubt stemmed from the fact that they were in a sense civil servants, paid for out of public funds and on a lower grade than Cabinet ministers.'

That is too harsh. Nevertheless, the BBC news department at the time was a fearful and unhappy place, thanks partly to the influence of one man, a New Zealander with the unfortunate name of Tahu Hole. Hole was an interesting man, who made no secret of the fact that he was gay – a brave course of action at the time – but his influence as a BBC executive was disastrous. Domineering towards his staff, and obsequious towards his superiors, he created an atmosphere of fear and nervousness. As news editor, Hole introduced a characteristically timid rule which remained in force in parts of the BBC for decades afterwards, that no item of news should be broadcast unless it was supported by at least two news agencies. This ignored the fact that in some places the agencies were often represented by the same freelance journalist.

But however cowardly Hole's regime was, the BBC satisfied neither Churchill nor Eden, nor the previous Labour government. Sometimes this was merely accidental, as William Clark's diary, reporting the unfolding of the Suez saga on Tuesday 7 August 1956, reveals: 'At ten I listened to the news, and the BBC failed to get it right. At 10.07 the PM rang up in a great state: "Are they enemies or just socialists?" I got after them and it all turned out to be pure muddle.'

As the crisis developed, it became more and more necessary for the

BBC to broadcast interviews and talks by people who did not agree with Eden's approach. On Wednesday 15 August, Clark was telephoned at the theatre to hear a complaint from Eden about 'an anti-government' programme the BBC was planning to broadcast the following evening: 'Could he stop it? I said no – at any rate he should not.'

In an outburst of anger, Eden contacted Sir Alexander Cadogan, the chairman of the BBC governors who had long been a close associate, and who, as a director of the Suez Canal Company, stood to lose or benefit personally from what the British government decided to do. This was not reported in the press at the time, though the clash of interests would nowadays be regarded as wholly unacceptable.

As chairman of the BBC, it was Cadogan's responsibility to protect its independence and integrity; yet he sympathized with Eden, and privately agreed with Eden's determination to attack Nasser. Although it was not his job to decide what the BBC could and could not broadcast, he made an agreement with Downing Street that the BBC would restrict itself to what he called 'straight news'. In other words, opinions and arguments about the Suez operation would not be broadcast. If the agreement had been implemented, it would have meant that the BBC would not have been able to interview people like Hugh Gaitskell. This would have been in direct contravention of the BBC's charter, of which Cadogan was supposedly the chief guardian.

On Thursday 13 September the governors agreed 'that the BBC should do nothing to underline the existence of party division and disunity at a time of crisis': precisely the response the Cabinet wanted. The broadcasters, for their part, felt they were committed to the principles set out in the late 1930s by J.B. Clark, the first deputy director of the BBC's Empire Service, and the man who later transformed it into the World Service: that news should never be suppressed on the grounds that it was 'inconvenient from a short-term political standpoint'. Now, for not the first or last time, the BBC's broadcasters found themselves at odds with the board of governors about the very essence of their job.

The other Clark, William, as Downing Street press secretary, was obliged to do what the Cabinet instructed; but he was increasingly worried by the way things were going. In his memoirs Harman Grisewood, the chief assistant to the BBC's director general, later wrote: 'I doubt if any career civil servant could have done what Clark did by tact and initiative both in restraining Eden and calming the BBC.'

By Tuesday 2 October the Cabinet was discussing the possibility of taking over the BBC Overseas Service. Presumably if the plan had gone ahead, the Information and Research Department would have been responsible for the BBC's foreign broadcasting, and audiences would have simply evaporated. It is curious how little, over the decades, British politicians of all parties have understood the value of impartial news reporting.

In fact, the board of governors was given a formal warning that the Foreign Office budget for the overseas services would be cut by a fifth. Cadogan and the governors protested: this would mean doing immense damage to Britain's voice overseas. But they accepted the stationing of a Foreign Office liaison officer at Bush House, who would supply the BBC with programme ideas and information, much of it garnered from the IRD and perhaps from intelligence sources.

However, broadcasters in the Overseas Service paid little attention to the liaison officer's snippets of information, and it did not help that he had a ludicrous name: J.L.B. Tichener, which meant he was universally known as Titchener of Tartoum. He stayed on after the Suez operation for some time, apparently forgotten about in his own ministry and with little heart for the job he had been sent to do. At the same time, the IRD sent one of its senior experts on the Middle East to broadcast black propaganda to the region, and particularly to Egypt, using a wavelength which had once been assigned to BBC broadcasts but had been discontinued. There was a feeble attempt to mimic the way the BBC introduced its programmes, in the hope that some listeners in the Middle East would think they were listening to the BBC itself.

In the days before the Suez operation began, with hostility mounting on all sides, Harman Grisewood was told that censorship and other controls would shortly be imposed – yet without the establishment of a new Ministry of Information, and with none of the meticulous planning which had ensured that wartime broadcasting had been a notable success. His memoirs reveal some of the tensions:

> Clark was finding it harder and harder to prevent the PM's anger from taking the form of sweeping changes. I asked what changes. William told me that the Prime Minister had instructed the Lord Chancellor to prepare an instrument which would take over the BBC altogether and subject it wholly to the will of the Government.

But the Lord Chancellor, Lord Kilmuir, dragged his feet and produced a paper which Eden thought was too protective of the BBC. Before he could produce another, the whole issue came to a head on one single issue: the right of the leader of the opposition to broadcast a reply to a prime ministerial address by Eden. Cadogan seems to have accepted the argument that Gaitskell had to have the right of reply, since the BBC's charter obliges it to be balanced.

Gaitskell's broadcast, on the evening of Sunday 4 November, was one of the best speeches he ever made.

> We're doing this all alone, except for France. Opposed by the world, in defiance of the world. It is not a police action; there is no law behind it. We have taken the law into our own hands. That's the tragic situation in which we British people find ourselves tonight.

It would indeed be a political disaster of major proportions; and within hours it had become so all-consuming that Eden and his ministers forgot all about taking over the BBC.

§

As the moment of war came close, Eden began ringing Fleet Street's editors and proprietors with increasing shrillness. Esmond Harmsworth, the owner of the *Daily Mail* and son of Lord Rothermere, came to dread the calls from Downing Street which woke him every day at 6 a.m., as Eden took issue with things he read in his morning newspaper.

The *Mail*'s chief leader writer, George Murray, managed to inject a more balanced atmosphere into the paper, giving Eden the *Mail*'s broad support, but allowing the views of his opponents a good showing. This, for instance, was Murray's Comment on 1 November 1956:

> This morning British soldiers, sailors, and airmen face battle and sudden death for their country. It is for all of us to uphold and support them by uniting behind the Government in the action they have taken.
>
> Many people disagree violently with that action. Time may give them justification. It may prove the

> Government to have been mistaken in intervening in
> the Middle East with France, and at this juncture.

That morning *The Times* editorial announced nervously: 'Doubts remain whether the right course has been taken now.'

These doubts were enhanced by a clear feeling that the Eden government had not been honest about Israel's involvement in the attack on Egypt. On 1 November the *Mail* carried a late item in a box on its front page, headlined

ISRAELIS CLAIM 1,000 CASUALTIES

Tel Aviv, Thursday. – Estimated Egyptian casualties are 1,000 dead, wounded, and captured, plus about 200 sailors who surrendered, say reports here.

The involvement of Israeli forces in attacking Egypt on Monday 29 October was something the British press preferred to ignore as much as possible. There was obvious collusion with Israel, though the British government maintained a blackout on the entire subject. In fact France and Britain had agreed on 13 October to ask Israel to attack Egypt, and at first the Israeli prime minister David Ben-Gurion had refused indignantly, until talked round by his adviser Shimon Peres. There was always an element of confusion, and William Clark's memoirs imply that the news of Israel's attack came as a surprise to Eden on the evening of 29 October. Nevertheless Clark writes that the journalists who rang him about it all suspected that Downing Street had known at the time of the usual afternoon briefing: 'I vigorously denied this though of course the suspicion was strong in my mind.'

If the prime minister's own press spokesman was unaware of it, it seems reasonable to suppose that the newspapers were in a genuine state of doubt about the extent of the collusion. But if one of the newspapers had carried out an investigation into Israel's reasons for joining in, it would have provoked a major scandal. It is very hard not to see this as a serious failure on the part of British journalism.

The invasion continued on its doomed way. As ever, Eden's timing was as bad as his judgement. The Suez campaign was launched just at the moment that the crisis in Hungary between an increasingly liberal government and its Soviet overlords reached its height. The tanks rolled into Egypt just as they were rolling into Budapest. It compounded the unwisdom of Eden's action, and meant that the attention of Western governments was fatally divided.

On Friday 2 November the *Mirror*'s headline was huge:

THE NAVIES CLOSE IN
Nasser bid to block the Canal is foiled

but alongside is an editorial which fills two whole columns of the front page.

MIRROR COMMENT ON EDEN'S WAR
'DISASTROUS FOLLY'
There is NO treaty, NO international authority,
NO moral sanction for this desperate action.

The *Mail*, by contrast, could have been reporting on an entirely different conflict that morning. Its readers might well have supposed it was reporting an Anglo-French victory; instead, it was an Israeli one.

BRITISH WIPE OUT 90 PLANES –
FRENCH HIT DESTROYER
Pincer fleets move in as Tel-Aviv claims big victory
NASSER'S ARMY ROUTED

Elsewhere on its packed broadsheet front page, the *Mail* found space to report at some length on Britain's rejection of a ceasefire proposal by John Foster Dulles at the United Nations, on Eden's victory by a record majority in a House of Commons vote of censure by Labour (whom the *Mail* almost invariably calls 'the Socialists' during the 1950s), the resignation of Anthony Nutting, a junior Foreign Office minister, more attacks on Egyptian airfields, the halting of a British raid to safeguard the lives of American and other civilians fleeing Cairo, and a denial that British forces were fighting with Israel. Down the left-hand column is another of George Murray's evenly balanced Comments:

> Britain is apparently not at war. She is engaged in a police
> action in the Suez area.

> This is what Sir Anthony Eden told the Commons yes-
> terday, and he is right. But although there is a distinction
> in definition there is none in fact.

Meanwhile the right side of the front page is devoted to events in Hungary. Under the headline

RED TANKS RING BUDAPEST

the *Mail*'s correspondent Jeffrey Blyth, who would shortly distinguish himself in reporting the fighting in the streets of the Hungarian capital, writes a tense account of a city waiting for the Russian onslaught.

By Monday 5 November, the day of the British and French assault on Port Said and other targets, the *Guardian* is calling for Eden's resignation. Suggesting that the Russians felt able to use greater force in Hungary because of the Anglo-French operation, the *Guardian*'s editorial reads:

> The first task in Britain is to change the Government. The
> present Prime Minister and his Cabinet must be removed.
> Sir Anthony's policy, however sincerely intended, has been
> hideously miscalculated and utterly immoral.

All the same, a story is a story. The *Mirror*, like the *Guardian*, might disapprove of the invasion of Egypt, but it sent its reporters to cover it with a certain zest. On Wednesday 7 November it carried a full-page story from one of its star reporters:

IN WITH THE RED DEVILS –
AGAINST ODDS OF 5 to 1
The Man from the Mirror is there

> Here is the first dramatic despatch from the Port Said battle
> area by Mirror reporter PETER WOODS, who parachuted
> into Egypt with British paratroops at dawn on Monday.

The article is a model of its kind: 'As I dropped towards an airfield runway strewn with barrels to keep us from landing I saw Egyptian troops in slit trenches point their rifles towards me and start shooting.'

Yet Woods, twenty-six at the time, says nothing of what happened to him when he landed. He had talked his way onto the plane by convincing a brigade major that he knew all about parachuting, even though he had never made a jump in his life. As he landed, he broke both his ankles; but with a good deal of self-control he does not mention this in his report, though he clearly has personal knowledge of the British field hospital set up on the airfield: 'A team of surgeons operated as the windows of their makeshift theatre were blown in and shrapnel splattered the walls.'

Peter Woods went on to read the news for BBC television, and became the first newsreader in Britain to appear in colour.

Perhaps the greatest of British post-war journalists, James Cameron, was characteristically opposed to the war; so was his paper, the *News Chronicle*. At the British headquarters in Cyprus Cameron took particular issue with the claim by the British and French governments that they were involved in a police action, not a war. In his memoirs he described how, at a press conference, he confronted General Sir Charles Keightley, the British commander, over the distinction.

> I said, well I'm buggered if I'm going to call it a Police Action. I'm going to call it a war. And Keightley said, 'If you do, we'll hold up your reports forever.' Which they did.
>
> But then, during a Press Conference, General Keightley himself used the expression 'limited war'. So I said: 'I see it is a war at last.'
>
> 'No it's not,' said Keightley.
>
> 'But you just said it was.'
>
> 'Did I?' asked Keightley. 'Did anyone else hear me say that?'
>
> 'Yes,' shouted about two hundred correspondents.

Cameron decided to go back to London, where he could call a war a war. But they wouldn't allow him to leave until it was all over.

It wouldn't be long. By Wednesday 7 November the *Mail*'s headline read:

CEASE-FIRE: CANAL OURS

It sounded good, but perhaps deliberately it masked the scale of the diplomatic defeat Britain, even more than France, had suffered.

At the United Nations, various leading Commonwealth countries, encouraged by the United States, had threatened to impose sanctions on Britain and France if they did not call an immediate ceasefire. The Americans had also hinted at a halt to oil supplies.

Worse by far was the possibility of a run on the pound, leading perhaps to the collapse of sterling. The British government, encouraged by the Chancellor, Harold Macmillan, believed that the Americans would come to sterling's aid by agreeing to a loan from the International Monetary Fund if the crisis became serious. Not only was this wrong, but the Cabinet, appalled, suddenly realized that Washington was orchestrating an attack on the pound. An immediate ceasefire, and agreement to a UN force to take over from the British and French, was the only way out.

It was a disaster; and William Clark put in his resignation. He was too honourable, and perhaps too naive, to survive long in the atmosphere of deceit and falsehood that Eden and his senior ministers had created.

Clark had been kept largely in the dark by Eden, because Eden knew he was against the entire Suez adventure. He had stayed on, even though he hated what he was doing, and he remained remarkably loyal to the Whitehall ethos that requires a civil servant to serve the government of the day whatever his or her personal opinions. Later, in a book called *Secrecy*, he delivered his verdict on the policy whose spokesman he had unwillingly been:

> Parliament, the public and the bureaucracy were not only
> unconsulted, not only surprised, they were deceived . . .
> Public opinion at home and particularly abroad was
> sufficiently potent that it could not be ignored, it had to be
> fooled. News management became news invention . . .

Within a matter of weeks Eden, too, did what the *Manchester Guardian* had recommended, and resigned. Neither British power nor the strength of sterling ever recovered from the Suez adventure. It was the lowest Britain had sunk to during the twentieth century. Harold Macmillan, who had argued for the invasion and misled the Cabinet on the likelihood of American support for the pound, took over from Eden. But the whole episode had taught Britain that it was no longer a great power, and that it would have to play a much more moderate role in the world.

17

LAVENDER LIST

It was, many people thought at the time, one of the best political speeches a British political leader had ever made:

> The Britain that is going to be forged in the white heat of this [scientific] revolution will be no place for restrictive practices or for outdated methods on either side of industry . . . In the Cabinet room and the boardroom alike, those charged with the control of our affairs must be ready to think and to speak the language of our scientific age.

Harold Wilson's speech at the Labour Party conference on 1 October 1964, a fortnight before the general election, was greeted with rapture by the press. Even the man from the *Daily Express*, whose house-style still obliged its journalists to call the Labour Party 'the Socialists', sounded a little awe-struck.

'Dr' Wilson wins mastery with technocrat vision

> [I]n 50 minutes he spread a canvas so wide and filled it so imaginatively that his audience was left gaping and gasping behind him . . . Mr Wilson foresees the new Britain as scientifically streamlined to make 'break-throughs' right and left in the application of science to industrial projects.

Wilson's words electrified the country. At forty-eight, he was young, he was classless, and he represented change. If he won the coming election, thirteen years of rule by upper-class, tweed-wearing, grouse-shooting Tory grandees would come to an end, and Wilson would lead Britain into the new age his speech foreshadowed. As with so much in his career, though, the reality surrounding the speech was less impressive. Ben Pimlott, in his biography of Wilson, reports that by 9 p.m. on the evening before it had to be made, Wilson had no idea what to put in it.

> 'I still don't know what to say,' he told Marcia [Williams]. 'I think I'll go to bed and do it early in the morning.' 'No,' she replied firmly, aware of the tight logistics of preparing a speech for the press, 'you will do it now.' 'What about?' asked the Party Leader. Marcia thought of [Richard] Crossman's suggestion [that he should talk about the importance of science]. 'Why not the Science Committee stuff?' she said.

They were up till six in the morning writing the speech.

On 15 October 1964 the country elected a sharp-minded, witty, pleasant-seeming man as its new prime minister. For a while this was how the press presented him. Lobby correspondents who knew he was a confirmed cigar-smoker, but smoked a pipe in public because it seemed more egalitarian, said nothing about it in the papers. Nor did they refer to the way his Huddersfield accent intensified when he spoke in public. Above all, they said nothing about his conviction that members of the press and his own party were conspiring to do him down.

One of Wilson's first tasks on becoming prime minister was to make himself more accessible to journalists than any of his predecessors. Editors and political correspondents were delighted; the relationship between them and the prime minister seemed manifestly to have changed. After Harold Macmillan and Sir Alec Douglas-Home, Wilson seemed like a breath of fresh air. He had a mocking wit, wholly in tune with the mordant satire which was the dominant tone of the early 1960s; in July 1961, for instance, he told the House of Commons, to the accompaniment of appreciative laughter from the Labour benches and the press gallery, 'I myself have always deprecated . . . in crisis after crisis, appeals to the Dunkirk spirit as an answer to our problems.'

Yet within three years of becoming prime minister, with economic troubles mounting, Wilson duly appealed to the Dunkirk spirit in order to rescue the country. By that time whatever respect and liking most of the Lobby had had for him had evaporated. Although he had served as a top civil servant, Wilson had an extraordinarily simplistic view of politics. He believed that the key to success was to influence the people who ran the newspapers: proprietors, editors, correspondents, columnists. He was, according to James Margach of the *Sunday Times*, enraptured by the role of being premier, captivated by the thrilling interplay of today's performance and tomorrow's headlines. Margach blames it on his loneliness and insecurity. Wilson, the grammar school boy who made it to Oxford, had no close friends, either before or during his time in Downing Street. Instead, he became dependent on a group of lively but often mildly questionable people: Joseph Kagan, whose Gannex macs Wilson had faithfully worn in public; Rudi Sternberg, a petrochemicals importer; and the property developer, Eric Miller. Kagan was imprisoned for fraud in 1980, and Miller committed suicide in 1977 while under police investigation – also for fraud.

There was considerable unease in Whitehall about the influence of Wilson's 'kitchen cabinet' – the small group of advisers whom his secretary, Marcia Williams, gathered round him; and there was Mrs Williams herself. The suggestion was constantly being made by journalists, sotto voce rather than in public, that there was something improper in Wilson's relationship with her. The rumours eventually proved to be untrue, but they were widely believed. There seemed to be something not quite right about Mrs Williams's official status, too: although she ran Wilson's Downing Street office and travelled with him on his visits to meet Ian Smith, as well as to Moscow and other world capitals, her name still appeared on the staff-list of Labour Party headquarters at Transport House as a shorthand typist.

The Tory press quickly overcame any brief attraction they might have felt for the new, classless prime minister. Wilson was presented as an economics wizard, yet Britain's economic position was getting worse and worse, and the devaluation of the pound was coming closer. Supposedly a man of the people, his relations with the unions were worsening. He was clever and manipulative, yet the Rhodesian Front leader, Ian Smith, outmanoeuvred him again and again in the battle to perpetuate white rule in Africa.

On 3 June 1965, Derek Marks of the *Express* caught the now habitual tone of much of Fleet Street:

> Have you ever seen such a shambles? But have you really?
> . . . The shameless fiasco over the Steel Bill in which, with
> the approval of Mr Harold Wilson, Mr [George] Brown gave

> a worthless pledge, has been followed by Mr James
> Callaghan's Finance Bill, the like of which has, mercifully,
> not been seen in modern times . . . Now, of course, the great
> question is: How long can Mr Wilson remain on the bridge
> with his feet awash?

Wilson had entered office expecting that journalists would like him, and support him; and when they did not, he felt betrayed. According to Margach, less than two years after coming to power, Wilson 'started huffing about "traitorous Lobby correspondents"' and began a campaign to damage his critics.

One of his early victims was the pleasant, scholarly figure David Wood, political correspondent of *The Times*. In late 1966 James Margach was a dinner guest at Chequers with Lord Thomson, the Canadian who owned Margach's newspaper, the *Sunday Times*, and was planning to buy *The Times*. Over coffee Thomson asked Wilson conversationally what he should do when he had taken it over. Wilson launched into a detailed diatribe, which showed how much attention he had devoted to the subject. 'Well, you can start by giving a golden handshake to four people on your staff, starting with the political correspondent, David Wood. Get rid of him first . . .'

He went on to attack Charles Douglas-Home, the diplomatic and defence correspondent, and then turned his attention to a range of other journalists, each of whom had criticized him. One was a drunk, he said; another had no understanding of politics; a third always got things wrong. Wilson took to lunching with Fleet Street editors and proprietors, and attacking their political correspondents. He complained about David Wood at four separate lunches with *The Times*. William Rees-Mogg, the paper's editor, responded in 1968 by making Wood political editor.

Wood's reporting was usually so accurate and fair that it is hard to see why Wilson should have singled him out for abuse. Perhaps it was simply that Wood did not treat him with enough respect. In *The Times* on 8 November 1965 he noted that Labour would soon be starting on an arduous session of major legislation, even though its majority was down to three and would probably drop further:

> On the face of things, it looks like madness or a bluff of
> surpassing impudence by a Prime Minister whom some

Conservative backbenchers still cannot see in any terms
other than as the cheeky chap of politics.

Only a year after winning the election, Wilson had few friends left in the
press. On the issue of Rhodesia and Ian Smith's efforts to maintain white
rule, even the *Daily Mirror* was critical. On 3 December 1965 it devoted
its front page to an editorial, under the headline

WATCH IT, HAROLD!

with a box alongside containing the words

You called the Rhodesian crisis your 'Cuba'.
It could be your Bay of Pigs.

The *Mirror*'s advice was to stop worrying about Rhodesia and sort out
his domestic problems.

Come home, Harold. The crisis is right here in Britain.
Would it be so disastrous, eventually, to hand over the
Rhodesian problem to the United Nations?

The *Express*, the *Mail* and the *Daily Sketch* openly supported Ian Smith;
the *Daily Telegraph* was more circumspect, but had no time for Wilson.
The Times sympathized with his predicament but gave him no support.
Only three daily papers tended to back him: the *Mirror*, the *Sun*, launched
by IPC in 1964 to replace the ailing *Daily Herald* and now a lively but
struggling centre-left paper, and the *Guardian*, which in the same year
had moved from Manchester to London.

Apart from David Wood, the journalist Wilson hated most was Nora
Beloff of the *Observer*. In article after article she pointed out his lack of
any firm political principle. Her three-part series on him in April 1966
remains one of the shrewdest accounts of Wilson's approach to leadership:

All the evidence, both from his present balancing acts and
from the earlier, so-called 'left-wing' phase of his career,
points in the same direction: on the traditional Left-Right
split, Wilson is uncommitted.

Nora Beloff was an easy target, a lone woman in the Lobby with few Fleet Street friends. Tiny and usually late, her hair unbrushed, her words and ideas flowed out in an unguarded torrent. But she was highly intelligent and fiercely independent. Born in 1919 into a famous family of Jewish intellectuals, she refused to become either a feminist or a Zionist. She joined the *Observer* in 1948, and was responsible over the years for a number of first-class exclusives, one of which was a series on the torture by French soldiers of women rebels in Algeria. Later she was based in Moscow and Washington, and in 1964, just as Harold Wilson was elected to power, she became the first female political correspondent in British history. A gentler, less intense woman would have had an easier time. But the Lobby was a crusty organization with little liking for change, and there was much resentment at the idea of a woman joining the club; especially one who could not take shorthand, and could scarcely use a typewriter. That she had been an eyewitness at some of the world's major events made her even less popular with a group who tended to think that Westminster was the centre of the universe. Although James Margach never admitted it in public, he and Nora Beloff, notionally two of the fiercest competitors in Fleet Street, had an arrangement which ensured that neither of them scooped the other. While foreign correspondents often adopted the same system, political correspondents never told their competitors about their exclusives. There was horror at the *Observer* when news of the arrangement came out. It all went to prove, the Lobby felt, that Nora Beloff wasn't a real journalist.

In fact she was a highly successful one, who simply refused to restrict herself to the narrow confines of the Lobby. On 17 April 1966 she became the first to reveal the role of Harold Wilson's shadowy 'kitchen cabinet', and of Marcia Williams herself. After the publication of Beloff's inside look at Downing Street, Wilson ordered his ministers not to speak to her in future. Obsessively, he kept copies of her articles, and would pull them out to show people how biased she was against him, sometimes hinting that he had her under surveillance. David Astor, who was both editor and proprietor of the *Observer*, reported him as saying, 'Of course, I know all the people she sees (mentioning several names). In fact, our people keep an eye on her just to see what she is up to.' Offices and rooms were mentioned in detail. When the names were subsequently checked back against Beloff's diary entries and notes they proved totally accurate. It was a curious thing for Wilson to say to her editor and Astor assumed he meant that people from the kitchen cabinet were spying on her. When Astor showed his disapproval, Wilson hinted that she might have been having an affair with a government minister in order to get her stories. This was certainly untrue.

Wilson was more successful in freezing out Anthony Howard. At the start of 1965 the *Sunday Times* appointed Howard as its Whitehall correspondent: an entirely new job for a British journalist, though already commonplace in the United States, which involved reporting on the activities of top civil servants rather than ministers. On 21 February 1965, a major article by Howard appeared in the paper, revealing the emerging power struggle between the newly created Ministry of Economic Affairs under George Brown and the Treasury, under James Callaghan.

A disturbing account of the disastrous effect of allowing two senior ministries to compete for control over the economy, Howard's piece showed that the dispute over economic control was not so much a ministerial row between Brown and Callaghan as a battle between two top civil servants, Sir Richard Clarke and Mr (later Sir) Douglas Allen. Outside advisers, such as Thomas Balogh who had been brought in as chief economic adviser in the Cabinet Office, were being completely sidelined by the career civil servants.

Wilson, infuriated by what he read, issued the firmest instructions that no minister, and no civil servant, was to speak to Howard about any subject whatever. Howard's rich flow of information died away to almost nothing, and his articles about Whitehall became fewer and briefer. When, the following year, the *Observer* offered Howard the job of Washington correspondent, he accepted gratefully.

Wilson's chief motive, apart from liking secrecy for its own sake, may well have been his increasing paranoia. Howard's articles might offer the dissidents a platform. Wilson was obsessed by the thought that potential rivals like Richard Crossman, Roy Jenkins or George Brown might gang up against him. Each night at around midnight, Wilson and members of the kitchen cabinet, in particular Marcia Williams, his press adviser Gerald Kaufman, and his informal security adviser, the absurd yet mildly sinister George Wigg, once a colonel in the Education Corps, would go through the first editions of the next day's newspapers with immense care, trying to work out who the sources of the various political stories might be.

During these sessions, Wigg would often call a correspondent or an editor and demand that some correction should be made. Over breakfast the following morning, the kitchen cabinet would meet again to see if the required changes had been made. If not, there would be angry calls to the newspaper involved. It all showed an extraordinary degree of sensitivity to criticism.

§

All British governments, to a greater or lesser extent, believe that the BBC wants to do them down. Their invariable mistake is to assume that this is on party political grounds. Conservative governments over the years have been certain that the BBC is staffed by left-wingers, or 'honeycombed with Communists', as Winston Churchill put it in 1953. Labour governments have been equally certain that the BBC is full of supercilious middle-class Oxbridge types, instinctively hostile to Labour.

The reality is different. For decades, news and current affairs broadcasters have tended to see it as their function to challenge power. They believe – and it is in some ways an arrogant belief – that they are the representatives of the ordinary viewer and listener, and that as a result they must always put the opposing viewpoint, in order to create a sense of balance. Broadcasters, therefore, are professional contrarians; and governments, always uncomfortably aware of how close they are to the rocks, see them as wreckers. The more stressed and anxious the government, the louder it will attack the broadcasters. Opposition parties are usually favourable to the broadcasters, knowing they are legally obliged to provide balanced news. That gives them a chance to get their voices heard. Yet directly the main opposition party wins an election and comes into government, its attitude to the broadcasters always seems to change at once. Even in a mature democracy like Britain's, governments often demand that the broadcasters should support their views, and cannot understand when they refuse.

In October 1964 Harold Wilson believed he could transform politics by using television to talk directly to the British people. He felt, in some ways rightly, that he was a natural television performer, and he made an effort to understand the technicalities of broadcasting. He also assumed that the good relationship he had built up with the BBC in opposition would continue now he was prime minister, but in fact it soon deteriorated.

During his first ten days in office, Wilson made two broadcasts at the BBC's invitation. He assumed this strike-rate would continue. But given his knife-edge majority and the likelihood that he would have to call another election soon, the BBC's board of management quickly decided that the whole delicate balance between government and opposition would be upset if Wilson were allowed to make too many broadcasts. Unlike smaller, more focused television news organizations, the BBC is vast, free-ranging, and has dozens of outlets, all competing with each other to produce better and better programmes. That is the BBC's glory; it is also one of the major causes of political friction. Within a year of Wilson's election, the annoyances were mounting up: interviews with left-wing union leaders with radically different views from those of the government, awkward and embarrassing questions to senior ministers, news items about the deteriorating economic situation. By now Wilson was certain the BBC was out to get him, and that it was biased towards the Conservatives.

Independent Television News was much more cooperative. Small, energetic and well funded, it stood to benefit from Wilson's dislike of the BBC. ITN did not see itself as being responsible for maintaining the historical independence of British broadcasting. Instead, it was responsible to its shareholders; and if ITN stole some of the BBC's plums, the shareholders would benefit. ITN's editor, Sir Geoffrey Cox, who had reported the Spanish Civil War for the *News Chronicle*, played up to Wilson's belief that ITN was more sympathetic than the BBC. During the election campaign of 1966 ITN agreed to take a part of Wilson's key speech live into its main news bulletin: something the BBC felt would be too favourable to Labour. In a poisonous green-room session after his final election broadcast, Wilson told several of the BBC's senior editorial staff that he had had two enemies during the campaign: the Tories and the BBC. And on the morning after the election, his exclusive interview was with ITN.

The BBC's only consolation came when Paul Fox, the head of the Corporation's election coverage, arranged for Desmond Wilcox to meet Wilson off the train. Wilcox had recently moved to the BBC from ITV's main current affairs programme, *This Week*, and Fox thought Wilson would not realize this. At Euston station he stood as far away from the other BBC team as possible; Wilson fell for the trick, and started talking to Wilcox on camera. So the BBC got its interview after all, but Wilson was even more annoyed and charged one of his rising young ministers to draw up a set of punitive measures.

Anthony Wedgwood Benn (who several years later announced he preferred to be known simply as Tony Benn) attacked its 'enormous accumulation of power', and said famously that broadcasting was too important to leave to the broadcasters. But there was no public support for any of this, and by the end of 1966 the campaign faded away.

Wilson was still determined to get his own back. When the BBC's chairman, Lord Normanbrook, died in June 1967 he appointed Lord Hill, the chairman of the Independent Television Authority. Hill and Sir Hugh Greene were bitter enemies, and inside the BBC it was assumed that he had been appointed in order to force Greene to resign, which he did in March 1969. Yet Hill quickly 'went native' and from being the government's Gauleiter, he became the head of the resistance movement; not that this made him any more popular with the BBC's staff.

When the next general election, held on 18 June 1970, was an unexpected defeat for Harold Wilson, he blamed the BBC. In February 1970 he had told the Cabinet that there was 'implacable enmity' to the government in the BBC's news and current affairs department. Perhaps it was the spirit of the time which was to blame. The decade from 1962 to 1972 was a time when young people were suddenly allowed a freedom and scope they had never previously been accorded. The BBC now gave young producers and presenters their heads. It made for exciting programmes and some remarkable output; it could also make for poor judgement and unnecessary confrontation with authority. On 17 June 1971, one day short of a year after Wilson's unexpected election defeat, the BBC transmitted a programme called, provocatively, *Yesterday's Men*. It was about the way seven senior members of the Labour government had adjusted to defeat. *Yesterday's Men* had all the advantages and attractions of being made by young men and women, and all the drawbacks; and it infuriated every leading figure in the Labour Party, including those who did not share Wilson's dislike of the BBC.

The key figure in the programme was David Dimbleby. At thirty-two he was still very much in his father Richard's shadow, a gentle, thoughtful young man who nevertheless had all the elder Dimbleby's fearlessness. The first part of his interview with Wilson for *Yesterday's Men* went smoothly. Then Dimbleby asked a question intended to be tartly amusing; coming from a journalist in his early thirties to an ex-prime minister of fifty-five with a highly developed sense of his own dignity and a grudge against the BBC, it was disastrous:

> Many of your colleagues have told us that they are suffering financially from being in opposition, but you are said to have earned between £100,000 and £250,000 from writing your book. Has that been a consolation to you over this time?

No one had warned Wilson that the programme he and his ex-Cabinet colleagues had agreed to take part in was to be so combative or so deeply personal; nor that it was to be called *Yesterday's Men*. Soon he was in full resentful flow, and inevitably dragged in the name of his rival, Edward Heath, who had famously bought a racing yacht, *Morning Cloud*, two years before. All Wilson's obsessiveness and resentment started to emerge.

> WILSON: Why do you come snooping with these questions? You have not put the question to Mr Heath. When you have got an answer from him, come and put that question to me. This last question and answer are not to be recorded ... I think it is disgraceful. I have never heard such a question. If this film is used or this is leaked, then there is going to be a hell of a row.

Directly the interview with Dimbleby finished, Wilson's press secretary Joe Haines made a furious complaint to Charles Curran, Sir Hugh Greene's successor as director general. Haines was an acidic former journalist whom Roy Jenkins, Wilson's Chancellor of the Exchequer, nicknamed 'Vinegar Joe'. Ben Pimlott, Wilson's biographer, wrote that he had 'an anti-Establishment chip, an acute, non-intellectual brain, and an excellent Labour Party feel'. With his dark shirts and black suits, his five o'clock shadow and his rimless glasses, he looked more like a gangster's minder than a senior government official.

The BBC quickly backed down. Angela Pope, the producer of the programme, agreed to cut out the offending question and Wilson's angry answer. But Wilson had been right about Lime Grove's habit of leaking stories about him. Exactly a month later, on 10 June, the story of the interview and Wilson's demands for cuts to it, was deliberately leaked to the press. Gleefully, every newspaper in London carried the news. The programme was due to go out in a week's time.

There were heavy threats of injunctions and libel writs from Wilson's formidable solicitor, Lord Goodman. In this case the press, which disliked the BBC as much as it disliked Wilson, sided almost unanimously with the BBC. Goodman tried to get photographs of Wilson's expensive new country house cut from the programme's title sequence. All this merely aroused extra interest in the programme. *Yesterday's Men*, interspersed with cartoons and songs, was clever and funny. It was also distinctly shallow, poking its finger into the eye of authority merely for the sake of it. It had succeeded in persuading a number of senior politicians to be interviewed for what they assumed would be a serious, balanced current affairs programme. It seemed like a betrayal of the BBC's values.

§

On 21 June 1968 the British newspapers were full of stories about Harold Wilson's plans for reforming the House of Lords, the rescue of a missing yachtsman, safe, well and heavily bearded, and the decision by the country's train drivers to reject a peace proposal. There were also reports about the continuing race problems in the United States.

There was no mention anywhere in the London papers of a small demonstration the day before in the Northern Ireland village of Caledon, in County Tyrone, about local authority housing allocation. A young Nationalist MP in the Northern Ireland Parliament, Austin Currie, staged a sit-in at a council house which had been allocated by Dungannon Rural District Council to a nineteen-year-old unmarried Protestant woman, Emily Beattie, the secretary of a local Unionist politician, despite the fact that there were many Catholic families with children on the waiting list. Of the fifteen houses in the development, only one was occupied by a Catholic family. Among the officers of the Royal Ulster Constabulary who arrived to evict the protesters was Emily Beattie's brother. The operation was carried out with unnecessary brutality.

This was one of the key moments in the start of the Troubles in Northern Ireland, which would last at least forty years, kill 5,500 people, involve half a dozen other countries in a wide range of different ways, and draw in every infantry unit in the British army. Before the violence effectively came to an end (though there were several serious incidents afterwards) the annual cost of Northern Ireland to the British Treasury was more than £3 billion. Meanwhile the Irish Republic was spending more than a quarter of its annual budget on security and border patrols.

The incident at Caledon, in other words, encapsulated several of the most characteristic features of the Troubles: blatant discrimination, instinctive violence, and the small-scale, almost personal nature of the mutual hatred. Northern Ireland had been the skeleton locked away in Britain's political cupboard ever since the treaty which established the Irish Free State came into force in 1922. The statelet which came into being consisted of the six counties of Antrim, Down, Londonderry (or Derry), Armagh, Fermanagh and Tyrone. Of these, only Antrim and Down had big Protestant majorities. In Derry and Armagh Protestants were slightly in the majority, while in Fermanagh and Tyrone Catholics predominated. Overall, the proportion of Protestants to Catholics was roughly two-thirds to one-third. Successive Ulster Unionist governments quietly encouraged political gerrymandering and outright oppression for more than forty years. The Royal Ulster Constabulary was a Protestant protection force, and behind it were the B-Specials, a paramilitary force of police reservists who were willing to use any brutality including murder to keep Catholics in their place.

These things went entirely unnoticed in the British press before the mid-1960s. No newspaper carried out an investigation into them. There was no traceable reference to the sectarian violence meted out to Catholics, no questioning of the constitutional sleight-of-hand that propped up an elected dictatorship in a distant corner of the United Kingdom. The press and the BBC maintained bureaux in Northern Ireland, but they were mostly staffed by Protestants who took the set-up there for granted. The discrimination against Catholics had no particular journalistic interest for them. Plenty of editors in London over the years must have known what was going on in the Province, but it did not constitute 'a story'. It was just the way things were there.

Life was pleasant for those with money, and there was no call to look below the surface. Journalists, like everyone else, prefer to let sleeping dogs lie. 'I feel guilty about it now,' a British-born reporter for a London newspaper said in 1972, when he celebrated ten years as Belfast correspondent, 'but honestly, if I'd tried to sell stories about political repression here before 1968, no one would have printed them.' It was only as 1967 gave way to 1968, and the civil rights campaigners in the United States were given more and more media attention in Britain and

Ireland, that Northern Ireland Catholics realized how similar their lives were to those of black Americans.

By the start of 1969 Northern Ireland had come to dominate the news. Reporting the violence there was dangerous, complicated, and required a great deal of energy; it was therefore a job for the young and willing. Although some news organizations sent older correspondents, particularly defence specialists, to Belfast, the day-to-day work was mostly done by men in their twenties; at this stage women reporters were still rare, and news desks were reluctant to send them to places where there was a chance of their getting hurt. Most of the reporters who were sent to Northern Ireland were inexperienced, and some had never done any serious reporting anywhere else. There was one advantage to this which was completely unforeseen: they looked at the situation with fresh eyes. Older correspondents slotted quickly into their familiar routines, talking to senior military and political figures, some of whom they would have known from other theatres of activity. But the newcomers headed for the streets, talking to eyewitnesses and neighbours and anyone they bumped into. There was a freshness and an accuracy of perception in their reporting and several – among them Simon Winchester and Simon Hoggart of the *Guardian*, Brian Cashinella and Robert Fisk of *The Times*, and Henry Kelly of the *Irish Times* – first made their names and reputations there.

Such reporters did not automatically accept, as some correspondents of an older tradition did, that the Royal Ulster Constabulary or the British army represented the bedrock of truth. On the contrary, they soon found that police and army accounts of violent clashes or, later, of car bombings, often bore much the same relation to reality as the Five O'Clock Follies, the daily US army briefings in Saigon, did to the daily battles in the paddy fields and forests outside that city. The police and army, they came to realize, had an axe to grind. As a result the Ministry of Defence, the Stormont government and Downing Street made regular complaints to editors in Fleet Street and the broadcasting organizations. Faced with the angry assurance of senior officials on the one hand, and the inexperience and youth of their correspondents on the other, not every editor behaved as well as he should.

In August 1971, after the imposition of internment in Northern Ireland, a BBC reporter waited at the gates of one of the main prisons in the expectation that some prisoners who had been picked up by mistake would be released. He interviewed half a dozen of them, and recorded their angry, shocked complaints that they had been subjected to inter-rogation methods by British soldiers which amounted to torture. They had been isolated, deprived of sleep, kept in metal tanks in very cold temperatures while unbearably loud 'white noise' was played to them. In some cases soldiers put iron buckets over their heads and beat on them with metal implements. All these allegations were later shown to have been true; yet one senior figure in BBC news and current affairs issued a personal instruction that none of these recordings could be used, because a senior official at the Ministry of Defence had given him an assurance that the claims were false. When it became clear that other news organ-izations had gathered similar stories and reported them, the interviews were at last broadcast. But the BBC's first instinct had been to believe the government official rather than side with a young and inexperienced reporter in suggesting that British soldiers had used torture on British citizens.

The contrast between the apparently authoritative statements of official spokesmen and the eyewitness reporting of journalists was at its most stark in the aftermath of 'Bloody Sunday' in Londonderry on 30 January 1972. The 1st Battalion, The Parachute Regiment, under the overall command of General Robert Ford, Commander of Land Forces in Northern Ireland, confronted a large anti-internment demonstration in the Bogside area of the city, and opened fire, killing twelve people outright. Another died in hospital later. The best account was written by Simon Winchester of the *Guardian*, who was now the paper's main correspondent in Northern Ireland and was close to the front of the demonstration when the shooting began. Winchester was twenty-seven, tall, bespectacled and with prematurely thinning hair: more of a scholar than an adventurer. He was lucky to survive Bloody Sunday unscathed, as his despatch showed. It was written in great haste for the next morning's newspapers, and shows it: there is little art or style about his words, which fall over themselves as he dictated his story down the phone line. It gives them even greater urgency.

> Paratroopers piled out of their vehicles, many ran for-ward to make arrests, but others rushed to the street corners. It was these men, perhaps 20 in all, who opened fire with their rifles. I saw three men fall to the ground. One was still obviously alive, with blood pumping

from his leg. The others, both apparently in their teens, seemed dead.

The meeting at Free Derry Corner broke up in hysteria as thousands of people either ran or dived for the ground. Army snipers could be seen firing continuously towards the central Bogside streets and at one stage a lone army sniper on a street corner fired two shots at me as I peered around a corner. One shot chipped a large chunk of masonry from a wall behind me.

An early news bulletin on BBC television, put together by an inexperienced reporter who was not himself an eyewitness, followed the army's version closely. Like many of the British and foreign journalists in Derry that day, he was working out of the City Hotel, not far from the Bogside where the shootings had taken place. Soon after his report had been shown on the early evening news, a message was passed to the hotel to say that if he was still in Derry an hour later he would be killed. He and his crew left at once.

The BBC man who compiled the main report for that night's 9.50 news was a much more formidable character. John Bierman was an ex-Royal Marine of thirty-two who had founded and edited the *Nation* in Kenya before coming back to work for the *Daily Express*, and then joining the BBC.

Both as a soldier and as a journalist, Bierman was thoroughly equipped to judge what had happened on Bloody Sunday. Directly he had obtained all the interviews he needed, he sent his film back to be processed, so that he could start the business of editing his report. The editor in London, realizing the importance of the story, told him his report could be as long as he wanted. At that time the longest news items lasted little more than two minutes; Bierman's report on Bloody Sunday was thirteen minutes long. There was no time to craft it properly, since it takes about an hour to edit a minute for television news. Most of what Bierman did had to be ad-libbed live on air; but it was so well done that it won an award at the Cannes Film Festival.

BIERMAN: The scene inside Catholic Bogside was as much a battlefield as anything I've witnessed . . . The first body I saw was that of a youth being carried out by another civilian with a priest in the lead, waving a bloodied handkerchief as a white flag. While the angry Bogsiders hurled bitter abuse in the direction of the paras, crouched behind their armoured vehicles some 150 yards away, I spoke to one of their priests, Father Edward Daly, curate of St Eugene's church nearby . . .

DALY: They just came in, firing at the people. There was no provocation whatsoever . . .

BIERMAN: Are you quite sure that nothing was fired at them first?

DALY: There was nothing fired at them, I'm absolutely certain of that. I can speak of this without any difficulty whatever, because I was there, I was just standing at the flats when they started the shooting first of all . . .

BIERMAN: Soon after I saw General Ford, Commander of Land Forces, and asked him for his version of what had happened.

FORD: Paratroops did not go in there shooting. In fact, they did not fire until they were fired upon, and my information at the moment is that the 1st Battalion fired three rounds altogether, after they'd had something between ten and twenty fired at them from the area of the Rossville Flats over there.

BIERMAN: They fired three rounds only?

FORD: My information at the moment . . .

BIERMAN: I believe that there are more than three dead. I certainly . . . I've seen three dead myself.

FORD: Well, they may well not have been killed by our forces.

British people were predisposed to believe that violence was always used first by the IRA and its supporters, and that British soldiers, if they opened fire at all, did so only in self-defence. General Ford, responsible for the behaviour of his soldiers that day, was a figure of considerable authority. Even so, his version did not seem particularly confident.

The lead story on the front page of *The Times* the following morning offered a careful compromise between the two versions of what had happened. *The Times*, as the leading establishment newspaper, was usually cautious about accusing British soldiers of wrongdoing, yet it is obvious from the wording and the treatment of the report that the editorial staff in London placed more credence on their own correspondent's eyewitness account than they did on the army's version. The main despatch was preceded by a brief hundred-word introduction, written by the paper's subeditors in London. It picked up some of the key words from the main report, and put the accusations by the march leaders before the army's account: an arrangement which made it clear *The Times* thought the likelier version was that of the march leaders, much as their own reporter indicated. Under the headline

13 civilians are killed as soldiers storm the Bogside

the introductory paragraph reads

> Thirteen civilians were shot dead in Londonderry yesterday as British troops stormed into the Bogside after thousands of anti-internment marchers had been dispersed at a city centre barricade. Civil rights leaders taking part in the march, which had been banned by Stormont, accused troops of indiscriminate firing but the Army said they were replying to snipers' fire and that the dead might not have been killed by soldiers.

The lead story bore a headline that was studiously neutral:

March ends in shooting
From Brian Cashinella and John Chartres
Londonderry, Jan 30.

Cashinella was a young, well-regarded correspondent, who had been close to the shooting when it happened, though not, it seems, quite as close as Winchester. Chartres was an older man, a defence specialist with good contacts among senior officers. The first half of the story is Cashinella's work:

> More than 200 heavily armed parachutists this afternoon stormed into the IRA stronghold of Bogside, Londonderry, and a hospital official stated tonight that 13 people had been shot dead and 17 others, including two women, wounded in a brief but fierce gun battle.

This reference to a gun battle contradicts the rest of Cashinella's account. It is not clear whether it was inserted by someone else for reasons of balance, or whether it found its way in through sheer haste.

> Bogsiders were tonight complaining that troops had fired on unarmed men, 'including one who had his arms up in surrender'. A photographer who was directly behind the parachutists when they jumped down from their armoured cars said: 'I was appalled. They opened up into a crowd of people. As far as I could see, they did not fire over people's heads at all.'

Chartres presumably contributed the sections of the story which gave the army's accounts. Several of the specific details quoted in *The Times* were never mentioned again, even at the Widgery Tribunal which examined the shootings and ended, many people felt, by whitewashing the army.

Lieutenant Colonel Derek Wilford, the parachutists' commanding officer, said later that two gunmen, who had been firing at his soldiers from a pile of rubble at the base of the [Rossville] flats, had been shot dead. He said no weapons had been found on the men but he was quite certain they were gunmen.

The response in London was varied. The news desks seem to have published their reporters' accounts in full, but the writers of comment columns and editorials, older and generally more establishment-oriented, often took a different line in the days that followed Bloody Sunday. Sensing that the army had not behaved properly, they nevertheless placed the real blame firmly on the marchers for provoking the massacre.

> The civil rights movement does not murder; it simply creates conditions favourable to the murders attempted by others and leaves the army in the last resort with no alternative but to fire.   – Daily Telegraph

> Who is really responsible for the 13 deaths in Ulster yesterday?
>   British bullets will be found in most of their bodies . . . but the blood is on the consciences of irresponsible political leaders and the fanatical IRA.   – Daily Mail

The Times, despite having acknowledged the contradiction between the eyewitness accounts and the army version, ended up by condemning the marchers.

> It must be presumed that those who are inciting the Catholics to take to the streets knew very well the consequences of what they are doing. Londonderry had a taste of those consequences last night.

Even the *Guardian*, which habitually took a stern line on human rights abuses in other countries, ran an editorial which seemed to suggest that the people who were shot down in the streets by the army were somehow themselves to blame. The *Guardian* has always been a remarkably democratic paper, and after a long debate a senior journalist with a Northern Ireland background and strong Unionist sympathies wrote the main editorial.

> The march was illegal. Warning had been given of the danger implicit in continuing with it. Even so, the deaths stun the mind and must fill all reasonable people with horror. As yet it is too soon to be sure of what happened. The army has an intolerably difficult task in Ireland. At times it is bound to act firmly, even severely. Whether individual soldiers misjudged their situation yesterday, or were themselves too directly threatened, cannot yet be known.

It was left to the *Daily Mirror* to make the one key point that no other newspaper had made: that soldiers were not the best people to maintain law and order in the streets of British cities. On Thursday 3 February, four days after the shooting, the *Mirror* came up with a set of proposals under the heading

HOW TO END THE KILLING IN IRELAND

It suggested replacing British troops with UN ones, which would probably have been disastrous and would certainly have been profoundly humiliating for Britain; opening talks on the constitutional future of

Northern Ireland, which (when combined with a withdrawal of British troops) would certainly have led to far more violence on the Protestant side; an end to internment, which was an essential requirement for any solution, since it had failed lamentably; and starting the move towards a political solution.

These two last points foreshadowed what the British government soon did. As a direct result of Bloody Sunday, Edward Heath announced two months later that he was withdrawing security powers from the Northern Ireland government, and then dissolved it altogether. Britain instituted direct rule. It was a remarkable change of course which made the long-term settlement in Northern Ireland and the effective surrender of the IRA a possibility. But no one was brought to justice for Bloody Sunday.

§

The relationship between the army and the media was often a hostile one. At times, British and foreign journalists working in Northern Ireland came to regard the army's version of events as little more reliable and authoritative than the Provisional IRA's. At a seminar held in Dublin in 1974, a well-known British journalist drew the distinction between the two like this:

> With the Provos, you know exactly what their line is and you can discount it. They lie about a lot of things, but you can pretty much always tell what those things are, because the Provos are a single-minded outfit with one clear aim that it's pursuing. The Army mixes up truth and lies so much that often you can't disentangle the two. And the trouble is, the mixture comes with such an apparent air of authority and realism because the soldiers are wearing the Queen's uniform and are officers and gentlemen.

Soldiers, like politicians and members of the security services, tend to have a Manichaean view of the world: if you are not demonstrably on their side, you are more than likely to be siding with their enemy. The concept of balance does not find easy acceptance among them, especially at times of conflict. Their view of public relations is a zero-sum game, in which anything short of complete support is seen as potential hostility. This is of course the natural attitude for soldiers who are fighting a war: if one of your men is uncertain of the value of the enterprise, or disinclined to follow orders, he is a danger to everyone else in the platoon.

But Northern Ireland wasn't a war; that was one of the mistakes that led to Bloody Sunday. It was something much more complicated and ill-defined – a battle for moral authority. That could not be won by a government which gave its forces carte blanche to sort the problem out, with no questions asked. The British authorities did many things over the years in Northern Ireland which detracted from their moral authority; but fortunately for them the Provisional IRA regularly used tactics which caused revulsion among everyone not emotionally committed to their cause. That decided the outcome.

Robert Fisk, who went to Belfast as the *Times* correspondent in 1972 and continued working there until 1976, was the kind of journalist tunnel-visioned soldiers dislike most. He had not the slightest interest in being 'helpful' – a word which military men use to mean something like 'doing their patriotic duty by being favourable to the armed forces'; instead, he was an obsessive ferreter-out of awkward facts. He was open about his hostility to people who killed innocent civilians, but made it clear he occasionally included the British army as well as the Provisional IRA in that category.

On 16 February 1976, Fisk revealed on the front page of *The Times* that British plain-clothes soldiers operating in Northern Ireland and the Irish Republic were using forged press cards and claiming to be freelance journalists. The army had always categorically denied that it did this. When *The Times* contacted the military press office in Lisburn and showed the forged press card which Fisk had obtained, it caused a certain amount of discomfiture. Then a statement was issued to say that the forgery had been produced more than eighteen months before.

The story was filled with the kind of minute detail Fisk habitually put into his reports ('the soldier was identified in the grill room of the Gresham Hotel by a member of the Royal Ulster Constabulary who was on holiday in the republic'), and was probably of far more interest to other journalists than it was to the general reader. In difficult places like Northern Ireland, where journalists wandered about unprotected, investigating stories and meeting contacts, it would obviously make their lives more dangerous if people suspected they might be undercover soldiers; though in truth many supporters of the IRA or the Protestant paramilitary groups believed that British journalists were likely to be working for the British government anyway. It was hard not to see the angry reactions from journalists' associations which followed as another example of the self-righteousness which so often characterizes the media.

As for the army, it found it difficult to understand why a journalist like Fisk would want to report such a thing; it was certainly not 'helpful', and would make things harder for army undercover operations in future. Might this kind of reporting not be explained by an in-built hostility, an instinct for subversion, a fundamental lack of loyalty and patriotism, on the part of the media? That, certainly, was the opinion of a great many soldiers. Eight days later, on 24 February 1976, Fisk wrote another front-page article for *The Times* which contained further revelations about the relationship between journalists and the army. It was headlined

Army regards press as destructive in Ulster, papers show

and quoted two confidential army memoranda, 'one of them a policy document sent to a senior military official at the Ministry of Defence in Whitehall'. They indicated that the army regarded the work of the British press in Northern Ireland as actively damaging to the military campaign there.

The problem with such revelations is that it is often hard to know how serious they are. All too often, the journalist merely opens a window halfway through a private conversation, and shuts it again before the reader can gauge how significant the speaker was, or what the response might have been. Were the memoranda a serious attempt to influence the Ministry of Defence's thinking, or simply the sound of frustrated senior officers letting off steam? It was impossible to know. Nevertheless, the leaked documents provided an insight into the way many mid-ranking and senior officers undoubtedly felt about the work of the media in Northern Ireland.

One passage, written by an unnamed lieutenant colonel at the army's Northern Ireland headquarters, sounded a particularly sour and personal note:

The desire of journalists to make a quick and lucrative reputation for themselves as war correspondents led to a style of individual arrogance quite unsuited to the reporting of a major tragedy like Northern Ireland.

Then came the habitual complaints: many journalists working in Northern Ireland have long since abandoned any pretence of separating news from comment so that reports from Northern Ireland often contained the personal views of journalists ... [T]his represents a dangerous situation ... Following shooting incidents in Northern Ireland it was commonplace for journalists to report local people as saying that men shot by the army were innocent, unarmed boys.

The pronouncements of suspect groups are treated as valid. Organizations with high-sounding names ... have no difficulty in finding space in newspapers or time on the air. Rarely are the sinister affiliations of these groups, or their infiltration by the IRA, mentioned by the reporters who propagate their views.

All these things certainly happened, and some were perhaps the result of bias on the part of a few journalists. Most were the result of something the lieutenant colonel does not mention: a kind of modishness, a general tone which pervaded many newsrooms. The minds of journalists, like those of most other people, run along tramlines, and if a particular kind of story or a particular kind of tone has been successful, then it will be delivered again and again in exactly the same way. There is no doubt that the British media regarded an exclusive story about wrongdoing on the part of the army more highly than one about wrongdoing on the part of the Provisional IRA. The IRA committed all sorts of crimes and atrocities, so it was no great surprise to find it had carried out more. By contrast, when the army's ethical standards fell below the level expected, it made much more of an impact at home. For a few journalists, too, there may have been the consideration that the army's revenge would be nothing worse than an official complaint and a certain amount of cold-shouldering. The Provisional IRA, by contrast, was likely to be much more threatening.

There were also, of course, plenty of European and American

journalists who knew there was credit to be gained at home from presenting the British army as brutal and stupid. From reporters like these the Provisional IRA could always expect an easy ride and some positive propaganda. So the lieutenant colonel was not necessarily wrong; he was merely being defeatist and unimaginative.

The army's main problem was that in Northern Ireland it had quite a lot to hide. In 1974 it was shown to have embarrassingly close links with men like the Littlejohn brothers, who carried out bank robberies in Dublin; the aim was to encourage the Irish government to take a stronger line against the IRA. The exact degree of the British army's involvement with Protestant death squads in the killing of IRA men has never been fully revealed, but it seems to have been considerable. The use of agents provocateurs, the links between the army and Loyalist groups which carried out bombing campaigns in both the North and South, the use of targeted murder as a weapon of war: these things, and others, were all revealed first by journalists, often by television journalists like Peter Taylor.

The lessons were embarrassingly simple: if you don't want bad publicity, don't do things that will look bad if they are made public. Yet from the army's point of view it all worked out reasonably well in the end. The anonymous lieutenant colonel quoted in Robert Fisk's exclusive was entirely wrong in his gloomy forecast:

> The critical point in the campaign will be when the terrorists have, through their political wings, won [British] withdrawal; when the Government's economic advisers start rationalising and recommend the cutting of losses; when the will to win and the moral fibre of the Government has been weakened by left-wing, anti-authoritarian [sic] press reports, depicting the terrorists as a down-trodden, ill-treated little child who only wants his freedom from a big bully.

On the contrary, successive British governments stuck with the policy, with the strong cooperation of the Irish government. The army learned new ways of combating the violence. A new and better police force took over. Sinn Fein politicians were brought into the system. Support for the Provisional IRA in the Catholic community was reduced to such low levels that in the end all but the most embittered and irreconcilable Republicans decided to hand over their weapons. A year after Fisk's exclusives about the use of forged press cards and the warnings about the dangers of the media, the army made it mandatory for every one of its units in Northern Ireland to be accompanied by a properly trained press officer whose job was to deal with the media. Not all of them were good, and a few were still spectacularly bad; but the overall improvement was soon noticeable. The army's instinctive terror of journalists began to fade. There was, in the end, no need for lieutenant colonels to hyperventilate about the bad press the army occasionally received.

§

When Edward Heath came to power in May 1970, he had as little as possible to do with journalists. Like Eden before him, he was too self-confident, as well as too distant, to believe he needed a good press. Most newspapers, including the *Daily Mirror*, had supported his decision to join the European Common Market in 1973, and he seems to have believed that he had the basic support of Fleet Street, whatever the day-to-day editorials might say. James Margach, political editor of the *Sunday Times*, who liked showing off his closeness to the great and powerful, thought a great many of Heath's problems were caused by his fundamental shyness: 'Sometimes he would be touching in his boyish anxiety, as for instance when he would write to me: "Dear James: Thank you so much for your kind references on Sunday. As ever. Ted."'

Once, when Margach went round to his flat for an interview, Heath settled his mind first by playing Chopin and Liszt on his piano for half an hour. He told Margach: '[I]t's the best way of getting that bloody man Wilson out of my hair.' For all his accomplishments as a soldier, a musician and a sailor, Heath remained sensitive about his lower-middle-class origins as the son of a jobbing builder.

He seemed not to understand that the Tory grandees had pushed for his selection as leader of the Conservative Party precisely so that he could match Harold Wilson's classlessness. When Edward du Cann, the subtle and not over-loyal chairman of the party, suggested to Heath that the image-makers should stress his background before the next election, Heath got him dismissed.

When he found himself facing a confrontation with the miners' union towards the end of 1973, he began inviting newspaper editors and their political correspondents to Downing Street for briefing sessions. Soon, as had happened with Eden fourteen years before, the editors started to realize that he was not interested in their views; the meetings were a chance for Heath to launch into monologues about his own policies. Presumably he thought that if he explained them better, the editors would be more sympathetic.

When that failed, he turned to more senior Fleet Street figures. At the height of the crisis over miners' pay he invited Sydney Jacobson, later Lord Jacobson, the editorial director of Mirror Newspapers, to come to Downing Street for a talk. Jacobson told James Margach later that he had found Heath depressed and lacking his usual self-confidence. Heath told him that the miners were making the dispute more and more political, and that the Communist Mick McGahey, the leader of the Scottish miners, had told him they wanted to see him out, and they were going to get him out. Did Jacobson think he should call an election?

Jacobson found himself in a strange position. He was in charge of a newspaper group which, though it had strongly supported Heath over Britain's entry into the Common Market, would be bound to campaign for Heath's defeat in an election. But he felt a real personal sympathy for the man sitting opposite him, and advised him strongly not to go to the country. All his experience, Jacobson said, showed that trying to focus an election onto one single issue – in this case, the question of whether the unions or the elected government should run the country – would fail. When Heath complained that he could not get his message across to the public, Jacobson said the *Mirror*'s political editor would conduct a major interview with Heath. It happened soon afterwards, and was published under the heading 'My Case – by Edward Heath'.

Heath clearly thought the *Mirror* had had a change of heart, and soon afterwards Heath invited Jacobson back and asked him outright who the paper would support in an election. Jacobson told him there could be only one answer. When Heath announced he would go to the country, the *Mirror* ran the scornful headline

Now he has the nerve to call an election

The election resulted in the first hung Parliament of the century. The Conservatives had won slightly more votes – 37.9 per cent to Labour's

37.18 per cent – but Labour had 301 seats to the Conservatives' 297: not enough for an overall majority, but enough to form a government. Harold Wilson had just squeaked in.

He was a different man from the Wilson who had bustled into Downing Street a decade before. Now he was lethargic, often ill, and had spells of memory-loss and vagueness. A member of his kitchen cabinet, Bernard Donoughue, noted in his diary how much Wilson was drinking: 'Brandy from midday till late evening, when he is slow and very slurred.'

Yet no newspaper made a single open reference to the decline in Wilson's physical and mental health. For all the frenzied talk of plots and conspiracies which filled Wilson's last two years as prime minister, the only serious conspiracy was one of total silence among those around him in covering up the fact of his unsuitability for office.

At the start of his new term in office, however, things seemed to go well. Joe Haines, Wilson's press spokesman, persuaded him to keep off the television screen. The members of the reconstituted kitchen cabinet agreed; perhaps they thought television would show up his declining powers. Wilson, they argued, should be seen as a distant, magisterial figure, above the fray. From March to July he rejected all requests from the BBC for interviews. Instead, he gave a long and relaxed interview to Granada's *World in Action* programme. The programme began with Wilson and his Cabinet colleagues coming down the steps into the garden of 10 Downing Street, then wandering around in small groups, supposedly discussing policy. In the interview itself he was folksy and approachable, the common man's prime minister. In his first two terms, he said, few of his Cabinet colleagues had any experience, so he had to do most of the work himself, like the one professional footballer in the side:

> I had to take corner-kicks and penalties, administer to the wounded and bring on the lemons at half-time and score all the goals myself. Now I will be the deep-lying centre-half, concentrating on defence, initiating attacks, distributing the ball for my star forwards. They'll score the goals, and, by Heavens, they are scoring goals.

Two years earlier, Wilson had given a number of briefings to senior journalists about his plans if he won the next election. His first priority would be to get rid of the Lobby, he told them, which was greeted by a real sense of disappointment as the journalists realized how little he had changed.

It was not until June 1975 that Joe Haines made the announcement that the briefing system was to end. Haines was widely disliked at Westminster, and many Lobby journalists assumed the idea was his. He certainly had no liking for the Lobby as an institution, and seemed contemptuous of many of its members. The newspapers reacted angrily, among them the *Glasgow Herald*. On 23 June 1975 it wrote: 'When governments slam doors but profess to conduct an open policy, it is time to be alert for sinister motives.'

Yet there was nothing more sinister to Wilson's motives than a desire to get even with the people who had failed to treat him as he wanted to be treated. Time and again journalists misunderstood Wilson because they failed to grasp the smallness of his motives.

Over the next few months, without Downing Street's briefings, the political correspondents flourished. The reporting of Westminster and Whitehall seemed just as well informed. The Lobby correspondents continued to work together, and often agreed on their stories as they had done before the change, so it is hard to tell what difference, if any, the loss of their briefings had on the quality of their reporting.

It is significant, though, that a change in the government's briefing arrangements should have led the *Glasgow Herald* and others to assume that something sinister was brewing. Wilson's last two years as prime minister were poisoned by such suspicions. The stories that were going round were legion: Wilson was a Soviet agent, and had been recruited during his trips to Moscow in the 1950s; a KGB colonel was in regular contact with Downing Street; senior government officials were involved in drug-taking or sex orgies; Wilson was dependent on Marcia Williams because she had been his mistress for years; sinister men with Eastern European names had enmeshed the British government in a web of corruption and espionage. None of these accusations had any substance to them, but they flourished in the climate Wilson had created. As for Mrs Williams, *Private Eye* came up with the sensational revelation that, far from being Wilson's mistress, she had had two children by a married Lobby correspondent, Walter Terry. There was indeed a hidden story in Downing Street, but it was not the one people imagined. Wilson was not unfaithful to his wife, and Mary Wilson and Marcia Williams were close friends.

Above all, the faint but unmistakable whiff of dubious financial dealings seemed to emanate from Downing Street. On 3 April 1974 the *Daily Mail* ran an arresting front-page exclusive which pushed the death of President Georges Pompidou of France and a major malfunction of the *QE2*'s engines in mid-ocean to the side-columns:

WHO FORGED WILSON'S SIGNATURE?
By HARRY LONGMUIR and BRIAN PARK

Mr Harold Wilson's name has been used – and his signature forged on a mysterious letter – to help push a £1 million land speculation ... Although people close to Mr Wilson, including his personal secretary Mrs Marcia Williams, were involved in the deal which was quite legitimate, Mr Wilson was in no way connected to it ... Involved in the site were: Mr Anthony Field, a friend of the Prime Minister, who was once called in to streamline his House of Commons secretariat. His sister, Mrs Marcia Williams. His other sister, Miss Peggy Field, former secretary to Mrs Mary Wilson ...

And Mr Victor F. Harper, an undischarged bankrupt, who was appointed as Mr Field's agent on the unusually high commission of £3,000 an acre.

The *Mail* might have to admit that Wilson was unconnected with the deal, but it all had a sleazy appearance. In fact his signature had been forged by a middleman, Ronald Millhench, who duly went to prison, and Field, who was a geologist not a businessman, made scarcely anything out of the deal. Nor was there anything illegal about it; but the fact that Labour had so often attacked land speculation made it doubly embarrassing.

Wilson was always loyal to his friends. Despite the advice of Joe Haines he came out fighting at Prime Minister's Questions in the Commons on the day of the *Mail*'s exclusive.

If you are trying to follow the smears of the Tory press, I will say this ...

If you buy land on which is a slag heap 120 feet high

> and it costs £100,000 to remove it, that is not land specu-
> lation in the sense we [the Labour Party] condemned it,
> it is land reclamation.

'Reclamation' became as much a joking term of abuse in newspaper columns, cartoons and in ordinary conversation, as his assurance about 'the pound in your pocket' not losing its value had been at the time of sterling's devaluation in 1967. Wilson was correct, technically, on both counts, but it simply didn't feel right; and he was judged accordingly.

Some days later, Wilson complained in the Commons about the 'intolerable degree of newspaper harassment' of Marcia Williams at her home, and said it was a cowardly way of attacking him and, through him, the government. Journalism in Britain was changing. There had been plenty of media scrums in the past, going back to the late nineteenth century; but nothing quite on this scale, directed towards someone who, no matter how well known, was only partially involved in a much bigger news story.

The shoving, sweating, shouting crowd of journalists, photographers and television cameramen which gathered to besiege the house which Marcia Williams was sharing with her sister Peggy was the harbinger of many similar attacks in the future. There was no doubt why Marcia Williams was subjected to this treatment. It was not because she was peripherally involved in a relatively small, not very edifying piece of speculation; it was because large numbers of people thought she was Harold Wilson's mistress.

Writs were issued against the *Mail*, the *Evening Standard*, the *Evening News* and the *Sun* (now owned by Rupert Murdoch, and unsurprisingly one of the leaders in Mrs Williams's hounding) as a result of the way they had handled the story. Yet, as the commentator Bernard Levin, a lawyer by training, pointed out in a column in *The Times* a few days later, on 9 April 1974, the press took another step away from its older, more polite habits, and kicked a hole in a legal convention which used to calm public debate once legal proceedings had started: the rule of sub judice.

> Not long ago, no newspaper which had received a writ
> for alleged libel arising out of something it had published
> would in any circumstances have gone on publishing
> further matter connected with the subject ... It might

> have been thought that the four writs . . . would stem the
> flood. Not a bit of it; the flood instantly increased, and
> though, obviously, all the newspapers – sued and unsued
> alike – were having due regard to the law of libel, as they
> had been from the original disclosures, it was more than
> ever clear that no one was being deterred by the sub
> judice rule.

The papers had realized that in a case of massive public interest, combining politics, the possibility of doubtful dealings, and sex, it was worth brushing legal niceties aside. A precedent had been set. Bernard Levin rather approved: '[T]he dam is down beyond any possibility of reerection, and I for one cannot help feeling that the floodwaters beyond, as they pour past the ruins, will have a beneficially cleansing effect.'

§

On 17 March 1976 the big headline on the front page of the *Sun* was

MARGARET AND TONY TO PART?

A box at the top of the page read

Soccer Tube train hit by bomb blast
SEE PAGE 7

referring to an explosion on the Underground carried out by the IRA (a common enough occurrence by 1976, so it did not generate any great media hysteria). The smallish column down the left-hand side of the page read

Odds on Big Jim!

It was in this way that the *Sun*'s readers were told that Harold Wilson had unexpectedly resigned as prime minister, and that the campaign to succeed him had begun. When a celebrity/Royal/human interest story takes precedence over political news of the first importance, you know that journalism's priorities have changed. It was the strongest evidence yet that the *Sun*'s arrival on the scene had begun to change the way newspapers reacted to the world around them.

Inside the paper, Anthony Bevins, one of the finest and most independent-minded correspondents in the Lobby, wrote a summary of the reasons for Wilson's decision which was entirely accurate: he had been leader and prime minister long enough, he wanted his successor to be given enough time to settle in before the next general election, he had a feeling that he might be growing stale and he wanted a fresh mind for the job.

It is strange that the news should have taken so many journalists by surprise, since it had been accurately forecast less than two years earlier. On 27 October 1974 the *News of the World* made the story its splash lead soon after the second of the two elections that year. The headline read

WILSON WILL HAND OVER TO JIM NEXT YEAR

forecasting not only that Jim Callaghan would succeed him, but even when it would happen: within eighteen months. Marcia Williams was said to have been the source for the story; Wilson had broken the news to her and Mary Wilson when the three of them went out for a long walk during a holiday on the Scilly Isles.

Four days later, on Thursday 31 October, Anthony Shrimsley in the *Sun* followed up the *News of the World*'s story and added more detail. He wrote, with a half-suppressed reference to Wilson's drinking habit, of the 'scenario which he has been rehearsing over the after-dinner brandy since 1970, that another 18 months as Premier would be enough'.

Wilson wanted a dignified, relaxed exit from power, to be announced on his sixtieth birthday. But the conspiratorial atmosphere that surrounded him made this impossible. Simon Hoggart wrote in the *Guardian* on 17 March 1976:

> Nothing was more typical of the man in office than the way he left it. Witty and thoughtful, courteous and savagely rude by turns, sometimes generous and sometimes contemptuous, he was often the statesman and sometimes the unwitting clown. The House of Commons never really loved him, but it did not half respect him . . .

> At the end, Mr Wilson said that he had told the Speaker
> months ago that he was leaving; and Mr Thomas said
> rapidly 'That's correct', as if he thought the House might
> doubt the Prime Minister's word.

It was a telling shot. The House, and the country in general, immediately questioned Wilson's word on this, just as they had about everything else. His account of his reasons for leaving office seemed much too tame and obvious; there must, people felt, be some deeper reason for his decision. All those associates with Eastern European names, all those visits to Moscow, all those accusations about Marcia Williams – might not the reason lie there? No one could remember a prime minister who wanted to walk out of the job before.

Plenty of investigative reporters looked into possible reasons for Wilson's resignation, but they came up with nothing worth risking a libel writ for. Only *Private Eye* seemed not to mind the dangers. The *Eye*, as most journalists called it, had established itself in a carefully selected niche from which it published many outrageous and often libellous stories, on the basis that most people realized it would only make them look silly if they sued. Its second editor, Richard Ingrams, who ran the magazine from 1963 to 1986, maintained, 'I can always seem to tell when something is right or not.'

His self-confidence gave the magazine an air of moral superiority. This was augmented by the much-repeated fact that Ingrams played the organ at his local church. Eventually he left his wife of thirty-one years for a much younger woman, but this was seven years after he had handed over control of *Private Eye* to Ian Hislop. Hislop managed to drop the moral air (though he too was a practising Anglican) and the magazine remained both funny and effective.

Under Ingrams, much of the *Eye*'s best material was provided by Auberon Waugh, who described the Diary he wrote for it from the early 1970s to 1985 as 'the world's first example of journalism specifically dedicated to telling lies'. The disclaimer gave Waugh, and the *Eye*, an extra if flimsy protection against the lawyers. When in December 1974 the allegation (which later proved to be true) surfaced that the disgraced former postmaster general in Wilson's Cabinet had been an agent of the Communist regime in Czechoslovakia, Waugh used it as an opportunity to attack Wilson on similar grounds.

There is not a shred of evidence that [John] Stonehouse was a Czech spy, apart from the first-hand evidence of his Czech spymaster. No wonder Wilson allowed him to stay in the government ... I have never attempted to hide my belief that Wilson is a Russian agent ... I think I would be prepared to back my intuition with a small wager. Perhaps I will place it with my old friend Ian Mikardo, the House of Commons bookmaker ...

Mikardo, a left-wing Labour MP, was believed by MI5 and others to have been a Soviet agent prior to 1967.

Such teasing accusations, sometimes true but often not, were gleefully lapped up by journalists and ordinary readers alike. In 1974 the writer Patrick Marnham, who worked for *Private Eye*, was handed a dossier on Wilson which he was told had come from MI5. The general thrust of the documents he used in his articles was that Wilson was a Zionist–Soviet agent; not an easy double function to carry out, one would have thought. In 1987 Peter Wright, a former MI5 officer, wrote his memoir *Spycatcher*, which made far-reaching allegations about Harold Wilson's supposed links with Soviet intelligence, and described MI5's activities in a very unflattering light. Sales were hugely augmented by Margaret Thatcher's decision to ban the book in Britain. The investigative journalist David Leigh examined the accusations at length in his book *The Wilson Plot*, published in 1988, and found nothing worth supporting. The leading academic expert on espionage, Christopher Andrew, who was given access to any of MI5's files that he wanted to see, made it clear in his authorized history of the service, *The Defence of the Realm*, published in 2009, that he did not believe Wright's accusations. He was certain, too, that Wilson was not a Soviet (or indeed a Zionist) agent. Apparently he just liked to keep questionable company.

For the most part, the newspapers' interest in Wilson faded. Each new accusation was reported, often with great attention, but it would soon be forgotten. The sinister air which had settled over Wilson turned to absurdity. Joe Haines wrote a memoir about his time in Downing Street, savagely attacking Marcia Williams, most memorably over the 'lavender notepaper' affair, when she supposedly gave Wilson a list of people (some thought to be highly unsuitable) he should include in his resignation honours. Haines even alleged that Wilson had asked his doctor to murder her, though when the BBC included this in a much later fictionalized drama about Downing Street under Wilson, Mrs Williams (now Lady Falkender) threatened to sue and the BBC settled out of court. The assumption was that Haines could not stand the accusation up.

Wilson himself briefed two young investigative journalists, Barrie Penrose and Roger Courtiour, who were looking into a possible South African involvement in some of the events of the 1970s. The meeting soon turned embarrassing. He told them:

> I see myself as the big fat spider in the corner of the room. Sometimes I speak when I'm asleep. You should both listen. Occasionally when we meet I might tell you to go to Charing Cross Road and kick a blind man standing on the corner. That blind man may tell you something, lead you somewhere.

It was a bizarre end to a bizarre period. In many ways it was better covered by the satirists of *Private Eye* than by the political correspondents of the newspapers, radio and television.

18

RISING SUN

At a celebration in the grimy surroundings of the *News of the World* machine room, on the evening of 16 November 1969, British journalism, and perhaps British life, was about to be changed for ever. The party was a small one: Rupert Murdoch, the thirty-eight-year-old Australian newspaper proprietor, his wife, Anna, the man Murdoch had chosen to be the editor of his new newspaper, Larry Lamb, his wife, Joan, and the bosses of the printing unions and their wives. Mrs Murdoch switched on the printing presses, and they began to roll. 'Here's to the *Sun*,' said someone and they all raised their glasses of champagne as the machines gathered speed.

The start was not particularly auspicious. After Murdoch and his party had left, the presses had to be stopped because of technical problems, and a million copies of the first Murdoch edition were lost. As for the paper itself, it had little of the flair it was to show later. The front page headline was

HORSE DOPE SENSATION

– scarcely much of a scoop. On page 2 an editorial welcomed the paper's new readers in unimaginative terms:

> Today's Sun is a new newspaper. It has a new shape, new writers, new ideas. But it inherits all that is best from the great traditions of its predecessors. The Sun cares. About the quality of life. About the kind of world we live in. And about people.

Page 3 is just another news page. On page 9 there is an exclusive but lacklustre interview with the prime minister, Harold Wilson, by the *Sun*'s political editor, Anthony Shrimsley. The centre spread shows pictures of the Rolling Stones relaxing during their latest American tour and wishing the *Sun* well. A nude blonde appears discreetly in a couple of the photographs; the day of the page 3 girl is almost exactly a year away still. Of the paper's forty-eight pages, ten are devoted to sport.

The first edition was distinctly unimpressive; so it took some foresight for a leader-writer at *The Times* the following morning to realize how successful the new arrival might soon become.

> Mr. Murdoch has not invented sex but he does show a remarkable enthusiasm for its benefits to circulation, such as a tired old Fleet Street has not seen in recent years. He has borrowed from the old Daily Mirror so many things, including its populist slogan 'Forward with the people'. There will be folks who will say that the slogan of the new Sun should be 'Backwards with the Boss' . . .

No one at the time could have foreseen, though, that the *Sun*'s new boss would become so successful that in twelve years he would be able to buy *The Times* itself.

It seems to have been anti-Semitism which helped Murdoch to start his newspaper empire in Britain: not anti-Semitism on his part, but on the part of the owner of the *News of the World*, which Murdoch had his eye on. Sir William Carr was a pleasant and convivial man, but suffered from the usual prejudices of his generation. Robert Maxwell, the aggressive entrepreneur born of Jewish parents in pre-war Czechoslovakia, heard rumours in the spring of 1968 that Carr was in financial trouble, and launched a hostile bid for the the *News of the World*. Carr was unwilling to sell to him, and on 20 October 1968 wrote an intemperate and rather nasty front-page article on the subject:

THE BATTLE FOR YOUR NEWSPAPER –
By The Editor

> Why do I think it would not be a good thing for Mr Maxwell, formerly Jan Ludwig Koch, to gain control of this newspaper which, I know, has your respect, loyalty and affection – a newspaper which is as British as roast beef and Yorkshire pudding . . . ?

Rupert Murdoch, in a manoeuvre which showed his remarkable business abilities, slipped into the gap, offered Carr a relatively small amount of money for the paper, and bought his first title. He proposed a clever package which allowed Carr to be the chairman of the new company for three months, then to hand over to Murdoch and become titular life president. Carr was satisfied, Murdoch was delighted, and Maxwell was left fuming on the sidelines.

The following year, in April 1969, the owners of the *Daily Mirror* group, IPC, offered the *Sun* for sale. A well-written, good-looking paper which supported the Labour Party and appealed to a more middle-class readership than the *Mirror*, its sales were down to 750,000 and still dropping. Robert Maxwell saw a second opportunity to buy himself a newspaper, and made an offer for it. Hugh Cudlipp, a first-class editor but at best a second-class businessman, was attracted. Maxwell, then a Labour MP, was not prepared to pay anything for the paper, but he was prepared to take on its losses; however, he would only be able to afford to do so if he could persuade the unions to agree to redundancies. There seemed no chance it would happen. But then Rupert Murdoch paid a flying visit to Rome to see one of the print union leaders, who was on holiday there. He promised there would be no redundancies if he bought the *Sun*, and won the backing of the union. Soon after, he did a deal with Hugh Cudlipp and got it for a remarkably low price: £50,000 for every year the *Sun* stayed afloat, for a maximum of seventeen years. Murdoch couldn't believe his luck. His first act as owner was to hire a former *Mirror* man as editor, with the plan of making the *Sun* into a better version of the *Mirror*. He chose Larry Lamb.

It took a few weeks to find its level, and then it started to pull away from the *Mirror*, which looked elderly and prim by comparison. Right from that moment, some of the *Sun*'s lasting qualities began to show themselves. There was the constant repetition of certain words in large type on the front page: LOVE, FREE, WIN and SEX were the ones the editor specified. There were free offers linked to sex, like the 'erotica kits' which consisted of champagne, oysters and vitamin pills. There were serializations of books like *The Love Machine*, with passages cleverly selected to increase in raunchiness through the week. There were, from the first anniversary of the *Sun*'s arrival onwards, naked girls on page 3. The first, on 17 November 1970, was relatively discreet – just a single nipple showed – but the text was characteristically aggressive-defensive.

BIRTHDAY SUIT!

> From time to time some self-appointed critic stamps his
> tiny foot and declares that The Sun is obsessed with sex. It
> is not The Sun, but the critics, who are obsessed. The Sun,
> like most of its readers, likes pretty girls. And if they are as
> pretty as today's Birthday Suit girl, 20-year-old Stephanie
> Rahn, who cares whether they're dressed or not?

The reasoning is odd, but if there is any purpose behind it, other than to
fill space, it seems to be intended to reassure men who genuinely suffered
from the pre- and post-war embarrassment about sex which was
commonplace in working-class Britain. The *Sun* was breaking down
inhibitions. As early as its second week it had evolved a philosophy: 'The
Sun is on the side of youth. It will never think what is prim must be
proper. It will never accept a code without reason. It will never urge
others to do so.'

Larry Lamb, whenever he was interviewed, insisted that it was all just
a bit of fun; there was nothing wrong or nasty about the *Sun*. Yet there
seemed too little that was spontaneous about it either; the whole enterprise had a distinctly manipulative feel. Moralists said it was like a
commercial version of Orwell's *1984*, where the state keeps the proles
quiet by feeding them pornography. What Murdoch was doing seemed
extraordinarily cynical.

But, for the moment, there was little or none of the naked, insulting
ferocity which the *Sun* would soon adopt in its articles, and particularly
in its headlines. In these early years, Rupert Murdoch had no great
interest in British politics. On the day of the 1970 election, in which
Edward Heath scored his surprise win, its headline was

THE SUN WOULD VOTE LABOUR

The decision was as limp as the headline. On the day of the February 1974
election the *Sun* plumped for the losing side again, announcing that 'Ted's
Tories look the better bet'. By the October election the *Sun* had no
opinion at all: 'The best answer is to vote for the candidates you would
like to see in a Government of all parties.'

That was the last time the *Sun* failed to have an opinion about British politics. In future its views would be loud, and sometimes abusive; and Murdoch would learn how to give the impression that he was a dominant political force in British life. He was so successful that, time and again, British prime ministers believed it.

The *Sun* phenomenon has been so divisive in British public life that it is hard to find any of its critics who will say anything in the newspaper's favour. Yet it succeeded in persuading large numbers of working-class people to read newspapers, at a time when the *Mirror* was losing readers fast, and the tabloid industry seemed to be dying on its feet. Many of the *Sun*'s readers had never read a daily newspaper before. For all its crudity, the *Sun* said things no other newspaper was prepared to say; and it said them in ways that stuck in people's memories.

It was Larry Lamb who first discovered how influential the *Sun*'s loud tones, sometimes mocking and sometimes angry, could be. In January 1979 Jim Callaghan went to an economic summit in the French West Indies, at a time when Britain was hit by freezing weather and a campaign of strikes by public sector workers. The entire tabloid press played up the contrast, with Callaghan dressed, like the other leaders, in brightly coloured tropical shirts while Britain shivered. Later, if such a thing had happened, the *Sun* would have led the pack with its abuse. Then, its headlines were factual, and much the same as those of other papers as they concentrated on the freezing weather and the strikes by rail workers, airport staff and lorry drivers:

SIBERIA SOCKS IT TO BRR-BRR BRITAIN

– Wednesday 3 January 1979

BRR! IT'S GOING TO GET WORSE!

– Thursday 4 January

SHOPPING PANIC – AIRPORT CHAOS

– Friday 5 January

MILES OF MISERY

– Monday 8 January

Over the weekend there had been long queues at petrol stations because the tanker-drivers were on strike. Life was indeed miserable. But when Callaghan returned to Heathrow two days later, on Wednesday 10 January, he made the immense mistake of giving the journalists at his airport press conference one of his habitual lectures – this time to stress that there was a world outside, and they shouldn't be so parochial. So when someone asked him about the 'mounting chaos', Callaghan said he didn't think 'other people' would share the view that there was mounting chaos. '[A]s regards domestic affairs, I'm trying to raise your eyes a little because, believe me, there are other issues in the world as well.'

It was probably the greatest mistake of his political career. Everyone pounced on the gaffe he had made – even the usually neutral BBC News. But Larry Lamb's summary of Callaghan's attitude the next morning fixed it in people's minds in three words:

CRISIS? WHAT CRISIS?

During the election campaign four months later, people often claimed to have seen Callaghan on television actually using the words. The *Sun* had discovered its political power at last.

§

Margaret Thatcher was elected leader of the Conservative Party in February 1975 by mistake. In its first round of voting, most members of the 1922 Committee of MPs clearly wanted to rap Edward Heath over the knuckles after he had lost the two elections of 1974, but they did not want to overthrow him altogether. The easiest way to punish him seemed to be to vote for his rival, since it was clear that she had no chance of winning. It was a gesture only. But as they trooped back from registering their votes, the MPs realized, as they consulted each other, that most of them seemed to have made the same gesture. Mrs Thatcher won 130 votes, Heath only 119. He resigned at once. In the second round, when she stood against the Tory grandee William Whitelaw, her bandwagon swept her on to an easy victory.

David Wood, the political editor of *The Times*, who had triumphantly survived the long years of Harold Wilson's dislike, greeted Mrs Thatcher's victory of 11 February 1975 in prescient terms:

These are early days to assert that politics, in and outside Westminster, will undergo a radical change with the emergence of Mrs Thatcher. But there must be speculation, with Mr Heath's removal and her accession, about the direction that Conservatism will take from now on.

The *Sun*, inevitably, put it shorter and sharper.

MARGARET BY A MILE!

No doubt Mrs Thatcher and her colleagues will quickly work out what Thatcher-type Toryism is really about . . . what Tories really stand for. What is important to all of us is that they should once again be clearly seen to be standing for SOMETHING.

But at first she did not impress. She was defensive about the limitations in her knowledge and her lack of experience, and that made her more aggressive. Her weekly meetings with the Lobby as leader of the opposition could be bad-tempered affairs, if the correspondents pushed her on subjects she knew little about: principally Europe. The Lobby system might encourage tameness and lack of competition, and it might lay the political correspondents open to spoon-feeding; but as they sat on rows of uncomfortable little grey plastic chairs in their panelled tower room, overlooked by the boards which carried the names of past officers of the Lobby, they were a formidable group, and easily irritated if they disliked someone. At first, they disliked Margaret Thatcher because they did not think she was up to the job. They had never liked Edward Heath either, but at least they had had respect for him. It was well over a year before the Lobby as a whole began to warm to her. 'I didn't enjoy myself very much at those early meetings,' she once said privately. 'Everyone seemed so hostile.'

Even so, the hostility never seemed to spill over into the political reporting. The political correspondents did not feel it was their job to make judgements about her abilities, simply about her policies. When she was prime minister and Neil Kinnock was leader of the opposition the correspondents took broadly the same view. The editors, the columnists and the leader-writers could be brutal about him, but the day-to-day reporting, even in the *Sun*, was several degrees fairer than what appeared on the other pages of their newspapers.

In Margaret Thatcher's case, most editors and their proprietors supported her. So although many Conservative MPs were highly critical of her, their complaints and criticisms were rarely reflected in the political reporting. Soon, Margaret Thatcher showed her remarkable ability to learn, and her weekly appearances in the tower at the top of the stairs became smoother. Although she was not by nature a humorous woman, she found that they responded very well to the occasional lightly amusing comment, and some Lobby correspondents had the impression that she would prepare two or three before each session. And she knew how to charm them, too. She had a way of touching people lightly on the arm and looking into their eyes which could be very effective on a jaded middle-aged journalist.

In the House of Commons she made an impact from her very first appearance at Prime Minister's Questions. Harold Wilson made the mistake of assuming that the best way to treat her was to patronize her.

THE PRIME MINISTER: Some of us are rather old hands at these matters.
MRS MARGARET THATCHER: What the Prime Minister means is that he has been around for a long time – and it looks it.

Even some Labour MPs could not resist laughing. It appeared to be a contrast between two entirely different generations: a trim, good-looking woman in her forties, against a bent, elderly figure who was close to retirement. Few people stopped to reflect that Wilson was only nine years older than Thatcher.

Early on, as a minister in the Heath government, she had shown a dislike for television, and perhaps even a fear of it. This was fairly general among politicians at the time; but Mrs Thatcher understood that television was a medium she would have to master. And she was fortunate in the man who now began to advise her. Gordon Reece was a sharply dressed, rather dashing television producer, with a sharp wit and just the right looks and attitude to attract her. Reece's association with Mrs Thatcher, which brought him a knighthood and a good deal of money, happened through a chance recommendation. In the early

1970s the Conservative Party was looking for someone to act as editor for its election broadcasts, and Gordon Reece's name came up. They worked together during the two 1974 elections, and she turned to him when she staged her campaign for the Tory leadership in February 1975.

He encouraged her to soften her appearance, even though the Red Army newspaper in Moscow had just given her a lasting nickname by calling her 'The Iron Lady', which she naturally revelled in. A voice coach from the National Theatre was hired to help Mrs Thatcher to lower the timbre of her voice, and to lose some of the 1940s 'proper speaking' which she had learned as a lower-middle-class girl at Oxford. These efforts were only partly successful, but they helped.

Reece's strategy was to use the tabloids and the lighter programmes on radio and television to project a view of Mrs Thatcher which would appeal to housewives in Labour households. During the 1979 election campaign he was widely quoted as saying, 'You have to appeal to ordinary voters, who are not very interested in politics', which meant that image was more important than facts or political arguments. This was and remains clearly true. The Gordon Reece approach had a dramatic effect on the nature of political communications for the rest of the twentieth century. Saatchi & Saatchi's poster campaign for the Conservative Party, with the slogan 'Labour Isn't Working' over the photograph of a long dole queue (which was actually a line of volunteers from Hendon Young Conservatives), has often been credited with winning Mrs Thatcher the 1979 election. The agency was appointed by Gordon Reece.

§

There was a good deal of tone-adjustment going on in Britain at this time. Old-fashioned grandeur and high-mindedness were no longer required. Upper-class accents, faux or otherwise, were starting to be muted. This, it slowly became clear, was only part of a wider, more demotic change in the media generally. Newspapers were beginning to understand from the success of the *Sun* that sharper, fiercer, more downmarket journalism was needed. Hugh Cudlipp's decision to put the *Daily Mirror* on a higher plane, with longer and more explanatory articles about politics and world affairs, was shown to be a disastrous wrong turn. A quickening pace, a shortened attention span, a retreat from high seriousness: these were some of the defining characteristics of journalism in the last two decades of the twentieth century. Not long after the process became evident in the tabloids, it spread to television. In 1978 the average clip of interview in a television news bulletin lasted 24 seconds, and the average length of a reporter's statement to camera was 31 seconds. Ten years later the average interview would last 13 seconds and a piece to camera 18. People did not seem to want more information; instead, they seemed to want to be given information which was easier to absorb.

Mrs Thatcher first appeared on *Panorama* a year after her election as leader of the Conservative Party. She was still very uneasy in the presence of television cameras, and both before and after she was distinctly hostile to the journalists who ran the programme. Afterwards, the audience responses to the programme were not particularly favourable. The entries on the telephone log included phrases like 'much too stiff' and, more curiously, 'not very intelligent'. Gordon Reece realized he would have to do something about it. Roger Bolton, then a relatively junior *Panorama* producer, is quoted as saying

> Gordon Reece would ask what would be the colour of the set, would there be flowers – he thought that was necessary – what sort of chairs did we plan? Normally a party leader's press secretary would be wanting to know about the areas for questioning for the interview. But I suppose Gordon Reece was the first such person in British politics to do his job properly; he took what I would regard as the depressing view that the image was more important than the message . . .

Soon he took the equally depressing second step: that Mrs Thatcher would shine more if she appeared less on the grand, high-minded current affairs programmes and went on more relaxed, popular programmes presented by people who asked softer questions. In January 1977, for instance, she was the guest on *Jim'll Fix It* with Jimmy Savile. It was the best way to appeal to the aspiring working-class and lower-middle-class voters who she was starting to realize would vote her into power.

These were not her ideas; Gordon Reece, in particular, understood the nature of what he insisted on describing as 'the market' much better than she did. Nor did she prefer to shy away from tough questioning; on the contrary, she always enjoyed a probing interview, and as long as it was conducted politely she thought much better of the interviewer as a result. But Reece saw that if she expended all her effort on the serious current affairs programmes she would be addressing only the relatively small proportion of the population interested in the details of policy. Put her on *The Jimmy Young Show*, a radio programme specifically directed at housewives, get her filmed as she went shopping or mopped the floor, and it would be far better for what he called her 'persona' than sitting in a studio talking about the fine detail of policy. She was an intensely serious-minded woman to whom policy details were of the greatest importance, yet she did go shopping when the cameras weren't with her, and was well aware of the cost of things; so much so that she was one of the few political leaders who could not be floored if a reporter asked her on camera the price of a dozen eggs or a packet of cornflakes.

Jim Callaghan realized he had to match Mrs Thatcher's popular appeal in order to have any chance whatever in the coming election. Yet things were not looking quite as bad as they had a few months earlier. The agreement he had reached with the Liberals, the so-called Lib-Lab Pact, protected his minority government against sudden defeat in Parliament. Inflation was coming down to single figures. Callaghan agreed to go on *Nationwide*, a popular programme of regional news from around the whole of Britain, to answer viewers' questions. Jolly, avuncular, easy-going, Callaghan was at his best, and his opinion poll ratings were improving.

Callaghan benefited, too, from the broadcasting of Parliament. Big audiences tuned in to hear him speaking confidently and jovially, while Mrs Thatcher, from the opposition front bench, had to shout to make herself heard. The *Observer*'s television critic Clive James wrote in January 1978:

> The hang-up has always been the voice. Not the timbre so
> much as, well, the tone – the condescending explanatory
> whine which treats the squirming interlocutor as an eight
> year old child with learning deficiencies.

Gordon Reece and the voice coach had done their best, but it wasn't enough. Her advisers, who previously assumed that she would win the next election easily, now watched as Labour cut the Tory lead in the opinion polls, and even managed to ease ahead by 2 percentage points.

On the evening of 27 January 1978 she staged a controversial fight-back. She chose Granada Television's *World in Action* programme, the most assertive current affairs programme of its time, for a long interview. She and her advisers believed the programme's instincts were much too far to the left, but they realized that if she came out fighting against hostile questioning she would get maximum attention. It worked.

The interviewer was Gordon Burns, a presenter who moved back-wards and forwards between entertainment and regional news reporting. Burns had a reputation as a sharp, terrier-like interviewer, without the grand pretensions of several of the big London-based current affairs figures. It was a shrewd choice on *World in Action*'s part.

GORDON BURNS: Considerable controversy and confusion in recent weeks about [a] possible new get-tough Tory policy over immi-gration; threats that you may well make major cutbacks on the level of immigrants allowed into this country. If you do get to power how severely would you cut the numbers?

MARGARET THATCHER, PC, MP: [T]here was a committee which looked at it and said that if we went on as we are then by the end of the century there would be four million people of the new Commonwealth or Pakistan here. Now, that is an awful lot and I think it means that people are really rather afraid that this country might be rather swamped by people with a different culture . . .

Much of the huge political row which followed centred on her use of the word 'swamped'.

There was criticism from all sides, including some Conservative MPs. Mrs Thatcher realized it had been a mistake, and in the House of Commons she made a highly uncharacteristic retraction: '[T]he media raised it, not me. I have given my views and I have been bullied and intimidated.'

The press spokesmen at Conservative Central Office quickly began putting out a different version to the Lobby. Mrs Thatcher, they whispered, was inclined to make up policy as she went along. In this case, she was shooting from the hip. Some of this spin was reflected in the reporting.

It has been strongly suggested that the use of the word 'swamped' had been fully discussed and agreed with her advisers before the interview; it had been used as a deliberate tactic. Contrary to what her press officers said when they were under pressure, Mrs Thatcher hardly ever 'shot from the hip' on important matters of policy. She always memorized her brief thoroughly; since this was her answer to the first question Gordon Burns asked her, it seems scarcely likely that she would have wandered away from the agreed line right at the start of the interview.

But large numbers of letters of support for her line on immigration came in, many of them from traditional Labour supporters. Five weeks later, there was a by-election in North Ilford, an Essex constituency where the extremist National Front was expecting to do well on the immigration issue. Many Labour supporters voted Conservative, and the Tory candidate beat the Labour candidate (the young Tessa Jowell) by more than 4,000 votes. Mrs Thatcher's populism attracted plenty of disapproval, but it clearly worked.

§

By this point, the *Sun* was Mrs Thatcher's most ardent supporter. On election day, 3 May 1979, it urged people, in language that seemed strangely unimaginative and dull, to

VOTE TORY THIS TIME
This is D-Day. D for Decision.
The first day of the rest of our lives.

The Sun today particularly wishes to address itself to the traditional supporters of the Labour Party and to those people who have not hitherto had the opportunity to vote in a General Election.

It sounds as stilted as a kidnap victim reading out a statement; the journalist and writer Matthew Engel has suggested that the reason for the dullness of the writing was the *Sun*'s nervousness that, faced with the paper's appeal to Labour voters to defect, the print unions would react in some characteristically savage way. They did. The typesetting of the front page that night was sabotaged, and Scottish, Irish and Northern English editions were all heavily delayed. By the terms of the remarkably supine agreement the newspaper owners had signed with the all-powerful print unions, the *Sun* had to pay its workers double to do the job again, even though they were the ones who had done the damage. It was a system which Mrs Thatcher and Rupert Murdoch between them would smash in a few years' time.

What counted that bright spring morning, right across the country, was the memory that Jim Callaghan had failed to stop 'the winter of discontent'; the phrase was a Larry Lamb adaptation from Shakespeare, and before it became an inescapable political cliché, it appeared first in a *Sun* editorial. There was a good deal of doubt still about Margaret Thatcher's abilities, and much dislike of her nakedly partisan approach to domestic politics. But she was not a failure at dealing with the one thing most people seemed to care about: the overweening power of the unions.

And in some ways she was a tougher, more determined woman than she had been. On the afternoon of 30 March 1979, the day after Callaghan had called the election, her campaign manager Airey Neave MP was murdered by the INLA, a splinter group of the Provisional IRA. Neave was driving his car out of the House of Commons car park; as it started to mount the ramp an explosive device, attached to the underside of the car and primed to go off when it reached a certain angle, blew up and killed him.

He had been an important influence on Mrs Thatcher; she had been his pupil when she was a young barrister, and during this election campaign, which he had run for her, he had been her adviser and close friend. His murder was a serious blow. Characteristically, she came out fighting. On *Nationwide* that evening she seemed close to tears, but they were tears of anger as much as grief. 'Some devil has got him. They must never, never, never be allowed to triumph. They must never prevail.'

Northern Ireland was to make its mark on the entire course of Margaret Thatcher's years in power. Many of the intense rows she had with the media centred on Northern Ireland in one way or another, and almost all of them were with television, rather than the newspapers. In July 1979, her fury reached its zenith when the BBC's evening current affairs programme, *Tonight*, decided to interview a spokesman for the INLA about its campaign, including the murder of Airey Neave. The Northern Ireland secretary, Sir Humphrey Atkins, asked the BBC not to broadcast the interview, but the BBC's director general, Ian Trethowan, decided to reject his request.

Journalists from several newspapers had interviewed INLA spokesmen, but Mrs Thatcher was only really concerned with television. Gordon Reece had taught her well: television was a far more powerful medium than print journalism. Most British television journalists would probably share the view that their job is to provide their viewers with as wide a range of information as possible. If that involved interviewing a self-confessed member of an organization that commits murder, so be it. One BBC editor told the *Guardian*, 'We're in the business of telling people as much as we possibly can – not of trying to tell them less.' Margaret Thatcher and her supporters took an entirely opposing view. They saw themselves as being at war with the IRA, and believed it was rank treachery to want to interview the enemy.

The BBC, whose management was habitually more cautious than its programme-making staff, often took her attacks more seriously than, perhaps, they should have. Mrs Thatcher, like most successful political and business leaders, was something of a bully. She had much more time for people and organizations if they stood up to her, while people and organizations who bent the knee could expect trouble. After leaving the BBC Ian Trethowan wrote about the question of political pressure in his autobiography, *Split Screen*:

> I felt what was important was not whether someone tried to bring pressure on the BBC, but how we responded. To dismiss all pressure seemed to me as foolish as automatically to give way to it. Sometimes those exerting pressure had a legitimate point. On the other hand there were times when we were palpably being pressed to depart from an honest, truthful policy, and there we had to stand firm.

That is a wholly accurate statement of the position which any big, politically embattled news organization finds itself in; but since it is so subjective, it is not much help as a roadmap for getting out of trouble.

Trethowan was an instinctively cautious man, conservative in his political opinions, and a close personal friend of Edward Heath. He had joined the BBC in 1963 after a career in newspapers and at ITN, then became head of network radio and finally, in 1977, director general.

When Airey Neave's widow wrote a letter to the *Daily Telegraph* to say how hurtful the INLA interview had been to her, and how upset she was that the interviewee should have accused her husband of being a torturer, Trethowan wrote in his letter of reply that the BBC had clearly misjudged the interview's emotional impact. He defended his decision to broadcast it, but without much conviction. In a later interview he said: 'With the benefit of hindsight, was I wrong to allow the INLA interview to be broadcast? Almost certainly, yes.'

That modifier, 'almost certainly', was characteristic of Trethowan. He was essentially a committee man, pleasant and thoughtful, but he lacked any great toughness of character. Trethowan's five years as director general were marked by a pattern which was familiar from the BBC's history: the BBC's managers, who had usually themselves been pro-gramme makers and shared the desire to produce good, telling reports, would at first agree the project and help to make it a reality. But they, unlike the programme makers, also had the responsibility of protecting the BBC's long-term interests and prospects of survival; and if a major row erupted the executives could sometimes be tempted to back down and start apologizing. Working out where 'to stand firm', in Trethowan's phrase, became a matter of personal character. Not surprisingly, any government was likely to find a combination of hard-hitting programme making and pallid compliance infuriating and hard to deal with; especially when opinion poll after opinion poll showed that the licence-fee payers sympathized more with the BBC than with those who wanted to clip its wings.

§

The subject of Northern Ireland continued to generate poison between the broadcasters and the government, with Trethowan and other senior administrators caught in the middle.

Panorama had a new editor: Roger Bolton, who had been the editor of *Tonight* when it had interviewed the INLA spokesman. He was a deceptively gentle man with views that were impeccably middle-of-the-road, a powerful hatred of violence and terrorism, and an ability to inspire a team of journalists. Directly he settled in at the *Panorama* offices he announced that one of his priorities would be to cover the most important news story of the day in Britain: Northern Ireland. He sent

Jeremy Paxman, then a reporter, David Darlow, a producer, and a camera crew to Dublin, where they made contact with the Provisional Sinn Fein office there; it was still a legal entity. Soon afterwards the team received an anonymous phone call: they were told to drive to the village of Carrickmore, across the border into Northern Ireland. There were no more details.

When they got there, they saw ten masked IRA men stopping traffic at a roadblock they had set up. It was a rather ludicrous business, but it had a point: a few days before, the British army had announced that it had cleared out the Provisional IRA from the border area. The BBC team filmed the scene for half an hour, then drove away. The following day they reported the incident to the security authorities, and took the film back to London, where the lengthy process of editing and scripting began. It was not until three weeks later that the *Financial Times*, whose Dublin correspondent was married to someone who came from the area, carried a small report about it at the bottom of page 8.

Unlike most prime ministers, Margaret Thatcher did not read the newspapers. 'They're only full of the same old stuff, and sometimes they can be upsetting,' she once told a group of journalists. Her new press secretary, Bernard Ingham, an intemperate John Bull-like Yorkshireman, used to produce a daily digest of the papers for her; and on the morning of 8 November 1979 he included the paragraph in the *Financial Times* about Carrickmore. Mrs Thatcher exploded with rage when she read it. She assumed, as did many other politicians and journalists, that the *Panorama* team had set up the whole incident.

As tends to happen in such cases, no one troubled to investigate what had really happened. Mrs Thatcher assumed instantly that she knew, and when she was this angry scarcely any of her ministers felt inclined to tell her to calm down and think again. It was, said one, like facing up to Elizabeth I in a rage. And once Downing Street had started creating a fuss about something, the newspapers didn't feel the need to do their own investigating. They sheltered behind Thatcher's coat-tails; unwisely, in the case of the *Daily Telegraph*, which started embroidering its account by claiming that the *Panorama* team had colluded with the IRA in setting up the roadblock incident. Roger Bolton sued and won; it is unwise to assume that a prime minister motivated by an upsurge of anger is always trustworthy as a source.

However, the Conservative tabloids knew Mrs Thatcher liked it when they poured scorn on the BBC and on 9 November 1979, the *Daily Express* wrote:

> Whether the BBC Panorama team actually organised the IRA to take over the village of Carrickmore or merely accepted the terrorists' invitation to film them doing so is immaterial. What is crucial – and crystal clear – is that a BBC film team happily consorted with enemies of the British people. It is as if, during the Second World War, a BBC crew had gone to film Nazis occupying the Channel Islands.

In fact, if it had been possible in Beaverbrook's day for an *Express* reporter and photographer to land on the Channel Islands and report back on the activities of the Nazis there, of course they would have done.

On the left as on the right, nothing about the Carrickmore incident was allowed to be what it really was: a series of more-or-less unrelated, chance events. Mary Holland, a radical critic of British actions in Northern Ireland, put forward a Nationalist spin in the *New Statesman*:

> The row about Panorama should be seen for what it is – an attempt to divert popular attention from the uncomfortable truth about Northern Ireland which the security forces know well and the BBC's report just might have pinpointed – 13,000 soldiers are now engaged in fighting a force in the province which the Army itself estimates as numbering between 300 and 500, and they are not winning the war.

For both sides, Carrickmore had to be a conspiracy emblematic of something sinister and, somehow, morally wrong.

While Trethowan was recuperating from a mild heart attack, his deputy, Gerard Mansell, was acting director general in his place. Mansell treated the Carrickmore incident as a simple breach of internal instructions. The right people had not been notified, so someone's head must roll. He selected Roger Bolton, as *Panorama*'s editor, to be the sacrificial victim. Bolton was to be sacked, and moved sideways into an administrative job.

Many leading management figures in the BBC were furious and they signed an unprecedented petition demanding that Bolton should keep his job at *Panorama*. The National Union of Journalists, represented in BBC current affairs by the formidable figure of Vincent Hanna, himself a BBC reporter, made a similar demand. It worked. Bolton stayed at *Panorama* for another six months, and then became editor of *Nationwide*. In the longer run, his career progressed. That of John Gau, the head of current affairs, did not. When it came to appointing a new head of BBC1, he was overlooked.

The entire episode centred on a programme which was never made. The pictures of the Carrickmore incident were shelved. No law had been broken, and certainly not the laws relating to treason. But the BBC's nervousness had allowed Mrs Thatcher's personal anger, augmented by the often synthetic anger of her ministers and the newspapers which supported her, to dictate its programme policy. Worse, it had allowed the British government to influence the careers of some of its leading figures, on the questionable excuse that not all the BBC's internal consulting systems had been followed. This was timidity in the face of government interference; and it would lead to more trouble later.

§

In her early years as prime minister, Margaret Thatcher saw herself as a rebel, single-handedly leading a revolution. Even among her own ministers she knew she was potentially isolated, with few real supporters. The majority of them would certainly have preferred an easier, less confrontational existence, getting on with the business of quietly governing the country. But if they had, the essential job of turning the country around would not have happened. She was ferocious because she had to be: if they had not been scared of her, plenty of her ministers would have been glad to push her aside at some convenient point. She needed a coalition of support to keep her in power: front-benchers and back-benchers, whether sincere or not, but also a network of supporters in leading institutions, and of course in Fleet Street. There were dozens of ways in which she could keep the loyalty of such people.

The editors of newspapers that supported her could expect invitations to Downing Street and Chequers, private briefings, help with overseas business interests, and, of course, knighthoods; Thatcher honours were handed out with as notorious a partiality as Wilson honours. It was firmly believed in the BBC that with one or two exceptions like Robin Day, who was given a knighthood, Mrs Thatcher had laid it down that none of the usual honours should be handed out for long-serving BBC employees. Certainly, during her time as prime minister, scarcely any BBC people were honoured. If true, it certainly fitted her notorious lack of generosity towards those she disliked.

To those she liked, or thought would be useful to her, however, she could be remarkably generous, especially with honours; her biographer, John Campbell, prefers the word 'shameless'. Most of the newspaper editors who gave her their unquestioning devotion were knighted: Larry Lamb of the *Sun*, David English of the *Daily Mail*, Nick Lloyd of the *Daily Express*, John Junor of the *Sunday Express*. There was no doubt that the honours were doled out purely as a reward for services rendered. Mrs Thatcher wanted unconditional worship, not necessarily for its own sake but because it shored up her position. The *Sun*, the *Mail* and the *Express* were all prepared to suspend their instinctive independence and supply it to her in large doses.

The one newspaper baron she could not reward in this way was Rupert Murdoch. By 1985 he had become an American citizen, in order to qualify as the owner of a television channel in the United States. But, instead of a knighthood, Mrs Thatcher was able to reward him in ways that meant a great deal more to him, and which would bring him large amounts of money. In some fields, this might be regarded as corruption; but not in politics or in journalism, where it has always happened over the years.

Rupert Murdoch was altogether different from most of the newspaper magnates who dominated British journalism during the twentieth century. Most of them had big political ideas they were determined to propagate, using their newspapers and the influence they had over public opinion and the political elite. Sometimes, as with Rothermere's *Daily Mail* in the late 1930s, the ideas threatened to damage the paper's commercial position. Murdoch's commercial position, by contrast, dictated the political ideas his editors were obliged to follow. There were general trends to Murdoch's political thinking, and they shifted further to the right as the years went on; but it was always clear that his papers would support whatever line Murdoch thought would help his group's profits.

As a result, Murdoch worked assiduously at creating a legend around himself and his media empire: that he was a king-maker. In reality, he simply sided with the candidate he assumed would win, and claimed the victory afterwards. The support of the Murdoch press would be offered only to those who had no real need of it. Mrs Thatcher won three elections to the accompaniment of loud support from the *Sun* and the other Murdoch newspapers (though she received least support in the most difficult election of the three, that of 1979); yet there is no doubt that she would have won all of them, even if Murdoch had, unthinkably, decided to come out against her. It was a conjuring trick; and as with most successful conjuring tricks, it succeeded because the audience decided to believe in it.

What Rupert Murdoch offered Mrs Thatcher was not just the loud support of his newspapers at election time: it was a constant, day-by-day flow of political propaganda in support of her approach and ideas, always loud and sometimes abusive, which masqueraded as news reporting. And the price Mrs Thatcher was willing to pay in return for this service was her agreement to allow Murdoch's business interests to thrive, without too much interference from the watchdogs whose job it was to protect the public against the concentration of control in the hands of media barons. This process reached one of its most questionable points in 1981, when the Canadian press baron Lord Thomson decided he could no longer afford to keep *The Times* and the *Sunday Times* afloat.

As Murdoch was the owner of two of Britain's best-selling newspapers, the *News of the World* and the *Sun*, his bid for *The Times* and the *Sunday Times* should have been cleared by the Monopolies Commission. Instead, the newly appointed trade secretary, John Biffen, decided that after the recent printers' strikes, which had affected both papers, they were not profitable. This was literally true at the time, but it did not take into account the fact that the *Sunday Times* was potentially a strong money-maker. It is unclear precisely who arranged things so that Murdoch's acquisition of *The Times* and the *Sunday Times* went through; but somebody certainly did.

Murdoch's success now gave him huge power, but it was not unprecedented. Lord Northcliffe had owned even more high-selling British newspapers: in the twelve years from 1896 to 1908 they included the *Daily Mail*, the *Sunday Despatch* (Britain's largest-circulation Sunday newspaper before the First World War), the *Daily Mirror*, the *Observer*, *The*

Times and the *Sunday Times*. But in 1990, during her last months in power, Mrs Thatcher again gave Murdoch an extraordinary gift to add to those he already had: the right to control satellite television broadcasting in Britain. In November, a matter of days before she resigned as prime minister, British Sky Broadcasting was formed by merging Murdoch's Sky Television with British Satellite Broadcasting – again, without reference to the Monopolies Commission, even though this gave Murdoch an unprecedentedly dominant position in the British media, greatly beyond anything Northcliffe had achieved. Once more, the rules had been skilfully evaded. British society and the political system were far less confident and strong than they had been in the early part of the twentieth century and Murdoch was able to use his newspapers not simply to influence British politics in the way he chose, but also to change society.

And not for the better. The *Sun*, in particular, had as clear an effect on British public discourse as it did on the noisy sexuality which was becoming more and more evident in British society. During the Thatcher years, the *Sun* turned coarse insults into the everyday language of political argument. Yet because she saw only what she wanted to see, Mrs Thatcher had no real idea of the true nature of the Murdoch effect. On a day-by-day basis, all she knew of the newspapers came from the brief press reviews Bernard Ingham prepared for her. He left out all details about the *Sun*'s non-political preoccupations. She knew about page 3, of course, but in spite of her strong dislike of indecency in any form, she preferred not to investigate. After a period of uncertainty about the course it should take, the *Daily Mirror* decided to follow the same route. The culture of soft porn, hard politics and celebrity gossip began to seep into the life of the country. And Margaret Thatcher, who disapproved of much of the *Sun*'s culture, encouraged it to happen.

The strange thing was that when Mrs Thatcher left office, although his newspapers grieved for her political passing, Murdoch himself seems to have paid it little attention. The man who had been able to see her or call her on the phone any time he wanted, who had been invited to spend Christmas with the Thatchers at Chequers several times, and who had attended various intimate family celebrations over the years in the position of a personal friend rather than a political ally, seems to have had little to do with her once she was out of power. Mrs Thatcher replied to this coldness with a silence of her own. In her memoirs his name is not even mentioned once. She had delivered British journalism and the British media to him on a plate; yet only three years later she had completely written him out of her life.

§

No one forecast the decision by the Argentine junta to invade the Falklands: not the SIS, not the CIA, not the Chilean secret service, and certainly not the British media. Argentina, like the rest of Latin America, was a blind spot for British journalism, and there was a submerged sense in every London newsroom that nothing seriously affecting British interests was likely to come out of it.

Small wars have small causes. A group of scrap-metal workers landed on South Georgia, a dependency of the Falklands, and raised the Argentine flag. They were observed by a British scientist who happened to be taking observations at the time. He alerted his base, who told Port Stanley, who told the Foreign Office.

The British government ordered the Royal Navy's Antarctic Survey ship *Endurance* to head for South Georgia with a detachment of Marines and two helicopters, in order to put pressure on the scrap-metal men to get permission for what they were doing from the British Antarctic Survey station nearby. The Argentine government, which had believed the British would simply stand by if Argentina took over the Falklands, now decided that this was part of a British military response.

In the early hours of 31 March 1982 the junta took the decision to send an armada of Argentine ships to the Falklands. A little over twenty-four hours later the captains of the various ships were told that their mission was to capture the islands. It took President Reagan a long time to raise President Galtieri in the Casa Rosada in Buenos Aires. He warned Galtieri that the invasion was not a good idea. 'You don't know her,' he was later reported as saying; 'she's a very difficult woman.'

The British government knew from intelligence sources directly the Argentine fleet set sail, and they guessed exactly where it was heading. As Mrs Thatcher's team of advisers gathered in the prime minister's office there was a good deal of gloom. Everyone knew that public opinion would demand that the government should try to retake the islands, and they were all aware of the considerable problems involved.

The distances were worryingly disproportionate: the Falklands were only 300 miles from Argentina, but they were 8,000 miles from Britain, and there were no regional bases whatever from which the British could operate. This meant that the task force would not have adequate air cover; the British would be able to deploy a maximum of 34 Harrier jump-jets, as against Argentina's 220 jet fighters, all of which could use their own bases. An article published soon afterwards in the United States Naval Institute Press stated with some certainty that it was a military impossibility for the British task force to succeed in retaking the islands.

The newspapers knew nothing of the meeting at the prime minister's office but they had already decided what was going to happen. On 3 April 1982, the *Sun* carried a picture of a hand grenade looking rather like a penguin and the words

BATTLE FOR THE ISLANDS

and, beside it, the huge headline

IT'S WAR!
Falklands seized
Three-hour battle
We'll strike back

Mrs Thatcher's first instincts, and those of most if not all of her Cabinet colleagues, were to make a fight of it. Her military chiefs, sharing the same views and knowing, too, that she did not appreciate too much caution at a time like this, all demonstrated a can-do attitude. They assured her that they could assemble a task force and retake the islands. The *Daily Mail* agreed, and it understood the dangers that the situation presented for Margaret Thatcher.

> Forcing Argentina to disgorge the Falklands is a bloody, hazardous and formidable enterprise. It can be done. It must be done. And Mrs Thatcher is the only person who can do it . . . If she flinches, if this bold venture fizzles out in vainglorious bathos, Margaret Thatcher, her Government, and the Tory Party will be sunk.

The *Daily Mirror* and the *Guardian* were the least enthusiastic about the war. The *Guardian*, in particular, was inclined to be rather patronizing about the whole affair. On Saturday 3 April it called it 'a sorry little episode', and said it had 'heavy comic opera overtones': a view that has tended to persist to this day on the left and in other countries – particularly the United States.

It took the *Guardian* until the following Monday, when it had been decided to gather an invasion fleet together, to remember that the Argentine junta was 'an altogether heinous regime' and to decide that, although 'it is natural to wish General Galtieri the bloodiest of bloody noses', it was still nervous. As in the Boer War, as in 1914, the *Guardian* was reluctant and worried, but in the C.P. Scott tradition, since British lives were at stake and the *Guardian* had decided that the enterprise was just, it would support it; but not enthusiastically. The *Mirror* seemed unwilling to support it at all. Its editorial was called

Might Isn't Right

and advised that

> [T]he main purpose of British policy now should be to get the best possible settlement for the islanders. We could probably throw the Argentines out of the Falklands, but for how long? Is Britain willing to spend hundreds of millions of pounds to keep in the area an army, navy and air force strong enough to repel any future invasions?

Not for the first time, the *Mirror* misread the public mood, and its stand on the war lost it tens of thousands of readers, while the newspapers on the right found that noisy support for the enterprise added hundreds of thousands of readers. The *Sun* gauged the mood a great deal better. But it added its own twist as well: the effete upper classes had failed the country. It was now up to 'men of iron' to surround the Iron Lady.

And so that Monday morning, when Britain was faced with a military challenge from a far-right South American dictatorship which had terrorized its own people and bled the country white with its corruption, the *Sun*'s editorial was an attack largely directed at the Foreign Office – no doubt in case it pressed for a negotiated settlement.

> Since the days of Chamberlain, it has been a safe haven for
> the appeasers. ITS CODE has been that of the Old Etonians
> and playing the game. ITS PHILOSOPHY has been: Never
> rock the boat. Never offend foreigners . . .

The *Sun*, which was already the most assertive newspaper in Britain,
identified the recovery of the Falklands as the issue on which it would
finally establish its dominance. Sensing its power, and the support it was
getting from Mrs Thatcher, it became louder and more aggressive than
ever. On Tuesday 6 April it wrote:

> The ailing Daily Mirror, which tried to pretend that there
> was no threat to the Falklands until the invaders had
> actually landed, now whines that we should give in to force
> and obligingly resettle the islanders. But our whole experi-
> ence with dictators has taught us that if you appease them,
> in the end you have to pay a far greater price.

'At home the worms are already coming out of the woodwork,' the *Sun*
added. The violently expressed, humiliating insult was now the paper's
weapon of choice. The following day, Wednesday the 7th, the *Sun* used
it again, with even more personal force. 'Out of the woodwork, like the
political termite he is, crawls No. 1 Left-winger Tony Benn to demand
the evacuation of the Falkland islanders.'

There is a menace to this, which represents a significant change in
the tone of public discourse in Britain. Not even the *Daily Mail* referred
to people it disagreed with as insects who deserved, presumably, to be
stamped on and killed; in the past that had been the kind of thing that
was associated with Communist or Fascist regimes. Until the 1970s, at
least, Britain prided itself on its calmness at times of stress, and on a tone
of politeness; these were characteristics which had come to be regarded,
at home and abroad, as typically British. It was foreigners who screamed
insults and abused each other in their newspapers; the British weren't like
that. Now the Murdoch press had finally put paid to such outmoded
conventions. They were the kind of things that Old Etonians clung to.
Playing the game was finished.

§

Given that the entire Falklands campaign was such an extraordinary success, it is easy to forget how nervous everyone intimately involved in it was. With hindsight, the British government, the Ministry of Defence and the Royal Navy, in particular, threw away opportunity after opportunity to present themselves well to the world. Mrs Thatcher explained why only British correspondents were allowed to travel with the task force: 'We certainly didn't want any foreigners reporting what we were doing down there!'

Such blinkered judgements ensured that one of the best-conducted wars of the century, carried out with textbook precision, would be regarded as petty and rather comic for ever after.

When the twenty-nine British journalists, photographers and cameramen who were selected to cover the expedition went aboard their ships, they came across an atmosphere of suspicion and outdated etiquette (they were told to bring dark suits with them, presumably for when they dined in the wardroom) which most of them found foolish and stifling.

They also faced a good deal of quiet hostility. Michael Nicholson of ITN, whose experience of war and world affairs was considerable, wrote afterwards that the feeling on board was that the press would always do the dirty because it was their instinct to do so. Brian Hanrahan, the BBC correspondent whose calm and balanced reporting would soon be accorded enormous respect, was not allowed to see the captain when he went aboard HMS *Hermes*. The ship's education officer was to be his liaison instead. Hanrahan and his colleagues were, however, eventually invited to a briefing with Admiral Sandy Woodward, who was in command of the task force, at which 'they would be told what they should and should not report'. It was, perhaps, just a figure of speech; but for the admiral to presume to tell journalists what they should report, as though they were sailors under his command, went down extremely badly.

Even by the arcane standards of the Royal Navy, this seems like a wholly unsuitable approach. Admiral Woodward seems to have been prepared to consider the possibility that some of the journalists reporting on the expedition were deliberately hostile. In some ways the Falklands campaign, brilliant though it was in military terms, showed the whole system at its worst: naive, sheltered from the real world, and lacking in self-confidence for anything except the job in hand. Perhaps, on consideration, it was better that no foreign journalists were allowed to follow the task force after all.

Some of this was endemic, and some was generated by the anxiety of the moment. In Britain and abroad, there was considerable scepticism about the likelihood that the task force could succeed. When Admiral Lord Hill-Norton was quoted in the *Financial Times* as saying he did not think a blockade of the Falklands would necessarily risk British casualties, it sounded like an attempt to keep spirits up at home. Inevitably, when their sources were gloomy, defence correspondents were likely to be gloomy too. Geoffrey Archer, the usually impeccably accurate correspondent of ITN, suggested on air that 'The decision of what to do when the fleet arrives is desperately difficult.'

He added that any attempt to recapture the islands could cause colossal loss of life. Christopher Wain, Archer's opposite number at the BBC, who as a former soldier had a considerable understanding of the capabilities of the weaponry used in the war – something that many journalists lacked – doubted whether it was really a good idea to interview so many former senior officers. But the three weeks that it took for the task force to sail down to the islands was an interminable time for the press and broadcasters, who felt obliged to speculate endlessly about what might happen at the other end of the journey. There was no doubt that this was what audiences and readers wanted. The sale of newspapers and the audiences for radio and television news programmes shot up; and in the absence of any combat and any hard facts, speculation filled the gap.

It was something of a relief, therefore, when the task force arrived in the South Atlantic and a new phase of the war began. It was on Saturday 1 May, when British Harrier jets made their first attacks on Argentine positions on the Falklands, that Brian Hanrahan got round the reporting restrictions with the lapidary sentence 'I'm not allowed to say how many planes joined the raid, but I counted them all out and I counted them all back.'

When Hanrahan's recorded voice-track was played by satellite from the South Atlantic into the BBC newsroom in London, the subeditors, producers and correspondents who heard it broke into spontaneous applause. His wording was the most elegant way imaginable around the official prohibitions; and there was general relief at the news that the British planes were unscathed.

THE SUN SAYS
Dare call it treason
There are traitors in our midst.

So wrote 'The Paper That Supports Our Boys' on 7 May 1982. The treason was not, as the innocent reader might have expected, that someone had betrayed some key detail of the Falklands task force to Buenos Aires. It was something that the patrician broadcaster Peter Snow, grandson of a general and the son of a senior army officer, had said on the BBC's *Newsnight* programme. Speaking off the cuff about Argentine claims to have caused British losses which the British authorities had not announced, he went on: 'Until the British are demonstrated either to be deceiving us or to be concealing losses from us, we can only tend to give a lot more credence to the British version of events.'

It could have been expressed more carefully, perhaps; but it was the sense that Peter Snow was speaking from a neutral rather than a British viewpoint that enraged Margaret Thatcher, the *Sun*, and a few dozen viewers. The belief that in time of conflict the entire country must be compelled to echo noisy patriotic sentiments or keep quiet was a survival from the period of total war in the first half of the twentieth century. But Britain was not in a state of total war against Argentina – it would have been ludicrous to suggest such a thing – and there was a small but very definite section of opinion in Britain which disliked the Falklands War; partly, perhaps, because of the exaggeratedly chauvinistic views of the *Sun*, the *Daily Express* and the *Daily Mail*.

The *Sun* editorial continued:

> We regard the freedom of opinion and speech as among our most ancient and precious rights. But with rights go responsibility and a duty to one's country. What is it but treason to talk on TV as Peter Snow talked, questioning whether the Government's version of the sea battles was to be believed? . . . A British citizen is either on his country's side – or he is the enemy.

This is foolish stuff, of course; the editorial is trying to make out that in a democracy if you do not support your government you are a traitor.

But it eventually becomes clear what the real purpose of all this is: attacking the BBC, of course, and shouting Margaret Thatcher's praise, certainly – but at the core it is something even closer to the proprietor's heart: scoring points against the *Sun*'s commercial rival, the *Daily Mirror*: 'What is it but treason for this timorous, whining publication to plead day after day for appeasing the Argentine dictators . . . We are truly sorry for the *Daily Mirror*'s readers.'

Despite this distasteful commercialism posing as national sentiment, it was the *Sun* whose coverage dominated the war. Not through its reporting, which was derivative and highly forgettable, not through its editorials, which were too savage to be worth remembering, but through the vibrant simplicity and force of its front pages, which have remained in the national memory when so much about the war itself is starting to fade. They genuinely represented the gut feelings of almost everyone in Britain who supported the enterprise – whether or not they would have admitted it, then or later.

STICK IT UP YOUR JUNTA
Britain sinks latest Haig plan for peace

– 20 April

HIGH NOON
Britain set to shoot Argies out of the sky

– 29 April

OUR DARKEST HOUR
24 die as jets blitz two ships

– 27 May

And of course the headline that only appeared on the front of the paper's first edition:

GOTCHA
Our lads sink gunboat and hole cruiser

– 4 May

It is often regarded as an example of the crassest brutality; yet the subheading shows that at the time of the paper's first edition it was thought that the *Belgrano* had merely been hit by the nuclear submarine HMS *Conqueror*: 'The ship was not sunk and it is not clear how many casualties there were.'

Roy Greenslade, who was assistant editor of the *Sun* at the time, maintains that the *Sun*'s editor Kelvin MacKenzie changed the headline to

DID 1,200 ARGIES DIE?

for later editions. Greenslade also said that Rupert Murdoch wanted to keep the 'Gotcha' headline even after it was known that there had been large loss of life, but MacKenzie insisted on dropping it. Nevertheless in after-years, perhaps in order to maintain his reputation, MacKenzie insisted that the fact that so many Argentinians had died was 'a bloody good thing'. He had never, he said, lost a moment's sleep over it.

The loss of life on board the *Belgrano* was not quite as terrible as at first thought – the Argentines put it at 378 out of a total crew of 1,042 – but it was still a shocking end to the comic opera view of the war. And though the decision of HMS *Conqueror* to fly the skull and crossbones when she returned to her home port of Faslane created considerable anger in Argentina, it was the kind of thing the *Sun* would have approved of.

Some of the best reporting of the war was done by Max Hastings of the *Evening Standard*, whose march into Port Stanley at the end was an act of derring-do which matched anything by the great war correspondents of the earlier part of the century. Perhaps the best single despatch was that of Michael Nicholson of ITN. His account of the sinking of a British ship attacked by Argentine fighters on Wednesday 9 June was printed in the next day's *Daily Express* under the headline

TRAGEDY OF SIR GALAHAD
'I vouch it was a day of extraordinary heroism'

[T]he Royal Navy Sea King and Wessex helicopter pilots and their crews ignored the flames. They ignored the explosions and ignored the ammunition erupting around them, and they flew their machines into the smoke to lift the queues of men waiting calmly. I watched one pilot steer his machine slowly and deliberately into the black smoke and hover. He was completely blinded, completely enveloped. I saw his crewman winching down to pick a man out of the sea. Three times I saw him go down: three times he brought men up through the blackness.

The Falklands War was a brilliantly fought campaign. But it was sullied by the foolish and intemperate accusations of treason by newspapers and politicians for anyone who disagreed with them. Worse, the government and in particular the Ministry of Defence failed to understand that proper facilities for good and effective reporting would have achieved much better results around the world. The Ministry of Defence understood the extent of the public relations disaster it had helped to create; and soon it began to improve its practices. Slowly, the Edwardian-seeming admirals and captains would eventually be made to understand that journalists didn't have to be enemies; they could even be rather useful.

§

After the Falklands, the *Sun* was Margaret Thatcher's heavy artillery. Her press spokesman, Bernard Ingham, had impressed on her that this was the newspaper which spoke most effectively to the conservative-minded working-class people whom she wanted to vote for her. The *Daily Mail*, providing her with support which was just as intemperate, addressed middle-class voters who had nowhere else to go. But the *Sun* could bring new people to her cause in large numbers.

At first, it was not hard. Labour had seemed determined to destroy itself over Europe and other issues, and the more timid middle-of-the-road MPs in the Parliamentary Labour Party, assuming that in the new Thatcherite era it would swing sharply to the left, ignored common sense and voted for Michael Foot, charming but elderly and unelectable, as the Party's leader to replace Jim Callaghan in 1980. In the election of June 1983, Labour, under Foot's leadership, was annihilated. But when Neil Kinnock replaced Foot as leader a few months later, Labour immediately appeared more formidable. In the wake of the Falklands War Mrs Thatcher was unbeatable, yet Neil Kinnock represented a genuine long-term threat; and the *Sun* went to work on him.

Kinnock often helped the process himself. On the day he was elected Labour leader, he went for a walk with his wife Glenys on the foreshore at Brighton for the benefit of the photographers, and was unlucky enough to fall over: something he never really forgave himself for. On 3 October 1983, under a photograph of Kinnock measuring his length on the Brighton shingle, was a report by the *Sun*'s political editor, Trevor Kavanagh. Kavanagh was a thoughtful and usually fair-minded man in the Lobby tradition, who was becoming an important figure in the paper's policy-making. He reported Kinnock's embarrassment amusingly but without any obvious animus.

SPLASH HIT!

Fiery Welshman Neil Kinnock made a splash hit with Labour yesterday. Whizz-kid Neil became the party's youngest-ever leader – on a day when he ran into a few problems too. Mr Kinnock walked it in the leadership stakes, by taking 71 per cent of the vote. But he failed to walk on the water when he took a stroll on the seafront at Brighton.

No newspaper writer would have done anything less. Kavanagh's story could have appeared in the *Mirror*, or, with some of the adjectives stripped out, in the *Guardian*. On the inside pages, though, the atmosphere was poisonous. This was where the editor, Kelvin MacKenzie, delivered his attack on Labour and the new threat to Margaret Thatcher which Kinnock seemed to pose. There were three stills of Kinnock's embarrassing fall side by side, captioned according to an ancient newspaper convention 'GOING ... GOING ... GONE', and an article that went:

Labour kicks off the conference with a new bust-up over the bomb
STILL ALL AT SEA

New Labour leader Neil Kinnock was swamped by a tidal wave of Left-wing fury last night ... as he shivered from a ducking in the sea.

> Mr Kinnock, who was soaked while posing for photographs on Brighton beach, was dramatically gagged in a row over defence policy ... In a contemptuous slap in the face for the Welsh golden boy, outgoing party chairman Sam McCluskie refused to call him to speak before the ballot was taken ...
>
> The vote means that Mr Kinnock is now saddled with a defence policy he is certain could lose Labour the next election just as it helped them lose to Mrs Thatcher in June.

Not a single phrase of this was entirely accurate. The atmosphere on the Left at Labour's Brighton conference was one of resignation and gloom, not fury. Hours after the trivial incident on the beach, he was certainly not shivering. He had not had a ducking in the sea, nor was he soaked: a wave had wet his legs. He was not gagged, dramatically or otherwise; the defence policy which was approved was certainly not what he wanted, but he abstained on it rather than voting against it. He knew, as did every political correspondent reporting on the conference, that things had changed inside the Labour Party after the election defeat that June. From now on the policies of the far Left would slowly be junked, and by the next election Kinnock would be able to fight on the kind of policies which would make Labour potentially electable.

But this article was not a piece of reportage, seeking to explain to the *Sun*'s readers what was going on inside the Labour Party; it was little more than propaganda, to tell them that even though Kinnock might look attractive and more electable, nothing had changed and the Left was just as powerful as it always had been. It was characteristic of the approach of the paper's second editor, Kelvin MacKenzie. Far more aggressive and openly right wing than his predecessor, Larry Lamb, MacKenzie created an atmosphere in which *Sun* reporters felt free to make up stories altogether if they seemed to be good ones. After the Falklands War there was an entirely invented interview with the Welsh Guardsman Simon Weston, who was badly disfigured in an Argentine attack. In an edition of the *Sun* which appeared on 1 March 1984, the day of the Chesterfield by-election in which the left-winger Tony Benn was standing, there was a story headlined

BENN ON THE COUCH

which quoted a well-known American psychiatrist as saying that Benn was insane, and discussing various supposed symptoms which he had exhibited. The psychiatrist quickly attacked the article and called the claims in it 'absurd'. Benn won the by-election. In January 1987 MacKenzie ran a story on the front page which accused the singer Elton John of having sex with rent boys. Not long afterwards the *Sun* accused him of having the voice boxes of his guard dogs surgically removed because they had kept him awake at night. It was hard to see why MacKenzie would launch attacks like these on a well-known figure, apparently at random, without even checking whether they were true. (When the *Sun*'s reporter went to Elton John's house the guard dogs barked ferociously.) At the time, other journalists attributed these things to a sense that with Murdoch and Thatcher backing the *Sun*, it could say and do anything it chose.

Most proprietors, faced with an editor who seemed at times to be completely out of control, would have sacked him because of the damage he was doing to the group's reputation. But for Murdoch, all that seemed to count was that the *Sun* was putting on readers. He rather liked MacKenzie, and gave him his continuing support. Certainly the fact that the *Sun* was given to publishing stories that weren't true did not seem to worry him overmuch. His own attitude to truth could be fairly semi-detached. In April 1983, the *Sunday Times* was preparing to publish Hitler's supposed diaries when the paper's editor, Frank Giles, discovered that Lord Dacre, the expert employed to verify the authenticity of the diaries, was starting to have his doubts about them. Giles contacted Murdoch, who famously answered, 'Fuck Dacre. Publish them.' Kelvin MacKenzie could not have expressed it better.

MacKenzie certainly did not introduce brutality and coarseness into Fleet Street, but he took it to new levels. Peter Chippindale and Chris Horrie, in their book about the *Sun, Stick It Up Your Punter!*, quote him as describing the typical *Sun* reader like this:

> He's the bloke you see in the pub, a right old fascist, wants to send the wogs back, buy his poxy council house, he's afraid of the unions, afraid of the Russians, hates the queers and the weirdos and drug dealers. He doesn't want to hear about that stuff.

'That stuff' being serious news. MacKenzie may have been right, but 'the right old fascist' he identified as his archetypal reader didn't necessarily vote Conservative at all. As James Curran and Jean Seaton point out in their book *Power Without Responsibility*, only 40 per cent of the *Sun*'s readers supported the Conservatives in the 1987 election. A generation later, Britain has moved on, and even in the pub the most avid *Sun* reader is more careful on many of these issues. Nor is the *Sun* racist or homophobic in the way it was in the 1980s. It has mellowed; and it is not, as a result, the force it once was under MacKenzie.

§

Rupert Murdoch changed the character of every single newspaper he bought; even the *News of the World*. When he met the senior staff there he told them, 'I didn't come all this way not to interfere.' One of the paper's editors is quoted by Curran and Seaton as saying, 'He would come into the office and literally rewrite leaders which were not supporting the hard Thatcherite line.'

And this was on a newspaper which absolutely no one read for its editorials. One of the main conditions on which he was allowed to buy *The Times* and the *Sunday Times* was that there should be strict guidelines set out in articles of association which guaranteed editorial freedom for the papers; these guidelines were to be policed by independent directors. Murdoch complied, to the extent that he never gave Frank Giles, the editor of the *Sunday Times*, a direct editorial instruction. He didn't need to. According to Giles, 'Murdoch, the paper spread out before him, would jab his fingers at some article and contribution and snarl, "What do you want to print rubbish like that for?" or, pointing to the byline of a correspondent, assert that "That man's a Commie."'

Under the fourteen-year editorship of Harold Evans, from 1967 to 1981, the *Sunday Times* was arguably the best newspaper in Britain, with some of the finest investigative journalists in the world on its staff. Directly Rupert Murdoch took it over, it started to become a different paper and over the years that followed many senior journalists chose to leave. Evans himself went to edit *The Times* in place of William Rees-Mogg, but he had such a torrid time there, with Murdoch breathing down his neck, that he only lasted a year.

His replacement at the *Sunday Times* was Andrew Neil, a thirty-four-year-old Scot, who was appointed in preference to the political columnist Hugo Young, whom a number of people on the paper's staff would have preferred. Neil would later mellow greatly, both in his attitudes and his politics; but in his early years as editor he was feared and disliked. He made no secret of his impatience with those from public school and Oxbridge backgrounds. Life was made deliberately unpleasant for anyone who did not easily fit in with the new system.

Neil, with Murdoch's enthusiastic backing, turned the *Sunday Times* into a strong supporter of Margaret Thatcher's policies. During the miners' strike of 1984–5 Neil regularly tried to persuade the paper's labour correspondent, Donald Macintyre, to write more favourably about the way the National Coal Board and the government were handling the dispute. Macintyre eventually left.

Every proprietor has the right to make his newspaper toe whatever line he chooses; it is one of the fundamental conditions of the system. The problem with the *Sunday Times* and *The Times* was that their standards declined as a result.

The Times in particular did not always seem to be properly independent in the years after Murdoch took it over, and its proprietor's political and commercial interests often seemed to impinge on its coverage. The distinguished foreign correspondent Robert Fisk, who worked for *The Times* in Northern Ireland and moved on to the Middle East, resigned from it in 1988 after he claimed that a controversial report he wrote about the shooting down of an Iranian Airbus by an American warship that year had been censored for political reasons.

Nevertheless there is another case to be made about Murdoch's control of *The Times*. When Lord Thomson put *The Times* and the *Sunday Times* up for sale, Murdoch's was the only bid which convincingly proposed keeping both papers alive. If any of the other would-be buyers had taken them over, the loss-making *Times* would almost certainly have been quietly ditched. Murdoch ensured that it survived and prospered. It might not have the quiet, almost somnolent authority it had before Murdoch came along, but it has remained an effective and thoroughly readable newspaper.

Most important of all, Murdoch used *The Times* as a battering ram to break down the power of the print unions. That power, cynically used, threatened to suck the life out of the entire national newspaper industry in Britain. Print workers were some of the best-paid employees in the country, often working such short hours that dozens of them, perhaps more, doubled as taxi drivers. There were many cases where union members staged ruinously expensive lightning strikes because they disagreed with something in that night's newspaper copy. Their power ensured that British newspapers were some of the last in Europe to use the wasteful, slow, labour-intensive linotype method, rather than being composed electronically.

The move by *The Times* to Wapping in 1986 was made possible by a carefully planned deceit, with Murdoch fooling the unions into thinking he was planning to start up a London evening paper, to be printed in Wapping. The printing works he built there was in fact big enough to produce all Murdoch's titles. He had secretly bought and installed the machinery to do the job, and had reached agreement with the electricians' union, the EETPU, for it to be manned by them rather than by the print unions.

When the printers went on strike, on 24 January 1986, the machines at Wapping went into production. By the time the dispute ended, just over a year later, on 5 February 1987, 1,000 people had been arrested in the daily and nightly picketing, and in the attacks on the armoured coaches which took people in and out of the Wapping site. More than 400 police officers and at least 100 civilians were injured. It was just as fiercely divisive as the miners' strike had been, though there was a great deal less public sympathy for the printers, whose actions over the years had been purely destructive. Yet many journalists found it hard to sympathize with Murdoch; and once it started to become clear that he would win in the long run, there was a distinct feeling of revulsion for him and his methods – even though journalists were the chief bene-ficiaries. The *Observer* refused to employ freelance subeditors who worked for *The Times*, and individual editors and reporters at ITN and the BBC often preferred not to interview *Times* experts for their reports.

Yet there was no doubt that by smashing the print unions Murdoch had given British newspaper journalism a new lease of life. At a time when newspapers were on the decline in America, they were facing a new period of success in Britain. On 7 October 1986 a new title, the *Independent*, was launched. For some years it had the reputation of being the best newspaper in Britain. It benefited, as every other London newspaper did, from the new conditions that Murdoch's battle with the unions had created. And it managed to recruit reporting and editorial staff from the Murdoch papers – men and women who did not want to be part of his crusade or face the poisonous atmosphere on the picket lines each day. This was scarcely a positive achievement for Murdoch, but it was part of the changes he wrought. So was the fact that there were just as many newspapers at the end of the century as there had been in 1950, and not all that many fewer than there had been in 1900. Although Murdoch did his best at times to kill off the opposition, in the ruthless fashion of the worst nineteenth- and twentieth-century press barons, he was also responsible for saving it.

19

WARS WITHOUT END

The correspondent who wrote the lead story in the *Daily Mail* of 20 November 1990 seemed to have no doubt:

MAGGIE: I'LL WIN IT IN ONE

> Mrs Thatcher stands poised to reassert her leadership of the Tory Party by a decisive first ballot margin, her campaign managers believed last night. They estimated that they had enough support among 40 'waverers' to give her a clear victory this evening, avoiding a result which would leave her a lame duck.

The Comment column alongside was a great deal darker and less confident:

> [T]he plotters in her own party in London are nerving themselves to replace her in a Palace of Westminster coup . . .
>
> House of Commons convention would have us call them all 'honourable' men. Posterity may find a rougher word for the Tories who would this day encompass the assassination of so great a Prime Minister.

That evening, Mrs Thatcher was in Paris for a magnificent ceremony marking the end of the Cold War between the West and the Soviet Union. The result of the first round of the leadership ballot, which pitted her against Michael Heseltine, the pro-European and former defence secretary, came through at 6.59 p.m. Paris time. Three minutes later the BBC's chief political correspondent, John Sergeant, was reporting live from the courtyard of the British embassy in Paris for the *Six O'Clock News* in London, waiting for Mrs Thatcher to emerge. Over his shoulder while he was speaking the viewers could see Mrs Thatcher, her burly spokesman Bernard Ingham and another official charging down the embassy steps towards him. The high drama of the moment turned into knockabout farce as Ingham shouldered Sergeant aside.

JOHN SERGEANT [trying to regain his balance]: Mrs Thatcher, could I ask you to comment?

MRS THATCHER: Just a moment. Good evening. Good evening, gentlemen.

INGHAM: Where's the microphone?

SERGEANT: It's here. This is the microphone. [Sergeant holds it out towards Mrs Thatcher]

MRS THATCHER: I am naturally very pleased that I got more than half the Parliamentary Party and disappointed that it's not quite enough to win on the first ballot, so I confirm it is my intention to let my name go forward for the second ballot.

PETER ALLEN, IRN: Isn't the ... isn't the vote against you, Mrs Thatcher, large enough for you to have to acknowledge ...

MRS THATCHER: Look, I have ...

ALLEN: ... that you no longer enjoy the confidence of the party?

MRS THATCHER: I have got more than half the votes of the Parliamentary Party. It was not quite the fifteen per cent above those of Mr Heseltine – I think it's about 14.6 per cent – so it means we have to go for a second ballot, so I confirm that I shall let my name go forward.

JOURNALISTS [speaking at once]: Prime Minister! Mrs Thatcher!

MRS THATCHER: I must go and do some telephone calls.

The following morning, with greater insight than it had shown the previous day, the *Mail* characterized her statement correctly:

> It was a political streetfighter's instinctive reaction. Shortly afterwards Mr Heseltine said the same thing. And so the struggle for power in the Tory Party, unprecedented in its lust for self-destruction, continues.

That forecast by Gordon Greig, the *Mail*'s political editor, was wholly accurate. The internecine savagery over Europe in the Conservative Party destroyed Mrs Thatcher's successor, John Major, and was to continue for twenty years. On the morning of 23 November 1990 the paper's headline had a savagery of its own:

TOO DAMN GOOD FOR THE LOT OF THEM

> Betrayed and rejected by her party, Margaret Thatcher gave up her party yesterday. She did so with the magnificent class that she alone of British politicians can produce.
>
> Margaret Thatcher had not always been magnanimous in victory, but in defeat, as she gave her last speech in the Commons, she was witty and even relaxed. 'Where were we? – I'm enjoying this!' she said at one point.

But if she stayed light and pleasant and amusing, up in the press gallery some of the correspondents were getting distinctly emotional. Her speech, wrote Colin Welch in the *Mail* that Friday 23 November, was absolutely heartrending.

> Why, was it so sad? No. Was it so awful? On the contrary, because it was so absolutely and uniquely and joyously exhilarating. What a woman! I must confess that there was a bit of exultant sniggering up here among the hacks, some of the Left-wing, others laughing lest they weep.

Welch was a figure from Fleet Street's past: anarchic (he once chaired an editorial meeting with his suit covered in spaghetti, presumably flung at him by the woman he had been lunching with; 'Careless waiter,' he explained), and with a fierce, fantastical humour that led him to found the Peter Simple column in the *Daily Telegraph*, which was populated by dozens of characters who represented everything Welch most loathed. As political correctness invaded London journalism, and smoking and lunchtime drinking were increasingly frowned on, Colin Welch and a group of colleagues kept up a resistance movement at their headquarters in the King and Keys pub in Fleet Street. It was the last stand of a dying breed: male chauvinist, deeply reactionary, probably racist, but always waspishly witty.

As for Mrs Thatcher, she left office at the lowest point in her popularity, and the judgement in much of the Conservative Party was that if she stayed she would lose them the next election. Yet in the days after her departure even journalists she had clashed with remembered her with respect. The BBC, for instance, broadcast a reminiscence from one of its senior correspondents about an interview he had done with her in November 1983, just outside New Delhi. She had gone to visit a British graveyard, and as they were walking together and talking, with the cameraman alongside filming them, Mrs Thatcher tripped and fell full-length on the ground.

> Bernard Ingham came running over, and bellowed and spluttered right in my face, 'These pictures will never be seen on air.' But down from about knee-level came a voice: 'Oh, don't be silly, Bernard, of course [he] can use them if he wants to.' Not a lot of politicians would have said that. And I didn't use the pictures of her tripping up: why should I? Everyone trips over sometimes; it's not some kind of political statement. To be honest, I thought that was magnificent. There were politicians who would go berserk if they thought you were going to use material like that. She didn't care. No; I had all sorts of run-ins with her, over the years, but it was impossible not to feel respect for her.

The right-wing journalist and author Paul Johnson, whose books became required reading for conservative Republican politicians in the United States during the 1990s and the first decade of the twenty-first century, was regarded by British colleagues who were further to the left as frequently wrong-headed. When, on 28 November 1990, the *Daily Mail* printed an article by him about Mrs Thatcher's successor, it headlined it:

A winner to put the Tories on top again.

> [T]he Thatcher revolution will continue, possibly even accelerate under John Major.
>   I also have a growing feeling that, after the tragic waste of sacking Margaret Thatcher at the height of her powers, we may have picked another winner.

Other, better informed and more insightful political journalists understood that John Major was essentially a centrist – an old-fashioned, pro-European, one-nation Tory. He had none of the aggressive self-belief that a true successor to Mrs Thatcher would have required. Somehow, he had managed to persuade her that he shared her views; a considerable achievement, of a sort. But privately he believed that Mrs Thatcher's approach had been too extreme, too divisive, and he intended to be milder. Only those true believers who, like Paul Johnson, were desperate for her influence to continue, convinced themselves that he was a Thatcherite. There was, Johnson wrote, 'a world to conquer and a great adventure beginning'.

The most immediate place to conquer was Iraq. On 1 August 1990, at a final crisis meeting between Kuwait and Iraq to debate Iraq's demand for urgent financial aid from Kuwait, the Kuwaiti crown prince, in a fit of anger, turned to his own side and asked: 'Why don't they [the Iraqis] send their wives out onto the streets to earn money for them?' It was a reference to the old stories that President Saddam Hussein's mother had been a prostitute. When he was told about this, Saddam went wild with fury and ordered the immediate invasion of Kuwait. He told his closest advisers: 'The Emir will not sleep in his palace tonight.' At two o'clock the following morning Iraqi tanks began rolling across the Kuwaiti border.

Immediately, a coalition of nations was gathered together to oppose the invasion and, if necessary, to force Iraq out of Kuwait by military means. There was a body of opinion in Britain which was opposed to intervening militarily, even when it was clear that Iraqi forces were engaged in widespread looting and murder. This opposition was not reflected in the great bulk of the British press, which was often noisily and sometimes ignorantly in favour of war; but it was expressed by one of the most famous British foreign correspondents of his day, Robert Fisk of the *Independent*, who had once been *The Times*'s man in Northern Ireland and who had subsequently received more awards for his journalism than just about any other British journalist.

Never willing to go along with the crowd, Fisk often annoyed his colleagues by criticizing their methods; he coined the terms 'hotel journalism' for those who stayed in the safety of their rooms to do their reporting, and 'rooftop journalism' to describe twenty-four-hour television reporting. As he rightly pointed out, this was usually conducted from the safety of a high building rather than in the streets below: the proper place for anyone seeking to explain to others what was really going on. Fisk's own reporting was sometimes questioned by other journalists, and it was not clear that he invariably eschewed the hotel room and the rooftop himself. But his criticism was salutary, and sometimes shamed others into doing a proper job. And he scored some brilliant successes, such as his three exclusive interviews with Osama bin Laden in Afghanistan, and although he lived openly in Lebanon for nearly thirty years he always spoke out bravely and honourably against the dictators in the region. To criticize Saddam Hussein or the elder President Assad of Syria while living unprotected in Beirut was remarkably courageous.

Fisk's article in the *Independent* of 9 August 1990, at the start of the build-up to the Gulf War, caused a sensation. It was clear he believed that the Western-led force preparing to establish itself in Saudi Arabia for a possible counter-invasion of Kuwait faced catastrophic defeat. Under the headline

History haunts the new 'Crusaders'

he wrote:

> To understand . . . why the young Americans and British who are now committing their lives in the sands of Arabia are in such danger. . . it is necessary to look at the Middle East through Arab rather than Western eyes.

Yet each of his predictions turned out to be wrong.

> [A] war against Iraq may well turn out to be a war against the Arabs themselves. Jordan could scarcely stand aside under such circumstances. Syria is already showing signs of sympathy with Iraq. President Mubarak of Egypt might not survive if he did not support Iraq in the event of war . . . [A]ll-out war would leave the West fighting on its own amid the dust and heat.

In fact, the entire strategic approach was a model of intelligent American diplomacy; a greater contrast with the invasion of Iraq by the second President Bush in 2003 would be hard to imagine. In 1990–1 the war against Saddam Hussein was not a war against the Arabs themselves, even though in the streets of Arab cities it was often hugely unpopular. Jordan did stand aside; Syria, far from showing sympathy with Iraq, sent troops to fight alongside the Americans and British; President Mubarak did not support Iraq in the event of war, and at the time of writing he has survived for twenty more years.

Robert Fisk has an enormous body of supporters around the world: people who admire his stand against ignorant Western neocolonialist approaches to the Middle East. Many professional journalists prefer his eyewitness reporting to his analysis; but his real value to British journalism is that he is a maverick who refuses to go along with the journalistic herd; and mavericks often force those around them to question their own assumptions.

In the last few months of 1990 a clear bias against understanding (to use the expression introduced by John Birt and Peter Jay into the debate about the values of television news in the late 1980s) established itself in the coverage of the coming war with Saddam Hussein. A few journalists, like Robert Fisk, thought it would be a disaster. The great majority accepted at face value the assessments of the United States, British and other governments, which, in order to keep popular support for the war at a high level, made Saddam Hussein's tatterdemalion regime out to be an immensely powerful and dangerous opponent. Every British newspaper repeated the line that Iraq's army was the fourth largest in the world, without any reference to its quality.

Saddam's Republican Guards were usually referred to as 'elite'; the general commanding them told a BBC correspondent in Baghdad off the record that the Guards were selected on the basis that they could swing their left arms in time with their right legs, and vice versa. Yet this was not the kind of information people in Britain seemed to want to hear. Editors were dubious about it, given that so many military experts (very few of whom had ever visited Iraq) seemed to have a high opinion of Saddam's army. One British correspondent, who spent more time in Baghdad than the rest, discovered that many of the supposedly highly trained Iraqi officers who volunteered to go to Kuwait to defend it from Coalition attack did so for three reasons. Firstly, it was far away from the dangerous atmosphere of Baghdad and other big cities, where agents of the Mukhabarat, Saddam's intelligence service, were always sniffing out treason. Secondly, no one thought there really would be a war, so it seemed entirely safe to volunteer. And thirdly, out in the desert discipline was greatly relaxed.

Few of the Western correspondents who were allowed to visit Baghdad were given any insight into this side of things. They were entirely confined to 'hotel journalism'; their movements were restricted, and their reports were subject to censorship by the Iraqi Ministry of Information. Yet when they returned to London, they found that suggestions about Iraq's lack of readiness and appetite for war were simply not wanted. A senior news editor at CNN's bureau in London, told about the real state of affairs in Iraq during a live television discussion, replied politely, 'I'm sorry – I just can't believe it.' BBC programme editors showed a powerful resistance to reporting of this kind, not on ideological grounds or because it might weaken public support for the confrontation with Saddam Hussein, but because no one else was reporting it. Journalists – especially in the BBC, which instinctively prefers a centrist, consensus approach – often feel uncomfortable if their work is not supported by the reporting of others.

Essentially the weakness and lack of fighting spirit of even the better-trained Iraqi forces was not revealed to the British and American public. As a result, when the ground assault began on 24 February 1991, public opinion was surprised to find it was not much better than a massacre. The Iraqis had inferior weapons and little will to resist. Most of them were only interested in giving themselves up as quickly as they could, and many of them died because they were unable to make it clear enough to the Americans and British that they wanted to surrender. The Iraqis did not even have numerical superiority to make up for their complete inferiority in equipment and morale.

The Western media, following figures issued by the Pentagon, had settled on a figure of around 500,000 for the Iraqi forces. In fact Iraq only had something like 300,000 properly trained troops, and they had to be divided into two parts to protect against the possibility of an invasion by the Turkish army in the north. By contrast the US-led Coalition was able to count on something like 540,000 soldiers.

The destruction of the column of trucks driven by the last Iraqi soldiers to leave Kuwait provided some ugly images of one-sided slaughter, and led President Bush to call a ceasefire in the campaign. The crew of the lorries were scarcely innocents. Most of them were the last wave of looters, delayed in Kuwait City because they had grabbed everything and sometimes everyone they could lay their hands on: an unknown number of people who died at the Mutlah Ridge were hostages, seized by the Iraqis for later ransom. Some of the others who died were intelligence officers who had been based at the Nayef Palace, the main torture and execution centre during the Iraqi occupation. Estimates varied of the number of people who died in the trucks at the Mutlah Ridge, as the American planes attacked again and again, but the general assumption was that it was in the low thousands. It took the meticulous efforts of the *Daily Telegraph* correspondent Robert Fox, who had distinguished himself with his reporting for the BBC from the Falklands, to find out the exact number. He was the only reporter among the hundreds covering the war who undertook the distasteful job of counting the burned and damaged bodies in each of the trucks; his total came to less than four hundred.

At roughly the time Fox was carrying out his body count, the American photographer Ken Jarecke, who worked for the Associated Press, was driving along the main highway from Kuwait City to the Iraqi border, past the Mutlah Ridge. He spotted a truck which had been destroyed by an American bomb; leaning out of it was the charred body of an Iraqi soldier, his facial muscles set in the terrible rictus laugh of an agonizing death, gripping on to the side of the truck. The American public affairs officer with Jarecke allowed him to take the picture, but back in New York the photograph, which in many ways summed up the way the war ended, was removed from the AP's domestic wire. This meant that it was not seen at all in the United States, though it was sent out to the rest of the world. In Britain the *Observer*, after some internal debate, decided to print it, over a sensitive article by Julie Flint headlined

The real face of war

A reporter entering Kuwait City passed a line of Iraqis shambling towards him with their hands tied behind their backs by American soldiers who had told them to walk south. Further down the road, a single figure brought up the rear – 'limping and dejected, a terrible example of the humiliated army ... He must have spent the night like that, unable to drink, eat or urinate, frightened and frozen,' the reporter wrote. 'I will always feel ashamed that I did not cut him free.'

Only the poorly armed conscripts, the cannon-fodder of Saddam's army, had been placed in the front line. The better-trained and better-equipped Republican Guards were held back for the inevitable uprisings which Saddam knew would greet his military defeat. They were waiting for the safer task of shooting down the city mobs which (urged on by President Bush, who then refused to help them) would rise up against Saddam in the Shi'ite and Kurdish areas. Yet much of the British media still chose to present the Gulf War as a magnificent feat of arms, achieved against alarming odds. Instead, it was merely a well-planned, well-executed operation by some of the best military machines in the world against a smaller, weaker and utterly demoralized Third World army. The correspondents of a century before would scarcely have recognized it as a battle; for them, it would merely have been organized slaughter.

§

It is not particularly easy, in an advanced democracy, to get public support for a war of intervention. It requires strong moral motivation. Governments have to make out a powerful case for going to war, and they then require the backing of most of the media. At such a time, honest reporting is not required – either by the government itself, or by the people who support (or sometimes by those who oppose) the war effort. Typically, the demand for truthful reporting returns only when the war is over; until then, emotions rather than facts are what is wanted. This is especially true when, in the inevitable way of wars, civilians are killed by the very countries who are claiming to defend the rights and lives of the innocent. The Gulf War of 1990–1, when public support was needed to sustain the seven-month effort to force Saddam Hussein to withdraw from Kuwait, provided a number of examples.

At around 7.20 Baghdad time on the evening of 13 February 1991, the twenty-eighth day of the war, an American 2,000-lb penetration bomb hit a specially constructed shelter in the well-to-do Baghdad suburb of al-Amiriyah. By this stage in the war the daily and nightly attacks had become so intense that there were scarcely any targets left untouched; some buildings in Baghdad had been hit twenty times or more, for lack of alternatives. Yet the al-Amiriyah shelter had survived unharmed; no doubt the Coalition's sophisticated satellites had spotted that every evening large numbers of civilians took refuge there. But for some reason, that Wednesday night the Americans took the decision to attack it. Over the following few days a number of justifications were issued: it was an Iraqi military command post, it was transmitting radio messages; there was reason to think that Saddam Hussein might be there. None of these excuses seems to have been true.

The reality was that up to 300 women and children, the families of senior government figures plus their friends and relations, used the shelter every night, and the Americans, studying their satellite pictures with the greatest care – those pictures which, we were often told, could read a car numberplate from space – must have known it. This must have been why they had not attacked it before. No one knows how many women and children died that night, burned and scalded and suffocated, but it was certainly the great majority of those who had gone to the shelter. If, in some change of fortune, Saddam Hussein had given the orders to bomb the shelter, knowing that up to 300 women and children were there, he would have been guilty of one of the worst war crimes of modern times. If the Americans held an inquiry into the bombing, which seems unlikely, its outcome was never reported. No apology was issued; there was never even an acknowledgement that this was not a suitable target.

A BBC correspondent, Jeremy Bowen, and the freelance cameraman he was working with, Rory Peck, heard the news of the attack as they waited in the lobby of the Al-Rasheed Hotel, where the foreign journalists were obliged to stay. Bowen was the archetypal foreign correspondent, raffish, amusing, brave and questioning. Peck, who was killed two years later in Russia, was a languid Anglo-Irish aristocrat who turned into one of the most fearless cameramen in the world: not always very good technically, but often the only one with the courage to cover the most frightening stories. They were taken with a group of other journalists to the shelter. Bowen described later how they saw burned body parts being brought out, and how after they went back the next day their shoes became coated with the liquid fat from the bodies of those who had been burned. No one interfered with their work or told them what to do: they filmed what and where they wanted.

The following morning's *Daily Mail* avoided any questions about why the Americans should have bombed the shelter, and instead blamed the loss of life on Iraq.

Were civilians deliberately put in bomb-target bunker?
VICTIMS OF SADDAM'S WAR

The White House [press secretary Martin Fitzwater] last night accused Saddam Hussein of sacrificing hundreds of women and children for a propaganda coup . . .

Stressing that the policy of the U.S. and the Allies was to avoid civilian casualties, he accused Saddam of killing civilians intentionally. 'Time and again he has shown a willingness to sacrifice civilian lives and property that has furthered his war aims,' Fitzwater said.

This was true; but the fact remained that the bombing of the shelter had been carried out by the Americans and had had horrifying consequences. The *Mail's* story was from correspondents in Saudi Arabia, Washington and London; it had no reporter in Baghdad. If it had, the *Mail* might not have accepted quite so easily the silly notion that Saddam Hussein had deliberately herded women and children into a bunker on the off-chance that the Americans would bomb them. With Iraq and Saddam Hussein, it seemed, anything could be alleged, anything believed. On page 2 the *Mail* ran a couple of headlines that read

Heartbreak toll of Saddam's war lust

Shameful that the civilians were there, says U.S. Army

On page 4, the *Mail* turned to the much more congenial business of attacking the BBC. Jeremy Bowen's report for the main television news the previous night had brought a storm of protest. Many viewers were clearly upset by the thought that more than 200 women and children had died the most terrible deaths, and were prepared to blame anyone rather than reflect on the true responsibility. The *Mail's* coverage employed precisely the same sort of terms and devices which it had used in its coverage of F.A. Voigt's commentary on the Spanish Civil War for the BBC almost exactly forty-five years before (see p.240).

Outrage as TV's bunker bomb bulletins 'show bias to Saddam'

'Switchboards were swamped with complaints', the *Mail* reported, though later it quoted ITN, which had also covered the bombed-out shelter, as saying that it had received a hundred calls, while the BBC had had twenty. Nothing, it seemed, had changed since. The *Mail* itself had received several calls: it quotes three complainants, including Mrs Judith Hamilton, forty-nine, from Hampton, south-west London, who was upset at having her evening disturbed: 'I find it disgraceful the way we are subjected to all these pictures of hardship from Iraq.'

The *Mail* obtained a memorable quote from a Conservative MP, Neil Thorpe. He maintained that the television reports were putting the lives of Allied servicemen at risk by putting pressure on the Allies not to bomb strategic targets in civilian areas. By the following day, Friday the 15th, more calls were coming in and the word 'treason' was inevitably starting to makes its appearance in the *Mail*.

> [P]ensioner Irene Bull, from Lymm, Cheshire, said: 'What they are saying in a time of war is practically treasonable.'
> '"BBC" obviously stands for the Baghdad Broadcasting Corporation,' said Julian Eynon, 32, a promotions consultant from Swansea.

Telling people uncomfortable truths about what was going on had, it seemed, become treasonable propaganda. The *Sun*, like the *Mail* unrepresented in Baghdad, went so far as to suggest that Saddam Hussein's propaganda machine had supplied English-speaking people for the BBC and ITN to interview after the bombing. (It took place in a well-to-do area where it was common to find people who spoke English.) In a war fought in a faraway country of which the British tabloid press knew little, ignorance and invention were commonplace.

§

During the first Gulf War the *Sun* took something of a back seat. This was no repeat of the Falklands: the main effort was American, and the British were restricted to playing a distinctly secondary role in it. The *Sun* was a cheerleader, but it took no part in influencing the strategy of the war, since that was not decided in Britain. Its reporters were kept away from the two areas that mattered: the front line and Baghdad. The *Sun*'s strength had always been in its domestic coverage, and since its political reporting was particularly strong, it had to wait until public attention in Britain turned back to politics. This happened within a year. John Major, trailing in the polls, decided to call an election for the beginning of April 1992.

It was hard to find anyone who thought the Conservatives had a chance of winning – except John Major himself, and some of the people around him. In the two weeks before the election, the *Spectator* was the only newspaper or magazine to suggest that he might after all win. The opinion polls were not disastrously against him, but he usually trailed by 4 or 5 percentage points. On 8 April, the day before polling day, the last opinion polls gave Labour a lead of about 1 per cent; yet, when the votes were counted, the Conservatives had a lead of 7.6 per cent over Labour. The turnout (at just under 78 per cent) was the highest since the 1964 election. There was a swing to Labour of 2.2 per cent, yet the Conservative share of the vote fell by only 0.3 per cent since the 1987 election.

There was a good deal of soul-searching afterwards – by market research groups, individual pollsters, newspapers, broadcasters and by the political parties themselves. The unsettling reason many of them came up with was that, because there was so much vituperation against John Major in the press and in public, a sizeable number of people who intended privately to vote Conservative pretended, if the pollsters asked them, that they would vote Labour. It became known as the Shy Tory Factor.

Other factors were suggested, including widespread public dislike of the American-style triumphalist election rally held by the leader of the Labour Party, Neil Kinnock, in Sheffield. But the *Sun*, and various Conservative MPs, were in agreement with its famous headline the day after the election:

IT'S THE SUN WOT WON IT
Truth hailed by Tories

Triumphant Tory MPs queued yesterday to say 'Thank You My Sun' for helping John Major back in to Number 10 . . .
    Even Labour admitted our double whammy had swung

don't-knows behind the Tories to give them a 21-seat
majority . . .
Winning Basildon MP David Amess got a majority of
1,480, a swing of only 1.3 per cent from Tories to Labour.
He told us yesterday: 'It was your front page that did it.
It crystallized all the issues.'

The front page in question, which appeared on the morning of the
election, scarcely had anything to do with issues; but it was rich in abuse.

If Kinnock wins today will the
last person to leave Britain
please turn out the lights

Kinnock's head appeared alongside the headline, inside a light bulb. It
was the culmination of a deliberate campaign which had begun on page
3, where instead of the usual bare breasts, a grossly overweight woman
of fifty-three appeared in her underwear, pulling down her bra-strap
provocatively, beside the headline

HERE'S HOW PAGE 3 WILL LOOK
UNDER KINNOCK!

All the evidence shows that people buy newspapers for a variety of
reasons, and do not necessarily take any notice of their political leanings.
The editorial column in the *Sun* is one of the least-read sections in the
entire paper. At this time, in 1992, almost half of all *Sun* readers were
traditional Labour voters; they read the paper because of its ebullience
and showmanship, not because of its political coverage.

Nevertheless, the *Sun*'s habit of heaping abuse on people it disliked
could not possibly be ignored, and must have undermined Kinnock's
chances. It had only a fringe effect on working-class voters; but in places
like Basildon, a key marginal constituency which tended to move between
Labour and Conservative, the *Sun* helped to cut the general 2.2 per cent
swing from Conservative to Labour by half – enough for the
Conservatives to win. Carefully thought-out political arguments would
certainly never have achieved that; nor did the simple exhortation to vote

Tory. The *Daily Star*, a feeble shadow of the *Sun*, read largely by men who were lower down the sociologists' scale than *Sun*-readers, also supported John Major in the 1992 election, but no one suggested it was the *Star* wot won it. Exhortation counted for little or nothing. The Shy Tory Factor showed how embarrassed many people were to admit they were thinking of voting for a party as unpopular as the Conservatives; the crude, personally abusive bludgeon which the *Sun* supplied helped to encourage them.

Though no commentator seems to have suggested it at the time on radio, television or in the newspapers, the 1992 election represented the most poisoned of chalices. If Neil Kinnock had won, he would certainly have suffered just as badly as John Major did from the events of Black Wednesday, 16 September 1992, when the pound fell out of the European Exchange Rate Mechanism. Instead, it was John Major's chances of a successful term in office that were destroyed. If he had lost the 1992 election, no one would have blamed him; it would have been said that the fault lay with Margaret Thatcher's continuing unpopularity. Still, John Major would not have been able to calm the party's angry divisions over Europe, which were still present nearly twenty years later, fuelled by the main anti-European tabloids, the *Sun*, the *Daily Mail* and the *Daily Express*.

As it was, by January 1994 the *Sun*, in an unusual fit of self-criticism, headlined an article

What fools we all were

for backing him before the 1992 election. The *Sun*, like the Murdoch group in general, was looking for someone else to back. Four months later, the unexpected death of the Labour leader John Smith on 12 May 1994 provided them with a candidate.

When Neil Kinnock stepped down as Labour leader, on 13 April 1992, he blamed the Tory press (by which he meant the *Sun*) as one of the reasons for his failure. This was slightly disingenuous, and was intended to deflect attention from the failings of his own campaign; but it came to be regarded within the Labour Party as a statement of fact. During John Smith's brief leadership, no approaches were made to Murdoch. He was still regarded with distaste by Labour members as a result of his battle with the print unions after *The Times* moved to

Wapping in 1986. John Smith's director of communications, David Hill, encouraged him to consider it, but no decision had been taken by the time of Smith's death.

Tony Blair was instinctively disposed to believe in the theory of Rupert Murdoch's dominant influence. His relationships with older men could be complex and significant; he seemed to respect them, and was skilful at wooing them and impressing them with his abilities. But as a leader, and a dominant one at that, he always had a tendency to deliver his allegiance to someone else.

On 15 July 1995 that allegiance was given, apparently unconditionally and apparently in perpetuity, to Rupert Murdoch. He flew 12,000 miles around the world to attend a conference of News International managers on Hayman Island, off the coast of Queensland, and delivered a speech which was intended as a courtship display to attract Murdoch's support. Taking off his jacket, but not his tie, he set out to show that he was a different sort of left-of-centre leader: so different that he was closer to Margaret Thatcher than she had been to the Conservative Party. The new Right, he said, meaning the Thatcher–Reagan alliance,

> got certain things right. A greater emphasis on enterprise.
>
> Rewarding not penalising success. Breaking up some vested interests.
>
> In that sense Mrs Thatcher was a radical, not a Tory.

This might have been news to Mrs Thatcher, but it seemed to win over Rupert Murdoch. By the morning of Monday 17 July *The Times* was reprinting Blair's speech virtually in its entirety, and running a curious article about it on the front page. Curious, because it seemed intentionally to play down the connection with News International.

'Radical' Blair lays claim to the Thatcher inheritance

> Tony Blair made a fresh grab for Tory clothes yesterday, saying that only a Labour Government could complete the social and economic revolution begun by Margaret Thatcher in the 1980s.

The article is almost halfway through before it explains that this remarkable speech was made 'to senior executives and editors from Rupert Murdoch's media empire', and there was no examination of the reasons why Tony Blair might have been speaking to such an audience. But it quotes Blair as saying of the rift between Labour and News International since the Wapping dispute, 'There have been changes on both sides. The past should be behind us.'

It worked. Murdoch certainly took to Blair as a result, but as ever, commercial interests lay behind the decision to back him; Major's government was too distracted by the endless in-fighting with its anti-European wing to be able to decide whether News International should be classed as a foreign company or a British one. Blair seemed much more likely to be favourable to Murdoch's empire, in return for its support; and that is what turned out.

On the morning of 18 March 1997, with a pomposity that it had rarely shown before, the *Sun* devoted its front page to

An historic announcement from Britain's No 1 newspaper
THE SUN BACKS BLAIR
Give change a chance

> The people need a leader with vision, purpose and courage who can inspire them and fire their imaginations.
>
> The Sun believes that man is Tony Blair. He is the best man for the job, for our ten million readers and for the country.

There was no room for anything on the page except the gigantic headline and a little box of text, accompanied by a photograph of an impossibly young-looking Tony Blair showing his teeth in a gleaming smile. Inside, there was a two-page-long article explaining why the *Sun* was now backing Blair. The Conservatives, it said with considerable justification,

> have become sloppy, divided and tired out. Their incompetence shines through and getting things wrong is the one

thing they consistently get right. The Tories lack direction and purpose. They have been tarnished with sleaze,
riddled with scandal, beset by foolishness and weakened
by division.

It was all true, but there was no recognition of the role the *Sun* itself had
played in the Conservatives' civil war, by consistently encouraging the
efforts of the Eurosceptics. Major had been increasingly worried that the
Murdoch papers were going to turn against him, and rang Kelvin
MacKenzie at the *Sun* to find out. MacKenzie supposedly told him: 'Well,
John, let me put it this way. I've got a large bucket of shit lying on my
desk and tomorrow morning I'm going to pour it all over your head.'

This is regularly quoted, and its accuracy has never been questioned.
Perhaps the crudity and sheer unpleasantness of it is its own guarantee
of truth, though it may be nothing more than the boast of a man anxious
to keep up his reputation for fearless brutality. Yet it makes clear the
contempt MacKenzie felt for the prime minister. He would never, of
course, have dared to speak to Margaret Thatcher like that; and if he had,
Rupert Murdoch would have sacked him on the spot.

The *Sun* might well have used very much the same tone of utter
contempt towards Tony Blair and New Labour if Rupert Murdoch had
ordered his newspapers to switch its support away from him. There was,
it seems, little Tony Blair would not do to ensure this did not happen:
including setting aside one of his pet projects. In 2005 Lance Price, a
media adviser to the Blair government and deputy to Blair's chief press
secretary, Alastair Campbell, provided an insight into the extent of
Murdoch's influence over the Blair government when he wrote a book
about his time in Downing Street, *The Spin Doctor's Diary*. He told press
interviewers:

Nobody ever said, 'We have to do this because Murdoch supports it.'
   But his views were always heard. And they were heard ahead of
many Cabinet ministers.

Price gave a particular example:

Blair was very keen to join the European monetary system, but at
every stage of the way he stepped back. And one of the main rea-

sons he pulled back was that Rupert Murdoch was vehemently opposed to closer links with Europe.

In other words, Murdoch was given powerful influence over one of the most important decisions the Blair government made during its ten years in power. There are few other examples during the entire twentieth century of a government shifting away from a major policy initiative because a newspaper proprietor disliked it; though there were other factors as well, not least the general unpopularity of the policy in the country at large. The balance of power had changed decisively; now it was the prime ministers who were wary of the press barons, not the other way round.

The extent of Tony Blair's willingness to make himself available to Rupert Murdoch surprised even Murdoch's own executives. They had, perhaps, been inclined to expect something more like the kind of relationship Murdoch had with Margaret Thatcher. She had certainly gone out of her way to bend the rules in Murdoch's favour, both in allowing his company to widen its already large newspaper ownership to take in *The Times* and the *Sunday Times*, and in letting him take over British Satellite Broadcasting and form BSkyB. These were examples of cross-media ownership which went against the spirit of competition and monopoly legislation and gave Murdoch his overpoweringly dominant position in British politics and journalism. But Murdoch always treated Mrs Thatcher with great care and respect, knowing that she was tough enough, and confident enough, to make life difficult for him.

Murdoch behaved differently to Tony Blair. At first, in particular, he seemed to expect that Blair would use his influence as Britain's prime minister to help Murdoch's business interests. In March 1998 Murdoch offered the Italian politician and media tycoon Silvio Berlusconi £4 billion for his Mediaset television network, but he became agitated about the possibility that the Italian government would step in and prevent the deal from going through. On Wednesday 18 March the Italian prime minister, Romano Prodi, had a telephone conversation with Tony Blair, in order to work out the schedules of some European Union meetings which Britain would chair. Prodi was surprised when Blair started talking about Mediaset and Rupert Murdoch's interest in it. The story was leaked by the Italians to the respected Turin newspaper *La Stampa*, which published the story on Monday 23 March in terms that were scarcely flattering to Tony Blair. When a Lobby correspondent asked Alastair

Campbell that afternoon if the report was true, Campbell dismissed it as 'crap'. As it turned out, the report was indeed wrong: the call had been placed by Prodi's office to Blair, not by Blair's office to Prodi. Everything else about it was entirely correct.

The nervousness which Blair seemed to show towards Rupert Murdoch was to some extent justified. No doubt the personal relationship between them was friendly: it was in both their interests that it should be. But as in the French proverb, it was Blair who did the kissing and Murdoch who presented his cheek to be kissed. The element of respect, of fear even, was obvious on Blair's side, but it certainly did not seem to be mutual. Eventually, Murdoch ceased to worry about going public with Blair's confidences. On 18 September 2005 a headline in the *Independent on Sunday* read:

Blair tells Murdoch: 'gloating' BBC is 'full of hatred for America'

Extraordinary attack on corporation's coverage of New Orleans disaster

Tony Blair has told Rupert Murdoch he believes the BBC's coverage of Hurricane Katrina was 'full of hatred of America and gloating'. In an extraordinary disclosure that will acutely embarrass Mr Blair, the world's most powerful media mogul revealed details of a private conversation that took place in New York on Thursday.

The full text of Murdoch's words was as follows:

Tony Blair – perhaps I shouldn't repeat this conversation – told me yesterday that he was in Delhi last week. And he turned on the BBC World Service to see what was happening in New Orleans. And he said it was just full of hate of America and gloating about our troubles. And that was his government. Well, his government-owned thing.

Murdoch, as always, had clear business reasons for breaking Tony Blair's confidence. The BBC's reputation in the United States had been growing considerably ever since the invasion of Iraq. More and more television stations were taking BBC reports, and half of all the hits on the BBC News website, now the most visited in Europe, were from Americans. Several leading commentators, among them the Middle East expert Juan Cole, were publicly comparing the BBC very favourably with Murdoch's openly right-wing channel Fox News. Tony Blair had made a private aside to Murdoch in support of their mutual friend President George W. Bush, whose feeble handling of the Katrina disaster had been widely criticized. But Murdoch decided to turn this to his own purposes – clearly without troubling himself about the consequences to Blair.

In public as in private, Tony Blair was charming and amusing, and in his early days in power he had managed to transform the whole self-image of the nation, lifting it out of the gloom of the John Major years. The Conservatives had been swept into oblivion. Labour seemed a young person's party, and Britain suddenly felt like a country for the young and enterprising. It was an important achievement – and much of that achievement belonged to Alastair Campbell.

Campbell was a complex figure, personally honest, remarkably bold, and surprisingly thoughtful. He was a thoroughgoing bully, like several of his predecessors in the job of prime minister's spokesman, yet anyone who stood up to him found it was worth doing; the flow of invective always seemed to fade away. His frankness could often be appealing, and he rarely seemed to go in for polite or social lying. What he thought, he said. That made him a rarity in journalism, and almost unique as a civil servant. Having been a journalist for much of his life, he had little respect for journalists and journalism; he knew from the inside how sloppy and imitative their work so often was. Campbell was never, it has to be said, a particularly impressive journalist, though he could be a first-class phrase-maker. His biographer, Peter Oborne, has pointed out that as political editor of the *Daily Mirror* he seemed to find remarkably few stories of any quality. Instead, Oborne says, Campbell's real talent lay in office politics:

Unlike Tony Blair, Campbell was a class warrior. Although he was a middle class boy, the son of a vet, he chose to see himself as working class, and found the atmosphere of faux upper class languor at Cambridge, when he got there, completely intolerable. This sense that life was a war between the classes only went underground when he joined Tony Blair's camp. As late as 9 May 1994 he wrote with great savagery about Prince Charles in

his column in the short-lived (and Murdoch-owned) newspaper *Today*.
He said, without drawing breath, that the prince was someone who:

> cannot hold his marriage together, does not see his own kids from
> day to day, delegates their upbringing to nannies and private school
> spankers, went to a Spanking Academy himself, needed the power
> of patronage to get into university, apparently wants to send his
> own sons to Eton, the Spanking Academy, whose advisers all come
> from similar establishments and are similarly ill-suited to speak
> about the real world, and who courts his mistress with lavatorial
> suggestions.

There is a great deal of hatred packed into that long (though unquestionably well-written) sentence. At other times, some of his hatred was
diverted towards John Major, whose education was a great deal less
distinguished than Campbell's, and whose background was humbler. But
Major was a Conservative, and Campbell did not hold with Conservatives. The abuse he heaped on him in his column in the newspaper
Today was as intense as anything that came from Kelvin MacKenzie in
the *Sun*. On 9 May 1994, for instance, he spoke of 'the piece of lettuce
who passes for Prime Minister'.

And because there was nothing underhand about Campbell, he was
almost equally abusive in person. On an early foreign trip, when Major
came back to talk to the journalists accompanying him on the plane,
Campbell said – no doubt for the benefit of his colleagues – 'Oh, sod off,
Prime Minister, I'm trying to do my expenses.' Some years afterwards (in
Today on 17 February 1994) he had the grace to admit that this had been
grossly rude: 'I realized the moment the words had formed in my mouth
that it was wrong to speak in this way, but it was too late.'

He would never have spoken like that to Margaret Thatcher; but
he neither respected nor feared John Major; and it merely confirmed
Campbell's contempt for him when Major did not respond or retaliate
in any way.

During another of Major's overseas flights, to Washington in the run-
up to the first Gulf War, Campbell claims to have found the evidence for
an even more spiteful little story: that Major wore his shirt inside his
underpants. In his column for the *Sunday Mirror* on 17 March 1991
Campbell wrote gleefully:

> Somewhere over the Atlantic, a jacketless Mr Major left his
> comfy quarters at the back of the plane to join the press for
> an hour or two. At one point I was standing behind him as
> he bent down to talk to someone. I noticed three layers of
> clothing – his trousers followed by what looked like the
> elasticated top of a pair of underpants, followed by his pale
> blue shirt closest to his skin.

This revelation sounds like the kind of thing that boys at one of Campbell's spanking academies might jeer at one of their social inferiors. It was something that could only have happened in Britain, with its dreary snobbish codes about what is, and what is not, socially acceptable. Campbell's revelation played an important part in the humiliating and demeaning of John Major. Everyone joined in, including the best and most inventive British political cartoonist, Steve Bell, who used a pair of underpants to symbolize, by synecdoche, Major's entire time in office. Perhaps, after Margaret Thatcher's years of domineering power, the class was taking the opportunity to rag the unfortunate supply teacher. But it was hardly very edifying.

Campbell was a strong hater, but he could also be a loyal devotee. When he worked for the *Sunday Mirror* he formed an admiration for the group's owner, the bullying, oversized Robert Maxwell, who was less of an instinctive newspaperman than an all-round entrepreneur but who saw in newspaper ownership a way to promote his business interests. Maxwell ran his businesses along idiosyncratic lines; he ordered his staff on pain of dismissal never to open mail addressed to him. But since he never opened them himself, the letters piled up alarmingly over the months. One weekend a small group of staff went in secretly to open them. Among various other things of importance they found two writs and a cheque for a million pounds.

Maxwell had been born Jan Ludvik Hoch, the son of Yiddish-speaking parents, in a small village in Slovakia in 1923. In 1939 he joined forces with another young Jewish Slovak, Victor Grosz, and headed off to fight for the Allies against Hitler. In the retreat to Dunkirk, Grosz said many years later that they captured a dozen or so German soldiers.

> Hoch took them round the back of a building, then he lined them
> up and started shooting them in the back of the neck. I couldn't

decide what to do, but a British officer came running round the
corner and started screaming at him. He was going to court-martial
him, have him shot, you know. But things were so chaotic it all got
forgotten about.

Later in the war Maxwell became a captain and was awarded the Military
Cross; no one ever doubted his tremendous courage. In 1988, however,
Joe Haines published a remarkably favourable biography of Maxwell.
Haines had been Harold Wilson's devoted press spokesman, and had now
swung his loyalties behind another dominant leader; Maxwell gave him
a job on the *Sunday Mirror*, but expected the same kind of treatment that
Maxwell himself gave to the leaders of Communist Eastern Europe in a
series of ludicrously flattering biographies. Maxwell let slip to Haines that
he had shot the mayor of a German town during the last days of the war
in Europe; a German tank had opened fire from the town on Maxwell's
platoon. As a result of Haines's book, the Metropolitan Police began
preparing a war crimes case against him for the Crown Prosecution
Service.

The case started coming to a head in October 1991. So did Maxwell's
own financial crisis. He was technically bankrupt, and had used hundreds
of millions of pounds from the pension funds of his various companies,
including the *Mirror*, to finance his corporate debt. On the night of
Monday 4 November 1991 Maxwell was cruising off the Canary Islands
in his yacht *Lady Ghislaine*. Although he had given up smoking cigars
some years before, on doctor's orders, he smoked one that night. At some
stage afterwards, he went overboard and his body was afterwards found
floating in the Atlantic. Although all sorts of evidence came out later that
he had been providing intelligence to the Israeli secret service Mossad,
and there were some who believed he had been murdered, it seems most
likely that, faced with so many terrible and humiliating possibilities,
Maxwell decided to end his own life.

When the news came through at Westminster, the amusing, slightly
acid-tongued political editor of the *Guardian*, Michael White, sought
out Alaistair Campbell, Maxwell's faithful supporter, in the House of
Commons press gallery and started goading him, apparently chanting
'Cap'n Bob, bob, bob, bob.' Campbell seems to have been genuinely
upset by Maxwell's death, and he was busy writing and making calls
about it. When White came back a third time to make the same joke,

Campbell punched him. 'It was,' Campbell told Jonathan Sale later in the *Independent*, 'a terrible punch, quite hopeless.' Stories about the fight circulated for a long time among the press, but the journalist, academic and commentator Roy Greenslade, a friend of Campbell's, later wrote in the *Guardian* on Wednesday 4 February 1998 that too much had been read into it. 'It was a silly spat that had more to do with Alaistair's and Michael's own relationship than a display of misguided loyalty to Captain Bob.'

Campbell was a man of quick emotions, to whom personal loyalty was important. In the *Daily Mirror* the following day, Wednesday 6 November, he described Maxwell as 'a big man with a big heart'; when the ugly facts started to come out, Campbell saw no reason to jump on the bandwagon of his detractors.

After he left Downing Street, people close to Campbell said he had become a more rounded, less angry figure, from whom many of the demons had been exorcized. Yet by comparison with some of the prime ministerial spokesmen from the past who have appeared in these pages, he seems louder and more aggressive, and at the same time smaller and diminished. His memoirs, though at first lively-seeming and exciting, giving the reader the feeling of listening at the keyhole, quickly pall and start to seem empty and almost degrading: to be told that the prime minister and his leading adviser use expressions like 'thin-skinned wankers', 'stupid twats' and 'self-important fuckers' does not, somehow, add to the stature of either man. As for his central role in presenting government policy, Campbell turned his office into a foghorn of command and abuse. It was certainly effective, and many people were cowed by it; but it is not the kind of achievement that is likely to be much admired in the future.

§

In his essay 'Media Control' the American academic and campaigner Noam Chomsky describes how, within six months in 1917, the administration of Woodrow Wilson (who had been elected the previous year on the slogan 'Peace Without Victory') had turned 'a pacifist population into a hysterical, war-mongering mob which wanted to destroy everything German, tear the Germans limb from limb, go to war and save the world'.

This was achieved, of course, through the medium of the press. Propaganda stories, many of them emanating from the British government, were picked up and embroidered and passed on to an American audience. Soon the newspapers were competing with each other to come up with accounts of atrocities. It is not difficult, if a sufficiently large section of the media is prepared to go along with it. And as Woodrow Wilson found in 1917, there are many reasons why the media are more than happy to do so. When he first entered government in 1997, as Minister without Portfolio in the Cabinet Office, Peter Mandelson, the first British politico to earn the American title 'spin-doctor' in the British press, was quoted in *Web of Deceit*, Mark Curtis's fierce critique of British foreign policy under Blair, as saying: 'Of course we want to use the media, but the media will be our tools, our servants; we are no longer content to let them be our persecutors.'

The first major example of this desire to control, rather than merely manage, came with the crisis over Kosovo, which began in 1998. The efforts of the ultra-nationalist President Slobodan Milošević of Serbia had cost tens of thousands of lives in the wars he had provoked against the other parts of the former Yugoslavia. The siege of Sarajevo, carried out by Bosnian Serbs with Milošević's strong support behind the scenes, had caused suffering on a large scale. The murder of more than 8,000 Muslim men and boys at Srebrenica by the Bosnian Serb army in July 1995 was the worst act of genocide in Europe since 1945, and although Milošević was not personally responsible he had created the climate in which murder on this scale could be committed. In 1998 he and his forces were moving into Kosovo, where, although it represented holy ground to Serbian nationalists, ethnic Albanians were in a large majority. It seemed reasonable to assume that there would be ethnic cleansing, and perhaps massacre, on a large scale.

The government of Bill Clinton in the United States had mostly done what it could to stay out of the wars in the former Yugoslavia, and its only intervention had been some ineffectual bombing raids. The Americans had put the blame for the lack of intervention on European inaction. The United Nations had done little more than look on. The demand, generated originally by the American media, for Clinton to get involved, had become stronger. Christiane Amanpour of CNN had made her name by debating America's inactivity over the siege of Sarajevo, and the *New York Times* and other papers were campaigning for a stronger line by Clinton.

He had problems of his own, however. The details of his affair with Monica Lewinsky were emerging, and there was much speculation in the US that he wanted to find a way to distract the nation's attention.

Tony Blair was probably not averse to the idea of protecting Albanian Kosovans (the correct term, 'Kosovars', was quickly adopted by those in favour of attacking Serbia, and became too loaded to be used by anyone who wanted to remain neutral) by joining in a NATO attack on Serbia. One of the passages which Downing Street wanted cut out of Lance Price's book was one where he said he felt Tony Blair had 'rather relished' sending people into action – in this case, ordering the RAF to bomb Iraq in 1998. Blair certainly had a strong belief in the need for the developed world to intervene in the developing world if necessary. Perhaps, too, he felt that being seen as a strong leader, sending in the nation's forces to help the innocent, would reinforce his political position.

The *Sun*, which Campbell and his colleagues increasingly favoured over the traditionally Labour *Mirror*, was thoroughly in favour of the NATO action. On 24 March 1999 its editorial was headed

Time to act

> Few of us know where Kosovo is. Probably even fewer care.
>
> But young British servicemen are about to risk their lives there. So will our allies, the Americans.
>
> Why is it any of our business what happens in Kosovo?
>
> For the same reason it mattered when the Nazis invaded Poland in 1939.
>
> Because countries like Britain, some of our European partners and America are the guardians of liberty and democracy. We fight for the oppressed.
>
> The Serbs are slaughtering innocent men, women and children in Kosovo.
>
> That cannot be allowed to go unchallenged.

The *Sun* wrote and did almost everything the Blair government could have wanted. It warned the British people to be ready for possible losses:

PREPARE TO PAY PRICE

PM warns Our Boys' lives are on line as Nato order Serb blitz

TOUGH TASK FOR THE ALLIES

Brit top guns could face a wall of lead

– Wednesday 24 March 1999

CLOBBA SLOBBA

Our boys batter butcher of Serbia in Nato blitz

Britain's brave Harrier pilots blitzed the Serbs last night as Nato launched a devastating air bombardment.

There was no question about the bravery of the pilots, but the attacks of the previous night were regarded in Belgrade as a damp squib. The immensely complex politics of corralling NATO's countries into an agreement to attack a country with which many of them had complicated relationships over the years meant that the NATO command at first ordered attacks on buildings and installations on the outskirts of Belgrade and other cities. There was no blitz, and the Serbs were encouraged to think that NATO was too scared to stage one. But the readers of newspapers like the *Sun*, which, perhaps in deference to Alastair Campbell's information machine, decided not to send their correspondents to Belgrade, were not told of this. Instead, the *Sun* put its efforts into stirring up British emotions. A piece by Mike Jones on 25 March 1999 read:

I SAW SERBS BUTCHER MOTHERS AND KIDS

I saw a three year old blown to pieces when a shell hit a truck he was travelling in . . .

Milosevic's troops hid in bushes down the only escape

road and butchered people with machine guns and mortar
fire as they tried to flee . . .

. . . Most vile of all, I also met a young girl and her two
year old sister who had endured barbarity which defies the
imagination of even the sickest mind . . .

This is how Milosevic treats his enemies.

No doubt all the things Mike Jones saw really happened. During the wars
in the former Yugoslavia every side committed atrocities, and the Serbs
were among the worst. But the specific incidents he writes about occurred
during the Bosnian war, and were done, not by Milošević's men but by
the Bosnian Serbs under the command of President Radovan Karadžić
and General Ratko Mladić. And although these men had the full, even
enthusiastic, backing of Slobodan Milošević in Belgrade, their campaign
against the Bosnian government was carried on separately, and Milošević
had no control over their day-to-day tactics.

Furthermore, the atrocities committed by the Bosnian Serbs in their
war were probably even worse than those carried out by Milošević's forces
in his wars. Early on in the Bosnian war, indeed, Milošević became nervous about the way the campaign was going. Karadžić and Mladić
ignored him, and his influence over them dwindled. None of this means
that Milošević was in any way guiltless overall. He was not; but he cannot
accurately be accused of the crimes listed in Mike Jones's article, since
the soldiers who carried them out were not in any sense his men. The
Sun, however, was out to create a mood of righteous anger, and presumably counted on the fact that most of their readers would not be
aware of the full complexity of Balkan politics.

A cartoon by Griffin above Jones's article was adapted from the
graphics of the popular 1970s television comedy *Dad's Army*, about
the wartime Home Guard, and showed arrows with British, American,
French and German flags pointing at Serbia. The caption was derived
from the programme's theme-song, and replaced Hitler's name with that
of Milošević:

'WHO DO YOU THINK YOU ARE KIDDING
MR SLOBBA'?

Beside the cartoon is an editorial:

Allies at last

> The Luftwaffe was in the air last night alongside
> British firepower and the Americans.
> At last. A genuine alliance attacks the Butcher of
> Belgrade.

The *Mirror* – for the time being it had dropped the word 'Daily', presumably in an attempt to compete with the *Sun* – was as open to stories about Serbian atrocities as the *Sun*, and just as vague about the details. On 27 March 1999 page 6 was largely taken up by a photograph of a sad little girl gazing at the camera, captioned

ESCAPE: This young massacre witness fled from brutal Serbs.

The story is headlined:

They came to her village and seized the fathers . . . 20 were killed as the Serbs took their revenge

Again, there is no indication which Serbs are being referred to: Milošević's men or the Bosnian Serbs. Nor is it clear which of the various wars during the previous decade the incident was part of. No matter: she had been recruited into the emotional propaganda effort which Downing Street was demanding. Neither the *Sun* nor the *Mirror* seemed at all interested in the facts; they wanted 'stories', rich in emotion, which would stir up their readers in support of the government's cause.

The Ministry of Defence in London announced on 10 May 1999 that it was setting up an intelligence unit of twelve people to compile a dossier of Serbian atrocities. It seems clear that this was a Downing Street initiative. Although there was no shortage of Serbian atrocities against ethnic Albanians in Kosovo the political requirement for the dossier quickly passed, and any results the team of investigators found received little attention. The British government seemed to have no great interest in human rights abuses per se; the interest was purely short-term, and purely for political purposes.

The only means by which NATO could exert real pressure on Serbia was from the air. President Clinton was not willing to send in ground troops, and he was probably right; Serbia, with its stubborn, fiercely nationalistic tradition, would have resisted as powerfully as it resisted the Germans in the Second World War. It had no effective response to NATO's bombs and missiles; but instead of the 'few days' which the American Secretary of State Madeleine Albright assured President Clinton were needed for the NATO action, it took eleven weeks before Slobodan Milošević agreed to give way. During that time the strains within the NATO alliance became intense, and sometimes looked as though they might pull the alliance apart.

There was an absurd faith by deeply non-military politicians in the effectiveness of a military solution. Neither Clinton nor Blair, or any of the other leading figures in NATO, paused to reflect that conventional bombing alone does not bring a country to its knees. Despite a half-century of evidence to that effect, the debate was largely unchanged from the 1930s, when unwarlike men like Stanley Baldwin and Neville Chamberlain assumed that mass bombing would bring total destruction and immediate surrender. That was the first mistake Clinton and Blair made. The second was to believe the myths propounded by the American defence industry about the pin-point accuracy of 'smart' bombs and missiles. And there was a third mistake: to assume that people in NATO countries would not find out anything about the effects of the bombing.

At first only about half a dozen Western journalists remained in Belgrade to report on the war. They were sometimes under threat from local Serbian militias, and faced the possibility of being thrown out of the country by the Serbian government. Yet they were left almost completely alone to report as they wished. Edited television reports were supposed to be passed by a Serbian censor, though in practice this was a restriction easily evaded. And it was possible to broadcast by mobile phone or satellite phone without any interference whatever. There was no system for providing Western journalists with government minders, and it was possible to travel anywhere in Belgrade and its outskirts alone and at will.

These things were probably not known to Alastair Campbell or the others in the Downing Street machine. They were busy briefing news-papers like the *Sun* about the Nazi-like qualities of Slobodan Milošević and his regime, and had probably come to believe it themselves. On

12 April 1999 the BBC ran a report on the effect of the bombing on local morale. It contained a number of 'vox pops' with passers-by, stopped at random, in one of Belgrade's main shopping streets.

> 'We used to like everything from West. Now we hate you.'
> 'We are all for Milošević now, even if we didn't like him before.'
> 'You British are the fucking slaves of fucking America.'

One or two of them spat as they spoke. This sort of thing was deeply unwelcome to the Blair government. It realized that the bombing campaign was not working as fast as expected, and began to be worried by the growing divisions within NATO. Perhaps, too, it was worried that people back at home would start to see ordinary Serbs as human beings, not unlike themselves. The demonization effect was wearing off.

Alastair Campbell and two of his assistants at Downing Street went into action, suggesting in the corridors and the fringes of briefing meetings that the BBC man had naively been taken in by stories told to him by Milošević's propaganda machine, which they seemed to endow with something of the same sophistication they themselves possessed. One of Campbell's people suggested that the Serbs had provided the BBC man with people to interview, and he either failed to realize this or had decided to go along with it and interview them anyway for reasons the Downing Street official said he preferred not to go into. Another official, possibly Campbell himself, told a political correspondent that the BBC correspondent's reports were openly pro-Serbian.

Tony Blair then told the House of Commons that the BBC man was working 'under the instruction and guidance of the Serbian authorities', which was a double untruth. He was heckled by a Labour MP. Afterwards, the BBC man sent an email to Alastair Campbell threatening to sue him personally unless he apologized; which he duly did, in pleasant and quite generous terms. The apology was reported a few days later by the *Sunday Telegraph*.

In his memoirs, Campbell quotes Tony Blair's private anger against the BBC man (who was, in fact, the author of this book): 'What a precious arsehole. Thinks he should swan around criticising as he pleases but if anyone speaks back it is an attack on civilisation as we know it.'

Yet in the next sentence the real reason for Blair's tension becomes clear: 'TB said if we didn't win this it was curtains for the government, and not just ours.'

Soon there was evidence that the accuracy of the pilots and the missiles that were being fired was not nearly as great as the politicians had been led to believe. There were attacks on hospitals, on housing estates, on a television station killing several cleaners, cameramen and a make-up lady, on a passenger train packed with people, on a large convoy of Albanian refugees, killing seventy-two men, women and children, on the Chinese embassy in Belgrade, killing three people, on the centre of a busy market town with cluster bombs, which exploded with horrifying effect, showering a crowd with jagged shrapnel. For an alliance fighting a humanitarian war against a savage dictator, NATO's use of so much high explosive was sometimes hard to defend; and it did NATO no good at all if there were credible witnesses on hand to report on the suffering and the loss of human life. Nor was the bombing at all effective. By the end NATO claimed that as a result of its 40,000 bombing sorties it had knocked out up to 40 per cent of Serbia's 280 elderly tanks (scarcely a strike rate to be proud of). Afterwards, though, the real figure became clear when NATO troops invaded Kosovo: it had destroyed just 13 Serbian tanks. It would have been cheaper to have offered Milošević $10 million for each of them, and saved a great many innocent lives.

Journalists in Belgrade, and there were soon plenty of them, made life harder for NATO, and particularly for President Clinton and Tony Blair. The Belgrade press corps included the *Daily Mail*'s David Williams, a correspondent of the old school. Like Ann Leslie, another of the *Mail*'s great foreign reporters, he showed that the *Mail* was still left with something of its old instinct for good, accurate, colourful eyewitness reporting. This was his despatch from Belgrade on 1 April 1999:

> The people of the Serbian industrial town of Kragujevac had listened from their bunkers as the Tomahawks thudded into the buildings on the edge of a military complex and felt the earth shake as the missiles tore through the brick and concrete to cut holes twenty feet deep in the ground. In their thousands, they walked past the devastated buildings on the edge of the base, peering into the dark waters filling the craters and spitting out their contempt for NATO.

Should people like David Williams have been there? Or should the reporting of the bombing have been done from Serbia's borders, and from London, where they would have been based at least in part on 'stories' handed out by Alastair Campbell's office? Several British politicians, heavily influenced by all the comparisons between Milošević and Hitler, thought the place of the journalists was standing four-square behind the government. Clare Short, the international development secretary, said:

> During the Second World War they would have said: 'Mr Hitler criticised the bombing from his bunker today' . . . This is worrying. Is this country capable now of taking military action when necessary to defeat monstrous evil?

The Foreign Secretary, Robin Cook, advised the British media to leave Belgrade because the Serbs controlled their activities; except, of course, that this was not what was happening. 'They have to come to a judgement as to whether they are prepared to accept the censorship that prevents you telling the truth about what is happening in Kosovo.'

The defence secretary, George Robertson, asked the *Today* presenter John Humphrys:

> Can you imagine, Mr Humphrys, if, during the Second World War, you had the opportunity to question ministers in that government day after day, and say, 'What happens if you are defeated on D-Day?'

These people seemed to think they were fighting the Second World War against Hitler alongside Churchill and Roosevelt, when in reality they were fighting a short action against a small, if unpleasant, dictatorship and using overwhelming force to do it, alongside Tony Blair and Bill Clinton. Simon Jenkins, in a calm, sensible article which struck a very different note from much of the (often artificial) emotion which surrounded the subject, wrote in *The Times*: 'Milošević is a nasty job of work, but he is not Hitler or Stalin. He does not merit a Third World War.'

What seemed to be missing, in so much of the 'our brave lads stick it to them' type of journalism, was any sense of reflection and balance. Martin Bell, himself one of the best war correspondents in the BBC's history, made the point in writing for *The Times*, which repeatedly defended the need for good on-the-spot reporting, that it was the duty of journalism to tell as much of the truth as it possibly could. In a free society, its function was not to worry whether this might be inconvenient for the government. Governments – including the government headed by Tony Blair and Alastair Campbell – often have a rather different approach to the truth: they see it as something to be used selectively in order to support a particular policy. Fine; but it should not be the job of journalists to help them. In a free society, it is the role of the press to tell people what is going on, as honestly as possible, and allow them to make up their own minds.

John Pilger and Phillip Knightley were two of the twentieth century's best-known journalists. Pilger, in 1978, persuaded the *Daily Mirror* to issue virtually a whole edition of the newspaper on a single subject: the killing fields of Cambodia. It is thought to be the only time an entire print-run of a newspaper has sold out. Knightley is the author of the examination of war journalism *The First Casualty*. In the April 1999 issue of *Press Gazette* Pilger and Knightley signed a letter, with others, criticizing the British press for 'largely' supporting the Kosovo war. Yet that was, perhaps, unfair. Even the *Sun*, which was the war's loudest supporter, gave Richard Littlejohn a full page to argue that NATO had been led into an unwinnable conflict by a priapic draft-dodger and a one-time supporter of CND. The *Guardian*, which also tended to support the war, with Hugo Young and Francis Wheen most strongly in favour, allowed Richard Gott and Seumas Milne to oppose it. *The Times*, despite the ownership of Rupert Murdoch, loudly defended the BBC's reporting from Belgrade, supported the war in its leading articles but allowed two of its best columnists, Matthew Parris and Simon Jenkins, to oppose it.

Another long-serving reporter watched the flow of Albanian refugees across the Kosovan border. It was his sixty-sixth year as a journalist, since he had joined the *Morning Post* in 1931 at the age of eighteen. William Francis Deedes was the only journalist to have been a Cabinet minister as well as a newspaper editor. He had a remarkable lightness of approach, and kept the air of innocence which led many people to believe that he had been Evelyn Waugh's model for William Boot in *Scoop*. Deedes attracted an entirely new generation of supporters when he appeared on the satirical quiz show *Have I Got News for You*. His last article, written only two weeks before his death in 2006 at the age of ninety-four, was about Darfur. In April 1999, however, he was reporting on the Kosovo war; and his words helped to emphasize the human side of the war, rather than the military side which attracted so much attention: 'Not even during the Second World War did I witness a scene of human anguish comparable to that which I saw yesterday on the Kosovan-Macedonian border.'

A century of reporting had seen extraordinary changes in the world. Yet it ended as it had begun, with some correspondents speaking out loudly, others willing to close their eyes to anything that didn't fit the official version, angry generals, government demands for greater support from journalists, and – just occasionally – the thoughtful, measured, sympathetic tone of a reporter who sees what it means for the ordinary human beings caught up in it all.

Conclusion

At the start of the twenty-first century the British press was still recognizably the same institution it had been at the start of the twentieth. Surprisingly few of the titles published then had disappeared, and the ethos of those which remained, or which had grown up in more recent years, had remained largely unchanged. It is hard to be altogether confident about the future of newspapers, just as it is about magazines, books, the music industry, television and so on; but at least they survived and often prospered throughout an entire century. It is worth noting that for the past thirty years this has been largely due to Rupert Murdoch, who has been so often accused of destroying good journalism.

There have been plenty of changes. At some point in the mid-1950s – it is tempting but probably not properly accurate to say it happened as a result of the Suez crisis – news stories in *The Times* and other serious newspapers routinely started to be interpreted by correspondents and reporters, rather than being merely outlined in brief factual terms. By that stage, political reporting had over the previous twenty years become much more important than parliamentary reporting: the doings of ministers were acknowledged to have greater value than their public speeches, or the speeches of backbenchers. In the 1980s, fuelled by a series of scandals about the Royal Family and the rise of the celebrity culture, the British press began a downward drive which led newspapers like the *News of the World* to publish material gained from illegal phone taps and other gross infringements of personal liberty and privacy. Some newspapers reached unpleasant depths of intrusion and bad taste. Others however refused to follow, and by the second decade of the twenty-first century the situation seemed a little better.

Individual newspapers managed to hold on to their essential characters. *The Times*, though much livelier than it was before it replaced the advertisements on its front page with news on 3 May 1966, remained instinctively conservative, unadventurous but reliable, concerned with precision in language, conscious that many people around the world still regard it as the mouthpiece of Britain's ruling elite. The *Guardian* was still recognizably the newspaper of C.P. Scott, radical but not too much so, a little predictable perhaps but with a liveliness of touch which Scott would probably have jibbed at. The *Daily Telegraph* was equally predictable: in 2000 as in 1900 the voice of the comfortable and established, the reasonably well-to-do, the people who had long since settled on their views and were not likely to change them at this stage in their lives.

Of all the newspapers in this study, the *Guardian* and the *Daily Telegraph* probably come out of it best. The Trust which controls the *Guardian*, and the traditionally light touch of *Telegraph* proprietors, who have mostly kept out of the paper's policy-making, have allowed them to present the world in their different ways in a fairer and less distorted way than the rest of their competitors. The *Independent*, launched on 7 October 1986 by three former *Daily Telegraph* journalists, Andreas Whittam Smith, Stephen Glover and Matthew Symonds, became for a time the best newspaper in Britain; and even after its financial decline, when the journalists on it worked for some of the worst pay-rates in Fleet Street because they believed in the principle of independent-minded journalism, it remained lively and well informed. Its Irish owner, Sir Tony O'Reilly, was careful not to manipulate its views or instruct its editors and writers what to say. The newspapers owned by the Canadian Lord Thomson of Fleet were good because of his refusal to interfere with the policy of his editors, and the *Sunday Times* under his ownership and the editorship of Harold Evans was probably the finest newspaper of the century.

The basic quality of any newspaper comes from its reporters. For reasons which have been examined in this book, reporters are generally a distinctly fallible lot; but if they are allowed to write about things as they see them, more or less free of the constraints which an intrusive proprietor places on their editors, the results are certain to be better. Intrusive proprietors have mostly been bad for the quality of British journalism: from Northcliffe, Rothermere and Beaverbrook to Richard Desmond and Rupert Murdoch, they have rarely made life easier for straightforward reporting, and sometimes a proprietor's ideas can be wrong-headed or even ludicrous. They may have to ensure the survival of the press, but they haven't necessarily helped the level of its reporting. Yet it is in the nature of empires to dissolve, and the worst newspaper proprietors have usually given way to feebler successors, whose grip on their newspapers has eventually loosened. There is no reason to think that this process will not continue.

It is noticeable that, over a period of a hundred years, many of the same issues keep coming up. The *Daily Mail*, after long years in which it was the newspaper which influenced the wives of *Times* and *Telegraph* readers, who in turn influenced their husbands, has reverted to its radical Tory roots and is in some ways more similar in 2010 to its old 1900 self: noisy, everlastingly complaining about the unfairness and unreasonableness and stupidity of things, fiercely anti-European, inclined to exaggerate the ills it feels strongest about, and strangely unmissable: in some ways the *Mail* is still the newspaper that most sums up the way British people see their world, just as it was in 1900.

In the first decade of the twentieth century, as we have seen, the *Daily Mail* carried regular articles with titles like

Remarkable Facts About The Criminal Alien

and drew connections between immigrants and the rise in London crime. Exactly a century later, the *Mail* led the way, with the *Sun* and the *Daily Express* closely behind, in turning the presence of foreign nationals in Britain into a major political issue. Sometimes the figures were exaggerated or merely wrong. On 8 September 2006, in an article as much a mixture of fact and opinion as anything it had written on the subject a century before, the *Mail* announced:

> Up to 80,000 bogus asylum seekers have been granted an 'amnesty' to live in Britain, it has emerged . . .
>
> They have been in the UK for so long the Government has decided not to even bother considering their claims.
>
> It is the latest shocking indictment of Home Office incompetence.

In 2006 a MORI poll found that readers of the *Daily Mail* and the *Daily Express* believed respectively that 19 per cent and 21 per cent of Britain's population was made up of immigrants. In reality it was 7 per cent – a third of the *Express* readers' imaginings.

The *Express* is probably the British newspaper which has changed most from its origins at the start of the twentieth century. In its great days it was the best and most exciting of all the British newspapers; no other British paper had the imagination to commission Leon Trotsky, newly arrived in exile in 1929, to write articles about Stalin's Russia, with headlines like

DRAMATIC REVELATIONS BY BANISHED REVOLUTIONARY

BITTER ATTACKS ON STALIN, HIS CHIEF ENEMY

THE USE OF FORCE OVER A REBELLIOUS PEOPLE.

The *Mirror* is a much reduced newspaper from the days when it sold 6 million copies a day, and influenced the thinking of large sections of the British working class: the paper Winston Churchill hated most. It has suffered both from imitating the *Sun*, and from not imitating it well enough. It finally seemed to lose its instinctive link with the Labour Party when Tony Blair decided to invade Iraq.

Yet strangely this has made it more like the newspaper it was in 1903, when it was founded. And although it has never regained its old self-confidence – the *Sun* has seen to that – it is more readable and less uncertain than it was in its embarrassing Piers Morgan years.

The *Sun* itself has also lost the fizz and sense of superiority it once had. It is probably still the dominant British newspaper, but it is no longer the force it used to be.

As for the BBC, it too is recognizably the same institution that it was on the day of its first broadcast, on 14 November 1922: highly principled, always slightly behind the times, an odd alliance of adventurous, creative programme staff and anxious management. Endlessly criticized by the press for the way it is structured and financed (though newspapers like the *Daily Mail*, the *Sun* and even the *Daily Telegraph* rarely explain that their proprietors would gain financially from any reduction in the BBC's services), regularly threatened by governments of all political hues, it nevertheless seems to be strongest in public favour when it is most under attack.

In 2009, after two years of relentless and often angry criticism of the

BBC in the press for a series of serious mistakes, an opinion poll for the *Newsnight* programme found that 76 per cent of respondents said they were proud of the Corporation. In the same year, as other British broadcasters faded and those in European and North American countries suffered major setbacks, the BBC finally emerged as the world's pre-eminent broadcaster, in terms both of audiences and programme quality. Funded by its audience and accountable to them, reporting on but reporting to the political world, the BBC never quite lost the sense of its own vulnerability, its air of standing by with an apology already drafted, just in case.

§

This book ends, as it began, with a superpower risking its reputation and strength by fighting a small war of choice, in the course of which its weaknesses and shortcomings became obvious. Some of the similarities between the Boer War and the invasion of Iraq are strangely close. Britain had no need to force a war with the Boers.

It did so in pursuit of an openly imperialist agenda: to take control over an important stretch of territory, the Boer Republics, together with their gold and diamond mines. The parallels with America's desire to stage a war of choice in order to overthrow Saddam Hussein, establish a friendly democracy in Iraq, and administer its oil production are strong.

By the end of the twentieth century Americans were starting to become aware that their world dominance was fading, and they talked loudly, just as the British had once done, to convince themselves and others that it wasn't happening. President Clinton's Secretary of State, Madeleine Albright, famously announced on NBC's *Today Show* on 19 February 1998, about the bombing of Iraq: 'If we have to use force, it is because we are America. We are the indispensable nation. We stand tall. We see further into the future.'

The Boer War led Britain to build concentration camps where thousands of women and children died. In 1996, when she was US ambassador to the United Nations, Madeleine Albright was asked on the CBS programme *60 Minutes*: 'More than 500,000 Iraqi children are already dead as a direct result of the UN sanctions. Do you think the price is worth paying?' Albright memorably replied: 'I think this is a very hard choice, but the price – we think the price is worth it.'

The British colonial secretary, Joseph Chamberlain, was already considering ways of provoking a war of conquest with the Boers when he made a speech reported in *The Times* on 1 April 1897:

> It is a gigantic task that we have undertaken when we
> have determined to wield the sceptre of empire. Great is
> the task, great is the responsibility, but great is the
> honour; and I am convinced that the conscience and spirit
> of the country will rise to the height of its obligations.

Soon after he had made up his mind to invade Iraq, in his State of the Union speech on 29 January 2002, President George W. Bush said: '[I]t is both our responsibility and our privilege to fight freedom's fight. We seek a just and peaceful world beyond the war on terror . . .'

Tony Blair, too, was given to speaking in a high-minded way. During a speech he gave in Chicago on 22 April 1999, at the height of the destructive bombing of Serbia which was killing hundreds of ordinary civilians, he said:

> [O]ur actions are guided by a . . . blend of mutual self interest and
> moral purpose in defending the values we cherish. In the end values
> and interests merge. If we can establish and spread the values of
> liberty, the rule of law, human rights and an open society then that
> is in our national interests too.

Soon, Tony Blair was presenting Saddam Hussein as an even more suitable target for his policy of spreading human rights and an open society by the use of military power. It required an even greater effort to persuade British public opinion about it. In private, British diplomats, senior civil servants and generals tended to be as strongly against the policy of attacking Saddam Hussein as many commentators were.

John Pilger, in the *Daily Mirror*, was only one of a number of columnists who objected to Blair's philosophy, writing as the war approached:

> Western governments have had a gift in the 'butcher of
> Baghdad', who can be safely blamed for everything . . .
> British obsequiousness to Washington's designs over

> Iraq has a certain craven quality, as the Blair govern-
> ment pursues what Simon Jenkins calls a 'low-cost, low-
> risk machismo, doing something relatively easy, but
> obscenely cruel'.

Pilger had been dropped by the *Mirror* in the Maxwell years, apparently on the grounds that the readership (in other words Maxwell himself, whose business interests in Soviet-bloc dictatorships were considerable) was bored by his chief theme of human rights. In 2002 Pilger was brought back to the *Mirror* by Piers Morgan, an editor who wanted to make it more of a newspaper and slightly less of a gossip sheet.

Morgan was an odd mixture of qualities. A less talented imitator of the *Sun*, he was obsessed, in spite of his new approach to news, with the culture of celebrity, and ultimately careless about facts (he was sacked for publishing a false story about British soldiers urinating on their Iraqi prisoners). Under him, the *Mirror*'s opinions were noisy and exaggerated: only four years before the paper decided it was uniquely evil to bomb Iraq and overthrow Saddam Hussein, it had thrown its weight behind the bombing of Serbia and the overthrow of Slobodan Milošević, apparently in order to stop him from coming and killing us:

No mercy for the butcher of Kosovo

> . . . [W]e have to do it. Not just to stop this carnage on
> Europe's doorstep but to prevent it spreading closer to our
> own shores.

– Wednesday 24 March 1999

As editor of the *Mirror*, Morgan seemed oddly naive: altogether an unlikely successor to men of the quality of Jack Nener, Richard Stott and Roy Greenslade. Nevertheless, once he had decided that the Iraq war was wrong, he followed through with courage and force. The line he took was summed up neatly in the headline to the paper's editorial on 21 March 2003:

Troops are heroes, the war's insane

It was a stand for principle which cost the *Mirror* dearly in terms of readers lost. By contrast Rupert Murdoch seems to have instructed all the newspapers in his empire to support the invasion of Iraq. His noisy, angry television news service in America, Fox News, was one of the war's strongest backers; but Sky News, his British television news station, was prevented by legislation and government regulation from taking political sides, and reported with verve and balance on the war; often, as in the Kosovo war of 1999, beating both ITN and the BBC despite its smaller resources.

In Britain, the *Sun* was the war's loudest supporter.

THE BRITS ARE COMING

News that will have Saddam trembling in his bunker . . .

10,000 of Our Boys bear down on Basra

A mighty force of 10,000 Royal Marine Commandos, Paras and Desert Rats stormed into Iraq last night with the southern city of Basra in their sights . . .

Thus the *Sun* on 21 March 2003. The tone is unmistakable across the years: it could be William Beach Thomas, the correspondent of the *Daily Mail*, reporting. But there are differences. Beach Thomas wrote about soldiers who were fighting a fierce enemy who were their equals; George Pascoe-Watson, the deputy political editor of the *Sun*, whose work this article was, reported on wholly superior British forces attacking an Iraqi army which was worse equipped than it had been in the first Gulf War, and whose morale was even lower than it had been then.

For the most part, Iraqi soldiers put up little resistance and are scarcely mentioned in the *Sun*'s story. Beach Thomas, who was also given to writing about 'Our Boys', did so from positions miles behind the front lines, but liked to give the impression he was up there with the fighting troops. George Pascoe-Watson did not do anything of the sort; he was at US Central Command in Qatar, nearly 400 miles away from Basra. Correspondents in the First World War scarcely ever saw German troops, except those who were taken prisoner, and their reports were almost exclusively about the doings of the Allies. Much of the reporting of the Iraq war was just as one-sided, though some British journalists and cameramen were in Baghdad: a dangerous place to be, directly the American troops entered town.

On 8 April 2003 Richard Littlejohn, the *Sun*'s main columnist at the time, pointed out that the hundreds of thousands of deaths predicted by the anti-war protestors had not happened. It was true at that point; the hundreds of thousands of deaths in Iraq were still to come.

> [T]he Not In My Name crowd and the Starbucks Strategists have got it hopelessly, ridiculously wrong.
>
> This isn't another Vietnam. It's not another Suez. They were wrong about Afghanistan – remember, the Americans were going to be involved in guerrilla war there for years to come.
>
> Now they're wrong about Iraq.
>
> We still don't know what may be in store, but we can be confident victory is assured.

As it turned out, the Iraq war was another Vietnam, and another Suez. America and Britain would be involved in guerrilla war in Afghanistan for years to come. And victory was not assured. Strange alliances were formed. The defence editor of the *Daily Telegraph*, John Keegan, found Tony Blair almost Churchillian, while those who opposed the war were 'the new appeasers'.

> Appeasement is certainly in the air and has taken possession of a large number of British opinion makers – perhaps a third of the Labour Party, all the Anglican bishops and even some generals and diplomats.

Keegan was influential in the United States, and it became a commonplace of debate there to use his analogy with the appeasers of the 1930s. As with Milošević, Saddam Hussein was presented as another Hitler, dangerous not only to his own citizens and his neighbours, but to us too. Yet 'appeasement' was used as little more than a term of abuse. No one was planning to offer concessions to Saddam, in order to buy him off, to persuade him not to attack us. As for the war itself, Keegan argued, most of the horror that had been generated about it was specious.

> Western armed forces are now so efficient and their weapons so precise that, as was demonstrated in Kosovo, even a very intense bombing campaign kills very few

> civilians and does the minimum of damage to the
> opponents' infrastructure.

The *Daily* and *Sunday Express* were both noisy cheerleaders for the war, unlike the *Daily Mail*, which showed both doubt and thoughtfulness. The *Express* titles had been bought in 2000 by Richard Desmond, the proprietor of various celebrity journals, soft-porn magazines and television stations, and his papers had been obliged to adopt various of his obsessions (he was strongly against the European Union, and seemed to believe that Diana, Princess of Wales, had been murdered by MI6). For Desmond, the fact that France and Germany were hostile to the plans to invade Iraq guaranteed his newspapers' support for it.

On 23 March 2003 the *Sunday Express* headlined its lead editorial

Huge gulf separates the EU outcasts from reality

> When Iraq is liberated from the yoke of its dictator, Britain
> and our allies within the EU will emerge with honour. The
> losers in moral terms will be those who gave succour to
> Saddam. We look forward to seeing the political map of
> Europe reshaped and our ties with the US strengthened.

Below, the second editorial was headlined in terms that were even more characteristic of the new regime at the *Express*:

Let evil family burn in hell.

The family was Saddam Hussein's. The *Express* had often said and done silly things over the decades, but it had always managed to hold on to a modicum of class. That seemed now to have gone.

Overall, people in 2003 assumed very much what they had in South Africa in 1899: the sheer power of the invading army would be so great that it would be successful at once; and such was the high-mindedness of the entire operation that the people who had been conquered would quickly fall in with the new regime. In both South Africa and Iraq the outbreak of guerrilla warfare took the occupying forces by surprise. The British in South Africa dealt with it in ways that some British politicians denounced as barbaric; the *Independent*'s Middle East editor, Patrick Cockburn, revealed with great courage how barbaric much of the war in Iraq was. Cockburn, the son of Claud Cockburn who founded and edited the *Week* in the 1930s (see Chapters 11 and 14), suffered from polio during his childhood in Ireland, and had a severe limp as a result. Yet he spent long periods of time in Iraq when it was the most dangerous country on earth, and provided arguably the best chronicle of the decline of the American and British operations there.

§

Why did Britain invade Iraq? Because America did. Ever since Suez (though not, interestingly, during the Vietnam War) it had been drummed into politicians, diplomats and soldiers that Britain must always stick with America. Why was so much effort invested in trying to show that Saddam Hussein had a large arsenal of weapons of mass destruction, and could use them at short notice? Because, as the headline on a column by Patience Wheatcroft in *The Times* of 21 March 2003 put it, 'We need to be frightened if we're to feel this is our war.' Downing Street, interpreting intelligence in ways that were later shown to be thoroughly questionable, did its best. On 3 February 2003, a month before the invasion of Iraq, Alastair Campbell (by now entitled 'Director of Communications and Strategy') gave journalists copies of a document called 'Iraq: Its Infrastructure of Concealment, Deception and Intimidation'; not, as it turned out, a particularly auspicious title. It contained a good deal of information about Saddam Hussein's weapons of mass destruction; but, as *Channel 4 News* quickly revealed, Dr Glen Rangwala of Cambridge University had discovered that much of the Downing Street report had been cut and pasted off the Internet without attribution from different sources, including an article in the *Middle East Review of International Affairs*. Even minor errors of spelling and punctuation were reproduced. *Spiked*, a thoughtful and entertaining online political magazine then edited by Mick Hume, called it 'the dodgy dossier', and the name stuck; it was even used wryly by Alastair Campbell himself. (Mick Hume had previously edited the magazine *LM*, which had been known as *Living Marxism*. It was driven out of business as the result of a controversial court case brought against it by Independent Television News, after it had questioned some of ITN's reporting in Bosnia.) But just over four months earlier the Blair government had published a more important document. On 24 September 2002 Parliament was recalled to discuss it. Entitled 'Iraq's Weapons of Mass Destruction: The Assessment of the British Government', it had the outward appearance of being the result of a serious government investigation, thoroughly based on intelligence sources; yet it was accused right from the start of having been produced for public relations purposes. Although it carried prominent references to the Joint Intelligence Committee, the real force behind it was Alastair Campbell, who was now arguably the most powerful figure in the government. The likelihood is that he drafted Tony Blair's foreword to the document, which contained the words 'The document discloses that his [Saddam Hussein's] military planning allows for some of the WMD to be ready within 45 minutes of an order to use them.'

The following morning, 25 September 2002, the *Sun*, under instructions from Rupert Murdoch to throw its entire weight behind Tony Blair and President Bush in their plan, now reaching an advanced stage to invade Iraq, picked up this detail and added its own emotionalism to it:

BRITS 45 MINS FROM DOOM

– Wednesday 25 September 2002

So did the *Daily Star*, which was owned by Richard Desmond, and in the normal way was disinclined to trouble itself with anything other people would regard as news of any kind.

MAD SADDAM READY TO ATTACK
45 Minutes from a Chemical War

It had a strong effect on the debate; indeed, the forty-five minute claim was probably more influential than any other in persuading public opinion in Britain that Saddam Hussein represented a serious threat to British lives. Yet in 2004 the Butler inquiry into the quality of the intelligence published in the run-up to the invasion destroyed the credibility of this claim. It reported that it came from a 'sub-source': '[P]ost-war validation by SIS [the official name for MI6] has raised serious doubts about the reliability of reporting from this new sub-source.'

Even 'sub-source' makes the origin of the report seem a little grander than he seems to have been. The Conservative MP and defence specialist Adam Holloway later claimed it was an Iraqi taxi-driver who had overheard two generals talking in the back of his cab.

Three days before the invasion took place the British government was told that Saddam Hussein had got rid of his weapons of mass destruction, but by then it was too late to stop the war. The fact that no weapons of mass destruction were found reignited the whole debate about the original reasons for the war.

At 6.07 on the morning of 29 May 2003, after the invasion was over, Andrew Gilligan, whom the *Today* programme on Radio 4 had hired to be its defence correspondent, was briefly interviewed by John Humphrys about a report he had compiled for that morning's programme. It would be broadcast a little over an hour later. The question-and-answer was unscripted. This is usual on *Today*, but it was a mistake on Gilligan's part, given the extreme sensitivity of the things he was planning to say.

JOHN HUMPHRYS: The government is facing more questions this morning over its claims about weapons of mass destruction in Iraq. Our defence correspondent is Andrew Gilligan. This in particular, Andy, is Tony Blair saying they'd be ready to go within forty-five minutes.

ANDREW GILLIGAN: That's right, that was the central claim in his dossier which he published in September . . . And what we've been told by one of the senior officials in charge of drawing up that dossier was that, actually, the government probably knew that that forty-five minute figure was wrong, even before it decided to put it in. What this person says, is that a week before the publication date of the dossier, it was actually rather a bland production . . . [T]he draft prepared for Mr Blair by the Intelligence Agencies actually didn't say very much more than was public knowledge already, and Downing Street, our source says, ordered a week before publication, ordered it to be sexed up, to be made more exciting and ordered more facts to be discovered.

JOHN HUMPHRYS: When you say 'more facts to be discovered'; does that suggest that they may not have been facts?

ANDREW GILLIGAN: . . . [I]t only came from one source and most of the other claims were from two . . . [T]hings are got wrong in good faith, but if they knew it was wrong before they actually made the claim, that's perhaps a bit more serious.

JOHN HUMPHRYS: Andrew, many thanks; more about that later.

There was indeed more about that later; a great deal more. Even before Gilligan's full report had been broadcast, Downing Street was already shouting down the phone. It argued that Gilligan's story was wrong from start to finish: that the dossier was not 'sexed up', that Downing Street had not interfered in the process, and that MI6 was happy with the forty-five minute claim. None of these things seems to be true. Yet it was the wider issue, of doubting the basic facts of the dossier, that seemed to concern Alastair Campbell and his colleagues. Some journalists within the BBC felt that Gilligan's allegation had been unwise, and very difficult to substantiate.

Nevertheless these words were not at first Downing Street's main target; it was nearly a month before Downing Street began to focus on what, precisely, Gilligan had said at 6.07 that morning. He himself admitted later:

None of this is to say that I shouldn't have been more alert at 6.07, or that we shouldn't have retracted that single two-way [interview]. But both I, and others more senior than me who remain at the BBC, are quite sure that to have done so would have made no difference whatever to the outcome of this saga.

By that stage, it seemed to many people both inside and outside the BBC to have turned into a vendetta. Campbell, who had been facing increasing numbers of stories that he was going to be pushed aside, seems to have lost his sense of judgement. The BBC's leading figures, its chairman, Gavyn Davies, its director general, Greg Dyke, and its head of news, Richard Sambrook, all saw it as an attack on the BBC's independence.

They were also reasonably confident about the truth of the story itself. The editor of *Today*, Kevin Marsh, had received a briefing from Sir Richard Dearlove, the head of MI6, and two of his colleagues in April 2003, which had led him to believe that MI6, did not feel the intelligence had supported the case for war against Iraq. Sir Richard spoke to at least one other senior BBC figure a little before this, and gave him the same impression. Then, just a few hours before Gilligan wrote his report, Kevin

Marsh met Clare Short, who had resigned from the Cabinet over the invasion of Iraq. She told him that no intelligence had been produced to demonstrate conclusively that Iraq was an imminent threat. These details did not come out at the controversial inquiry held by Lord Hutton into the affair, since Hutton did not call Kevin Marsh as a witness; even though his evidence might have been of considerable importance to the BBC's case.

Gilligan was always regarded in the BBC as an outsider, someone who was not imbued with the kind of qualities the BBC likes to regard as its own. There was a feeling among some people in the BBC that because he failed to own up to his mistake in saying the government 'probably' knew that the forty-five minute detail was wrong, Gilligan himself had set in train the entire disastrous course of events: the suicide (assuming it was that) of his chief source, Dr David Kelly; the Hutton inquiry into Kelly's death, which seemed to many people inside and outside the BBC to be grossly biased in favour of the government; the resignations of the chairman and director general; and the easing out or pushing aside of just about everyone who had any responsibility of any kind for what happened: including Richard Sambrook, the head of news, and Gilligan's immediate boss, Kevin Marsh.

Yet without Alastair Campbell's remarkable behaviour, which seemed almost unstable – forcing himself live onto Jon Snow's *Channel 4 News* to complain about the BBC, for instance, in what turned out to be one of the most compelling interviews ever shown on British television – the whole affair could easily have been allowed to fade away.

The BBC's handling of the Gilligan affair was a reaction among its topmost management against the meekness which it perceived that the Corporation had so often displayed over the decades. This time it defended itself and its broadcasting with courage; the problem was, the broadcasting had been faulty. As a result, this turned out to be the wrong battle to fight.

The two men at the top of the BBC, Gavyn Davies the chairman and Greg Dyke the director general, both had something to prove. The *Daily Mail* and other newspapers hostile to the Corporation had often stressed that both men had had strong links with the Labour Party in the past; now, both of them were keen to show that they were fiercely protective of the BBC's independence against a Labour government. An article in the press by a senior BBC journalist also played its part in their thinking.

Written not long before the Gilligan affair erupted, it argued that the government – any government – had a perfect right to put pressure on the BBC if it chose; what mattered was that the BBC should be tough and unequivocal in defending itself and its standards.

Both Davies and Dyke took this advice to heart. On Wednesday 2 July 2003, at the height of the row with Downing Street, Gavyn Davies was the speaker at a lunch for media people at a central London restaurant. He stood up and announced that although he could not answer questions about the Gilligan affair, 'If you're asking me did we do anything wrong – no, we didn't.'

The BBC's key decision-makers during the crisis, who included Richard Sambrook, were all well aware of the old tradition of the pre-emptive cringe, and none of them wanted to return to it. Sambrook was a shrewd and thoughtful man, who was popular with his department. He believed the BBC had an overriding duty to support its journalists when they came under attack. But in this case there was a problem. Gilligan's most important accusation was that the government had claimed that Saddam Hussein could fire his weapons of mass destruction within forty-five minutes, knowing that this was false. The only convincing source for this would have been either someone very close to Tony Blair at the time, or else someone at the top of the intelligence community. Richard Sambrook assumed at first that Gilligan's source had been of this quality; he was only disabused of this after he had made his assumption public, as he made clear in his evidence to the Hutton inquiry:

Q: Mr Gilligan also referred, in his evidence this morning, to the fact that on Radio 4, on 26th June, you described his source as a senior and credible source in the Intelligence Services. Was it right that there was a conversation between you and Mr Gilligan shortly after that broadcast?

A: My recollection is that it was the morning of Friday 27th when Andrew Gilligan told me the identity of his source; and at that point it became clear to me he was not a member of the Intelligence Services.

This was a severe blow to the BBC's entire case. Gilligan's sole source was Dr David Kelly, who, though very well-informed, could not possibly have been a reliable authority on what the prime minister had known and when he had known it. The fact that later evidence, at the inquiry into the Iraq war chaired by Sir John Chilcot, which opened in 2009, appeared to support Gilligan's general thesis, did not alter the basic fact that Gilligan had gone a great deal further than his information at the time permitted. The BBC had selected the wrong ground on which to defend its independence.

The first formal complaint about Gilligan's 6.07 broadcast came from a fairly junior Downing Street figure, who pointed out, reasonably enough, that Gilligan had not given the government the proper right of response. Her letter read:

> 'Today' continued to run these allegations at the top of every news bulletin, without any reference to the firm denial provided voluntarily by Downing Street after we first heard the story. This absence of any balancing comment continued despite our duty press officer calling the programme no less than four times.

It was some time later before Alastair Campbell, who was on an early flight to the Middle East that morning, grasped the full force of Gilligan's accusation. The crisis grew worse over the days that followed, and by Thursday 26 June, Campbell, now beside himself with fury, demanded a full apology by that evening. Later, the feeling grew within the Corporation that Dyke's big mistake had been to respond to this arbitrary deadline. Previous directors general – John Birt, for example – would probably have replied that they could not give an answer so quickly, but that they would carry out a full investigation and reply once it had been properly completed. If Dyke had waited, the absence of a proper source for Gilligan's accusation would have become much more clear.

On Wednesday 24 January 2004 Lord Hutton finally published the findings of his inquiry into the circumstances surrounding the death of Dr Kelly. Alastair Campbell, Tony and Cherie Blair and a few people close to them, showed a degree of delight which was widely regarded as unseemly. Even the *Daily Mail* showed a degree of shock that its old whipping-boy should have been dealt with so harshly. The following day its main editorial read:

> We're faced with the wretched spectacle of the BBC chairman resigning while Alastair Campbell crows from the

summit of his dunghill. Does this verdict, my lord, serve
the real interest of truth?

Divided between its twin dislikes, the Labour government and the BBC,
the *Mail* found it hated the government even more. The *Independent*
carried one of the most effective front pages in its brief history. The top
half read simply and in small letters

WHITEWASH? THE HUTTON REPORT

The absence of a screaming headline made its effect all the stronger. Only
the Murdoch press rejoiced openly in Hutton's judgement. Both *The
Times* and the *Sun* had predicted his findings accurately. In the case of
the *Sun*, its political editor, Trevor Kavanagh, revealed all the main
findings of the report on the morning of its publication. There was a
mildly ludicrous inquiry into the leak, which after seven months failed
to find the source. Most people had assumed from the morning of the
Sun's exclusive that it must have been Downing Street, but this was never
confirmed.

The heart of Hutton's judgement lay in one paragraph, which said
that the BBC's Governors, who were ultimately responsible for the BBC's
conduct, should have recognized more fully than they did that their duty
to protect the independence of the BBC was not incompatible with giving
proper consideration to whether there was validity in the government's
complaints, no matter how strongly worded by Mr Campbell, that the
allegations against its integrity reported in Mr Gilligan's broadcasts were
unfounded and the Governors failed to give this issue proper consideration.

But if there was undeniable truth to some of this, other passages in
the judgement were more questionable: for instance that the general
public would have understood Gilligan's famous phrase that the
government's dossier had been 'sexed up' as meaning that the government had openly lied about Saddam Hussein's weapons of mass
destruction rather than merely exaggerated its claims about them.

This assumption is open to doubt. Hutton, at seventy-two, was an
unlikely authority on contemporary English. Like many older Northern
Ireland Protestants of upper-middle-class stock, he still pronounced the
word 'mass' (as in 'weapons of mass destruction') in late-Victorian

fashion, as though it had an 'r' in it: 'marss'. And yet an essential part of his judgment on Gilligan's reporting was based on his idiosyncratic interpretation of one of the most up-to-date expressions in the language.

Perhaps the most balanced and accurate judgement on the whole affair came a few days later from Martin Kettle in the *Guardian*. On Tuesday 3 February he wrote:

> Too many newspapers invested too heavily in a particular preferred outcome on these key points. They wanted the government found guilty on the dossier and on the naming, and they wanted Gilligan's reporting vindicated. When Hutton drew opposite conclusions, they damned his findings as perverse and his report as a whitewash. But the report's weakness was its narrowness, and to some extent its unworldliness, not the accuracy of its verdicts.

Hutton's findings failed entirely to convince public opinion; and Tony Blair's instinct for grasping the national mood, which had often been so sure, seemed to have deserted him on this occasion. In any major dispute between government and the BBC, people have always tended to support the BBC; and it was particularly so in this case.

Gavyn Davies, the BBC's chairman, resigned immediately. Greg Dyke, under pressure from the board of governors, resigned the next day. The acting chairman, the former Conservative chief whip Lord Ryder, infuriated most of the BBC's staff by making an unreserved apology to the government; this time the cringe was no longer pre-emptive. But he was not speaking for the staff. Eight days after the Hutton report was published, the *Daily Telegraph* ran a full-page advertisement which read, in part:

> **The following statement is from BBC employees, presenters, reporters and contributors. It was paid for by them personally, not the BBC itself.**

> Greg Dyke stood for brave, independent BBC journalism that was fearless in its search for the truth. We are resolute that the BBC should not step back from its determination to investigate the facts in pursuit of the truth.

Alastair Campbell left Downing Street in August 2003, while the Hutton inquiry was still at its height. Political journalists reported that it was because Tony Blair realized he was no longer acceptable as the frontman for the British government. In spite of the damage Campbell had tried to do to the BBC, it employed him in 2008 to make a television documentary about his history of mental illness. Some people in the Corporation suggested, probably wrongly, that this was a refined form of revenge.

§

One of the most annoying things about journalists is that they often contrive to have the last word. In 1902 it was Edgar Wallace, the *Daily Mail* correspondent, who defied Lord Kitchener and broke the news of the peace treaty with the Boers. On 21 November 2009 Andrew Gilligan's name appeared on the front page of the *Daily Telegraph*, over a huge lead article headlined

Iraq report: Secret papers reveal blunders and concealment

The 'appalling' errors that contributed to Britain's failure in Iraq are disclosed in the most detailed and damning set of leaks to emerge on the conflict.

By Andrew Gilligan

> . . . Tony Blair, the former prime minister, misled MPs and the public throughout 2002 when he claimed that Britain's objective was 'disarmament, not regime change' and that there had been no planning for military action.

Journalism does not necessarily make good history. It can often be mistaken, and it is easily deceived. Sometimes it deliberately does the deceiving. But the justification for good reporting, as Martha Gellhorn once said, is that it's the only real way of explaining to people what their world is truly like.

Bibliography

This is an unavoidably long book, and to prevent its becoming even longer and more bulky I have made the precise sources available on the Pan Macmillan website as a free ebook download. They can be found at the following location: www.panmacmillan.com/unreliablesources. At the same time, I have tried to signal in the text where most of the details in question come from ('In his autobiography, so-and-so wrote . . .'). My primary sources being newspapers and broadcasts, I have given the date and provenance of each quotation where it appears. Everything else has been shepherded onto the website. I apologize sincerely to the purists and traditionalists for dealing with the important matter of sources in this peremptory fashion.

Books and Other Sources Consulted

General

Andrew, Christopher. *The Defence of the Realm: The Authorised History of MI5*. Allen Lane. 2009.

Brendon, Piers. *The Life and Death of the Press Barons*. Secker & Warburg. 1982.

Briggs, Asa. *The BBC: The First Fifty Years*. Oxford University Press. 1985.

Curran, James, and Seaton, Jean. *Power Without Responsibility*. Routledge. 1988 and later editions.

Engel, Matthew. *Tickle The Public: One Hundred Years of the Popular Press*. Gollancz. 1996.

Gilbert, Martin. *Winston S. Churchill, The Official Biography*. Vols. 1–8. William Heinemann. 1966–93.

Griffiths, Dennis. *Fleet Street: Five Hundred Years of the Press*. British Library. 2006.

Horrie, Chris. *Tabloid Nation: The Birth of the* Daily Mirror *to the Death of the Tabloid*. André Deutsch. 2003.

Hudson, Miles and Stanier, John. *War and the Media: A Random Searchlight*. Sutton Publishing. 1997.

Knightley, Phillip. *The First Casualty: the War Correspondent as Hero, Propagandist, and Myth Maker from the Crimea to Vietnam*. André Deutsch. 1975.

Koss, Stephen. *The Rise and Fall of the Political Press in Britain. Vol. 2: The Twentieth Century*. Hamish Hamilton. 1984.

Morison, Stanley. *Official History of The Times, 1935–52*.

Orwell, George (Orwell, Sonia and Angus, Ian eds). *The Collected Essays, Journalism and Letters of George Orwell*. Secker & Warburg. 1968.

Seaton, Jean and Pimlott, Ben (eds.). *The Media in British Politics*. Avebury. 1987.

Smith, Anthony (ed.). *The British Press Since The War*. David & Charles. 1974.

Williams, Francis. *Right to Know: The Rise of the World's Press*. Longmans, Green. 1969.

1. The Voyage of the *Dunottar Castle*

Atkins, J.B. *Incidents and Reflections*. Christophers. 1947.

Dickson, W.K.-L. *The Biograph in Battle: Its Story in the South African War Related with Personal Experiences*. T. Fisher Unwin. 1901.

Farwell, Byron. *The Great Boer War*. Allen Lane, 1977.

Hammond, J.L. *C.P. Scott of the Manchester Guardian*. Bell. 1934.

Kruger, Rayne. *Goodbye Dolly Gray: The Story of the Boer War*. Macmillan. 1977.

Pakenham, Thomas. *The Boer War*. Weidenfeld & Nicolson. 1979.

Stead, W. T. *Character Sketches*. John Haddon. 1891.

2. The Boer War

Baden-Powell, Robert. *Sketches in Mafeking and East Africa*. Smith Elder & Co. 1907.

—— *Adventures and Accidents*. Methuen. 1934.

Davey, Arthur. *The British Pro-Boers 1877–1902*. Tafelberg. 1978.

Erskine Childers and Amery, L.S. (eds.). *The Times History of the War in South Africa, 1899–1902*. Sampson, Low, Marsten & Co. 1907.

Gardner, Brian. *Mafeking: A Victorian Legend*. Cassell. 1966.

Hales, A.G. *Campaign Pictures of the War in South Africa, 1899–1900: Letters from the Front*. Cassell. 1900.

Hamilton, Angus. *The Siege of Mafeking*. Methuen. 1900.

Headlam, Cecil (ed.). *The Milner Papers*. Cassell. 1933.

Hobhouse, Emily. *The Brunt of the War And Where It Fell*. Methuen. 1902.

––––––– *Boer War Letters*. Human & Rousseau. 1984.

Kinnear, Alfred. *To Modder River with Methuen*. J.W. Arrowsmith. 1900.

Koss, Stephen (ed.). *The Pro-Boers*. University of Chicago Press. 1973.

Lane, Margaret. *Edgar Wallace: The Biography of a Phenomenon*. Heinemann. 1938.

Marlowe, John. *Milner: Apostle of Empire*. Hamish Hamilton. 1976.

Neilly, Emerson. *Besieged with B.-P.* Blackwood. 1901.

Steevens, G. W. *With Kitchener to Khartoum*. Blackwood. 1898.

––––––– *From Cape Town to Ladysmith: An Unfinished Record of the South African War*. Blackwood. 1900.

Wallace, Edgar. *Writ in Barracks*. Methuen. 1900.

––––––– *Unofficial Despatches*. Hutchinson. 1901.

3. Aliens

Dangerfield, George. *The Strange Death of Liberal England*. Constable. 1936.

Holmes, Colin. *John Bull's Island: Immigration and British Society 1871–1971*. Sheridan House. 1988.

Rumbelow, Donald. *The Houndsditch Murders and the Siege of Sidney Street*. Macmillan. 1973.

Sebag Montefiore, Simon. *Young Stalin*. Weidenfeld & Nicolson. 2007.

4. All-Highest

Bourne, Richard. *Lords of Fleet Street: The Harmsworth Dynasty*. Barrie & Jenkins. 1990.

Cecil, Lamar. *Wilhelm II, Vol. 2: Emperor and Exile, 1900–1941*. University of North Carolina Press. 1996.

Elliott, B. J. *Bismark, the Kaiser and Germany*. Longmans. 1972.

Le Queux, William. *The Invasion of 1910: With a Full Account of the Siege of London*. Foreword by Lord Roberts. Eveleigh Nash. 1906.

———— *Things I know about Kings, Celebrities and Crooks*. E. Nash & Grayson. 1923.

5. Wrong Turn

Brook-Shepherd, Gordon. *Victims at Sarajevo: The Romance and Tragedy of Franz Ferdinand and Sophie*. Harvill Press. 1984.

Feuerlicht, Roberta Strauss. *The Desperate Act: The Assassination of Franz Ferdinand at Sarajevo*. McGraw-Hill. 1968.

Steed, Henry Wickham. *Through Thirty Years, 1892–1922: A Personal Narrative*. 2 vols. Heinemann. 1924.

6. Defence of the Realm

Brown, Malcolm (ed.). *The Wipers Times*, introduction by Ian Hislop. Little Books. 2006,

Cook, Sir Edward Tyas. *The Press in War-Time*. Macmillan. 1920.

'Ephesian' (Carl Eric Bechover Roberts). *Lord Birkenhead: Being an Account of the Life of F.E. Smith, First Earl of Birkenhead*. Mills & Boon. 1926.

Fussell, Paul. *The Great War and Modern Memory*. Oxford. 1975.

Fyfe, Hamilton. *My Seven Lives*. Duckworth. 1928.

Gibbs, Philip Hamilton. *Realities of War*. Heinemann. 1920.

Grigg, John. *Lloyd George: From Peace to War, 1912–1916*. HarperCollins. 1997.

———— *Lloyd George: War Leader, 1916–1918*. Penguin. 2003.

Machen, Arthur. *The Bowmen, and Other Legends of The War*. Simkin, Marshall and Hamilton. 1915.

Palmer, Roy. *'What a Lovely War': British Soldiers' Songs from the Boer War to the Present Day*. Michael Joseph. 1990.

Ponsonby, Arthur. *Falsehood in War-Time*. George Allen & Unwin. 1928.

Repington, Charles à Court. *The World War, 1914–1918: Personal Experience*. Constable. 1920.

Rowland, Peter. *David Lloyd George: A Biography*. Macmillan. 1976.

Thomas, William Beach. *A Traveller in News*. Methuen. 1925.

The Wipers Times, A Facsimile Reprint of the Trench Magazines. Herbert Jenkins. 1918.

7. This Bloody Business

Ashmead-Bartlett, Ellis. *The Uncensored Dardanelles.* Hutchinson. n.d.
Cocks, Frederick Seymour. *The Secret Treaties and Understandings.* Union of Democratic Control. 1918.
Gibbs, Philip. *The Battles of the Somme.* Heinemann. 1917.
——— *The Germans on the Somme.* Darling & Son. 1917.
——— *Now It Can Be Told.* Harper. 1920.
Graves, Robert. *Good-bye To All That.* Jonathan Cape. 1929.
Hamilton, Gen. Sir Ian. *Gallipoli Diary.* 2 vols. Arnold. 1920.
Harris, J. P. *Douglas Haig and the First World War.* Cambridge University Press. 2008.
John, Angela V. *War, Journalism and the Shaping of the Twentieth Century: The Life and Times of Henry W. Nevinson.* I. B. Tauris. 2006.
MacDonald, Lynn. *Somme.* Michael Joseph. 1983.
MacDonagh, Michael. *In London During the Great War: The Diary of a Journalist.* Eyre and Spottiswoode. 1935.
Middlebrook, Martin. *The First Day on the Somme.* Allen Lane. 1971.
Price, Morgan Philips, (Rose, Tania ed.). *Dispatches from the Revolution: Russia 1916–18.* Pluto Press. 1997.
Smuts, Jan Christian, the Younger. *Jan Christian Smuts, by his son.* Cassell. 1952.
Steel, Nigel and Hart, Peter. *Passchendaele: The Sacrificial Ground.* Cassell. 2000.
Tomlinson, H. M. *Old Junk.* Andrew Melrose. 1918.
Wilson, Trevor (ed.). *The Political Diaries of C. P. Scott, 1911–1928.* Collins. 1970.

8. Black and Tans

Bennett, Richard. *The Black and Tans.* Spellmount. 2000.
Edwards, Owen Dudley. *1916: The Easter Rising.* MacGibbon & Kee. 1968.
Gleeson, James. *Bloody Sunday.* Davies. 1962.
Levenson, Leah. *With Wooden Sword: A Portrait of Francis Sheehy-Skeffington, Militant Pacifist.* Northwestern University Press. 1983.

Marreco, Anne. *The Rebel Countess: The Life and Times of Constance Markievicz*. Phoenix Press. 2000.

McKenzie, Frederick Arthur. *The Irish Rebellion: What Happened and Why*. C. Arthur Pearson. 1916

McMahon, Paul. *British Spies and Irish Rebels: British Intelligence and Ireland, 1916–1945*. Boydell Press. 2008.

9. The Coming Man

Chisholm, Anne and Davie, Michael. *Beaverbrook: A Life*. Hutchinson. 1992.

Kershaw, Ian. *Hitler*. Allen Lane. 2008.

Price, Morgan Philips (ed. Rose, Tania). *Dispatches from the Weimar Republic: Versailles and German Fascism*. Pluto Press. 1999.

Taylor, S. J. *The Great Outsiders: Northcliffe, Rothermere and the Daily Mail*. Weidenfeld & Nicolson. 1996.

Tobias, Fritz. *The Reichstag Fire: Legend and Truth*. Secker & Warburg. 1963.

10. The Cause

Delmer, Sefton. *Trail Sinister: An Autobiography*. Secker & Warburg. 1961.

Gerahty, Cecil. *The Road to Madrid*. Hutchinson. 1937.

Hastings, Selina. *Evelyn Waugh*. Sinclair-Stevenson. 1994.

Preston, Paul. *The Spanish Civil War 1936–39*. Weidenfeld & Nicolson. 1986.

——— *The Politics of Revenge: Fascism and the Military in Twentieth-Century Spain*. Unwin Hyman. 1990.

——— *We Saw Spain Die: Foreign Correspondents in the Spanish Civil War*. Constable. 2008.

Langdon-Davies, John. *Behind the Spanish Barricades*. Secker & Warburg. 1936.

Page, Bruce, Leitch, David and Knightley, Philip. *Philby: The Spy Who Betrayed a Generation*. André Deutsch. 1968.

Philby, Kim. *My Silent War*. MacGibbon & Kee. 1968.

Rankin, Nicholas. *Telegram from Guernica: The Extraordinary Life of George Steer, War Correspondent*. Faber. 2003.

Salter, Cedric. *Try-Out in Spain*. Harper Brothers. 1943.
Steer, George Lowther. *The Tree of Gernika*. Hodder & Stoughton. 1938.
Thomas, Hugh. *The Spanish Civil War*. Eyre & Spottiswoode. 1961.
Voigt, F.A. *Unto Caesar*. Constable. 1939.
Waugh, Evelyn. *Scoop: A Novel About Journalists*. Chapman & Hall. 1938.

11. Abdication

Cockburn, Claud. *In Time of Trouble*. Rupert Hart-Davis. 1957.
Cockburn, Patricia. *The Years of 'The Week'*. Macdonald. 1968.
Cooper, Duff. *Old Men Forget*. Rupert Hart-Davis. 1957.
Cudlipp, Hugh. *Publish and be Damned!* Andrew Dakers. 1953.
Donaldson, Frances. *Edward VIII: The Road to Abdication*. Weidenfeld & Nicolson. 1978.
Nicolson, Harold. *Diaries & Letters 1930–1939*. ed. Nigel Nicolson. Collins. 1966.
Warwick, Christopher. *Abdication*. Sidgwick & Jackson. 1986.

12. Appeasement

Bartlett, Vernon. *I Know What I Liked*. Chatto & Windus. 1974.
Boothby, Robert. *Recollections of a Rebel*. Hutchinson. 1978.
Cockett, Richard. *Twilight of Truth: Chamberlain, Appeasement and the Manipulation of the Press*. Weidenfeld & Nicolson. 1989.
Faber, David. *Munich: The 1938 Appeasement Crisis*. Simon & Schuster. 2008.
Hadley, W.W. *Munich Before and After*. Cassell. 1944.
Hubble, Nick. *Mass-Observation and Everyday Life: Culture, History, Theory*. Palgrave Macmillan. 2006.
Kershaw, Ian. *Making Friends with Hitler: Lord Londonderry and the Roots of Appeasement*. Allen Lane. 2004.
Low, David. *Low's Political Parade*. The Cresset Press, 1936.
——— *Low Again*. The Cresset Press. 1938.
——— *Low's Autobiography*. Michael Joseph. 1956.
Margach, James. *The Abuse of Power*. W.H. Allen. 1978.
Olson, Lynne. *Troublesome Young Men: The Churchill Conspiracy of 1940*. Bloomsbury. 2007.

Pimlott, Ben. *Labour and the Left in the 1930s*. Cambridge University Press. 1977.

—— *The Political Diary of Hugh Dalton*. Jonathan Cape. 1986.

Price, G. Ward. *The Year of Reckoning*. Cassell. 1939.

Rock, William R. *British Appeasement in the 1930s*. Hodder Arnold. 1977.

Self, Robert. *Neville Chamberlain*. Ashgate. 2006,

Williamson, Philip, and Baldwin, Edward. *The Baldwin Papers: a Conservative Statesman, 1908–1947*. Cambridge University Press. 2004.

13. First Blood

Allingham, Margery. *The Oaken Heart*. Michael Joseph. 1941.

Barnes, John and Nicholson, David (eds.). *The Leo Amery Diaries*. Hutchinson. 1980.

Beachcroft, T. O. *Calling All Nations*. BBC. n.d.

Boyle, Andrew. *Poor, Dear Brendan: The Quest for Brendan Bracken*. Hutchinson. 1974.

'Cato'. *Guilty Men*. Victor Gollancz. 1940.

Dimbleby, Jonathan. *Richard Dimbleby*. Hodder & Stoughton. 1975.

Edelman, Maurice. *The 'Mirror': A Political History*. Hamish Hamilton. 1966.

Faber, David. *Speaking For England: Leo, Julian and John Amery – The Tragedy of a Political Family*. Free Press. 2005.

Hickman, Tom. *What Did You Do In The War, Auntie?: The BBC At War, 1939–45*. BBC Books. 1995.

Lukacs, John. *Five Days In London: May 1940*. Yale Nota Bene. 2001.

McLaine, Ian. *Ministry of Morale: Home Front Morale and the Ministry of Information in World War II*. Allen & Unwin. 1979.

Murrow, Edward R. *This Is London*. Simon & Schuster. 1941.

Roberts, Andrew. *The Holy Fox: A Biography of Lord Halifax*. Weidenfeld & Nicolson. 1991.

Talbot, Godfrey. *Ten Seconds From Now: A Broadcaster's Story*. Hutchinson. 1973.

Thomson, George Pirie. *Blue Pencil Admiral: The Inside Story of the Press Censorship*. Sampson Low, Marston & Co. 1947.

Waugh, Evelyn. *Put Out More Flags*. Chapman & Hall. 1942.

14. Dunkirk To The Blitz

Bell, Amy Helen. *London Was Ours: Diaries and Memoirs of the London Blitz*. I.B. Tauris. 2008.

Calder, Angus: *The Myth of the Blitz*. Pimlico. 1994.

Calder, Ritchie. *The Lesson of London*. Secker & Warburg. 1941.

Campion, Garry. *The Good Fight: Battle of Britain Wartime Propaganda and The Few*. Palgrave Macmillan. 2008.

Cross, Arthur, Tibbs, Fred and Seaborne, Mike. *The London Blitz*. 3Nishen Publishing. 1987.

Collier, Richard. *The Sands of Dunkirk*. Collins. 1961.

Donoughue, Bernard, and Jones, G.W. *Herbert Morrison: Portrait of a Politician*. Weidenfeld & Nicolson. 1973.

Jackson, Robert. *Dunkirk: The British Evacuation, 1940*. Barker. 1976.

James, T.C.G. *The Battle of Britain (Air Defence of Great Britain: vol. 2)*. Routledge. 2000.

Ministry of Information. *The Battle of Britain, August–October 1940*. HMSO. 1941.

15. Censorship and Enterprise

Barber, Noel. *Sinister Twilight: The Fall and Rise Again of Singapore*. Collins. 1968.

Beevor, Anthony. *D-Day*. Viking. 2009.

Burchett, Wilfred G. *At The Barricades: Memoirs of a Rebel Journalist*. Quartet Books. 1981.

Collier, Richard. *The Warcos: The War Correspondents of World War II*. Weidenfeld & Nicolson. 1989.

Daniell, Raymond. *Civilians Must Fight*. Doubleday, Doran & Co. 1941.

Hack, Karl and Blackburn, Kevin. *Did Singapore Have To Fall? Churchill and the Impregnable Fortress*. Curzon. 2003.

Hamilton, Nigel. *Monty: Battles of Field Marshal Bernard Law Montgomery*. Hodder & Stoughton. 1994.

Horne, Alistair and Montgomery, David. *Monty: The Lonely Leader, 1944–45*. HarperCollins. 1994.

Lewis, Nigel. *Exercise Tiger: The Dramatic True Story of a Hidden Tragedy of World War II*. Prentice Hall Trade. 1990.

McMillan, Richard. *Miracle Before Berlin*. Jarrolds. 1946.

Monks, Noel. *Eyewitness*. Muller, 1955.

────── Eyewitness: Journal of a World Correspondent. Shakespeare Head. 1956.

Moorehead, Alan. *African Trilogy: Mediterranean Front, A Year of Battle, and The End In Africa*. Hamish Hamilton. 1945.

────── *A Late Education: Episodes in a Life*. Hamish Hamilton. 1970.

Morrison, Ian. *Malayan Footsteps*. Faber & Faber. 1942.

Williams, Francis. *Nothing So Strange: An Autobiography*. Cassell. 1970.

16. Suez

Bosanquet, Reginald. *Let's Get Through Wednesday: My 25 Years With ITN*. Michael Joseph. 1980.

Clark, William. *From Three Worlds*. Sidgwick & Jackson. 1986.

Cockerell, Michael. *Live From Number Ten: The Inside Story of Prime Ministers and Television*. Faber & Faber. 1988.

Cockerell, Michael, Hennessy, Peter and Walker, David. *Sources Close To The Prime Minister: Inside the Hidden World of the News Manipulators*. Macmillan. 1984.

Cameron, James. *Point of Departure: An Attempt at Autobiography*. Oriel Press. 1978.

Evans, Harold. *Downing Street Diary: The Macmillan Years, 1957–63*. Hodder & Stoughton. 1981.

Grisewood, Harman. *One Thing At A Time*. Hutchinson. 1968.

Moran, Lord. *Winston Churchill: The Struggle for Survival, 1940–1965*. Heron Books. 1966.

Shaw, Tony. *Eden, Suez and the Mass Media: Propaganda and Persuasion During the Suez Crisis*. I.B. Tauris. 1995.

Thorold, Algar Labouchere. *The Life of Henry Labouchere*. Constable. 1913.

Woollacott, Martin. *After Suez: Adrift in the American Century*. I.B. Tauris. 2006.

17. Lavender List

Butler, David. *The Trouble With Reporting Northern Ireland: The British State, the Broadcast Media and Nonfictional Representation of the Conflict*. Avebury. 1995.

Donoughue, Bernard. *Prime Minister*. Jonathan Cape. 1987.

Haines, Joe. *The Politics of Power*. Jonathan Cape. 1977.

——— *Glimmers of Twilight: Murder, Intrigue and Passion at the Court of Harold Wilson*. Politico's. 2003.

Marnham, Patrick. *The* Private Eye *Story: The First 21 Years*. André Deutsch. 1982.

McKittrick, David, and McVea, David. *Making Sense Of The Troubles*. Blackstaff Press. 2000.

Penrose, Barrie, and Courtiour, Roger. *The Pencourt File*. Secker & Warburg. 1978.

Pimlott, Ben. *Harold Wilson*. HarperCollins. 1992.

Rolston, Bill (ed.). *The Media and Northern Ireland: Covering the Troubles*. Macmillan. 1991.

Rose, Peter. *How The Troubles Came To Northern Ireland*. Palgrave Macmillan. 1999.

Seaton, Jean. 'Yesterday's Men'. *Contemporary British History*, Vol. 11 issue 2, summer 1997.

Williams, Marcia. *Inside Number 10*. Weidenfeld & Nicolson, 1972.

18. Rising Sun

Campbell, John. *Margaret Thatcher: Iron Lady*. Vintage. 2007.

Chester, Lewis and Fenby, Jonathan. *The Fall of the House of Beaverbrook*. André Deutsch. 1979.

Chippindale, Peter and Horrie, Chris. *Stick It Up Your Punter!: The Uncut Story of the* Sun *Newspaper*. Simon & Schuster. 1999.

Evans, Harold. *My Paper Chase: True Stories of Vanished Times*. Little, Brown. 2009.

Giles, Frank. *Sundry Times*. John Murray. 1986.

Haines, Joe. *Maxwell*. Macdonald. 1988.

Hanrahan, Brian, and Fox, Robert. *I Counted Them All Out And I Counted Them All Back: The Battle For The Falklands*. BBC. 1982.

Hart-Davis, Duff. *The House the Berrys Built*. Hodder & Stoughton. 1990.

Hastings, Max and Jenkins, Simon. *The Battle For The Falklands*. Michael Joseph. 1983.

Leapman, Michael. *Treacherous Estate: The press after Fleet Street*. Hodder & Stoughton. 1992.

Porter, Henry. *Lies, Damned Lies and Some Exclusives*. Chatto & Windus. 1984.

Shawcross, William. *Rupert Murdoch, Ringmaster of the Information Circus*. Random House. 1992.

Thatcher, Margaret. *The Downing Street Years*. HarperCollins. 1993.

Trethowan, Ian. *Split Screen*. Hamish Hamilton. 1984.

Wolff, Michael. *The Man Who Owns The News: Inside the Secret World of Rupert Murdoch*. Random House. 2008.

19. Wars Without End

Campbell, Alastair, and Stott, Richard (eds.). *The Blair Years: Extracts from the Alastair Campbell Diaries*. Hutchinson. 2007.

Cockburn, Patrick. *The Broken Boy: The Extraordinary Story of a Life Split in Two*. Jonathan Cape. 2005.

––––– *The Occupation: War, Resistance and Everyday Life in Iraq*. Verso Books. 2006.

Curtis, Mark. *Web of Deceit*. Vintage. 2003.

Greenslade, Roy. *Press Gang: How Newspapers Make Profits from Propaganda*. Macmillan. 2003.

Jones, Nicholas. *Sultans of Spin*. Victor Gollancz. 1999.

––––– *The Control Freaks: How New Labour Gets Its Own Way*. Politico's. 2001.

Oborne, Peter. *Alastair Campbell: New Labour and the Rise of the Media Class*. Aurum. 1999.

––––– *The Rise of Political Lying*. Free Press. 2005.

Price, Lance. *The Spin Doctor's Diary: Inside Number 10 with New Labour*. Hodder & Stoughton. 2003.

Index

and Kosovo war 533, 537, 538–9, 548
relationship with Murdoch and influence
    of 522–3, 524–7
support of by the *Sun* 523–4
Bloody Sunday (1972) 170–1, 445–50
Blücher, Field Marshal 71
Blunt, Dr Alfred 266–7, 268
Blyth, Jeffrey 428
Boer War (1880-1) 1
Boer War (1899-1902) 5, 6–7, 8–19, 20–46,
    48, 547
    'Black Week' (1899) 22–3, 25
    British casualties 19, 24
    concentration camps and deaths of Boers
        in x, 8, 40–4, 547
    cult of 'Tommy Atkins' 39, 40
    demonstrations against 8
    filming of by Biograph camera 15–16
    guerrilla campaign and reporting on
        second stage of war 36–9, 41, 552
    imperialist agenda 11, 12, 13
    Kimberley siege 25–7
    Ladysmith siege 27–8, 29
    Mafeking siege 28–9, 30–5
    medical care for soldiers 23–4
    origins 10–12
    peace negotiations and signing of
        agreement 44–5, 562
    press support of 11, 12, 13, 14
    replacement of Buller with Roberts 24
    revolution in reporting 8, 15
    shooting of British wounded by Boers
        story 39–40
    shortcomings of British army in 18
    similarities with Iraq war 547–8, 552–3
    treatment of Africans at Mafeking and
        racism in reporting 32–4
    and Wilhelm II 77, 80
Bolín, Luis 250
Bolsheviks 157–61, 198
Bolton, Roger 476, 482–3, 484–5
Boothby, Guy 57
Boothby, Robert 280
Borah, William 214
Bosanquet, Reginald 422
Bosnian Serbs 532, 535
Bosnian War (1992) 90, 535

Botha, Louis 35
Bowen, Jeremy 516, 517
Bowen-Colthurst, Captain 183, 184
Boy's Own Paper 29
Bracken, Brendan 309–10, 349, 361, 390
Bradford *Telegraph and Argus* 267, 271
British Expeditionary Force (BEF) 125, 130,
    314, 326, 334–6, 343, 346
British Sky Broadcasting *see* BSkyB
British Union of Fascists (BUF) 206, 290–1
British United Press 371
Brook, Sir Norman 407
Brooks, Collin 293
Brown, Douglas 372
Brown, George 437
BSkyB 488, 525
Buchan, John 131, 132–133
    Greenmantle 131
Buchanan, Sir George 111
Buchanan-Allen, Revd D.S. 241
Buller, General Sir Redvers 1, 3, 4, 16, 17, 24
Burchett, Wilfred 396–7
Burdett-Coutts, William 23
Burgess, Guy 416
Burleigh, Bennet x, 20–2, 35, 40, 43
Burma 373
Burns, Gordon 478
Bush, President George W. 527, 548
Butler Inquiry (2004) 554

Caballero, Francisco Largo 228
Cadett, Thomas 252, 253
Cadogan, Sir Alexander 285, 298, 423, 424,
    425
Cairo summit (1943) 371–2
Calder, Peter Ritchie 360–1
Callaghan, Jim 437, 463, 471–2, 477, 480, 498
Cambodia xi, 541
Cambon, Paul 103
Cameron, James 429
Campbell, Alastair 524, 525–6, 527–9, 538,
    553
    and Gilligan affair 556–7, 449
    hatred of Major 528–9
    leaves Downing Street 562
    and Maxwell 529, 530–1
    memoirs 531

Acknowledgements

Every effort has been made to contact the copyright holders of material reproduced in this book. If any have been inadvertently overlooked, the publishers will be pleased to make restitution at the earliest opportunity.

'Fight to a Finish' copyright Siegfried Sassoon by kind permission of the Estate of George Sassoon.

Excerpt from *The Uncelestial City* by Humbert Wolfe (© Humber Wolfe 1930) reproduced by permission of PFD on behalf of the Estate of Humbert Wolfe.

Illustrations

British Cartoon Archive, University of Kent: 38 (Cartoon by Steve Bell, reproduced in the *Guardian*, 1994), 40 (Cartoon by Charles Griffin, reproduced in the *Sun*, 1999)
Corbis: 16 (Sean Sexton Collection), 18 (Hulton-Deutsch Collection), 23 (Bettmann)
Daily Express/British Library: 9
Getty Images: 4, 8 (Popperfoto), 10, 12, 13, 14, 17, 19–21, 24, 29, 30–31 (Time & Life Pictures), 33–35, 39
Mary Evans Picture Library: 1, 3, 5
Mirrorpix: 26, 27
National Portrait Gallery, London: 2
Press Association: 11, 32, 36, 37, 41
Rex Features: 6, 7, 22 (Photo by C.J. Tavin./Everett)
Richard Busvine: 25
The Wipers Times, Little Books, 2006: 15